TO THE PRIESTS, OUR LADY'S BELOVED SONS

18th English Edition
"Pro manuscripto"

Cover: Marienfried (Germany), Sept. 2, 1985: Don Stefano Gobbi during an outdoor cenacle with priests and laity of the M.M.P. (Foto Weber)

Printed in the United States of America

". . . I obtained from God for the Church the Pope who had been prepared and formed by me.

He has consecrated himself to my Immaculate Heart and has solemnly entrusted to me the Church, of which I am the Mother and Queen.

In the person and the work of the Holy Father, John Paul II, I am reflecting my great light which will become stronger, the more the darkness envelops everything."

January 1, 1979

1st	English Edition:	May	1974	
2nd	English Edition:	Mar.	1977 –	10,000 copies
3rd	English Edition:	Oct.	1977 –	20,000 copies
4th	English Edition:	Apr.	1978 –	40,000 copies
5th	English Edition:	July	1979 –	30,000 copies
6th	English Edition:	June	1980 –	40,000 copies
7th	English Edition:	Mar.	1983 –	60,000 copies
8th	English Edition:	Mar.	1985 –	30,000 copies
9th	English Edition:	Mar.	1987 –	50,000 copies
9th	Edition–Revised:	Dec.	1987 –	5,000 copies
10th	English Edition:	May	1988 –	50,000 copies
10th	Edition–Reprint:	Dec.	1988 –	30,000 copies
11th	English Edition:	May	1990 –	100,000 copies
12th	English Edition:	Sept.	1991 –	50,000 copies
13th	English Edition:	Sept.	1992 –	40,000 copies
14th	English Edition:	July	1993 –	50,000 copies
15th	English Edition:	June	1994 –	75,000 copies
16th	English Edition:	Apr.	1995 –	100,000 copies
17th	English Edition:	Nov.	1996 –	100,000 copies
18th	English Edition:	Feb.	1998 –	100,000 copies

It is hereby stated that the messages contained in this book must be understood not as words spoken directly by Our Lady, but received, in the form of interior locutions, by Don Stefano Gobbi. Their publication is in conformity with the directives published by Pope Paul VI on the 14th of October, 1966.

This noncommercial edition is being distributed free of charge. Therefore no one is authorized to request payment, contribution or offerings. Those who wish to make a contribution to help cover the cost of printing and distribution may send an offering to the National Headquarters of the Marian Movement of Priests in their respective country.

Imprimatur:

There is nothing contrary to faith or morals in this manuscript.

+ Donald W. Montrose, D.D.
   Bishop of Stockton
   February 2, 1998
   Presentation of the Child Jesus

El Cardenal
Bernardino Echeverria Ruiz, OFM.

After reading and deeply meditating the messages given by Our Lady to Don Stefano Gobbi, I consider it a privilege not only to be able to give the Imprimatur to this edition of the book, "To The Priests Our Lady's Beloved Sons", but also to take this opportunity to recommend the reading of these messages. They will contribute to the spread of devotion to Our Lady.

Bernardino Cardinal Echeverria Ruiz O.F.M.

Archbishop Emeritus of Guayaquil
Apostolic Administrator of Ibarra

February 2, 1998
Feast of the Presentation
of the Child Jesus

Publisher's Note

In the message dated December 31, 1997, the Blessed Mother tells Fr. Gobbi that she will no longer be giving him any public messages. This 18th edition, therefore, will be our final edition. The book will, however, be reprinted as the need arises.

The one great change in this text compared to former editions concerns capitalization and punctuation. The Italian punctuation was followed but sometimes made the text somewhat difficult to understand. We have weeded out unnecessary commas, semi-colons, etc., but always with a view of maintaining, as closely as possible, the precise meaning of the original Italian text. Changes were also made to correct typographical and grammatical errors which had been noted by the book's readers over the years. We trust that these changes will make its reading easier and its understanding more complete.

The entire book has been re-typeset; hence, those of you who have older copies of the book will notice that the page numbers do not correspond with those in prior editions. This is because the extra spaces between paragraphs have been eliminated in certain instances where it was judged that the same thought or idea was being continued from the previous paragraph.

The following lists the general areas in which the text was modified. When necessary, an explanation for the change is given:

1) Capitalization: In proofreading the book, we realized that there was a lack of uniformity in the capitalization of certain words. Since this is a book which contains a religious vocabulary, many words had been capitalized, and we realized that the overuse of these capitalized words tended to make the reading more laborious. For this reason, we adopted a system of capitalization that, while being in agreement with the best American usage, still maintained the proper capitalization of religious words. We have tried to be consistent in this regard throughout the book.
   Examples:
   a) In his Gospel, St. John the Evangelist identifies the Second Person of the Holy Trinity as the "Word of God." To differentiate the "Word" from its other connotation, "word" is used in lower case when it refers to the "word" of the Scripture.
   b) Names and words referring to the Blessed Trinity - Father, Son, and Holy Spirit - or their Being *personified* (i.e. Wisdom referring to God) have been capitalized. However, when a word such as wisdom signifies an *attribute* of God, it has not been capitalized.

c) Titles of Mary have remained capitalized, i.e. Mother of Mercy; Mediatrix of Grace; Gate of Heaven; the Woman Clothed with the Sun, etc. Spouse, Daughter and Mother have also been capitalized when referring to Mary.

d) Immaculate Heart, Heart of Jesus and Heart of Mary are always capitalized to differentiate them from the hearts of her priests and beloved children, etc.

e) "My M(m)other's heart / love" have been changed to "my motherly heart / love" when these could be misconstrued as referring to her mother, St. Ann.

N.B. Many of the above changes in capitalization were also made so as to facilitate their differentiation in the Concordance.

2) Punctuation and typographical errors.

3) In comparing with the original Italian text, we found that the translation of certain words and passages should be changed for clarity. In many instances, this could be achieved by rearranging the sentence structure. In other cases, certain words were changed to better capture the nuance of their meaning in Italian.

4) All biblical citations have been referenced, except when repeated in the same message. Oftentimes, the biblical quote, when translated from the Italian, is not verbatim as it appears in standard biblical translations. In these instances, the citation refers the reader to this passage in Scripture by adding *cf.* before the reference, as in the example which follows: (cf. Lk 2:4-5).

5) As a final note, we have given no preference to so-called "all-inclusive" language. We have tried our best to render a literal translation from the Italian, remaining as faithful to the original language as possible and not adding to or deleting from the messages in any way.

We hope that the changes in pagination and other minor discrepancies will not be too much of an inconvenience for those who are following along using former editions of the book. All of the modifications listed above were made in consideration of benefiting you, the reader. Your understanding is appreciated.

Rev. Albert G. Roux
National Director for the
United States of America

NOTE FROM THE SPIRITUAL DIRECTOR

(From the 21st Edition of the original Italian text)

The twentieth [Italian] edition of the present book, published in April of last year, is already exhausted. Many requests are still coming in from everywhere. This fact calls for reflection. As I have already observed in the note to the previous editions, this book responds to a deeply felt need on the part of souls and to a real necessity in the ecclesial life of today.

But there is something more.

From the reading of the most recent messages, which develop a line of thought common to the whole book, one comes to comprehend that in them are described the signs of the times in which we are living and a way in which one can achieve an authentic interpretation of them in the light of the Holy Spirit.

— First of all, the profound crisis of faith already foretold by Our Lady at Fatima, and which today has become more critical and widespread, is clearly described. The continual spreading of errors in every segment of the Catholic Church brings one to the conviction that we are living the time of the great apostasy of which Saint Paul writes in his Second Letter to the Thessalonians, chapter two, verse three. Hence from here comes the constant, concerned and even anguished admonition of the messages to walk along the way of the true faith, following Mary, the faithful Virgin to whom we entrust ourselves in a special way by the consecration to her Immaculate Heart.

— Then comes an ample description of the situation of the interior disunity of the Church, caused by the contestation against the Pope and the rejection of his Magisterium. The painful wound, caused by the schism of Archbishop Lefebvre is nothing more than a sign of much deeper division, even if not as yet open and proclaimed. Hence comes the continuous invitation of the messages to a courageous, humble and strong unity with the Pope who has been given by Jesus Christ the task of feeding the flock, of presiding over it in love, of being the foundation of the whole Church, and of keeping it in the security of the faith and of the truth, following Mary who is the Mother of unity.

— Moreover, there is brought out in bold relief the fact that today theoretical and practical atheism, diffused on a world-wide scale, has constructed a new atheistic and materialistic civilization, bringing about a general justification of sin, which is no longer looked upon as a moral evil, but extolled through the media of social communication as a positive value and a good. Thus there is spread about the general practice of living in sin, of no longer confessing it and of reducing the demands of Christian life to the communitarian and social plane, forgetting one's personal duty to live in the grace of God and to walk along the road of sanctity.

From here comes the constant summons of the messages to the obligation of conversion, in an ascetical effort to fight against sin and to walk along the way of prayer, of penance and of the daily exercise of the theological virtues of faith, hope and charity and all the moral virtues, especially those of humility, of purity and of obedience, following Mary who is for all an example and model of holiness.

— Finally, there is the continual and clear reference to the apocalyptic nature of the times we are living in, and this, in truth, is the aspect of the messages which most disconcerts and even scandalizes many. But why should this surprise us? Are there not many signs which perhaps indicate that we are indeed living in such times?

I submit for the reflection of all some significant words which Pope Paul VI spoke in 1977, one year before his death, and which are recorded in the book, "The Secret Paul VI," by Jean Guitton:

"There is a great uneasiness, at this time, in the world and in the Church, and that which is in question is the faith. It so happens now that I repeat to myself the obscure phrase of Jesus in the Gospel of St. Luke: 'When the Son of Man returns, will He still find faith on the earth?' It so happens that there are books coming out in which the faith is in retreat on some important points, that the episcopates are remaining silent and these books are not looked upon as strange. This, to me, is strange. *I sometimes read the Gospel passage of the end times and I attest that, at this time, some signs of this end are emerging.*

"Are we close to the end? This we will never know.

"We must always hold ourselves in readiness, but everything could last a very long time yet. What strikes me, when I think of the Catholic world, is that within Catholicism, there seems sometimes to pre-dominate a non-Catholic way of thinking, and it can happen that this non-Catholic thought within Catholicism, *will tomorrow become the stronger.* But it will never represent the thought of the Church. It is necessary that a *small flock* subsist, no matter how small it might be." (Pope Paul VI)

So why be scandalized if Mary, Mother of the Church, is intervening today in a very strong way, to form for herself a little flock which will remain faithful to Christ and to his Church?

It is my wish that whoever takes this book in hand may be assisted to become a part of this faithful little flock which Our Lady is forming each day and guarding in the secure refuge of her Immaculate Heart.

January 1, 1996
Solemnity of Mary
Mother of God

For an exact and balanced interpretation of the messages contained in this book, it is recommended that a meditated reading of the whole introduction be made.

For All My Priest-Sons

"Whatever I communicate to you, my son, does not belong to you alone, but it is for all my priest-sons, whom I love with predilection.

Above all it is for the priests of the Marian Movement of Priests whom I love most tenderly and whom I want to form and lead by the hand to prepare them for their great mission.

Therefore gather together in a booklet whatever I have told you... You are not to concern yourself in any way with all that has respect to its printing; your confessor will provide for everything.

And this booklet is to be disseminated as quickly as possible among priests; it will be the means through which I will bring them together from all sides and with which I will form my invincible army.

Remain ever in my Heart, and trust in me, O my son!"

August 29, 1973

PREFACE

THE MARIAN MOVEMENT OF PRIESTS

PART ONE
ORIGIN—SPREAD—SPIRITUALITY

ORIGIN

On the 8th of May, 1972, Don Stefano Gobbi was taking part in a pilgrimage to Fatima and was praying in the little Chapel of the Apparitions for some priests who, besides having personally given up their own vocations, were attempting to form themselves into associations in rebellion against the Church's authority.

An interior force urged him to have confidence in the Immaculate Heart of Mary. Our Lady, making use of him as a poor and humble instrument, would gather all those priests who would accept her invitation to consecrate themselves to her Immaculate Heart, to be strongly united to the Pope and to the Church united with him, and to bring the faithful into the secure refuge of her motherly Heart.

Thus a powerful cohort would be formed, spread throughout every part of the world and gathered together, not with human means of propaganda but with the supernatural power which springs from silence, from prayer, from suffering and from constant faithfulness to one's duties.

Don Stefano asked Our Lady interiorly for a little sign of confirmation. She gave it to him promptly, before the end of that same month, at the Shrine of the Annunciation in Nazareth.

The origin of the Marian Movement of Priests stems from this simple and interior inspiration which Don Stefano received in prayer at Fatima.

Concretely, what was he to do? In October of the same year, a timid attempt was made, by way of a gathering of three priests, for prayer and fraternal sharing, in the Parish of Gera Lario (Como); a notice of the Movement was given in some papers and Catholic reviews.

By March 1973, the number of priests inscribed was about forty. In September of the same year, at San Vittorino, near Rome, the first national gathering took place, with twenty-five priests taking part, out of the eighty already enrolled.

Beginning in 1974, the first cenacles of prayer and fraternal sharing among priests and faithful took place. These gradually spread throughout Europe and every part of the world.

By the end of 1985, Don Stefano Gobbi had already many times visited the five continents to preside at the Regional Cenacles, involving a good 350 air flights and numerous journeys by car and train. He has conducted 890 cenacles, of which 482 took place in Europe, 180 in America, 97 in Africa, 51 in Asia and 80 in Oceania.

This gives evidence of how the Movement has, throughout these years, spread everywhere in an astounding way.

SPREAD

The Marian Movement of Priests has succeeded in expanding in a silent and extraordinary way. In practically all the countries of Europe, America, Asia, Africa and Oceania, national directors have at this time been appointed and entrusted with the task of gathering the membership and assisting in the formation of cenacles.

To them has been entrusted the task of appointing the various regional and diocesan directors, taking every care that all be carried out with greatest fidelity to the spirit of the Movement.

In view of the autonomy which is given to each of the national centers, it is difficult to give a precise numerical picture of the M.M.P. But this is not of great importance, as there is question of a "spirit" which escapes external controls and which becomes a reality in the measure in which each priest, who belongs to it, seeks to live daily his consecration to Mary.

If one were to judge from the letters of inscription, members would now number about three hundred bishops and more than sixty thousand priests, coming both from the diocesan clergy and from all the orders and religious congregations. As to the laity, since there is no formal inscription we cannot give even an approximate figure, although they certainly number in the millions.

Moreover, it is consoling to note the existence of a large segment of priests who are sympathetic; although they have not yet been inscribed in the Movement, they demonstrate their solidarity with it in various ways and on various occasions. I believe they are more numerous than those who have been actually inscribed. If they live the spirit of the Movement, though they are not registered, they are already doing what is essential.

Although, almost imperceptively, we have become a numerous company, it still happens that many priests do not know their confreres who live quite close to them and are also members of the Movement. This happens in areas where the M.M.P. is just beginning, but it also happens in some other places. The reasons for this are the scanty organization we make use of—and this will remain one of our traits— and secondly, a certain reserve (given that we are concerned with a spiritual choice and a commitment that is mainly interior) which makes us unwilling to hand over lists and addresses to just anyone who asks for them.

And yet, we are everywhere witnessing the following astounding phenomenon: Our Lady is seeing to it that, through cenacles of prayer and brotherhood, her priests get to know one another, help one another, love one another as brothers and become a cohesive force throughout the entire clergy.

Through the consoling reality of the communion of saints, those priests who have already preceded us into eternal life seem still active members and closer to us than ever. Among them are some cardinals (the first of whom to enroll was Cardinal Giacomo Lercaro, then Archbishop of Bologna), many bishops (we recall, among others, Bishop Joao Venancio Pereira, formerly Bishop of Leiria and Fatima, who enrolled in 1973 and died in 1985) and now more than five thousand priests who enriched their last years of intense apostolate or of sickness by accepting Our Lady's invitation and by living it in the M.M.P. Of these, it is good to recall a Servant of God, Father Gabriele Allegra, a well-known biblical scholar and translator of the Holy Scriptures into Chinese, whose last work was a translation into Chinese of "To the Priests, Our Lady's Beloved Sons."

In its wide and rapid spread, the M.M.P. has encountered fewer difficulties than one would have feared. As its characteristic is fidelity to the Church and obedience to legitimate superiors, where these (especially at the episcopal level) have shown themselves sympathetic and encouraging, things have proceeded with greater facility. On the other hand, it has been a question of exercising patience in knowing how to wait, in those situations where Authority has been undecided or indifferent.

We are constantly aware of the watchful and enlightening presence of Our Lady, above all as she guides "her" Movement: she comforts in difficulties and keeps enthusiasms on course; she teaches how to assume with courage the liberty of the children of God, while at the same time preventing from taking positions not in accordance with, or in outright rebellion to, superiors—a thing which is obviously in flat contradiction to the second fundamental principle of the Marian Movement of Priests: love for the Pope and the hierarchy united with him.

SPIRITUALITY

(a) What the Marian Movement of Priests Is

The M.M.P. is a little seed planted by Our Lady in the garden of the Church. Very quickly it has become a great tree which has spread its branches into every part of the world. It is a work of love which the Immaculate Heart of Mary is stirring up in the Church today, to help all her children to live, with trust and filial hope, the painful moments of the purification.

In these times of grave danger, the Mother of God and of the Church is taking action, without hesitation or uncertainty, to assist first and foremost the priests, who are the sons of her maternal predilection.

Quite naturally, this work makes use of certain instruments; and in a particular way Don Stefano Gobbi has been chosen. Why? In one passage of the book, the following explanation is given: "I have chosen you because you are the least apt instrument; thus no one will say that this is your work. The Marian Movement of Priests must be my work alone. Through your weakness I will manifest my strength; through your nothingness I will manifest my power." (July 16, 1973)

The M.M.P. is not therefore just a laudable association with a lot of statutes and directors, set in motion by some fervent priest or soul, but a "spirit," as our Holy Father John Paul II happily and intuitively perceived. It is something impalpable, but very strong and very much alive, as are the gifts of God, and it has as its main purpose the living out of the consecration to the Immaculate Heart of Mary. For priests, to entrust themselves to Mary is to become more aware of their own consecration, made to God, on the day of their baptism and their priestly ordination.

The M.M.P. becomes a reality not by numbers, or the resonance of names, or the efficiency of organization, but in the measure that one listens to Our Lady and cooperates with the work of the Holy Spirit, to the glory of the Most Holy Trinity.

He belongs to the spirit of the Movement who, whether inscribed or not, consecrates himself to the Immaculate Heart of Mary, seeking to live accordingly and to carry on his work in obedience to, and for the good of, the Church and who helps the faithful in living their entrustment to Our Lady.

It is a Movement open to all priests, diocesan or religious, without distinction of age or office..There are priests inscribed in it who are happy in their work and filled with zeal, and there are some who are embittered because of negative experiences either in their personal lives or in the apostolate.

The heart of Our Lady is open to all her sons; her arms gather and bring together her priests without distinction or partiality. The choice of predilection is not one made on the part of Our Lady, who addresses herself resolutely to everyone: "Whatever I communicate to you, my son, does not belong to you alone, but it is for all my priest-sons, whom I love with predilection." (August 29, 1973) The choice is made on the part of those who voluntarily accept the motherly invitation.

Whoever wishes to join the Movement and be kept informed of its activities, may send in writing his declaration of membership to the proper national or regional center or, if these do not yet exist, he may send his request to Italy to the:

Movimento Sacerdotale Mariano
Via Terruggia, 14
20.162 Milano, Italy

However, this enrollment means nothing if interior adherence is lacking. And this is all the more true of a willingness to live, and to bring others to live, the consecration to Our Lady.

It is well to remember that Our Lady is speaking not only to those who are enrolled in the Marian Movement of Priests, when she speaks to her beloved sons, but to all those bishops and priests who have entrusted themselves to her and who strive to live as her consecrated ones.

This pledge of total consecration to the Immaculate Heart of Mary gives priests a profound sense of trust and serenity. To believe, in each and every concrete situation, that Our Lady is always near, anxious to help us as much and even more than any mother, gives a feeling of security, even amid the personal sufferings and uncertainties of the days in which we live.

And so, we arrive at the very core of the evangelical message, that is, trust in the providence of God, which brings us to accept every circumstance of life with the filial confidence of little children who abandon themselves completely to his fatherly love.

Thus, the past is left to the infinite mercy of the Heart of Jesus; the future is awaited as a gift from Providence, coming to us through the hands of the Mediatrix of all Graces; and the present is lived with joyous zeal, like children playing or working under the eyes of their mother.

(b) The Characteristic Commitments of Its Spirituality

There are three commitments which characterize the spirituality of the Marian Movement of Priests: consecration to the Immaculate Heart of Mary, unity with the Pope and with the Church united to him, and the leading of the faithful to a life of entrustment to Our Lady.

The pages which illustrate the spirituality of the Movement are taken from Circulars 21, 23, and 24 of Don Stefano Gobbi.

-1- *Consecration to the Immaculate Heart of Mary*

We are living in difficult, insecure and painful times. Today the Red Dragon is ruling in the world and has succeeded in building up an atheistic civilization. Man, puffed up by technical and scientific progress, has put himself in the place of God and has built up a new secular civilization. This radical rejection of God is the real chastisement of modern-day society.

As God is the Savior and Jesus Christ alone the Redeemer of man, humanity of today can only be saved on the condition that it returns to the Lord. Otherwise it runs the danger of destroying itself by its own hands.

But how can it be saved if it obstinately continues to reject God who alone can lead it to salvation? It is here that Mary's role, in view of her motherhood, enters in. Mary is the Mother of Jesus and has been constituted by Jesus as the true Mother of all men. And therefore Mary is also Mother of the men of today, of this rebellious humanity, so far away from God.

Her motherly task is that of saving it. And Our Lady, in order to be able to save it, wishes to become the way of its return to the Lord. She acts in all manner of ways and gives herself much to do in order to bring about this return. This is the reason for her many extraordinary manifestations, which have become so numerous today: she wants to make us understand that our heavenly Mother is present and is at work in the midst of her children.

She wishes to act in person, but not directly. She is able to act through those children who consecrate themselves to her Immaculate Heart, who entrust themselves to her completely, in such a way that she can live and manifest herself in them. She wants above all to work through the priests, because they are her sons of predilection.

It is typical of the spirituality of the M.M.P. not to formulate a doctrine of the consecration which is, in any case, already known in the Church, but to suggest that one learn it by the experience of everyday life. For this purpose, it sets out an itinerary which leads to the perfection of entrustment to Our Lady and which develops through four successive stages: that of accustoming oneself to living with Mary, of allowing oneself to be interiorly transformed by her, of entering with her into a communion of hearts, and lastly of reliving Mary.

The consecration to Our Lady (which is demanded as the first commitment for belonging to the M.M.P.) is therefore the path which leads to a specific goal, that of allowing Mary to live and work in us. "I want to love with your heart, to gaze with your eyes, to console and encourage with your lips, to assist with your hands, to walk with your feet, to follow your bloodied footprints and to suffer with your crucified body." (July 1, 1981)

Now we can understand why Our Lady asks for consecration to the Immaculate Heart for anyone who wishes to belong to her cohort. She herself wants to live and act in her consecrated children, in such a way that they become an expression of her sorrow and of her motherly love, and work untiringly to lead all men back to God.

Thus present-day humanity will be able to reach salvation along the road of the motherly love of Mary, who becomes the channel through which the merciful love of Jesus can reach all people. The consecration to the Immaculate Heart of Mary is directed solely to the consecration of the world, that is to say to the complete return of the world to the perfect glorification of the Lord.

From this we can also understand why Pope John Paul II sees, in the act of consecration or entrustment to the Immaculate Heart of Mary, the most efficacious means of obtaining the gift of divine mercy upon the Church and upon all humanity. *(Dives in Misericordia, 15)*

Thus light is also shed upon the profound significance of that act, often criticized by some, which he frequently repeats with fervor and intimate joy of soul; the act, that is, of his personal consecration to Mary. We understand, then, what he is doing in every part of the world when, during his frequent apostolic pilgrimages, he goes to the most famous shrines in order to consecrate to the Immaculate Heart of Mary the local Church in which he finds himself.

The profound reason is that the Pope sees, in the consecration to the Immaculate Heart of Mary, the most powerful means of obtaining the precious gift of the merciful love of Jesus upon the world of today!

" . . . Oh, *how deeply we feel the need of consecration* for humanity and for the world: for the contemporary world! . . . *Oh, how painful* therefore is everything which, in the Church and in each one of us, is opposed to holiness and consecration! . . . Blessed be all those souls who obey the call of eternal Love. Blessed be those who, day by day, with unexhausted generosity, welcome your invitation, O Mother, to do what your Jesus says, and give to the Church and the world a serene witness of a life inspired by the Gospel." (Consecration to the Immaculate Heart of Mary by John Paul II, made on March 25, 1984)

-2- *Unity with the Pope and with the Church United to Him*

The Church is both divine and human, and in its human dimension, it is fragile and sinful and thus has great need to do penance. The Church is the light of the world, *"Lumen Gentium,"* but often the evils of the world in which it lives become the maladies which attack the human dimension of the Church. This has been proven by nearly two thousand years of its history.

Today the Church is living in a world which has built up a new secular civilization. The spirit of this world, or secularism, which has entered into its interior, has caused the state of great suffering and of crisis in which the Church finds itself. This is the famous "smoke of Satan" spoken of by Pope

Paul VI of venerable memory.

Secularism, at the intellectual level, becomes "rationalism" and, at the level of life, it becomes "naturalism."

Because of rationalism, there is today the tendency to interpret the whole mystery of God and the deposit of revealed truth in a purely human way, and thus often the fundamental dogmas of the faith are denied and most serious errors are spread about in a hidden and ambiguous way. Sometimes these errors become taught even in Catholic schools and little or nothing survives of Divine Scripture or even the Gospel of Jesus.

"You have made a gospel of your own with your own words." (September 25, 1976)

Because of naturalism, there is the practice today of giving great value to one's own personal actions, to efficiency and to the setting up of programs in the apostolic sector, forgetting the primary value of divine grace and that the interior life of union with Christ, that is of prayer, must be the soul of every apostolate.

From this originates the gradual loss of the awareness of sin as an evil and the neglect of the sacrament of Reconciliation, which has now spread throughout the whole Church.

Against these errors, which are ensnaring the integrity of the faith in a subtle and dangerous way, Cardinal Joseph Ratzinger, Prefect of the Sacred Congregation for the Doctrine of the Faith, has spoken out clearly with his famous interview, published in the book, "The Ratzinger Report."

But the Magisterium of the Pope has also frequently spoken out powerfully and insistently.

So then, one spontaneously asks oneself: how is it that the Church has not yet emerged from this profound crisis of its faith? The persistence of the crisis within the Church up to the present time comes only from its interior disunity. Because of this, not everyone today is listening to and following what the Pope, together with his Magisterium, is pointing out.

Our Lady has obtained for the Church a great Pope, consecrated to her Immaculate Heart and whom she herself is leading along all the roads of the world, in order to spread the light of Christ and of his Gospel of salvation and to strengthen everyone in the faith, both pastors and the flocks entrusted to them. But, about the Pope, there is often a great void: his Magisterium is not supported by the whole Church and often his word falls upon a desert.

And yet the renewal of the Church takes place only through its interior unity. The road to be followed is still that of full union of all the bishops, priests, and faithful with the Pope.

Here we find explained the profound reason for the second commitment of the Marian Movement of Priests. Our Lady is asking of us today to be an example to everyone in this unity. An example in loving the Pope, in praying and suffering for him, in heeding and spreading the teachings of his Magisterium, and especially in always obeying him in everything.

Our Lady desires that there be a return among the clergy to the humble and powerful exercise of the virtue of obedience!

Naturally obedience to the Pope, who is the point of reference and of unity with the bishops, implies the unity of obedience with the pastor of one's own diocese and with one's own superiors.

-3- Leading the Faithful to Entrustment to Our Lady

From the very beginning of this Movement there was an awareness that the religious and faithful were being called to take part in it. In fact, the third commitment on the part of a priest of the M.M.P. is that of leading the faithful, entrusted to his pastoral care, to consecration to the Immaculate Heart of Mary.

"But these priests must now begin to act; through them I want to return to the midst of my faithful, because it is with them, gathered about my priests, that I want to form my invincible cohort." (November 1, 1973)

This explains why the M.M.P., which sprang up in the first place for priests, opens out also upon the vast world of the laity, thus giving rise to the Marian Movement.

(c) The Marian Movement

The Marian Movement is made up of all those non-clerical religious and of the faithful who have committed themselves to live a life of consecration to the Immaculate Heart of Mary, in serene union with their priests and their bishops. They are not bound together by any kind of juridical bond and can freely carry on their work within those ecclesiastical associations to which they belong.

As members of the Marian Movement, they commit themselves to the experience of a life totally entrusted to Our Lady, that they may be assisted by her to remain faithful to their own baptismal consecration and to become witnesses of communion and unity, constantly striving for conversion through prayer and penance.

-1- *Living Their Baptism*

In the act of consecration for the members of the Marian Movement, set out at the end of the book, we read: "By this act of consecration we intend to live, with you and through you, all the obligations assumed by our baptismal consecration." These words bring out clearly how a member of the faithful, who makes the consecration to the Immaculate Heart, is assisted by Our Lady especially in living out today the obligations assumed at the time of baptism. It is natural that, in these times, the Christian, immersed in a world which is so secularized, finds it very difficult to live out his baptismal consecration.

Baptism brings about a radical transformation: it communicates grace and divine life itself and makes us into the image of Jesus Christ, whose brothers we become and whose life we must relive in our own.

At the present time, through all the means of social communication, the Christian is easily made use of and even manipulated by the world in which he lives in such a way that often, almost without noticing it, he absorbs and shares the values which are opposed to those taught by Christ.

Thus today how many baptized persons there are who, in their everyday life, come to betray their baptismal consecration! And so Our Lady asks that the faithful consecrate themselves to her Immaculate Heart, as a specific commitment of the Marian Movement and then, as a mother, gently leads them to live out their baptism, in complete fidelity to Jesus and to his Church.

-2- *Witnesses of Communion and of Unity*

Again, it is said in the act of consecration of the laity: "We promise you to be united with the Holy Father, with the hierarchy and with our priests, in order thus to set up a barrier to the growing confrontation directed against the Magisterium, that threatens the very foundation of the Church."

This is a characteristic commitment, which marks every member of the faithful who belongs to the Movement, and urges him to become ever an instrument of communion, of peace and of unity.

In this period of its purification, the Church is living through times of grea suffering. The M.M.P. desires above all to share fully in the sufferings of the Church, drinking together with her the chalice of much bitterness. For this reason it is never called to act by way of criticism or judgment and, much less, by way of condemnation. And therefore, it has nothing to do with, and in fact totally rejects, those means taken by many today who publicly, even through the press, criticize Holy Mother Church in a bitter and mischievous way.

We must never pour vinegar on open and bleeding wounds. The only help the Movement wants to give to the Church is that of love, a filial and merciful love.

"I will bring you to love the Church very much. Today the Church is going through times of great suffering because it is loved less and less by its own children. Many would like to renovate it and purify it solely by criticism and by violent attacks on its institution. Nothing is ever renewed or purified without love!" (November 9, 1975)

The specific commitment of the Marian Movement consists in leading the faithful to be witnesses of love for the Church today: a love which must become concrete in a faithful and passionate presence, to share in its sorrow and bear with it its great cross; a love which above all brings us to be, in every circumstance, instruments of coherence and of unity, and thus to contribute to healing the Church of its many deep and painful lacerations.

-3- Commitment to Conversion

In the act of consecration for the laity, it is further affirmed: "We pledge to bring about in ourselves that interior conversion so urgently demanded by the Gospel." Our Lady asks of the faithful also, who belong to the Movement, a daily commitment to conversion along the road of prayer and penance.

For this, as an attentive and concerned mother, she helps them flee from sin, to live in the grace of God, invites them to frequent confession, to an intense Eucharistic life, to always observe the Law of God, with a particular commitment to live the virtue of purity especially on the part of young people and those who are engaged to marry, and conjugal chastity within the sacrament of Matrimony, according to the doctrine of Christ, recently reaffirmed by the Magisterium of the Church. And this becomes so necessary in our day in order to counteract a shameless impurity which has spread everywhere and in order to help make the world cleaner and more beautiful.

Let the faithful be a good example "...by an austere manner of life, by repudiating styles which are ever increasingly provocative and indecent, by opposing in every way possible the spread of immoral literature and entertainment and this continual flooding from a sea of filth that is submerging everything. Let them be an example to all by their purity, their sobriety and their modesty. Let them flee all those places where the sacred character of their person is defiled. Let them form about the priests my faithful cohort, my great 'White Army.' " (November 1, 1973)

There are now tens of millions of lay people from every part of the world who have joined the Marian Movement, and often it is from them that the priests receive good example, concrete assistance and precious encouragement.

(d) The Cenacles

It can be said that the M.M.P. is at work in all the areas of ecclesial life in which its members find themselves personally engaged: from religious houses to parishes, from the theological sector to the pastoral, and from the field of spirituality to the apostolate of the missions. The more a priest lives the spirit of the Movement, the more he commits himself enthusiastically to the initiatives of the Church and makes them his own. But at times the Movement develops within the life of the Church, with an activity proper to itself, which is that of bringing the priests and the faithful together in gatherings of prayer and fraternal sharing, called "cenacles."

-1- Regional, Diocesan and Family Cenacles

Regional and diocesan cenacles always develop in union with the bishop of the place who either takes part personally or, at times, gives his assent and blessing. These cenacles offer an enviable opportunity of experiencing, in a concrete way, prayer offered together and genuine fraternity, and are a great help to all in overcoming doubts and difficulties in order to continue with courage along the arduous road of consecration.

From among those priests who have taken on the task of bringing their confreres together, directors of the Movement have been selected at the national, regional, and diocesan level. From the directors of each country, very comforting accounts have been received. In these we find assurance that the cenacles have continued to develop increasingly.

Family cenacles are today particularly providential, in view of the serious break-up of family life. In these, one or more families of the Movement gather together in the same house. The rosary is recited. There is a meditation on the life of consecration. Also there is fraternal sharing during which mutual problems and difficulties are discussed. There is always, made as a group, the renewal of the act of entrustment to the Immaculate Heart of Mary. It has already become evident that Christian families have been helped by these family cenacles to live today as true communities of faith, prayer and love.

-2- The Structure of the Cenacles

The structure of the cenacles is quite simple. In imitation of the disciples who were gathered together with Mary in the Cenacle of Jerusalem, we come together:

- To Pray with Mary

The cenacles must, above all, be gatherings of prayer. But this prayer must be made together with Mary.

It is for this reason that one of the characteristics that is common to all the cenacles is the recitation of the holy rosary. Through it we invite Our Lady to join us in our prayer; we pray together with her, while she herself unveils to our souls the mystery of the life of Jesus.

"Your entire rosary, which you recite in the Cenacle in accordance with the urgent request of your Mother, is like an immense chain of love and salvation with which you are able to encircle persons and situations, and even to influence all the events of your time. Continue to recite it, and multiply your cenacles of prayer..." (October 7, 1979)

During the cenacles, we should help each other to live the consecration to the Immaculate Heart of Mary. This is the way we should do it: by accustoming ourselves to Our Lady's way of seeing, feeling, loving, praying and working. The pause for meditation which is made during the cenacles must serve this purpose. There are other times and places for reflections concerning *aggiornamento* which are likewise indispensable for all.

Usually this space of time is given over to a communal meditation from the book of the Movement. It is not therefore within the spirit of the Cenacle to spend this time listening to learned conferences or cultural updatings. Otherwise we would run the risk of getting away from that atmosphere of simplicity and of familiarity, which makes our gatherings so fruitful.

- To Create Fraternity

Lastly, in the cenacles we are all called to take part in the experience of a true fraternity. Is this not perhaps one of the most beautiful experiences, which always occurs in every Cenacle? The more we pray and allow time for the action of Our Lady, the more we experience as well an increase of mutual love among ourselves.

"Why do I want them to come together in cenacles with me?...To love each other and to live in true brotherhood in the company of their Mother. It is necessary today that my priests know each other, that they help each other, that they truly love one another, that they be as brothers brought together by their Mother. There is today too much loneliness, too much abandonment for my priests!... I do not want them to be alone: they must help each other, love each other, they must feel as—and really be—brothers." (January 17, 1974)

To the danger of loneliness, today particularly felt and dangerous for priests, here is the remedy offered by Our Lady: the Cenacle, where we gather together with her to get to know, love and help each other as brothers.

(e) A Help for the Church

At the end of this first part of the preface in which we have sought above all to explain the origin, spread, and spirituality of the Marian Movement of Priests, we ask ourselves naturally this question: But what significance has this Movement in the Church today? Among the very many associations which are at work at every level, what is its function in the life of the Church? To this question it seems to me that I should give this simple response: the M.M.P. is a help which our heavenly Mother is offering to the Church today, that it may become aware of her motherly presence, be consoled in the midst of great sufferings, and feel itself ever surrounded by the love and prayer of so many of its children.

By means of the M.M.P., Our Lady wishes to offer to the Church a strong help in overcoming the painful crisis of the purification through which it is living at this time. Because of this crisis, it can be seen that religious orders and congregations, once flourishing, are now going through times of particular difficulty.

Through her work, Our Lady wishes to assist everyone to overcome with her the present moments of suffering and, therefore, invites first the priests and then the religious and faithful to consecrate themselves to her Immaculate Heart and to be most faithful to the Pope and to the Church. The reason why the Movement does not have any juridical existence is that the aforementioned assistance can more easily be accepted by everyone. In this there lies its weakness because, not having any juridical form, it finds itself unable to seek any official approbation which could help it on its way. But this is also its strength because, as it does not impose any associative bond, it makes it easy for priests and religious to belong to it.

If we compare the Church to a great tree, I would say that the role of the M.M.P. is not to add another branch to the many which it already has, but that of infusing it with a secret strength which, coming from the Immaculate Heart of Mary, spreads through all its branches. And thus each one is assisted to develop according to its proper function and particular form, imparting to all a greater strength and beauty.

If then one wishes to know which is the most striking quality of the Marian Movement of Priests, it seems to me that I would have to say: *its essential poverty.* The Movement is so poor that it does not even have an official existence. And, not having any existence, quite naturally it cannot in any way be catalogued. Sometimes we smilingly say among ourselves: we are now more than sixty thousand priests and tens of millions of faithful, who belong to the Marian Movement of Priests, but nowhere can one find the proof that we exist.

The Movement is so poor that it cannot even own its own material resources, nor is it able to accept legacies or goods. It lives only from offerings sent to it by Divine Providence to meet the heavy expenses of printing and distributing the books. But even in this matter, each national center manages its affairs autonomously in regard to the life of the Movement, according to the means which Divine Providence places at its disposal.

The Movement is poor in terms of human support, even in those things which could bring it comfort and joy in the midst of the inevitable difficulties which it encounters. Such could be particular recommendations on the part of superiors, praise and encouragement from ecclesiastical authority, and various other such marks of approval.

The sure support which Our Lady wishes to give us is her Immaculate Heart, and the only letter of recommendation is that which is to be found written in the life of each priest who has been consecrated to her, that he may thus be assisted in attaining holiness.

This radical poverty of the Marian Movement of Priests *must be loved, blessed and lived by each one of us,* because it is the poverty of Mary herself which is reflected in her work. It is the poverty of the Queen of Heaven who hides herself beneath the clothing of a simple housewife. It is the poverty of our Mother, immaculate and completely full of grace, which is revealed in her so simple and normal way of living in the perfect service of her spouse, Joseph, and her divine Son, Jesus.

The poverty of Mary should always be reflected in this work of hers, because the Marian Movement of Priests must also exist, spread and work *only at the service of—and as a perfect service of love for—the Church.* This is why the Movement must not even have an existence of its own: it can only live within the life of the Church and at the service of the Church.

In this way, the Church can be truly helped to carry its great cross in these bloody moments of its purification. And it is supported in its journey toward its greatest splendor, by the light which the Immaculate Heart gives to it by means of so many of her beloved children.

"Through you who have responded, my light spreads ever more in the Church. And thus the Church takes on vigor, confidence and a new impetus in the evangelization and salvation of all nations." (November 14, 1980)

PART TWO
THEOLOGICAL CRITERIA
FOR AN UNDERSTANDING OF THE BOOK

Some people are under the impression that the Marian Movement of Priests is identified with the book, "To the Priests, Our Lady's Beloved Sons." That is to say, the Movement and the book are one and the same thing. This is erroneous. The fact is, the M.M.P. is distinct from the book.

The Movement is a work of Our Lady, and it consists essentially in calling priests to a consecration to her Immaculate Heart, to a great unity with the Pope and with the Church and to directing the faithful to a renewed Marian devotion.

As can easily be seen, it is a simple matter to set out the points which characterize the Movement, and so when one lives according to them he actually belongs to the Movement even though, hypothetically, he may never have heard of the little book. In this sense, the Marian Movement of Priests is distinct from the book.

But when one begins seriously to live out these commitments, one naturally feels the necessity to ask the question: How must I live them? Who will give me the assurance that I am living them? What is the road that I must travel? The book gives the answers to these questions, because it traces out the itinerary which one must follow in order to live out in a concrete way the consecration to the Immaculate Heart of Mary.

Can then the M.M.P. do without the book? In theory, yes, but in practice, absolutely no. The Movement is the work of Our Lady, and she herself has chosen the book as an indispensable instrument for its diffusion and for a genuine understanding of its spirit.

"Even the little book is only a means for the spread of my Movement. It is an important means which I have chosen because it is small. It will serve to make known to many this work of my love among the priests." June 24, 1974)

At this point it seems useful to me to pause a bit in order to explain the origin and the literary form of the book, its merits and limitations and, above all, to trace out some criteria of sound theology which are necessary for its exact understanding. In this inquiry we have made use of the considerable help provided by Circulars 16 and 18 of Don Stefano Gobbi and in particular by the introduction to the previous edition.

(a) Origin and Form of the Book

Starting in July 1973, Don Stefano began to note down some limpid and strong thoughts which sprang up in his soul. In obedience to his spiritual director, he undertook to gather them together in a little book, which numbered but a few pages, and thus he managed to prepare the first edition which was presented at a gathering of priests of the Movement, which took place at the end of September of that same year. Its reception on that occasion was rather negative. Why such a rejection, despite the fact that its contents could be deemed to be in perfect conformity with what was perceived, in prayer and in discussions, to be the way of the Marian Movement of Priests? For the same reasons many find it difficult to accept the book today.

—First of all, because it lacked ecclesiastical approval. Such an approval had not been requested, as there was question then of a small publication in non-commercial manuscript form, and because writings of this nature are exempt in virtue of the *"mote proprio"* of Pope Paul VI, dated October 10, 1966.

—And then, because of the literary form in which it was presented. In fact, it provided the Movement with spiritual guidance as traced out by Our Lady herself, through the mystical phenomenon called "interior locutions," and it is with this aspect that priests are usually uncomfortable.

—And especially because, with so many messages circulating about today (of which it is permissible to think that some are pathological in origin and others of doubtful authenticity), it was feared that, by presenting a book of this nature, one would find it exposed to insurmountable obstacles and grave difficulties along the way, especially on the part of ecclesiastical authorities.

This hesitation was however gradually overcome by a great and ever-increasing acceptance of the book on the part of priests, religious and faithful and by the multiplication of translations everywhere into the principal known languages.

Everyone became aware, at first with a certain amount of surprise and then with a profound joy of soul, that it was a very small and limited means, but one chosen by Our Lady, for the spread of the Movement throughout every part of the world. The book in fact is an instrument, humanly speaking quite limited, of which our heavenly Mother has willed to make use in order to draw to herself priests and the faithful entrusted to their care. Once attracted to her motherly Heart, priests and faithful will be brought by her into the intimacy of the Heart of Jesus, to live in the heart of the Church, his Mystical Body.

If one takes up this book with respect and meditates upon it with simplicity of heart, he will become aware of hearing a living word, sweet as honey and sharp as a sword. In it is set forth a spirituality based on Revelation and the life of the Church, by means of such luminous pillars as Saint John the Evangelist, Saint Francis of Assisi, Saint Francis de Sales, Saint Louis de Montfort, Saint John Bosco, Saint Therese of Lisieux and Saint Maximilian Kolbe. We can verify its validity only if we put it into practice; from its fruits you will know the quality of the tree.

The book is not organized into well-defined and connected chapters. This is because the Marian Movement of Priests itself is understood more clearly in its demands and richness little by little as Our Lady makes it known through the writings of Don Stefano Gobbi. She herself is defining, spreading, and establishing the M.M.P., now in every part of the world, in a manner which is as discreet as it is magnificent.

(b) Merits and Limitations of the Book

The merits and limitations of the book come from the fact that it is a simple but precious instrument for the Marian Movement of Priests.

-1- *It Is a Precious Means for Its Spread.*

The M.M.P. has now spread into every region, and it has always reached there by means of the book. It has been spontaneously translated into the principal languages and has thus been able to offer priests the possibility of knowing the urgent invitation of Our Lady to consecrate themselves to her Immaculate Heart.

From all the continents, priests, drawn by Mary's motherly invitation, have responded by joining the Movement, have entrusted themselves to her, and have begun to gather together in cenacles. In this way, the work of Our Lady has succeeded in spreading everywhere and has reached even the most distant and remote parts of the earth. Whenever Don Stefano goes to even the most unknown parts of the world to take part in cenacles, he has the happy surprise of finding the Movement already spread there and thus cannot but recognize that the means of such a diffusion has always been the book. The book therefore serves, in a marvelous way, the purpose of making the Marian Movement of Priests known everywhere.

-2- It Is a Precious Means of Understanding Its Spirit

Meditation on the contents of the book often brings about a true transformation in souls. It helps one live the spirit of the consecration and sometimes gives priests the impression that it has responded to their particular needs. It encourages them to overcome difficult circumstances and leads them gradually to do everything with Mary, by means of Mary, and in Mary.

Thousands of letters of enrollment, sent in by priests to the various national centers, attest to this fact. I cite by way of confirmation some excerpts from three letters which I have received from priests.

From an Italian priest: "I have your book, which was made known to me by my bishop, now deceased. He read the book regularly and had it always in his hand. When his eyes became weak, I had the duty of reading him a few pages. They delighted him and helped greatly to bolster up his spirit. He found in them a source of joy and fervor."

From a missionary in Brazil: "My fear is that of coming to a halt, and this for a number of reasons. These can be described in brief as those simple temptations which, in one way or another, are my daily food. But then, after meditating on the contents of the book, I renew my act of abandonment to the Immaculate Heart of Mary and, little by little, my confidence is reborn. How I would like to live the awareness of being Mary's very own property."

From a country in Central America: "I am a priest who was laicized fourteen years ago. Having been swept away by a grave crisis in faith and in my moral life, I no longer prayed. I am a professor in a large university. Your book came into my hands but for many months I did not read it, thinking it to be an ordinary run-of-the-mill book of Marian devotion.

But I finally felt a desire to open the book, which I had not until then touched. I don't know what happened inside of me. From the first page, there was awakened in me a growing desire to read more and more, an eagerness and a renewed love for Jesus and for his Church. I then remembered something that I had learned in the seminary: to Jesus through Mary. I prepared myself all through the month of November and, on the eighth of December, I made my act of consecration to the Immaculate Heart."

The undeniable merits of the book consist, therefore, in the contributions it succeeds in making to the spread and the understanding of the spirit of the Marian Movement of Priests.

-3- The Limitations of the Book

The limitations of the book are obvious and can be summed up in the fact that it is an undeniably humble and small instrument. Its poverty and littleness can be seen in a number of ways.

First of all in its form: it is presented to us in fact under the form of interior locutions, and this can be for many a stumbling block to its acceptance. But for whom? Generally speaking, for those who tend to reject any form of supernatural intervention, because they accept only that which passes through their own rational judgment. Such moreover can be persons who are good, well-trained and cultured but who have a mentality which is too adult and thus they stop short, scandalized, before the extreme littleness of this instrument.

It is also in its content that its littleness stands out. Indeed the book is not a treatise in either theology or Mariology, nor does it set itself forth as a complete compendium of Marian devotion. And neither does it develop, in a systematic way, the biblical and theological reasons which favor the spiritual experience of consecration to Mary. And these are, however, of considerable weight and value as is proven in de Montfort's *Treatise on True Devotion.*

It sets out, in extremely simple language, that which our heavenly Mother desires today of her beloved sons, the priests. It is a matter of pages chosen from a diary, the content of which however is in accord with revealed doctrine and the teaching of the Church. It has the flavor of a colloquy between a mother and her children, in a style which, on first contact with the book, may appear to be too saccharine in some instances and too harsh in others. Some themes come back again and again with the insistence of a hammer, while others are almost ignored.

We do not have before our eyes a work which has been composed at a writing table and which develops according to a prearranged scenario. In order that disappointment may not lead to the rejection of the book, we should keep in mind that everything that each priest should know is necessarily taken for granted. Namely, for his interior life, for his apostolate and for living in communion with the whole Church and the world, the priest must draw upon Revelation and the Magisterium, as well as the sources of sound philosophy, theology, literature, asceticism, and mysticism.

In fact the theological basis of the M.M.P. is constituted by the whole Marian doctrine contained in Sacred Scripture, illustrated by the Fathers of the Church and expounded by the Magisterium of the Church. The book does not seek to be a compendium of this because there already exist within the Church institutions which specialize in this task.

Nothing however is more contrary to the truth than the idea, held by some, that in the Marian Movement of Priests one finds the type of priest who is allergic to sound theological science or is sentimentalist or over credulous. On the contrary, it can be calmly asserted that among those who have enrolled in the Movement there are priests who are outstanding in the area of culture, others who are in positions of great responsibility, and others who are assigned to more humble posts. Each of these has his own qualities and limitations, but all of them are among the most interiorly balanced of people.

A priest in Ireland has made the observation that one finds in the book a compendium of the doctrine of de Montfort concerning consecration, the way of spiritual childhood of Saint Therese of the Child Jesus and the implementation of the message of Fatima. It is for each one to verify this for himself.

It seems to me that one does indeed find here such a synthesis because, in order to live the consecration to Mary, it is necessary to offer oneself to her in a slavery of love which is fulfilled in concrete terms by living as a little child entrusted to her Immaculate Heart in such a way as to allow oneself, with utter docility, to be nourished, clothed and led by her at every moment.

At this point, if at no other, one can ask a very interesting question: Why has Our Lady wished to choose so small and limited an instrument? "You have not understood, my son, that I have chosen foolishness to confound wisdom, and weakness to vanquish strength." (September 27, 1973) The whole secret is right here!

But this is the very secret of the Gospel. Jesus did not condemn the learned and the wise, but He thanked his Heavenly Father for having hidden from them the mysteries of his reign and for having revealed them to the little ones.

Certainly every member of the Marian Movement of Priests has the duty of reading and meditating upon what is contained in the little but precious instrument, which is the book, if he wishes to live his act of consecration to the Immaculate Heart of Mary and thus to contribute to the carrying out of her motherly plan of salvation and of mercy.

(c) Theological Criteria for Its Understanding

The Interior Locution

-1- Leaving to everyone the freedom to hold to his own convictions in this matter, it can be credibly affirmed with considered certainty that what are represented to us in this book are "interior locutions." But alas, mystical theology is too little known so that some phenomena are either under- valued to the point where they are scoffed at, a *priori*, or else they are over-valued to the extent that they are considered on a par with official Revelation.

One forgets that grace makes us true sons of God and that Mary is truly our Mother. One fails to keep sufficiently in mind that prayer is not a monologue but a dialogue, the greater part of which should be left to the heavenly participants. We know that God has infinitely possible ways of communicating with his children, selecting for each one the form that is most adapted to him, over and above the official means known to everyone.

-2-What is an interior locution? First of all, it is necessary to make clear that it is not something strange or sensational, but a mystical phenomenon present in the life of the Church and described in manuals of spiritual theology. It is not a censorial communication with Jesus, Our Lady or the saints such as takes place in authentic apparitions. Here one does not see with the eyes, hear with the ears, nor does one touch anything. Nor is it simply a good inspiration, that light which the Holy Spirit normally causes to pour down into the minds and hearts of those who pray and live by faith.

In the case of an authentic phenomenon, the interior locution is that gift by which God wishes to make something known and to help someone carry something out as well as the outward clothing of this gift, in terms of human thoughts and words, according to the style and the way of writing of the person who receives the message.

The person becomes an instrument of communication, while still maintaining his full freedom, which is expressed in an act of assent to the action of the Holy Spirit. While receiving the word from the Lord, the person's intellect remains, as it were, inactive: that is to say, it does not search for thoughts or for a way to express them as, for example, would be the case when one is writing a letter or preparing a demanding discourse.

-3- Saint John of the Cross calls locutions, or formal supernatural words, those distinct words which the spirit receives not from itself but from another person, sometimes while it is recollected and sometimes when it is not. ("Ascent of Mount Carmel," Book 2, Chapter 28, note 2) Tanquerey defines locutions or supernatural words as manifestations of divine thought heard by the interior or exterior senses. ("The Spiritual Life," Book 3, Chapter 3, No. 1494)

One could therefore give interior locutions this definition: "They are very clear words perceived by the person who receives them as though they were being born from the heart and which, taken together, form a message."

The summons from heaven is almost always unforeseen: it is the Lord, or Our Lady, or the angels, or the saints, who take the initiative as regards the time and the content of the message.

-4-To discern authentic locutions from those that are spurious, or which are the fruit of deliberate deceit, or of morbid autosuggestion, or of downright satanic interference, there are norms which are fairly precise. The literature on this matter is neither rich nor up-to-date. The writings of the great mystics (Saint John of the Cross, Saint Theresa of Avila, Saint Ignatius, Saint Catherine of Genoa, Saint Catherine of Siena) are helpful as are the studies and treatises of spiritual theology of Tanquerey, Royo Marin, A. Poulin, Garrigou-Lagrange, etc.

Less easy to measure is the weight of the human element in which the ineffable Word of God becomes clothed, in order to arrive at a clear understanding of what is essential and universal in the contents of the message, in a word, what is of God.

One hears it said frequently that the messages, such as those contained in the book, are too frequent and wordy. A comparison is made with the style of the Gospel and of the apparitions which have been approved by the Church, while we forget that we are dealing here with manifestations of the Word of God which are very different, not only in the matter of authority but also of modality.

In our respect for each person and his freedom, why should we be obliged to make an exception only for God, as though He must ask permission of us and conform Himself to our tastes in the choice of places, times, modes and instruments for communicating with his children?

There is need to grow in the spirit of wisdom, so as to rejoice with Jesus as He exclaims: "I thank you, O Father, because you have hidden your secrets from the learned and wise, while you have revealed them to little children," and to exult with the spirit of our heavenly Mother as she sings: "The poor He has filled with good things and the rich He has sent away empty-handed."

The Interior Locutions in the Book

In the specific case of the book, "To the Priests, Our Lady's Beloved Sons," it is good to keep in mind these theological criteria which can be of help for a deeper understanding of it.

-1- That which comes from God brings with it a profound sense of peace and inspires greater humility and confidence in our relationship with Him; it helps us detach ourselves from what is wrong and to do good in a spirit of simplicity and constancy; it respects our freedom and that of our neighbor. Whoever writes and works in the name of God edifies by his sense of balance, of humanity, of strength of soul, even within the framework of his human limitations and defects.

If some passage in this book should bring uneasiness, it would be better to put off its reading for a better occasion rather than to cause oneself to become distressed.

-2- God can and wants to communicate, at each moment of history, with his children living on earth. It is possible for us Christians to know whether something we meet up with is truly the work of God by measuring its content with Revelation which is faithfully guarded and infallibly given to us by the Magisterium of the Church.

In our case, the message taken as a whole, and likewise each of its parts, is to be read and lived in the context of Christian doctrine. The purpose of these locutions is that of leading priests, more easily and steadily, to holiness of life, keeping in mind that:

a) The motherhood of Mary, with those rights and duties that follow upon it for her and for me, have to do with me personally.

b) Our Lady, who is the most humble and pure of all creatures, is not an end in herself, but she is a mother who begets and raises her adoptive children, bringing to completion the work accomplished in her Son Jesus. The goal then is solely the glorification of the Most Holy Trinity to which a priest who strives to fulfill his vocation is called.

c) As Mary is Mother of the Church, the historical context of her action and of our response is obedience and flawless unity with those who exercise the ministry of authority in the Church, namely the Pope, our respective bishops and our legitimate superiors.

d) Because the priest is a man dedicated to God for the sake of man, he feels himself duty bound to communicate to his faithful the joy, the richness and the obligations of the consecration to Our Lady which he, in the first place, has made and lived.

–3– While there is no question of age, of human gifts, of prestige and still less of past personal experience, be these positive or negative, in order to be received into the M.M.P., anyone who would want to enter it in a spirit of sectarianism would be totally ignorant of its nature. Within the Church there is an element which remains immutable, and there are exterior forms with which the word and the life of the Church are clothed and which, like clothing, can change with time.

Those who are incurably nostalgic for the times that have gone confuse the ancient, which is always valid, with the old, which can be changed. So also those who search hungrily for new experiences seem to know a little more than the Eternal Father. And they have an urge to solicit initiatives from the Holy Spirit, as though the salvation of each soul did not move along the one single track of prayer and penance.

–4– As the components and the expressions of doctrine and of Christian life are varied and complex, there is no intention, in these writings, of undervaluing, much less of condemning, any of them. If some expressions, for example, about contemporary theology seem strong, it must be understood that the point is not being made against theology as such but against the less than prudent way in which it is presented by some dissenting theologians and—which is still worse—against the way in which their teachings are so readily accepted by others.

Another example: some themes, such as those of a social or pastoral nature, are not treated expressly. For one thing, the book, not being an encyclopedia, cannot give answers to each and every question. And for another, those who truly entrust themselves to Our Lady do not just hold discussions in seats of learning but actually live and resolve concrete pastoral and social problems. We have only to call to mind Don Bosco, Don Orione and the present Pope himself.

-5- As regards the phenomenon of interior locutions recorded in the book, Don Stefano, in a completely normal way, neither in a trance nor in ecstasy, writes without interruption and without mental fatigue, without re-thinking or correction, that which he perceives interiorly, without paying any particular attention to it, according to the richness and the poverty of his own style and temperament, even when it is a question of bringing out truths previously unknown to the subject, or even before they were recognized as such by him.

From the writings of Don Stefano Gobbi, a preferential choice has been given to those pages which bring out best the total entrustment to Our Lady, in an atmosphere of evangelical spiritual childhood. As regards the validity of these writings, the classical and traditional criteria have been adhered to:

—correspondence with revealed truth;
—an enduring attitude of humility and obedience;
—some confirmations, humbly asked of God;
—the subject's calm availability and the peace which precedes and follows the divine communication.

What has been considered, however, as a positive sign is the enormous good which the M.M.P. has already achieved in the souls of tens of thousands of priests, many of whom were in situations of crisis, and the good that has been accomplished among very many of the faithful. From the wonderful fruits that have been produced, it can be deduced that the cause is to be found only in the spiritual light which flows from the Holy Spirit, through the intercession of the Immaculate Heart of Mary, into the minds and hearts of those who take this book into their hands.

-6- Since, in this period of considerable transformation for the Church and for the world, there is a multiplication of cases of persons who are said to be privileged with charismatic gifts such as visions, locutions, the gift of healing, etc., the M.M.P. takes this attitude:

—It does not make any bond of unity with (to the point of identifying itself with) any association, person or fact which takes on supernatural aspects. It recognizes that it has no right either to approve or to condemn because this task falls to the Church. It leaves each priest free to conduct himself, in his own personal life, in the way prudence suggests to him, always however in perfect obedience to ecclesiastical authority.

—When, on the other hand, there is question of revelations which contain doctrine not in conformity with the Magisterium or of persons who clearly depart from what characterizes normal human behavior and Christian balance, it must put its members on guard that they might remain completely faithful to the Church.

—When there is question of persons or events which the Church has been pleased to approve, the M.M.P. respects to the utmost the choices and tastes of each one, even though it cannot prescind from what has taken place at Fatima, which is a fact of universal importance not yet well understood and still less witnessed to, even though it has been officially accepted by the Church. We have only to recall Popes Paul VI and John Paul II, who journeyed as pilgrims to the Cova da Iria.

(d) Useful Advice for the Reader

-1- As is obvious, those who belong to the M.M.P. must accept first of all the entire patrimony of Revelation in the light of the official Magisterium. On the other hand, they are free to accept, or to give no importance to, or to reject writings and happenings which are generically called "private revelations."

Since mystical doctrine and history is little known, it is easy to fall into one of two forms of free and easy fanaticism. One is to preconceivedly deny and ridicule everything from the outset. The other is to accept naively everything without any discernment.

Therefore one must avoid two extremes:

—childish credulity which does not carefully scrutinize the person or the event, in order to verify its credibility on a human plain, let alone on the supernatural. The instruments of God, even in their littleness and poverty, always exhibit a note of dignity and of purity and the signs of the Holy Spirit, which accompany every true apostle are not lacking to them.

—haughty superficiality which rejects or directly opposes that which, on the contrary, might be a work of God. In concrete situations, one loses sight of that which one respects in theory, namely, the absolute freedom of God and of all heaven to communicate with us, pilgrims here on earth.

-2- In reading this diary, which for many priests has already become a book for daily reflection, each sentence must be accepted with discernment, that is, according to the true meaning that is derived from the whole context.

Let us consider, for example, Our Lady's advice to give up newspaper and television. For some, this may be interpreted literally. For many priests, it means, rather, not wasting precious hours, following programs that are frivolous and tendentious and refraining from reading world events as interpreted in a materialistic sense, on the part of much of the present-day means of social communication.

Another example can be found in the frequent expressions, that at first sight can leave us uneasy, in which it is affirmed that the triumph of the Immaculate Heart of Mary coincides with the coming of the glorious reign of Christ. These expressions are of course to be interpreted in the light of what is taught in Sacred Scripture (Revelation 20, 1-7) and the authentic Magisterium of the Church. In this regard, let us keep before our eyes the frequent references which, in his first encyclical, *"Redemptor Hominis"* and in other important documents, Pope John Paul II makes concerning the Church of the second Advent which awaits the second coming of Jesus.

-3- Another piece of advice lies in the invitation to accept the character of this book for what it is, a humble instrument. Our Lady wants it that way, written in a style chosen by Providence which, as Saint Paul teaches, chooses what is weak and poor in the eyes of the world, to confound earthly wisdom and diabolical strength.

-4- Because of the poisonous air we breathe and the astuteness of the devil who can play nasty tricks on us, we ought not become hung up over the occasional sweetness of the style. Priests who have accustomed themselves to the educative action of Mary testify that she acts with sweetness but with firmness. It is with good reason that the Eternal Father entrusted to her his only-begotten Son that she might generate Him in his human nature and educate Him for Calvary. If Our Lady takes us up with gentleness, it is because she loves us as a mother and that she may then place us, without any rebellion on our part, upon the wood of the Cross, transforming us into the image of Jesus Crucified. This is a far cry from sentimentality!

-5- Even the numerous references to the evil times in which we are living and the painful future which awaits us must always be interpreted in their proper perspective, which is that pointed out by Sacred Scripture. How many times and in how many ways has the Lord threatened to punish his people, precisely in the attempt to urge them along the road of conversion and of return to Him! One thinks, for example, of the preachings of the prophet Jonah, sent by God to announce the destruction of the city of Niniveh.

Many have come to a halt, perplexed with the prophetic character in which some of the messages are clothed. And they have asked themselves the question: Is what is written indeed true? Will what is foretold in fact take place? And if they do not turn out to be true, what credibility can then be given to the words of the message? From an attentive reading of the book a most appropriate answer to all these questions can be found. It is this:

"Don't be delayed, therefore, by the predictions I give you in the effort to make you comprehend the times in which you are living. Like a mother, I am telling you the dangers through which you are going, the imminent threats, the extent of the evils that could happen to you, only because these evils can yet be avoided by you, the dangers can be evaded, the plan of God's justice always can be changed by the force of his merciful love. Also when I predict chastisements to you, remember that everything, at any moment, may be changed by the force of your prayer and your reparative penance. Do not say therefore: 'How much of what you predicted to us has not come true!' Instead, give thanks with me to the Heavenly Father because at the response of your prayer and consecration, your suffering, and on account of the immense suffering of so many of my poor children, again He alters the period of justice, to permit that of the great mercy to come to flower..." (January 21, 1984)

-6- One must possess a solid evangelical maturity, preventing us from either disdaining or underestimating, a *priori,* a book such as this, or from overestimating it. It will give, in other words, a proper sense of respect for the experience which the message transmits to us and of the interior freedom with which it should be received. The perception that no word and no message are the Word itself, and the consciousness that in phenomena such as locutions a good deal of the subjective and human element can be introduced, should not on principle make these phenomena radically suspect. There is need to observe and evaluate, as Saint Paul says, and to retain whatever of good you can gather or extract. We should therefore take up a book of this kind with a reasonable amount of respect.

But this respect should be allied to a sense of freedom, which comes from the ability to put the "messages," which such books intend to transmit, in their proper place. It has been said and repeated: the words of Our Lady which have been made known here are neither a new Gospel nor a new faith. They lead us to discover, according to their typical resonance and outlook, the Gospel and the faith.

Hence, even a book like this can be accepted according to its measure of truth and can thus lead to the Truth which is Christ, and be a most suitable way of living, as authentic evangelical "children," this relationship with the Mother of the Lord and our Mother.

-7- This invitation to a simple and open faith in our relationship with the Mother of Christ and of the Church provides us with a sort of magnetic line of force according to which the compass of our Christian life and personality can orientate itself. This line of force must be found in the Mariological teaching of the Church which, for example, was set out for us in the Second Vatican Council. *(Lumen Gentium,* Chapter VIII)

No locution, not even such as are gathered together in this book, could take the place of, or be put on a par with, an official public statement of the faith of the Church, from which the complete physiognomy of Mary and her mission will become apparent. Within the Church we must also bring and show forth a childlike manner in our relationship with Her, and hence also in our apostolic life and mission.

Mary is in the Church and leads to Christ in the Church: to that Church which has recently expressed itself in the Second Vatican Council and which has supplied us with pastoral goals which a priest must make his own. It is in this sign of the total docility of faith that Mary leads us to live the mystery of the Church, thereby accepting and disposing ourselves to accept its ministerial and apostolic dimension as well.

Even a priest, and in particular a diocesan priest, will not be able to find in this book everything that is entailed in his priestly life and mission. But sooner or later he will be able to find there a perspective, a point of view, a unifying element and a driving force for his priesthood, and above all for his personality as a Christian. And this will not be to the detriment of the attention he must give to the pastoral care of his Church, nor to the detriment of the proper attention he must give to solid theology.

–8– Finally, one last piece of advice for anyone approaching a reading of this book. One should pay more attention to its substance than to its form, and should take it up without any preconceived ideas but with humility and simplicity of heart. It should be read without presumption or avidity. One should reread it, meditating upon it calmly and lovingly. And then move on to verify it in his daily life, experiencing in a personal way what Our Lady is asking and promising.

The tens of thousands of priests who, throughout these years have done so, have never regretted it. More than that, they are praying to Our Lady that others may follow in the same path.

Don Stefano Gobbi

Milan, February 2, 1986
Feast of the Presentation
of the Child Jesus

TO THE PRIESTS, OUR LADY'S BELOVED SONS

be greatly abandoned; they will carry the cross with him even when, as did my Son, he will have to climb the road of Calvary.

o   Near the Pope on the cross and with me, the Mother, I want to find his dearest friends: the priests of my Movement.

p   — *Comforters*, because they will alleviate his abandonment and his suffering and will not be afraid to share, as he does, the same fate that today awaits those whom I have prepared for the ultimate sacrifice for the salvation of the world.

q   — *Defenders*, because they will always be faithful to him and will combat all those who challenge and calumniate him.

r   At Fatima I foretold of these moments which would come upon the Holy Father, but I also promised him my special assistance and my protection. I will defend him and assist him through you, my priests.

s   You must be my cohort, ready to fight for the Church and the Pope. Thus you will remain faithful to the Gospel, and through you I will gain my great victory."

24
October 31, 1973

From the Hands of My Adversary

a   "...By means of my Movement, I will snatch many of my priest-sons from the hands of my Adversary.

b   Many of them are in darkness and in the greatest of desolation because they have betrayed Jesus and the Gospel.

c   But I will bring them to see my light and to hear my voice, and they will once again become my dearest sons. I myself will bind up their wounds; I will heal them, and I will make them invulnerable to any further falls.

d   I am the Mother, and I want to save them because they are my children.

e   Therefore, no one should feel lost; no one should despair. My Immaculate Heart is preparing this great return of my dearest sons."

My Faithful Cohort

a   "I want every priest of my Movement and every priest who has consecrated himself to me to pray, suffer and work in order to bring me back once again into the midst of my faithful.

b   Today more than ever, he who finds me will have found life and will receive salvation from the Lord.

c   My Adversary fears only this. He will make every effort to remove me even further from the hearts of my faithful, in order to keep me even more obscured in the Church. He is now engaging in his greatest battle against me, the decisive one, in which one of us two will be defeated forever.

d   At the moment, from many indications, it seems as though my Adversary is the victor; but the time of my greatest return and of my total victory is at hand.

e   In the decisive battle, I want my priest–sons to be with me. They will be led by me; they will be docile to my orders, obedient to my wishes, responsive to my requests.

f   Since by their consecration they have allowed themselves to be possessed by me, I will manifest myself in them, and through them I will act to strike at the heart of my enemy and to crush his head with my heel.

g   But these priests must now begin to act; through them I want to return to the midst of my faithful, because it is with them, gathered about my priests, that I want to form my invincible cohort.

h   Of the faithful, who are supporters of my Movement, I ask:

i   — *That they consecrate themselves* in a special way to my Immaculate Heart, without being concerned for external or juridical bonds, but only for giving themselves completely to me, so that I may dispose freely of their whole being and arrange their whole life according to my plans.

j   They must let themselves be led by me, like little children. They must begin again to pray more, to love Jesus more, to adore Him more in the mystery of the Eucharist, so that He becomes the sun which illuminates their whole life. What joy and what a gift of love will Jesus in the Eucharist communicate to these faithful who are consecrated to me!

k   Let them recite the holy rosary every day so as to hasten my great return.

l   *— That they be faithful to the Pope and to the Church united with him,* by a total obedience to his commands, anticipating and seconding his desires, spreading his teachings, defending him from every attack, ready to fight even to the shedding of their blood in order to remain united to him and faithful to the Gospel.

m   There will soon come a time when only those who are with the Pope will succeed in keeping the faith of my Son and being preserved from the great apostasy that will be spread everywhere.

n   *— That they must observe the commandments of God* and carry out everything that my Son Jesus has taught so that they may be his true disciples. Thus they will be a good example to all.

o   Let them be just that, especially by an austere manner of life, by repudiating styles which are ever increasingly provocative and indecent, by opposing in every way possible the spread of immoral literature and entertainment and this continual flooding from a sea of filth that is submerging everything.

p   Let them be a good example to all by their purity, their sobriety and their modesty.

q   Let them flee all those places where the sacred character of their person is defiled. Let them form about the priests my faithful cohort, my great 'White Army.' Through them my light will once again shine in the midst of the great darkness and my immaculate whiteness in the midst of so much corruption of death.

r   These faithful children of mine will be called by me and formed for this great task: to prepare this world for the great purification which awaits it, so that at last a new world may be born, completely renewed by the light and the love of my Son Jesus, who will reign over all."

The Demon Fears and Hates Them

a   "The serious accident that happened last night, O son, should convince you that my Adversary has now been unleashed upon you and that he is trying in every way to do you harm. But I will always be with you, and he will not be able to touch even a hair of your head or to graze you with even the slightest physical scratch. I am for you a mother, kind and jealous, vigilant and terrible against the Evil One who wants to do you harm. I will send my angels to guard and protect you from every danger and from every snare which the Evil One sets for you…

b   Let all the priests of my Movement know how much the devil dreads them and hates them and how much they will have to suffer because of his plots.

c   Now the Evil One is beginning to suspect something… And he will rage about with ever increasing fury. But I will be with my priests to protect and defend them.

d   They will not be touched, not even a hair of their heads, because they are my beloved sons and I am now forming them and bringing them up; I am preparing them so that they will be strong and invincible at the hour of the decisive battle.

e   I love them; I keep them in my Heart, one by one. I protect them; I bless them."

27   *November 27, 1973*
Anniversary of the Apparition of the
Blessed Virgin Mary to St. Catherine Labouré

Only for My Son Jesus

a   "I want all the priests of my Movement to rely on me as little children. They must no longer think of themselves; I want to take care of them myself. I will grant all their requests and satisfy their deepest desires.

b   They must no longer live for themselves, not even as regards their priestly activity, which absorbs them so much, tires them, and consumes them, but leaves them empty and far from me.

c   On the contrary, they must live only for my Son Jesus, carrying out the Gospel to the letter. For this, they must live only for me, with me. I alone will be able to form them to an ever greater unity of mind and of heart with my Son Jesus; I will have them act solely for Him, as though led by the hand by me and under the sweet influence of my inspiration.

d   They will then be still doing the same things, but in how different a manner! And because these same things will be done by them in union with me, I will manifest myself in them, and through them I will be able to carry out my great plan of salvation.

e   But it is necessary for me that these priests become ever increasingly *mine*: in silence, in prayer, in humility, in equanimity. How beautiful it is when they speak of me, but it is even more pleasing to my Heart when they live me.

f   I want to live again in them so as to be once again as Mother in the midst of my children. Let them be docile, humble, and kind toward all, especially toward those who are furthest away, who are lost, who are despairing.

g   I want to give them my Heart; for this they must accustom themselves to live always in my motherly Heart. Let them worry about nothing. For the rest, for all the rest, I myself will provide so that my great and loving plan may be realized."

28   *December 1, 1973*
First Saturday

The Spirit of Rebellion Against God

a   "Begin this new liturgical year with much prayer.

b   In my Heart you will find the safe refuge from the many troubles of the life of today.

c   Troubles, anguish and tribulation are bound to increase from day to day, because humanity, redeemed by my Son, is withdrawing ever more and more from God and transgressing his laws.

d   The Demon of Lust has contaminated everything. My poor

children, how sick and stricken you are!

e   The Spirit of Rebellion against God has seduced humanity; *atheism* has entered into so many souls and has completely extinguished the light of faith and love.

f   This is the Red Dragon spoken of in the Bible. Read it, my sons, because the present times are those of its realization! How many of my children are already victims of this error of Satan!

g   Even among my priests how many there are who no longer believe; and yet, they still remain in my Church, true wolves in sheep's clothing, and they are bringing to ruin a countless number of souls!

h   Nothing can now hold back the hand of God's justice, which will soon be roused against Satan and his followers, as a result of the love, the prayer and the suffering of the elect.

i   Times of great indescribable tribulation are in preparation. If men only knew, perhaps they would repent!

j   But who has listened to my messages, who has understood the meaning of my tears, of my motherly requests? Almost no one, but a few unknown souls thanks to whom the chastisement has again been put off.

k   But this year will not end before a great sign is accomplished. Pray, pray, pray, O you souls chosen by me and prepared so maternally by me.

l   Above all, you, my priests: forsake vain and superfluous things. These are times of emergency; you must live only with me, in me, for me.

m   Be vigilant; be ready. Soon I will have need of you, because the time of my triumph has arrived."

29   *Dongo (Como, Italy); December 19, 1973*

The Triumph of My Immaculate Heart

a   "This morning, my son, you came with your mother to my Shrine, before the image of Our Lady of the Tears, which you have always loved and venerated from your earliest childhood, to celebrate Holy Mass on the ninth anniversary of your priestly ordination.

b   This is a gift that I have wanted to make to you: your returning on this day with your mother, before me who have always
looked upon you with eyes filled with special love, who have
chosen you from your infancy and have always led you by the
hand. Never have I abandoned you, even when my Adversary
attacked you and snatched you from me, and was then sure of
having conquered once for all.

c   Because of this you have had to suffer much; you have had to
walk often in darkness and abandonment, almost despairing that
I had heard your wails and your cries for help.

d   But all this was part of my great plan; you seem now to have
some glimpse of it, and your heart is filled with joy. But that
which is most beautiful, most important, my son, is yet to come.

e   I have chosen you and prepared you for the triumph of my
Immaculate Heart in the world, and these are the years when I
will bring my plan to completion.

f   It will be a cause of amazement even to the angels of God, a
joy to the saints in heaven, a consolation and great comfort for all
the just on earth, mercy and salvation for a great number of my
straying children, a severe and definitive condemnation of Satan
and his many followers.

g   In fact at the very moment when Satan will be enthroned as
lord of the world and will think himself now the sure victor, I
myself will snatch the prey from his hands. In a trice he will find
himself empty-handed, and in the end the victory will be exclusively my Son's and mine. This will be *the triumph of my Immaculate Heart in the world.*

h   If all the priests of my Movement only knew with what care
they have been chosen and molded by me to prepare them for
this great task!

i   Every detail of their life — even the most insignificant — has
a precise and profound meaning. Therefore let each one become accustomed to read with me in the stupendous book of
their own existence.

j   I will give them the gift of wisdom of heart, and they will
understand with me the reason for all that concerns them: the
reason for much of their lack of understanding, the reason for
their sufferings, the reason for those times when they were aban-

doned, and even the reason for their falls.

k   Oh, how many moments of darkness and of agony they must
have had to experience in their lives, these beloved sons of mine!

l   But these have been for them necessary and fruitful moments:
because I was thus able to take greater possession of them; because I could detach them from their way of seeing, from their
way of feeling, from their easy attachment to things, to results, to
goodness as such, to success, so that they would learn to be mine,
to live only for me by carrying out my wishes.

m   I have wanted them to have, as it were, the impression that
they were good for nothing, to be considered of little value. I
have given them the great gift of humility of heart, of childlikeness of spirit, so that they might feel themselves as mine alone
and thus lose their dependence and reliance on everything else
but me alone.

n   Yet it will be with these poor children of mine, mocked and
trampled on, that I will realize my great plan.

o   That is why each one must entrust himself totally to me at
every moment. I will speak to them and tell them my desires.

p   Do not be afraid of the difficulties and the misunderstandings
you will encounter along the way. I will always be with you, and
you, in spite of everything, will always be joyous.

q   To win the battle which is approaching, I want to give you a
weapon: *prayer*.

r   Forget everything else, and form the habit of using nothing
but this weapon. The crucial times have come, and there is no
longer any time for certain vain and superfluous things. There is
no more time for useless discussions; there is no more time for
chatter and projects: *this is the time for prayer!*

s   Priests of my Movement, offer yourselves to me so that I myself, in you and with you, may always pray and intercede with
my Son for the salvation of the world.

t   I have need of you and of your prayer to realize the great plan
of the triumph of my Immaculate Heart."

30

The Caress of a Mother

a "...How I love you, my son, and what love of predilection I have for you! You must accustom yourself to understand this in so many little things, in so many circumstances which are hardly noticed, such as today: the splendid bright day which I have given you; the blue of the clear skies, the luminous brightness of the snow caressed by the sun, the color of my heavenly mantle under which I ever protect you; the white of my most pure robe with which I wish to cover you.

b These simple things are like the caress of a mother for you... Entrust yourself more and more to me; do you not see that now I alone am your life?

c Pray now for your brothers: for the priests of my Movement. Today, whatever you ask for them I will grant you.

d Pray; profit from this time of rest to enter more deeply into my Heart. Transform every moment of your day into a colloquy with me. I want to hear your voice, my son! Turn everything into a prayer."

31

My Church Will Be Renewed

a "My son, you must be the comforter of my Immaculate Heart. For this you must live each moment outside of yourself, indifferent to all your personal problems.

b If you love me, if you are all mine, if you are my consoler, how can you still have problems of your own? How can you still want or desire anything?

c I have given you the dimensions of my Heart, and what is mine must be yours; my desires must be your desires, my concerns and sufferings must be yours as well!

d Henceforth, you will be happy only if you remain always and at every moment in my Immaculate Heart.

e   How many thorns afflict my Heart: the souls which stray from my Son, even from among the faithful, become more numerous every day. Those who only yesterday were good and generous souls, swept away by the general confusion, become timorous, insecure and as though paralyzed.

f   The most painful thorns are those caused me by the most loved and especially chosen of my children, the priests.

g   Along with those who, like Judas, daily betray my Son Jesus and his Church, how numerous now are the wavering, the doubting, the unfaithful! They celebrate Holy Mass, they administer the sacraments and they no longer believe...

h   Their sacrileges have now reached that limit which cannot any longer be exceeded without abusing the very justice of God.

i   If these unfaithful sons of mine only knew the horrible trials which await them, oh, perhaps they would repent!... On the contrary, they go heedlessly to meet their great chastisement, and at the decisive moment they will be taken unprepared.

j   And so you understand, O my son, why I am now so active among the faithful souls from among my priests.

k   I will call them, and they will answer me; I will cover them with my immaculate mantle, and they will be invincible. Jesus will pour out upon them the Spirit that filled my soul, and they will be transformed.

l   I will give them my Son Jesus, as only the Mother knows how, and they will listen to Him alone; they will love Him alone; they will faithfully announce Him according to the Gospel. And through them my Church will be entirely renewed.

m   What must I do — you ask me — to spread this Movement of priests throughout the world?

n   Remain solely in me, always, at each moment in prayer. I will do everything myself, O my son, because this is my hour.

o   I ask you only to believe, to pray, to suffer, to let yourself be led by me by the hand, and you will soon see my marvels. Even now you are able to learn many things from the year that is about to end.

p   With me you will make no mistake in reading the true signs of the times, of these times which are so very distressful, and yet so blessed by me!"

34

32

They Become Intoxicated with Emptiness

a   "Begin this new year with me, in prayer.

b   At this moment how many there are who are celebrating the arrival of the new year with amusements which are for the most part empty and offensive to the great dignity of creatures who are loved and redeemed by my Son!

c   They become intoxicated with emptiness, these poor children of mine, and how unhappy they are!

d   As for you, keep watch; pray also for them. With the new year, the decisive moments draw near; great events await you. And so begin the new year on your knees, praying with me, O my son.

e   With the coming year, my Movement will develop beyond all expectations. Will this be enough for your little faith so that you may come to believe more and to entrust yourself to me?..."

1974

CENACLES OF LIFE WITH ME

My Heart Will Be Your Refuge

a   "Today, I want to lead you by the hand like a mother; I want to lead you ever deeper into the depths of my Immaculate Heart. My Heart must be as a refuge for you, in which you ought to live and from which you ought to contemplate all the events of this world.

b   If you live each moment in this refuge, you will always be kept warm by my love and that of my Son Jesus.

c   Every day that passes, this world will plummet deeper and deeper into the coldness of egoism, of sensuality, of hatred, of violence, of unhappiness.

d   Before the great darkness, the night of atheism which will envelop everything will descend upon the world.

e   It is especially then that my Immaculate Heart will be your refuge and your brightness. Fear neither the cold nor the darkness, because you will be in the Heart of your Mother, and from there you will point out the way to a great multitude of my poor wandering children.

f   But my Heart is still a refuge which protects you from all these events which are following one upon another. You will remain serene; you will not let yourself be troubled; you will have no fear. You will see all these things as from afar, without allowing yourself to be in the least affected by them.

g   'But how?' you ask me. You will live in time, and yet you will be, as it were, outside of time. My Immaculate Heart, O my son, is like a part of paradise in which I want to enclose my beloved sons in order that they may be preserved from the great events which await you, so that they may be consoled by me, prepared by me, directed by me for the great and approaching moment of my triumph!

h   Remain therefore always in this refuge of mine!"

Cenacles of Life with Me

a   " '*When two or three are gathered in my name, I am there in the midst of them,*' (Mt 18:20) thus spoke my Son Jesus.

b   When two or more priests of my Movement are gathered together on my account, I also am in the midst of them. I manifest myself to them and through them, especially when these priests are joined in prayer.

c   It is therefore necessary that these priests of my Movement begin to meet each other and to gather together. It is not necessary that they come together in great numbers: even two or three are enough. These gatherings must constitute real and true cenacles.

d   Now that my Movement of priests is spreading everywhere, these cenacles must be multiplied.

e   There is no need of organization. Everything should be simple, spontaneous, quiet and fraternal. Where two or more priests of my Movement come together because of me, *there is the cenacle.*

f   In the Cenacle, there were the Apostles with Mary, the Mother of Jesus. In these cenacles, I want the priests of my Movement to be gathered with me, the Mother of Jesus, and Mother most special for them.

g   Why do I want them to come together in cenacles with me?

h   — *To remain with me,* so that I myself can nourish and form them and cause them to grow in perfect consecration to me, so that they may truly be my priests alone, and in them and through them, I may once again manifest myself.

i   — *Above all to pray with me*: when my priests pray, united with each other and with me, how efficacious is their prayer!

j   For it is then that I myself accomplish in them my maternal task of interceding before God for all my children.

k   To be united among themselves and with me in the celebration of Holy Mass, in the recitation of the Liturgy of the Hours, and in praying the holy rosary: this is my prayer!

l   The rosary is the weapon that I give to these children of mine to fight the great approaching battles which await them.

m   — *To love each other* and to live in true brotherhood in the company of their Mother. It is necessary today that my priests know each other, that they help each other, that they truly love one another, that they be as brothers brought together by their Mother.

n   There is today too much loneliness, too much abandonment for my priests!…

o   I do not want them to be alone: they must help each other, love each other, they must all feel as — and really be — brothers.

p   — *To await the decisive moments* which are drawing ever closer. The time is near when some of my poor priest–sons, tricked and seduced by Satan, will come out in the open and set themselves against my Son, against me, against the Church and the Gospel.

q   Then the cohort of my priests, prepared and led by me, are to come forth into the open to proclaim with courage and before everyone the divinity of my Son, the reality of all my privileges, the necessity of the hierarchical Church united to, and under the leadership of, the Pope and all the truths contained in the Gospel!

r   Many priests, uncertain and, as it were, overwhelmed by the tempest, will follow your example and return along the road of salvation. For the present, prepare yourself with me during this time of waiting.

s   Let your gatherings be *true cenacles* of life with me, of prayer, of brotherhood, and of waiting…"

35   *January 23, 1974*

The Sign That I Will Give to Each One

a   "Do not be concerned about all that is necessary for the spread of my Movement. I myself will provide for everything.

b   I want my priests to live always and only in the greatest trust in me. They must expect everything from me, even whatever concerns their life and their means of sustenance.

c   My priests will have to be poor in imitation of my Son Jesus, but they will never lack whatever is necessary to live, and to live with dignity.

d   I am the Mother, and I will take care even of this. I will do great and extraordinary things, even miracles, when it is necessary.

e   But my priests must be neither eager nor preoccupied about what concerns food and clothing. As little children, they should leave it up to their Mother to provide.

f   On the other hand, let them be solely and always concerned about the salvation of so many of my children who, more and more each day, are being lost and falling into the hands of Satan. Do they not feel my great motherly sorrow which is growing ever greater?

g   Let them live solely with me, to console the Heart of my Son Jesus. Jesus, at this time, must be consoled. Let it be my priests who will be the consolers of his Most Sacred Heart!

h   Let them live solely and always looking to me, remaining with me, loving with me, praying through me. From the way they allow themselves to be possessed by me, they will be recognized as priests of my Movement.

i   This will be the sign that I will give to each one, so that the life of each one may be truly transformed!"

36
Rome (Italy); January 28, 1974
Feast of St. Thomas Aquinas

What a Mother Can Do

a   "How happy I am, my son, with the gathering which took place here with the twelve priests of my Movement! It is a little seed which soon will become a tree and from here, my beloved city; it will spread out its branches over the whole Church, throughout the whole world.

b   Have you not noticed how, through you, I myself spoke to the hearts of my priests? They have received an extraordinary grace which will transform their whole life. They will now be apostles of my Movement...

c   Oh, always let yourself be led by me; then you will see what the Mother can do for her sons."

37 *February 10, 1974*

Rely on Me Alone

a   "You must be more attentive, O my son, in order to remain always in my Immaculate Heart, and not let yourself be taken up or discouraged by things, especially when these are independent of your will.

b   You are in a hurry. You would like my Movement to spread more rapidly, and that the booklet would not encounter so many difficulties in its reprinting.

c   How much of the human there is in your desires! It is necessary that I, in a motherly way, purify you, if you want me to lead you to that perfection which is pleasing to my Heart.

d   Rely only on me and not on human means; entrust yourself only to me. There is one thing that you can always do, and which is the only thing that I want you to do at each moment, because it is so useful to me for the Movement: your prayer, your suffering, your trust in me.

e   This is what I ask of you: that you let yourself instead be divested of all other preoccupations. *This is not one of many movements, but it is my Movement,* my son. So then let me act!

f   All my priests must act this way. I will make them understand by causing every human means in which they had placed their trust to come tumbling down. They must entrust themselves to me alone. I know that this asks much of human nature. But I want the priests of my Movement to be *mine alone.*

g   If they do not accustom themselves now to seek me alone, to listen to me alone, and to entrust themselves to me alone, how are they going to find me at the moment of the great tempest when everything will be plunged in darkness? Let them accustom themselves as of now to see me as the light of their every action!"

Let Them Live Out the Trust of the Present Moment

a   "How I am present, O my son, each moment of your day… You are no longer alone. You always have with you the Mother who leads you by the hand, who clasps you to her Immaculate Heart.

b   Everything that happens to you has been prearranged by me for your good. Learn to entrust yourself to me ever more and more.

c   Even the moments of obscurity, of suffering and of misunderstanding are prearranged so that you may grow and become strong along the way of perfect consecration.

d   Learn to see me even in obscurity; learn to feel my presence even in abandonment, O my son; learn to do everything with me, in me. Give me your whole self completely, at each moment.

e   Your past does not exist. I now see you only in my Heart; *you are mine.* Do give me the present moment with generosity: for me this is all that matters, because I can make use of it for my designs.

f   Oh, if all the priests of my Movement only knew how much I have need of them! Let them offer me each moment of their existence with perfect surrender, so that I can make use of them according to my wishes!

g   Since they have consecrated themselves to me, they belong to me; they are mine. If they are mine, they can no longer belong to themselves; they can no longer possess anything that is not my very self.

h   So then why do they still think of the past? Why do they still make plans for the future? Let them truly give themselves to me with perfect abandonment. Let them live the trust of the present moment! Only when these children of mine surrender themselves completely to me and are in my hands like little babies, will I be able to work my wonders by means of them.

i   O my priests, allow yourselves to be truly possessed by me, so that I can again act through you and return to the midst of all my children!"

It Is Time That I Myself Gather Them Together

a   "Let yourself be led by me, my son, and you will see marvels happening around you: one of these is that which you are living through today... X is an example of all the priests of my Movement. What love he has for me and for my Son Jesus! How he lives for souls; how many he saves!

b   This is a humble place, a place of little things, almost unnoticed by most. And yet it is here and no place else that today my presence is to be found.

c   Even today I like to reveal myself to my children in places similar to those in which I lived with my Son Jesus: Bethlehem, Nazareth. Yes, even today I choose poverty, simplicity, littleness, and the ordinary in order to manifest myself.

d   I know this can be a difficulty for many; and yet, this is necessary for those who wish to encounter me. It is necessary to be little and that all feel themselves to be just what they are before me: *just little children.*

e   The little child never looks at himself, but gazes so intently at his mother. It is the mother who looks at her little child. She is the one who, looking at him, can say to him: 'Oh, how beautiful you are; how precious you are; how good you are!'

f   ...Today for you, here in this very place, something is really being born. It is like a small seed, but it will spread itself out, grow and become a great tree. For you, there has been a meeting here today: you have found a brother. But for a long time he has been made ready by me! You see, from long ago I have been fashioning this priest, through suffering, through misunderstandings, through solitude; oh, how I have accustomed him to that interior humility and to that childlikeness of spirit which is so pleasing to my Immaculate Heart.

g   Now I look upon him with satisfaction; he is only a little child in my arms, and I can carry him and make use of him as I wish. Such is one of my priests; such are all my priests.

h   Called by me long ago, long ago they have answered. Nourished by me, fashioned and guided by me, now they let themselves be led with docility.

i   It is time that I myself gather these children of mine from all sides. With them I must form for myself an invincible cohort.

j   They meet each other; they look at each other, and it seems as though they had always known each other. They feel themselves to be really brothers. I give you as gifts, one to the other.

k   Love one another, my beloved sons; be united; look after each other; help each other! Oh, how happy the Mother is when she sees you all gathered together as good brothers in her house…"

40

It Will Begin with My Priests

a   "You ask me if I am pleased. Oh, you do not know, my son, the joy that you give me! It is a mother's joy to be with her children. My paradise is that of being close to each one of you. The priests are children whom I love in a special way because, by their vocation, they are called to be Jesus.

b   It is my duty to form the image of my Son in them. I never abandon them; I never leave them alone.

c   Let them not become discouraged because of their defects or their falls, because they too are so very frail, I am Mother. My greatest delight is to forgive because, afterwards, I can show an even greater love.

d   These children of mine should not be afraid to give themselves to me completely. They are now living in times of great confusion; in many of them faith in my Son and trust in me is diminishing. Bad example is everywhere increasing, and how discouraged are many of them becoming… This is the time to call on me, to yearn for me; this is all I am waiting for in order to reveal myself to them.

e   That which most touches my Heart is to hear them cry like little children. Can a mother not be moved before her little child who is crying?

f   Behold: when everything will have come tumbling down, all that will remain will be the strength of their tears that will compel me to intervene in an amazing and terrible way. And my triumph will begin with these beloved sons, my priests.

...You will have to become accustomed to seeing ever greater and greater things. My Immaculate Heart is an inexhaustible channel of mercy and forgiveness and can no longer hold back the flood of this fire. Soon God will begin to cause torrents of pardon and mercy for these poor children of his and mine to gush through the whole world."

41

Great in Love

a "Today you had something like a sign: a confirmation of how much I love you, my son. I permitted that up to the last moment everything would be contrary to what I had told you beforehand; and then, in an almost miraculous manner, it turned out just as I had promised.

b This is because I want you to grow in *trust* in me. You must let yourself be led by this trust without ever offering resistance, but rather being, as it were, carried and guided by it every moment of your day. Raise yourself up ever higher and higher, until you live habitually in my Immaculate Heart.

c Then this being habitually in me will be for your soul like the air which will permit you to breathe and to live.

d Every priest who is consecrated to my Immaculate Heart and who belongs to my Movement is called to live this way.

e My Heart is sometimes saddened to see that some children who are consecrated to me are not *totally mine*. They do not give me everything. Why do they still keep something back? From now on they must possess nothing, nothing at all: they must simply be little children, the smallest of my children.

f Because I call them to be great in love, in holiness, in heroism, they must become the smallest of all. Oh, my priests are not yet, all of them, my little children, but I will make them so, because it is only in this way that they can grow in *trust* for me.

g When they are perfect in spiritual childhood, when their only concern is to let themselves be led by trust in me, then they will be ready for my great plan.

h My children, let yourselves be formed and fashioned by me. Without you or others being aware of it, I will transform you completely; I will give you great gifts of love; I will call you to an ever deeper union with God and with me.

i This is why I ask you to entrust yourselves to me; if this giving of yourselves is not perfect, you bind my hands, and I will not be able to act according to my wishes. Oh, give yourselves completely to me, O generous and dearly beloved children of mine!"

42   *March 23, 1974*

I Give You the Joy of the Cross

a "Let yourself be led by me at every moment, my son, and you will find peace... even in sorrow, even in abandonment, even in contradictions, even when you seem to feel that you are powerless to do good.

b You would like to, and you cannot, because this does not depend on you; you would like to, and yet you cannot, because you meet with difficulties which you cannot overcome alone. You would like to, and yet you cannot, because, one by one, all those human supports on which you counted so much fail you.

c Even for me and for my Movement, how many times you would have liked to do something, and you cannot... Oh, this inability to act, this experience of your own fragility, and the patience which you must exercise, and this waiting — how much this costs you at times; how it makes you suffer; how it purifies you.

d Indeed, you will know joy even in sorrow; moreover, you will offer for my joy each of your sufferings, even the smallest. And I will accept it as a gift which the little child makes to its Mother, and I will change it immediately into joy for you.

e However, the joy that I give you is deep; it is not superficial; it is peaceful; it never brings agitation. It is for you, my son, *the joy of the cross*: the joy of remaining always in my sorrowful Heart to experience all its indescribable motherly sadness.

f I want to bring all the priests of my Movement to this joy. They must know how I completely change and transform their existence, taking literally the gift which they made to me by their consecration.

g   I will lead them, these little children of mine, very far in love, in suffering, in the joy of the cross!

h   Those moments are approaching when I will be able to act, for the salvation of the world, through the sufferings of my priest-sons... From them I want trust, prayer, simplicity, silence..."

43   *March 27, 1974*

Place Them in My Maternal Heart

a   "Gather these sons of mine together. This is the time for them to get to know each other, to meet each other, to love each other.

b   You are in me, and when you speak in these gatherings I am *truly present* in the midst of you. Even though you do not see me, I am not only spiritually but really and truly present. And I will give you sure signs of this presence of mine.

c   Each one will be aware of it; and his life will be gently changed, and his soul will be delicately touched with my motherly caress. Therefore, my son, you should not seek anything else; you should not be concerned about anything but remaining ever in my Immaculate Heart.

d   What joy and comfort you give to your Mother, O my son! Bring to me all these beloved sons of mine. Gather them into my cohort; place them all in my maternal Heart."

44   *April 1, 1974*

Let Them Offer Me Their Sufferings

a   "The road on which I lead you is difficult, my son, but it is the one that I have ever been preparing for you.

b   With what difficulties and what sorrows it is strewn! But you must not be discouraged. Why do you feel so frightened? What are you afraid of? Let yourself be led by me; remain always in my Heart.

48

c   Give me all the difficulties which you encounter, all the sufferings and the abandonment which you experience. Nothing comforts my Immaculate and Sorrowful Heart more than a suffering which is offered to me out of love by my priest-sons.

d   Even Jesus willed to offer to the Father all his sufferings through and with me. And it was thus that, offering my Son freely to the Father, I became true Co-redemptrix.

e   Let these children of mine offer me all their sufferings, all their misunderstandings, all their difficulties. This is the greatest gift that they can make to me, because thus they allow me to carry out in time — in this, your time! — my task as Mother and Co-redemptrix. I will save many souls redeemed by Jesus, but at present so far away from Him, because my sons, together with me, will pay for them.

f   Oh, all I want of them is prayer and suffering. This is how they will really comfort my Heart and respond to the great plan of mercy which I am about to realize through them."

45

I Will Give Them This Water

a   "Do you not understand that, as the parched earth cries out for a drop of dew, so also my Church has long been awaiting this work of mine which I am carrying out among my priests?

b   Indeed the priests of my Church are today the most prepared, the most desirous of accepting it. The confusion and the numerous defections of these recent times have, as it were, parched the souls of these sons of mine. They have so much need now of pure water, crystal-clear water, to quench their great thirst!

c   I myself will give them this water.

d   For this reason you must become more and more available in my hands; let yourself be led completely by me, who have great plans. From now on you must free yourself from all other obligations...for the sake of my Movement.

e   My son, gather together from all sides my beloved sons. They need so very much to know each other, to meet each other, to love each other deeply as brothers, to help one another, to encourage one another in walking always in simplicity and abandonment along the difficult and painful path of these times.

f   I will be with you; do not fear. As Mother, I will provide everything for you: home, clothing, and food, as only the Mother knows how.

g   I will lead you to a complete emptiness of all human support and to a more total abandonment, so that you may at last learn to do that which pleases me most and that which I am always asking of you: entrust yourself to me alone; let yourself be always led by me; expect everything, and ask everything of me.

h   What joy my motherly Heart feels when you ask me for something. Ask me for everything for your brother-priests, these sons so loved by me, and you will obtain everything, because my Immaculate Heart has already begun its great triumph in them!"

46   *Lourdes (France); April 30, 1974*

My Beloved Children

a   "Have you become aware of the great tenderness my motherly Heart feels for all these children of mine? I reveal myself especially to the little and the innocent.

b   If you only knew how much my Heart loves and cherishes *purity*. This is a virtue which makes souls open to receive a special influx of my love, which enables them to see me, to feel my presence with them.

c   This is the time when I am drawing all these privileged souls to myself, so that they may be protected and kept unharmed, by me and by my Son Jesus.

d   All the sick and the suffering whom you see everywhere, these too are my privileged children. They remind you of the value of suffering, of the necessity to suffer.

e   But, more than all others, my beloved children are *the priests*. In striking them, my Enemy has truly struck at my Heart.

f   This has been permitted by God for the sake of his great designs which are as yet unknown to you; however, this wounded and sorrowful Heart of mine is preparing the greatest return of my straying and wavering priest-sons.

g   For this I bless in a special way all you priests of my Movement. You are the soothing balm for this wound of mine, my comfort in this great sorrow; you are the instruments personally chosen by me for my great triumph!"

47   *May 20, 1974*

The Prayer of My Priests

a   "As each day passes, I want you to be ever closer to my Heart: far from human vicissitudes and the events which so convulse the world and disturb my Church, so that you will remain with me alone.

b   I want you with me *in prayer*. These present moments are so important and grave that they demand much, very much prayer on the part of my priests. The prayer of my priests is necessary for the salvation of the world.

c   Holy Mass must be celebrated well, and it must be lived by my priests. The Liturgy of the Hours must be for them a summons to consecrate every moment of their day to me.

d   The rosary should be a time of conversation with me. Oh, they must speak to me and listen to me, because I speak softly to them, as a mother does to her little children.

e   But even every action of their day can become a prayer. And this happens when they let the Spirit within them — which still today laments with ineffable groanings — cry out invoking God as a Father.

f   Seek the Father; cry out to the Father; yearn for the Father! For yourselves and for all my children.

g   The sufferings of your day will dispose you to be prompt to enter into continuous prayer.

h   The moments which are approaching are more serious than you can possibly imagine. And so I want to prepare you so that at the opportune moment you will all be ready.

i   This is why I call you to prayer."

The Work I Am Accomplishing

a "For all that pertains to my Movement, let yourself be led only by me. You will receive light little by little; this will be assured you through your confessor and spiritual director.

b At the present time you do not see, my son, all that my Immaculate Heart wants to do through you and through my Movement.

c I want things this way for many reasons. First of all, you must remain always poor, humble and simple, considering yourself as the least of my children. Then you must become accustomed to letting yourself be led by the hand and always by me. At *every moment you must expect everything from me.* This is the way I want the consecration which you have made to me to be truly lived out.

d Do not rely on other charisms or on other confirmations; do not look to other works or other plans. This is the work which I am carrying out in the Church through you.

e For this you will receive everything from me; walk in simplicity and total abandonment. Never let your heart be troubled.

f No external interference will ever be able to harm this work of mine which I am jealously bringing to birth for the salvation of my Church.

g In this, consider yourself as *a nothing,* truly incapable of anything, because that, O son, is just what you are. But in the measure you offer your utter nothingness to me; I will be able to act and operate according to my plans.

h Prepare yourself now to also suffer a bit; I want you to be always more and more my own, and soon I will purify you. But this will be in order to give you a greater love than you could ever imagine, O my son..."

49   *June 8, 1974*

I Want to Make Jesus Live Again

a "You must remain more attentive to my voice, my son, and

let yourself be led by me with much docility. It is also good that you form the habit of writing all that I cause you to hear in your heart.

b   I know that this costs you much, yet it is thus that you please me, because you are more and more obedient to your confessor and spiritual director. He will receive from me the gift of understanding what should be made known, since this will be beneficial to many of my sons. He will also know what should be kept secret. For your part, write an account of everything in all simplicity…

c   I will accustom you to depend on me at each moment; oh, but in a manner so simple and spontaneous, as a child does in the arms of its own mother.

d   At every moment I will tell you what I want of you; thus it will be I myself who will do everything in you and with you. You will always act, as it were, under my sweet motherly inspiration.

e   And thus you will grow continually in a life united with me. My life will be your life. It will become painful and insupportable for you to live even for a moment outside of me.

f   My son, you see how I have accepted with pleasure and taken at your word the gift of your consecration which you have made to me!

g   Certainly you are small; you do not have great qualities; you get frightened over nothing; you are almost afraid of your own shadow! And yet, I have considered the intensity and the love of your total gift.

h   Your nothingness, which you have offered completely to me, will be transformed and made great by my motherly Heart.

i   My beloved priests, give me all your nothingness; give me your whole selves!

j   Oh, do not look to yourselves any longer. I want even your miseries, your defects and your failures!

k   Give me everything with great love, and I will transform it all in the burning furnace of the most pure love of my Immaculate Heart. I myself will transform you into most faithful replicas of my Son Jesus.

l   It is Jesus whom I want to make live again in the priests who are consecrated to me, these priests of my Movement. It is Jesus living in these priests of mine who will again save my Church at the very moment when it will seem to be sinking.

m   If you only knew, my sons, the designs which I have upon you, you would leap for joy! This is why I say to you: Give yourselves to me completely, your whole priesthood, without fear. Abandon yourselves to me..."

50

In the Furnace of the Heart of Jesus

a   "Before leaving this place where I have wanted you to be for a time of rest and of prayer and to give you graces which you will understand later, I want to manifest to you once more all the benevolence and the predilection of my motherly Heart.

b   Here you have been very closely united with the one whom I love and hold especially dear and whom I myself give to you as an elder brother for the sake of my Movement.

c   How he loves you, this beloved son of mine! He is one of the greatest gifts that I give you, and you will understand this later on… He will be called upon to wear himself out on a cross of true martyrdom, a martyrdom of love and of pain, which will make him into a living copy of my crucified Son.

d   Let him not be troubled over the difficulties that surround him. They are allowed by God for his sanctification. Let him always pronounce his generous and total *yes*. This is so necessary and pleasing to me.

e   And thus I will have him live always in my motherly Heart, and there he will taste such great, such very great sweetness.

f   Oh, my sons, if the Mother has thus kept you together for so long, it is because she has great designs upon you.

g   I place you in the burning furnace of the Heart of my Son. I press you both to my own motherly Heart, and I bless you."

51

I Have No Need of Human Means

a "...The Movement goes forward when you offer me your prayer and your suffering.

b I have no need of human means. Even the little book is only a means for the spread of my Movement. It is an important means which I have chosen because it is small. It will serve to make known to many this work of my love among the priests.

c But to adhere to it depends entirely on correspondence to a special grace which I will grant to each one. And this you can obtain through your prayer, my son, through your love, through your suffering, and even through your inability to act.

d Remain with me always."

52

I Accept Your Crown of Love

a "...Now I have made known to you the dimensions of my motherly Heart. Every instant of your existence has been prepared by me so that through you I can manifest myself more and more.

b You have at last found your post: my Heart. Rest, my son, on this Heart. Pray, console; and then let me do everything for you.

c My Heart is surrounded by a crown of thorns. Oh, my son, how sharp and painful these thorns have become in these recent times! I am continually being pierced by them.

d Now you ask me for this crown of thorns. How can the Mother offer the crown of her great suffering to her little child? Nevertheless, I accept your desire, the gift of your love.

e And so now, I will have you share in my great sufferings. For this, very gently, I will make you more and more capable of suffering, and I will make you resemble more and more my crucified Son.

f I accept the *crown of love*, the Movement of my priests. They form about my Immaculate Heart a triple crown, as it were, which truly brings about a soothing of all its wounds.

g — *A crown of lilies*, by their purity. Oh, I know that many of these sons of mine have had to undergo the violent attacks of my Adversary and that often they have fallen and that many have lost their innocence.

h They must not become discouraged, these sons of mine. I my self will clothe them with my purity, giving them back their innocence. My innocence will be theirs, and as the fruit of my special predilection, they will be made like me, immaculate.

i — *A crown of roses*. What is the rose if not the most beautiful symbol of love? That is why, from among all the flowers, I am called upon by you as the 'mystical rose.' Oh, these priest-sons of mine must have only one great love: Jesus and souls!

j They cannot love anything else. They must live and let them selves be consumed only by this great love. For this, I myself will purify them through great sufferings, I will detach them from everything, and I will lead them by the hand along the road of my motherly predilection.

k — *A crown of cyclamens*. These are tiny and fragrant flowers, which grow only in the coolness of the woods; it is necessary to climb up high to find them.

l They signify the love that my sons must have for me. They must truly be all mine, my little children who always expect everything from me.

m But they will not be completely my little children if they do not climb the summit of spiritual childhood, a gift which I make to my priest-sons who consecrate themselves to my Immacu late Heart.

n In this way my Immaculate and Sorrowful Heart will be truly consoled, and the many thorns will cause me less pain because of the great joy you give me.

o For the rest I myself will provide because this is my hour, and I have prepared you all for this hour..."

My Triumph and That of My Children

a "Walk in simplicity. I am leading you by the hand, and you should follow me always. Let yourself be led by me; let yourself be nourished and cradled by me like a little child in my arms.

b Since Satan has today deceived the greater part of humanity by pride and by the spirit of rebellion against God, it is only through humility and littleness that it can now encounter and look upon the Lord.

c Caused by the rebellion against God, by this pride which comes solely from Satan, it is the flood of the denial of God and of atheism which truly threatens to seduce a great part of humanity.

d This spirit of pride and rebellion has likewise contaminated part of my Church. Even those who should be a light for others have been deceived and seduced by Satan and are now nothing more than shadows walking in the darkness of doubt, of uncertainty and of lack of faith.

e They now doubt everything. My poor children, the more you search for light by your own selves and through your own strength, the deeper you will plunge into darkness!

f You must return today to simplicity, to humility, to the confidence of little children, in order to see God. For this, I myself am preparing this cohort: my priests, whom I will cause to become littler, ever littler, so that they may be filled with the light and the love of God.

g Humble, small, abandoned and trusting, they will all let themselves be led by me. Their weak voice will one day be changed into the roar of a hurricane, and, joining the victorious cry of the angels, it will resound in a powerful cry throughout the world: 'Who is like God? Who is like God?'

h Then will come the conclusive defeat of the proud, and my triumph and that of my little children."

I Will Lead You by the Hand

a   "Continue, my son, your life of simple and filial abandonment. Live always in greatest confidence in my motherly action.

b   Do not let yourself be caught up with things; do not become anxious. I tell you once again: no outside interference will be able to harm this work of mine.

c   I am making known to you how I want this work done, and I myself will lead you by the hand to realize this plan of mine. Bit by bit, I will detach those who are to help you from every thing — even from what they consider good and useful for my Movement — and I will lead them along the road of perfect abandonment and of the accomplishment of my will.

d   They will be personally called by me to this detachment; from them I expect total submission.

e   O my son, if you only knew with what care I am molding my priests, just as I am molding you yourself! Entrust yourself ever more completely to me; let yourself be led by me. You will see how the Mother knows how to do all things well in your place!"

The Decisive Moments Are Near

a   "Today you have remained constantly close to my Heart; you have prayed for your brother-priests who belong to my Movement. This has been a day of special graces for all of them; I have made my presence felt, close to each and every one of them. I must make these sons of mine ever more and more my very own. I must detach them as quickly as possible from everything in order to cause them to become only and completely the possession of my Son Jesus. If only you knew, son, how much I love them, how much I clasp them to my Heart, one by one!

b   The decisive moments are very near... A little while longer and then, together with them, with the littlest of my babies, I will crush the head of Satan and his many followers, and I will obtain the victory, which has already been announced!"

Fatima (Portugal); August 15, 1974
Solemnity of the Assumption
of the Blessed Virgin Mary into Heaven

In Heaven to Be More a Mother

a   "Today is my feast: all Paradise exults and the Most Holy Trinity rejoices at the reflection in me of its most pure light.

b   Even with my body, I am in heaven so that I can be more a mother: the Mother of all.

c   Today I want you with me at Fatima. You have not returned there since the time when, through you, my Movement was born. Bring me all these priests of mine in order to make with them a crown of love which you will place about my Immaculate Heart...

d   Continue to walk deprived of all assistance and in this abandonment. Do not be afraid; I myself am leading you by the hand and clasping you to my Heart. In this way, I can now make use of you as I wish, and never before as now are you the instrument chosen by me for the spread of my Movement."

My Reign

a   "...You will soon see in all its splendor the great design which the Mother has upon you. You will be always my little child who does not know how to say anything or to do anything other than to remain with me, speak with me, and let yourself be used by me.

b   I will manifest myself in you. You will also have to suffer because many — in good faith — will place obstacles in the way of my motherly action. But in the end they will understand and will become my most docile sons.

c   Today the Church and all Heaven acclaim me as Queen. My Son Jesus has given me this crown of glory.

d   If you only knew, my son, what great glory and what comfort is given to me when I reign as sovereign in your heart! The hearts of all my priests must be the kingdom where I may reign. Thus, very soon, my motherly Heart will triumph in all my children!"

57

Pray for the Holy Father

a   "Spend these days in continuous prayer; make your spiritual exercises with me… Upon your descent from this mountain, I myself will lead you here and there, that you may gather my priests into my Movement.

b   Pray also for the Holy Father. There are grave and painful moments approaching for him, and I myself want to give him the comfort of your filial affection and of your prayer."

58

No One Passes Beyond This Point

a   " 'I want to bring you to a detachment from everyone and to an absolutely total abandonment.' These words of mine, my son, I repeat to you today so that in the present difficulties you will not become discouraged. You are grieved at the fact that some have separated themselves, by organizing a new association of priests who honor and love me, without considering what I myself am doing through you.

b   But if it is I myself who am taking hold of you and leading you, who am causing you to do each thing, how can these sons of mine please me more fully when they do not accept me in the work that I am carrying out? Poor children of mine, because what they are doing is done in good faith and with the intention of honoring me, they will soon understand what path they must follow in order to honor me. There are many ways, but there is only one path for my beloved priests: that of my Immaculate and Sorrowful Heart.

c Here I want them all to be like little children. For this they must learn to be silent, not to become agitated, not to organize themselves, not to act. They must be little children who pray and love, little children who suffer with me, for me and in me for the salvation of all my children.

d Oh, this is for my Church the hour of greatest confusion. The Pope speaks and points out the faith with assurance, and he is left alone and unheeded by almost everyone.

e There are also speaking today false prophets, who announce the Gospel by betraying it, and these are listened to and followed! And they bring disorder and confusion among the most faithful children of my Church.

f You priests consecrated to me, set up once again a strong barrier of defense *together with the Pope*. Do not leave him alone; form with him the last line of defense, the last trench for the defense of my Son and of my Church.

g I am with you, and no one passes beyond this point; and from here I will begin my battle for my greatest triumph!"

59

October 23, 1974

Prayer and Docility to My Voice

a "...I have already told you many times what you must do, and I now repeat it: just pray and remain always in my Heart in prayer. I will look after the Movement myself.

b You are not to let yourself become worried about any preoccupations... I myself am calling together and uniting the priests from all sides, and they, these beloved sons of mine who have been nourished and formed by me, are all heeding my call.

c Have you not seen how the declarations of membership are now coming from all parts of the world?

d Tell X that there will be more and more for him to do for my Movement. Therefore he must accustom himself to do less and less on his own and to leave the action to me alone. He must pray, pray much, and I myself will be his light…

e   The booklet should be the only means of spreading [the Movement]. Do not look at its weakness because it is willed by me.

f   I do not want any propaganda, but only prayer and docility to my voice. I am pressed for time. The decisive times have come, and my army is now ready and awaiting my orders.

g   I bless you all from my Heart."

60

October 29, 1974
Feast of Blessed Michael Rua

How Much You Have Need of a Mother!

a   "I am always near you; let yourself be led by me, without looking to anyone or anything.

b   As I have said to your heart many a time, human events are constantly getting worse and worse. Men have forgotten God; many obstinately deny Him. How many there are now who ignore Him in practice!

c   This poor, poor generation whose sorry lot it is to be so polluted and corrupted by the Evil Spirit, who has risen up against God to repeat again his challenge: 'Non serviam: I will not serve; I will not acknowledge God!'

d   My sons, how much you have need of the Mother! She alone can understand and help you. She alone can heal you. She alone can, by divine plan, snatch you from the hands of Satan and save you. Have recourse to me still, and I will be your salvation.

e   To realize my plan of salvation for all poor humanity, I am gathering together my priests from all parts of the world… They must be docile to my voice and respond, each and all, to the gentle invitation of my motherly Heart.

f   I who have triumphed over all errors and heresies, everywhere, will again, with the cohort of my beloved sons, triumph over the greatest error which history has ever known: the error of atheism which has now drawn away from my Son almost all humanity.

g   Write this, my beloved son: these are now the years when I will realize my greatest triumph.

h   Humanity, renewed by much suffering and by a great purification, will re-consecrate itself completely to the worship and the triumph of God, through the triumph of my Immaculate Heart."

61   *November 19, 1974*

The Altar on Which They Will Be Immolated

a   "...And yet, how I am molding you and transforming you, my son! Are you not now aware of how completely I live and act in you? It is difficult for you to understand, my son, and yet it is a reality. In a priest who has consecrated himself to my Immaculate Heart, it is I who live, work, suffer, pray and act.

b   Take your own life for example: other people, from outside, will say, 'How he has changed; it no longer seems to be he!' But as for yourself, do you not really feel that you are a different person? Your tastes, your desires, your aspirations and even your deepest interests, how changed they are! Consider how formerly you longed for success, and now it seems that even life is burdensome to you. How you used to make plans and projects for tomorrow, and now it seems that the future does not interest you at all. How often, even unconsciously, you have sought yourself...

c   Now something is really changing: it is I who am living and working in you. Your heart beats in unison with mine; your mind follows my thoughts; your words repeat my voice; your hands repeat my gestures: you are, as it were, born again in me.

d   As for one, so also for all the priests of my Movement. All little children, nourished, kissed, caressed and cradled by me.

e   So that I may place them all, with much love, on the wood of their cross, I must prepare them for this ineffable and painful moment. They, like my Son Jesus, will have to be immolated on the cross for the salvation of the world.

f   Let them entrust themselves therefore to me like little chil-

dren. The Heart of their Mother will be the altar on which they
will be immolated, victims acceptable to God for his triumph."

62

The Sign Which God Gives

a "My beloved sons, do not let your hearts be troubled. Why do
you doubt? Why do you look with uncertainty at the present
and the future in search of the sign which I have predicted to
you?

b There is only one sign which God gives to the world and to
the Church of this day: *I myself.*

c I alone am announced as a great sign in the heavens: this Woman,
Clothed with the Sun, with the moon as a carpet under her feet
and twelve stars as a luminous crown about her head.

d My victory over the Red Dragon has been foretold and over
atheism which is triumphing and apparently victorious today.
This victory will be obtained through the triumph of my Immaculate Heart in the world, and I will achieve this victory
through the priests of my Movement.

e For the present, do not look for any other prodigies in the
heavens: this will be the only prodigy!

f For this reason, prepare yourselves in prayer, in suffering and in
complete trust in me. The decisive hours of the battle are near,
but I am already declaring in advance that the great sign of my
victory is you, O priests consecrated to me whom I am gathering together in the Church of which I am the Mother."

63

Revealed to the Little Ones

a "You have come, my son, before my image, which you have
venerated with special love since your childhood and which even

then was a sign of my special predilection.

b   You have celebrated Holy Mass to console my Immaculate and Sorrowful Heart and for all the priests of the Marian Movement of Priests.

c   Have no fear. I myself am gathering these sons from all parts of the world into *my cohort*; all are now responding to my call!

d   If now and then you meet up with some obstacles, with difficulties or with misunderstandings, offer everything to my Heart.

e   I have already told you, and I repeat again, that no external interference will be able to harm this work of mine. It is the sign that I am today giving to my Church.

f   At the moment of its greatest confusion, on the very eve of events which will upset the faith of so many of my children, this is the sign which I will give: *My very self!*

g   I, the Mother of the Church, am personally intervening and initiating my work of salvation. I am initiating it thus: with simplicity, in hiddenness, and in such a humble manner that most people will not even be aware of it. But this, my sons, has always been the way your Mother has acted.

h   Therefore, in order to recognize this action of mine, you must have the eyes of a little child, the mind of a little child, the heart of a little child. You must again become simple, humble, recollected, poor, innocent. You must truly become once again *those little children* to whom alone will be revealed the plans of God, the mysteries of the kingdom of God.

i   Thus the interior space of your souls will be brightened, and your hearts will be truly transfigured because I myself will imprint my image upon them.

j   Your hearts will be my kingdom, and through you, the priests of my Movement, I will give the Church of today a sign — which will become clearer and clearer and perceived by all — of my presence, of my assistance and of my action which is destined for the victory and the triumph of my Immaculate Heart."

Moments of Anxiety

a   "Spend these hours of vigil with me, my son. Forget everything else, and do not let yourself be taken up with anything else…

b   Relive with me these moments of anxiety and painful apprehension when my spouse received a refusal at each request he

c   made for hospitality for *this night* — pain and apprehension not for ourselves, but for my Son Jesus who was about to be born. Every refusal given to us was a refusal given to Him.

d   Many times during the day He had, so to speak, knocked at the door of my Heart. The time had come for his birth, and I, the Virgin, *was now*, as a Mother, to give Him to all humanity.

e   But humanity had no place to receive Him. Every door which closed opened a new wound in my Heart which opened itself more and more to beget in love and pain — in this pain — my Son Jesus.

f   And thus there was no welcome for Him but the poverty of a cave and the warmth of an ox and the young donkey which had carried us throughout the day.

g   Relive with me these hours of vigil, my son, that you may understand that it is *your poverty* alone that has drawn down upon you the predilection of my Son Jesus who has given you the gift of being a priest especially beloved of my Immaculate Heart.

h   Your poverty which makes you only and always such a little child; your *total poverty*: of goods, of attachments, of ideas, of affections. To be poor means precisely to possess this nothingness. It is this nothingness which attracts God's pleasure and which is alone capable of receiving it.

i   Priests whom I cherish, you must all be poor in this way. This is why I ask you to be as little children.

j   Then I will always be able to lead you by the hand, and you will let yourselves be led with docility. You will listen only to my voice, because you will not be filled with other voices and other ideas.

k   And the voice and the ideas which I will communicate to you will be those of my Son. How clear then for you will all the Gospel be! The Gospel of my Son will be your only light, and you, in a Church filled with darkness, will give the full light of the Gospel.

l   You will not be rich in other affections. Your only affection will be *mine*, that of your Mother. And I, as your Mother, will bring you to love my Son Jesus with a total love. I will lead you to such a degree of love that you will not be able to live without Him. I will make love for Him your very life, and He will truly be able to live again in you!

m   My beloved sons, this is why I need your poverty, your humility, your docility.

n   Do not be afraid if the world does not understand you and does not accept you; there is always the Heart of the Mother which will be your home and your refuge."

65
December 26, 1974
Feast of St. Stephen

The Power of the Spirit

a   "...Saint Stephen was truly a little child. What candor illuminated his soul, what purity his unshakeable faith in my Son, and what strength his whole person!

b   He conquered everyone with his glance, with the purity of his faith, with the power of his love. After Jesus, he was my first child whom many times I clasped to my Heart... I knew that he had to be the first one to die, after my Son Jesus. And with what tenderness did I encourage him so that he would become stronger and stronger.

c   And when he fell, killed, they brought him to me, and I again clasped him to my Heart... Oh, it was, as it were, the same scene as at Calvary!

d   ...You too are called to be a *crown*: the crown of my Immaculate and Sorrowful Heart.

e   As upon him, so also upon you I pour out the fullness of my Son's love so that no one will be able to resist this grace. The Holy Spirit will sweep you along like a little feather on the wave of his fullness.

f   Each of the priests of my Movement will be this *crown of love* for me. A crown of lilies, of roses and of cyclamens, all these little children of mine. But no one will be able to resist the power of the Spirit which I will obtain for them.

g   Oh, and even they — in great part — will be called to the ultimate testimony. But their blood will wash and purify this world, so that from it a new world may be born, renewed in love and consecrated anew to the triumph of God!..."

66
December 31, 1974
Last Night of the Year

The Seed Is Beginning to Germinate

a   "End this year and begin the new year with me, my son, close to my Immaculate Heart, in prayer.

b   *Prayer of thanksgiving* for all that I have done this year for my Movement, accepting those most precious things you offered me for it: your prayer, your suffering, your complete trust in me.

c   It is in this way that the invitation, sent out by me, has now reached all my chosen ones throughout the world. Thus the seed has been sown and is already beginning to germinate.

d   With the coming year it will mature and blossom into so marvelous a spring that it will be a great joy and comfort for all my children.

e   *Prayer of propitiation* for so many of your brothers who await this new year amidst amusements, simply straining to forget things and to enjoy themselves, and often they offend the Heart of my Son and my motherly Heart.

f   With the new year, the decisive events will begin: at a moment when a great part of humanity will least expect them.

g   Now my cohort is ready for the battle and soon the entire Church will witness this struggle between me and him who has always been my Adversary: Satan, who has seduced a great part of humanity and who has corrupted and led astray so many children of my Church.

h   Prepare, son, by incessant prayer; this is what I want of you. Live always in my Immaculate and Sorrowful Heart. Each day that passes, this Heart will be more and more your only light. I bless you for *this time* which has still been granted you for the spreading of my Movement...

i   Priests, look only to me because the days when all that I predicted will take place, word for word, are very near. O priests specially beloved by me, offer yourselves each and all, upon my Immaculate Heart, as a *clean oblation* for the sacrifice with which this world must be renewed in blood, that it may be purified and made ready for the birth of a new world, illumined by the light and the love of my Son Jesus!"

1975

BE JOYOUS

Faithful to My Voice and That of the Pope

a   "...How I appreciated the Holy Mass in honor of my Immaculate and Sorrowful Heart which you celebrated this morning in my venerated Shrine!

b   You came as on a pilgrimage of prayer, reciting the rosary and singing hymns in my honor.

c   I have already manifested to you how delighted I am, and you are aware of this, especially at the moment when I stopped you and, through you, blessed all the priests of my Movement, in particular those who are the farthest away geographically: those of the German, the French and the English language, those in faraway America, and those in the missions of Africa and Asia.

d   At that moment, in every part of the world, all my priests felt me close to them: my sons who on this first Saturday of the month and of the year are spiritually united in honoring my Immaculate Heart.

e   My beloved sons, what joy and what comfort you give to my motherly Heart! You are at last answering with your generous *yes* to what I asked at Fatima for the salvation of the world.

f   Your *yes*, O priests consecrated to my Heart, was the one thing I was waiting for in order to begin to act. Now, with you, I will begin my work!

g   First of all, this Movement of mine will spread everywhere. I will bring together from every part of the world my beloved priests who, as it were, impelled by the irresistible force of the Holy Spirit, will respond and will gather together in the cohort of my priests who are called to remain faithful solely to the Gospel and to the Church.

h   When the time comes for the terrible encounter with those priests who are bearers of error and who will range themselves against the Pope and my Church, dragging a great number of my poor children toward their perdition, you will be my faithful priests.

i   In the darkness which the Evil Spirit will spread everywhere, in the midst of the many false ideas which, propagated by the

Spirit of Pride, will be asserted and followed by almost everyone, at that moment when everything in the Church will be called into question, and when even the Gospel of my Son will be proclaimed by some as a legend, you, my consecrated priests, will be my *faithful sons*: faithful to the Gospel, faithful to the

j   Church, and the strength of your fidelity will come from your habit of entrusting yourselves to me alone and of remaining docile and obedient solely to my voice.

k   Hence, it will not be the voice of this or that theologian, nor the teaching of this or that person — even though he gain widespread approbation — but my voice alone which you will listen to, O my sons.

l   And my voice will repeat to you gently only that which the Pope and the Church united to him will proclaim.

m   Faithful to my voice and that of the Pope, you will be the cohort prepared by me to defend his person, to disseminate his unheeded teachings, to comfort him in his abandonment and his solitude.

n   You also will be persecuted: the time will come when you will be the only light left burning, and thus, through your fidelity to the Gospel and your sufferings, you will be able to point out the way of salvation to a vast number of souls. And through my intervention, this light of yours will never be completely extinguished.

o   My specially loved ones, be aware of my presence as Mother at the side of each one of you. Now the days are passing, and the great moment is approaching. This is the hour when I am gathering you together from each part of the world to enfold you all in my Immaculate Heart.

p   With the help of your prayer and your immolation, I will be able to begin the battle and win my great victory."

68

The Time Left to You

a   "Prepare, my son, to bring together again these sons of mine.

Follow the directives which I have already made known to you.

b   I must hasten, and I desire that the priests of my Movement be once again reunited before the great tempest.

c   — *To pray together:* as in the Cenacle, I, the Mother, gather you together in prayer. O priests specially chosen by me, return to prayer. I *have need* of your prayer.

d   Pray with me and through me, with that prayer which is so simple and yet so efficacious and which is the prayer I asked of you: *the holy rosary.*

e   Pray well: with humility, with simplicity, with abandonment, with trust. Do not be any longer concerned about other things; you must no longer become troubled by other disturbing problems...

f   In great numbers, souls are straying far from God and rushing down the road of depravity which is daily becoming more violent and inhuman. Now any action of yours, or any action undertaken by you alone, to restrain them is no longer sufficient. They are one step from their eternal damnation. I alone, through a motherly and miraculous intervention, will be able to save them at the last moment.

g   This is why *I need* your prayer!

h   My priests must be, at every moment, in this priestly attitude: close to my Heart in prayer for the salvation of the world.

i   Discussions, feverish activity, taking on the problems and the ways of acting that are in vogue at this time but which dissipate and waste your energies, these are all the disturbing tactics of my Adversary who today succeeds in ensnaring everything and everybody.

j   You, my beloved sons, will never be seduced by him, because you are consecrated to my Immaculate Heart. Therefore, you will always be *my priests* alone, who pray with me without ceasing so that the great apostasy will be in part contained and the great and imminent chastisements be at least mitigated.

k   — *To love each other as brothers,* gathered about your own Mother. What grief my motherly Heart experiences every day in seeing that even amongst themselves priests today no longer love each other, nor do they help each other! Egoism has smothered every impulse of fraternal charity, and in the souls of many of my sons, there is only coldness and darkness.

l Love one another, my beloved sons! Seek out each other; be united with each other; help each other to be faithful priests: faithful to the Pope, to the Gospel and to the Church.

m Do not be worried if at present everything concerning the faith seems to be in ruin. Not one word of the Gospel of my Son is to be denied. All must be taken in its intended sense if you wish to remain in the truth.

n You yourselves must be the living Gospel in order to oppose with your light the great darkness which is growing ever denser throughout my Church.

o — *To remain with me*: in these gatherings all will experience my special presence. And because time is pressing, I will make myself perceptible to each one in an extraordinary way...

p There must be many more of these gatherings. The time left at your disposal is now short. Everything must be done well, so that the spirit of my beloved sons be prepared, but without their becoming fearful."

69

February 15, 1975
Anniversary of the Apparition
of the "Virgin of the Poor" at Banneux

The Joy of Making You Grow

a "My dearly beloved son, why are you troubled? Why do you sometimes lose your peace of mind?

b All that has happened to you these past days was arranged by me in order that you would really detach yourself from everyone, even from those persons who are especially loved by me and by my Son Jesus.

c You are so little that, without your noticing it, you end up by attaching yourself to them and depending on them. And your attachment becomes all the stronger, the closer these souls are to me.

d You have no need of anything but their prayers and their sufferings, and this is what I ask of them for you and for my Movement. And you should reciprocate with your prayer and your great brotherly love. This is sufficient. Anything else is not from me; for you, anything else is vain and superfluous: it is truly a waste of time...

e   My beloved sons, let yourselves be truly detached from everything! See: it is not your defects, your falls or your great limitations that prevent you from being totally mine and available for my great plan. Oh, no! On the contrary, these are a great gift to you because they help you to realize how little you are and to remain little. They give you, so to speak, measure of your littleness.

f   It is your attachments which make up the only obstacle which prevents you from being totally mine. How many ties you still have, my sons! Ties to your own self, to other persons however good and holy they be, to your activities, to your ideas, to your feelings. And I will break them, one by one, so that you will be mine alone.

g   With each day that passes, I will liberate you from your attachments, and I will make you more and more free, little, trusting and surrendered, until you are totally mine and my Immaculate Heart is in fact your only good. Then I will be able to act in you and carry out my work as Mother, which is that of making each one of you into a living copy of my Son Jesus. Entrust yourselves to me without fear. Every pain that you feel because of a new detachment will be soothed by me with a new gift of love. Each time that you detach yourself from a creature, you will feel your Mother closer to you.

h   My little children, let me have the joy of making you grow!"

70   *March 15, 1975*

Without Thinking of Tomorrow

a   "...Live each moment in me, without thinking of tomorrow, without ever worrying about what you must do. I will guide you by the hand at each moment...

b   For a little while yet you will walk in light, but soon everything will be plunged in darkness. Then I myself will be your light and will guide you in carrying out that which my Immaculate Heart desires.

c   To do this, beloved sons, I must ask of you that which your human nature finds most costly: I ask you to live without thinking of tomorrow, without being preoccupied about the future.

d   Do not ask me:'What shall we do? How should we conduct ourselves? Is the great purification near? What will be the outcome for us?'

e   Live, with perfect love and perfect abandonment, the present which I — moment by moment — arrange for you, my little babes.

f   For this, accustom yourselves not to look at things but to me alone. Do not consider what is awaiting you, the deeply distressing events of these times of yours. Do not consider what many are doing today against my Son and against me and what they are preparing to do against you.

g   The hour of darkness is approaching, the hour when you must drink the chalice which my Son has prepared for each one of you. But do not even think of this hour, that you may not be caught up in fear and anxiety.

h   Look only to my Immaculate Heart: take refuge and warm yourselves here, strengthen yourselves here. Feel yourselves in safety here!

i   Abandon yourselves completely and without reserve in this Heart; then only will you correspond to the great plan of salvation which my Heart has in each one of you, my little children."

71

March 28, 1975
Good Friday

The Way of the Cross

a   "The reason why I have wanted you here today, far from all preoccupations and activities, is that you might remain alone with my Son Jesus...

b   The path along which I wish to lead my beloved sons, the priests who are consecrated to my Immaculate Heart and who belong to the Movement, is *that of the Cross*.

c   I want them all on the Cross with my Son, in prayer and in suffering. This is the road that Jesus took to carry out the work of redemption and to save all men.

d   This is the road which the priests called to form my cohort must follow, in order that men redeemed by my Son, but snatched from Him by Satan, may yet be saved today through a special intervention of this motherly Heart of mine.

e   *The way of the Cross*, my little children, is the only way that I have traced out for you because it is that which your Mother has first traveled, together with her Son Jesus.

f   Journey along it without fear, because you will be led by the hand, by me, enheartened by my motherly tenderness.

g   Journey along it with me, in my Immaculate Heart; near your cross you will thus feel the presence of your Mother who will comfort and help you.

h   This road *must be traveled* by you, because only in this way can you become similar to my Son Jesus in all things. My duty is that of making you *in every way* similar to Him.

i   Now that I have detached you from everything to make you ready to do the Will of the Father, and formed you once again into little children to make you priests according to the Heart of Jesus, the time has come when you are being called to climb Calvary with Him.

j   This is the hour of Calvary for my Church, for the Holy Father, and for all the priests who want to be faithful to my Son and to the Gospel.

k   But it is also, beloved sons, your most beautiful hour for which I have prepared each one of you for a long time. Say with me: 'Yes, Father, your Will be done!' (cf. Mt 26:39)

l   Even if this hour is one of darkness, you are called by me to reflect the light of the Will and the plan of the Father. You will be called to bear witness to the fatherhood and the merciful love of God.

m   This then is your hour, and this is why I am calling you to nothing but prayer, suffering and a total immolation of yourselves. Forget every other preoccupation, and entrust yourselves to me; and by your great love, second this plan of my Immaculate Heart."

Do Not Grieve Me by Your Doubt

a   "My most beloved son, you have now almost completed the work which I have entrusted to you.

b   Take refuge now in my Immaculate Heart: I want you here to strengthen you and to protect you at the time of the terrible trial.

c   My beloved sons, priests consecrated to my Heart, listen again to the voice of your Mother who is gently admonishing you that you may be prepared for the great events which are now weighing upon the world.

d   Be truly and *only mine*; give yourselves to me without reserve. After you have been consecrated to my Immaculate Heart, let there be no other concern within you but to allow yourselves to be led by me as little children.

e   Think no longer of your past.

f   There are some among you who are still dwelling upon their past, feeling again the pain of the many wounds which I have healed, and they are, as it were, impeded from giving themselves totally to me. They are impeded by this thought: 'Is it possible that I — after all my shortcomings and infidelities — could be truly chosen and especially loved by the heavenly Mother?'

g   O my children! My Heart overflows with tenderness for you precisely because you are small and weak, because you have sometimes fallen, because you feel yourself to be so frail.

h   By yourselves, my little children, you would never be able to surmount that which is awaiting you, and this is why I want to enfold you in my Immaculate Heart. I myself will be your security and your defense.

i   There are some among you who are still caught up in the temptation of doubt and criticism. After all I have done for you!…

j   Do not grieve my Heart by your doubt, by your incredulity. Have you not yet learned to let yourselves be guided by me? Overcome this temptation by prayer.

k   From my priests, I want only prayer and confidence in me. Every moment which is not spent by them with me in the most complete abandonment is, as it were, lost to them and taken away from me, and this deeply grieves my motherly Heart.

l   The time has come when some of my priest-sons are preparing to openly oppose my Son, myself, the Pope and the Church.

m   I will then be no longer able to recognize them as my children; I myself will come down from heaven to place myself at the head of the cohort of my beloved sons, and I will crush their plots.

n   After a great upheaval and the purification of the earth, my Immaculate Heart will sing of its victory in the greatest triumph of God.

o   It is for this moment, my beloved priests, that I have called you one by one from all parts of the world and have made you ready.

p   This is no longer a time for doubt and uncertainty: this is the time of battle!

q   Each one of you should let himself be enfolded by me in my Immaculate Heart."

73

June 7, 1975
Feast of the Immaculate Heart of Mary
First Saturday

Respond to My Supreme Call

a   "Once again write what I will dictate to your childlike heart, chosen by my Immaculate Heart.

b   Be ever more docile and obedient to your spiritual director. Entrust yourself to him completely. I will give him the necessary light to understand what I want of him for the realization of my plans.

c   Do not fear, my most beloved son. Why do you become troubled and sometimes lose your peace of mind?

d   You are in my Heart; live habitually enfolded in my motherly Heart. Feel all its serenity and all the tenderness it has for you!

e   Live, my son, so that I may pour out, upon you, all the tenderness of my Immaculate and Sorrowful Heart…

f   Whoever looks at you, listens to you or passes by you should be able to sense in his soul a touch of this supernatural perfume of mine and the tenderness which my motherly Heart has for all her children.

g   And so I want you to be truly detached from everyone. Do not seek other voices or other supports. Do you not see that I myself am speaking to you and leading you? My Immaculate Heart will be your only comfort, and from this Heart will come all your encouragement.

h   As for the rest, leave it to me. This is my work alone, and no one will touch it, because I am jealous of it with the very jealousy of God. This work is willed by me for the great triumph of God and the conclusive defeat of Satan.

i   Do not become uneasy if you find that movements inspired by souls to whom I have revealed myself are springing up here and there: on the contrary, all is part of my great plan. And so each thing must be in its place.

j   Your place is the Marian Movement of Priests. Through my priests, an immense number of the laity will again be consecrated to my Heart and entrust themselves completely to me. With simplicity and without organization, let them give themselves to me as a little child gives himself completely to his own mother.

k   My children, the battle has already begun, and I ask you only to respond to my supreme call.

l   Be my priests; be solely priests of prayer. Do not waste any more time, because the time left to you is far too precious. Pray the holy rosary often and well. Live and spread the Gospel of my Son Jesus.

m   Pray for, help and defend the Vicar of Christ: the Pope. Be poor; be little; be humble: be nothing other than my little children who form a crown of love about my Immaculate and Sorrowful Heart.

n   Today, one by one, I bless you; I embrace you, and I enfold you in this Heart of mine.

o   Never, even for an instant, feel yourselves alone and without me. Sons consecrated to my Heart, I am your Mother who today gives you the gift of her habitual presence at the side of each one of you."

Your Heaviest Cross

a   "How often I tell you: remain always in my Heart and fear nothing. Never become preoccupied, even concerning my Movement; all I want of you is prayer, suffering and a most complete surrender to me.

b   At this time, I have not wanted to put you to the test. You are so little and so completely mine that your Mother cannot leave you alone, not even for an instant...

c   I have wanted you to taste just a *little drop* of the great bitterness which overwhelms my Heart because of so many of my poor priest-sons of whom Satan has now taken complete possession...

d   My poor sons, what anguish they cause me!

e   Priests of my Son, they no longer believe in my Son and continually betray Him; priests called to be ministers of grace, they now live habitually in sin: their life is an uninterrupted succession of sacrileges. Priests sent to proclaim the Gospel of salvation, they have now become propagators of error. Priests chosen to save many souls, they lead so very many souls along the road of perdition.

f   This is the hour when the abomination of desolation is truly entering into the holy temple of God.

g   They are no longer the salt of the earth, but a salt without savor, corrupted and nauseating, good only to be strewn on the ground and trampled underfoot by everyone. They are no longer the light on the candlestick, but darkness which makes the night even more obscure.

h   They are all poor ailing priest-sons of mine, because they have fallen under the dominion of Satan...

i   My beloved son, how can my Heart not be submerged in an infinite sea of sorrow?

j   Priests of my Movement, you beloved sons of my sorrowful Heart, what must you do in order to save all these priests who are so ill and so much in need of my motherly help?

k   *Help them*, without ever judging them. Love them always. Do not condemn them; this is not your role. Love them by your suffering, by your witnessing, by your good example.

l　Be an example to them by defending, even exteriorly, your dignity. You should never abandon the ecclesiastical garb, thus obeying the will, time and time again expressed, of the Vicar of my Son, the Pope.

m　*Pray for them.* A great force of prayer is needed to obtain from the Heart of Jesus the conversion and repentance of these poor sons of mine. You have been chosen by me for the triumph of my Immaculate Heart in the world. But this triumph will begin with the salvation of many of these poor priest-sons of mine who have gone astray.

n　Form an unbroken chain of prayer and of love to ask for their salvation and that my Immaculate Heart may become, especially for them, the most secure refuge.

o　*Suffer* with the Pope, with the bishops, with the faithful priests.

p　This is the cross which Jesus now asks you to carry: to live side by side with brother-priests who no longer believe, who spiritually are no longer alive, who betray the Gospel, who are *unfaithful servants* and yet remain in the Church to be ministers of this infidelity. This is for you the heaviest of crosses, but it enters into a greater plan of mine. The decisive events have already begun, and the one you are living through is the beginning of these.

q　This scandal will become even greater and more serious. You will be called upon to suffer more and more, because this veritable apostasy from the Gospel will one day become general in the Church, before the great liberating purification.

r　Therefore, no longer fix your attention on time; do not be even reckoning on the time of my triumph. Live simply in surrender and trust, like my little children, in my Immaculate Heart."

Serene in This Time of Your Repose

a   "Enter, my dearly beloved son, into my Immaculate Heart: this is the place of your repose.

b   Spend these days constantly with me, in my company. I wanted you here again this year: in the midst of these little children of mine, humanly speaking a little frail and more needy, and therefore dearer to my Heart.

c   Be only and ever my little child, in need of everything, rejoicing to receive everything from me in all simplicity...

d   This way I have of talking to you may astonish the grown-ups, but it is very natural and simple for my little children.

e   The sun, the sea, nature: all is a gift to you from the Heavenly Father; all is made holy by the presence and the joy of my Son Jesus.

f   In times of anguish, how comforting for the Heart of my Son was this nature, prostrate, as it were, at his feet: the sun with its light, the charming countryside of Galilee with its flowers, with its songs with its warm and golden harvest and the lovely mirror of the great lake.

g   Everything spoke in harmony, as it were, with the great prayer of my Son Jesus, with his ardent thirst for solitude, with his natural desire of living in the company of his Father.

h   How many today, on these same shores, live forgetful of God, submerged in a new paganism, and offend Him, ungrateful for this great gift of his.

i   But here, in these same places, many of my little children love and console Him.

j   Your presence, my son, should be like an *act of reparation*. It must therefore be a presence of love and of prayer, a presence of life with me.

k   So also is the presence of the priests of my Movement in the world of today: consecrated to my Immaculate Heart, they are offered by me to the Father as *a sign of reparation*.

l   For this reason, the more sin will increase, the more their love for God will grow; the more filth will submerge everything, the more their purity will become limpid and shining; the more apostasy will spread, the more heroic will be the witness of their faith, even to blood.

m   In this way they will be a sign of reparation: by their love, by their fidelity, by their purity.

n   And it will be due to these little children of mine, consecrated to my Heart, that evil will not prevail. On the contrary it will, in the end, be defeated.

o   For this purpose they have been all chosen and prepared by me for this great purification of the earth.

p   From this place I bless you all with an abundance of graces, including your spiritual director whom I have placed at your side and whom I am making an increasingly docile instrument in my hands for the realization of my plans, and including also these little children of mine who are keeping you company.

q   Pray, rest, work, love: even these days of yours form part of the great plan which I have in your regard. So then, enter serenely into this time of rest."

76

Behold the Handmaid of the Lord

a   "Consider, my son, the good that the Mother wants for you.

b   You are now becoming accustomed to doing everything with me; you are coming to realize how at each moment I lead you to do what I desire of you. It is the Mother's Heart which is carrying you; here you now experience how all your anxieties cease.

c   Priests so dearly beloved by me, I want you all to abandon yourselves to me in this way.

d   Do not think about yourselves any longer; do not be worried about anything; let yourselves be carried by me, one and all.

e   I need only your trust; I want only your complete abandonment to me.

f   Satan fears only this: an army of priests consecrated to my Immaculate Heart and completely abandoned to me.

g   He knows that through them I myself have accepted the challenge which he has again dared to hurl at my Son, and he now senses that his defeat is at hand.

h　To his renewed gesture of pride and rebellion by which he has now seduced the whole of humanity, I will again repeat through my little children: '*Behold the handmaid of the Lord; be it done unto me according to your word*.' (Lk 1:38)

i　And then will come the final defeat of Satan and of his many followers, through the triumph of my little children in my Immaculate Heart.

j　Do not ask me when this will take place, because I have already initiated this triumph."

77

Feast of Our Lady of the Snows

The Priests Are Responding to Me

a　"Remain serene; have confidence in me, even for what pertains to the spread of my Movement.

b　Do not be anxious over the many requests for the little book over these past months, to which, through no negligence on your part, it has been impossible to answer.

c　Let us suppose that with a perfect organization we could send out immediately all the booklets requested. Do you think that this would be sufficient for the spread of my Movement? No, my son, because the booklets, once they had arrived at their destination, could be put away in a drawer by those who receive them, without being read; or even if read, they could leave the reader completely indifferent.

d　*My motherly action is the only thing necessary* for the spread of my Movement. It is my action alone that prepares souls to receive this gift of mine, that determines for each one the moment when this will be given, that gives a special grace by which my words can be understood and can produce in souls that marvelous reality which they express.

e　This is why I ask you insistently to support my action with *your prayer*. This is what I am always asking of you because this, and not technical perfection, is what is necessary for me.

f   Tell X that I look upon him with delight when he is working for my Movement, as I know that he is already taken up by so many other occupations.

g   But in order that my sorrowful Heart might be consoled by him and that he himself might live in the intimacy of this Heart, I ask his generous soul for *more prayer*, more moments of silence and of living with me…

h   Of you, my dearest son, I ask prayer, suffering and silence.

i   *Silence*, above all, concerning our intimacy.

j   Do not speak about what I am doing for you, so as not to curb my action and delay the plan of my Immaculate Heart. Tell everything only to your confessor and spiritual director.

k   You see how I myself have brought you to a great intimacy with me, but your brothers are still on the way. Therefore, they are not yet able to understand.

l   Of you I always expect *prayer and suffering*.

m   The announcement of my Movement has now reached all parts of the world, and those priests consecrated to my Immaculate Heart are all responding to me.

n   However, it is necessary that these sons of mine walk under my guidance, without ever halting. Not one of them must be mediocre. I want to lead them all, in my Immaculate Heart, to the summit of sanctity.

o   If you only knew how much Satan tempts and obstructs them, torments and discourages them.

p   Remain always in my Heart and on the cross for their sakes: your prayer and your suffering will help them to grow in holiness.

q   On the cross and in my Immaculate Heart, at my side, you will then be constantly helping those who are your brothers and my beloved sons."

78   *August 13, 1975*

Satan Breaks Loose

a   "…You are aware that I am always near; sometimes my motherly action absorbs, as it were, your own activity, and you live habitually recollected in my Immaculate Heart.

b   You are here in this place where my Son Jesus resides, and where I also am present…

c   Why have I wanted you up here?

d   To help you climb your cross, my little one. I will give you great gifts of love and of pain. Only in this way will you be able to help your brother-priests to grow in holiness and to become priests after the Heart of Jesus.

e   It is true, you have consecrated them all to my Immaculate Heart; they are now mine; they belong to me, and it is my duty to form them as the priests that Jesus wants them to be.

f   But if you only knew, my son, how human they still are: attached to themselves, to pleasures, to the esteem of others, to the goods of this world, to their own way of looking at things. They still doubt me, my son, and they doubt you and the mission that I myself have confided to you.

g   Satan torments them, sifts them violently, seduces them with pride and greatly discourages them! He bites furiously at my heel; he hurls himself with rage at my little children; he knows that soon it will be the faithful priests, and I with them, who will crush his head forever.

h   I have wanted you up here because it is here that your Calvary begins… From this place I bless all the priests of my Movement, in every part of the world; I am the Immaculate Conception, the Fount of Mercy."

79

August 23, 1975
Feast of St. Rose of Lima

You Will Have Them Walk Toward Me

a   "Be at peace once again in my Immaculate Heart. How much you have suffered these past days: the darkness, the obscurity, the doubt. In a certain sense, you have tasted even the bitterness of being abandoned!

b   At these moments it seems to you that you have lost your way; you call on me, and it seems to you that I am far away, that all is an illusion. On the contrary, never as in these moments, never as at this very moment, my son, am I so close to you and do I clasp you so close to my Immaculate Heart and gaze on you with such tenderness and love.

c   I need this suffering of yours: all I want of you is prayer and suffering. And then I will give you new light and new serenity; you will rejoice and be strengthened and thus made even more ready to be placed again upon your cross.

d   Only when you will be lifted up on your cross will you be able to help all the priests of my Movement to be that which my Immaculate Heart wants them to be.

e   What a long road these sons of mine must still travel, and you will give them your hand and have them walk toward me... For my Movement of Priests, I will manifest myself through you; you are the instrument chosen by me for this mission. This must be understood by everyone in order to avoid any confusion what-soever with which my Adversary will attempt to obscure my work. Those who will accept it through you will receive the gift of my most pure light..."

80   *September 12, 1975*

Little to Others, Great to Me

a   "I have chosen you precisely because of your littleness, your poverty. Jesus looks with pleasure and with predilection on the small, the pure of heart, the simple.

b   Be ever thus!

c   And so never look at yourself, because I will make you the gift of leaving you with your faults.

d   My Son Jesus does not love you for what you can do, but for yourself. He loves you just as you are. It is not your merits but only his love which draws Him strongly to you.

e   I also, your Mother, love you just as you are: even with your defects, as long as you are always striving to correct them. And if they give you a true measure of your littleness, even they will help me to make you more my own.

f   Priests of my Movement, do not fear if you sometimes feel far away from the ideal which I am proposing to you. Your humility, your trust and your good will suffice for me.

g   I am forming a cohort of priests who will perhaps never be perfect, but they will certainly be *all mine*.

h   The perfection which I will build in them will be interior and hidden: little to others, great to me. They will even be despised and persecuted by many, but in their soul they will always have my joy.

i   I want you to offer me these flowers, my son, on this feast day of mine.

j   I bless you; I bless you all with gratitude and thankfulness."

81

September 15, 1975
Feast of Our Lady of Sorrows

Offer and Suffer with Me

a   "My very dear son, through the entreaty and wish of my dying Son, I became your true Mother.

b   I am the Mother of all.

c   By the privilege of my bodily assumption into heaven, my Immaculate Heart never ceases to beat with love for you.

d   Thus it has never ceased to be saddened and pained by so many of my children who continue to do evil and who walk on the road of perdition, making useless all the suffering of my Son Jesus and mine.

e   To be sure, I am in heaven: I am perfectly happy close to my Son, in the light of the Most Holy Trinity, in the eternal joy of the angels and saints. But my duty as Mother still binds me to you and keeps me close to you on this earth.

f   If I am your Mother, all your pain is mine as well.

g   And so it is that in my Heart I truly feel the repercussions of all the bitterness, all the misery and all the great suffering of the world.

h   If I am your Mother, I cannot help but suffer for my children, for all, especially those who are farthest away, who are most in need, and above all for my poor children who are in sin.

i   If I am the Mother, I cannot help but suffer for those who are sinners, for all of them, because I desire that they all return to the Heart of my Son Jesus and to my motherly Heart.

j   I who am happy in heaven am grieving on earth, close to you, my poor afflicted children.

k   Priests of my Movement, beloved sons of my sorrowful Heart, do you wish to accept my gentle invitation to suffer with me?

l   Often I am, as it were, surprised to see with what anxiety — and sometimes even with such great human curiosity — you scrutinize the future. You often on occasion ask yourself: 'But when will this purification take place?'

m   There are even some who, in my name, believe that they can indicate the dates of events and exact occurrences, and they forget that the hour and the moment is a secret hidden in the merciful and fatherly Heart of God.

n   The Mother cannot put time limits on her motherly admonition or her merciful expectation.

o   And so I say to you, beloved sons, do not scrutinize the future, and thus, neither anxiety nor discouragement will take hold of you! Live only in the present instant, in complete abandonment, close to my Immaculate Heart, the present instant which the love of the Heavenly Father puts at your disposal, my little children...

p   Before the Father — the omnipresent Father — only the present moment counts: not the past nor the future because this time is not yours.

q   Live then each moment upon my Heart in prayer. Share my suffering, privileged sons of mine. At the time when the whole world was once for all redeemed and purified, the Father accepted the Son's divine suffering together with my human suffering of the Mother.

r   Your suffering, my sons, is truly contributing to the purification of the earth.

s   If the chastisement comes, it will be only as an ultimate and solemn demand for suffering to bring about the renewal of the world and the salvation of so many poor children of mine.

t   But nothing contributes so much to the triumph of my Immaculate Heart as a priestly heart which suffers. In you, my sons, it is Jesus who continues his mission of purification. Only his blood can wash away all the evil, all the hatred and all the sin of the world.

u   And so, now that the moment of the purification is here, you will be called upon to suffer more and more. For you, my sons, this is the hour of the cross. But you will suffer with me, with your Mother who begot you under the Cross.

v   Be ever with me, in the present moment which the Father gives you: to offer and to suffer in the Heart of your sorrowful Mother."

82

October 7, 1975
Feast of Our Lady of the Rosary
Anniversary of the Victory
of the Blessed Virgin Mary at Lepanto

What It Means to Be a Mother

a   "My son, you have come here only because I wanted you here, and you have seen my marvels.

b   You have seen where my special favor is always directed: upon the little ones, the poor, the suffering, the sinners.

c   Wherever there is suffering, there also is my predilection.

d   If you knew what it means to be a mother!...

e   If you could but succeed in understanding this, you would no longer fear anything: it is my maternity that saves you.

f   The justice of the Father has determined that the sufferings and the death of the Son are to pay for your redemption. The love of the Heart of the Son has determined that his Mother is to bring you to salvation.

g   Priests so dearly loved by me, it is for this reason that I say to you: *Do not be afraid; it is the Mother who is preparing each thing for you.* Do not be anxious; leave all your worries in my Heart...

h   Be prepared to see my greatest marvels. Today you recall one of my victories, but soon you will all be witnesses of my greatest triumph.

i   My cohort is now ready, and the time has come. With the weapon of prayer, of the rosary and of your trust, it is now the time to enter into battle.

j   Soon, my sons, a new date will be celebrated. The entire Church will flourish anew under the most pure mantle of your Mother."

Be Joyous

a   "I have chosen you, my son, for this simple reason: because you are the poorest, the smallest and the most limited. Humanly speaking, you are the most destitute.

b   I have chosen you because in your past life my Adversary had almost succeeded in claiming a victory. In your life, I have had you live, as if by anticipation, the experience of what I myself will do at the moment of my great triumph.

c   My Adversary will one day think that he is celebrating a complete victory: over the world, over the Church, over souls.

d   It will be only then that I will intervene — terrible and victorious — that his defeat may be all the greater when he is certain in his conviction that he has conquered once for all.

e   What is in preparation is so extraordinary that its like has never happened since the creation of the world. That is why everything has already been predicted in the Bible.

f   The terrible struggle between me, the Woman Clothed with the Sun, and the Red Dragon, Satan, who has now succeeded in seducing many even with the error of Marxist atheism, has already been foretold to you. The struggle between the angels together with my children and the followers of the dragon led by the rebellious angels has already been foretold to you. Above all, my complete victory has already been clearly foretold.

g   You, my sons, have been called to live through these events.

h   It is now the time for you to know this, that you may be consciously prepared for the battle. This is now the time for me to begin disclosing part of my plan.

i   First of all, it is necessary that my Enemy have the impression of having conquered everything, of having everything now in his hands. This is why he will be permitted to penetrate even into the interior of my Church, and he will succeed in plunging the sanctuary of God into darkness. He will reap the greatest number of victims from among the ministers of the sanctuary.

j   This will in fact be a time of great falls on the part of my beloved sons, my priests.

k   Satan will seduce some of them by pride, others by love of the flesh, others by doubts, others by unbelief, and still others by discouragement and loneliness.

l   How many will have doubts about my Son and about me and will believe that this is the end of my Church!

m   Priests consecrated to my Immaculate Heart, my beloved sons whom I am gathering together for this great battle, the first weapon that you must make use of is *trust in me.* It is *your complete abandonment to me.*

n   Conquer the temptation of fear, of discouragement, of sadness. Distrust paralyzes your activity and greatly benefits my Adversary.

o   Be serene; be joyful!

p   This is not the end of my Church; what is in preparation is the beginning of its total and marvelous renewal!

q   The Vicar of my Son, in virtue of a gift I grant to him, is already able to foresee this, and though living in the present moment of sadness, he invites you to *be joyous.*

r   'To be joyous?' you ask me, all surprised.

s   Yes, my sons, in the joy of my Immaculate Heart where I enfold you all. My motherly Heart will be for you the place of your peace, while outside the most violent storm is raging.

t   Even if you have been wounded, even if you have fallen many times, even if you have doubted, even if at certain times you have betrayed your calling, do not become discouraged, because *I love you*!

u   The more my Adversary will have sought to rage about you, the greater will be my love for you.

v   I am the Mother, and I love you all the more, my sons, for your having been snatched away from me.

w   And my joy is to make each one of you, priests beloved of my Immaculate Heart, sons so purified and strengthened that from now on no one will ever again succeed in snatching you from the love of my Son Jesus.

x   I will make of you living copies of my Son Jesus.

y   And so be content, be confident and be totally abandoned to me. Remain always in prayer with me.

z   The weapons that I will use to fight and win this battle will be your prayer and your suffering.

_A And so then, yes, you too will be on the cross with me and with my Son Jesus, close to his Mother and yours. And then I myself will do everything, because God has arranged that this be my hour, my hour and yours, O sons consecrated to my Immaculate Heart."

84

Your Silence

_a "How many times I repeat to you: you will meet with sufferings and misunderstandings, but never obstacles! This is my work; no one will touch it.

_b My angels have already begun the battle; at my orders they are bringing these sons of mine together from all parts of the world. My Heart knows what means to use to reach them; I find my greatest joy when they answer *yes* to me.

_c Many feel so small and unworthy; they are conscious of so many past infidelities and weaknesses, and they are rather perplexed in taking this step.

_d The *yes* which they say to me makes my Heart leap for joy.

_e Count now how many of these yeses there are; calculate how much joy is given to my Immaculate Heart!

_f This complete offering of yours is the only thing I ask of you, my sons: the offering of yourselves with your limitations, your weaknesses and your inabilities.

_g I need this in my plan.

_h If I have asked for no juridical structure for the Movement, it is precisely because I want it to be spread in silence and hiddenness.

_i The second weapon which you must use, after your trust and abandonment of yourself to me, is your prayer and your silence.

_j *Interior silence*: let it be the Mother who speaks within you.

_k She will repeat softly to your childlike heart all the Gospel of Jesus. She will give you once again a taste for his word.

_l You will not listen to other voices or other words: you will

hunger and thirst for his alone, and thus you will be formed in the school of the word of God.

m   *Exterior silence*: let it be the Mother who speaks through you. I am so eager to do this, if you will let me act freely within you.

n   In order that I may speak, I need your silence. Some of you find it difficult to understand this. Yet this silence is so necessary, even for your own word.

o   Some of you believe that even for my Movement it is necessary to do, to write, to act. Yet your silence is so necessary for the spread of my Movement, according to the plan which has already been clearly outlined by my Immaculate Heart.

p   Speak always by your life. Let your life be your word. Then it will be I myself who will speak in you and through you. Then your words will be understood and received into the hearts of your listeners.

q   Today when the spoken word is the weapon used by my Adversary to seduce all humanity, I ask you to oppose him with your silence.

r   Thus it will again be the Spirit who will speak in you, and by means of the Spirit, making use of you, the whole world will be completely renewed."

85   *October 30, 1975*

I Am Calling Them All

a   "Have you seen how I place in your path the priests called by me to consecrate themselves to my Immaculate Heart? Your task, my son, is to gather them together and to entrust them all to me.

b   These sons of mine have now such great need to be consoled and encouraged. And this is why I am always present in these gatherings. The souls of these sons of mine will thereby rejoice, and they shall all be consoled.

c   The time has come when I will make myself more manifest in the Church, through increasingly greater signs.

d   *My tears* are shed in many places to call everyone back to the

96

sorrowful Heart of the Mother.

e   The tears of a mother succeed in moving the most hardened hearts. But now my tears, even tears of blood, leave many of my children completely indifferent.

f   *My messages* will become all the more frequent, the more the voice of the ministers refuses to proclaim the truth.

g   Because so many priests have abandoned their trust, how many of my children are now suffering from a true spiritual famine of the word of God.

h   The truths which are most important for your life today are no longer preached: heaven which awaits you, the Cross of my Son which saves you, sin which wounds the Heart of Jesus and mine, hell into which innumerable souls are falling every day, the urgent necessity of prayer and penance.

i   The more sin spreads like a pestilence and causes the death of souls, the less it is talked about. Today some of my priests even deny its existence.

j   It is my duty as Mother to give nourishment to the souls of my children; if the voice of the ministers is stilled, the Heart of the Mother will open up more and more.

k   Following now upon my interventions, the time has come *when I must make myself present in person and act in the Church whose Mother I am.*

l   I want to act through you, O priests consecrated to my Immaculate Heart. This too is part of my plan.

m   The Evil One, my Adversary from the beginning, is now in the process of seducing a great number of priests, and he is working among them and gathering them together against my Son, against me and against the Church.

n   I am personally intervening and calling together into my cohort the priests who are determined to remain faithful. *I call them all* to consecrate themselves to my Immaculate Heart and to take refuge in me.

o   The struggle will be especially between me and the ancient Serpent whose head I will, in the end, crush. And so I now ask of you only those things which, according to your human way of looking at things, seem small and insignificant.

p   As day by day propaganda increases, as well as the clamor of the enemies of God who are succeeding in winning everything over to themselves, all I ask of you is to respond with your *trust* and total *abandonment*, with *prayer*, with *suffering* and with your *silence*.

q However, whatever you offer to my Heart will become in my hands a terrible weapon with which to fight and to win this battle.

r To the haughty cohort of the arrogant who rebel against God, I will reply with the cohort of my little, humble, despised and persecuted sons.

s And through you the victory will belong, in the end, to the humble 'handmaid of the Lord.'" (Lk 1:38)

86

November 9, 1975
Dedication of the Basilica of St. John Lateran

Live Your Consecration

a "...You were chosen by me to make everyone — and especially your brother-priests — understand the wealth and the wonders of my Heart.

b At Fatima, I pointed to my Immaculate Heart as a means for the salvation of all humanity. I pointed out the way of return to God. But I was not listened to.

c Now I want to offer you my Immaculate Heart as your only refuge in the very painful moments that await you.

d Day by day your sufferings will increase. The crisis, now under way within my Church, will grow deeper to the point of open rebellion especially on the part of many of my sons who share in the priesthood of my Son Jesus. The darkness, which is indeed already growing denser, will deepen into night throughout the world.

e Marxist atheism will contaminate everything; like a poisonous fog it will penetrate everywhere and will bring many of my children to death of faith.

f It will subvert the truth contained in the Gospel. It will deny the divine nature of my Son and the divine origin of the Church. Above all, it will threaten its hierarchical structure and attempt

98

to break down the Rock upon which the edifice of the Church is built.

g   This is the time when I want to pour out the mercy of my Heart upon all my children, to save them through my motherly love which always understands, helps and pardons.

h   I want to act through you, O priests especially chosen by me.

i   In order that I may do this, you must be totally at my disposal. I will be able to act in you to the extent that you allow yourselves to be possessed by my gentle motherly action.

j   You do this through your consecration to my Immaculate Heart: it is the only thing necessary for you to do in order to belong to my priestly Movement.

k   Make it; renew it often, and especially, my sons, *live this consecration of yours!*

l   How much comfort you give to my sorrowful Heart when, in your gatherings, coming together for concelebration, you renew all together the act of consecration to my Heart!

m   If you live your consecration, your life will be truly transformed: I will accustom you to my way of seeing, of thinking, of praying, of loving.

n   I will communicate my spirit to you and will make you ever littler, more simple and more humble.

o   I will bring you to trust always and only in God. And the more that doubt and denial increase, the more you will find your certainty in Him, and you will bear witness to this.

p   I will bring you to love the Church very much. Today the Church is going through times of great suffering because it is loved less and less by its own children.

q   Many would like to renovate it and purify it solely by criticism and by violent attacks on its institution. Nothing is ever renewed or purified without love!

r   I will bring you to love the Pope with a deep filial love; the Mother will lead you to carry his cross with him and to share his sufferings.

s   Where are they now, those priests who are close to the first priest, to this first son whom the Mother loves with special tenderness?

t   Let it be you, O priests consecrated to my Immaculate Heart, who are closest to the heart of the Pope.

u   Pray for him; suffer with him; be always with him! Listen to him; put his instructions into practice; spread his unheeded teachings!

v   In the darkest hours of night, this will be the only light left burning. You will be illumined by this light, and, led by me, you will spread it throughout the world, so full of darkness.

w   It will also be with the weapon *of your fidelity* that I will fight and win the battle.

x   For this reason, my sons, I invite you to take refuge completely in my Immaculate Heart."

87   *November 25, 1975*

These Hours Will Be Shortened

a   "My plan, O son, is now being accomplished.

b   The decisive events have begun, and you will be called to suffer more and more.

c   I have need of *all your sufferings*: this is the most precious weapon that can be used in this battle of mine. So I ask you to be prepared to suffer, to get ready to climb Calvary with Jesus and me, to offer yourselves to the Father as victims chosen by me and long prepared with motherly care.

d   In fact, as your Mother, I have gathered you all into my Immaculate Heart. Here is your refuge, the altar on which you will be immolated for the salvation of the world.

e   Do not let your hearts be troubled, my sons. Give yourselves to me at every moment! The time of desolation and abandonment of my Church has come. It will be abandoned especially by many of its ministers and its own children.

f   It will be scoffed at, betrayed and given into the hands of him who is its enemy and who wishes to destroy it. It will be some of its own ministers who will hand it over to its executioners.

g   Prepare yourselves with me to live out these moments. Everything has already been arranged by the Father. This is the chalice which you must drink to the dregs.

h   You too will be scoffed at, betrayed and persecuted with the Vicar of my Son, the Pope. Many will have to give their lives and shed their blood. The others will remain to be consumed as a holocaust, by living through these moments of great suffering which are in preparation for the purification of the earth. Thus you will be my light in the great darkness.

i   But this most severe trial, my beloved sons, will be of short duration. Through my special intervention, these hours will be shortened. And soon there will shine forth upon a renewed world the triumph of my Immaculate Heart."

88

I Will Be Victorious

a   "I am the Immaculate Conception!

b   I came from heaven, my sons, and at Lourdes I recalled that truth which the Church had but a short time before officially defined.

c   By a privilege I am exempt from all sin whatsoever, even from that original sin which each one of you contracts at the moment of conception.

d   I was preserved from sin because, in this humble creature, the Most Holy Trinity wanted its wondrous plan to be reflected, whole and entire.

e   I was preserved from sin and filled with grace because I was chosen to become the Mother of the Word [1] and destined to give you my Son Jesus. And my Son Jesus has given me to each one of you as your true Mother.

f   Therefore my motherly plan for you is to clothe you in my own immaculateness. I want above all to heal you from the evil that makes you so ugly: sin.

g   My beloved sons, priests consecrated to my Immaculate Heart: from the beginning I have been announced as the enemy, the antagonist and the Conqueror of Satan, the father and the first artificer of all sin.

---

[1] (W)ord refers to the Second Person of the Most Holy Trinity.

h   My mission is to fight and defeat Satan, to crush his head with my heel.

i   I conquered in the beginning when the Trinity proclaimed me as the sign of sure victory, at the moment when all humanity had fallen under the bondage of sin. 'I will put enmity between you and the Woman; between your offspring and hers. She will crush your head as you make an attempt on her heel.' (Gen 3:15)

j   I conquered when, by my *yes*, the Word was made flesh in my most pure womb and when on Calvary my Son Jesus offered Himself on the altar of the Cross.

k   In Him, who has redeemed you all, my total victory was accomplished.

l   I have continued my battle throughout the long years of the Church's pilgrimage on earth: its greatest victories have been due to my special motherly action.

m   But when, in this last century, my Adversary wanted to challenge me and begin a struggle which, through *the error of atheism*, would have seduced and deceived all humanity, from heaven I appeared upon earth as the Immaculate One to comfort you, because it is, above all, my duty to fight and to conquer the Evil One.

n   And in this century, while atheism has organized itself as a force spread out for the conquest of the whole world and the complete destruction of my Church, I again appeared from heaven to tell you not to fear, because in this terrible struggle I will be the victress: 'In the end my Immaculate Heart will triumph!'

o   You, my poor sons, are the ones most knocked about in a struggle which is, above all, between me and my Adversary, the Ancient Serpent, Satan, the seducer and the artificer of all evil.

p   For this reason, before telling you of the battle, I have, as Mother, invited you to seek a safe refuge. Take refuge in me; entrust yourselves completely to my Heart.

q   *My Immaculate Heart*: now you understand, my sons, why it is the greatest gift which the Heavenly Father offers you.

r   *My Immaculate Heart*: it is your safest refuge and the means of salvation which, at this time, God gives to the Church and to humanity.

102

s   The special intervention of this Heart of mine is the work which I am carrying out in my Church to call all priests, my beloved ones, to take refuge in me.

t   Do you see how Satan has now entered into the interior of the Church? How he deceives, corrupts and drags off so many of my poor priest-sons?

u   This is then the hour when I will personally intervene.

v   I have called you to trust, to complete abandonment and to consecrate yourselves totally to my Immaculate Heart. I have revealed my plan to you, and I have indicated the arms which I have selected for this battle.

w   Now, my sons, I reaffirm to you that *I alone will be the victress*. This victory of mine has already begun, and soon it will shine forth upon the entire Church and upon the whole of renewed humanity, when Satan will once again be crushed by the power of my virginal foot."

89

December 24, 1975
The Holy Night

Do Not Fear

a   "This is the holy night, my most beloved son, and so live it in my Heart.

b   I want to have you share completely in my love, in my motherly anxiety at the moment when, caught up in a light from heaven, my Son Jesus is born into this world. He is born of me, his Mother in a virginal and miraculous manner.

c   It was deep night. Deeper still was the night which enveloped humanity, enslaved in sin and beyond hope of salvation. The night also enveloped the Chosen People, who no longer responded to the spirit of their election and were not ready to receive their Messiah.

d   On this night so deep, the Light appeared; my little Infant was born. At a time when no one was looking for his coming, when there was no place open to receive Him…

e   Unexpected, unwelcomed, rejected by humanity — and yet, at this moment redemption begins for humanity — my Jesus is born to redeem all men from their sins.

f   Thus the light rises in the midst of such great darkness, and my little Child comes to save the world.

g   He is born in poverty and in the pain of this rejection, and his first cries are but tears of mourning: he feels the rigor of the chill, as the whole world envelops Him in its cold.

h   My Immaculate Heart gathered the first tears of the divine Child. They were mingled with those of my own Heart, and I wiped them away with my motherly kisses.

i   On this holy night, as I again give you my Son, I say once more: *Do not fear,* Jesus is your Savior.

j   Now, more than ever, the world is plunged in darkness; the coldness of hatred, of pride and of unbelief envelops the hearts of men. Even the Church is disrupted by a profound crisis, and even many of its priests have doubts about my little Child.

k   O my Church, receive with joy the coming of your Jesus: He is living in you because He wants to save all these poor children of mine!

l   Priests consecrated to my Immaculate Heart, *do not fear.* Today I announce to you great tidings of joy for all: my Son Jesus is your Savior. You were all redeemed by Him; now you can all be saved by Him.

m   *Do not fear:* as my Heart has given you the Savior, so now in these times my Immaculate Heart gives you the joy of his salvation.

n   Soon the whole world, which is pervaded with darkness and which has been snatched from my Son, will at last rejoice over the fruit of this holy night.

o   The triumph of my Immaculate Heart will be realized through a new birth of Jesus in the hearts and the souls of my poor wandering children.

p   Only have confidence, and do not let anxiety or discouragement take hold of you. The future that awaits you will be a new dawn of light for the whole world, now at last made clean.

q   On this night, close by the humble crib of my Child, I feel the loving presence of these dear sons of mine, these priests consecrated to me, and together with my Son Jesus whom I clasp to my Heart, I thank and bless you all."

The Gift Which I Give to the Church

a   "Spend the last hours of this year close to my Immaculate Heart in prayer.

b   So closes a year which has been a year of grace and of mercy: the Holy Year, 1975.

c   Many of my children have accepted the invitation of the Vicar of Christ and have come from all parts of the world to receive the great pardon.

d   Other children of mine have passed this year in complete indifference, immersed only in their earthly interests.

e   A great many others have not heard this invitation; on the contrary, they have deliberately closed their souls to the great mercy of my Son Jesus.

f   Among these, alas, there have also been some priests.

g   This is the sign of the truth of what I have often caused you to perceive in your heart.

h   Satan is maneuvering more and more openly in my Church. He has now associated many of my priest-sons with himself, deluding them with the false mirage that Marxism proposes to all: exclusive interest in the poor, a Christianity engaged solely in the building up of a more equitable human society, a Church which would be more evangelical and therefore disengaged from its hierarchical institutions.

i   This real division within my Church, this real apostasy on the part of so many of my priest-sons, will become accentuated and thus develop into a violent and open rebellion.

j   This is why, my dearly beloved sons, I have now completed my work in the course of this past year. As I foretold to you a year ago, my Movement has spread everywhere and has blossomed into a wonderful spring for the whole Church. My work has expanded throughout the whole world; the cohort of my priests is now ready.

k   I will still continue this motherly action of mine, which will become daily more apparent and strong, for the triumph of my Immaculate Heart.

l And so spend the last hours of this year in prayer. Unite your prayer to that of all my beloved sons. In every part of the world, they will hear during these hours my invitation to gather in prayer with me and to draw close — all of them — to my Immaculate Heart.

m What now awaits you, my most beloved sons, is nothing less than your complete sacrifice for the salvation of the world and the purification of the earth.

n The time which the Father still leaves at your disposal is too precious: do not waste it! You should live every moment with me, in my Heart.

o Do not look to the future; live only the present which your Mother prepares for you.

p May the evil which is increasing ever more and more and appearing to submerge everything neither disturb nor discourage you. Very soon, I myself will gather up all the good that is to be found in the whole world, and I will lay it up in my Heart to offer to the justice of God.

q Begin the new year with me, my beloved sons. You are the warp and woof of my plan; the loving design of your Mother; the gift that I give to the Church, to comfort her in the passion and apparent death that awaits her, before her wondrous renewal through the triumph of my Immaculate Heart in the world!"

1976

YOU MUST BE LITTLE

A Sign of Contradiction

a   "Do not be troubled, my sons, if you are not understood by some and if on the contrary you are openly criticized and persecuted. My Heart permits this to accustom you not to rely on any creature, but on me alone. Beloved sons, lean on my Immaculate Heart alone.

b   Let yourselves be carried just as the baby Jesus let Himself be carried in my arms to the house of the Father. He presented Himself in the temple to be offered to the Lord on this mother's Heart of mine.

c   At the moment when I entrusted Him into the hands of the priest, the old prophet Simeon revealed that the Mother had been chosen by God for this offering: 'He is destined to be a sign of contradiction and a sword, O Mother, will pierce your soul.' (cf. Lk 2:34–35)

d   You also, my little children consecrated to my Immaculate Heart, you will be called today to be *this sign of contradiction*.

e   *By your life*, which will be, purely and simply, a living Gospel. Today the Gospel of my Son Jesus is believed in less and less, and even in the Church there are some who tend to interpret it in a human and symbolic manner.

f   You will live out the Gospel to the letter: you will be poor, simple, pure, little and totally given over to the Father.

g   *By your word*, which will repeat ever more loudly and clearly the truth which my Son Jesus has come to reveal to you.

h   Do you see how many of your brother-priests betray this truth, in the attempt to adapt it to the mentality of the world, impelled by a false illusion of being better understood, listened to by more people and more easily followed? No illusion is more dangerous than this.

i   Always announce the Gospel that you live with fidelity and clarity! Your speech must be: 'Yes, Yes – No, No.' (cf. Mt 5:37) Everything else comes from the Evil One. Therefore let yourselves be guided and led with docility by the Church.

j   See how the Pope is now announcing this truth with power and how his voice falls more and more on barren soil!

k   My motherly Heart is again pierced by a sword as I see how the Holy Father, this first of my beloved sons, is abandoned even by his brother-priests and left more and more alone.

l   You, O priests consecrated to my Immaculate Heart, must be the voice which spreads throughout the whole world whatever the Vicar of my Son announces again today with firmness, for the salvation of my poor misguided children.

m   *By your witness,* which must be a light and example for all the Church. It has been ordained by the Father that yours be a witness which will become more and more painful. I repeat, my sons; the road upon which I am leading you is that of the Cross.

n   Do not fear if you become increasingly the target of misunderstandings, criticisms and persecutions. It is necessary that this happen to you because, as was my Son Jesus, so also are you being called today to be a sign of contradiction.

o   The more you are followed, the more you will be rejected and persecuted.

p   When they attack your person or my Movement, answer with *prayer,* with *silence* and with *forgiveness.*

q   You will soon be called upon to struggle openly when my Son Jesus, myself, the Church and the Gospel are attacked.

r   Then only, led by me by the hand, should you come out in the open to at last give your public witness. For now, continue to live with simplicity, by entrusting yourselves, each and all, to the care of my motherly Heart."

92

February 11, 1976
Feast of Our Lady of Lourdes

The Perfume of Your Purity

a   "Today, my beloved sons, I receive with joy the perfume of your purity, and I place it on my Immaculate Heart to offer it to God as a sign of reparation.

b   How much filth submerges this poor humanity, urged by me to set itself free from sin: 'Come and drink of this water I give you; come and wash at the fountain!' (cf. Jn 4:14)

c   Do you see how, every day, many of my children remain defiled with this filth which is spreading more and more and dragging countless numbers of souls to their death? How can even many of my poor priest-sons escape from this tide of filth?

d   I am the Immaculate One: I am purity.

e   Take refuge in my Immaculate Heart.

f   Even though the surroundings in which you live become more and more submerged in this impurity, you must breathe in only my heavenly perfume.

g   I have come down from heaven to make of you, sons consecrated to my Heart, my heaven on earth. In you my light is reflected. Thus through you many souls will again be drawn by my candor, and they will spread the perfume of my virtue.

h   The Pope has given you the signal for turning the tide of this moral battle.

i   *Listen to him! Defend him! Console him!*

j   The outrage which was recently perpetrated against his person and the insults which are increasingly being hurled against him deeply pain my motherly Heart.

k   This tide of filth has finally reached to his very feet! But you must set up an embankment about the feet of this angelic Pastor, of the gentle 'Christ on earth.'

l   By a special intervention on my part, carried out through you, this diabolical wave of rebellion and of filth, unleashed against the Pope, will stop at his feet. And the greatness of his innocent person will appear intact to all."

93

March 7, 1976
First Sunday of Lent

The Perfect Consolers

a   "My sons, be the perfect consolers of my Son Jesus. Never as at the present time has his divine lament been so often repeated: 'I looked for comforters, and I found none!' (Ps 69:20) Why does my Son ask if there is anyone who is able to console his Heart?

b   Jesus is God, but He is also man. He is perfect man. His Heart beats with divine and human love: in Him is all the fullness of love. His is the Heart which has loved most, which has suffered most, which is sensitive to the delicacies and the manifestations of affection, as it is to outrages and offenses.

c   The Heart of my Son is now, as it were, submerged in the great sea of human ingratitude.

d   How much it still loves you! It continues to beat with love for you, and it receives only offenses and sins.

e   To you He has revealed the secret of the Father, and He has led you back to Him. And now humanity has rebelled by the very rejection of God.

f   The flood of atheism is the thorn which now makes the Heart of my Son Jesus bleed continuously.

g   And you, O priests, are all my privileged sons because you are the most painful and loving fruit of the predilection of my Son Jesus.

h   You are called by divine plan to be his ministers, his apostles, his consolers.

i   Why then do so many of you again betray Him today?

j   Why do many of you again flee today and leave Jesus and the Church all alone?

k   Why are so many of you again sleeping today? And that sleeping is often the very work in which you allow yourselves to be caught up and overwhelmed.

l   That sleeping is also the way in which you seek to adapt yourselves to the world, and to succeed in being agreeable to, as well as accepted and understood by, this world. That sleeping is everything which humanly weighs you down.

m   Where are my sons who again today are willing to keep watch? In prayer:'Watch and pray lest you give in to temptation!' In the suffering of this new hour of agony for my Church:'The spirit is willing but the flesh is weak!' (Mk 14:38)

n   I am now calling you, my beloved sons; I am gathering you together from all parts of the world, as a mother hen does her chicks. I am gathering you all into my Immaculate Heart.

o   Can the Mother remain indifferent to the great abandonment and the great sorrow of her Son?

p And so then, understand that my duty is above all to console Him.

q Therefore, I want you all consecrated to my Heart to make you all into perfect consolers of the Heart of my Son Jesus."

94

Mother of Jesus, and Yours

a "Priests consecrated to me, my sons, this is the reason why *you have need of me* to become perfect consolers of my Son Jesus.

b At the moment when, overshadowed by the light of the Spirit, I uttered my *yes* to the Will of the Lord, the Word of the Father, the Second Person of the Most Holy Trinity, descended into my most pure womb, in the expectation of my maternal collaboration, to receive from me his human nature and thus become also man in the divine Person of my Son Jesus.

c Do you see how God entrusted Himself completely to this human creature of his? The reason is to be found in the mystery of the love of God.

d What moved God to stoop down to me was the profound sense I had of my littleness and of my poverty, as well as my perfect availability for the accomplishment of the Will of the Lord.

e God could have chosen many other ways to come to you, but He chose to select mine.

f And therefore, this way now becomes necessary for you to reach God.

g The first thing that I ask of you, sons, is your unconditional *yes*, and you say this by your consecration to my Immaculate Heart.

h And then I ask you to entrust yourselves to me with the greatest confidence and most complete abandonment.

i Your *yes* and your complete availability will allow your Mother to act.

j As with great love I formed the human nature of the Word, so too I will form in you, my sons, that image which corresponds more and more to the plan which the Father has for each one of you. The plan which God has for you, my beloved sons, is that you be priests according to the Heart of Jesus.

k   I am the Mother of God because I was chosen to bring God to men; I am your Mother because I have the duty of bringing to God those men redeemed by my Son and entrusted, each and all, by Him to me.

l   I am, therefore, the true Mother of Jesus and your true Mother as well.

m   On this day, when all Heaven exults in the contemplation of the mystery of the Incarnation of the Word, you too must rejoice while meditating on this mystery of the love of your Mother.

n   It is not given to everyone to understand this mystery of love; it is given only to the pure of heart, to the simple, to the little, to the poor. Go forward thus, my beloved ones, and you will always be consoled and encouraged more and more by me."

95

April 3, 1976
First Saturday

Your Light Will Shine Resplendently

a   "My beloved sons, today I accept with joy the homage that you give to my Immaculate Heart.

b   Let your hearts never become troubled.

c   Obscurity is descending ever more and more upon the world wrapped in the chill of the denial of God, of hatred, of egoism, of rebellion against God, of impiety.

d   The cup of iniquity is almost full, and the justice of God demands atonement.

e   I need you, my beloved sons, to form you into victims worthy of being offered to the divine Justice.

f   And so you will be called more and more to suffer. The hours of agony and passion are drawing closer to you.

g   Do you see, sons, what is happening even in the Church? Errors are being spread more and more and have taken hold of even the good; infidelity is spreading increasingly among the ministers of God and the souls consecrated to Him; even the hierarchy is impaired in the bond of charity and in its unity.

h   Above all, the Vicar of my Son Jesus is left more and more alone! He is calumniated, even in a most vulgar and blasphemous way; he is criticized and challenged and left more and more alone by my own sons.

i   You must share his lot with him: this is for him and for you the hour of Gethsemane.

j   Live it with me, in my Immaculate Heart.

k   You are the crown of love woven by me to place, as a source of comfort, about the Heart of my Son Jesus and of his Vicar on earth.

l   Therefore I ask you again for prayer, suffering and silence.

m   But your light must shine ever more and more brightly as the darkness envelops everything.

n   And yours will be the light of my presence in this most severe trial. And my motherly and merciful intervention will then become manifest to all."

96

April 13, 1976
Holy Tuesday

Look at My Crucified Son!

a   "Beloved sons, look at my crucified Son.

b   Look at his face stained with blood, his head crowned with thorns, his hands and his feet pierced by nails, his body which has been made an open wound by the scourges, his Heart pierced by a lance.

c   My beloved ones, look at my crucified Son, and *you will be faithful priests.*

d   How many of you have gone no further than to merely consider his word. They have wanted to penetrate and understand it only with their own human intelligence and have thus inadvertently fallen into most serious errors.

e   It is not with human intelligence alone that the word of my Son is to be read. He thanked the Father for having hidden the mysteries of his kingdom from the wise and prudent of this world to reveal them to the little ones.

f It is above all with interior humility and full docility of the soul that his word is to be read and understood.

g For this reason, my Son has entrusted its authentic interpretation only to the Magisterium of the Church, and this, to accustom you to this difficult, and yet so necessary, attitude of humility and interior docility.

h If you remain united to the Magisterium of the Church, and if you remain humble and attentive to what the Church points out to you, you will always keep within the truth of the word of Jesus.

i Today error is being spread more and more within the Church, and it seems that there is no longer any barrier that can contain it. It is spread about especially by many theologians; it is propagated by my poor priest-sons.

j How can you now, in the Church, be sure of being preserved from error?

k Look at my crucified Son, and you will be faithful.

l My Son who, God though He was, became obedient even to the death of the Cross.

m Look at his thorns; look at his blood; look at his wounds: they are flowers blossoming from the pain of his obedience.

n My beloved sons, now that darkness covers all things, you are being called to bear witness to the light of complete obedience to the Church: to the Pope and to the bishops united with him.

o And the more you witness to this complete obedience to the Church, the more you will be criticized, ridiculed and persecuted.

p But it is necessary that yours be an increasingly painful and crucifying witness in order to help many of my poor children to remain, even today, in truth and in fidelity."

97

April 16, 1976
Good Friday

See if There Is a Greater Sorrow

a "Beloved sons, behold my sorrow. See if there is a greater sorrow than mine!

b　My Son Jesus, abandoned by all, scourged, crowned with thorns, climbs Calvary with difficulty, carrying the heavy Cross on his poor shoulders.

c　He is unable to walk: He totters. There is not one gesture of pity: only hatred, hostility and indifference surround Him.

d　It is at this moment that the Father gives Him the comfort of his Mother. Think, my beloved sons, of the comfort and of the pain of this encounter.

e　Oh, the glance of my Son at that moment!… In my Heart there opened a wound which has never healed.

f　See the sorrow of your Mother as she contemplates her Son crucified, agonizing and slain.

g　Sorrow for Him who was dying; sorrow for you.

h　Now my Son continues his passion in his Mystical Body which is the Church.

i　Today I think again of the villainous gesture made by *Judas in betraying Jesus.* I feel again the same pain at the betrayal which so many of my priest-sons perpetrate every day.

j　O priests, my beloved sons, why do you still betray? Why do you still persist in your treason? Why do you not repent? Why do you not return?

k　And *Peter, who three times denies* my Son out of fear…

l　How many of you, for fear of not being understood, appreciated or esteemed, still deny the truth of the Gospel: 'I do not know that Man!'? (Mt 26:72)

m　And *the Apostles who run away* and leave Jesus alone for the whole of this long Friday!…

n　How many of you run away and abandon my Church. Some leave the Church to follow the world; others remain in the Church and, to please the world, abandon it in their minds and hearts.

o　The Church is not loved by many of you. The Vicar of my Son finds himself in a state of isolation which grows ever greater.

p　The bishops united with the Pope feel in their souls the thorn of this solitude: they are increasingly criticized, challenged and abandoned by their priests.

q　John remains. He stays with the Mother.

r　Priests of my Movement, you at least stay with the Church and with me, your Mother.

s   Look well at my sorrow, and suffer with me. In this hour of
Calvary for the Church, you will thus be the sign of my presence — the one and only comfort which the Father gives it, in
this moment of its passion and its martyrdom."

98   *May 3, 1976*

You Will Be Capable of Loving

a   "Beloved sons, let your hearts never be disturbed by the attacks against my Movement, which are becoming increasingly
frequent.

b   This is my work alone, and it corresponds to a special plan of
my Immaculate Heart.

c   Difficulties, misunderstandings and sufferings are permitted
by me that this work of mine may be purified yet more.

d   I want it to be purified of every human element that it may
thus reflect only my most pure light.

e   I want to cover all my beloved sons, the priests consecrated to
my Immaculate Heart, with this most pure light.

f   This is why I ask you for complete detachment from all persons, that I may give you true purity of heart. Every human
attachment to yourselves, to creatures and to the world beclouds
your interior purity.

g   Of course I cannot ask you to live apart from the world. It is in
accord with the Will of my Son that you live in the world, but
without being of the world.

h   You should live in the world in such a way as to belong solely
to my Son Jesus.

i   You must belong solely to my Son Jesus to bring the whole
world to Him and thus lead souls to salvation.

j   This is the kind of sympathy that you should have for the
world: the only kind desired by my Son and still proposed to
you by the Church today.

k   Many of my sons are today being drawn into numerous errors and becoming alienated from my Son and from me, by this
false way of understanding how you should live in the world.

l   How many of my poor priest-sons have ended up by being

totally of the world and have become its prisoners.

m   My Son Jesus saved this world above all when, to be faithful to the Will of the Father, He detached Himself from everyone to be raised up from the earth and hung upon the Cross.

n   You will begin to bring back many souls to my Son when, like Him, you also will be raised up from the earth. You must become accustomed to being raised up even now, spiritually speaking, by interior detachment from everyone.

o   Thus you will possess true purity of heart. And you will be truly capable of loving, even to the supreme test.

p   You will always be carried by your Mother, who knows where and how to lead you, that in each one of you the design of the Father's Will may be realized."

99
May 13, 1976
Anniversary of the First Apparition at Fatima

Consecrate Yourselves to My Immaculate Heart

a   "Today, my beloved sons, recall my coming down upon this earth, in the poor Cova da Iria in Fatima. I came from heaven to ask you for the consecration to my Immaculate Heart.

b   Through you, priests of my Movement, what I had then asked is now being realized. You are consecrating yourselves to my Immaculate Heart and leading souls entrusted to you to this consecration which I desire.

c   Since that day how much time has passed! It is now fifty nine years.

d   The Second World War, foretold by me as a punishment allowed by God for a humanity which alas did not repent, has also taken place.

e   Now you are living in that period of time when the Red Dragon, that is to say Marxist atheism, is spreading throughout the whole world and is increasingly bringing about the ruin of souls.

f   He is indeed succeeding in seducing and casting down a third of the stars of heaven.

118

g These stars, in the firmament of the Church, are the pastors: they are yourselves, my poor priest-sons.

h Has not perchance even the Vicar of my Son affirmed to you that it is the dearest friends, even the confreres of the same table, the priests and the religious, who are today betraying and setting themselves against the Church?

i This is then the hour to have recourse to the great remedy that the Father offers you to resist the seductions of the Evil One and to oppose the real apostasy which is spreading more and more among my poor children. *Consecrate yourselves to my Immaculate Heart.*

j To everyone who consecrates himself to me I again promise salvation: safety from error in this world and eternal salvation.

k You will obtain this through my special motherly intervention. Thus I will prevent you from falling into the enticements of Satan. You will be protected and defended by me personally; you will be consoled and strengthened by me.

l Now is the time when my call must be answered by all priests who want to remain faithful.

m *Each one must consecrate himself to my Immaculate Heart,* and through you priests many of my children will make this consecration.

n This is like a vaccine which, like a good Mother, I give you to preserve you from the epidemic of atheism, which is contaminating so many of my children and leading them to the death of the spirit.

o These are the times that I myself foretold; this is the hour of the purification. Heed the requests of your Mother, and entrust yourselves to me with all confidence and the most complete surrender."

100

May 28, 1976

Follow Me on the Path of My Son

a "Beloved sons, listen to the voice of your Mother who calls you gently to follow her.

Follow me along the path of prayer.

b   Many of my children are on the point of being eternally lost in these decisive moments, because there is no one to pray and sacrifice himself for them.

c   You must pray for them. Help me to save your brothers!

d   This is the hour of error, which is succeeding in entering everywhere and especially in seducing many of my priest-sons.

e   Do not be astonished if you see fall those who, still only yesterday, seemed the most faithful and most secure.

f   You will see fall even those who set themselves up as teachers of others.

g   Do not be surprised if, in this battle, those fall who did not want or did not know how to use the weapon that I myself gave you: my prayer, the simple and humble prayer of the holy rosary.

h   It is a simple and humble prayer, and therefore it is most efficacious in combating Satan who today is leading you astray especially by ostentation and pride.

i   It is my prayer because it is offered with me and through me. It has always been recommended to you by the Church and also by the first of my beloved sons, the Vicar of Jesus, with words that moved my motherly Heart.

Follow me along the path of suffering.

j   You have now arrived at the moment of your immolation; you are being called to suffer more and more.

k   Give me all your suffering. Today it is the misunderstandings, the attacks, the calumnies of your brothers. Tomorrow it will be persecutions, imprisonment, condemnations on the part of atheists and enemies of God who will see in you the obstacles that must be eliminated.

l   Walk with me, and follow me along the path of my Son Jesus, along the way of Calvary, along the way of the Cross.

m   Never as in these moments will you have to live so profoundly that which is the vocation of every Christian: 'He who wishes to come after Me must deny himself, take up his cross and follow Me!' (Mt 16:24)

n   Follow me, beloved sons: today it is necessary to follow your Mother if you want to travel without fear the path of my Son Jesus."

120

Say with Me Your Yes

a   "There is another thing I ask of you, beloved sons: your life. These are times, my sons, when I must ask of some of you the gift of your very lives.

b   The hour of martyrdom is in preparation, and the Mother is gently leading you to the moment of your immolation.

c   *Do not look any longer at this world:* look to me; look upon the face of your heavenly Mother.

d   I am reflecting upon you the light of paradise which awaits you, and at the hour of trial, you will be strengthened and encouraged.

e   *Do not look to creatures* who, misled and corrupted by Satan, will hurl themselves upon you with hatred and violence.

f   And yet, my beloved sons, you have always loved and done good to all; you have always sought to help everyone.

g   And now the chill of hatred and ingratitude is spreading all about you.

h   Do not be afraid. This is the hour of Satan and of the power of darkness.

i   Do not fear: take refuge in my Immaculate Heart.

j   In this motherly Heart you will be warmed and consoled. Here is the source of your joy and the secret of your confidence.

k   In this Heart you are little children whom I am forming in interior meekness so that, at the invitation of my Son who is associating you in his Sacrifice, you may respond with a *yes.*

l   Say it with me, my beloved sons, this *yes* of yours to the Will of the Father. Then very soon you will see appearing the dawn of a new world, washed and purified by your reparative offering."

Your Most Necessary Witness

a   "Be ever more docile in my hands, beloved sons.

b   Your life will be truly mine alone, if at every moment you offer me your interior docility.

c   How many priests there are today who do not obey, who are in rebellion, who no longer observe any kind of discipline!

d   Your interior docility will bring you to a more complete discipline in respect to the norms and directives of the Church.

e   You suffered today when you saw, in this place consecrated to me, what a great number of profanations there are and how many sorrows are inflicted on my motherly Heart. Children who come to me dressed so indecently and who manage to pass freely at the very feet of my venerated image…

f   Share in my sorrow, and make reparation for these true profanations that are being committed every day in this place consecrated to me.

g   Unfortunately the most responsible are the priests. You see how they themselves dress in all sorts of ways, sometimes in ways that are so shocking that they even scandalize the faithful themselves.

h   And yet the existing discipline of the Church obliges these sons of mine to wear the ecclesiastical garb. But who any longer observes this discipline? Few, and they are for this reason all the more thought of as backward and old-fashioned.

i   This question of garb is just a small example, but it is indicative of a sad reality: today lack of discipline, disobedience and intolerance of any norms is spreading among priests, who are nevertheless still the sons of my maternal predilection.

j   You at least, O priests consecrated to my Immaculate Heart, be an example by your interior docility and your obedience to the discipline of the Church.

k   This is today the most urgent and necessary witness that you can give.

l   Only thus can you spread about you the example and the fragrance of my Son Jesus. You will be chosen instruments for the return of many priests to their duty of giving that good example, which is one of the most important exigencies of your own ministry."

103

In the Spirit of Filial Surrender

a   "Son of my maternal predilection, do not let yourself be distracted by things and by human vicissitudes. Remain always close to my Heart in prayer!

b   I am arranging everything for you as your real Mother: the persons you are to meet, the circumstances in which you find yourself and what you are to do. And so accustom yourself to live trustfully in the present moment which the Father gives you and the Mother prepares for you.

c   Sons consecrated to my Immaculate Heart, you should all live in the spirit of filial surrender, with the most complete confidence in your Mother's action.

d   A priest, who consecrates himself to my Heart, draws upon himself this predilection on my part, which becomes stronger and more evident and which the soul comes to perceive with greater and greater clarity.

e   It is I myself who, with you, am enabled to carry out in a more complete manner my function as Mother. I am thus able to act through you because, by your consecration to my Immaculate Heart, you truly place yourselves like little children in my arms.

f   Thus I speak to you, and you can hear my voice. I lead you, and you let yourselves be guided by me, with docility.

g   I clothe you with my own virtues; I nourish you with my food. You are more and more interiorly drawn by the perfume of this motherly action of mine which makes you little, poor, humble, simple and chaste.

h   Above all, I bring you gently before the divine Person of my Son Jesus present, as in heaven, in the sacrament of the Eucharist. You acquire from me a taste for prayer. Prayer of adoration, prayer of thanksgiving, prayer of reparation.

i   The more the coldness of desertion and silence surrounds my Son Jesus, present among you in the Eucharist, the more I myself gather the voices of my beloved sons so that, united with my voice, there may be composed even here on earth a melody of love to be offered to the Heart of my Son for his consolation.

j   This is the army that I am preparing; this is the cohort of my priests that I am now gathering from all parts of the world. A hidden cohort of little children consecrated to my Immaculate Heart, whom I am making more and more like myself, that Jesus may offer them to the Father as a sign of reparation and atonement.

k   Therefore I say to you again: pay no attention to all the evil which is spreading more and more and flooding everywhere. Disregard also the great evil which Satan is succeeding in spreading even in the Church.

l   Turn your gaze to me alone, and consider the great good which, in silence, your Mother is accomplishing by drawing an ever increasing number of priest-sons to her Heart.

m   Close your eyes to everything else, and open them only to this marvelous reality. This is why I ask you again, sons, to live in the spirit of filial abandonment and of your most steadfast confidence in my Immaculate Heart."

104

July 26, 1976
Feast of Sts. Joachim & Ann

My Time

a   "My time, beloved sons, is not measured by days. My time is measured only by the beating of my motherly Heart. Each beat of this Heart marks a new day of salvation and of mercy for you, my poor children.

b   And so I invite you to live only in trust.

c   Your time must be measured by trust in the merciful love of the Father and in the action of your heavenly Mother.

d   My parents, Ann and Joachim, whom the Church calls to mind today and holds up to you as examples, lived in this trust.

124

e   All the saints and the friends of God lived in this trust.

f   The Almighty, in carrying out his plan in every age, always made use of this trust alone.

g   Often He realized it even against everyone's expectation, at a moment when no one thought it possible. This is how the great plan of God was accomplished through these two poor and humble creatures, whom He called to prepare for the birth of your heavenly Mother.

h   And your Mother was called to hope against the very evidence of things and to place her complete trust only in the word of God. Thus she became the Mother of the Word and gave you her Son Jesus.

i   Now I have announced to you the triumph of my Immaculate Heart and the necessary and painful purification which must precede it.

j   I have also told you that this is the time of the purification and that these are the years of my triumph. But do not search out the moment, scrutinizing the future and counting the years, the months and the days. In this way you would be caught up by anxiety and agitation and would truly waste your time, which is so precious.

k   My beloved sons, my time is not to be measured in this way, but only *by your trust in me,* who am preparing you to be instruments chosen and formed by me to bring about at this time the triumph of my Immaculate Heart."

105

July 31, 1976
Feast of St. Ignatius of Loyola

Your Difficulties

a   "Follow me, beloved sons, in complete trust, and do not let yourselves be troubled by the difficulties which you encounter on your way.

b   These difficulties are permitted by God to help you grow in your life of perfect consecration to my Immaculate Heart.

c   They detach you from your way of seeing and thinking, from your tastes and attachments, and little by little, they bring you to see and think only according to the Heart of my Son Jesus.

d   After each difficulty I see the life of Jesus increase in you: and it is this that gives such great comfort to my motherly Heart.

e   Have you not become aware, my sons, of how, under my personal influence, your life is truly changing?

f   It is the *interior difficulties* of the soul which cause you most pain.

g   You are mine, and yet you feel attracted to the world; you are clothed in my own purity, and yet you experience the affliction of temptations of the flesh. Some of you complain and would like to be free of this.

h   And yet, my beloved sons, how much this interior difficulty which you are experiencing makes you grow in detachment from your own selves!

i   Never look at yourselves. The less beautiful you look to yourselves the more beautiful you will look to me and my Son Jesus.

j   It is my mantle that covers you. It is my own purity which causes you to shine.

k   Then there are the *exterior difficulties*. These are the ones in the midst of which you find yourselves: misunderstandings, criticism. Sometimes I permit even scorn and calumny.

l   My Adversary makes special use of this last mentioned, above all, to strike at you and discourage you.

m   And you, how are you to respond? As Jesus did: by silence, by prayer, by living in intimate union with the Father.

n   In the light of the Father, all that is not true, all that is not good, all deceit and all calumny dissolve of themselves like mist in the sun.

o   And since you are in my Immaculate Heart, there is nothing that can touch you.

p   Anyone who would intentionally do you harm will not succeed in striking you; anyone who acts in good faith will see the light even before the evil reaches you.

q   And you will walk in peace, even in the midst of the tempest of the present moment.

r   Then there are also the *difficulties of your time*. Beloved sons, with what care you have been formed and prepared by me for your time!

_s These difficulties are also permitted by me that they may make you ever more docile instruments in my hands for the plan which I am realizing at this time.

_t Atheism which is spreading throughout the world, the crises which continue to expand within the Church, error which is being disseminated everywhere: these are the waves of the great tempest.

_u You are being called to be my peace in this storm.

_v And so walk in serenity, walk in tranquility, walk in trust. Thus the more obscurity descends, the more you will be my light; and if the storm increases day by day, you will be ever more and more my peace. You will give to each one, at every moment, the sign of my motherly presence among you."

106

Only with the Pope

_a "Today from every part of the world comes that homage which is so pleasing to my Immaculate Heart, the homage of those priests who are consecrated to me, of you, sons of my maternal predilection.

_b Let yourselves be led by me, and you will not feel the weight of your daily difficulties.

_c I want you in my arms, all of you given over to my Immaculate Heart, that you may thus walk toward the goal which I have set for each one of you.

_d I have already pointed out what this goal is: to make of you priests according to the Heart of Jesus.

_e You must be truly Jesus today for the men of your time.

_f *Jesus who speaks*: thus you will speak only the truth. The truth contained in the Gospel and guaranteed by the Magisterium of the Church.

_g Today, as darkness descends upon everything and error spreads more and more in the Church, you should direct all people to that fount from which Jesus causes his words of truth to issue

forth: the Gospel entrusted to the hierarchical Church, that is to
h say, the Pope and the bishops united to him – not to individual priests, not to individual bishops, but only to those priests and bishops who are united with the Pope.

i Today, how deeply wounded and afflicted is my Heart of Mother of the Church by the scandal, even of bishops who do not obey the Vicar of my Son and who drag a great number of my children along the path of error.

j And therefore, you should at this time proclaim to all by your words that Jesus has made Peter alone the foundation of his Church and the infallible guardian of truth.

k Today whoever is not with the Pope will not succeed in remaining in the truth.

l The seductions of the Evil One have become so insidious and dangerous that they are succeeding in deceiving almost anyone.

m Here even the good can fall.

n Here even the masters and the wise ones can fall.

o Here even the priests and the bishops can fall.

p Those will never fall *who are always with the Pope*.

q This is why I want to make you a disciplined and attentive cohort, obedient and docile even to the desires of this first of my beloved sons, the Vicar of my Jesus.

r *Jesus who acts*: you must above all relive Jesus in your life and be a living Gospel.

s For this I will make you ever poorer, ever more humble, ever purer, ever smaller.

t Do not be afraid of entrusting yourselves completely to me. I am his Mother and yours; and I know how to do only one thing for you, and that is to help you to be born and to grow up like other little Jesuses for the salvation of all my children.

u When this cohort of priests is ready; then it will be the time for me to crush the head of my Adversary, and the renewed world will experience the joy of the triumph of my Heart."

107

August 15, 1976
Solemnity of the Assumption
of the Blessed Virgin Mary into Heaven

Live in Paradise with Me

a   "Live, my beloved sons, there where I am: in paradise, assumed body and soul, to share fully in the glory of my Son Jesus.

b   Always associated with Him through my role of Mother on this earth, I am now in paradise associated in the glory of the Son, who wants the Mother at his side, having given me a glorified body like his own.

c   Here is the reason for this extraordinary privilege of mine.

d   As by my *yes* I made it possible for the Word of God to assume his human nature in my virginal womb, so also by my *yes* I entrusted myself to the action of my Son Jesus, who assumed your Mother into the glory of heaven, body and soul.

e   Mine is a transfigured and glorified body, but a real body, my beloved sons. Mother and Son are now together in paradise forever.

f   But I am also your real Mother, and thus I can love you not only with my soul, but also with my glorified body.

g   I love you with this mother's Heart of mine which has never ceased to beat with love for you.

h   Beloved sons, you also should be living there where I am: *live in paradise with me.*

i   It is true; you are still on this earth of sorrows, and often you experience all its weight and suffering.

j   But why, while still living in this land of exile, do you not also live, even now, there where your Mother is? Live in paradise with me, and do not let yourselves be attracted by the world, nor imprisoned by this earth.

k   Today there is a tendency which is extremely false and dangerous: that of looking only at this earth. It is as though we are afraid that, if we look at paradise, we will be drawn away from the duties of daily life. Live in paradise with me, and then you will live well, even on this earth!

l   Carry out here below the plan of the Heavenly Father, and you will create true happiness all about you.

m   The more you look to the Father and live with me, the more will you labor on this earth for your own good and the good of all.

n   Paradise — that is, the real one — can never be found on this earth.

o   How he deceives and seduces you, this Adversary of mine who in his fury tries to prevent you from coming up here to be with my Son and with me!

p   Paradise is found only in the light of the Most Holy Trinity, with my Son Jesus and with me.

q   The angels and the saints are illumined by this light, and they rejoice in it. All paradise is resplendent with this light.

r   Live then while searching for, cherishing and gazing upon this paradise which awaits you, my beloved sons.

s   And here below, *live in the paradise of my Immaculate Heart.*

t   Then you will be serene and deeply happy.

u   You will always be littler and more abandoned, poorer and more chaste.

v   And the littler, poorer and more chaste you become, the more you will be able to enter into the paradise of my Immaculate Heart, where time is now marked by the beating of a Heart which knows no stopping."

108

August 22, 1976
Feast of the Queenship of Mary

Your Queen and Your Leader

a   "*I am your Queen.*

b   The power of the Father, the wisdom of the Son and the love of the Holy Spirit, in the light of the Most Holy Trinity, have confirmed me forever in my function of maternal royalty.

c   This is my crowning glory.

d   It is my universal royalty: Mother of the Son, Queen with the Son.

e   *I am your Leader.*

f   I am calling you, my beloved sons, to gather you all into my cohort, of which I myself am the Queen and the Leader.

g   Therefore *there should be no leader* among you: you are all brothers, united in love that must grow ever more and more.

h   If anyone wishes to become the greatest, let him become truly
the least.

i   Only he who loves the most, who serves the most, who listens
to me the most, who becomes ever smaller to the point of disappearing in my Immaculate Heart is the one whom I myself will
make ever greater.

j   *I am your Leader.*

k   You therefore, my beloved ones, must listen to my voice, be
docile to my teachings and above all be prompt and obedient to
my orders.

l   I want to make of you sons who want to obey, who always
know how to obey.

m   Obedience and docility: this is the livery in which I wish to
attire you.

n   I will give my orders through the voice of him whom my
Son has appointed to govern his Church: the Pope with the hierarchy united to him.

o   How my motherly Heart is wounded and saddened today to
see that some priests and even some bishops no longer obey the
orders of the Vicar of my Son Jesus!

p   Every kingdom divided against itself is destined to defeat and
ruin.

q   These poor sons of mine who do not obey and who rebel are
already victims of the most subtle and insidious kind of pride
and are walking towards their death.

r   How Satan, my Adversary from the beginning, is succeeding
today in deceiving and seducing you!

s   He makes you believe that you are guardians of tradition and
defenders of the faith, while he causes you to be the first to make
shipwreck of your faith and leads you, all unaware, into error.

t   He makes you believe that the Pope is denying the truth, and
thus Satan demolishes the foundation on which the Church is
built and through which the truth is kept intact throughout the
ages.

u   He goes so far as to make you think that I myself have nothing to do with the Holy Father's way of acting. And so, in my
name, sharp criticisms aimed at the person and the work of the
Holy Father are spread about.

v Priests, sons of my maternal predilection, be prudent, be attentive, be enlightened because the darkness is invading everything.

w How can the Mother publicly criticize the decisions of the Pope, when he alone has the special grace for the exercise of this sublime ministry?

x I was silent at my Son's voice; I was silent at the voice of the Apostles. I am now lovingly silent at the voice of the Pope: that it might be disseminated more and more, that it might be heard by all, that it might be received into souls.

y This is why I am very close to the person of this first of my beloved sons, the Vicar of my Son Jesus.

z By my silence, I am helping him to speak.

A By my silence, I am lending strength to his own words.

B Return, return, my priest-sons, to love, obedience and communion with the Pope!

C Only in this way can you belong to my cohort, of which I am the Queen and Leader.

D Only in this way can you hear my orders, which I will give through the very voice of the Pope.

E Only in this way can you fight along with me for the assured victory; otherwise, you are already marching toward defeat.

F Beloved sons, if you consecrate yourselves to my Immaculate Heart and entrust yourselves to me completely, I will cover you with my own brightness, and you will always be filled with light. I will clothe you with my interior docility, and you will be ever obedient; I will thus make you instruments fit for this battle of mine, and you will see in the end my royal victory."

109

September 8, 1976
Feast of the Nativity of the Blessed Virgin Mary

You Must Be Little

a "Look, O sons, at your Mother, as a little infant. Because I was little, I was pleasing to the Most High.

b The exemption from all stain of sin whatsoever which I enjoyed, by privilege, from the first instant of my conception, gave me the true measure of my littleness.

c   Little, because a creature of God and chosen beforehand to be the Mother of the Word.

d   Little, because I received everything from God.

e   Little, because I was overshadowed by the power of God who covered me with his greatness.

f   My richness is therefore only that of the little and poor: humility, faith, abandonment, hope.

g   Today the Church invites you to contemplate your heavenly Mother at the moment of her birth.

h   Look, my beloved ones, at this infant Mother of yours, and learn to be little.

i   You must be little because you are my children, and therefore you should live the same life as I.

j   You must be little to become docile instruments in my plan and to draw upon yourselves the good pleasure of my Son Jesus.

k   How Jesus loves you, my dear sons! Indeed He loves you because you want to be little, poor, simple and humble.

l   You must be little to oppose Satan who is succeeding in leading people astray by pride and arrogance.

m   Do you not understand that he will never succeed in leading you astray or in deceiving you if you remain humble?

n   You must be ever littler because your Mother wants you entirely for herself: she wants to feed you, to clothe you, to carry you in her arms.

o   You must be little because in this way you will always say *yes* to the Will of the Father.

p   Say with me your *yes*. Thus in you I will repeat the *yes* of my perfect docility to the Will of God.

q   And lastly, you must be little to form this humble heel which Satan will try to bite, but with which I will crush his head.

r   You must therefore be ever littler if you wish to prepare for the greatest triumph of my Immaculate Heart."

This Is Why I Speak to You

a   "If you are little, you will always hear my voice.

b   My beloved sons, do not let yourselves be misled by the many voices which are heard today. My Adversary deceives you with ideas and confuses you with words.

c   You are, as it were, being submerged by a sea of words which grows ever greater and covers everything. The event of the Tower of Babel described in the Bible is now being repeated. You are now reliving the drama of the confusion of tongues.

d   Your own words confuse you. Your own voices hinder you from understanding.

e   It is now more than ever necessary to listen to my voice. *This is why I speak to you.*

f   *I speak to you* to help you recover from the confusion, created today by your own words. Hence, as Mother, I gently lead you to listen to the one Word of the Father. This Word was made flesh and life in my most pure womb. My Heart opened to welcome it and guarded it as a precious treasure.

g   *I speak to you* because today it is necessary to listen to his word. It is necessary to welcome it and to guard it jealously.

h   It is only the word of my Son that I want you to hear. Today his voice has become, as it were, drowned out: it is the Word of the Father; it is my Son Jesus who is no longer heard.

i   His word, so clearly contained in the Gospel, is, as it were, submerged by so many other human voices. You have made a gospel of your own with your own words. You, my beloved sons, should listen to and announce only the word of my Son, just as it is set down in his Gospel.

j   The Church speaks to you. But each one wants to have his own say as to what she is telling you, and thus insecurity and confusion spreads about. And the Church is more than ever torn by this real confusion of tongues.

k   *I speak to you* to tell you what sort of word you should listen to today in the Church: that of the Pope, and that of the bishops united with him.

l   The darkness grows ever deeper, and I speak to you to be your light. Error spreads, and I speak to you, my beloved sons, because you are called to remain in the truth, you the ministers of the word, you the heralds of the truth.

m   The future looks distressing, and I speak to you to urge you to be confident and completely abandoned, in my motherly Heart.

n   A deafening uproar of voices brings greater and greater confusion to everything. And I speak to you to implore silence, suffering and prayer.

o   *I speak to you* to ask of you today those things which are most precious to me. Each day I gather up your prayer and your suffering, and they are deposited by me in the chalice of my Immaculate Heart and are offered to the justice of God which seeks to be appeased.

p   Hence today everything can still be saved: *and this is why I speak to you!*

q   Beloved sons, do not close your hearts to my words.

r   The plan of the Father has made much of what awaits you depend on whether my words are harkened to or rejected.

s   The purification can still be set back or shortened. Much suffering can still be spared you.

t   Listen to me, sons, with simplicity. If you are little, then you will hear me and heed me. Little children understand very well the voice of the Mother.

u   Happy those who still listen to me. They will now receive the light of the truth and will obtain from the Lord the gift of salvation."

111
November 8, 1976

Look at Your Mother!

a   "Look, son, at your heavenly Mother. See how beautiful she is!

b   She is the Father's masterpiece of beauty. She is the cradle of the Son. She is the delicate tapestry of the Holy Spirit. She is the enclosed garden in full bloom, where the delight of the Most

HolyTrinity has grown ever greater.

c   Look only at your Mother! Thus my beauty will cover you. I want to clothe you in my heavenly mantle; I want to clothe you with my purity; I want to surround you with my own light.

d   You feel little, and this is true. You feel poor, and you see yourself full of defects; it seems to you that you have nothing to give me.

e   Oh, your love is enough for me! I do not want anything else of you...

f   You cannot understand at this time, but in heaven you will contemplate, in yourself, the glory of your Mother and the summit of love to which Jesus, with her, has brought you.

g   It seems to you as though Jesus is hiding Himself to put his Mother before Him. But this is because He wants it to be she who loves Him in you!

h   It seems to you that you always have the Mother before you. I see that it is Jesus Himself who leads you to me, because in this way you will give to his Heart that joy which others cannot give Him.

i   Do not talk; be more and more silent with everyone. Never become discouraged because of your defects. I love you so much, son; I look at your heart, not at your character. And when by impulse you make mistakes, how great is the joy you give me if immediately you humble yourself and ask forgiveness. Offer me your wounds. Give me always a *yes*, and no longer think anything of yourself. I want to be the one who thinks of everything..."

112

The Time of the Purification

a   "Listen to my voice, and let yourselves be led by me, beloved sons. Thus my own life will increase in you, and you will spread my light all about you.

b   It is now becoming ever more necessary and urgent to spread

136

the gentle invitation of your Mother throughout the world.

c   This world is constantly drawing further and further from God and no longer pays any attention to the word of my Son Jesus. Thus does it fall into the darkness of denial of God and into the deceitful mirage of being able to do without Him.

d   It is as if you have even succeeded in building a purely human civilization, obstinately closed against any divine influence whatsoever.

e   God, in his infinite majesty, cannot but hold in disdain this humanity which has gathered itself together in opposition to Him.

f   Thus the cold of egoism and pride spreads ever more and more. Hatred prevails over love and daily claims its countless victims, victims known and unknown, violence against innocent and defenseless creatures who, at every moment, cry out for terrible vengeance before the throne of God.

g   And more and more, sin continues to pervade everything.

h   Where today is there a place where sin does not exist? Even those houses consecrated to the worship of God are profaned by the sins that are committed in them. It is the persons who are consecrated, the very priests and religious, who have lost even the sense of sin. Some of them, in their thoughts, their words and their way of life, sacrilegiously allow themselves to be led by Satan.

i   Never before as today has the Devil succeeded so well in seducing you.

j   He seduces you through pride and thus brings you to justify and legitimize moral disorder. And after you have fallen he succeeds in smothering within you the voice of remorse which is a true gift of the Spirit, which calls you to conversion. How numerous now are my poor children who for years have stopped going to confession!

k   They are rotting in sin and are eaten up with impurity, with a devouring attachment to money, and with pride.

l   Satan has now pitched his tents even among the ministers of the sanctuary and has brought the abomination of desolation into the holy temple of God.

m   It is necessary, then, that the Mother speak to you and lead you by the hand. Her duty is above all that of guiding you in the struggle against the infernal dragon.

137

n So I say to you: these are the times of the purification; these are the times when the justice of God will chastise this rebellious and perverted world, for its salvation.

o The purification has already begun within the Church: pervaded with error, darkened by Satan, covered with sin, betrayed and violated by some of its own pastors.

p Satan sifts you like wheat; how much chaff will soon be blown away by the wind of persecution!

q From now on, my presence among you will become more continuous and more apparent. You yourselves will experience it more and more, as from every part of the world I am already calling you and gathering you together in the cohort of my priests, that you may all be guided by me in the battle which has already begun."

113
December 4, 1976
First Saturday

Of What Are You Afraid?

a "My beloved sons, be ever more docile, and allow yourselves to be led by me with complete confidence.

b In the darkness of this hour of trial for the Church, you are called by me to walk in the light.

c The light shines forth from my Immaculate Heart and comes to you to envelop you and illumine your path.

d Stand firm; never again must you doubt! Your road is safe because it has been marked out for you by your heavenly Mother. How much my motherly Heart is saddened by the doubt and mistrust which is taking more and more hold of the souls of so many of my priest-sons! Why do you doubt? Of what are you afraid?

e Jesus redeemed you from the Evil One at the very hour of his triumph: 'This is the hour of Satan and of the power of darkness.'
(cf. Lk 22:53)

f My Son Jesus gave you life for ever at the very hour when He was slain on the Cross.

g At the moment of his death, He set all of you free from death.

138

h   My Church, of which I am the Mother, lives again the life of Christ and is now called to tread the same path He trod.

i   Of what, then, are you afraid?

j   Of a world that has hurled itself with violent hatred against you? Of Satan who has succeeded in making his way into the heart of the Church and of reaping his victims from among its very pastors? Or of the error which menaces it, or the sin which darkens it more and more, or the infidelity which floods it?

k   This, my beloved sons, is for my Church still the hour of Satan and of the power of darkness.

l   It will be also immolated like Christ on the Cross and be called to die for the salvation and the renewal of the world.

m   And since this is the hour of your purification, it is above all the hour of your suffering.

n   Could it perhaps be this that you fear?

o   But what if the Father has called you now, one by one, from all eternity for this hour? And what if your heavenly Mother has long since chosen you and prepared you for this hour?…

p   Live then in serenity of spirit and without fear, even in the midst of the anxieties and threats of your time.

q   And so I say again: do not be always peering into the future to see what is going to happen. Live only the present moment with trust and complete abandonment, in this Heart of mine."

114

December 24, 1976
The Holy Night

I Ask the Gift of Your Love

a   "Beloved son of my Immaculate Heart, spend these hours of vigil with me: in prayer, in silence, in attentiveness to your heavenly Mother.

b   Today, as of old, is the birthday of my Son Jesus; today, as of old, my dear sons, you should prepare for his coming.

c   With my spouse, Joseph, a just and chaste man, humble and strong, chosen by the Father to be of precious assistance to me especially during these moments, I completed the last stage of a most fatiguing journey.

d   I felt the fatigue of the journey, the sharpness of the cold, the uncertainty of the arrival, the insecurity of what might be lying ahead of us.

e   And yet I dwelt, as it were, far from the world and the things of the world, all absorbed in a continual ecstasy with my Child, Jesus, whom I was about to give you.

f   My sole support was trust in the Father; the sweet expectation of the Son lulled me; in the Spirit, I was filled only with the fullness of love.

g   As Mother I thought of a house, and the Father prepared us a shelter; I dreamt of a cradle for my little baby, and even then the manger was ready; on that night all paradise was contained within a cave.

h   And when fatigue had seized upon us and the continual refusal to receive us had worn out our human endurance, then the cave was ready for the light. And in the light of a heaven which opened to receive the great prayer of the Mother, my virginal bud opened in the divine gift of the Son.

i   With me, my beloved sons, give to his Heart the first kiss. Feel with me its first beat. Be the first to look into his eyes.

j   Hear his first cry of weeping, of joy, of love.

k   He wants only your comfort.

l   He asks for your gift of love.

m   Enwrap his little limbs in love; He has so much need of warmth! All the coldness of the world surrounds Him. Only the warmth of love comforts Him.

n   Since that time, each year the Church renews this mystery. Since that time, my Son is ever being born again in hearts.

o   And today, also, there is a world which rejects Him and, in great part, closes its door to Him. Just as in those days, the great ones ignore Him.

p   But the hearts of the little ones open to Him. The longing of the simple is appeased. The life of the pure is enlightened.

q   On this holy night, my beloved sons, I want to entrust my Child to you.

r   I lay Him down in the cradle of your hearts. Let the great fire of your love increase. With Him I must enkindle all the love of the world."

140

True Poverty of Spirit

a   "Spend the last hours of this year, which the Immaculate Heart of your heavenly Mother has made extraordinary for you by its graces and gifts, in prayer and interior recollection.

b   I myself have wanted you here and have led you to this house which I have been preparing for you for some time. You are here in silence and in prayer: you listen to me; you speak to me; you call upon the Father with me. You have close to you this brother of yours who loves you so much and who, in my Heart, deeply cherishes you.

c   Your heavenly Mother sees with eyes that are different from yours: hers is a regard of light and of love. For me, that person is great who is considered a nobody and of no value in the eyes of men.

d   This house, which is hidden and unknown and attracts no attention, is now the place of my presence, and it is here, and nowhere else, that I have wanted you to spend these holy days with me.

e   Accustom yourself to see everything with the same eyes as your Mother. Always regard with pleasure and very special love those whom the world ignores and disdains.

f   May your heart always consider those to be greater whom men consider as nobodies and of no worth: the poor, the small, the humble, the suffering, the unknown.

g   Even among your brother-priests you should feel closer to those who are overlooked and considered as nothing. Oh, if you only knew what precious treasures to my motherly Heart are all these beloved sons of mine whom no one esteems.

h   Give them to me on this last night of the year: offer them to me, one by one. What comfort their love brings to my Immaculate Heart! How their hidden beauty makes amends for the sorrow caused to my Heart by those who consider themselves great and esteemed, and who spend their lives seeking every kind of human recognition.

i   True poverty of spirit is the gift I make to him whom I call. It is emptiness which draws my love. It is the wavelength on which my voice can be heard and understood.

j　　Be always poor in this way, that you may see each new day through my eyes and give me to him who, in poverty, has awaited me for so long."

1977

IN EVERY PART OF THE WORLD

Walk in My Light

a   "Begin the new year with me, my beloved sons, on this day when the Church invites you to contemplate my divine maternity.

b   As my Son Jesus entrusted Himself totally to me, to find in his Mother a safeguard and protection, so too should you let yourselves be led in security by your heavenly Mother.

c   What will this year be like? What events await you?

d   My beloved sons, you should not have to trouble yourselves over what awaits you, if you accustom yourselves to live each moment in my motherly Heart.

e   Each day, humanity is drawing further and further away from God, and men in ever growing numbers persist in turning away from his Law.

f   Because of this, with the new year the darkness will become more dense, and the calamities and sufferings that await you will become greater.

g   Even in my Church the crisis will become more acute because my most urgent call to prayer, to conversion and to penance will be listened to less and less.

h   Unfortunately, there will be many priests among those who do not heed my voice.

i   Consequently, the pastors will have less light, and the flock will be scattered along the roads of insecurity and division, of error and apostasy.

j   Pastors of the Church, become once again that which my Son Jesus wishes you to be!

k   Once again, be zealous and ardent only for the salvation of souls; once again, be strict guardians of the truth of the Gospel!

l   Once again, follow Jesus to Calvary, and do not let yourselves be misled or distracted by the world to which you often conform your life!

m   My beloved sons, the more this darkness will descend upon the world and into the Church, the clearer will be the light which will shine forth from my Immaculate Heart to show you the way.

n Walk in this light. Thus you will always be filled with light.

o In you who are following me, my Immaculate Heart has already today achieved its triumph.

p The triumph of the Heart of the Mother is won in the souls and the lives of her faithful children.

q In them it is good which triumphs at the very moment when evil is spreading everywhere. While sin tries to pervade everything, the grace and the love of God triumph in them; if error succeeds more and more in corrupting minds, they bear witness to the truth.

r If division tears the Church, they love her and live for her unity; if the Vicar of my Son is more and more left alone and abandoned, they draw close to him with greater love to become his constant comfort and defense.

s Yes, at this very moment when my Adversary is now triumphing everywhere, my Immaculate Heart also has its triumph in the lives of my beloved sons.

t So do not fear if you are beginning a year which will be even more difficult and painful: the more you see darkness enveloping everything, the more brilliant will be the light of my presence among you.

u Consequently, I ask you to begin this new year with me confidently and without fear. My Son Jesus will always be with you, and with Him, in your company, will be his Mother and yours."

117
January 13, 1977

I Will Teach You to Love

a "My very dear son, I love you. I love you so much! It pleases you to hear this repeated to you; it pleases my motherly Heart to say it to you more and more often.

b From now on, it should be love alone that guides you at every moment and in each of your actions.

c Love for the Father, for the Son and for the Holy Spirit — love for this Divine and Most Holy Trinity which, dwelling within your soul, impels your heart towards an ever greater love for your heavenly Mother as well.

d   It is in my Immaculate Heart that your Mother will form you to an ever greater and purer love for God.

e   No creature has ever been able to love the Lord as has your heavenly Mother.

f   The Spirit of the Father and of the Son begets in you a great thirst for perfect love, and thus your soul is inclined spontaneously to seek the Heart of the Mother.

g   I will teach you to love God and your neighbor ever more and more. I will give to your heart my own capacity to love. I will help you to divest yourself of every other yearning, to bring you to a simple, continuous and pure act of love.

h   And thus you will realize your vocation…

i   My only joy is to bring you to love, so that my own Heart may love, within yours, the Most Holy and Divine Trinity."

118   *Rome (Italy); January 15, 1977*

You Will Be Completely Renewed

a   "My Church, beloved son of mine, has become now more than ever the target at which my Adversary directs his rage in an increasingly violent manner.

b   The Vicar of my Son Jesus has had a foreboding of this decisive hour of combat, and so he has solemnly proclaimed me to be Mother of the Church.

c   As I am the true Mother of Jesus, so also am I the true Mother of the Church which is his Mystical Body. And as Mother I look today upon this Daughter of mine with apprehension and with a sorrow that is constantly growing.

d   My Heart is again pierced by a sword to see the Church more and more violated by my Adversary.

e   Satan has truly penetrated within it, and every day he is harvesting his victims, even from among its very pastors. He has succeeded in obscuring its light with the darkness of error which endeavors to pervade everything.

f   The Vicar of my Son is at times cut off, as it were, from his own children whom he must nevertheless guide, and the cross of this suffering of his becomes daily greater.

g   Among those who surround him, there are those who sometimes do not act out of love for him, but who are moved rather by a spirit of pride and a thirst to dominate.

h   Satan is trying to strike even the hierarchy in its bond of love and unity.

i   How many pastors are there today who do not love and help each other?

j   Many of them criticize and often obstruct each other, seeking only to get further ahead more quickly, trampling underfoot at times the most elementary demands of justice.

k   Even in the case of important problems which regard the life of the Church and souls, how many are there who, in their love for truth, demonstrate unanimity of thought and action?

l   And as a consequence these priests, these sons of my maternal predilection, may find themselves left to their own resources.

m   Thus an increasing number are led astray by the general confusion, become the victims of error and wander far from my Son Jesus and the truth of his Gospel.

n   Thus their light becomes extinguished and the faithful walk in darkness. How many there are among them who now live habitually in sin, and who turn a deaf ear to my pressing invitations to conversion! They even try to justify themselves, adapting themselves to the mentality of the world which today legitimizes even the most serious moral disorders.

o   How many of my priest-sons no longer pray? They are swallowed up in activities and no longer have a moment to pray.

p   This poor Church of mine! As Mother I draw near, my Daughter, and I find you so sick! It would seem as though you are close to death…

q   How profound is your affliction and your abandonment! More and more each day, my Adversary strikes at you in those pastors who betray you and those priests who become unfaithful servants.

r   This grave malady of yours, this apparent victory of my Adversary over you, is not however unto your death! It is for the greater glorification of God.

s   I myself, as Mother, am helping you in this agony of your most painful purification. I take you into my motherly arms and press you to my Immaculate Heart.

t   As Mother, I pour balm on your wounds and await the hour of your complete healing. I myself — when the time comes — will heal you.

u   You will be more beautiful! You will be totally renewed and completely purified at the moment when, through the new life that will be yours, the triumph of the Heart of Jesus and of my Immaculate Heart will shine forth throughout the whole world."

119

I Am Carrying You in My Arms

a   "Behold the mystery of love of my divine motherhood: as Mother, I entrust my Child to the hands of the priest, and in Him I adore my God who enters into the glory of his house.

b   Every provision of the Law is fulfilled: the offering, the sacrifice, the ransom. A Child is confided to the priest: for him He is only one among many.

c   But to him who possesses the heart of a child is revealed the mystery of the Father. The Holy Spirit comes down upon a poor old man lost in the crowd. The arms of the old man reach out to embrace with love the promised Messiah, the awaited Savior of Israel.

d   My spouse, Joseph, and I look on in astonishment.

e   For the first time, the mystery is made manifest, and a human voice proclaims it.

f   It is not revealed to the doctors and the priests.

g   It is manifested to an old man and to a woman, to people who are humble and poor in spirit. Thus is the future design anticipated: '...this Child will be set as a sign of contradiction, for the salvation and the ruin of many.' And for me, the Mother, 'a sword will pierce your soul.' (cf. Lk 2:34-35)

h   When, come of age, He will begin his mission, this same fact will be repeated.

i   He is driven out of the synagogue and obliged to flee; his message is rejected by the great ones: the doctors of the Law, the scribes, the priests.

j   This official rejection, like a sword, pierces my motherly Heart.

k   But Jesus is welcomed by the poor, the sick and the sinners. His voice reaches down into the hearts of the simple. And my motherly sorrow is assuaged by the response which the littlest ones know how to give my Son.

l   The little ones are for Him the gift of the Father. The little ones are his thanks which He returns to the Father, the little ones who alone understand the mysteries of the kingdom of heaven.

m   My beloved sons, become today my little children. My Church must open itself to the action of the Holy Spirit.

n   This edifice is built on columns that defy the centuries and against which hell cannot prevail: the college of the Apostles founded upon Peter, which is perpetuated till the end of the world through the bishops in union with the Pope.

o   But today, such profound darkness seems to pervade this edifice: it is necessary that the Spirit make it all resplendent again with a totally new light. For this I am gathering together from every part of the world the cohort of my beloved sons: that the Holy Spirit may transform them and prepare them to carry out today the great plan of the Father.

p   Again this design is entrusted to the sorrow and the love of my Immaculate Heart; and so, I ask you to consecrate yourselves to my Heart. I ask you to become little children, so that I may carry you all in my arms.

q   As I did with my Child Jesus, so too with you I present myself in the holy temple of God, and I offer you as a holocaust to the Father to satisfy his divine justice.

r   Do not be troubled if again today I receive the rejection of the great ones. For nonetheless, my voice is being welcomed more and more by the little ones. It will be only with these children of mine that I will achieve my triumph of love."

Pure of Mind, of Heart, of Body

a   "Look, beloved sons, at your heavenly Mother who appears on earth in the lowly grotto of Massabielle.

b   You should look more to your immaculate Mother. You should have a firmer belief in this apparition of mine.

c   I come from heaven to show you the road to follow: that of prayer and of penance. I come from heaven to give you, my sick children, the medicine you need in order to be healed: go, and wash at the fountain!

d   Wash yourselves at the spring of living water which flows from the pierced Heart of my Son Jesus and which the Church still gives you today through the sacraments, especially that of Reconciliation.

e   Wash yourselves often at this fountain because you have need of it to be purified of sin and to heal the wounds which evil leaves in your lives.

f   Wash yourselves at this fountain that you may become always purer. Your immaculate Mother, dear children, casts about you her heavenly mantle and gently helps you to live the virtue of purity.

g   I want you pure in mind, heart and body.

h   *You must first of all be pure in mind.*

i   In thought, you should seek and do only the Will of the Lord. Your mind should be completely open to receive his light. Do not defile it by attachment to your way of thinking, to the way in which the majority of men think today. Do not obscure truth with error.

j   My Adversary, today more than ever, leads you astray by pride in order to corrupt that purity of your mind which alone permits you to receive the word of God with humility and to live it.

k   And then by means of the widespread corruption and immorality which is everywhere propagated and glorified, he attempts to corrupt your chastity of thought.

l   Close the eyes of your body to this evil, and your soul will open itself to receive my most pure light.

m   Only the chaste in mind can continue to keep themselves upright and strong in the faith. And so, walk along the road of this corrupted world to spread only my light from heaven, and to the multitudes, which each day are seduced by error, give the good example of remaining firm in the truth of the faith.

n   *I want you pure of heart* to be truly capable of loving. Your love should be supernatural and divine. All inordinate attachment to yourselves or to creatures bedims its interior purity.

o   You ought to love my Son Jesus, and souls for love of Him. Can one love one's neighbor and not love God? Today there is this tendency, so false and so widespread even among many of my children: to seek to love one's neighbor while ignoring God.

p   You can always do good, and help your neighbor. But for your love to be supernatural and perfect, it must begin with God. Love the Most Holy Trinity with the Heart of my Son Jesus, and among yourselves love each other as He has loved you. In this way your love will always be more pure, and you will be capable of truly loving your brothers.

q   Only he who is chaste of heart can open himself to a great capacity for loving and can live the virtue of charity.

r   Today still, it is the pure of heart who can see God and, in his light, understand and love all men.

s   *I want you pure in body.*

t   You have made the offering of your chastity to God. This is a virtue which you should live with particular consciousness. To-day this is done only with difficulty because of the errors which are becoming constantly more widespread, and which tend to diminish the value of your true consecration.

u   How many of my beloved sons have given up living their priesthood, because the Holy Father has required that celibacy still be maintained today!

v   But how many others remain and no longer observe it be-cause either they believe it to be outmoded, or they believe it to be something transitory, or they even feel interiorly that it is unjustified and no longer obligatory…

w   And thus, how numerous today are my priest-sons who live habitually in impurity!

x   Begin anew, my beloved sons, to relive, in your bodies, the virginity of my Son Jesus, and the stigmata of his passion: your priestly body should be a crucified body. Crucified to the world and to its seductions.

y   Be, once again, pure of body because one day it will rise again, spiritual and purified, to enjoy the light and the life of God.

z   Your body is not destined for the sepulchre, where it will be laid to corrupt, but for paradise into which it will enter, risen again, that it may live forever.

A   It is, above all, through this chastity of yours that you are able today to bear witness to your hope for the paradise which awaits you.

B   Today, your immaculate Mother calls all of you to be chaste in mind, heart and body in order to live the virtues of faith, charity and hope.

C   Thus it will be Jesus in you who again loves and saves his brothers and yours."

121
Mexico; February 18, 1977

In Every Part of the World

a   "If you are pure, my beloved sons, you can see my light. In the darkness which daily becomes deeper, a ray of light shines forth from my Immaculate Heart and comes right to you. Look at my light; it is the light given you by your Mother!

b   How much you have need of it, especially today!

c   No one listens to you any longer; few still understand you and help you. Many, having become victims of atheism, hate and disparage you; even among the faithful many criticize you and do not accept you, and more and more, you remain alone.

d   Who can understand you and help you? Who can console you? Your heavenly Mother.

e   For you I leave heaven again; for you I set out on the roads of the world; for you I pray and ask help of many generous souls.

f   And when you come together among yourselves, I join in your prayer as in the Cenacle: your souls open to the light of the Spirit and to the consolation of the Mother.

g   This happens in every part of the world. And today I have again given you proof of this in this new continent, to which I have led you to gather together my beloved sons. Have you seen with what joy they opened their hearts?

h   Yes, I want you to be all gathered together in my Immaculate Heart because today, more than ever, you have need of being consoled and encouraged. The greatest joy of the Mother is that of comforting the children of her maternal predilection."

122 *March 10, 1977*

Your Martyrdom of the Heart

a   "The confusion grows greater even within the Church and now spreads to every part of the world. The first to be stricken are the priests. Each day, the number of those who allow themselves to be misled by the error which leads to infidelity grows greater and greater.

b   In the name of progress, some priests have become nothing but ministers of the world and live according to the world.

c   For prayer they have substituted a feverish activity; for mortification, the constant seeking after comfort and pleasures; for holiness, a progressive yielding to sin, especially impurity, which is becoming more and more committed and justified.

d   They have become walking corpses, whitened sepulchres who still call themselves priests, but whom my Son Jesus no longer recognizes as such.

e   And these are indeed sometimes the most esteemed, those who have succeeded in achieving success and those who have been placed in positions of responsibility.

f   Those who have remained faithful are generally the most persecuted, the most ignored, and sometimes intentionally ostracized.

g   Thus the darkness spreads, and the smoke of Satan seeks to cover everything; each day the apostasy grows greater.

h   How great is your suffering, beloved sons, O priests consecrated to my Immaculate Heart!

i   Your suffering will of necessity grow greater as the great apostasy spreads more and more.

j   This is your martyrdom of heart for which I am preparing you all. Upon my motherly Heart, let each one offer his interior immolation to the Father.

k   Accept, to its very dregs, this hour of darkness. Live this martyrdom of the entire Church, invaded by the night. Remain faithful and confident, now that infidelity becomes more widespread and extolled.

l   Say *yes* to the Father and to your heavenly Mother, who is gently preparing you to live without fear, through those terrible moments which are now awaiting you."

123   *March 21, 1977*

The Angel of Consolation

a   "Never become discouraged.

b   As Jesus in the Garden of Gethsemane, you too are being assailed by the temptation of fear. Offer this to the Father and continue trusting.

c   At every moment, your heavenly Mother is close to each one of you. She is at your side to help you suffer and to comfort you in your great abandonment.

d   With you, the whole Church is living through this hour of trial.

e   The Holy Father, the Vicar of my Son Jesus, who never before has received so many blows from all sides and been so abandoned, even by some of his own, is today living through this hour.

f   I, the Mother, am, for the Pope, the angel of consolation.

g   I am such, through you. I offer him the chalice of my Immaculate Heart, and in it is all the love of his priests, my beloved sons.

h   Thus, through me, you are his comfort before the great trial which is awaiting you all and for which I have long been preparing you."

154

124

With Me Beneath the Cross

a   "Today, beloved sons, I am bringing you with me to Calvary; with me beneath the Cross of my Son, where I became your Mother.

b   *Here I want to teach you to love.*

c   There is no greater love than to give one's life for those whom one loves. Look at my Son Jesus who is dying on the Cross for you. He is dying because He is giving his life. He is giving his life out of love.

d   My motherly Heart feels Him dying, and it is pierced by all his horrible agony.

e   My motherly love unites with his in loving you; my sons, learn from us always to love thus!

f   *Here I want to teach you to suffer.*

g   My Son Jesus has become nothing other than the Man of Sorrows. He no longer bears resemblance to a man; He is crushed under the weight of suffering, cruelly beaten, outraged, humiliated. He suffers without complaint; as gentle as a little lamb, He is nailed to the Cross.

h   Behold the path along which I am calling you today: that of Calvary which you must tread with docility and meekness.

i   Do not seek to escape this trial; do not beg for human consolation. You will always find the Heart of your Mother who will help you to say *yes* to the Will of the Father.

j   *Here I want to teach you to be silent.*

k   The word of my Son is silent in these final moments. Now He speaks with his life. This is the supreme witness to the Will of God.

l   Thus the last word of his life comes forth: a word of pardon for all and of complete abandonment to the Father.

m   Learn today especially to be silent. Create a silence within yourself in order to hear only his divine word.

n   Create silence about yourself. Do not reply to the criticisms and the calumnies of him who does not accept you.

o   Give no answer to the sneers and the offenses of him who persecutes you. Judge no one.

p   In the moments that await you, you will be called upon more and more to keep silent. You will speak by your life. And for you too, from this life of yours on the Cross, will come forth the word of love for all men and of complete abandonment to the Will of the Father."

125 *April 23, 1977*

Do Not Let Yourselves Be Led Astray

a   "My beloved sons, do not let yourselves be led astray by the world in which you live.

b   *It misleads you by word.*

c   Never before as today has the word become an instrument of truly diabolical seduction. Speech is used to ensnare. Speech is used to spread error. Speech is used to hide the truth.

d   Thus things which are real transgressions of the natural law and the Law of God are proposed as values and conquests of the human mind.

e   Errors are propagated as new ways of understanding the truth.

f   Even in the explanation of the word of God, the most serious errors are propagated. The Pope speaks and is no longer listened to. People continue along the same road and plunge deeper and deeper into the darkness which error spreads everywhere.

g   Today my Adversary is seducing you especially through the mind.

h   Answer with your humility, your docility and your obedience. Look only to my Son Jesus, who is the Truth.

i   *It misleads you with images.*

j   Never have immorality and obscenity been so widespread and so extolled as in your days.

k   In the name of this false way of understanding the value of freedom, every moral aberration is justified.

l   Indeed they begin with the little ones, betraying the innocence of so many souls. And thus many end by being infected

156

almost without noticing it.

m   As for you, answer by looking to me alone. Thus you will see the evil which surrounds you without gazing upon it. And you will go forward keeping your eyes on my Son Jesus who alone is your way.

n   *It misleads you by works.*

o   The works of the world have never been so evil as in these times. It has rejected God and walks in the darkness of this refusal. There is no longer the capacity to love, no longer the capacity to walk in the light.

p   Where are those who still manage to live as true children of God?

q   How it seduces you, above all today, this world in which you live!

r   Because of this, I ask you to follow only my Son Jesus, who is your life. He ascended into heaven to help you to live here below while nevertheless keeping your eyes on paradise. He ascended into heaven to help you to be in the world, while not being of the world.

s   You will not let yourselves be misled by this world if, led by me by the hand, you follow at every moment Jesus, your Truth, your Way and your Life."

126

My Plan

a   "This is my hour. No one will be able to obstruct my plan, which I have long since been preparing for the salvation of the Church.

b   It is you, O priests, sons of my maternal predilection, who are the strategic elements of this plan.

c   My plan can be carried out only through you.

d   Nevertheless, it is not for you to know it in detail. It is enough that it is known by me, as I am your Leader. You must all obey my orders with docility and let yourselves be led by me. Do not ask me where I am leading you.

e   I shall place each one of you at his proper post. Each one must look only to doing his own part well. For the rest, do not concern yourself or be preoccupied about it.

f   It is for me to arrange everything according to the plan prepared long ago by my Immaculate Heart, in the light of the wisdom of God.

g   Some of you will be called to stand *in the line of action*.

h   They will be given the light and the strength to overcome the attacks of those who will endeavor to destroy all the truth contained in the Gospel of my Son Jesus. In your mouth will be found the two-edged sword with which to unmask error and defend the truth.

i   In one hand you will have the crown of the rosary and in the other, the Cross of my Son to whom you will draw souls in increasingly large numbers in the measure that the battle becomes more intense and more decisive.

j   You will be clad in the fire of the most pure light of the Holy Spirit with which to burn away all the darkness of error; through you, the truth will in the end conquer.

k   Others will be called to stand *in the line of support*.

l   They will have to pray and suffer much. From many of these, I will have to ask a suffering so great that it will culminate in the offering of their own lives.

m   I will grant them the comfort of my habitual and extraordinary presence. My Immaculate Heart will be the altar on which they will be immolated for the salvation of the world.

n   My priest-sons, I am now calling you from every part of the world. And each one of you has been assigned to his post, in this battle which has already begun. I am pressed for time. Let yourselves be assembled by me; let everyone answer with a *yes*. Thus I will be able to place each one at his proper post, that which your Mother has already prepared for you. Only then will I have completed my plan and will the cohort of my priests be ready."

My Battle

a   "Let yourselves be led by me, beloved sons. My battle has now already begun.

b   I will begin to strike at the heart of my Adversary, and I will act especially there where he now feels that victory is assured.

c   He has succeeded in seducing you through pride. He has managed to pre-arrange everything in a most clever fashion. He has bent to his design every sector of human science and technique, arranging everything for rebellion against God. The greater part of humanity is now in his hands. He has managed by guile to draw to himself scientists, artists, philosophers, scholars, the powerful. Enticed by him, they have now put themselves at his service to act without God and against God.

d   But this is his weak point.

e   I shall attack him by using the strength of the little, the poor, the humble, the weak.

f   I, 'the little handmaid of the Lord,' shall place myself at the head of a great company of the humble to attack the stronghold manned by the proud. (cf. Lk 1:38)

g   The only thing I ask of all these sons of mine is that they consecrate themselves to my Immaculate Heart and let themselves be possessed by me. Thus in them it will be I myself who will act.

h   And my victory, through them, has already begun.

i   Even in my Church, Satan seems to have now succeeded in winning everything over.

j   He feels secure because he has succeeded in tricking you and misleading you:

k   — by error which has spread everywhere and is even proclaimed by many of my poor priest-sons;

l   — by infidelity which is dressed up as culture and modernization, in an endeavor to make evangelization more up-to-date and acceptable. Thus the gospel which some preach today is no longer the Gospel of my Son Jesus;

m   — by sin, which is more and more committed and justified. Often it is precisely priestly and religious lives which have become veritable cesspools of impurity.

n Over this Church, which seems about to sink, Satan desires to dominate as the decisive victor. I shall strike him to the heart by turning his own victory to the cause of the triumph of my Immaculate Heart.

o I shall avail myself of the darkness which he has spread everywhere, to choose the souls of the littlest of my sons, and I shall give them my own light.

p Thus everyone will be led by this very obscurity to seek salvation in the light which issues from my Immaculate Heart. And all the triumph of my Adversary will have only served to help many souls to take refuge in my motherly Heart.

q I will call upon my priests to give witness to their faith, even to the point of heroism. By their example they will help the souls of many of my poor wandering children to return to the path of fidelity.

r I will bring my beloved sons to great holiness so that, through them, reparation may again be made for all the sins of the world. And thus it will be still possible to save many of my lost children.

s This is why Satan has now such great fear of me!

t But I have now moved into action with the cohort of my little children. Nothing will be able to stop me until my victory is complete in every detail. Thus, at the very moment when everything will seem lost, Providence will bring about the triumph of my Immaculate Heart in the world."

128

July 8, 1977

The Snares of My Adversary

a "Allow yourselves to be led by me, beloved sons, with the greatest trust in my Immaculate Heart.

b To be submissive to my commands, to form my invincible cohort, you must resist the snares of my Adversary who never as in these times has unleashed such attacks upon you.

c He desires to bring you to lack of confidence, to discouragement. He causes you to suffer from his deceitful and cunning tactics.

d He even brings you to doubt that you have been really chosen by me and loved by me, so effectively does he convince you of your wretchedness and make you feel the extent of your human fragility.

e   To bring you to this paralysis of mind and thus render you ineffective, he will turn upon you with every kind of temptation.

f   Be attentive, my beloved sons; these are the snares of my Adversary.

g   This is the secret weapon which he uses against you. This is the venomous bite with which he strives to wound my little heel.

h   Your Mother desires now to lay bare his plot and to put you on your guard against his snares.

i   *You are my lilies,* and for this reason my Adversary often torments you with impure images, fantasies and temptations.

j   Remain serene and confident! Never, as in these moments, has all your purity shone so dazzlingly and inviolate before God and your heavenly Mother, because it is born of a gift which you renew by an act of your will, in the midst of the greater suffering of your entire being.

k   From every snare which Satan sets for you, you will emerge purer, more beautiful and more renewed. And the suffering which you undergo is used by me as a terrible weapon to snatch from my Adversary many of your brother-priests whom, for years and years, he has held prisoners and slaves.

l   *You are my roses* which should give off the fragrance of love only for my Son Jesus and for me.

m   Because of this, he will lay snares for you by presenting to your heart creatures to which, imperceptibly, he will seek to bind you. Here again, his action is always deceptive. Often he presents you with creatures that are good, even virtuous, even endowed with extraordinary gifts, but which can nevertheless constitute an obstacle to your act of love for my Son Jesus, an act I would like to make ever more pure, unceasing and perfect.

n   Even the slightest attachment to any creature is enough to prevent your act of love from being that which my Immaculate Heart desires it to be! And in this way your souls become darkened by shadows which prevent you from receiving and understanding all the light that I give you and which you need in order to make up my crown of love.

o   Oh, my beloved sons! Come to me, all of you, because you are so little, so insecure, so helpless! Come, because you are my little babes, because you have such need of me to walk along the way of perfect love!

p   *You are my cyclamens* by reason of your interior littleness, by the childlikeness of your spirit.

q   Satan ensnares you by causing you to feel like adults, sure of yourselves, and by causing you to set the basis of your security in your own selves, in your own ideas, your own actions. And because confidence and self-abandonment are qualities of the humble, he tempts you more and more with doubt and lack of confidence in my action in your regard.

r   He tries to convince you that it is you who should do, you who should organize, you who should act, that everything depends upon you alone.

s   And you constantly toil all the harder, and you do not let me act.

t   And so I cannot lead you any further because you are thus no longer capable of being docile.

u   If you do not remain little in this way, my designs cannot be realized.

v   Therefore, my beloved sons, I wanted to expose for you the traps with which my Adversary will constantly seek to trick you and lead you astray.

w   Respond always and only with heroic trust in me. That is all I need from you, my little children, to crush the head of my Adversary, while he will attempt to bite my heel, by laying snares for you, my dearest sons."

129   *Hermitage of Montegiove (Italy); July 14, 1977*

United in Love

a   "You are here, my beloved sons, on this mountain with me in prayer. This is a continuous cenacle, as was the one in Jerusalem, after the return of my Son Jesus to his Father.

b   Here too, I am always in your midst. I am united with you in prayer to help you to pray well, to encourage you to intercede unceasingly for all my poor children, straying but not yet lost. I will save them too, through you; for this, your prayer is necessary to me.

c   I am here to help you love one another always more and more. It is the Mother who kindles in you the desire to know one another, who impels you to love one another, who invites you to unite; it is the Mother who each day builds up an ever greater unity among you.

d   I am here to form you to a life of union with me. Because, through your consecration, you have entrusted yourselves to me, I can now truly live and manifest myself in you, especially when, as priests, you speak to my children.

e   It is the Holy Spirit who suggests everything to you. But it is the Mother who gives word and form to all that the Spirit prompts you to say, so that you may reach the hearts and minds of those who listen to you, according to their capacity to receive and their spiritual need.

f   Now you are here with me, and I watch over you with a love that is ever more motherly. I have truly great plans for you.

g   I am entrusting many of my priest-sons to you. Help me to make them grow in this life, by your prayers, by your generous and apostolic activity, and by your suffering which will increase.

h   Gather them together in cenacles of life with me: they are awaiting you as the parched earth groans and awaits a drop of dew.

i   Walk united in love, led by the hand of your heavenly Mother, of whose close presence you will become strongly aware, as you go down from this mountain. I now enfold you in my Immaculate Heart. And I bless you, one by one."

Your Docility

a   "My beloved sons, with docility let yourselves be formed by me. With your consecration to my Immaculate Heart, you have entrusted your priesthood to me. You have put it in a safe place.

b   But in so doing, however, you have only taken the first step, even though it is a very important one. Now I myself, as Mother, am committed to make each one of you just what my Son Jesus desires you to be.

c   The second step you must take is to allow yourselves to be formed by me, in a way which is different for each one of you.

d   It is my duty as Mother to form you in a very particular and personal way. Even the paths along which I am leading you differ among themselves, but they all bring you to the same goal, that set for each of you by my Son Jesus.

e   Pay no attention to how I am forming you; do not ask me where I am leading you; do not seek to know beforehand the path which I have marked out for you. Your duty is to second my action with your docility.

f   *An interior docility* which leads you always to say *yes* to me and to seek only to carry out my will in whatever you do. You now know the will of your heavenly Mother:

g   — I want you humble, silent, recollected and burning with love for Jesus and souls. Only thus will you become great in my eyes;

h   — I want you trustful, abandoned to me and without human preoccupations. Even wanting to 'act' for my Movement can become a human preoccupation. Only thus can your mind see the great work which I am doing in you and through you;

i   — I want you mortified in your senses, persevering in prayer, and gathered about Jesus in the Eucharist like living lamps of love. Only thus will you feel me close to you;

j   — I want you ever purer; thus you will finally be able to see me. You will see me with the eyes of the soul, if you close the eyes of the body to the vanity of this world.

k   Your life will be transformed by me, as gently and firmly I lead you to sanctity. Only if you cooperate with my action will you be able to escape the danger of coming to a halt or of allowing your fervor to grow tepid, after your act of consecration to me.

l   *An exterior docility* which now leads you to be examples of obedience which is lived out and witnessed.

m   Obedient to your Mother who speaks to you and who brings you, by her word, to obedience to the Pope and the Church united with him. Every day my motherly Heart is lacerated anew by acts, even public, of real disobedience to, and rebellion against, the Pope.

n   Your obedience ought to be like mine: humble, conscious, perfect. In this way you will cooperate with my action, as a second phase, so to speak, begins for my Movement.

o   Now that in all parts of the world you are responding to me by allowing yourselves to be enclosed in my Immaculate Heart, I must as quickly as possible make you into faithful copies of Jesus Crucified.

p   You have answered me with a *yes*; now I ask you to respond to my action with your exterior and interior docility. Only in this way can you resist the ambushes which my Adversary lays for you and respond to my great plan of love."

131 *July 29, 1977*

Enter My Garden

a   "Let yourselves be led, beloved sons, into the depths of my Immaculate Heart. Enter my garden. In it is reflected the most pure light of the Divine Trinity.

b   *The Father* finds herein his design intact and perfectly realized. Here therefore all creation is resumed and contained, to sing with me the eternal praise of its Lord and Creator. It is the place where the Heavenly Father receives his greatest glory from his creature.

c   *The Son* finds here his habitual dwelling place. My Heart is the house where the Word was formed in his human life; it is the refuge where Jesus withdrew to find aid and comfort.

d   Here He also brought his first disciples, that they might be strengthened and receive, each and all, his very own imprint. In this garden they grew, little by little, according to his divine plan; they became more humble, purer, more generous, stronger. Here they were well cultivated until each one attained that resemblance to Jesus which He Himself desired.

e   It was also the altar on which my Son was immolated, the chalice which received his blood, which opened itself to the moaning of his wounds, which was opened wide to the great gift of his dying Heart.

f   He desired that this garden of his should also become yours; and so, He gave you his Mother.

g   *The Holy Spirit* is the only Gardener within my enclosure. He has overshadowed me with his light of love; He has filled me with all his gifts; He has embellished me with his grandeur and has made me his Spouse.

h   In my Immaculate Heart this divine prodigy has taken place.

i   My garden is his exclusive property: it is the Holy Spirit who waters it and gives it light; it is He who causes the most beautiful flowers to spring up; it is He who gives them their color and fragrance; it is He who brings therein whom He wills.

j   No one can enter unless He Himself opens to them: no one walks therein unless He leads them forward.

k   If you but knew, my beloved sons, the gift you have received by consecrating yourselves to my Immaculate Heart!

l   It is the Holy Spirit who has brought you into my garden. And through your heavenly Mother, He is now cultivating you, embellishing you with his gifts, and enriching you with all the virtues.

m   This is how you are growing in holiness, becoming more and more priests according to my design, and moving forward that you may be introduced by Him into the depths of my Immaculate Heart, wherein shines brilliantly all the glory of the Most Holy Trinity.

n   Remain, then, forever in my garden."

132

Love Always

a   "Remain in my Immaculate Heart. Always. Then at each moment, I myself will accomplish everything in you.

b   Never consider yourselves. Accept your littleness with humility and meekness. Say to the Lord: 'I am your smallest child. I know my poverty, and I thank you.'

c   And then, love. You can love more if you are truly the littlest.

d   Love always. All that Jesus and I desire of you is love. Nothing else is yours, but the beating of your heart is yours.

e   Hearts of my beloved sons, beat with love only for my Son Jesus, for me and for souls! Then you will be, even here on earth, my perfect joy."

133

My Property

a   "If you remain in the garden of my Immaculate Heart, you become my property. Thus, no one can any longer take you away from me, because I myself am your defense; you should always feel safe.

b   You must no longer fear either Satan, or the world, or the frailty of your nature.

c   Certainly you will experience that seduction and that temptation which the Lord permits as a test to allow you to experience the extent of your weakness.

d   But I will defend you from the Evil One, who can do nothing to harm those who are part of my property.

e   Then gently I cultivate you till each one of you becomes that kind of garden in which, as in mine, the divine splendor of the Trinity can be reflected.

f   I form you with maternal solicitude. With my own hands, I root out from you whatever might, in any way, be displeasing to the Lord.

g   The Spirit in whom I am clothed is like a fire which consumes everything within you, so that there remain not even a shadow which might bedim that beauty to which your heavenly Mother wishes to bring you. I want to make you a most pure transparency of God.

h   And then, I am strengthening in you those virtues which are like roots on which depends any possibility of your growth: faith, hope and charity. Round about these, I am giving you, as ornaments, all those other virtues which have made your Mother beautiful in the sight of God.

i   And in the measure that you open yourself more and more to the light of God, I am sprinkling upon you the balm of my perfume: humility, confidence, self-abandonment.

j   Thus you grow, O flowers cultivated by me in my garden, because you receive the beauty and the perfume of your Mother.

k   Then, accompanied by the angels and the saints of paradise, and with the prayer of the souls in purgatory, I present myself each day before the throne of God to offer Him ever larger bouquets of these flowers from my garden.

l   When you have become like this, then all the Church will become my garden, in which the Divine Trinity will take delight in being reflected.

m   The Father will rejoice to see the design of his creation perfectly realized in it. The Son will dwell with you, into whose midst the reign of the Father has already come. The Holy Spirit will be Life Itself, in a world reconsecrated to the glory of God.

n   This will be the triumph of my Immaculate Heart."

134

August 24, 1977
Feast of St. Bartholomew, Apostle

The Decisive Move

a   "My beloved sons, look with my eyes at the world in which you live.

b   See how my Adversary has taken possession of everything: never before as in these present times has the world become so

168

completely his kingdom over which he exercises his power as ruler.

c And souls, the victims of his enticement, are daily being lost in ever greater numbers.

d I want to save them through an extraordinary intervention of my maternal love. For this, I need you; I need your love.

e Love, with my own Heart, these poor children whom Satan and sin have already led to their death. Love above all those who have strayed the furthest: even those who deny God and who reject and oppose you; even those who are victims of vice, hatred and violence.

f They have become docile instruments in the hands of Satan, who is using them as he wishes, and often they act only under the impulse of his malevolent influence.

g But even these have been redeemed by Jesus; even these are my children. They are the sickest children and therefore have the greatest need of me.

h You are the ones who must love them, in me and for me. Let your love be pure and without reserve; let it be my very own love.

i Even if it seems that they do not respond to you, such is really not the case; your love is already a force which is drawing them from the dominion of Satan! It is already a light which cuts through the darkness in which they find themselves; it is the most precious help that you can give them to lead them to salvation.

j You must be mine, and I shall use you to bring back home all those children whom my Adversary has snatched away from me to make them subjects of his dominion.

k I want all these lost children of mine to come back, through you, and enter the enclosure of my garden: thus they will again be saved!

l I am in a hurry, beloved sons, because the times have arrived. I am pressed for time because the battle, already under way, has a plan which is in the process of being fully realized.

m My decisive move, which will bring about the victory, is you, beloved sons: I need all your love to snatch from the hands of my Adversary all those children whom he has taken for himself.

n   Only when they all have entered into the garden of my Immaculate Heart will it be understood that my triumph is nothing more than the triumph of love in the world."

135

I Have Been Pointing Out the Way to You

a   "Remain ever in my Immaculate Heart, beloved sons. I must, as quickly as possible, form you to be such as Jesus wishes. I am pressed for time, and I am asking ever greater things of you.

b   Let yourselves be led by me. Never become afraid: let all of you answer with a *yes*. For years I have followed you, day by day. For years I have been pointing out the way to you.

c   Travel this road with me. I am leading you along it that, at the moment of greatest darkness, you may find there my light. Do not let yourselves be drawn aside by vain curiosity; do not look for other confirmations.

d   This way, which I have pointed out to you, will be your only confirmation. Journey ever along it, and never allow yourselves to become wearied. Live whatever I have told you. I have spoken in order to be listened to.

e   You are listening to me when you put into practice all the things that I have told you.

f   Keep them in your heart, against him who tries to suggest doubts and uncertainties to you.

g   Put them into practice if you wish to prove to yourself and to others the truth of my words. Only in this way can you go forward along the road which I have traced out for you and will you be able to draw close to me. Only in this way will you become poorer, more docile, littler — you who have been called to be the beloved sons of this Mother of yours, whom today you venerate as a little child.

h   Courage; have confidence and patience! You will be granted a little time more in which to assist me in saving and making amends. And then, for the great evil, will begin the hour of defeat."

It Is Not Given to All

a   "It is not given to all to understand my plan, but only to those whom I call.

b   My beloved sons, for how long have I been forming you, following you and leading you to prepare yourselves to answer this call! From your very mother's womb, I have received you into my Immaculate Heart, and in life, I myself have arranged everything for you.

c   Your whole life has been a tapestry of my love. And now this design must be completed as quickly as possible for the good of all.

d   Few have been called to this: but through them, the Mother wants to offer the possibility of salvation to all her children.

e   See how many of them are hurrying along the road to perdition! Who is there to help them? Who is there to hold them back?

f   You see how so very many of them, while still young, are already reaping the works of death, almost before they are able to sow. The world in which they live has poisoned and killed them.

g   How many generous souls today have been swept away by this darkness which has pervaded the whole Church!

h   You are experiencing again my own sorrow by your having also met here some brother-priests who no longer believe. They continue to exercise their ministry. They are teachers who teach error; they are the blind who lead others into blindness.

i   Share my own sorrow in this place from which progressivism and apostasy are spreading throughout this country and many parts of the world.

j   It is from here that my Adversary has gone into action, but it is also here that, as a sign of reparation, I have wanted to bring together today with me in prayer the priests of my Movement.

k   It is not given to everyone to understand my great plan. This is the hour when all who are called should respond to me.

l   Soon you will have no more time, because the number which the Heavenly Father has determined will have been completed."

The Miracle of the Sun

a   "Beloved children, walk in trust.

b   Today you recall with joy the sign which, sixty years ago, I gave in this place chosen by me to manifest myself. You call it the miracle of the sun.

c   Yes, children, even the sun, like all creation, obeys the laws established by its Creator. But sometimes it can act otherwise when God requires this.

d   Even the sun, like all the beings in creation, behaves in obedience to the laws of God.

e   Through this miracle, I have desired to indicate to you that my victory will consist in leading men back to a docile obedience to the Will of our God.

f   But the sun is the source of light. The earth blossoms and opens to its warmth; you live on this earth by the light which it gives you. Your activity begins with its rising, and with its setting your work comes to a stop.

g   I have thus wanted to indicate to you that my victory will consist, especially, in making the light shine again upon the world and the Church. The world will be enlightened anew because it will offer itself completely to the adoration and the glorification of God.

h   In the Church, once the darkness of error, infidelity and sin by which she is presently eclipsed has been entirely dissipated, the light of truth, of grace and of holiness will shine forth once again. Jesus will be so resplendent in the life of the Church that she herself will be the very greatest light for all the nations of the earth.

i   But the greatest victory of my motherly and Immaculate Heart will be to cause Jesus to shine in the souls of all my children.

j   Some of those present in this place today are thinking: 'What a great marvel it would be if the miracle of the sun were to be repeated!'

k   But every day I repeat it for each one of you: when I lead you along the pathway of my Son, when I help you to be healed of sin, when I lead you to prayer, and when I form you to holiness, it is the light of this sun that I cause to shine ever more brightly in your souls and your lives: the sun of *my Son Jesus*.

l   And so the miracle of the sun which took place here was but a sign. The eyes of those present perceived this extraordinary phenomenon which caused many to believe in the action of your Mother whose duty it is to set burning in the hearts of all men the light of Jesus, the true Sun of the world."

138

Doubts and Perplexity

a   "Do not be surprised, beloved sons, that my Adversary does everything he can to obstruct this work of mine.

b   His favorite weapon is to sow doubts and perplexity about what I am doing in the Church. He tries to base these doubts on reasons which are seemingly solid and justifiable. Thus he instills a critical attitude toward whatever I tell you, even before you have received and understood my words.

c   You happen to hear of certain brothers of yours who are cultured men and often even experts and masters in theology, who reject those things I tell you, because they sift all my words with their minds, which have already been filled with the richness of their culture. And so they find insurmountable difficulties precisely in those phrases which are so clear to the simple and small.

d   My words can be understood and accepted only by one whose mind is humble and well-disposed, who has a simple heart, and whose eyes are clear and pure. When the Mother speaks to her children, they listen to her because they love her. They do whatever she tells them, and thus they grow in knowledge and life.

e   Those who criticize her even before they have listened to her, and those who reject what she says before putting it into practice, cannot be her children. These people, even though they increase in learning, cannot grow in wisdom and life.

f   I tell you this so that you will not be troubled if you hear that even the learned and the teachers find difficulty in my words, while everything appears so clear and simple to whomever I call to be little. Look to your heavenly Mother who knows very well where and how to lead you so that the plan of her Immaculate Heart may be fulfilled. Do not allow yourselves to be either discouraged or surprised by the doubts and the perplexities which can even increase, without however being prejudicial in any way to my great work of love."

139

Everything Is About to Be Accomplished

a   "Everything is about to be accomplished according to the plan of God. Your Mother wants to enfold you in her Immaculate Heart in order to make you fit for the perfect fulfillment of the divine plan.

b   In it shines forth the triumph of the mercy *of the Father* who wants to lead all his wandering children along the path leading back to Himself who so eagerly awaits them.

c   Through it there is actualized the great hour of the merciful love *of the Son* who desires to purify completely with his blood this world, which was redeemed by Him on the Cross.

d   With it comes the time *of the Holy Spirit*, who will be given you by the Father and the Son in ever increasing superabundance, to lead the whole Church to its new Pentecost.

e   All is about to be accomplished that the Church may issue forth from the great suffering of its purification more beautiful and luminous in a renewed world.

f   Let everything that happens to you be viewed in this light. Let every single detail of the time in which you live be placed in the context of this wonderful design.

g   Do not stop to consider the ever thickening darkness, the sin which has been set up as the norm of human action, the suffering which is mounting to its peak and the chastisement which this humanity is preparing with its own hands.

h   These are the painful aspects of a great design. Do not be afraid; the hour has arrived, and all is about to be accomplished! As never before you must allow yourselves to be enfolded in my Immaculate Heart and live with confidence and abandonment in the Will of the Most Holy Trinity who will, in this hour, reflect upon the whole world its great glory. And finally, be prepared to live out, with me, this hour, so great and so painful!"

140

The Immaculate One at Your Side

_a   "I am your immaculate Mother.

_b   Let all of you, in every part of the world, today lift your gaze towards me to contemplate me in the glory where, through a singular privilege, the Most Holy Trinity has placed me.

_c   *I have never known sin.*

_d   My Son Jesus willed to make the first and most beautiful fruit of his redemption shine forth thus in me.

_e   As his blood makes it possible for you to be washed from every stain of sin, so too has He given me the privilege of never being contaminated by it from the first instant of my conception.

_f   He has wanted me to be 'all fair' that He might find in me a worthy gateway through which to come to you.

_g   My beloved children, let yourselves be drawn always more and more by your heavenly Mother, if you wish me to help you be set free from sin, which is the only true evil which can befall you and which distorts the image of my Son Jesus, which alone should shine in each one of you.

_h   It is on this day that I draw close and say to you: 'Do not be afraid; fear nothing, because you have your immaculate Mother at your side!'

_i   I have pointed out to you the goal to which I wish to lead you.

_j   I have marked out the road.

_k   I have called you from every part of the world, and I have

enfolded you in this Immaculate Heart of mine.

l I have even foretold to you what is to happen.

m And now, on this day, I am inviting you to entrust yourselves completely to me, without fear and without apprehension.

n If I have told you that, in the greatest darkness, the light will come to you from my Immaculate Heart, I have wanted in this way to inform you that, at the decisive moments, I myself will suggest everything to you.

o I will tell you whom you must follow in order to be faithful to the Vicar of my Son Jesus and to my Church.

p I will confirm you in what you must say to remain in the truth. I will point out to you those whom you ought to fear and what roads you can follow to avoid dangers, while, for him whom I will lead up Calvary to be immolated, I myself will arrange everything beforehand.

q *I am the Immaculate One who is at your side*: in these moments of your purification I will make my presence felt in an extraordinary way, because great indeed is this battle which we must fight against Satan, sin and all the great army of evil.

r For this, I am asking only that you entrust yourselves to me, and, as of today, you will begin to see my wonders!"

141

December 24, 1977
The Holy Night

You Too Beget My Son

a "My beloved sons, bend with me over this manger where my Son, just born, is still shivering from the cold and uttering plaintive cries.

b Let us together adore Him, for He is the true Son of God!

c You are especially dear to me because you are his priests. You have received a power which makes you very much like your heavenly Mother.

d When you celebrate Holy Mass, *you too beget my Son.* Jesus truly makes Himself present in the consecrated Host by means

176

of the words of the priests.

e   Were it not for you, my beloved sons, my Son could not become present in the sacrament of the Eucharist.

f   In the Eucharist Jesus is truly present with his Body, with his Blood, with his Soul, with his Divinity.

g   You priests renew the reality of his birth in time.

h   Again today, as then, this coming of his is wrapped in mystery.

i   Then, a cave received Him; now, it is the stone of an altar. The tender features of a baby veiled his divinity; now the white appearance of bread hides Him.

j   But just as then, in the little Baby, so too now in the consecrated Host, the real presence of the Son of God is to be found.

k   On this holy night, my motherly Heart is once again torn to see how widespread, even among priests, are the doubts concerning the divine presence of my Son Jesus in the mystery of the Eucharist.

l   And thus indifference towards the sacrament of the Eucharist spreads, adoration and prayer are snuffed out, and the sacrileges of those who approach it in a state of mortal sin increase day by day.

m   Alas, even among priests the number of those who celebrate the Eucharist without any longer believing in it is increasing. Some of these deny the real presence of my Son Jesus; others would restrict it to the time of the celebration of Holy Mass; and still others reduce it to a presence that is merely spiritual and symbolic.

n   These errors continue to spread despite the fact that the doctrine has been clearly reaffirmed by the Magisterium, especially the Pope.

o   The time will come when, unfortunately, this error will have even more supporters; and in the Church, the perfume of adoration and of the Holy Sacrifice will be, as it were, extinguished. And thus the abomination of desolation which has already made its way into the holy temple of God, will reach its culmination.

p   It is for this reason that, on this holy night, I want to gather together in my Immaculate Heart all my beloved sons scattered throughout the world.

q   I invite you to bend with me over the altar where you too will beget Jesus in the Eucharistic mystery. Adore Him with me; heap love upon Him with me; console Him with me; thank Him with me; with me, make reparation for the offenses, the coldness and the great indifference with which He is surrounded. Together with me, defend Him with your life, ever ready to shed your blood for Him.

r   And so, in this night so dark, Jesus will once again, through you, cast his light upon this world which his merciful love still wants saved!"

142

The End of a Period

a   "Most dearly beloved son, spend with me the last hours of this year which has been for my Movement truly extraordinary in view of its graces.

b   Sixty years have passed since I appeared in the poor Cova da Iria in Fatima to bring my important message to men.

c   My message is now more urgent and timely than ever.

d   *Timely,* because never as in these moments has humanity found itself so close to the brink of its own destruction; and *urgent,* because that which the justice of God has decreed is now in the process of being quickly realized.

e   Beloved children, let all of you heed the anguished appeal of your Mother: turn back along the road which leads to God through prayer and conversion.

f   Today I offer you again the means which the Father is giving you to help you return to Him: my Immaculate Heart. All of you must consecrate yourselves to this Heart and entrust yourselves to the arms of your heavenly Mother.

g   During this year which is about to end, I have been able to hold back the chastisement because of the prayers and sufferings of many of my children. Your *yes* has enabled me to add strength to my action of maternal intercession on your behalf.

h   Jesus has again willed to entrust to his Mother and yours the ultimate possibility of intervening to lead you to salvation and to alleviate the great suffering that awaits you.

For this I have need of your prayer, of your suffering, of your life. The hour which is closing this year is marking the end of a period which the mercy of God has granted to this rebellious humanity, before the terrible moment which is about to arrive."

1978

YOUR PUBLIC MISSION

143

It Will Begin with the Church

a   "Today the whole Church looks with great hope to its heavenly Mother.

b   With filial tenderness and unlimited confidence, the Vicar of Jesus, the Pope, this victim who is offering himself more and more on the cross for the salvation of the world, is praying to me. Today he is invoking me for the peace of all humanity. Turning to me with incessant prayer, he is especially asking this peace for the Church of which he himself has solemnly proclaimed me to be the Mother.

c   All my children scattered throughout the world are invoking me: the innocent little ones, the young who as never before are suffering from this uncertainty and darkness, the poor, the sinners, the sick, the aged, the exiled, the straying.

d   And you my beloved sons, priests consecrated to my Immaculate Heart, are calling upon me with special fervor.

e   Today I want to tell you that I welcome your prayers and am placing them on the altar of the justice of God.

f   In this new year I will carry out even more vigorously my work of maternal mediation between you and my Son Jesus…"

144

You Can Love Us This Way Too

a   "My dearly beloved son, turn with serenity to the Heart of Jesus.

b   If you knew how much He loves you, how He looks on you with predilection! Do you know why? Because you continue to be so small, so poor, so full of defects…

c   Cast everything into the burning furnace of his Heart, and everything will be burned up in his merciful love: your sins, your weaknesses, your defects.

d   In the end, nothing of yourself will remain: the good you do will be our work alone. You will offer us that gift which is, to us, the most precious and which we always want from you: your love.

e   *You can love us this way too*: in littleness, in poverty, in your truly great misery.

f   Do not become discouraged when you find that you promise me something and then do not keep it...

g   You have however offered me your sorrow and regret for your error and my motherly Heart leaps for joy because of this.

h   Nevertheless you should also strive to observe whatever I ask
i   of you and to keep to what you promise me: silence with everyone, prayer, suffering and the greatest confidence in me.

j   These intimate sufferings, these secret humiliations of yours, make you similar to my crucified Son. Let yourself be made more and more like Him by your heavenly Mother, who wants to adjust you well upon the cross, that cross which my Son Jesus has prepared for you..."

145

Rome (Italy); January 21, 1978
Feast of St. Agnes

Help Me, O Sons

a   "With each day that passes, beloved sons, your numbers increase. My action for the renewal of the Church and for the salvation of the world is becoming stronger and more evident.

b   Never as in the present time has your heavenly Mother been so concerned and, as it were, anguished. I draw close to the hearts of my beloved sons and ask each of you with maternal insistence to come to my aid.

c   *Help me, O sons!*
d   Your Mother has now need of your help.
e   Are you not aware of how I am summoning you from all sides, gathering you together and pleading with you? I am imploring you with signs which are becoming greater and more numerous: my tears, my apparitions, my messages.

f   I am now no longer able to restrain this poor world from plunging itself to the bottom of the abyss. And this is its greatest punishment, for if it touches the bottom it will destroy itself.

g It will indeed be destroyed and consumed by the fire of unbridled egoism and by the hatred which will drive one person against the other. Brother will kill brother; one nation will destroy another in a war of unheard-of violence which will claim countless victims. Blood will flow everywhere.

h *Help me, my beloved sons,* to keep this world from falling into the abyss! Help me yet save many of my poor lost children.

i With your little hands give strength to the merciful hands of your heavenly Mother. For this I ask you all to heed my anguished appeal.

j Each new priest who unites himself to my Immaculate Heart gives your Mother new strength to lead you all to salvation. And so let your only concern be always to answer with a yes to whatever I ask of you.

k I will be asking greater and greater things of you, as the need for my extraordinary intervention on your behalf grows more pressing."

146

You Will Be Immolated in the Temple

a "I am carrying you in my arms, beloved sons, and you should simply let yourselves be carried by me. And so I ask you to become little children. You are my tiniest babes.

b And this is the measure of your littleness: that of Jesus who, forty days after his birth, is carried to the temple in the arms of his Mother. His eyes look into mine, and He feels at peace. He sees nothing else, and He sleeps, cradled on my Heart, while the joy of giving peace, repose and love to the Child grows within me.

c *Beloved sons, you too should let yourselves be carried by me.* Thus will you become my perfect joy. Only in this way can you feel secure.

d   And so in the cold, which more and more is chilling everything, you feel the warmth of my motherly affection; midst the insecurity which is now taking hold of everyone, you feel the shelter which my arms offer you. In the darkness which is becoming deeper, here for you is my light.

e   You too should look into my eyes, at the light which God gives you through your Mother.

f   I carry you in my arms to the temple of God; you, the ministers of the Lord, you, the guardians of his temple.

g   It is a temple that is now profaned, that appears to be crumbling.

h   The columns of truth seem to be cracking, and many pastors are victims of the gravest errors!

i   Everything is contaminated by sin which seeks to cover even the altar. Sacrileges are increasing, and the cup of divine justice is now full.

j   *You will be immolated in the temple.* Blood can still wash away every stain; with it my Church will be purified.

k   It is for this that the Mother is at your side.

l   With complete abandonment, let yourselves be carried by me. Do not look about you; do not search for shelter or protection. In my Immaculate Heart, all is about to be fulfilled in regard to each one of you."

147   *February 10, 1978*

Only Then Will You Understand

a   "How pleased I am that you have come on a pilgrimage of love and prayer to my famous shrine, where you have begun the gatherings for my beloved sons of Sicily! You have come to console the sorrowful Heart of your immaculate Mother.

b   I have accepted the gift of your love and have wrapped it around my Heart as a splendid crown which you are making for me with the priests whom you are gathering from all parts of the world. Thank you for the joy which you give me!

c   You have also had a sign. This is its meaning: the light will now be going out everywhere. Those whom I have called are now taking refuge in my Immaculate Heart. This is where you will still be able to see; this is the shelter where you will be able to gather together; this is the path which will lead you to God.

d   Darkness will descend upon the Church and will become even more dense after your heavenly Mother has come to get the soul of the first of her beloved sons, Pope Paul VI, who is consummating on the cross his supreme sacrifice.

e   As long as he lives, thanks to his grievous martyrdom, I can still hold back the arm of God's justice. But after his death, all will come crashing down.

f   The Church will be, as it were, submerged in error which will be embraced and propagated, and thus apostasy, which already long since has been spreading like an oil stain, will reach its peak.

g   The pastors and the flock entrusted to them will be struck; for a short while, the Lord will permit that the Church will be as though abandoned by Him.

h   The darkness will grow deeper over the world, which will reach the extremes of its perversion. The more perverted it becomes the more obstinately it will advance along the roads of rebellion against God, of idolatry, of blasphemy and of impiety.

i   Thus by its own hand it will draw down upon itself all that which divine Justice has decreed for its total purification through darkness, through fire and through blood.

j   This will be the hour of the martyrs who, in great numbers, will shed their blood and of the remnant who will envy those they see persecuted and slain.

k   Only then will you understand all that I have done for you...''

148

You Must Prepare Yourselves Now

a   "From every part of the world, beloved sons, I gather you together today in my Immaculate Heart.

b   With humility, you have accepted the invitation to entrust your lives to me, and now at every moment I myself will be your defense.

c   You have also consecrated your priesthood to me: I take upon myself the duty of making it daily more and more conformable to the loving design of the Eucharistic Heart of Jesus.

d   You have given me your hearts. I will put in the place of your hearts, filled with sin, my Immaculate Heart, and thus I will draw down upon you the power of God which will form in each one of you my Son Jesus in all his fullness.

e   To this end, accede to whatever your immaculate Mother now asks of you.

f   I ask of you docility, prayer and suffering.

g   *Be, first of all, more and more docile.* Only thus can I nourish, clothe, lead and form you.

h   These are the times when I am working the greatest wonders in hiddenness and silence. I am working my greatest miracles in the hearts and the souls of my beloved sons.

i   Without you or others noticing it, I am leading you to great holiness.

j   I am giving you my own spirit; and thus, the Spirit of the Father and the Son will be irresistibly drawn to descend upon you as He descended upon me, and He will transform you completely. You will become great in love, in virtue, in sacrifice and in heroism.

k   And thus you will be ready for my plan.

l   *Pray more, beloved sons.*

m   Never give up the prayer of the Liturgy of the Hours, your daily meditation, and your frequent visits to Jesus present in the Eucharist.

n   The Sacrifice of the Holy Mass must be lived interiorly by you, in your life and at the moment of its celebration. It is above all at the altar that each of you comes to be like Jesus Crucified.

o   Never neglect the recitation of the holy rosary, this prayer which I hold so dear and which I came down from heaven to ask of you. I taught you to recite it well, by passing the beads of the rosary through my fingers, as I joined in the prayer of my little daughter to whom I appeared in the grotto of Massabielle.

p   When you recite the rosary, you invite me to pray with you, and each time, I truly join in your prayer. And so you are children who pray together with your heavenly Mother. And it is for this reason that the rosary becomes a most powerful weapon to be wielded in the terrible battle which you are called to wage against Satan and his army of evil.

q   *Offer me also your sufferings:*

r   — your interior sufferings, which are so humiliating to you, because they come from the experience of your limitations, your defects and your numerous attachments. The smaller and the more hidden the sufferings which you offer me, the greater is the joy which my Immaculate Heart experiences.

s   — your exterior sufferings, which my Adversary often provides for you, as he hurls himself at you with rage and fury, all the more violently because he foresees that you will be used by me for his definitive defeat.

t   Some he torments with temptations of all kinds, some with doubt and mistrust, others with aridity and weariness, others with criticism and derision, and others with even the most serious calumnies.

u   Respond in only one way: by offering me the suffering you experience, and have confidence, confidence, confidence in your heavenly Mother.

v   If I have always been near you, I am especially so at times such as these, with all the tenderness of my motherly love.

w   Do not be afraid! I repeat: be mine, and Satan will not touch you. You are in my garden, and no one will be able to snatch you from my Immaculate Heart..."

149

March 3, 1978
First Saturday

You Will Be Consoled

a   "Beloved sons, look to your Mother. Enter into the refuge which her love has prepared for you. Rest in my Immaculate Heart.

b   How great is the toilsome work which you must complete! You are treading a path which, from day to day, becomes rougher and more difficult.

c Often you are tempted to stop because of weariness, aridity and the obstacles you encounter. Never must you stop. Let yourselves be led always by the hand of your heavenly Mother.

d You are journeying today along the difficult path of purification.

e Is there still a long way to go? When will it end? Must we suffer much? What will happen to each of us, and who will reach the finish-line?

f These are the questions you often ponder.

g Yes, sons, the most painful part of the journey is still ahead of you, and it will still be some time before all is accomplished.

h To avoid becoming exhausted, take refuge in my Immaculate Heart. It is the garden which the Trinity has prepared for Itself and for you. For Itself, because in it is reflected its most pure light, and it is the place where God is most glorified. For you, because you have need of this delightful garden, especially in these times in which you are living.

i You have need of it:

j *for your rest*. Beloved sons, enter into this rest. I myself will then bind up your wounds, mend your tattered garments, prepare you the food that will restore you, and help you to grow stronger;

k *for your consolation*. You are the littlest of children whom I am now gathering from all parts of the world and who, with great generosity, are answering my call to suffering and to the cross. Do not become sad if your suffering has to become even greater. In my arms and in my Immaculate Heart, you will be consoled. And you will be given by me that which others will not be able to understand or taste;

l *for your immolation*. Grow each day according to my motherly plan, as I heap my tendernesses upon you and embellish you with my own virtues.

m My work is silent and hidden, but it is transforming you interiorly and drawing down upon you the good pleasure of the Lord.

n When you are ready, I will then gather you up and bring you to adorn the garden of God with the angels and the saints. How many of you I have already brought up here to paradise, and they form a most beautiful crown of glory about my Immaculate Heart!..."

The Hour of Darkness!

a   "My beloved sons, remain in my Immaculate Heart and live with me the moments of your painful passion, which has now begun. You too are to live it as did my Son Jesus.

b   You are entering into that time which the Father has prepared that his design might be realized.

c   Today, at the beginning of this Holy Week, you too should say your *yes* to the Will of the Father. Say it with Jesus, his Son and your Brother, who still offers Himself each day for you.

d   This is the hour of Satan and of his great power.

e   *It is the hour of darkness!*

f   The darkness has spread to every part of the world, and just when men are deluding themselves of having reached the peak of progress, they are walking in the deepest darkness. Thus all is darkened by the shadow of death which is slaying you, of sin which is imprisoning you, and of hatred which is destroying you.

g   The darkness has pervaded even the Church. It is spreading more and more, and each day it is reaping victims from among her very chosen sons.

h   Seduced by Satan, how many of them have lost the light which enables them to walk along the right path: that of truth, of fidelity, of the life of grace, of love, of prayer, of good example, of holiness!

i   How many of these poor sons of mine are even now abandoning the Church, either criticizing and challenging her, or even going so far as to betray her and deliver her into the hands of her Adversary!

j   'Is it with a kiss, Judas, that you betray the Son of Man?' (Lk 22:48)

k   Even you, today, are betraying with a kiss the Church, the Daughter of your heavenly Mother!...

l   You still belong to her, and you live for her; you exercise her ministries, and you are often even her pastors.

m   Each day you renew the Eucharistic Sacrifice, administer the sacraments, and proclaim her message of salvation...

190

n And yet some of you are selling her to her Adversary and striking her to the heart by corrupting the truth with error, by justifying sin and living according to the spirit of the world, which thus through you enters into her interior, threatening her very life.

o Yes, with a kiss, you, my very own poor sons, are again today betraying my Church and delivering her over into the hands of her enemies.

p And so she too will soon be dragged by you before him who will do all he can to exterminate her. She will once again be condemned and persecuted. She will again have to shed her blood.

q Priests consecrated to my Immaculate Heart, beloved sons whom I am gathering together from all parts of the world to form you into my cohort, if this is the hour of darkness, *this must also be your hour:*

r *The hour* of your light, which ought to shine more and more brightly;

s *The hour* of my great light, which I am giving to you in an extraordinary manner, that you may all walk together to meet my Son Jesus, the King of love and of peace who is now about to arrive."

151

March 24, 1978
Good Friday

How Much Blood!

a "Beloved sons, today live with me on Calvary.

b Stay with me beneath the Cross.

c How much my Son Jesus suffers: He is pierced with nails; He is hung upon the gibbet; He is completely covered with wounds and blood. His body is shaken by spasms of excruciating agony, while all about Him the abuse and mockery grows louder.

d Yet He utters no word of complaint: He prays; He suffers; He listens; He is silent; He offers Himself up.

e With the life which He is giving, He is saying his perfect *yes*, to the Will of the Father.

f   My motherly Heart is called to repeat with Him this *yes*, which I already gave at the moment when the Word was placed in my most pure womb.

g   Thus my Son becomes, Himself, the Victim and the Priest, the altar and the offering by this bloody Sacrifice of the new and eternal Covenant. Kiss, with me, his bleeding wounds.

h   How much blood my eyes have seen today! His hair is soaked with it, his face is bathed in it; his hands and feet are torn, and his whole body is marked with deep wounds.

i   Now his blood runs down the wood of the Cross and waters the earth. This is the blood of my Son which washes away all the sin of the world. This is the blood of the true Lamb of God who is being immolated for your salvation.

j   Today his blood can again purify this world.

k   His blood and yours, my beloved sons! Because through you Jesus truly lives again. With you He renews his Sacrifice of the eternal Covenant. In you He immolates Himself again each day, as Victim and Priest, altar and offering.

l   By his blood and yours the Church will be purified. By his blood and yours the whole world will be renewed.

m   Do not be afraid if today I want you all with me on Calvary: you are in my motherly Heart, and here you too must learn to pray, to suffer, to be silent, to offer yourselves up.

n   Thus am I preparing you for your priestly immolation.

o   Say your *yes* to the Will of the Father.

p   Say it with me, your heavenly Mother, who have long been preparing you in the same way that I prepared my Son Jesus..."

152

April 10, 1978
Easter Season

You Will Be the Witnesses

a   "Your heavenly Mother is in paradise, taken up in glory even with her body, now transfigured. She is now sharing, in a way which is for the present unique and not granted to any other creature, in that which my Son has prepared for you.

b   Close to the Father, Jesus has already prepared a place for each

192

one of you. Walk each day on this earth looking to Jesus, who is now sitting at the right hand of the Father.

c   The love of the Father and the Son has been given you by them that you may fulfill here below the plan which God, in his eternal wisdom, has already determined for you.

d   The place which Jesus has prepared for you in heaven corresponds to the plan which each of you must realize here on earth, under the powerful influence of the Holy Spirit.

e   And that which the Holy Spirit accomplishes in you, O sons consecrated to my Immaculate Heart, *is my own plan.*

f   Therefore Jesus, while preparing a place for you in heaven near the Father, has completely entrusted you on this earth to the action of his Mother and yours.

g   You are fulfilling the plan of God only if you correspond to my maternal action which is gently transforming you.

h   In fact I want to bring you all to reproduce in your life the perfect image of your heavenly Mother.

i   For this, I am causing you to become little, and to become ever littler, till each of you reaches the point of utter nothingness of his own self. I turn all your misery into a thing of value, because it is this alone which irresistibly draws down upon you the all-merciful predilection of my Immaculate Heart.

j   I am leading you to docility, to trust and filial abandonment by causing everything in you and about you in which you might put your trust to collapse.

k   I am nourishing and clothing you; I am caressing you and leading you with firmness toward the perfect realization of my motherly plan.

l   When I see my image reproduced in you, I will be able to give each of you my spirit and fill you with the fullness of my love. I will clothe you in my immaculate garment and embellish you with all my virtues.

m   Then all that is mine will also be yours, and I will, at last, be able to live again in you.

n   It will be I myself, living in these littlest children of mine, who will bring to completion the work which the Most Holy Trinity has entrusted to me, that its greatest glory may shine forth over the world.

o   And you will be witnesses of all that the Immaculate Heart of a Mother, who is nothing other than merciful, can do in these years to lead all her poor wandering children to salvation."

153

My Hour Has Come

a   "See my marvels everywhere in the world! My beloved children are responding with ever increasing generosity, and I am bringing them together in my cohort, which is now drawn up for battle.

b   In this great nation too, you are daily meeting with priests in cenacles of prayer and brotherly sharing.

c   You have accepted my invitation and are gathering together.

d   My duty is to bring you together, to form you and to prepare you.

e   *The hour of the great battle has come!*

f   At my orders you must now give evidence by word and example of your fidelity to Jesus, to the Gospel and to the Church.

g   Soon all will see the Church flourishing again and being renewed under the action of your heavenly Mother.

h   You must continue in docility, humility and confidence.

i   *My hour is come!*

j   I will give my spirit to all my little children so that I myself, through you, may again today live and work.

k   Thus all the world will see the loving plan which the Immaculate Heart of your heavenly Mother is carrying out for the coming of the reign of my Son Jesus."

The Whole Church in My Refuge

a "I have brought you here today to this great nation of a new continent to celebrate the feast of my Immaculate Heart.

b You are in the city that was bathed with the blood of the first Japanese martyrs, and you find yourself in the very place where a terrible weapon, in one single instant, killed thousands and thousands of my poor children.

c Near you is the church over which the atomic bomb exploded.

d My little child, this place and this day are for you a sign, and through you, I want to pass it on today from this place to all my beloved children.

e What happened in this place could soon happen in every part of the world if my children do not accept my invitation to return to God.

f *Look at my Immaculate Heart*: it trembles and is anguished at the fate that now awaits you if you do not accede to the urgent request of your Mother.

g Return, my children, never before so threatened and in such great need, return to your God who awaits you with the mercy and the love of a Father!

h Observe his Law; do not let yourselves be seduced by sin. Do not offend my Son Jesus any more; He has already been too much offended!

i The time now left you is short: my hour has come, and I myself am intervening to save you.

j *Enter into my Immaculate Heart*: it is the refuge which the Mother gives you. In it you will find all that I have prepared for you in order to pass through the terrible hours of purification through which you are now living.

k The whole Church must now enter into my refuge: with the Pope, the bishops, the priests and all the faithful.

l It is for this reason that I am leading you to all parts of the world. The time has come when the small remnant, who will remain faithful and with whom Jesus will bring about the realization of his reign, must enter, in its entirety, into my Immaculate Heart.

m   Whoever does not enter into this refuge will be carried away by the great tempest which has already begun to rage.

n   *Comfort my Immaculate Heart.*

o   Never as in these present times has my Heart been so utterly pierced by a crown of thorns: these are the sins, the ingratitude, the sacrileges, the desertions and the betrayals, especially on the part of my beloved sons and of consecrated souls.

p   Often I cannot enter some of their houses because they close the door on me and do not want me.

q   From being gardens of God, some of them have become swamps in which Satan covers and corrupts everything with filth.

r   *Beloved sons, console me in my great sorrow!* Thus you will draw out the thorns, pour balm on my wounds, and form about my sorrowful Heart a most beautiful crown of love.

s   Through you, your heavenly Mother again today wants to save all her lost children.

t   And so, what you are experiencing here is a sign which I am giving you. From it you will be able to understand how, through the death and sacrifice of a few, your Mother is preparing a new life for all."

155   *Hong Kong; June 12, 1978*

This Immense Nation

a   "Look at this immense nation from which the very idea of God has been officially expunged.

b   Hundreds of millions of my poor children have thus been educated from childhood to do without God. And often they are good and generous children, though deprived of the true light which alone can give joy and hope to their lives.

c   Think of all the great suffering that covers this immense land…

d   I assure you that what I already foretold you at Fatima has truly come to pass: Russia has spread its errors throughout the whole world. The Lord has made use of godless nations to chas-

tise the Christian peoples who have left the path marked out by
my Son Jesus.

e   Now that you are living through those events of which I have
foretold you, what must you do, my poor children, to run for
shelter?

f   *First of all, have recourse to prayer.* Pray more; pray with greater
confidence; pray with humility and absolute self-abandonment.

g   Especially, recite the holy rosary every day.

h   By your prayer, you prevent error from becoming even more
widespread; you hold in check the action of the Evil One; you
move to the counter–attack, and you limit, more and more, his
capacity to act.

i   And in the end, through your prayer, you are able to gain the
victory: it will be God alone who will conquer, through you.

j   *Offer up the holocaust of your suffering.* The hours through which
you are living are truly difficult and painful. That which is awaiting you is suffering such as the world has never known.

k   Yet, through this holocaust, you are able to save those who are
seeking your ruin, and you are able to do good to those who are,
for you, a scourge.

l   Thus, even these great nations which have openly rebelled
against God and have become a veritable scourge for all humanity can, in the end, be saved."

156

Rome (Italy); July 13, 1978
Anniversary of the Third Apparition at Fatima

Your Public Mission

a   "My beloved sons, you are gathered here with me in a cenacle
of prayer and love.

b   I have called you from many parts of the world, and you have
come. Now you are making your spiritual exercises that during
these days I may form you and prepare you for what awaits you.

c   All that I have for some time now foretold you is about to
come to pass.

d   Therefore, the plan that I have for each of you must be carried out as quickly as possible.

e   You have consecrated yourselves to the Immaculate Heart of your heavenly Mother. So you have a part to play in my own plan which is that of defeating Satan, the first artisan of sin and of every evil that has spread throughout the world.

f   Walk with me, and thus you yourselves will be, in the world, the immaculate light which will conquer the darkness of evil and sin.

g   That is why I have summoned you all to enter into the intimacy of my Heart in order to work this veritable transformation in you.

h   You are also here in the city where the Vicar of Jesus, the first of my beloved sons, the Pope, lives, suffers and is offering himself in sacrifice.

i   I wanted you near him to help him now in the final and most painful stage of his journey.

j   In you and through you, I myself am present beneath the cross on which the Holy Father is living out the hours of his agony.

k   It is for this reason that the Immaculate Heart of your heavenly Mother, in the cenacle, has always directed you, through prayer and love, towards his white-clad person.

l   You have ever before you my Son Jesus who looks upon you with special favor. It is Jesus who is present under the white appearance of the Eucharistic bread.

m   Yours is a true Eucharistic cenacle: your prayer, your love and your life are directed to Jesus in the Eucharist.

n   You are being called more and more to become the apostles and new martyrs of Jesus, present in the Eucharist.

o   And so you must increase your reparation, your adoration and your life of piety.

p   The Eucharistic Heart of Jesus will work great things in each of you.

q   Be docile: this is what pleases me more, and costs you more.

r   Be docile: this is what you often do not succeed in being, and your heavenly Mother is saddened when so much good will is met, in practice, with so little docility.

s   I have chosen you for a plan which you will fully understand later on.

t   Just as for the Apostles the Cenacle preceded the fullness of their mission even to martyrdom, so also it will be for you.

u   The time for your public mission has now arrived. Gather my beloved sons together; advance together with me in the life I have traced out for you.

v   *This is the hour of your witness!*

w   In the Immaculate Heart of your heavenly Mother, go now into all parts of the world to carry out the mission which my Son Jesus has entrusted to each one of you."

157   *Czestochowa (Poland); July 28, 1978*

A Sign for All

a   "I have brought you to this country which has been consecrated many times to my Immaculate Heart and of which I have been officially proclaimed Queen. From my shrine I am watching over it; I am protecting it, consoling it, strengthening it and defending it.

b   It has become my property because it has been entrusted to me through the consecration of each one to my Immaculate Heart. Its sons are conscious of this, because they renew it often and live it.

c   See how the Church here is alive and flourishing, although it has been persecuted for many years and in many ways! The seminaries have not enough space for all the young men who wish to become priests; the churches are filled with faithful; the priests wear the ecclesiastical garb. All prayer is centered about Jesus in the Eucharist, which is venerated, loved and exposed for public adoration.

d   What is happening in this country is a sign for the whole Church. If the request I made at Fatima for all to consecrate themselves to my Immaculate Heart had been accepted, what has taken place here would also have taken place everywhere in the world. I would have obtained peace for the world and, for the Church, its greatest sanctification.

e   On the contrary, the world is plunged into a desert of hatred and violence, and the Church is living through a period of great desolation.

f   But, my beloved sons, this is my hour!

g   Through you, my priests, I now call all to consecrate themselves to my Immaculate Heart. In this way, you give your heavenly Mother the opportunity of intervening to bring the Church to its greatest splendor and to prepare the world for the coming of the reign of my Son Jesus."

158

August 5, 1978
Feast of Our Lady of the Snows
First Saturday

In the Heart of the Church

a   "My beloved sons, look with my eyes, and you will see how the Church is being renewed interiorly, under the powerful action of the Spirit of God.

b   This does not yet appear externally because of the great coldness which covers her and the great darkness which pervades her. She is now living through the most painful moments of her purification.

c   Assisted and comforted by her Mother, the Church is now climbing the arduous road to Calvary, where she must again be crucified and immolated for the good of many of my children.

d   But enter with me into the heart of the Church! Here the triumph of my Heart has already taken place.

e   It has taken place in the person and the life of the Holy Father, who is being led by me to the summit of sanctity through his daily immolation which will bring him to a veritable martyrdom.

f   It has taken place in the lives of my beloved sons who are consecrated to my Immaculate Heart. Their number increases from day to day. See, the light increases within them, as does love, faithfulness, holiness and heroic witnessing to the Gospel.

g   Even in their littleness, my light shines forth in them. Led and formed by me, they will be the new apostles for the renewal of the whole Church. They are in the Heart of the Church and of your heavenly Mother.

h This triumph has taken place in the lives of many consecrated souls who, drawn by my gentle and powerful action, have again come to live their religious vocation with generosity, following and imitating Jesus, chaste, poor and obedient even to the death of the Cross.

i It has taken place in the souls and lives of many of the faithful who have responded with exemplary enthusiasm to the invitation of your Mother and have now become good examples to all.

j In all these children of mine, the triumph of my Immaculate Heart has already taken place: and they thus form, as it were, the heart of the renewed Church.

k Through them my action has begun, and but a short time remains before my complete victory, because when this vitality has been sent out by the heart into all parts of the organism, then the whole Church will flourish anew.

l Under the powerful action of the Spirit of God, its soil will open up to put forth its greatest growth, and there will be in the Church a greater splendor than has ever existed. She herself will become a light to all the nations of the earth who will turn to her, to the glory of God!"

159　　　　　　　　　　　　　　　　*August 9, 1978*

The Death of the Pope

a "Tomorrow, my very dear son, you will end this brief period of repose.

b I wanted you here again with your spiritual director and these children, so weak and limited, humanly speaking, but whom my Heart loves in a special way.

c It is only littleness and weakness that draw upon you my motherly predilection. You have lived with them in great simplicity.

d You have spent this time in prayer, in interior recollection and in union with me.

e With me, you have also spent these moments of sorrow which the Church is going through because of the death of its supreme pastor, the Vicar of my Son Jesus, Pope Paul VI.

f He was, in truth, a great gift made by the Heart of Jesus to the Church.

g His mission has been accomplished. As on this earth you have been very close to him through prayer and through your love, so now from paradise he will be close to you to help you carry out your mission through the powerful assistance of his intercession..."

160

Your New Birth

a "Share, beloved children, in the joy of all the Church which today venerates that mystery of love which is the birth of your heavenly Mother. With it, the plan of your salvation begins to take form.

b Life is given to me that it might be given by me to Him who is Life, to the Word of the Father, who assumes human nature in my virginal womb in order to be born of me in time.

c All Heaven exults in this mystery; the angels and saints share in your joy, my children who are still pilgrims on this earth.

d Look to your heavenly Mother. I am at your side at every moment. From my Immaculate Heart rays of light and of grace are ever issuing forth and showering upon you in every part of the world.

e Thus I enlighten and beget you, nourish and form you, guide and sustain you. Each day, you too share in the mystery of love which is your new birth given you by your Mother.

f Come to me, all of you, my beloved children, because you have need of me.

g The Church too is now living through her great trial, and what is awaiting her is something she has never known before.

h I am watching over her and arranging everything for her good. And now the Heart of my Son Jesus has given her a new chief pastor in the person of Pope John Paul I. Love him; listen to him; defend him; follow him, because he will have to suffer for the Church.

i The days of her trial are all numbered, and in my Immaculate

Heart I am preparing for her as well the moment of her new birth in time. She will be more beautiful and radiant, holier and more godlike, after the great trial of purification.

j   And so I am calling you all today to gather about the cradle of your infant Mother. Learn from me to grow in littleness and trust, in humility and greater abandonment to the love of the Father."

161

October 13, 1978
Anniversary of the Last Apparition at Fatima

The Hour of the Apostles of Light

a   "I am your immaculate Mother, who am at the side of each one of you, my beloved sons.

b   My plan is about to be fulfilled because the triumph of my Immaculate Heart has now come to pass.

c   You are being prepared by me to be the apostles of this time. You are therefore the apostles of light in this hour when darkness is enveloping all things.

d   Live in the light.

e   Walk in the light. Spread the light which comes from my Immaculate Heart.

f   As your heavenly Mother, I have been preparing you for years in silence and leading you by the hand.

g   Thus, while my Adversary was casting darkness over the Church and reaping victims from among many of her very pastors, I was preparing secretly, in my Heart, the new Church, all of light.

h   It is the same Church, but a renewed Church in which the glory of the Most Holy Trinity will shine forth resplendently, and in which Jesus will be adored, honored, listened to and followed by all.

i   Thus the Church will shine gloriously with a great light such as has never been known since the time of the Cenacle to this very day.

j   Today you are commemorating my coming down to earth in

203

the humble Cova da Iria, and the miracle of the sun which, prostrate at my feet, so to speak, testified to you that this is my hour, the hour of your Mother clothed in light.

k   Today I am announcing to you that this is also your hour.

l   The hour of your witness.

m   The hour of your public life.

n   The hour of the apostles of light.

o   With vigor and courage, spread everywhere the light of truth, the light of grace, the light of holiness.

p   It is the light of my Son Jesus, who has shown you the way to reach the Father through perfect docility to the action of his Spirit of Love.

q   Soon, nothing more will remain of the great darkness which has obscured the Church. After her great suffering, she will, at last, be ready for her rebirth: the new Church of light..."

162   *October 17, 1978*

The New Pope, John Paul II

a   "...Have more confidence and trust in your heavenly Mother: pray and live with her; never again be fearful!

b   I am leading and protecting you, I am at your side at each moment; what I ask of you is silence, prayer and confidence. I ask little and humble things of you because you must walk along the path of littleness and humiliations.

c   Today you have prayed for the new Pope whom my Immaculate Heart has obtained from Jesus for the good of his Church. He is a son especially loved by me because he has consecrated himself to my Heart from the beginning of his priesthood.

d   Unite yourself, through love and prayer, with all the priests of my Movement, whom I myself am bringing to an ever greater love for the Pope and for the Church united with him.

e   You must support him with prayer, with your love and with your fidelity. You must follow him, carrying out to perfection whatever he determines for the good of the Church. In this, be a good example to all.

f   You must defend him at those times when my Adversary lets loose his fury upon him, deceiving those of my poor children who oppose him.

g   With the Holy Father whom Providence has today given you, I bless you, my beloved sons throughout the whole world, chosen by my Immaculate Heart for the hour of its great triumph."

163

Do Not Feel You Are Alone

a   "Do not feel you are alone!

b   In the battle to which I am calling you, many of your brother-priests whom I have already brought up here to paradise, are also taking part.

c   This is the lot which awaits my beloved sons: my Immaculate Heart, about which they will, for all eternity, form its most beautiful crown of glory.

d   Do not feel you are alone! There also belong to my cohort the saints of heaven and your brothers who are still being purified in purgatory, offering to me their prayers and sufferings.

e   All those priests who, during their earthly life, responded to my invitation, listened to my voice and consecrated themselves to my Heart are now in paradise as lights which shine resplendently about your immaculate Mother.

f   They are still very close to you; they are helping you to carry out my plan; they are supporting you by their invisible presence, defending you from evil and protecting you against the many perils in the midst of which you live.

g   Do not feel you are alone! Along with these brother-priests of yours, your heavenly Mother's angels of light are also at your side. They are preparing you for your perfect offering, just as they prepared my Heart to say yes to the Will of the Lord.

h   They encourage you at the moment of your priestly immolation.

i   For you also, my little ones, the hour has come. And so, heaven and earth are united today in this extraordinary communion of love, of prayer and of action at the orders of your heavenly Leader.

j　　The plan of my Immaculate Heart is now being carried out, because my Son Jesus is on the point of achieving his greatest victory through the coming into this world of his glorious reign."

164

Fatima (Portugal); November 25, 1978
Vigil of the Solemnity of Christ the King

My Motherly Action

a　　"Beloved children, let yourselves be led by me at each moment, and always second the desires of my Immaculate Heart.

b　　In silence and hiddenness your heavenly Mother is now carrying out her great loving plan.

c　　This is the hour of my battle. With you, I have now begun to attack my Adversary precisely where he seems to have, for the moment, won a victory.

d　　Where Satan has demolished, I am building.

e　　Where Satan has wounded, I am healing.

f　　Where Satan has conquered, I am achieving the greatest triumph.

g　　In this, my motherly action becomes visible to all.

h　　I am Mother, and my action comes from the depths of my Immaculate Heart to help all those children who are at present in great difficulties.

i　　Above all, my love wishes to manifest itself in an extraordinary manner to those who have strayed and who are in grave danger of being eternally lost.

j　　It is in this motherly action of mine that there shines forth all the love of God, who wishes to let pour out upon the world the torrents of his merciful love.

k　　The time has come when the desert of this world will be renewed by the merciful love of the Father who, in the Holy Spirit, desires to draw all to the divine Heart of the Son so that his reign of truth and grace, of love, of justice and peace may at last shine in the world.

l　　The Church and the world will thus be able to attain a splendor which they have never before known.

m　　And that his mercy might shine forth all the more, God has entrusted the preparation of this renewal to my motherly action.

n It is my desire that the time be shortened, because each day many souls are being eternally lost!

o How many souls are going to hell...because people no longer pray, because sin increases and reparation for it is no longer made, because error is followed with such ease!

p I can shorten the time of the great purification through you, the apostles of light of my Immaculate Heart..."

165

Mother of the Church

a "I am the Immaculate Conception!

b My beloved children, I am your Mother, all fair. Today the Most Holy Trinity causes its most pure light to be reflected in me so that, through me, all paradise, with the choir of angels and saints, may sing to God his very greatest glory.

c And the whole Church, also, looks to its immaculate Mother with tremendous hope.

d *I am the Mother of the Church.*

e Today there shine forth from my Immaculate Heart luminous rays of love and grace which I am pouring out upon my children: upon the Pope, the bishops, the priests, the religious and all the faithful.

f Have great confidence in the special action of your immaculate Mother. I gaze upon you with that tenderness with which a mother looks at her sick children who are therefore so much more in need of her.

g Your real malady is sin. Each day it brings many of my poor children to eternal death...

h It is sin which obscures the face of my beloved Daughter, the Church, whom I want to be resplendent, without wrinkle and all fair in imitation of her Mother. Today sin is spreading like a mysterious illness, and with the force of a plague it has caused many of my poor children to fall into the deepest darkness.

i   This is a time of suffering for the Church because infidelity is spreading, and compromise with the spirit of the world has succeeded in misleading even some of those who carry great responsibilities.

j   *I am the immaculate Mother of the Church.*

k   I myself have begun my work of maternal assistance through those who are answering my urgent appeal to fight sin, to pray, to suffer, to love and to make reparation.

l   Through them I am able to heal many of my sick children and to lead them back to true love for Jesus, who was born of me for the salvation of all.

m   Every day there are many who are answering me with a yes, especially among my beloved priests.

n   *I am the victorious Mother of the Church.*

o   Through the cohort of my priests, I have already begun my victorious action, which will cause my Immaculate Heart to shine resplendently over the entire world.

p   This will be the triumph of mercy and of pardon.

q   I am bringing together my good and docile children, that they may build up with me that which the Evil One and his followers are tearing down.

r   It is in this way that the renewal of the Church and the world has already begun. It is taking place in silence, because noise is not becoming to the action of your heavenly Mother. It is taking place in hiddenness and humility.

s   But with each day that passes, it will become more apparent and complete. The more my children respond to the gentle invitation of their immaculate Mother, the shorter the time of the battle will be and the sooner the hour of the great victory will come.

t   And so today I bless all those priests, scattered throughout the world, who have responded with a *yes* to my invitation and have thus begun to form part of my loving plan."

His Second Coming

a   "My beloved children, I am gathering you here with me, close to the poor manger, waiting to place in it my newborn Child.

b   This is the holy night. You are spending it in prayer and recollection. You are spending it with me.

c   In this night, darkness covers everything, and silence has now dimmed every sound; when suddenly a new light pours forth from heaven, and the festive voices of angels resound along the deserted roadways of the world.

d   The desert of the world opens to receive its God who is born of me in his human life.

e   His second coming, beloved children, will be like the first. As was his birth on this night, so also will be the return of Jesus in glory, before his final coming for the last judgment, the hour of which, however, is still hidden in the secrets of the Father.

f   The world will be completely covered in the darkness of the denial of God, of its obstinate rejection of Him and of rebellion against his Law of love. The coldness of hatred will still cause the roadways of this world to be deserted. Almost no one will be ready to receive Him.

g   The great ones will not even remember Him, the rich will close their doors on Him, while his own will be too busy with seeking and affirming themselves...

h   'When the Son of Man comes, will He still find faith on the earth?' (Lk 18:8) He will come suddenly, and the world will not be ready for his coming. He will come for a judgment for which man will find himself unprepared. He will come to establish his kingdom in the world, after having defeated and annihilated his enemies.

i   Even in this second coming, the Son will come to you through his Mother. As the Word of the Father made use of my virginal womb to come to you, so also will Jesus make use of my Immaculate Heart to come and reign in your midst.

j   This is the hour of my Immaculate Heart, because the coming of Jesus' glorious reign of love is now in preparation.

k   Beloved children, just as I did, you too must prepare yourselves to receive Him!

l   This holy night is a sign and a grace for you. I am gathering you together close to his poor manger to fill the vast emptiness which humanity has made for Him..."

1979

THE SIGNS OF THE PURIFICATION

The Plan of Merciful Love

a "Beloved children, I am close to you at the beginning of this new year. Have confidence in my Immaculate Heart!

b Enclosed within my Heart is the plan of the merciful love of my Son Jesus, who wants to lead the world back to the Father for the perfect glorification of God.

c The world is not lost, even though it is now walking along the road of perdition and of its own destruction. Through a trial which I have foretold to you many times, it will in the end be saved by an act of the merciful love of Jesus, who has entrusted you to the action of your heavenly Mother.

d Sin still covers the earth; hatred and violence are erupting everywhere; the greatest crimes are crying out daily for vengeance in the sight of God.

e You are beginning a year during which all will be particularly aware of the powerful hand of God, which will be stretched out over the world to help it through the irresistible force of his merciful love.

f And so, my children, events which you cannot imagine are awaiting you.

g But there are also the prayers of the good, the sorrows of the innocent, the hidden sufferings of many, the tears and supplications of numerous victims scattered throughout the world. Through them, I have hastened the time of my extraordinary intervention.

h The Church, my beloved Daughter, is now emerging from a great trial because the battle between me and my Adversary has been waged, even at her very summit. Satan has attempted to infiltrate to the very point of threatening the rock on which the Church is founded, but I have prevented him from doing so.

i Precisely when Satan was under the illusion that he had conquered, after God had accepted the sacrifice of Pope Paul VI and of John Paul I, I obtained from God for the Church the Pope who had been prepared and formed by me.

j He has consecrated himself to my Immaculate Heart and has solemnly entrusted to me the Church, of which I am the Mother and Queen.

k   In the person and the work of the Holy Father, John Paul II, I am reflecting my great light which will become stronger, the more the darkness envelops everything.

l   Priests and faithful consecrated to my Immaculate Heart, children whom I have gathered from all parts of the world into my cohort for the great battle which awaits you, unite, all of you, about the Pope, and you will be clothed in my own strength and in my marvelous light!

m   Love him; pray for him; listen to him! Obey him in all things, even to wearing the ecclesiastical dress according to the desire of my Heart and his will which he has already made known to you. Offer me the suffering you may experience if, because of this, you are sometimes ridiculed by your own confreres.

n   For the Church too, which has a sure guide in the person of the Pope, the time of purification will be shortened, in accordance with my loving plan.

o   This then is your hour, the hour of the apostles of my Immaculate Heart.

p   Spread courageously the Gospel of Jesus; defend the truth; love the Church; help all to flee sin and to live in the grace and the love of God.

q   Pray; suffer; make reparation!..."

168   *January 28, 1979*

The First Sign: Confusion

a   "Beloved children, take refuge in my Immaculate Heart.

b   The glorious reign of Christ will be preceded by a great suffering which will serve to purify the Church and the world and to lead them to their complete renewal.

c   Jesus has already begun his merciful work of renewal with the Church, his Spouse.

d   Various signs indicate to you that the time of purification has come for the Church: the first of these is the confusion which

213

reigns there. This in fact is the time of its greatest confusion.

e   Confusion is spreading within the Church, where everything in the field of dogma, liturgy and discipline is being subverted.

f   These include truths revealed by my Son and which the Church has defined once and for all, through her divine and infallible authority.

g   These truths are unchangeable, as the very truth of God is unchangeable. Many of these form part of real mysteries in the strict sense of the word, because they are not and never can be understood by human intelligence.

h   Man must accept them with humility, by an act of pure faith and firm trust in God who has revealed them and proposed them to men of all times, through the Magisterium of the Church.

i   But now there is spread abroad a most dangerous tendency of wanting to penetrate and understand everything — even mysteries — to such a point that only that part of the truth is accepted which can be understood by human intelligence. There is a desire to unveil the very mystery of God.

j   Any truth which is not understood by reason is rejected. There is an inclination to propose all revealed truth in a new and rationalistic way, under the illusion of making it acceptable to all.

k   Thus truth is being corrupted with error. Error is being spread in a most dangerous way, namely, as a new and modern way of understanding the truth, and it ends by subverting the very truths which are the foundation of the Catholic faith.

l   They are not denied openly, but they are accepted in such an equivocal way that doctrine is most seriously compromised by error in an unprecedented manner.

m   As a result, talk and discussion go on and on; but there is no longer any belief, and the darkness of error spreads.

n   The confusion which tends to prevail within the Church and to subvert its truths is the first sign which indicates to you with certainty that the time of her purification has come.

o   The Church is in fact Christ who is living mystically in your midst.

p   Christ is the Truth. The Church must therefore always shine with the light of Christ who is the Truth.

q   But at present, its Adversary has succeeded, through his subtle

and deceitful works, in bringing much darkness into its interior.
r   And today the Church is darkened by the smoke of Satan.
s   Satan has first of all bedimmed the understanding and the thinking of many of my children, seducing them through vainglory
and pride, and through them he has darkened the Church.

t   You, beloved sons of your heavenly Mother, you, the apostles
of my Immaculate Heart, are being called today for this purpose:
to fight by word and example that the truth may be more and
more accepted by all. Thus the darkness of confusion will be
defeated by the light.
u   For this reason, you must live the Gospel of my Son Jesus to
the letter.
v   You must be, purely and simply, the living Gospel. Then you
must proclaim to all, with strength and courage, the Gospel which
you live. Your words will have the power of the Holy Spirit who
will fill you and the light of the wisdom given you by your heavenly Mother..."

169

The Second Sign: Lack of Discipline

a   "Contemplate your heavenly Mother as she presents herself
at the temple to offer her little Child.
b   He is the Word of the Father, made man; He is the Son of God
through whom the universe was created; He is the awaited Messiah to whom Prophecy and Law have been directed.
c   And yet, from the very moment of his human conception, He
becomes obedient in all things to the Will of the Father: 'Behold,
I come to do your Will, O God.' (Heb 10:7) And from his very birth,
He submits Himself to all the prescriptions of the Law: after
eight days, the circumcision and today, after forty days, the presentation in the temple.
d   Just as every other first-born, mine also belongs to God, and
He is ransomed by the prescribed sacrifice. From the priest, He
returns to my arms that He might be offered anew by me through
the wound of my Immaculate Heart, already pierced by a sword;

and thus, our *yes* to the Will of the Father is pronounced together.

e   Beloved sons, when I appeal to you to become littler, in my arms, it is to make you like my Child, Jesus, through docile and perfect obedience to the divine Will.

f   Today my Heart is wounded anew by seeing so many of my beloved sons who live without docility to the Will of God, because they do not observe and often openly disdain the laws proper to their priestly state.

g   Thus lack of discipline is spreading in the Church and reaping victims, even from among her very pastors.

h   This is the second sign which indicates to you that, for the Church, the final time of purification has come: a lack of discipline which has spread throughout all levels, especially among the clergy.

i   *It is lack of discipline* to be wanting in interior docility to the Will of God, a lack of discipline which is manifested by the flouting of those obligations which are proper to your state of life: the obligation to pray, to give good example, to lead a holy and apostolic life. How many there are, among the priests, who allow themselves to become absorbed in excessive activity and who no longer pray! They habitually neglect the Liturgy of the Hours, meditation and the recitation of the holy rosary. They limit their prayer to a hurried celebration of Holy Mass.

j   And so my poor sons become interiorly empty and no longer have the light and strength to resist the many snares amidst which they live. They thus become contaminated by the spirit of the world and accept its way of life, share its values, take part in its profane manifestations, allow themselves to be conditioned by its methods of propaganda and, in the end, come to adopt its very mentality. And so they end up by living as ministers of the world, according to its spirit which they justify and propagate, thus provoking scandal amongst many of the faithful.

k   From this springs the growing rebellion against canonical norms which regulate the life of priests, and the recurring objection to the obligation of sacred celibacy, desired by Jesus as expressed by his Church, and which has at this time been once again strongly reaffirmed by the Pope.

216

l   *It is lack of discipline* to disregard with ease the norms which the Church has laid down for the regulation of liturgical and ecclesiastical life.

m   Today each one tends to direct himself according to his own tastes or free choice, and with what scandalous facility are violated the norms of the Church, which have been reaffirmed again and again by the Holy Father, such as the obligation for priests to wear the ecclesiastical dress!

n   Alas, sometimes the first to continue disobeying this prescription are the pastors themselves, and it is their bad example which then fosters lack of discipline in all sectors of the Church.

o   This disorder, which is spreading in the Church, indicates to you with clarity that the final moment of her purification has come.

p   What must you do, beloved sons of your heavenly Mother, apostles of light of my Immaculate Heart?

q   Let yourselves be carried in my arms, as my tiniest babes, and I will make you perfectly docile to the Will of the Father.

r   Thus to everyone you will give a good example of perfect obedience to the laws of the Church, and your heavenly Mother will be able to make use of you to restore order in her house so that, after the suffering, the triumph of her Immaculate Heart may shine forth in the Church."

170

February 11, 1979
Feast of Our Lady of Lourdes

The Third Sign: Division

a   "I am your immaculate Mother.

b   I appeared on earth, in the poor grotto of Massabielle, in order to point out to you the road you must walk in these difficult times.

c   It is my road: that of purity, of grace, of prayer, of penance.

d   It is the road which my Son Jesus has already pointed out to you, to lead you all to the Father in his Spirit of Love. You have within you his own Spirit which causes you to cry out to God as Father because He has shared his divine nature with you.

e   Walk the road of love. Make place within you for the Spirit of Love which is bringing you, in life, to be more and more united.

f   Love one another as Jesus has loved you, and you will become truly one. Unity is the perfection of love.

g   And so Jesus has desired that his Church be one, to make of her the sacrament of God's love for men.

h   Today my Immaculate Heart trembles and is anguished to see the division within the Church.

i   This division, which has penetrated the Church, is the third sign which indicates to you with certainty that the final moment of her painful purification has come.

j   If, in the course of the centuries, the Church has many times been torn by division which has led many of my children to separate themselves from her, I nevertheless obtained from Jesus the singular privilege of her interior unity.

k   But in these times, my Adversary has, with his smoke, succeeded in darkening even the light of this divine prerogative of the Church.

l   *This interior division* is manifesting itself even among the faithful who often set themselves one against the other, in an attempt to defend and better promote the truth. Thus the truth is betrayed by even them, as the Gospel of my Son cannot be divided.

m   This interior division sometimes even leads priests to set themselves against priests, bishops against bishops, and cardinals against cardinals, for never before as in these times has Satan so succeeded in finding his way into their midst, rending asunder the precious bond of their mutual love.

n   *This interior division* is expressed by the tendency to leave to himself and to abandon, so to speak, the very Vicar of Jesus, the Pope, who is a son particularly loved and enlightened by me.

o   My motherly Heart is wounded to see how the silence and neglect of my children often envelop the words and actions of the Holy Father, while he is increasingly struck and impeded by his adversaries.

p   Because of this interior division, his very ministry is not sufficiently supported and furthered by the whole Church whom

Jesus has wanted to be united about the successor of Peter.

q My motherly Heart grieves to see how even some pastors refuse to let themselves be guided by his enlightening and trustworthy words.

r The first way of being separated from the Pope is that of open rebellion. But there is also another way, more subtle and dangerous. It is that of proclaiming one's unity openly, but of dissenting from him interiorly, letting his teaching fall into a void and, in practice, doing the contrary of what he says.

s Oh, Church, Mystical Body of my Jesus, in your painful journey to Calvary, you have reached the eleventh station, and you see yourself wrenched and torn in your members, which are again nailed to the Cross!

t What must you do, my sons, apostles of my Immaculate and Sorrowful Heart? You must become a hidden seed, ready even to die for the internal unity of the Church.

u And so I am leading you each day to a very great love for, and fidelity to, the Pope and the Church united to him. For this reason I am now letting you share in the anxiety of my motherly Heart; for this reason I am forming you in the heroism of sanctity and leading you with me up Calvary. Through you also, I will be able to help the Church emerge from her painful purification, so that in her all the splendor of her restored unity may be manifest to the world."

171

March 3, 1979
First Saturday

The Fourth Sign: Persecution

a "Remain, all of you, in the refuge of my Immaculate Heart, and you will find your peace and interior serenity.

b My beloved sons, the storm which I foretold at Fatima has now unleashed its fury for the purification of the Church and all the world. This is the hour of the Father's mercy which, through the love of the Son's divine Heart, is made manifest at the moment when everyone's suffering is at its greatest.

c   The fourth sign, which indicates to you that the culminating period of the Church's painful purification has come, is persecution. The Church is in fact being persecuted in various ways.

d   *She is being persecuted by the world* in which she lives and journeys, pointing out to all the way to salvation. The real enemies of God are those who set themselves deliberately against God, in order to lead all humanity to live without Him; it is they who are persecuting the Church more and more.

e   Sometimes she is persecuted in an open and violent manner; she is despoiled of everything and prevented from preaching the Gospel of Jesus.

f   But in these times, the Church is often subjected to an even greater ordeal; she is persecuted in a subtle and painless manner, by being deprived bit by bit of the oxygen which she needs to live. Then an attempt is made to bring her to compromise with the spirit of the world, which thus enters into her and affects and paralyzes her vitality.

g   Collaboration is often brought about through a most subtle form of persecution; an outward show of respect for her has become the surest way to strike her.

h   A new technique has been discovered by which she can be put to death with no outcry and without shedding blood.

i   The Church *is being persecuted also from within*, especially at the hands of those sons of hers who have reached a compromise with her Adversary. He has succeeded in seducing even some of her very pastors. Some of these are even knowingly collaborating in this plan of interior and hidden persecution of my Church.

j   My beloved sons are being called to the trial of finding themselves sometimes obstructed, pushed aside and persecuted by some of their own confreres, while those who are unfaithful have free scope for their action.

k   The same hours of suffering that my Son Jesus lived through are awaiting you too, beloved sons: the hours of Gethsemane, when He experienced the interior agony of being abandoned, betrayed and denied by his own…

l   If this is the road trodden by the Master, it is also the road which you too must tread, you his faithful disciples, as the purification of the entire Church becomes more painful.

m   Have confidence, beloved sons, apostles of my Immaculate Heart!

n   No other trial will serve so much to bring about the complete renewal of the Church as this interior persecution. In fact she will emerge from this suffering purer, more humble, more enlightened, stronger.

o   You must be ready to suffer more and more, the closer the final moment of purification comes. And so I have wished to prepare a safe refuge for you.

p   In my Immaculate Heart you will be consoled and formed in the virtue of fortitude, as you become more and more aware of the presence of your heavenly Mother at your side. She will gather up all your sufferings, as beneath the Cross she did those of Jesus, because she must now carry out once again for the Church her maternal function as Co-redemptrix, and lead back to the Father all the children who have gone astray."

172

March 9, 1979
A Friday of Lent

Your Liberation Is Near

a   "Beloved sons, consider with me the signs of the times in which you are living. The hearts of men have grown cold, and the world has become a desert.

b   But you should have all the more confidence in your heavenly Mother! Look, with me, at the times in which you are living, and you will see the signs of my extraordinary intervention.

c   When the first buds appear on the trees, you reflect that winter is now coming to an end and that a new spring is near.

d   I have pointed out to you the signs of the cruel winter through which the Church is now passing, by way of a purification which has now reached its most painful peak. The Spouse of my Jesus appears again covered with wounds and obscured by my Adversary, who appears to be celebrating his complete victory.

e   He is certain that he has won the victory in the Church, by the confusion which has subverted many of her truths, by the

221

lack of discipline which has caused disorder to spread, by the division which has attacked her internal unity and by the insidious and hidden persecution which has crucified her anew.

f But see how, in this most cruel winter of hers, the buds of a renewed life are already appearing. They tell you that *the hour of your liberation is near.*

g For the Church, a new spring of the triumph of my Immaculate Heart is about to burst forth. She will still be the very same Church, but renewed and enlightened, made humbler and stronger, poorer and more evangelical through her purification, so that in her the glorious reign of my Son Jesus may shine forth for all.

h She will be the new Church of light, and even now her branches can be seen sprouting with many new buds: these are all they who have entrusted themselves to their heavenly Mother; you also are among them, you apostles of my Immaculate Heart.

i All of you are these buds, my little children, who have consecrated yourselves to me and who live by my own spirit.

j You are these buds, you faithful disciples of Jesus, who are desirous of living a life of contempt for the world and for yourselves, in poverty, in humility, in silence, in prayer and mortification, in charity and in union with God, while at the same time being unknown and scorned by the world.

k The time has now come for you to emerge from your hiddenness and to go out and enlighten the earth. Present yourselves to all as my sons, for I am always with you. Let faith be the light which illumines you in these days of darkness, and let it be zeal alone for the honor and glory of my Son Jesus which consumes you.

l Fight, sons of light, few though you still be! Many will follow in your footsteps and will become part of my cohort, because the hour of my battle has now come.

m In this most cruel of winters, it is you who are the buds which are burgeoning forth from my Immaculate Heart, and which I am placing on the branches of the Church, to tell you that her most beautiful springtime is at hand.

n This will be for her like a new Pentecost.

o Beloved sons, look with my eyes at the times in which you are living.

222

p   Persevere in prayer, in suffering and in hope because the hour of your liberation is near."

173

Your Interior Equilibrium

a   "I am the Mother of the Incarnate Word.

b   By my *yes* I offered to the Father my personal co-operation in his plan of salvation.

c   From the bosom of the Father the Word was placed in my maternal womb to assume from me his human nature. I became the true Mother of Jesus.

d   This *yes* to the Will of the Father blossomed in my soul as the fruit of a long and silent preparation.

e   Behold the road your Mother traveled to reach this ineffable moment: that of humility, of trust, of filial abandonment, of silence, of intimate and profound union with God.

f   Already from my childhood, I offered myself completely to the Lord, putting myself as a slave at his service in perfect virginity, in hiddenness and in prayer.

g   My soul opened itself to an ever greater light, and my life was formed in detachment from all creatures in order to love the Lord perfectly, by fulfilling his will and listening to his word. I fostered within myself a relish for seeking, for gathering in and for treasuring only the word of God.

h   When the Father decided to place his Word in my virginal womb, He found your Mother ready to welcome Him with love and joy, being only intent upon the perfect fulfillment of the divine Will.

i   My beloved children, contemplate your Mother at the moment of her annunciation, as with her Heart and her lips she says her *yes* to the Will of the Lord.

j   You too should learn always to say *yes* to whatever the Lord now asks of you through the voice that comes to you from the Immaculate Heart of your heavenly Mother. You must no longer doubt! Do not seek elsewhere. Do not beg for confirmations or encouragement.

k   I have arranged, through this work of mine, that your support should be founded solely in my Immaculate Heart. I will cause every support to collapse about you, and I will not allow you to put your trust in purely human encouragement or approval.

l   My children, from you too I desire littleness, humility, hiddenness, silence and trust.

m   You must tread the same road as your heavenly Mother: that of intimate union with God, of detachment from all creatures and of perfect service to the Lord. I am bringing you to say *yes* always to whatever Jesus asks of you. How few there are, even among those specially chosen by me, who know how to say *yes* to Jesus!...

n   Tread with me the road which I am pointing out to you and along which I am leading you, letting yourselves be guided with docility and filial abandonment. I am training you to listen to the word of God that it may be received, understood, loved and treasured by you, and put into practice.

o   In these times of purification, many are led astray by other words. In fact, my Adversary succeeds in seducing even the good by false manifestations of the supernatural in order to bring about deception and confusion on all sides. He will succeed in working many prodigies which will beguile the minds of even the good.

p   As for you, remain within the refuge of my Immaculate Heart, and there listen to the word of God which the Church guards, interprets and proclaims. Never before as at the present time has the Pope had such light with which to lead you along the road of clarity and truth.

q   Within my Immaculate Heart I will build up your interior equilibrium, my beloved sons, because today you have need of being ever more prudent and well-balanced.

r   This equilibrium will be a sign to all of what your heavenly Mother is doing in you and will assure the Church of finding in you faithful and wise sons..."

Near My Son and My Sons

a   *"Today my place is here: near my Son who is suffering.*

b   The Will of the Father so disposed that I would not be near
Jesus during his interior agony in Gethsemane, because the very
absence of the Mother would make his abandonment more complete.

c   'If it is possible, let this chalice pass from me.' (cf. Mt 26:39) But in
my soul, during the night, I remained ever near my Son.

d   Through prayer and suffering, I truly shared in all his agony in
order to comfort and help Him, by uniting my *yes* to his in
saying: 'Father, not my will but yours be done.' (cf. Mt 26:39) And
when the angel was sent to Him from heaven to comfort Him,
he passed by me also, in order that I might place in his chalice all
the love of my motherly Heart.

e   *Today my place is here: near my Son who is dying.*

f   The meeting takes place on the road to Calvary, after Jesus has
been betrayed, denied and abandoned by his own. Of the twelve,
there remains only one, whom I take by the hand to encourage
him and to give him strength to remain with us. The condemnation is written on the scourged body of Jesus, and the thorns
cover his eyes with blood.

g   It is here that I meet my Son: I am at his side to help Him die.
I feel the nails which pierce his flesh, the tearing of his body
hung on the gibbet, his labored breathing; I hear his voice as it
grows weaker with words of prayer and pardon, and He appears
to me to be dying.

h   But I continue to live, beneath the Cross, with a pierced Heart
and a wounded soul, still miraculously alive because, as Mother, I
must help my Son to die. No one will ever understand the
hidden mystery of this moment.

i   *Today my place is here: near my buried Son.*

j   And now my sorrow bursts forth as a flooding river bursts
through all its embankments. My tears bathe his face, my laments cradle his body, and with my hands I close the deep
wounds, while my Immaculate Heart becomes his first sepulchre.

225

k Then when night casts a veil over all things, the vigil begins for the Mother. I am here, recollected in the faith which has never deserted me, in the hope which completely illumines me and in prayer which has become continual and unceasing as though to mark the passing of time which for me no longer has either day or night.

l The fervent prayer of the Mother penetrates heaven and is accepted by the Father who, to shorten my anguished wait, anticipates the moment of the resurrection of the Son.

m *My place is here: near my risen Son.*

n When Jesus comes to me in the light of his glorified body, receives me in his divine arms and bends down to kiss the wounds of my great sorrow, I understand that my mission on his behalf has been accomplished.

o I am beginning my maternal mission for you, for the Church which has been born of his great suffering and mine.

p *Today my place is again here: near all my sons.*

q Till the end of the world, I will always be close to you, sons begotten of the death of my only Son.

r Above all, I am with you during these moments of darkness and suffering, when you are being called to live out what Jesus endured during his redemptive passion.

s I am always near you to help you to suffer, to die and to rise again, until the plan of the Father be fulfilled, and with Jesus, you too may rejoice in the glory of his kingdom of life."

175
May 13, 1979
Anniversary of the First Apparition at Fatima

The Woman Clothed with the Sun

a "I have come from heaven to reveal to you my plan in this struggle which involves everyone, marshaled together at the orders of two opposing leaders: the Woman Clothed with the Sun and the Red Dragon.

b I have shown you the road you must take: that of prayer and penance. I have called you to the interior conversion of your life.

226

c   I have also prepared a refuge for you that you may be brought together, protected and strengthened during the present tempest which will become even more violent. The refuge is my Immaculate Heart.

d   I am now announcing to you that this is the time of the decisive battle. During these years, I myself am intervening, as the Woman Clothed with the Sun, in order to bring to fulfillment the triumph of my Immaculate Heart which I have already begun through you, my beloved sons.

e   Sufferings will be asked of you, but in my Immaculate Heart, you will be called to taste as well the intimate joy of my motherly love.

f   The darkness will grow deeper, but the ray of light which comes from my Heart to show you the way will become even stronger. Sin will cover everything, but you will be helped by me to clothe yourselves in divine grace which must become ever more resplendent within you that you may give a witness of holiness to all.

g   Listen to my voice with humility and docility..."

176

Garabandal (Spain); June 14, 1979
Solemnity of Corpus Christi

Jesus in the Eucharist

a   "My beloved sons, continue to walk trustingly along the road on which your heavenly Mother is leading you. My plan is about to be fulfilled through you who have responded to my motherly invitation.

b   Second my action, the purpose of which is to transform you interiorly, in order to make you all priests according to the Eucharistic Heart of Jesus. The triumph of my Immaculate Heart cannot take place except in the triumph of my Son Jesus, who will reign once again in the hearts, the souls and the lives of each person and nation: in all humanity.

c   But as Jesus is truly in heaven, so also is He truly present on earth in the Eucharist: with his Body, his Blood, his Soul and his Divinity.

227

d   His glorious reign will shine forth above all in the triumph of his Eucharistic Person, because the Eucharist will once again be the heart and center of the whole life of the Church.

e   Jesus in the Eucharist will become the summit of all your prayer, which should be a prayer of adoration, of thanksgiving, of praise and of propitiation.

f   Jesus in the Eucharist will once again be the center of all liturgical action, which will unfold itself as a hymn to the Most Holy Trinity, through the continual priestly action of Christ which will be carried out in the Eucharistic Mystery.

g   Jesus in the Eucharist will once again be the center of your ecclesial gatherings, because the Church is his temple, his house which has been built above all that his divine presence may shine forth in your midst.

h   Beloved sons, in these present times the darkness has alas obscured even the tabernacle; around it there is so much emptiness, so much indifference, so much negligence. Each day, doubts, denials and sacrileges increase. The Eucharistic Heart of Jesus is wounded anew by his own, in his own house, in the very place where He has taken up his divine dwelling in your midst.

i   Become again perfect adorers and fervent ministers of Jesus in the Eucharist who, through you, makes Himself again present, immolates Himself anew and gives Himself to souls.

j   Bring everyone to Jesus in the Eucharist: by adoration, by communion and by a greater love.

k   Help everyone to approach the Eucharistic Jesus in a worthy manner, by cultivating in the faithful an awareness of sin, by inviting them to present themselves for the sacrament of Holy Communion in the state of grace, by educating them in the practice of frequent confession, which becomes necessary before receiving the Eucharist for those who are in mortal sin.

l   Beloved sons, build a dam to hold back the flood of sacrileges. Never before as in these present times have so many communions been made and in such an unworthy manner.

m   The Church is deeply wounded by the multiplication of sacrilegious communions! The time has come when your heavenly Mother says: enough!

n   I myself will fill up the great void about my Son Jesus, present in the Eucharist. I will form a barrier of love about his divine presence. I myself will do this through you, beloved sons, whom I wish to set up as a guard of love round about all the tabernacles of the earth."

177

San Miguel (Azores); June 23, 1979
Feast of the Immaculate Heart of Mary

In My Immaculate Heart

a   "Even in this remote archipelago you see my wonders. Today, from every part of the world, I am gathering you all into my Immaculate Heart. It is the refuge which your heavenly Mother has prepared for you.

b   Here, you will be safe from every danger, and at the moment of the storm, you will find your peace.

c   Here, you will be formed by me according to the plan which the Heart of my Son Jesus has entrusted to me. Thus each one of you will be helped by me to carry out in a perfect manner the divine Will alone.

d   Here, I will give your hearts the capacity of love of my Immaculate Heart, and thus you will be formed in pure love for God and neighbor.

e   Here, each day I beget you to your true life: that of the divine Grace with which my Son has filled me, in view also of my motherly function on your behalf.

f   I am nourishing you, my beloved children, with this most pure milk, and clothing you with all my virtues. I am forming you interiorly and transforming you, because I am sharing with you my beauty and reproducing in you my image.

g   Thus your life is becoming daily more conformable to my motherly plan, and the Most Holy Trinity can reflect its light in you and receive greater glory.

h   My time has now come: this extraordinary intervention of mine must be clearly recognized by all.

i   Therefore it is my desire that the feast of my Immaculate Heart be once again celebrated throughout the Church, with the devotion and liturgical solemnity that had once been deter-

229

mined by the Vicar of my Son when times were very tempestuous.

j   Today everything is becoming worse and plunging headlong toward a most painful ending.

k   And so it must be apparent to the Church what that refuge is which I, the Mother, have prepared for all: my Immaculate Heart.

l   With the Holy Father, this beloved son of mine who is shedding upon the Church the light which comes from my Heart, I encourage you all and bless you."

178

Fatima (Portugal); July 1-7, 1979
International Cenacle of Priests of the M.M.P.
Coming from the Five Continents

In This Cova da Iria

a   "I have called you from every part of the world, and you, beloved sons, have replied with generosity to my maternal invitation.

b   You have come here in great numbers to this Cova da Iria, where I manifested myself from heaven, to give you a message of assurance and of salvation for these difficult days in which you are living.

c   United with you spiritually are all my beloved sons now scattered throughout all the parts of the earth.

d   Why have I wanted you here this year?

e   To press you all to my Immaculate Heart.

f   What can a mother do when a great danger menaces her children? She can gather them in her arms and shut them up in a safe place, where they will be defended and protected.

g   And here is the shelter that I am giving you, the protection that you need: *my Immaculate Heart.*

h   In these days, I want to enclose you and all my beloved sons in the refuge of my Heart, to give your filial hearts the same dimensions as mine, and thus to transform you into an ever more perfect image of your heavenly Mother.

i   The time has come when all of you must live, without doubts or reservations, the consecration which you have made to me.

j   For this reason, I wish to put in the place of your little hearts, filled with sin, my Immaculate Heart, so as to give you my own capacity to love and thus transform the life of each one of you.

k   And finally I have wanted you here to give each of you my spirit, in such a way that I might truly live and work in you. The time has come when I wish to manifest myself through you to the whole Church, because the time of the triumph of my Immaculate Heart has come.

l   I am your heavenly Leader.

m   I have wanted you here to gather you into my cohort, drawn up for battle, because now is the hour to go with me into combat.

n   Do not be afraid, apostles of my Immaculate Heart, beloved sons of your heavenly Mother.

o   At the orders of the Vicar of Jesus, go into every part of the earth, and spread the light which comes from my Heart.

p   Soon you will understand fully the great gift which I have given to each one of you during these days; then you will all come to know why I have wanted you all here this year at Fatima, in a cenacle which has been full of extraordinary graces for you and for all my sons scattered throughout every part of the world."

179

July 29, 1979

Your Response

a   "Beloved sons, each moment I look at you with the eyes of a mother, because I want from all of you an ever more perfect response to the desires which I have already made known to you in many ways.

b   Only thus can you be ready for my great plan of love.

c   Only thus can you be made use of by me for the battle which has begun.

d   Only thus can you really form part of my cohort of which I am the Queen and the Leader.

e   In order that my plan may be carried out, I must also be able to count on the response of each one of you.

_f_   Let your response be generous, persevering and without reserve.

_g_   You must respond to the great gift which I have given you, letting yourselves be nourished, formed and led docilely by me.

_h_   Respond to my pressing invitation to be priests of prayer, focusing your every action on giving souls the light of the divine life of which you are ministers and dispensers. All your priestly prayer should be offered with me, on the altar of my Immaculate Heart.

_i_   Respond to my motherly invitation to suffer. It is thus that I make you ever more similar to my crucified Son that you may cooperate personally in his work of redemption. It is through your sufferings, my beloved sons, that I can intervene in order to spare much suffering on the part of many of my poor wandering children.

_j_   Respond to my invitation to walk towards that holiness to which I want to lead each one of you, because only thus can you be apostles of my Immaculate Heart, called to illumine the earth with the light of Christ, which must shine forth in your persons, in your lives and in all your apostolic actions.

_k_   It is in this way, beloved sons, that the whole Church can be renewed. And then, through you, my great plan of love can be accomplished for the triumph of my Immaculate Heart, which is the triumph of the merciful love of God in the world.

_l_   On your response depends whether I will be able to count on you in the great battle against Satan and his powerful army, which has already begun.

_m_   I have told you that each of you has his post, prepared by me, a post which is unique and irreplaceable.

_n_   Do not ask me what your post is, or how I am making use of you, or where I am leading you, because the particular role which each one must carry out has, through my motherly love, been assigned to each and all of you. And in silence and humility, each one must carry out this role to perfection.

_o_   And so you must entrust yourselves to me with absolute confidence; you must believe in me, and you must let yourselves be led by me with docility and filial abandonment, without allowing yourselves to be stopped by doubts, or by the disbelief of those who surround you, or by your own desires, sometimes excessive, or by your curiosity which makes you want to know that which, for the present, you ought not to know.

p   I am your Queen and your heavenly Leader, and I am bringing you together in my cohort, as I clothe you in my own invincible strength, terrible against my enemies.

q   So now, you must obey my orders.

r   Some are, however, still uncertain and insecure. They stop to ask confirmation and encouragement, and thus their response is neither prompt nor complete.

s   This is now the time for you to be confident, because the time to go into combat has come. Soon each one of you will understand the great task to which you have been assigned, by the special predilection of my Immaculate Heart. For now, beloved sons, I ask of each one a response without reserve, so that my great plan of love may be accomplished, and your battle waged according to my orders."

180

The Five First Saturdays

a   "Beloved children, I look on you with motherly predilection, and from all parts of the world, I am enclosing you more and more in my Immaculate Heart.

b   These are the hours of battle, and therefore those weapons which I have prepared especially for you must be made use of:
— the consecration to my Immaculate Heart,
— the frequent recitation of the holy rosary,
— and the practice of the five first Saturdays of the month in reparation for the offenses committed against my motherly Heart.

c   During these Saturdays, I invite you to unite yourselves with me in the prayer of the rosary, in the meditation of its mysteries, in confession, in taking part in Holy Mass and in a communion of reparation.

d   To my daughter, Sister Lucy, I promised special protection at the moment of death and to obtain the graces necessary for salvation for all my children who, harking to my requests, will have devoutly carried out the practice of the five first Saturdays.

e   At this time, when the danger of being eternally lost is so grave, bring souls to safety by entrusting them to the particular protection of your heavenly Mother.

f   Today, reparation on the part of my children must also increase, because there is an ever increasing number of offenses committed against my Immaculate Heart, by insults against my Immaculate Conception, against my perpetual virginity, against my divine and universal motherhood and against my images and because, above all, the souls of the little ones are being alienated from me.

g   Through you, this filial and loving crusade of reparation must spread and grow.

h   Let the first Saturdays of every month be for you real encounters of reparative prayer and a generous response to the request which I have made of you. Above all, the religious and the faithful consecrated to my Immaculate Heart should, on these days, gather in cenacles of life with me.

i   Now, as the battle grows more violent, I must provide moments of spiritual peace and repose for all. In these cenacles you will enter into my repose because, by praying and making reparation with your heavenly Mother, you will be consoled and strengthened by me.

j   Thus, I will receive greater reparation from you, and you will receive new strength and light from your Mother, to walk along the difficult road of these times of yours."

181

August 22, 1979
Feast of the Queenship of Mary

Faithful, Prompt and Obedient

a   "I am your Queen.

b   I am calling you, my beloved children, to become, each and all, faithful, prompt and obedient subjects.

c   You are being faithful when you always do what I ask of you, when you listen to my voice, and when you let yourselves be led by me with docility.

d Your faithfulness should increase each day, by your perfect fidelity to the duties of your particular state.

e In this you should be a good example to all.

f Whoever is faithful to me, makes of their life a mirror in which I can reflect my image and spreads about them the perfume of all my virtues.

g Whoever is faithful, moves ahead with confidence and abandonment along the road which I have pointed out, without looking to any creature, without waiting for human approval, without seeking support or encouragement, but, entering more and more into the depths of my Immaculate Heart, they allow themselves to be led by me along the way of the cross until they reach the summit of Calvary.

h The degree of your fidelity, which I desire to bring to the point of heroism, will be able to be measured by how you know how to suffer, to be silent and to offer things up.

i You are being prompt when you carry out my orders readily and without hesitation.

j During these years, I have pointed out to you the road you must take. Why do you not follow it with confidence and trust? Why do some of you come to a halt, still uncertain and insecure?

k My Adversary succeeds in bringing you to a halt with doubts, and paralyzes you with mistrust. I have already shown you my battle-plan, as I have formed you and led you by the hand to prepare you for the great battle which awaits you.

l You are being prompt when you make use of the weapons which I have given you: prayer, your priestly prayer, the frequent recitation of the holy rosary, suffering, and your priestly immolation.

m You must now be prompt to answer to the orders of your Queen, because you are about to enter into a most painful and decisive period.

n Very soon all could come to pass. You will be called to live through serious moments, following him whom God has placed at the head of my cohort, the Vicar of my Son Jesus who, with strength and courage, is advancing toward his perfect immolation for which I have long been preparing him, ready to give his very life for me and for you.

o   You are being obedient when you give to all a witness of perfect docility to the norms which the Church prescribes for priests.

p   This is your livery, and I want you all to be clothed in it to make you invulnerable in combat: your silent, humble and perfect obedience.

q   Obedient to the Pope, to the bishops united with him and to the norms which regulate your priestly life.

r   I want you to be disciplined in everything, even in the smallest things. Say always and with promptness your yes to the Father who calls you to follow his Son Jesus who, for your sake, made Himself a perfect example of obedience even to death on a cross.

s   If all are faithful, prompt and obedient, I will be able truly to reign in each one of you. And through you I will be able to reign also in the whole world, preparing the way on which Christ the King is about to come to restore in your midst his glorious reign of love."

182   Altötting (Germany); September 8, 1979
Feast of the Nativity of the Blessed Virgin Mary

An Anguished Appeal

a   "In the most venerated sanctuary of this great nation, so exposed to dangers, I have wanted you today to celebrate the feast of the birth of your heavenly Mother.

b   In your person, I bless all my beloved sons scattered throughout the whole world. I have led you everywhere to gather into the refuge of my Immaculate Heart all those priests who, swept away by the tempest which has now been unleashed, are running the great danger of being lost.

c   How many of my beloved sons are now responding with ever greater generosity and are consecrating themselves to my Immaculate Heart!

d   All of you must hasten to entrust yourselves to me! Follow the example and the pressing invitation given you by the Vicar of my Son Jesus, who knows all and who perceives that the painful event, of which for years now I have been foretelling you, is now close at hand.

e   Yes, a little longer, until the time which the Father has ordained will be complete, and then the battle between me and
my Adversary will break out in all its fury and enter its final
phase.

f   I have prepared many of you for the supreme test. In my arms
you will be immolated like little lambs so that, with the blood of
Jesus, yours too may serve to purify the Church and to renew
the world.

g   Others will have to undergo persecutions and sufferings such
as you cannot now imagine. But have confidence because I will
be at the side of each one of you, in an extraordinary way, to help
you to fulfill my plan to the very last detail.

h   I must hasten, and I am making to you now, as it were, a last
and anguished appeal.

i   Answer, each one of you, and entrust yourselves to me.

j   Be little, docile, humble, poor.

k   Be the most beautiful flowers about the crib of your infant
Mother, who smiles on you and blesses you all."

183   *Nijmegen (Holland); September 29, 1979*
Feast of the Holy Archangels

The Angels of the Lord

a   "You have just ended a cenacle with these sons of mine, so
dear to me, who are suffering because of the torn and confused
situation in which my Church here finds herself.

b   Unite your anguish with mine, and be the expression of the
maternal benevolence with which I look upon them, receive
them, comfort and lead them.

c   Pay no attention to the fact that they are few in number and,
for the most part, frail because of age or poor health. They are
nevertheless so faithful and generous that they console the great
sorrow of my Immaculate Heart.

d   To me they are very precious treasures. And through them,
even here, how numerous are the children who are responding
to my invitation, entering into the refuge of my Heart and are
now being formed by me, in heroic fidelity to Jesus and his
Church.

e   Thus in this very place where my Adversary has begun his work of subtle destruction of the Church, I am replying to the challenge and forming my cohort.

f   It is a cohort of the little, the poor and the humble whom I am gathering into my Immaculate Heart to give them my spirit of wisdom, that the pride of those who allow themselves to be seduced by false knowledge and the spirit of loftiness and vainglory may be defeated.

g   Once again today, by means of this, my work, out of the mouths of babes and sucklings the Lord is receiving perfect praise.

h   With you also, are the angels of the Lord; I am their Queen, and they are ready to follow my orders, because the Most Holy Trinity has entrusted the work of the renewal of the Church and the world to my Immaculate Heart.

i   Saint Michael is at the head of my entire heavenly and earthly cohort, which is now drawn up for battle. Saint Gabriel is at your side to give each one of you the very invincible strength of God, and Saint Raphael is healing you of the numerous wounds which you often bring upon yourselves in the great struggle in which you are engaged.

j   Be ever aware of the angels of God who are at your side and invoke their help and protection often. They have great power to defend you and to rescue you from all the snares which Satan, my Adversary and yours, sets for you.

k   Their protection will now intensify and will be particularly experienced by you, because the time of the great trial has come and you are about to enter upon a period of greater anguish than you have ever before experienced.

l   Under my command, become aware of the angels of the Lord at your side, who will be your defense and your guide so that each of you will be able to carry out what I have determined for the triumph of my Immaculate Heart."

184

Lourdes (France); October 7, 1979
Feast of Our Lady of the Rosary
Anniversary of the Victory
of the Blessed Virgin Mary at Lepanto

Your Rosary

a   "Here also, I have brought you to gather many priests, religious and faithful into cenacles of prayer and life with me.

b   I am truly present in these cenacles, and I am joining in your prayer.

c   By this prayer, you offer your heavenly Mother a powerful force in intervening for the salvation of many of my poor straying children and in disposing the painful events of your time according to the motherly plan of my Immaculate Heart.

d   Your entire rosary, which you recite in the cenacle in accordance with the urgent request of your Mother, is like an immense chain of love and salvation with which you are able to encircle persons and situations, and even to influence all the events of your time.

e   Continue to recite it, and multiply your cenacles of prayer, thus responding to the invitation which the first of my beloved sons, the Vicar of Jesus, has so urgently made to you.

f   I am now able to make use of the power that comes to me from your prayer, and I want to intervene as Mother to shorten the time of the trial and to comfort you in the sufferings which await you.

g   Everything can still be changed if you, my children, listen to my voice and unite yourselves, through prayer, with the unceasing intercession of your heavenly Mother.

h   For this reason, here, where I appeared as the Immaculate One, I ask you again to continue with greater generosity and perseverance in the recitation of the holy rosary.

i   The rosary is the prayer which I myself came down from heaven to ask of you.

j   By it you are able to lay bare the plots of my Adversary; you escape from many of his deceits; you defend yourselves from many dangers which he puts in your way; it preserves you from evil and brings you ever closer to me, because I am able to be truly your guide and your protection.

k   As has already happened in other critical situations, so also today, the Church will be defended and saved by its victorious Mother, through the power which comes to me from you, my little children, by means of the frequent recitation of the holy rosary.

l   *Take courage, beloved children!* Pray, have confidence, and enter into the refuge of my Immaculate Heart, that you may form part of my victorious cohort.

m   This is my hour, and soon the whole Church will be brought to a new splendor by her whom you invoke as Queen of Victories."

185

November 21, 1979
Feast of the Presentation of the Blessed Virgin Mary

In the Temple of My Heart

a   "Beloved sons, contemplate your heavenly Mother as she is being brought to the temple to offer herself in the perfect service of the Lord.

b   Although, from the very moment of my conception, I was already prepared for the sublime mission which had been entrusted to me, yet even for me a time of silence and more intense prayer was necessary.

c   In the temple, my soul opened itself to the light of the Spirit, who led me to the love and the understanding of his word. Thus, I was brought interiorly to participate in the most hidden mysteries, while the true meaning of divine Scripture became ever clearer to me.

d   In the temple, my body was offered in an act of continual holocaust to the service of God, which was carried out by me in prayer and in the joy of fulfilling perfectly the humble tasks that were entrusted to me.

e   In the temple, my Heart opened itself to an act of pure and uninterrupted love of the Lord, while detachment from the world and creatures prepared me, each day more and more, to pronounce my perfect *yes* to his divine Will.

f   Priests, whom I so love, today you too must enter into the temple of my Immaculate Heart!

g   Now that my time has come, it is necessary for you also to enter into a time of more intense recollection and fervent prayer, which will prepare you to carry out your important mission.

h   In the temple of my Heart, your soul will be filled with divine wisdom, which I am now giving you in greater abundance, that you may shine forth ever more brightly and shed your light in these days of darkness. Thus, you will help many of my poor wandering children to return to my motherly arms.

i   In the temple of my Heart, your body will be purified in the fire of innumerable trials, in such a way that it may be conformable in everything to that of my Son and your Brother, Jesus.

j   Jesus wants to live once again in you, in order to realize at this time the great plan of his merciful love and to prepare for the coming of his glorious reign.

k   For this, He assimilates your mortal body into his glorious body, so that you in Him might participate ever more fully in his glory, and that He in you might share in your sufferings by means of your human frailty.

l   Once again, through you, Jesus returns to act, to work, to love, to suffer and to immolate Himself for the salvation of all.

m   In the temple of my Immaculate Heart, your heart too will be purified, to be formed by me to a pure and incessant act of love for the Lord. I am leading you on the road of perfect love, that you too may follow your Mother in saying your *yes* to the divine Will.

n   For this, you must enter into the temple of my Heart. You have need of silence and of prayer, of detachment and of renunciation. Thus the design that God has on you will be revealed to you, and you will be free and ready to accomplish it to the end.

o   Only in this way can the great mission which I have entrusted to you be accomplished by you.

p   Take courage, my little children! My time has now come. And so, today, in the temple of my Heart, I want to offer you all to the Most Holy Trinity, in an act of supreme reparation and of maternal supplication."

The Desert Will Blossom

a   "You are on the eve of your departure for Africa, for this great continent which I love with such a special love, because so many of my children live in great want and therefore have need of my motherly tenderness.

b   Go, and give to all the light which comes from my Immaculate Heart. Go forth with me in prayer, in love and in trust.

c   Each day, your Mother will cause torrents of grace and mercy to gush forth from the Heart of her Son, torrents which will water the earth and purify souls.

d   Beloved sons, you have been called by me to be, today, the workers of this divine wonder.

e   I want to act through you.

f   I want to manifest myself to the world through you. By means of you, I want to give my light to souls.

g   And so I have called you from all sides to consecrate yourselves to my Immaculate Heart, that I may give you the grace to live habitually in me, and thus fill your little hearts with the plenitude of my love.

h   Love all your brothers with my Heart, especially those who have lost their way today and are in great danger of being eternally lost.

i   Love above all those who are furthest away, the sinners, the atheists and those who are rejected by everyone; love even the persecutors and the executioners. Say with love, 'Father, forgive them for they do not know what they are doing.' (Lk 23:34)

j   For those who hate, those who kill, those who work violence, those who do evil, those who blaspheme, those who give scandal, bear only love and say, 'Father, forgive!'

k   How many of these brothers of yours you will one day find in paradise, drawn on the way of salvation by the irresistible force of your love!

l   For this, I have called you to prayer.

m   Your priestly prayer, offered with me and joined to your suffering, has incalculable power. Indeed, it has the capacity to bring about a far-reaching chain reaction for good, in which the good effects spread and multiply everywhere in souls.

n   Through it, you will always be able to reestablish equilibrium and to equalize the balance of the scale of God's justice.

o   Precious is your life of prayer: the Liturgy of the Hours, meditation, the holy rosary, but above all the lived-out celebration of Mass which truly renews the Sacrifice of the Cross.

p   Oh, what weight Holy Mass has to compensate for, and to destroy, the evil which is daily brought about by so many sins and by such a widespread rejection of God!

q   And so I have called you to trust.

r   Now that darkness covers everything and the forces of evil are being unleashed with horrible fury, you must above all grow in trust.

s   God alone ever has been, and still is, in every circumstance, the victor. God conquers especially when He appears defeated.

t   Therefore you must today imitate your heavenly Mother in exulting in God and in singing his immense mercy.

u   You must believe that the light will always shine, even in those times when the darkness will become deeper still. And the Light is Christ, and He must shine through you, his faithful disciples, prepared and molded in my motherly Heart.

v   A great wonder is about to be accomplished in your time, even though for the present it is happening in silence and mystery.

w   In the struggle between the Red Dragon and the Woman Clothed with the Sun, in which heaven and earth are taking part, the heavenly powers and those of hell, your Mother and Queen is each day accomplishing an important step in the realization of her victorious plan.

x   Therefore I say to you: soon the desert will blossom, and all creation will become again that marvelous garden, created for man to reflect in a perfect manner the greatest glory of God."

Look at the Heart

a   "Even in this great continent, where I am bringing you for the first time, you see everywhere the wonders of my Immaculate Heart.

b   Look at the heart of these children of mine: they are so poor, so simple, and they love and honor me so!

c   Like all the very poor people in general, they are the most defenseless and the most exposed to being exploited by others. And so especially here, there is increasing activity on the part of my Adversary, who never, as in this continent, has unleashed his fury in such a violent and dangerous manner.

d   Through you, I want to offer today to these children of mine the secure refuge and the maternal protection of my Immaculate Heart.

e   Here also you are aware that my Movement has spread spontaneously everywhere. This is yet another confirmation that it is solely my work and that I act in silence and hiddenness. I continue to choose as my preferred instruments those whom no one notices, and who know how to be silent, to pray, to suffer and to love.

f   In this way, I can accomplish the marvels of love of my Immaculate Heart here also, among these children of mine who are suffering so much and in such need, who are so simple and good, and therefore so dear to me.

g   Have you observed how many of my beloved sons live amid such poverty, solitude and lack of understanding? And how they have managed to share completely in the painful life of so many of their African brothers?

h   Love each and every one of them, these beloved sons of mine. You yourself must be the expression of my motherly tenderness for them.

i   Look at the heart of this whole people, and there you will find stamped the seal of love of your heavenly Mother.

j   Look at the Heart of your heavenly Mother, and you will find gathered there, in ever increasing numbers, children of every continent. The whole world is now held in my merciful hands, for the coming triumph of my Immaculate Heart."

188

Mother of All

a "Today I am spreading my immaculate mantle over all the earth and gaze upon you all with a mother's tenderness.

b On this day, I find you here in this small nation of such a great continent. What poverty, what simplicity, what goodness have you not encountered everywhere!

c I have caused you to love all these brothers of yours with the heartbeat of the Heart of Jesus and that of my own motherly Heart.

d Here too, you have met many of my beloved sons and daughters who have spent their whole lives amidst sacrifices and renunciations, in order to bring the tidings of the Gospel to this land.

e And through them how very many have entered and become part of the Church and of the one and only flock under the care of the one sole Shepherd. Look before you at the immense spring which is in preparation.

f Many of them are nevertheless still living in the error of paganism or belong to religions other than the true one which has been revealed to you by Jesus, the Eternal Word of the Father, to whom He desires to lead you all in his Spirit of Love.

g These also must the heavenly Mother, together with Jesus, lead to the fullness of the truth, as even now I gather all into my Immaculate Heart.

h I am the Mother of all.

i Especially of those who are furthest away, who are still walking in darkness. And in particular, I am the Mother of those who are poorest, simplest, most abandoned and most vulnerable.

j And today, on the feast of my Immaculate Conception, I have wanted you here in prayer, in recollection and in suffering, to

245

hold cenacles everywhere with me, so that you might be an expression of my maternal love and of my predilection for all these children of mine.

k   Thus here too, the triumph of my Immaculate Heart takes place daily, as the reign of Jesus extends more and more in hearts and souls bearing the standard of peace, of love and of joy.

l   With the Pope, the first of my beloved sons, I today bless all my children, especially those who are living in this great continent of Africa."

189

How Great a Light

a   "This is the holy night. Beloved sons, gather about me to welcome my divine Child.

b   There is so much darkness all about.

c   And yet, an ever increasing light shines within the cave. And now it appears entirely from heaven, while the Mother is deeply absorbed in prayer.

d   How great a light descends from the bosom of the Father into the virginal womb of the Mother, who opens herself to his gift, to Life.

e   And completely enveloped in this divine light, I behold for the first time his body: his eyes, his cheeks, his lips, his face, his arms, his hands; I feel his little Heart which has scarcely begun to beat. Each beat is a gift of love which now will never again be quenched.

f   There is so much cold about us: the severity of the cold and the frost of those who have shut all doors on us.

g   But here, within the cave, there is a pleasant and welcome warmth. It is the shelter that this poor place offers us; it is the warmth of little things; it is the help which a little straw gives us, and a manger which offers itself as a cradle...

h   No place is so warm, now, as this most chilly cave. And the Mother bends happily over her Baby who has been given you by the Father, over her Flower finally come to bloom, over her Heaven now forever opened, over her God who has been awaited for so long.

i   And my tears mingle with my kisses, while I gaze enraptured on my Son and my God, who has been born of me on this holy night.

j   There is still a great night lying over the world. There is a great cold freezing hearts and souls.

k   But the light has now conquered the darkness, and love has forever defeated all hate.

l   My beloved sons, on this holy night, keep watch in prayer. In my Immaculate Heart, remain in readiness.

m   His glorious return is now near. And new light and great fire will renew this world."

190

Your Last Hour

a   "Beloved sons, keep watch with me in prayer and trust.

b   This year, which has been for each of you one of extraordinary graces and gifts on the part of your heavenly Mother, is coming to a close.

c   From my Immaculate Heart, I have poured out upon you each day torrents of light and love. And thus I have nourished and clothed you, prepared and strengthened you.

d   Under my motherly and silent action, you have grown in your life of consecration, and in imitation of your Mother. You have become littler, more humble and docile, more trusting and strong.

e   I gaze on you, one by one, with motherly tenderness, sons singled out and nurtured by me in the garden of my Immaculate Heart, to be offered to the glory of the Most Holy Trinity.

f   In the course of this year, I have snipped many from among you to take them up here into paradise, to form a great crown of glory for Jesus and myself.

g   You, on the other hand, are still to remain on this earth and to prepare yourselves to carry out whatever has already been prepared for each one of you, according to my plan of love.

h   You are now in your last hour: the hour of the great battle, the hour of the great immolation, the hour of the great victory.

i   But everything has already been prepared for you by me. Even the time has been measured in accordance with the beating of my Heart, which no longer knows time. Here, all has already been accomplished which, in time, is yet to take place.

j   Here, I see you all at the end of the journey which you have yet to complete, living and sacrificing yourselves for the glory of God. Here, I see you already in the glory which awaits you, at the end of your painful sufferings.

k   You also should think of yourselves as being in the light of my Immaculate Heart, and live serene and content.

l   Live in joy, because your names have already been written in heaven..."

1980

YOUR VICTORIOUS MOTHER

191

Your Victorious Mother

a   "Priests, whom I am calling from every part of the world to enter into the refuge of my Immaculate Heart, sons so loved by me and so exposed to dangers, begin this new year with great trust in your heavenly Mother!

b   Today the Church invites you to contemplate me and to venerate me as the Mother. I am truly the Mother of Jesus, and I am truly your Mother. I am your Mother because I have given you my Son Jesus.

c   So it is that the feast of Christmas becomes truly the feast of your whole life.

d   Because I am the Mother of Jesus, I have been able to become your Mother also. And as I carried out well my motherly duty in regard to my divine Son, so too must I now carry it out well in regard to you, my sons.

e   It is in the joyous mystery of my motherhood that the source of your trust and your hope, at the beginning of this new year, is to be found. You are now being called to enter a time in which great sufferings await you.

f   First of all, my Church will have to suffer as it is called to a more intense and painful process of purification.

g   I am close to it at every moment to help it and comfort it. The more the Church must ascend Calvary, the more will it feel my help and my extraordinary presence. It must now enter into the precious moment of its redemptive passion, in preparation for its most beautiful rebirth.

h   It is for this moment that, in my Immaculate Heart, a sure help has been provided for you: it is the Vicar of Jesus, the Pope, whom I have given you that he might be loved, listened to, and followed by you.

i   For him also, the hours of Gethsemane and of Calvary are now drawing near, and you, my beloved sons, must be his comfort and his defense.

j   The world too is beginning to live through its most dramatic and painful hours.

k   In this new year, many things that I foretold you at Fatima will come to pass.

l   Do not fear; have confidence!

m   At the most violent hour of the storm, you will see my great light grow brighter and more apparent: the Woman Clothed with the Sun, with the moon at her feet and about her head a crown of twelve stars!

n   This is the sign of my victory and yours!

o   It is your victorious Mother who today, with the Pope, the first of her beloved sons, gathers you all into her Immaculate Heart and blesses you."

192   *January 22, 1980*

A Great Net of Love

a   "Walk in trust.

b   The times foretold by me have come, and so you must leave to me all preoccupation.

c   I am your heavenly Mother, and I am at the side of each one of you.

d   I am protecting and leading you.

e   I am sheltering and defending you. Do not be worried about what is going to happen to you, because everything has already been arranged in my motherly Heart.

f   Humanity is now on the brink of that destruction which it could bring upon itself by its own hand. Indeed, that which was predicted to you by me at Fatima, concerning the final closing of this age of yours, has already begun.

g   How can I any longer hold back the hand of divine Justice, when the perversion which humanity has reached, as it walks along the road of obstinate rebellion against God, becomes greater day by day? How many nations could be involved and how many people killed, while many others would have to undergo unspeakable sufferings!…

h   Famine, fire and great destruction: this is what the scourge, which is about to strike humanity, will bring you!

i   Beloved sons, heed, all of you, my urgent request; because my Immaculate Heart trembles: it is in anguish at the fate which awaits you.

j   *Pray more and more.*

k   Pray together with me, through the recitation of the holy rosary.

l   Pray and do penance that the times be shortened, and that the greatest possible number of my children may be eternally saved.

m   Pray that suffering may serve to convert all those who have strayed far from God.

n   Pray that you may never doubt the love of the Father, who always watches over you and provides for you, and makes use of suffering as a means of healing you from the sickness of corruption, of infidelity, of rebellion, of impurity, of atheism.

o   I now ask you for more prayer.

p   Multiply your cenacles of prayer.

q   Multiply your rosaries, recited well and in union with me. Offer me also your suffering and your penance.

r   I ask you for prayer and penance for the conversion of sinners, that even my most rebellious and most distant children may return to God, who awaits them with the merciful eagerness of a Father.

s   And then, together we will form a great net of love that will envelop and save the whole world.

t   Thus my motherly and supreme intervention can be extended everywhere, for the salvation of all who have gone astray."

193

February 2, 1980
Feast of the Presentation of the Child Jesus
First Saturday

Offered to the Glory of God

a   "Beloved sons, let your heavenly Mother present all of you today to the Lord, upon her Immaculate Heart.

b   The more complete the offering of yourselves which you make to me through your consecration, the better can I fulfill my motherly task, which is that of offering you to the perfect glorification of the Most Blessed Trinity.

c   In the temple of Jerusalem, I first offered my Child, Jesus, according to the prescriptions of the Mosaic Law. And now I must

252

also offer each of you, my little children, according to the Will of my Son Jesus who, before dying on the Cross, entrusted you to me.

d   Beneath the Cross, and by the Will of Jesus, I became the true Mother of each one of you. And in what does my duty as Mother consist if not in offering you to the perfect glory of God?

e   *I offer you to the glory of the Father.*

f   As in your heavenly Mother, He wishes to see shine forth in you with increasing brilliance the great design He has imprinted on the masterpiece of his creation; thus is He able to receive today from you, his little children, his perfect praise.

g   *I offer you to the glory of the Son.*

h   He wants to see realized in you, his brothers, his own likeness in such a manner that he can live once again through you and love, pray, suffer and work in order that the Father may be ever glorified in you.

i   And thus the Son lives again perfectly, through you.

j   *I offer you to the glory of the Holy Spirit.*

k   He communicates Himself to you to bring you into the very heart of the divine life and to transform you into burning flames of love and zeal, in order to shed his most pure light everywhere.

l   And seeing you in the motherly arms of his Spouse, who is reproducing her image in you, He is drawn to come down in fullness upon you and to communicate Himself to you just as He communicated Himself to her. Thus the Holy Spirit is being given to you increasingly as a gift by the Father and the Son.

m   In the temple of my Immaculate Heart, I offer you all today to the glory of the Most Holy Trinity.

n   I offer you as a sign of reparation, as a sign of motherly supplication and as a sign of perfect glorification, that God may receive this poor straying humanity and, through the great power of his merciful love, come to the aid of the world, purified by your reparative offering. Thus, by the Spirit of the Lord, the whole face of the earth will be renewed."

Under My Immaculate Mantle

a   "I look upon you, beloved sons, with my eyes of mercy.

b   This is the gaze of your heavenly Mother, which follows each one of you in every part of the world.

c   My motherly gaze falls upon you today with special pleasure and draws you gently to enter, each and all, under the protection of my immaculate mantle.

d   I want to bring you together in love which must grow constantly greater among yourselves, to the point of making you truly one.

e   Thus, I can give you to my Son Jesus to accomplish, according to his most intimate desire, that which He left you as his testament: 'As I and You, O Father, are one, so also may they be one in Us.' (cf. Jn 17:21)

f   And where can this unity be built up each day if not in the Immaculate Heart of your Mother, who loves you all and who is leading, gathering and uniting you?

g   I want to heal you of sin and of the consequences which it leaves in you: that sense of weakness and instability which so often casts you down and discourages you.

h   You feel so frail and insecure, so uncertain and fearful of again becoming victims of the evil that surrounds you.

i   You will not fall back into sin if you live ever under the immaculate mantle of your heavenly Mother!

j   Here, I heal your injuries, I pour balm on your painful wounds. I give you food that nourishes you, and I clothe you in my most beautiful garments; with maternal firmness I mold you and lead you to sanctity.

k   Through you I call all my children, this day, to take refuge under my mantle, especially those who have wandered far from Jesus and from me, who have allowed themselves to be carried away by the present storm and now find themselves in great danger. They have, for that reason, greater need of my motherly help.

l   And so, let no one despair; let no one feel abandoned by me.

m   The hour has come when the love of your immaculate Mother will shine forth resplendently for all."

With Jesus in the Desert

a   "Beloved sons, in this period of more intense prayer and penance, you too should go with Jesus into the desert. Offer yourselves with Him for the perfect carrying out of the Father's plan. Prepare yourselves for the important mission which awaits you, because my time has come and I must count with certainty on each one of you.

b   My plan does not correspond with yours, and my ways are not yours. You will be able to understand my plan and walk in my ways, only if you have a pure heart.

c   Blessed are the pure of heart because they will be able to see.

d   In the desert, your hearts will be made ever purer by me that, in the light of wisdom, you may see the plan of the Father and, as did Jesus, you too may dispose yourselves to carry it out, drinking to the last drop the chalice which has already been prepared for you.

e   For this, your hearts will have to be still more purified by me. The desert is the place where I bring you for this, my motherly work of purification.

f   *In the desert, Jesus suffered* hunger and thirst, the cold of night and the great heat of day.

g   In the desert, where I am leading you, you will feel great hunger and thirst solely for the word of God, while you will experience something like a nausea for all other words.

h   I will have you experience both the painful cold because of sin which has descended upon the world to make it cold and barren, as well as the burning heat of the Spirit of God who will diffuse everywhere the flame of his love so that all things may be renewed and all may thus flourish once again.

i   *In the desert, Jesus lived alone* and, with Him, I will bring you to interior solitude, detaching you from your own selves, from creatures, from the world in which you live and from your occupations, so that you may listen to the voice of the great silence.

j   It is only in the cradle of this great silence that your heart can be formed in the pure and perfect love of God and neighbor.

k   *In the desert, Jesus prayed* to the Father without cease. And so, with Jesus, I am leading you to prayer which must become unceasing and continuous.

l   Pray always: with your life, with your heart, with your work, with your pain, with your weariness, with your wounds.

m   Oh, dear sons, it is only in the desert that your heavenly Mother can train you to have a taste for prayer, that in this way you may perceive always at your side the Father who loves you, leads you and protects you.

n   *In the desert, Jesus was tempted.*

o   In this desert, into which I am leading you, you too will be tested by the fire of innumerable temptations and afflictions, and your faithfulness and confidence will be put to a great test.

p   My Adversary has been given a period of time in which to tempt you. Thus he will set snares for you in all sorts of ways with pride, with lust, with doubts, with discouragement, with curiosity. You will be sifted like wheat, and many will be allured by his dangerous deceits.

q   Follow Jesus in ever rejecting his seductions; above all be on the watch because today there are many false christs and false prophets, who are seducing many souls and bringing them to perdition.

r   Do not be discouraged, my dear sons, I am at your side to point out to you the snares of my Adversary and to help you overcome his seductions. Thus I am strengthening you with the word of God, which was the light that, during her life, guided your heavenly Mother.

s   In the desert, as was Jesus, you too will be prepared for the mission which you must carry out.

t   For this, your hearts must become purer; you must feel hunger and thirst for the word of God; you must pray and suffer in order to say, with your Brother Jesus, upon my Immaculate Heart: 'Father, your Will alone be done. You have taken delight in neither holocausts nor sacrifices; but you have prepared a body for me. O God, I come today to do your Will.' " (cf. Heb 10:5-7)

My Yes and Yours

a   "Beloved sons, contemplate your heavenly Mother today, at the moment when she said her *yes* to the Will of the Lord.

b   This yes blossomed in my soul as the fruit of much silence:

c   — *An interior silence,* in which I habitually lived, disposing me to seek only the word of God. In the most profound silence, the Word communicated Himself to my soul, while my mind opened to receive Him and my Heart closed itself in its jealous custody of Him.

d   — *An exterior silence,* which withdrew me from clamor, from distractions and from the events that were taking place about me, in order to recollect myself for the perfect acceptance of the Will of God, which I sought to fulfill in my humble and ordinary manner of living.

e   Thus silence hid the great plan of the Father, and when this was made known to me, yet still in silence I had to guard it jealously within my Heart.

f   My motherly assent was therefore invisible and secret, since the Father alone awaited it and received it.

g   My *yes* blossomed from my Heart also as the fruit of *much prayer.*

h   Now my life was completely an encounter of love with the Father, who, in secret, revealed to me ever more and more the mysterious plan of the Word, who was to become flesh in my virginal womb.

i   I understood the true meaning of Sacred Scripture, and everything became clearer to me, concerning that to which I was being called. It was my duty to prepare myself to give my flesh and my blood to the Word of the Father, who was to make Himself incarnate in my womb in order to offer Himself on the Cross as a sign of salvation for all.

j   And so my *yes* was also a complete *assent to suffer,* because at that moment I welcomed into my virginal womb all the suffering of the Son.

k   With my soul I saw, even before He was born, the wounds in his hands and his little feet, and the horrible gash in the Heart, even before I felt its beating. I saw Him stretched on the Cross, even before contemplating Him, newborn, in a crib.

l   Beloved sons, contemplate your heavenly Mother today, at the moment when she spoke her *yes* to the Will of the Father. You also are called to repeat it now, that the designs of the Father for you may be fulfilled. I welcome into my Immaculate Heart your *yes*, which each of you pronounces today. This *yes* must come to blossom in you as the *fruit of much silence*.

m   Keep in your heart the word of the Father; guard in the secret of your soul the plan which the Mother is revealing to you.

n   Withdraw yourselves from the noisy clamor of the world. Shield yourselves from that surge of words and images, which sweeps everything before it and contaminates it. At the present time, almost no one knows how to keep this interior silence. It is in this way that my Adversary succeeds in leading you astray and in profaning hearts and souls.

o   Say your *yes* that the Will of the Father may be accomplished. In this way, you are called to penetrate ever more deeply into his own secrets.

p   You do this by your prayer, which brings you to communicate with God.

q   And thus you are able to become, today, the very voice of God, his word lived out. At the present time, Jesus asks only this of his priests, while He is being betrayed by many of them, who misuse his very own divine words.

r   Pronounce with me your *yes to the cross*, dearest sons of mine, because for you also the hours of the passion and of Calvary have come.

s   As in my virginal womb I received the Word of the Father, so also I enclose each one of you today in my Immaculate Heart, while I already contemplate you at the moment of your offering of reparation.

t   Your *yes*, my little children, within the *yes* which your heavenly Mother continually repeats, with joy, to her God!…

u   Then, in you also, the Will of the Father can be fulfilled, and my Immaculate Heart will become the altar upon which you will be immolated for the salvation of the world."

In His Greatest Abandonment

a   "Beloved sons, remain today with me beneath the Cross.

b   I am at the side of Jesus, who is dying, to envelop all his immense suffering with my motherly love. And I become totally associated with Him in the drinking of the bitter chalice of his great abandonment.

c   Not here beneath the Cross are those friends and disciples; not here are all those who were helped by Jesus in so many ways.

d   His divine gaze is dimmed because of this interior and so very human bitterness. And my motherly gaze opens out and ranges about, searching among those present for someone to offer to Him, to appease his painful thirst for love: 'I sought consolers, but I found none.' (cf. Ps 69:20)

e   Not here beneath the Cross is that crowd who sang hosannas, or the people who received Him rejoicing, or the multitudes fed by Him with his bread.

f   There is here a group of poor children, blinded by hate and driven to inhuman ferocity by their religious leaders, to make the ingratitude yet more bitter for Him, and his abandonment more complete.

g   Thus, for his pain there is scorn; for his falls, contempt; for his wounds, insults; for his immolated body, outrage; for the moans of his agony, blasphemies; for the supreme offering of his life, contempt and rejection.

h   The Heart of my Son is rent by this great abandonment, even before this is done by the lance of the Roman soldier.

i   The Heart of the Mother is wounded by a sorrow so great that it cannot be assuaged by the presence of a few faithful persons.

j   Not here beneath the Cross are his twelve Apostles. One has betrayed Him and already taken his own life; another has denied Him and is weeping, far away; the others have scattered and are filled with great fear.

k   But one at least has stayed with me: little John.

l   I hear his innocent heart beating; I see his fear, the fear of a bewildered little child; his sorrow, the sorrow of a sincere friend; and I press him to my Heart to support him in the help which he is called to give me.

m   From the Cross, the gaze of Jesus, who is about to die at the moment of his supreme abandonment, is fixed intently upon the two of us and is illuminated by an infinite love:'Woman, behold your son!' (Jn 19:26)

n   And, beneath the Cross, where my Son has just died, I press to my Immaculate Heart my new child, who has just been born in such great pain.

o   Thus, all is accomplished!

p   Here, beneath the Cross, where I begot you, I want you today, beloved sons of mine.

q   At the moment when the Church is being called to live out the hours of her passion and her great abandonment, you are the sons I give her, that she may be consoled and helped by me.

r   And so, with John, stay all of you, beneath the Cross of Jesus, close to your sorrowful Mother, that the Father's plan may be fulfilled!"

198

Rome (Italy); April 24, 1980
Easter Season

Have Confidence

a   "Do not let your heart be troubled. Have confidence in Jesus, risen and ascended to the right hand of the Father, where He has already prepared a place for each one of you.

b   Beloved sons, have confidence also in your heavenly Mother. My plan is enclosed within the Heart of the Blessed Trinity.

c   *I am the Virgin of Revelation.* In me, the masterpiece of the Father is realized in such a perfect manner, that He can shed on me the light of his predilection. The Word assumes his human nature in my virginal womb, and thus can come to you by means of my true function as Mother. The Holy Spirit draws me, like a magnet, into the depths of the life of love between the Father and the Son, and I become interiorly transformed and so assimilated to Him as to be his Spouse.

d   Through me, the great plan hidden in the very mystery of God is made manifest.

e   My Son Jesus is the manifestation of this mystery. In Him alone dwells the fullness of the divinity.

f   Through Him, all humanity is led back to full communion with the divine nature itself. Only with Him, can the great plan of the Father be accomplished.

g   *Have confidence, beloved sons!* In these present times, so dense with darkness and threats, look to your heavenly Mother. I will reveal to your souls the secret of the Word, become flesh in my maternal womb.

h   I will bring you to the full understanding of Sacred Scripture. Above all, I will read to you the pages of its last book, which you are living. In it, everything is already predicted, even that which must still come to pass. The battle to which I am calling you is clearly described, and my great victory is foretold. For this reason, I repeat: do not fear; have confidence! In my Immaculate Heart, you will experience the joy and the peace that, even today, my risen Son gives to all of you."

199
Salzburg (Austria); May 8, 1980
"Supplica" to the Blessed Virgin of Pompei

The Same Dimensions As the World

a   "You see here also the marvels of my Immaculate Heart. What a generous response I am receiving from my beloved children, especially from so many of the faithful who listen to me, love me and allow themselves to be led docilely by me!

b   Have you seen how so many have come together, from every part of this nation, to take part in cenacles of prayer and to renew their consecration to my Immaculate Heart?

c   By means of them, my Heart grows ever larger to receive in ever increasing numbers my more needy children, so exposed to dangers.

d   From every part of the world, they are hastening to enter into this refuge, which has been prepared by your Mother. Here they become illumined by my light, strengthened by my action, comforted by my motherly love and prepared according to my plan.

e   And now my Immaculate Heart has the same dimensions as the world. It embraces all poor humanity, redeemed by my Son Jesus, and now so menaced by my Adversary, who has succeeded in extending his domain in it.

f   And so, I am offering you, as a sign of salvation, the love of my Immaculate Heart, which has expanded to tremendous proportions to receive all my poor children, in need of my maternal intervention.

g   My Heart is stretched out like a great tent of peace and salvation, to gather you in from the stormy waves which would submerge the world!"

200

Cologne (Germany); May 13, 1980
Anniversary of the First Apparition at Fatima

The Times of Battle

a   "This is my great battle!

b   What you are seeing and what you are living through forms part of my plan, hidden in the secret of my Immaculate Heart.

c   The Most Holy Trinity has entrusted to me the task of leading its army in the terrible struggle against Satan who, as ever, is the most astute and ruthless enemy of God.

d   God has entrusted the carrying out of his victorious plan to me, the littlest slave of the Lord, because the spirit of pride and rebellion may still be conquered by the humility and obedience of your heavenly Mother.

e   My Adversary has dared to attack the Most Holy Trinity, obscuring its great work of love and of glory.

f   He has obscured the work of the Father, by seducing other creatures to rebellion against God, by means of the spread of atheism to a degree that mankind has never before known.

g   To render fruitless the redemptive work of the Son, he has attempted to bedim his Church with error which has entered into her interior, and with infidelity which has spread like a terrible cancer. He keeps aflame the confrontation with the Pope, whom Jesus set in the Church as the center of unity and as the guardian of truth.

h   He has obscured the work of the Holy Spirit, succeeding in extinguishing the light of divine life in many souls, through sin. It is readily committed and even justified by many; and by some, it is no longer even confessed.

i   But the Woman Clothed with the Sun who has begun her great battle, continues to wage it each day through you, my faithful little cohort.

j   By means of you, I want to restore to its splendor the work of creation, of redemption and of sanctification, in such a way that the Most Holy Trinity will receive the greatest degree of glory.

k   Do not become disturbed by the darkness which has spread about, because this is part of the plan of my Adversary; it is on the other hand part of my own victorious plan, namely, that of dispelling the darkness so that the light may everywhere return.

l   And the light will shine resplendently throughout creation when it will once again sing the love and glory of God, following on the defeat of every form of atheism and of proud rebellion.

m   The light of truth, of fidelity and of unity will once again shine fully in the Church. My Son Jesus will manifest Himself fully in such a way that the Church will become light for all the nations of the earth.

n   I will make the light of grace shine in souls. The Holy Spirit will communicate Himself to them in superabundance, in order to lead them to the perfection of love...''

201

June 14, 1980
Feast of the Immaculate Heart of Mary

A Torrent of Water

a   "Beloved sons, today is your feast because it is the feast of the Immaculate Heart of your heavenly Mother, to whom you have consecrated yourselves.

b   Spend it in recollection, in prayer, in silence, in trust.

c   I have now imprinted my sign on the forehead of each one of you. My Adversary is no longer able to do anything against those who have been signed by their heavenly Mother.

d   The Star of the Abyss will persecute my sons, and therefore they will be called to ever greater sufferings; many will have to offer even their own life. It is with their sacrifice of love and of pain that I will be able to achieve my greatest victory.

e   I am the Woman Clothed with the Sun, I am in the Heart of the Most Holy Trinity.

f   Until I am acknowledged there where the Most Holy Trinity has willed me to be, I will not be able to exercise my power fully, in the maternal work of co-redemption and of the universal mediation of graces. For this reason, as the battle between me and my Adversary entered its decisive phase, he tried by every means to obscure the mission of your heavenly Mother.

g   In order to succeed in dominating the earth, the Red Dragon has set out first of all to persecute the Woman Clothed with the Sun. And the serpent has spewed out a torrent of water from his mouth at the Woman in order to submerge her and sweep her away.

h   What is this flood of water if not the ensemble of these new theological theories, by which an attempt is being made to bring your heavenly Mother down from that place where the Most Holy Trinity has put her? Thus it has been possible to obscure me in the souls, in the life and in the piety of many of my children, even to the point of denying some of those privileges with which I have been adorned by my Lord.

i   To take flight from this great torrent of water, the 'wings of a great eagle' were given to the Woman, and thus she was able to find a place for herself in the desert. (Rev 12:14)

j   What is this desert if not a place which is hidden, without noise, set apart and arid?

k   This place, hidden and silent and made arid by so many struggles and so many wounds, in which the Woman now finds a place for herself, is the soul and the heart of my beloved sons and of all who have consecrated themselves to my Immaculate Heart.

l   I am accomplishing the greatest prodigies in the desert in which I find myself. I carry them out in silence and hiddenness to transform the souls and the lives of these sons of mine who have entrusted themselves completely to me.

m   Thus each day I make their desert blossom within my garden, where I can still carry out my work fully and where the Most Holy Trinity can receive perfect glory.

n   Sons, let yourselves be transformed by my powerful action as Mother, Mediatrix of Graces and Co-redemptrix. Do not fear, because in the desert of your heart I have taken refuge and have set up my permanent dwelling place.

o   Live in joy and confidence, because you have been marked with a seal by me and have come to form part of my property.

p   Today I gather your little hearts into the immense, Immaculate and Sorrowful Heart of your heavenly Mother who watches over you with delight and blesses you together with the Pope, the first of my beloved sons, who sheds such great light upon all the Church."

202
Fatima (Portugal); June 29, 1980
Solemnity of Sts. Peter and Paul

The Desert Where I Withdraw

a   "Today I have wanted you here in Fatima, to conclude the cenacles which, during this year, I have been able to hold throughout Europe. My sons, I have accepted the generous response which you have made to me everywhere.

b   This is my hour. This is also the hour of your battle, because the victorious action of the heavenly Leader, the Woman Clothed with the Sun, will become more and more manifest.

c   But for half a time yet, I must remain withdrawn in the desert. Here I work the greatest prodigies, in silence and hiddenness.

d   You are the desert where I withdraw, you sons consecrated to my Immaculate Heart: that desert is your heart made arid by so many wounds, in a world flooded with rebellion against God and his Law, marked with hatred and violence which spreads menacingly.

e   Your parched hearts, your thirsting souls, sons: this is the place where the heavenly Mother now sets up her refuge.

f   Because of my presence, this desert is transformed into a garden, cultivated by me with special care.

g   Each day I water the aridity of your hearts with the tenderness of my immaculate love, the aridity of your souls with the grace with which I am filled because, as Mother, I must distribute it to all my children.

h   Then I bind up your wounds with heavenly balm, I clean you by helping you to set yourselves ever freer of sins, of your numerous defects and of inordinate attachments. In this way I prepare and make fertile the soil of my garden.

i   Then I sow in you the seeds of love for my Son Jesus, that it may spring up and blossom in an ever more perfect and luminous way. And in his Spirit of Love I cause you to open to the sun of the Father's good pleasure, so that thus the Most Holy Trinity may shine resplendently and be reflected in the heavenly dwelling place, built in my Immaculate Heart.

j   And thus you grow, cultivated by me, as little flowers which open only to sing the glory of God and to spread everywhere the splendor of his love.

k   I give you also the colors and the fragrance of my virtues: prayer, humility, purity, silence, trust, littleness, obedience and perfect abandonment.

l   Grow and develop, while each day I transform your desert into the most beautiful garden, guarded jealously by me..."

203

The Work of Co-Redemption

a   "Assent to my plan, beloved sons, and allow yourselves to be formed by your Mother. Thus I am able, more and more, to associate you with my maternal work of co-redemption.

b   Jesus is the only Redeemer because He alone is the mediator between God and men. He has however willed to take into partnership in his redemptive work all those who have been redeemed by Him, so that the merciful work of his love may shine forth in a greater and more wonderful way.

c   Thus you, who have been redeemed, can co-operate with Him in his redemptive work. He in you, who are so intimately united with Him so as to form his very Mystical Body, can gather in your day the fruit of what He accomplished once for all on Calvary.

d   I am for you the perfect model of your co-operation in the redemptive work accomplished by my Son. In fact, as Mother of Jesus, I have become intimately associated with Him in his work of redemption.

e   My presence beneath the Cross tells you how my Son has willed to unite the Mother completely to all his great sufferings, at the time of his passion and his death for you.

f   If the Cross was his scaffold, the pain of my Immaculate Heart was like the altar on which my Son offered to the Father the Sacrifice of the new and eternal Covenant.

g   As Mother of the Church, I was also intimately associated with Jesus in the accomplishment of his redemptive work, which is carried out in the course of history, by offering to all men the possibility of accepting that salvation which He obtained for you at the time of his bloody immolation. Thus the more numerous they are who attain salvation, the more fully is the masterpiece of his divine love realized.

h   My motherly task is that of helping my children in every way to attain salvation; and today still, it is that of co-operating in a very special way in the redemption accomplished by my Son Jesus. My role as true Mother and Co-redemptrix will become manifest to all.

i   I want to carry out this action today through you, my beloved sons. This is why I have wanted to withdraw myself into the desert of your life, where I have set up my safe refuge.

j   In this way I mold you as Mother so that, through you, I may carry out the great work of co-redemption. And so, I call you to prayer, to the perfect offering of yourselves, to suffering, to self-immolation.

k   I lead you along the way of the cross, and gently I help you to climb Calvary in order to transform you all into sacrificial vic-

267

tims, pleasing to the Father, for the salvation of the world.

l   This is the time of my silent action. In the desert of your life, I daily work the great prodigy of transforming you more and more, that Jesus Crucified may again live in each one of you.

m   When this work of mine is completed, the greatness of the loving plan which I am now carrying out will become apparent to the whole Church. My merciful work of co-redemption has now become more necessary and urgent than ever.

n   The task which the Most Holy Trinity has entrusted to me will be acknowledged by all; I will be able to exercise my great power fully, so that the victory of my Son Jesus may shine forth everywhere, when He will restore, through you, his glorious reign of love."

204

Mediatrix of Graces

a   "Beloved children, I am the Mediatrix of Graces. Grace is the very life of God which is communicated to you. It springs from the bosom of the Father and is merited for you by the Word who, in my virginal womb, became man to share with you that same divine life, and for this He offered Himself as a ransom for you, becoming thus the one and only Mediator between God and all humanity.

b   From the bosom of the Father, grace, in order to reach you, must therefore pass through the divine Heart of the Son, who communicates it to you in his Spirit of Love. Just as a ray of light, which passes through a window, assumes its shape, color and design, so too divine grace, merited by Jesus, can come to you only through Him, and it is for this reason that it reproduces in you his own image, the very same image which shapes you ever more and more to his own person.

c   Divine life can reach you only in the form of Jesus, and the more this increases in you, the more you are assimilated to Him, in such a way that you can really grow as his little brothers.

d   By means of grace, the Father communicates Himself to you ever more and more, the Son assimilates you, the Holy Spirit transforms you, bringing about a relationship of life with the Most Holy Trinity, which becomes ever increasingly strong and active. Within souls who are in grace, it is the Most Holy Trinity Itself which takes up its dwelling place there.

e   This life of grace has also a relationship with your heavenly Mother.

f   As I am truly the Mother of Jesus and your Mother, my mediation is exercised between you and my Son Jesus. This is the natural consequence of my divine motherhood.

g   As the Mother of Jesus, I am the means chosen by God by which my Son can reach you. In my virginal womb this first act of mediation of mine is carried out.

h   As your Mother, I was the means chosen by Jesus that through me all of you may reach Him.

i   I am truly the Mediatrix of Grace between you and my Son Jesus. My task is that of distributing to my little children that grace which flows out from the bosom of the Father, is merited for you by the Son and is given to you by the Holy Spirit.

j   My task is that of distributing it to all my children, according to the particular needs of each one, which the Mother is very good at knowing.

k   I am ever carrying out this duty of mine. However I can carry it out fully only in the case of those children who entrust themselves to me with perfect abandonment. I am above all able to carry it out in respect to you, my favorite sons who, by your consecration, have entrusted yourselves completely to me.

l   I am the way which leads you to Jesus. I am the safest and shortest way, the necessary way for each one of you. If you refuse to go along this way, you run the danger of being lost in the course of your journey.

m   Today many have wished to put me aside, considering me an obstacle in reaching Jesus, because they have not understood my function as Mediatrix between you and my Son.

n   And so, never before as in these present times, are so many of my children running the risk of not being able to reach Him. The Jesus whom they meet is often only the result of their human research, and corresponds to their aspirations and desires; he is a Jesus formed according to their measure: he is not Jesus, the

Christ, the true Son of God and of your immaculate Mother.

o   Entrust yourselves to me with confidence, and you will remain faithful, because I will be able to carry out fully my work as Mediatrix of Graces. I will take you each day along the way of my Son, in such a way that He may increase in you to his fullness.

p   This is my great work, which I am still carrying out in silence and in the desert. Under my powerful action as Mediatrix of Graces, you are ever more transformed into Christ, that you may become fit for the task which awaits you. Forward then, with courage, along the way traced out by your heavenly Mother..."

205   *August 8, 1980*

The Powerful Weapon

a   "You are here in the place which I have prepared for you, for your rest. You have spent these past days in the unity of prayer and life with X, whom I have given you as your little brother, upon whom I have great designs for this work of mine.

b   My beloved sons, how great is the love and the sorrow of my Immaculate Heart!

c   I look upon you with great tenderness. My light penetrates your life, your soul, your heart, your existence.

d   How many difficulties you must overcome: how many sufferings await you each day! Pain has become for you your daily food; and thus often you are brought to discouragement and distress.

e   Live in the immaculate love of my Heart. Be little, poor, humble! Accept, as a gift, your fragility. Never seek either to affirm yourself, or to stand out above the others. The way along which I am leading you is that of hiddenness and of humiliation.

f   Don't be curious to know what is awaiting you, but, at each moment, live in perfect love. Then you will be able to give yourself ever more for souls, because as you begin to do each thing there will be a corresponding help of the Lord, proportioned to your work. Go forward with courage, without ever

270

stopping, carrying your cross, as your Brother Jesus did on his journey to Calvary, along a way which seemed impossible and out of proportion to the little strength that remained to Him.

g   Your mission is sublime, and you must not let it come to a stop through weakness or human discouragement.

h   My time has come, and soon I will leave the desert, in which I find myself, for the decisive phase of this battle of mine. I therefore have need of you and of the powerful weapon of your love, pure, priestly love! Open your heart to the dimensions of my Immaculate Heart, and then we will trace out a great path of light, along which my poor wandering children will be able to be led back and to be saved."

206

August 15, 1980
Solemnity of the Assumption
of the Blessed Virgin Mary into Heaven

My Glorified Body

a   "I am your Mother, assumed into heaven.

b   Today I gaze on you all with these merciful eyes and I enclose you in my Immaculate Heart, which never ceases to beat with love for you.

c   I am the Woman Clothed with the Sun. My glorified body is a sign for you of my complete victory. The eternal sun of grace and love now illumines, penetrates and surrounds my glorified body, intimately associated in glory with that of my Son Jesus.

d   From my Heart flows the fountain of my light, with which I wish to envelop and illumine this world filled with darkness. Hasten along in the wake of my immaculate light, let yourselves be drawn by the exquisite fragrance of my glorified body!

e   Beloved sons, in order to succeed in drawing you away from me, my Adversary now rages against you with great fury. He succeeds in sweeping down from the sky a third of the stars, and you too are these stars in the firmament of the Church. But how much greater is the number of those whose splendor becomes bedimmed!

f   Thus he ensnares you in every way; he fights you often through those souls who are closest to you and most loved by you, in order to bring you to discouragement, so as to extinguish in you the zeal and the fervor of your apostolic action.

g   Step out with perfect trust in your heavenly Mother.

h   Seek the answer for your thirst for love solely in my Immaculate Heart. Here you will not experience any disappointment. Here you will be led to the heroism of love. Here all your wounds will be bound up and healed, and you will receive new strength and new enthusiasm to spend yourself for souls.

i   My Immaculate Heart has a great design upon you, a design which is being realized at this very time.

j   Look to paradise into which your Mother has been assumed, and live on earth letting yourself be guided and led by her. Thus you will shed my light, and you will contribute ever more and more to the triumph of my maternal love in the souls and the lives of so many of my children infected with evil and hatred.

k   The desert of your life will blossom in my garden, and you will spread about you the fragrance of all those virtues which here below adorned the soul and the body, now glorified, of your immaculate Mother."

207   *New York City (New York, U.S.A.); September 2, 1980*

The Rock of the Great Division

a   "I have wanted you here today in this great city of this continent to begin cenacles, which you will be able to hold in many other states of this immense nation.

b   Beloved sons, this is your hour. I am calling you all to fight along with me the final phase of the battle. Your Mother is on the eve of her greatest victory.

c   In you I have chosen the smallest and poorest child, and I am taking you to every part of the world to gather all into my Immaculate Heart. By means of you, I now receive from all sides the homage of your lives consecrated to me, and I fill your hearts with pure love for Jesus, so that you may thus save a great number of souls.

d   I accept your suffering, and I heal your many wounds. I love you with a motherly and merciful Heart. I have special love for you because of your extreme littleness and fragility. I am leading you because it is your duty to carry out the most important task at the moment of the decisive struggle.

e   Look at the great light which my Immaculate Heart has given to the Church: it is the first of my beloved sons, Pope John Paul II. From this time on this light will become much stronger, as the struggle becomes more bitter.

f   This Pope is a sign of my extraordinary presence at your side; he is becoming the stumbling-stone for all my enemies and the rock against which the great division will take place.

g   He has been even here and has spoken with firmness, but how few they are who follow his trustworthy and inspired teaching!... Even some of my beloved sons continue to ignore him, and thus slip into a greater darkness and the Church in this country becomes so ill and wounded.

h   May you, sons consecrated to my Immaculate Heart, be living examples of love for, of fidelity to, and of full unity with the Pope. Thus you will draw a great number of poor, confused children along the road of unity and of salvation in the true faith.

i   Within a short time the apostasy will become manifest; only those who will be with the Pope will be saved from the threat of shipwreck in their faith. With him, I bless you all, and I encourage you to walk in trust and in filial abandonment."

208   *Inverness (Florida, U.S.A.); September 8, 1980*
Feast of the Nativity of the Blessed Virgin Mary

He Will Come to You As Fire

a   "Today, my beloved sons, you are gathering here in great numbers; you come from the most distant states of this nation to spend two days of cenacle with me.

b   This is the time to gather together with me in prayer and in love, which must increase in your midst, so as to make you completely one.

273

c   Through your persevering with me in prayer, I will be able to prepare you to receive the gift of the Holy Spirit, who wants to communicate Himself to you in an ever fuller way. This is his hour, because through his powerful loving action the whole world will be purified and renewed.

d   He will come to you as an ardent and burning fire; He will come as witness of my Son, who has never been so despised and betrayed in his person and in his words.

e   He will come to lead back the world to the perfect glorification of the Father. Prepare yourselves to receive this great gift, which my Immaculate Heart has obtained for you.

f   I am your infant Mother. Look upon me in order to become littler. Your littleness is my great strength.

g   Gather together today about my cradle, and offer yourselves to me as little flowers, having the fragrance of love and of trust. And let us second together the Will of the Father, so that what He has ordained for the salvation of the world, may soon be fulfilled."

209
Chicago (Illinois, U.S.A.); September 15, 1980
Feast of Our Lady of Sorrows

The Sufferings of the Church

a   "I am your sorrowful Mother.

b   The sword, which pierced my Heart beneath the Cross, continues to wound me through the great suffering which the Church, the Mystical Body of my Son Jesus, is living through at the present time.

c   All the sufferings of the Church are in my Immaculate and Sorrowful Heart. It is in this way that I still carry out today my maternal duty, begetting in pain this Daughter of mine, to a new life. For this reason the function of the Mother becomes ever more important at the present time of its painful purification.

d   All the sufferings of the Pope, the bishops, the priests, of consecrated souls, and of the faithful are enclosed in my motherly Heart.

e   I too share with you in living out these hours of great pain.

And the passion of my Son continues in his Mystical Body.

f Today, with Him, for the Church I relive the very hours of Gethsemane, of Calvary, of the crucifixion and of his death.

g Have trust and patience; have courage and hope! Soon from our pain will rise a new era of light. The Church will again flourish, under the powerful influx of the love of God..."

210

A Great Design on This People

a "Look at this immense archipelago, and see how my work has also spread here, in an extraordinary way.

b You behold my marvels in every part of the world. I have also revealed to you the times and the places where the triumph of my Immaculate Heart is being realized.

c Look at the hearts and the souls of all these children of mine: they are so faithful to Jesus, so devoted to me, and so united to the Church. Through them the light of my Heart is spreading through all the countries of this continent.

d I have a great design on this people. They please me with their simplicity, their devotion, their great poverty, their humility and patience.

e I am the Mother of all peoples. I look at the hearts of nations, to gather the seeds of good and to make them blossom in the garden of my Immaculate Heart, that I may save them in greater numbers, at the time of the decisive trial, when some of these will disappear from the face of the earth.

f I look with tenderness and with joy at these children of mine, and I bring you into their midst to hold cenacles of prayer and to renew together the consecration to my Immaculate Heart.

g Your coming is a sign of my special presence at their side. Give to me all the crowns of fragrant flowers with which they encircle you. They are signs of the great crown of love, which my children from every part of the world are now offering me, to take from me the painful crown of thorns. With you are the guardian angels, who lead you into the light, so that my garden

275

may soon be filled with flowers.

h And then the Church and the world will see the masterpiece of love, which for the present I am jealously guarding in my Immaculate Heart."

211

Do Not Sin Any More

a "Today you are gathering here, in a cenacle of prayer, and re-calling my final apparition at the Cova da Iria which was confirmed by the miracle of the sun.

b From this land, dear to me for the love and devotion with which I am loved and venerated, I make again to the world the anguished appeal which I made on that same day at Fatima and which summarizes, in a few words, the message which I came from heaven to communicate to you.

c Do not sin any more!

d Do not offend any more my Son Jesus, who has already been too much offended. Return to God by your conversion, along the way of prayer and of penance.

e Alas, this message of mine has remained unheeded. And thus humanity has continued to hasten along the road of rebellion against God, in the obstinate rejection of his Law of love. Thus it has come even to the denial of sin, to the justification of even the gravest moral disorders, in the name of a falsely conceived liberty. Thus Satan, my Adversary, has succeeded in making you fall into his seduction.

f Many have thus lost the awareness of sin, and so, it is more and more committed and justified. The sense of guilt, which is the first step to take along the road of conversion, has practically disappeared.

g Even in those countries of the most ancient Christian tradition, the great crime of killing children still in their mother's womb has gone so far as to be legitimized. This crime cries for vengeance in the sight of God.

h This is the hour of justice and mercy. This is the hour of chastisement and salvation. The heavenly Mother intercedes before God for you because never, as in the present time, have you been so menaced and so close to the supreme test.

i   For this reason I beg you to repent and to return to God. Through you, sons especially chosen by me and consecrated to me, my apostles in these latter times, I want this anguished appeal to reach to the very limits of the earth.

j   From this blessed nation, upon which I have a great design of love and of light, I gather you all into the refuge of my Immaculate Heart."

212   Sydney (Australia); October 19, 1980
Feast of St. Paul of the Cross

The Marvels of Love and of Light

a   "I have brought you even to this new continent, to have you meet so many of my children, some of whom have come expressly for this from New Zealand and the most distant islands.

b   You see how my Movement has spread everywhere… Now this light enwraps every part of the world; there is no place to which the sweet invitation of your Mother has not yet been brought. I have made use of you, the smallest and the poorest of my children, to make of you a messenger of peace, of mercy and of salvation.

c   My time has now come. The painful hours foretold by me have arrived. The great prodigy of the Woman Clothed with the Sun, who has decided to hasten the time of her victorious intervention, will be made manifest.

d   And so you see that everywhere my triumph has already begun. My motherly Heart triumphs in the hearts of those children, who, on every side, answer me by saying *yes*. They are the littlest, the humble, the poor, the unknown.

e   In the heart of my children, who have accepted the invitation and have each day offered themselves to the love and the perfect glory of Jesus, the triumph of my Immaculate Heart is being prepared. Through them the glorious reign of Christ will soon come in all the fullness of power, of light and of victory."

The Way of Unity

a   "You see how my Adversary has succeeded in extending his dominion here, inducing so many of my children to get along without God, seducing them with the venom of atheism and of neo-paganism.

b   Never before as in these present times and in these places must the Church, which Jesus founded as a united body, present itself in all the power of its unity, that the light of the Gospel may reach out to all who are wandering.

c   I am the way of unity.

d   It is the Mother's role to lead back to mutual love, to concord and esteem, and to full communion all those who, by means of Baptism, have been incorporated into the very life of my Son Jesus.

e   Some have wanted to put your heavenly Mother aside, precisely in the deceptive prospect of making the reunification of Christians easier. This on the contrary has brought about a new and more serious obstacle. In fact, disunity has entered into the very interior of the Catholic Church.

f   A true reunification of Christians is not possible unless it be in the perfection of truth. And truth has been kept intact only in the Catholic Church, which must preserve it, defend it and proclaim it to all without fear.

g   It is the light of the truth which will draw many of my children to return to the bosom of the one and only Church founded by Jesus.

h   A true reunification of Christians is not possible except in the perfection of love.

i   And who, better than your heavenly Mother, can help you to love, understand and have compassion for each other, to know and esteem each other? For this reason a true reunion of Christians is not possible without an effort towards interior conversion and purification, in order to attain solely the fulfillment of the divine Will.

j   This is the divine Will for you: that all may be one. And who better than I can help her children travel along this difficult road?

k   I am for you the way of unity. When I am accepted by the whole Church, then, as Mother, I will be able to reunite my children in the warmth of one single family.

l   For this reason, the reunion of all Christians in the Catholic Church will coincide with the triumph of my Immaculate Heart in the world. This reunited Church, in the splendor of a new Pentecost, will have the power to renew all the people of the earth.

m   The world will believe in Him whom the Father has sent and will be completely renewed in his Spirit of Love..."

214

Mother of the Poorest

a   "I have wanted you to come also to this great country to hold cenacles, to gather together in ever greater numbers my chosen ones, all these children of mine, in the refuge of my Immaculate Heart.

b   Most of them, however, are still living in ignorance of the Gospel, which my Son Jesus has taught you with the command given to the Apostles, and passed on to you, to go and proclaim the Good News to all the people of the earth.

c   How many of these are still in the darkness of paganism or belong to other religions and therefore are in need of being led to the fullness of the truth, which is present only in the Catholic Church, founded by Jesus to bring the Gospel of salvation to all nations!

d   In no other place as this have you seen, however, how many of my children live in conditions of extreme misery and immense poverty. How many of them have neither home, nor work, nor food, nor clothing and, dressed in scanty rags, spend their lives on the sidewalks along the roads, where they suffer and die in the midst of general apathy and indifference.

e   Your coming is a special sign for them of my presence at their side, and of my painful motherly anxiety. I am the Mother of those who are ignored and abandoned by all.

f   Today I take all their suffering into the immense sorrow of my Heart. I pour balm upon their wounds, and I greatly value all the sufferings of these poor children of mine: the suffering of those who do not yet know Jesus and walk in darkness; the suffering of those who are cast aside and experience no help from anyone: the suffering of those who possess nothing; the suffering of those who live and die on the sidewalks along the roads, without anyone stopping to bring them help.

g   I am the Mother of the poorest of the poor, of the most miserable, and my Immaculate Heart wants to bring them the help that they need: help to reach Jesus and to accept his Gospel of salvation — brought by so many of my missionary sons and daughters who, for this purpose, are expending their whole lives here, and I am helping them to live with the dignity of sons of God, by a more becoming and human existence.

h   I am now making myself the voice of these poor children of mine, who have no voice, to repeat to all: think of these brothers of yours, of those who even today are dying of hunger and need. Give to these little ones of mine that which you have in abundance! Do not busy yourself with gathering riches, when those goods which your Creator has put at the disposition of all should be distributed among all.

i   I am the Mother of all, but especially of those who are poorest. I gather up their suffering and I bless it and I join it to the prayer of those who plead for the coming of the reign of Jesus, through the triumph of my Immaculate Heart. It will be a reign of truth and grace, of love and justice, and my poor children will have the best place in it."

215

The Power of the Gospel

a   "What you have lived through here, my little son, is for you a sign that this is my hour, and that the heavenly Leader has now gathered together her cohort from every part of the world.

b   Each day, in different dioceses, you have met in cenacles with hundreds of my beloved sons and with tens of thousands of religious and faithful, making in the cathedrals your consecration to my Immaculate Heart.

c   Through you who have responded, my light spreads ever more in the Church. And thus the Church takes on vigor, confidence and a new impetus in the evangelization and salvation of all nations.

d   Look at this immense nation and the huge number of my children, who still do not know Jesus and who walk in darkness, in the expectation that for these also the light of truth and grace may shine forth. This is the time when the Gospel of salvation must be announced to all the peoples of the earth.

e   And the Gospel must be preached to every creature, just as Jesus preached it to you, as the Holy Spirit gave it to the Church.
The Gospel must be kept today to the letter.
The Gospel must be lived today to the letter.
The Gospel must be preached today to the letter.

f   The attempt, undertaken by many, to explain the Gospel in a purely human manner, to ignore its historical and supernatural content, to reduce to natural interpretation that which is contained in it of a divine or miraculous nature, has brought about the weakening of its message and the enfeebling of the efficacy of its proclamation.

g   The power of evangelization is in its fidelity and its authenticity. It is not in the adapting of the message of Christ to the various cultures, but in the bringing of all cultures to Christ that the duty of evangelization, entrusted to you, is carried out.

h   How many of these children of mine would already belong to Christ, if today the power and the impact of evangelization were not weakened!

i   I am for you Mother and Teacher. Just as I accepted, guarded and lived the word of God, so too today I cause it to be accepted, guarded and lived by all of you, my little ones. The divine word must therefore be lived and proclaimed by you to the letter.

j   And so I want to communicate to all of you an enthusiasm for the Gospel. Illumined by its light, announce it to all the peoples of the earth! I am Mother and Teacher of all peoples, and the triumph of my Immaculate Heart cannot come in all its fullness, until I have brought them all to my Son Jesus.

k   Live in my Immaculate Heart, and give Jesus to all the peoples of the earth. Soon the deepest desire of my Son will be fulfilled, and, from every part of the five continents, under my guidance, all will hasten to enter into and become part of the one flock under the one Shepherd.

l   For now, I look with motherly tenderness on these children of mine, still far away, and through you I now bless them all and enfold them in my Immaculate Heart."

216
December 8, 1980
Solemnity of the Immaculate Conception

Great Mercy

a   "Beloved sons, I gather you all today under my immaculate mantle. It is the shield with which I cover you, to shelter you from every attack in the great battle to which I call you. You must gird yourselves once again with this powerful shield, which I give you for your defense and your salvation.

b   How numerous today are the snares of my Adversary who appears to be reaching the peak of his great offensive! In every way and by the most subtle means, he seeks to seduce you, if only he can succeed in striking your soul, in wounding you with sin, so as to draw you away from Jesus, who is your only Savior.

c   The whole of humanity is defiled with this invisible venom, and now needs to be healed by the merciful love of Jesus. He will manifest Himself to you in an extraordinary manner, through the intervention of your immaculate Mother.

d   The weapon, which I give you to fight with, is the chain which joins you to my Heart: the holy rosary. Beloved sons, recite it often, because it is only with your priestly prayer, gathered into my Immaculate Heart that I will be able, in these times, to move — to force, so to speak — the great mercy of the Lord to manifest itself.

e   At the hour when all will seem lost, all will be saved through the merciful love of the Father, which will be made visible through the greatest manifestation of the Eucharistic Heart of Jesus.

f   The standard, under which I rally you, is that of Jesus Crucified, which must be displayed by you because, even for your perverse generation, there is no other salvation but in the Cross of Jesus.

g   With the rosary in one hand and the standard of the Crucified in the other, fight as of now the decisive phase of the battle.

h   This maternal intervention of mine is also being powerfully implored through the confident prayer of the first of my beloved sons, the Pope, who has called upon the mercy of God on your behalf.

i   This powerful cry of his has penetrated heaven and has moved my motherly Heart to hasten the time of victory…

j   For this I now gather you into my cohort, and I give you the shield, the weapon and the standard for the battle. I strengthen you all, and I bless you."

217

December 24, 1980
The Holy Night

About the Crib

a   "Beloved children, this is the holy night. Spend it with me in prayer, in silence, in recollection, in waiting.

b   The day which I have spent, with the precious help of my spouse, in covering the final stage of an exhausting journey, has now gone by.

c   This has been the longest day of my life. But in the evening, as we enter the city which should receive us, every door is closed. At every request of ours a new refusal is ready for us.

d   And so the cold, which has so benumbed my members, begins to enter my soul and, like a painful sword, wounds me in the very depths of my life.

e   I must give you the Expected of the nations, at the very moment when no one receives Him. Love is about to be born, and the chill of egoism shuts the hearts of all. Only the compassion of one poor soul points out a nearby cave.

f   In the darkness and the cold, near a manger on which a little straw has been placed, the divine prodigy takes place.

g   The stars, the song of the angels, the light which pours down from heaven, but about the crib there is only the warmth of two human hearts which love, the heart of my most chaste spouse and my virginal motherly Heart.

h   But for the Child who is born, the warmth of this love is enough.

i   Beloved children, on this holy night, I want you all with me, about the crib of my divine Child.

j   Once again the doors of the houses are closed. The nations are in rebellion against the Lord who comes and plot to fight against his royal dominion.

k   The greatest cold envelops the hearts of men. It is so cold in the world today! This is the coldness of hatred, of violence, of unbridled egoism. It is the coldness of the lack of love which kills.

l   But on this holy night, about the crib, with my Heart and that of my spouse, Joseph, I want all your little hearts also.

m   Together let us love; let us pray; let us make amends; let us warm up by our love the baby Jesus, who once again is born for you. Your hearts, which love, are for Him his only comfort, his great comfort.

n   Through you, formed in the Immaculate Heart of the Mother, this little Babe wants to open the whole world to love…"

218

The Greatest Cry

a   "Beloved children, spend the last hours which close this year with me in prayer.

b   Your time is measured by the beating of my Immaculate Heart, which is shaping its plan of love and salvation. Each day, each hour is scanned and arranged according to this motherly plan of mine.

c   The moments you are living through are moments of emergency. This is why I have called you all to a more intense prayer and to live with the greatest trust in the merciful love of your Heavenly Father.

d   The golden door of his divine Heart is about to open, and

Jesus is about to pour forth upon the world the torrents of his mercy. These are floods of fire and of grace, which will transform and renew the whole world.

e   On the waves of sufferings, never before known to this day, and of prodigies never before accomplished, you will reach the safe haven of new heavens and a new earth. An era of grace, of love and of peace is about to be born from the painful days in which you are living.

f   And so I invite you to end this year on your knees, uniting yourselves spiritually with the Pope, the first of my beloved sons, who is now suffering and praying so much, to implore the mercy of God upon the world.

g   May your prayer be a powerful force of intercession and of reparation. Let it be the greatest cry which has ever been heard, strong enough to pierce heaven and to constrain the Heart of Jesus to pour out the fullness of his merciful love.

h   For this, watch and pray with me. My hour and yours has now come. It is the hour of justice and of mercy."

1981

THE LIGHT AND GLORY OF THE LORD

The Only Possibility of Salvation

a   "Begin this new year in the light of my divine maternity. I am the way along which peace will come to you.

b   The inability of the men of today to establish peace, is caused by their obstinate denial of God. So long as humanity continues to go along the way of rejection of God and of rebellion against his Law, you will have no peace. On the contrary, egoism and violence will increase and wars will follow upon wars, ever more cruel and bloody.

c   As has been many times foreseen, a third world-wide war, which will have the terrible capacity of destroying the greater part of the human race, can take place, if men do not seriously resolve to return to God.

d   The Lord is ready to pour out upon even your straying and so very threatened generation the floods of his mercy, only on the condition that this generation return with repentance to the arms of its Heavenly Father.

e   I myself have sung of his divine mercy, which extends to all generations of men who acknowledge the Lord, and the one and only possibility of salvation for you is in this return to the love and fear of God.

f   On the first day of the new year, on which you venerate the joyful mystery of my divine maternity, I direct to you, my poor sons, my merciful eyes. With an afflicted soul and an anguished voice, I implore you to return to God, who awaits you with that love with which the father, each day, awaited the return of the prodigal son...

g   I invite you to a loving crusade of reparative prayer and to works of penance. Together with me implore of God the grace of return for so many of my estranged children.

h   Multiply everywhere cenacles of prayer to compel the mercy of God to descend, as a dew, on the immense desert of this world. And prepare yourselves to see that which human eyes have never before seen. I am the way of peace. Through me, all humanity is called to return to God, because only in its complete return can my motherly Heart triumph..."

The Light and Glory of the Lord

a　"Entrust yourselves to me, beloved sons, with complete abandonment and with the greatest confidence in your immaculate Mother. As I did my own Child, Jesus, I take you too today into my arms, to present you each day in the temple of the Lord.

b　Let yourselves be offered by me to God, on the altar of my Immaculate Heart:

c　*To be his light,* which must ever shine more and more in the midst of the darkness which has recently covered the earth.

d　The light shines, even though the darkness still does not want to receive it. This light must shine through you, my beloved sons, because this forms part of your priestly mission.

e　Spread about you the light of the truth which is contained in the Gospel, which is the very light of my Son Jesus.

f　My motherly duty is that of making Jesus live in each one of you, to his very fullness. Never before as in these difficult times is it so necessary that all priests be Jesus alone, lived and living, to

g　be once again the light of all nations: his merciful eyes in your eyes; his divine Heart in your heart; his soul in your soul; his love in your love, to spread everywhere in the Church the fullness of this light.

h　*To be his glory,* which through you must be reflected in every part of the world.

i　At the same moment, in fact, in which humanity is experiencing the greatest rejection of God in all history, you are being immolated on the secret altar of my Immaculate Heart, to sing today the glory of the Father, the mercy of the Son and the love of the Holy Spirit:

j　— The glory of the new people of Israel, called to prepare humanity for the return of Jesus;

k　—The glory of the renewed Church, which will experience its new Pentecost of fire, of grace and of light;

l　—The glory of a new humanity, purified in the great tribulation, now ready to live the ineffable moment of its complete return to the Lord.

289

m   This is a grave hour, my dear sons. Therefore live out each day, with love and faithfulness, the consecration which you have made.

n   Allow yourselves to be always carried in my arms as my little Jesus, leaving everything to your heavenly Mother, that for each one of you also the plan of the Father may be fulfilled."

221

February 11, 1981
Feast of Our Lady of Lourdes

I Look Upon You with Pleasure

a   "Beloved sons, you are called today to carry out a great task, which has been prepared for you in all its details by your immaculate Mother.

b   For years I have traced out the road for you. I have taken you by the hand, and I have led you, supporting you and teaching you to take one step after the other, just as a mother does for her children.

c   How many times I have taken you in my arms, after each fall; how many times I have bound up your painful wounds and have given you strength in your great weakness!

d   How many times, without your even having been aware of it, have I intervened personally to rescue you from the dangerous snares which my Adversary and yours sets each day for you!

e   And now I look upon you with the pleasure of the Mother, who sees herself reflected and lived by her children.

f   My cohort is ready; my hour has come; my battle is already in its final phase...

g   Walk in this light of purity. You must spread about you only the fragrance of my Son Jesus and of your heavenly Mother, who never knew sin.

h   Let the fragrance of the very life of God be in you: the fragrance of the grace which clothes you, of the wisdom which enlightens you, of the love which leads you, of the prayer which sustains you, of the mortification which purifies you.

i   Do not be troubled by the assaults of my Adversary, who rages at you with fury to rob you of the precious virtue of purity, which is mine and which I give — to those sons who respond to me and consecrate themselves to my Immaculate Heart — as a sign that they belong completely to me. No one will snatch you from my heavenly garden, in which I have gathered you with such care.

j   In it, grow every day more beautiful and pure, to sing to all the glory of the Father, who is pleased to be reflected in you, of the Son who wants to be perfectly relived by you, of the Holy Spirit who gives Himself to you with inexhaustible abundance. And thus, many of my poor sons, who are today in such great need of grace and purity, will be able to run and wash themselves at the fount of that immaculate love which is both mine and yours!"

222

Mortify Your Senses

a   "Beloved sons, accept the invitation to conversion which the Church offers you especially at this time of Lent.

b   At this time your heavenly Mother asks of you works of penance and of conversion. Prayer should always be also accompanied by fruitful interior mortification.

c   Mortify your senses, that you may exercise dominion over yourselves and over your unruly passions.

d   Let the eyes be truly mirrors of the soul. Open them to receive and to give the light of virtue and of grace, and close them to every evil and sinful influence.

e   Let the tongue free itself to form words of goodness, of love and of truth, and therefore let the most profound silence always surround the formation of each word.

f   Let the mind open itself only to thoughts of peace and mercy, of understanding and salvation, and never let it be sullied by judgment and criticism, much less by malice and condemnation.

g   Let the heart be closed firmly to every inordinate attachment to self, to creatures and to the world in which you live, that it may open itself only to the fullness of the love of God and neighbor.

h Never as at the present time have so many of my fallen sons need of your pure and supernatural love, in order to be saved.

i In my Immaculate Heart I will fashion each of you in the purity of love. This is the penance which I am asking of you, dear sons; this is the mortification which you must perform, in order to prepare yourselves for the task which awaits you and flee the dangerous snares which my Adversary sets for you.

j In purity, in silence and in fidelity, daily follow your heavenly Mother, who leads you along the same road as Jesus Crucified.

k It is the road of renunciation and complete obedience, of suffering and of immolation.

l It is the road of Calvary which you also must travel, carrying your cross each day and following Jesus to the consummation of the pasch. ¹ And thus you will also put at my disposal a great power of intercession with which I will be able to break open the golden gate of the Heart of my Son and pour out the fullness of his mercy..."

223

"Yes, Father"

a "Beloved children, entrust yourselves to me, and I will bring you to perfect docility to the Will of the Father.

b Just as it was for my Jesus, so too on the plan for the life of each one of you it is written: 'Behold, I come to do your Will, O Lord.' (Heb 10:7)

c Your heavenly Mother wants today to help you fulfill well — and only — the divine Will. This is the Will of God: your sanctification!

d By the gift of your sanctity, you place on the altar of the Lord a powerful force of intercession and reparation. For how many evils, how many sins reparation is offered each day on the part of my beloved sons who, led by their heavenly Mother, journey

---

¹ (l) (P)asch in Hebrew means: Immolation of a lamb, sacrificed and consumed as in the Passover meal. In the case of Jesus, He is the Lamb of God sacrificed and consumed. Used in the lower case, (p)asch is meant to signify the priests being the lambs of God sacrificed and consumed for the salvation of others.

along the painful way of their own sanctification!

e Do not look at the great evils which are still perpetrated and spread about by the highly refined means of social communication.

f Under the ashes of the immense desert, to which this poor world has today been reduced, many new buds of life and salvation are sprouting. These are the lives, hidden and unknown but how precious, of my priests and of all those children whom I lead, each day, along the road to sanctity.

g Let your *yes* to the Will of the Father be realized in your daily effort to shun and to free yourselves from sin, to live in grace and in the fullness of love; in the effort to recollect yourselves in the intimacy of prayer and of life with Jesus, of reflection and of the understanding of his divine word; in the interior suffering in the face of the great abandonment and the solitude in which man today finds himself.

h *Yes*, Father, to your Will, that as in heaven, so also on this earth, your Will alone may be done.

i *Yes*, Father, that as in heaven, so may it be done on earth, abandoned as it is and never before so threatened as today.

j *Yes*, Father, to your scorned love, to your outraged presence, to your spurned word.

k *Yes*, Father, to the gift of your immense mercy which shines forth in your Son whom, through the *yes* of the Virgin Mother, you have once for all given us, Jesus–salvation, Jesus–life, Jesus–truth, Jesus–fount of divine mercy, Jesus–perfect fulfillment of the divine Will.

l May your *yes*, beloved children, be placed in the *yes* which the heavenly Mother forever repeats to her God: for the soon-to-come triumph of my Immaculate Heart in the triumph of mercy and love, of truth and justice..."

Today His Passion Is Repeated

a   "Beloved sons, live with me today the passion of my Son Jesus.
Each day this painful passion is repeated.

b   Enter, with me, into the depths of his divine Heart to savor all
the bitterness of his chalice: the abandonment by his own, the
treason of Judas, all the sin of the world which crushes Him under an impossible and deathly weight. As He is crushed in this
olive-press, the drops of blood escape, trickling down his body
and falling to irrigate the earth.

c   How heavily, even today, weighs on his Heart the ease with
which so many turn their backs on Him, to follow the ideas of
the world, or the ways of those who still reject and deny Him!

d   How many of his disciples daily sleep the slumber of indifference, of interior mediocrity, of doubt, of lack of faith!

e   Again the blow which the servant dealt to his face is repeated,
and that other still more painful one, the blow which his soul
receives from the High Priest, as he accuses and condemns Him:
'You have heard the blasphemy! Since He proclaimed Himself
the Son of God, He deserves death.' (cf. Mt 26:65-66)

f   There is another secret Sanhedrin which, every day, judges
and condemns Him, often made up of those who, among his
people, are invested with power.

g   The attempt to recognize Him only as man continues: the
tendency on the part of many to deny his divinity, to reduce his
divine words to a purely human interpretation, to explain all the
miracles in natural terms and even to deny the historical fact of
his resurrection.

h   It is this trial which is still going on; it is the same ignoble and
unjust condemnation which is being repeated.

i   See Him before Pilate, who tries Him and who has the grave
responsibility of passing judgment on Him, and who would like
to save Him… But out of cowardice he subjects Him to cruel
violence: the horrible scourging, which lacerates his innocent
flesh and transforms his body into a single bloody wound, the
crown of thorns, the condemnation and the impossible climb to

Calvary...Then the scaffold of the Cross, the agony and his death, with his Mother nearby, called to die with Him in spirit!

j   Beloved sons, live with me in silence, in prayer and in suffering these precious hours of the passion being repeated in the Church, which is his Mystical Body; it is being renewed in each one of you, called to be the ministers of his love and of his sorrow.

k   Together with me, suffer the judgment of the world, the rejection, the persecution and the condemnation on the part of a society which continues to deny its God and to walk in the darkness of perversion, of hatred and of immorality.

l   Together with me, carry your heavy cross each day. Pour out, with love, your blood. Allow yourselves to be placed on the altar of his very scaffold.

m   Meek as lambs, allow your hands and your feet to be also transfixed with nails: love, forgive, suffer and offer yourselves to the Father, with love, for the salvation of all.

n   And then let your Mother place you in the new sepulchre of her Immaculate Heart, at the moment when the whole Church is called to live mystically this passion of condemnation and of death, in expectation of the hour of the resurrection..."

225
Lome (Togo, West Africa); May 13, 1981
Anniversary of the First Apparition at Fatima

I Have Come Down from Heaven

a   "You are journeying along the roads of many of the countries of Africa, of this great continent so dear to my Heart for its poverty, its simplicity and the goodness of so many of its children.

b   This is the time when all are bound to become aware of my special motherly presence.

c   Give to all that light which comes from my Immaculate Heart. Give it especially to my dear missionary sons, whom I love with immense tenderness.

d   I, who gather up their every tear, who wipe away every drop of their sweat, who measure with joy their fatigue and count, one by one, their painful steps, how can I not express my motherly predilection for these sons who, for Jesus, have chosen to live here, amongst so many of their poor brothers, abandoned and still far from the Gospel in the midst of great sacrifices and much renunciation?

e   The light of my Immaculate Heart now embraces all areas of the world, and my plan for the salvation and the comfort of all stands out with ever increasing clarity.

f   For this I appeared at Fatima to three little children.

g   I have come down from heaven to join you in your journey. Be aware then of the presence of your heavenly Mother at your side. It is a silent and serene presence. She wants to bring strength to your weariness; she sustains you in your work; she defends you from many dangers and leads you each day to carry out well whatever the Father has disposed for you, that the Most Holy Trinity may today be better glorified.

h   I have come down from heaven to manifest myself, through you, along all the roadways of the world: along those traversed by the poor and the desperate, along those grievous roads of the sinners and the wanderers, along those of the sick, the agonizing and the dying.

i   To all those you meet anywhere along the way, you must give the light of my Heart and the tenderness of my motherly love.

j   For this I want to form you ever more and more to the gentleness of love, to attentiveness to others, to complete availability to each and every one you meet along your way.

k   I have come down from heaven to live once again in you and to love with your heart, to sustain with your labor, to save through your sufferings many of my children who have gone astray and, never before as today, have such need of firm assistance.

l   Along all the roads come to your heavenly Mother. My Immaculate Heart is the refuge which gathers you all from all sides, to bring you to the God of mercy and of salvation.

m   With you and through you, I want to manifest myself, to save my children who are in such great need. For this I come down again from heaven to this poor suffering earth."

"Come, Holy Spirit!"

a "I am the Spouse of the Holy Spirit.

b My powerful function as Mediatrix between you and my Son Jesus is exercised above all in obtaining for you in superabundance, from the Father and the Son, the Spirit of Love.

c By this divine fire, the Church must be renewed and transformed. By this fire of love, the whole world will be made new. At his powerful life-giving breath, new heavens and a new earth will at last be opened!

d In the cenacle of my Immaculate Heart, dispose yourselves to receive this divine Spirit.

e The Father gives Him to you to associate you intimately in his very own life and that the image of the Son, in whom He has made to repose all his pleasure, may shine forth in you ever more perfectly.

f Jesus gives Him to you as the most precious fruit of his redemption, as witness of his Person and of his divine mission.

g Even in this distant land in which you find yourself today, brought here by me, to hold cenacles with so many of my children, you see the Gospel already spread, through the precious work of the missionaries.

h Today the whole world must be brought to the fullness of the truth, to the Gospel of Jesus, to the one Church willed and founded by Christ, and this is achieved by the Holy Spirit.

i The Church must be opened to his divine fire in such a way that, completely purified, it will be ready to receive the splendor of his new Pentecost, in preparation for the second, glorious coming of my Son Jesus.

j Today I invite you all to enter into the cenacle of my Immaculate Heart in the expectation of receiving in fullness the Spirit of Love which is given to you as a gift by the Father and the Son.

k My Immaculate Heart is the golden doorway through which this divine Spirit passes to reach you. And so I invite you to

repeat often: 'Come, Holy Spirit, come by means of the powerful intercession of the Immaculate Heart of Mary, your well-
beloved Spouse.' "

Valdragone (San Marino); July 1, 1981
                          Cenacle with the Directors of the M.M.P.

This Is the Hour of My Victory

a   "Beloved sons, you are here in my house which I have prepared for you, and you are spending these days in a continuous
cenacle of prayer and of brotherly sharing, together with your
heavenly Mother.

b   I am always with you. I join in your prayer, and I present it to
the Father through my Son Jesus; I help you to know and love
each other, and I lead you to the perfection of love. I pour balm
on your wounds, and I give you strength in your weakness. My
wounded Heart is consoled, and my sorrow is transformed into
joy by you, my little children.

c   But why have I wanted you here again this year? Because the
struggle between your heavenly Mother — the Woman Clothed
with the Sun — and her Adversary, the Red Dragon, has now
entered into its conclusive phase.

d   What has taken place in these recent months has a profound
significance, following on what has already been predicted re-
garding this time of purification in which you are now living.

e   In the spirit of wisdom, know then how to read the signs of
the times in which you are now living. For this reason I have
called you and brought you up here, and given you strength because my great plan must now be accomplished.

f   But I can accomplish it only through you.

g   And so I await from you a complete response to my will. No
more doubts, no more hesitation, no more uncertainty. How
many of you my Adversary has paralyzed with these subtle and
dangerous weapons of his!

h   Do not look to those about you; pay no attention to the criticisms you hear, to the skepticism which often surrounds this
work of mine. Not to all is it given to understand my plan.

i   To you, my little ones, this has been granted by the Father through Jesus who, in his Spirit of Love, has placed you in the cradle of my Immaculate Heart.

j   *Only in my Immaculate Heart is the source of your security.*

k   Here you are prepared by me for the great struggle which awaits you.

l   Here you are trained by me in prayer, because this is the weapon with which you must fight. Pray more. Pray always. Every action of yours must truly be a prayer. Live your Mass, which immolates you each day with Jesus. Pray well the Liturgy of the Hours, which consecrates to God the rhythm of your day. Recite the holy rosary with love and joy. Meditate on my words, which I have communicated to you these past years. They will bring you to understand the Gospel, which must today be lived by you and announced to all.

m   You cannot come down from this mountain without being transformed by me into living victims, offered by the Holy Spirit to the Father, for the salvation of the world and for the imminent coming of the glorious reign of Jesus.

n   Here you are being helped by me to suffer. And now, the cradle of my Immaculate Heart becomes an altar, upon which I immolate you each day, in order to appease divine justice and that the mercy of God may descend, like a rain, to renew the world.

o   For this, you are called to great suffering, following the first of my beloved sons, the Pope, who now, bathed in his own blood, is following the path that leads to Calvary along which, together with him, your heavenly Mother is leading you.

p   Here you are, above all, being formed by me to the perfection of love. All your brothers in the Movement are spiritually close to you, and during these days, extraordinary graces are being poured into the hearts of my beloved sons scattered throughout all parts of the earth.

q   The time has come when I wish to live in you and to manifest myself to all through you.

r   I want to love with your heart, to gaze with your eyes, to console and encourage with your lips, to assist with your hands, to walk with your feet, to follow your bloodied footprints and to suffer with your crucified body.

s This is the hour of the final battle; it is therefore also the hour of my victory. And so I have called you once again, and you have responded and have come to this cenacle, where we are praying together, loving and invoking the Holy Spirit, whom the Father will give you in superabundance through the Son, that you may soon see new heavens and a new earth."

228

August 15, 1981
Solemnity of the Assumption
of the Blessed Virgin Mary into Heaven

Refuge of Sinners

a "Today Paradise rejoices in contemplating the glorified body of your heavenly Mother, in whom the splendor of the Most Holy Trinity is reflected.

b You too look upon me, and I will shed my light on you. In times of temptation, struggle and discouragement, look upon me, and you will be encouraged and aided.

c When you happen to fall or to feel the weight of defeat, when you are overwhelmed by evil and sin, come to me, and I will give you support.

d Today, looking with eyes of mercy on my sinful children, I say: I am your heavenly Mother who invites you all to gather together under my immaculate mantle, to be protected and led to Jesus, your Savior.

e *I am the refuge of sinners!*

f At the moment when the fury of my Adversary is unleashed, and succeeds in sweeping away so many with the power of evil which is triumphing, I invite you, my beloved sons, to offer yourselves and to pray for the conversion and the salvation of all sinners.

g You yourselves be, with me, the refuge of sinners, of the poor, the sick, the desperate, the little, the abandoned. From my glorified body I reflect my light upon your mortal body; from my Immaculate Heart I communicate my love to your ailing hearts; from my blissful soul I cause the fullness of my grace to descend upon your wounded souls. And so I now transform you, because I want to be, also through you, a refuge for all my poor sinful children.

h   Come then to me, and I will console you and lead you along the safe road which takes you up here to paradise, where, in the light and the joy of God, you will attain the goal of all your earthly existence."

229   *São Paulo (Brazil); September 4, 1981*
First Saturday

Mother of Mercy

a   "You have come once again to the largest country of this vast continent, to hold cenacles with my beloved sons and with all who have heeded my invitation and consecrated themselves to my Heart.

b   The Church will become more and more aware of the powerful assistance which the merciful love of my Immaculate Heart gives it.

c   *I am the Mother of Mercy.* And my presence today wants to become stronger there where the Adversary has done greater damage and brought about greater devastation.

d   I am entering into the enclosure of the Church, which is so desolate, and there I am gathering the broken flowers in order to repair them, and those that are withering to give them back new life, and those that are bent over to straighten them up. I am trying to make beautiful once again this garden, which should blossom and give forth fragrance solely for the love and glory of Jesus. Here also, where the Adversary has so violated the Church, I want to exercise mercy in an extraordinary way.

e   And I am making use of you, my poor child, whom I have set up as the sign of merciful love, because you have been called to bring to everyone confidence in my motherly Heart.

f   Encourage, console, strengthen your brother-priests. See how they are suffering! They are, as it were, abandoned and so discouraged, as a flock without shepherds, they who are called to be shepherds of the flock.

g   I want to be, with Jesus, their loving and understanding shepherdess. Let them follow me into the safe refuge which I have prepared for them: my Immaculate Heart. Bring light and strength to my poor children, bewildered as they are in the midst of the confusion in which they are living. Strengthen them in the faith and in their complete obedience to the Pope and to the hierarchy united to him, and confirm them in the truth; entrust them all to me, by the sincere and generous consecration of themselves to my Immaculate Heart.

h   I am pressed for time. Never as at the present time have you had such need of your heavenly Mother! For this reason, I desire to manifest myself through you. The time left to you is short. That you may be protected and defended, hurry — all of you — under the mantle of the Mother of Mercy."

230
Brasilia (Brazil); September 8, 1981
Feast of the Nativity of the Blessed Virgin Mary

By the Power of the Little Ones

a   "Gaze today upon your infant Mother. Learn to be little. If you do not change and become as little children, you cannot understand my plan. Its power lies in weakness, and its realization takes place each day in silence and hiddenness.

b   With the power of the Holy Spirit, which sets afire and renews everything, the kingdom of God will come to you through the way of littleness and humility.

c   If your heart is pure, it can open itself to the Holy Spirit, who comes to give witness in glory to the triumph of my Son Jesus. If your mind is docile, then you can understand and accept this invitation of mine.

d   By the power of the little ones, my proud Adversary will be defeated, and the whole world will be renewed. Therefore, all of you, gather today about the cradle of your infant Mother, and repeat with me to the Lord: 'In my littleness I was pleasing to the Most High. God has looked upon his servant in her lowliness, and thus He who is mighty has done great things in me; holy is his name.'" (cf. Lk 1:48-49)

231 *Ponta Grossa (Paraná, Brazil); September 15, 1981*
Feast of Our Lady of Sorrows

Mother of All Sorrows

a "I am your sorrowful Mother. Mine are all your sorrows.

b At the present time, for you also sufferings and afflictions are increasing, because you are living at a period of time when the hearts of men have become cold, closed up by a great egoism.

c Humanity is continuing to hasten along the road of its obstinate rejection of God, despite all my motherly admonitions and the signs which the mercy of the Lord continues to send it.

d Thus the chill of sin, of hatred and of violence spreads increasingly, and the easiest victims are the most defenseless of my children and those most in need of protection.

e How numerous today are the poor, the disinherited, and those who live in conditions of inhuman misery, without steady work, without means of livelihood; and how numerous are those who daily drift away from God and his Law of love, swept away by the powerful cohort of those who teach atheism!

f Humanity is living in a desert, barren and cold, and never before as now is it so threatened.

g The pain of humanity is enclosed within my Immaculate Heart.

h Today more than ever, I am the *Mother of All Sorrows* and tears are falling from my merciful eyes. Listen to me, and do not withdraw yourselves from the love of your sorrowful Mother who wants to lead you all to salvation.

i Beloved children, at this time you are becoming the sign of my immense sorrow. In your hearts carry, with me, the suffering of the world and the Church, in this its new hour of agony and of redemptive passion. It will be only from this suffering of ours that a new era of peace for all can be born."

303

Queen of the Angels

a   "In the struggle to which I am calling you, beloved sons, you are being especially helped and defended by the angels of light.

b   *I am the Queen of the Angels.* At my orders, they are bringing together, from every part of the world, those whom I am calling into my great victorious cohort. In the struggle between the Woman Clothed with the Sun and the Red Dragon, the angels have a most important part to play. For this reason, you must let yourselves be guided docilely by them.

c   The angels, the archangels and all the heavenly cohorts are united with you in the terrible battle against the Dragon and his followers. They are defending you against the snares of Satan and the many demons who have now been unleashed with furious and destructive frenzy upon every part of the world.

d   This is the hour of Satan and of the power of the Spirits of Darkness. It is their hour, which coincides with the moment of their apparent victorious action. It is their hour, but the time which they have at their disposal is brief, and the days of their triumph are counted.

e   Therefore they are setting dangerous and fearful snares for you, and you would not be able to escape them without the special help of your guardian angels. How many times each day they intervene to rescue you from all the treacherous maneuvers which, with astuteness, my Adversary undertakes against you!

f   This is why I call upon you to entrust yourselves more and more to the angels of the Lord. Have an affectionate intimacy with them, because they are closer to you than your friends and dear ones.

g   Walk in the light of their invisible, but certain and precious, presence. They pray for you, walk at your side, sustain you in your weariness, console you in your sorrow, keep guard over your repose, take you by the hand and lead you gently along the road I have pointed out for you.

h   Pray to your guardian angels, and live out with trust and serenity the painful hours of purification.

i   Indeed, in these moments, heaven and earth are united in an extraordinary communion of prayer, of love and of action, at the orders of your heavenly Leader."

An Interior Wound

a   "Today you are at Lujan, in the most celebrated shrine of this great country, where I am so loved and venerated. With a cenacle, you are commemorating my last apparition at Fatima, which took place on this very day in 1917.

b   The entire plan which I am now carrying out was revealed to you at that time. You are entering into the most difficult and decisive period of time. You are living through the last years of this century in which a great part of the battle between your heavenly Leader and her Adversary has already taken place.

c   You are now living out its conclusive phase. For this reason I am preparing you each day, through confidence and prayer, to live through the most painful hours of all.

d   With the anxiety and concern of the Mother, who sees how great the danger is through which you are passing, I beg you again to return to God who is awaiting you all to give you his forgiveness and his fatherly love.

e   *See with how many signs* I accompany this anguished appeal of mine!…With messages I have given and apparitions I have granted in many parts of the world, with my numerous weepings, even with blood, I want to make you understand that this is a grave hour, that the cup of divine justice is now full.

f   An interior wound has been inflicted on my motherly Heart as I see that these extraordinary signs are neither believed in nor accepted.

g   What more can I do for you, my poor children, so menaced and exposed to danger?

h   In a final attempt to save you, I am giving you the secure refuge of my Immaculate Heart. I am calling you from every part of the world, through this work of mine, to enter into this refuge by way of your consecration.

i   And you, my little one who are led and guided by me, go into every part of the world to bring to all my motherly call. My hour has come…

j   Raise up to the Father a powerful cry of supplication and reparation. From the divine Heart of the Son may rivers of mercy descend upon this world which, through the powerful action of the Holy Spirit, will be entirely renewed that in this the glory of God the Father may shine forth."

234 *Santiago (Chile); October 22, 1981*

Peace Will Come to You

a   "In this country too, which I love so much, you have gone everywhere to hold cenacles with my priests and with many other children of mine. How much love and how much devotion to me you find along all the roads of the world!

b   The most generous response to my motherly invitation comes from the poor, the little, the humble, the suffering, the sinners. The thorns of my sorrow are thus transformed into flowers and the tears into a smile.

c   Each day I see you increasing in numbers and in generosity, and from all sides the sound of your prayer, ever more pleasing, reaches me. How very dear I hold the rosary, which you recite so often in answer to the urgent appeal of your heavenly Mother!

d   How I welcome with joy your response to my sorrowful plea to consecrate yourselves to my Immaculate Heart, in the midst of the great indifference of the majority of my poor children.

e   Together we are fighting, and each day, you will add new forces to my cohort, for the victory which has already been announced.

f   *From my Immaculate Heart, peace will come to you!*

g   At the moment when everything will seem lost, it is then that you will see the extraordinary prodigy of the Woman Clothed with the Sun, who will manifest herself in all her power.

h   The darkness will be conquered by a light which will cover the whole world; the cold of hatred, by the fire of love; the great rebellion against God, by a universal return to his merciful fatherly love.

i   Yes, my beloved sons, you will also have to suffer, and some of you, in my Immaculate Heart, will be immolated, but through your generous response the time of the great trial will be shortened.

j   More quickly than you yourselves could think, there will come to you the reign of love and of peace of my Son Jesus, to whom alone is due honor and power and glory for ever and ever."

235

The Communion of Saints

a   "I am the Queen of all the saints. Today you are bid to lift up your eyes here to paradise, where so many of your brothers have preceded you. They are praying for you and helping you, so that the reign of Jesus, which in heaven is the cause of our joy and glory, may soon come also upon earth.

b   May this living communion with all your brothers who are already in paradise become ever more intense. The communion of saints must be lived out still more fully at these times, because there is only one Church in which my Son Jesus lives and reigns and is glorified by his brethren, who are still struggling, or suffering, or rejoicing in eternal beatitude.

c   As you go about, bringing my invitation everywhere and gathering my children into my cohort, how greatly you are assisted, protected and defended by your brothers who have already arrived up here!

d   They form a crown of light about my Immaculate Heart. Each one of these lights is reflected on each of you and illumines and guides you on your journey.

e   Your heavenly Mother wants to strengthen the bonds of love which unite you to heaven, so that you may daily benefit from the communion of saints, and go forward united with them."

The Great Trial

a "You are gathered here for a continuous cenacle of one week, and my beloved sons have come from the most distant parts of Mexico, this land which loves me so much and which I am protecting with special solicitude and which I am defending from the many evils which are today menacing it.

b I am your sweet and merciful Mother. Many years ago, I imprinted my image on the cloak of my little Juan Diego, to whom I appeared; today I want to imprint my image in the heart and the life of each one of you.

c You are thus signed with the seal of my love, which distinguishes you from those who have allowed themselves to be seduced by the Beast and bear his imprinted blasphemous number. The Dragon and the Beast can do nothing against those who have been signed with my seal.

d The Star of the Abyss will persecute all those who are signed with my seal, but nothing will be able to harm the souls upon whom I myself have impressed my image. By the blood which many of them will have to shed, divine justice will be appeased, and the time of my victory will be hastened...

e By your prayer, your suffering and your personal immolation, I will bring my plan to completion. I will hasten the time of the triumph of my Immaculate Heart in the reign of Jesus, who will come to you in glory. Thus a new era of peace will begin, and you will at last see new heavens and a new earth...

f I have great designs on you. Respond, each and all, with generosity! In this extraordinary cenacle, I have obtained for you from the Father, through Jesus, the gift of the Holy Spirit. He will transform you into 'apostles of these last times.'...

g Give me your prayer, your suffering and your trust. Do not be afraid if my Adversary attacks you with terrible snares, to lead you to discouragement.

h You are my very little children, my beloved sons, my apostles. Your light will increase day by day, and you will be a source of guidance and safety at the time of the great tribulation.

i   Pray, most dearly beloved sons, because for your homeland, as for all the world, the great trial has come."

237   New York City (New York, U.S.A.); December 8, 1981
Solemnity of the Immaculate Conception

On the Road of Perfect Love

a   "You are here today, on the feast of my Immaculate Conception, to conclude by a great cenacle this long and extraordinary journey, which has been strewn with true miracles of grace from my Immaculate Heart.

b   I am the Immaculate Conception.
c   I am your all-beautiful Mother.
d   I am the Woman Clothed with the Sun.

e   Being without the least shadow of sin, even of original sin, from which I was preserved by a singular privilege, I could reflect completely the plan which the Father had in the creation of the universe. Thus, in a perfect way, I could give the greatest glory to the Lord.

f   Because I was all-beautiful and full of grace, the Word of the Father chose me as his dwelling place, and, stooping to my extreme littleness, through a divine prodigy of love, He descended into my virginal womb; He assumed his human nature and became my Son. Thus I became truly the Mother of Jesus and your true Mother.
g   Because I am truly your Mother, Jesus has entrusted to me the mission of begetting you constantly into his likeness, by leading you along the road of love, of divine grace, of prayer, of penance, of your interior conversion.

h   In this daily struggle against Satan and against sin, my place is that of victorious Leader.
i   I am today the Woman Clothed with the Sun, who is doing combat against the Red Dragon and his powerful army. The Holy Spirit gives strength and vigor to the great cohort of my little sons.

j   Jesus is awaiting the moment to establish, through you, his reign of love, to carry out the Will of the Father in a perfect way. He will thus lead back all creation to its pristine glorification of God...

k   Go forward with the very greatest confidence. Follow the light of your immaculate Mother.

l   I am covering you with my very own splendor; I am clothing you with my virtues; I am signing you with my seal; I am revealing to you the secrets of divine wisdom; *I am leading you each day along the road of perfect love.* From your mouths, little ones, may the Most Holy Trinity receive today praise and glory. You are the greatest joy of my Immaculate Heart: you are already part of my victory. Today I am casting my light upon you all; I am protecting you; I am consoling and blessing you."

238

In the Cradle of Suffering

a   "Beloved sons, watch with me in prayer and in expectation. This is the holy night.

b   At the moment when the greatest silence envelops everything, there unfolds upon earth the great prayer of the Mother, which penetrates heaven and opens it to send down upon you my divine offspring.

c   I look into his eyes; I feel the beating of his little Heart; I stroke, with my motherly hands, his little hands. I place Him in the cradle, made of a poor manger, in the penetrating chill of the night and the cold which closes the hearts of all.

d   The cradle in which I place my heavenly Child, on this holy night, is formed from the suffering and the pain of all. For this Christmas also, the prayer of your heavenly Mother becomes more intense. It embraces the suffering of all and the desperation of many of my children.

e   I look at the sufferings of the Polish people, who have all been consecrated to me and who, in recent days, have been repeatedly

310

entrusted to me by 'my' Pope. They are living through the dramatic hours of their Calvary and carry the cross of a mortal suffering.

f   I look, with motherly apprehension, upon their children who are suffering from cold and hunger, upon their young people who have been imprisoned and deported, upon their families which have become broken up, upon their men who are carrying on an unequal struggle to defend their human rights, upon their women who again are shedding so many bitter tears.

g   On this Christmas day, the people of Poland, so loved by me, are becoming a warning sign for all and a symbol of that which now awaits poor humanity.

h   In the cradle of this immense suffering, I am today placing my heavenly Child.

i   Pray that the hearts of all may open to Him. Throw open wide the doors to Jesus Christ who is coming. At the moment of your greatest tribulation, from his birth will stream forth abundant light for a new birth of all humanity."

239

A Gentle and Sad Voice

a   "Spend with me, in prayer and in profound silence, the last hours of this year which is about to end. You will then hear in your heart the gentle and sad voice of my motherly lament.

b   And you will see many tears fall from my merciful eyes. And you will notice that the beating of my Immaculate Heart becomes more anxious and anguished.

c   Because, in my motherly Heart, you will feel beating the heart of the whole Church, never before so violated by its Adversary and betrayed by its own children; the heart of your homeland, never so threatened in its life and liberty; the heart of all poor humanity, now on the point of living the painful moments of its terrible trial. You are on the threshold of grave and painful events. In my Heart, your own preoccupation, anxiety and bewilderment is now reflected.

d   Turn your gaze, this night, to your immaculate Mother. In my motherly Heart, your prayers and sufferings are offered by me at each moment to the justice of God, as a sign of reparation and supplication for all. Thus, by the mercy of the Father, each new day and each new year is made ready for you.

e   May the new year, which is now about to be born, open up upon this straying world the road of your return to the God of salvation. The great hour of justice and of mercy is about to open upon the world. For this reason I bid you, beloved sons, to spend on your knees, in prayer and reparation, these very precious hours of this last night of the year."

1982

I AM A CONSOLING MOTHER

I Am the Mother of Consolation

a   "Today you are beginning a new year in the light of my divine maternity. On this first day, the Church invokes me as Mother and asks that I extend my motherly protection to all.

b   Today you also unite in asking God for the gift of peace. And you beg for it through the intercession of her whom you call the Queen of Peace.

c   Peace is the greatest gift of the Lord, which was lavished upon you appropriately on Christmas day.

d   The Infant Jesus, whom you see, so frail, at the moment of his birth in Bethlehem, is the eternal Prince of Peace. His name is 'Peace'; his gift is peace; his mission is that of bringing peace to all.

e   'Glory to God in the heights of heaven, and peace on earth to men of good will' (Lk 2:14) — this is what the joyous angels sang, about the crib on the night of his birth.

f   *Peace between God and men* — and it was for this that the Word of the Father became incarnate in my virginal womb, was born in Bethlehem and sacrificed Himself on Calvary.

g   *Peace amongst all men* — because you are all children of God, true brothers of Jesus and of each other. In living out your brotherhood lies the source of peace among men. Because the gift of peace is found only on the road of love, which one journeys by observing the laws of God and his Commandments. In these, we are taught to love God, ourselves and our neighbor; with these is built that harmony which is founded upon justice, upon truth and upon love. As long as the God of peace is not accepted, but on the contrary men continue obstinately to deny and reject Him, they will not even be able to safeguard the demands of respect for human and civil rights.

h   If the laws of the Lord are not observed, but on the contrary are more and more openly violated, humanity will run along the road of confusion, of injustice, of egoism and of violence. This is the reason why humanity is menaced with war and suffering. How much suffering I see scattered over all the roadways of the world, as this new year begins!

i The sufferings of little ones who have no food or help, of youth abandoned and deluded, of men whose dignity is trampled upon and who are made into tools of domination and tyranny, of women who mourn over the destruction of their homes...

j Humanity is close to the danger of a new world war. How great is my anguish over that which awaits you, my poor children, so threatened by hunger, by war, by hatred and by violence.

k Take shelter today under the mantle of your immaculate Mother! Never, as in these times, have I felt the motherly need of bringing you comfort in your sorrow, confidence in your discouragement, hope in your disillusionment and safety in your tribulations.

l You will now be constantly aware of the consoling presence of your heavenly Mother! It will become stronger as the sufferings you must undergo become greater, now that you are entering into the most painful period of the great purification.

m *I am the Mother of Consolation.* You are becoming aware of my great comfort, which will give you courage and protection, especially as you live through the bloody hours of the trial, which has been foretold by me for so long. And so, I am covering you all today with my mantle; I am gathering you into the refuge of my Immaculate Heart; I am stirring up your confidence and spirit of filial abandonment; and I am giving you my blessing."

241

The Light of Love and of Hope

a "Today I am gathering you all on the altar of my Immaculate Heart, dear sons scattered throughout every part of the world, and I am presenting you, with love and joy, in the temple of the Lord.

b Here, you are offered to his glory. Here, you are immolated for the salvation of all. For how long now have I been calling you to respond to my loving plan!

c As the hearts of men become closed because of the coldness of unbridled egoism, hatred, violence and inability to love, I want the light of my motherly love to shine through you.

d   You, my children, are being offered by me to the Lord, in order to spread this light everywhere. Love all my children ever more and more, with my own motherly tenderness. From among them, be especially kind and merciful to those who have lost their way, who are far from God, who are often the unconscious victims of sin and of evil, of corruption and of violence. Never so much as at the present time have I wanted to assist and save, through you, all my poor sinful children, who are running the danger of being lost.

e   Here, you are also being immolated for the perfect glorification of God. This world is experiencing such a rebellion against God as has never before been experienced in the whole course of its history. It is running the danger of self-destruction and menaced with ruin and death.

f   Beloved sons, let yourselves be offered on the altar of the Lord, as docile and meek lambs, for the salvation of the world. For this reason, I am bringing you all today into the temple of the Lord to present you, as a hymn of perfect glorification, to the Most Holy Trinity. Your little voices will become strong, like the roar of a hurricane, and joined to the powerful victory-cry of the cohorts of angels and saints, they will go out through all the world to proclaim everywhere, 'Who is like God? Who is like God?'

g   You have been called to live through pains and sufferings without number. Today, through you, I want to encourage and console my children. At the time of the great tempest, the Mother wants to gather her children in her arms, that they may be consoled. Together, we will live through the agonizing hours of the purification; together we will pray, suffer and trust in the mercy of the Father.

h   Together we will be tested; together we will also be consoled. For the present, through you, my beloved sons, I want to spread throughout the world the light of hope, of trust in God and of my motherly consolation."

The New Jerusalem

a   " 'How often have I yearned to gather your children, as a mother bird gathers her young under her wings, but you refused me. If only you had known the days of your peace!' (Mt 23:37)

b   I hear again the sorrowful lament of my Son Jesus. How often have I, too, as Mother, called you to gather you under the wings of my motherly love. And now, the days of the tribulation have come.

c   My requests have not been accepted. My extraordinary interventions have been given no credence. An attempt has been made to nullify everything that I have done these years in order to meet your needs and free you from the dangers that hang over you.

d   Just as in Jerusalem all the prophets were put to death, just as in this city the very Son of God, the Messiah promised and awaited for so many centuries, was rejected, abused and condemned, so also today in the Church, the new Israel of God, the salvific action of your Mother, the heavenly prophetess of these last times, is too often obstructed by silence and rejection.

e   In so many ways have I spoken, but my words have not been harkened to. In many ways I have manifested myself, but my signs have been given no credence. My interventions, even the most extraordinary, have been contested. O New Jerusalem, Church of Jesus, true Israel of God! How often have I yearned to gather all your children, as a mother bird gathers her young …If you had known the days of your peace!

f   But now, great tribulations will come upon you. You will be buffeted by the wind of a tempest and a hurricane; of the great works built in you by human pride, not a stone will remain upon a stone.

g   O New Jerusalem, accept today my invitation to conversion and interior purification. And thus the new era of justice and holiness can shine forth upon you; your light will spread to all the nations of the earth. And my Son Jesus will establish in your midst the glorious reign of love and peace."

Yes to the Gospel of Jesus

a   "Beloved sons, I want you at my side at that ineffable moment of my life, when the Archangel Gabriel had announced to me that I had been chosen to become the Mother of the Word, the Son of God, the long-awaited Messiah.

b   That which is known to you is nothing compared to that which your heavenly Mother experienced at that moment. That which is narrated in the Gospel of Luke is part of an event which truly took place; it is a true account, not a legend or a literary form.

c   The Archangel truly came to me, and his light, more resplendent than the sun, completely filled my poor little house in Nazareth: my eyes saw it; my ears heard his gentle voice; there was a real conversation between us. To my questions, there were his replies; to my interior apprehension, his serene and comforting explanations.

d   It was also through his precious assistance that my mind was opened to understand the plan of the Father, that my Heart was opened to receive the Word of God, and my life was united in a perfect manner to the Holy Spirit whose most beloved Spouse I became.

e   And it was the Archangel who received my *yes* and placed it upon the heavenly altar, for the perfect glorification of the Most Holy Trinity and for the greater joy of all the angelic hosts, whose Mistress and Queen I became at that moment.

f   Beloved sons, say your *yes* today to the Will of the Father, your *yes* to the Gospel of the Son, your *yes* to the love of the Holy Spirit. In these times, the Will of the Father is not being accomplished, and the action of the Holy Spirit is being impeded, because the Gospel of Jesus is not being accepted.

g   Often, a purely human interpretation is given to it, an interpretation which tends to exclude any supernatural intervention whatsoever. How many of its events are thus explained as legends or literary forms! Never before has the great mystery of God been given such a banal and paltry interpretation. As a result of this, the faith of many has become extinguished, and grave errors are spreading more and more throughout the

Church.

h   You will remain in the true faith only if you will give your full assent to all that is said in the Gospel of Jesus. Announce it to the letter; live it to the letter.

i   Be living gospels; and then, the plan of the Father will be accomplished, and the fire of the love of the Holy Spirit will purify this world. Let your *yes* as obedient children be placed within the *yes* which your heavenly Mother repeats continually to her God.

j   Then you will understand the mysteries of the kingdom of God, which are hidden from the proud and the mighty, but revealed to the little ones."

244

April 9, 1982
Good Friday

This Is How I Found My Son

a   "Draw near, beloved sons, to the fount of grace and mercy, which gushes forth from the pierced Heart of Jesus Crucified. Today, let yourselves be led with me up Calvary that we may live, together, through the painful and precious hours of his agony.

b   He is nailed to the Cross, about midday, after having reached, with great difficulty, the summit of Golgotha.

c   His body is crushed with suffering: the scourging has covered Him with bleeding wounds; the crown of thorns has surrounded his head with rivulets of blood which trickle down and disfigure his face; his Heart is overwhelmed by the immense weight of ingratitude; his eyes, so lively and penetrating, are now obscured by the veil of treason and abandonment...

d   This is how I found my Son, on the road to Calvary, on the Friday of his passion. John is there with me, and, beneath the Cross, we live out together the tremendous hours of his agony.

e   We see the nails transfix his hands and feet, his tormented body; we hear the impact of the Cross in the earth, which causes Him to start with pain, his moans of distress, his silent prayer, the loud cry to Heaven, the throbbing of his Heart as it gives its final beats.

f   O my beloved ones, with me and with your brother, John, live beneath the Cross on which my Son has been hung and on which He is agonizing and dying, out of love, and for the salvation of all.

g   This is how I find the Church today, the Mystical Body of Jesus Crucified. She too is climbing Calvary, carrying a heavy cross; she too is experiencing the hour of such abandonment and of betrayal; her body, also, is being tormented by the scourges of the sins which strike at it and by sacrileges which open up deep wounds in it...

h   And still, the Church looks upon this lost humanity with motherly and merciful eyes, and trustingly makes her way to the summit of Golgotha, for her crucifixion and agony.

i   This is how I find my Daughter today. I am close to her in the painful hour of her Good Friday. With John, who is living again in each of my beloved sons consecrated to my Immaculate Heart, together let us be willing to help her in this, her agony.

j   Let us kiss her hands, again transfixed; let us cover with love her body, again stripped bare; let us pour balm upon her numerous wounds; let us surround with prayer and hope the bloody moments of her crucifixion.

k   In the sure expectation of her resurrection, by the work of the Holy Spirit, she will again be completely renewed and know a wondrous splendor. For her too, the Good Friday of her passion will certainly be followed by a joyous Easter and a new Pentecost of grace and of life."

245   *Munich (Germany); May 13, 1982*
Anniversary of the First Apparition at Fatima

Look to the Pope!

a   "With the first of my beloved sons, Pope John Paul II, who has come today on a pilgrimage of love and prayer before my image in the very place where I appeared, I want you all to be spiritually united, gathered around your heavenly Leader, the Woman Clothed with the Sun.

b   *Look to the Pope: he gives an example of prayer.*

c   His life, which belongs entirely to me, has been molded by me in the spirit of incessant and trusting prayer. His voice penetrates heaven and, united with my maternal intercession, brings down, still today, a shower of graces upon this lost humanity.

d   You too, together with the Pope, must form a strong barrier of prayer to obtain the conversion of sinners, a return to God on the part of many straying children, peace for this humanity which is so threatened and a true and interior renewal for all the Church.

e   Pray often, using the holy rosary, which I came here also to ask of you. If the most grave problems for the Church and for the world have not yet been successfully resolved, despite all the human means which have been taken, this is a sign for you that you must now put all your trust in the power of prayer.

f   *He gives an example of fidelity.*

g   He is faithful to the mandate received through his succession to the Chair of Peter; he is faithful to Jesus Christ whom he announces by word and the witness of his life. Thus the light which he spreads everywhere is one and the same with the light of the Gospel.

h   You must all be united with him in giving witness to the life of my Son Jesus and in announcing faithfully the truth of his Gospel. The Pope is often surrounded by a great void and by loneliness. His words are those of a prophet, but often they fall upon an immense desert.

i   You must be a powerful echo of his word which must be more and more propagated, listened to and acted upon. Until this light is once again enkindled, walk behind him in the secure wake of this great brilliance, because soon the darkness may become even greater upon the world and the Church.

j   *He gives an example of fortitude.*

k   He is going forward everywhere without fear, with the power that comes from his great love as universal Pastor and as Vicar of my Son Jesus. He fears neither criticism nor obstacles; he does not halt before threats and attempts upon his life. Led and defended by me, he proceeds along the way that I have pointed out to him, like a trusting child that always allows itself to be led by the hand. And thus each day he climbs his painful Calvary, carrying a great cross for the good and the salvation of all.

321

l   What he is now living through has already been foretold him by me. Remain ever with him, beloved sons whom I am gathering from every part of the world into the refuge of my Immaculate Heart, and carry with him today the great cross of the whole Church. Today you are now being called to be immolated, that the plan of the Father may be fulfilled.

m   Have confidence and hope. Have courage and patience. The hour of justice and of mercy has begun, and soon you will see the wonders of the merciful love of the divine Heart of Jesus and the triumph of my Immaculate Heart. And so, from the Cova da Iria where, on the 13th of May 1917, I came from heaven to reveal myself to you and to walk with you, together with my Pope, the first of my beloved sons, I bless you all in the name of the Father, and of the Son, and of the Holy Spirit."

246   *Blumenfeld (Germany); May 30, 1982*
Solemnity of Pentecost

The Hour of the Holy Spirit

a   "In the cenacle of my Immaculate Heart, prepare yourselves to receive the fire of the love of the Holy Spirit, which will lead my Church to live the joyous moment of its Pentecost and which will renew the whole face of the earth.

b   This is its hour. It is the hour of the Holy Spirit who, from the Father and by means of the Son, is given to you ever more and more as a gift, as a sign of the merciful love of God who wants to save mankind.

c   By the fire of the Spirit of Love, the work of the great purification will be quickly accomplished. The Church groans as it awaits his merciful work of purification.

d   Through interior sufferings and by means of trials which will bring it to relive the bloody hours of the passion through which my Son Jesus lived, the Church will be led to its divine splendor.

e   It will be healed of the wounds of error, which have spread like a hidden cancer and which threaten the deposit of faith. It will be cured of the leprosy of sin, which obscures its sanctity. It

322

will be purified of all those human elements, which separate it from the spirit of the Gospel.

f It will be deprived of its earthly goods and purified of many of its means of power, that once again it may become poor, humble, simple and chaste. In its pastors and its flock, it will again be crucified, that it may give perfect witness to the Gospel of Jesus.

g Through the power of fire and of blood, the whole world will also be renewed. Humanity will return once again to the glorification of the Father, through Jesus, who will at last have established his reign in your midst.

h This is, then, the hour of the Holy Spirit. He will come to you in all his fullness, by means of the triumph of the Immaculate Heart of Mary, his most beloved Spouse."

247
Split (Yugoslavia); June 19, 1982
Feast of the Immaculate Heart of Mary

In You the Mother Is Glorified

a "Enter into the refuge of my Immaculate Heart. This year, I have called you from every part of the world and you, my little ones, have responded with generosity and have entered into the garden which your Mother has prepared for you. You have listened to my voice and you have accepted my call.

b And now, through you, I have formed my victorious cohort. With how many snares has my Adversary sought to impede your response to my anguished appeal. He has not succeeded because I have always intervened to defend my plan of love.

c Thus, despite all the snares of Satan and the difficulties that have been encountered, my call has gone out to the very limits of the earth. And from the five continents, my children have hastened in very great numbers to enter into the secure refuge of my Immaculate Heart. Today I gaze upon you with delight and love.

d *In you, the Mother is glorified,* because I am able to offer you all to the perfect glorification of the Most Holy Trinity. Thus, in these times of rebellion against God, through you, the Mother

323

can offer her hymn of glory to the Lord.

e   Not to the great, or the powerful, or the rich, or the proud is it given to understand my voice and to penetrate the mystery of my Heart. It is granted to the little, to the poor, to the humble servants of the Lord. With them, I have formed my cohort. And now, the time of preparation is complete. Now we must enter into the moments of the conclusive battle.

f   Humanity has reached that time when it is to live through the bloody hours of the great scourge, which will purify it through fire, hunger and devastation.

g   The Church will be purified by the blood of Jesus and by your blood and by the fire of the Holy Spirit, and it will be totally healed of the wounds of infidelity, of hypocrisy, of impiety and of apostasy.

h   The time has come when the task which the Most Holy Trinity has entrusted to my Immaculate Heart in this age must be acknowledged by the world and the Church. I embrace you all and bless you."

248

The Secret of My Immaculate Heart

a   "Beloved sons, I have brought you again up this mountain, for a week of continuous cenacle with me, your heavenly Leader. I want to reveal to you the secret of my Immaculate Heart, in order to have you share in the mystery of my maternal love.

b   Never as in these present times has my Heart trembled with a most pure love for those whom Jesus entrusted to me when I stood beneath the Cross on which He was about to die.

c   The Church today has need to feel itself loved by me. Humanity today has need to feel itself loved by me. My poor sinful and wandering children have need today of feeling themselves loved by me.

d   *I want to love through you.*

e   I want to help humanity, the Church and all my children through you who are called to enter into the mystery of my

Immaculate Heart. For this, I am bringing about an ever deeper union between my motherly Heart and your hearts, my beloved priests.

f   The luminous ray which shines forth from my Heart will spread to all parts of the world. It will be like a strong anchor to which all will be able to cling, with confidence, in order to be saved at the moment of the decisive test.

g   *I want to suffer through you.*

h   I will expand your heart that you may also be able to understand the mystery of my motherly suffering. See if there is today any suffering greater than mine: my Son Jesus is outraged, despised; He is again abandoned and betrayed by his own... The sacrileges, which are constantly increasing, make up a new crown of thorns, which surround the tabernacles scattered throughout all parts of the earth.

i   The Church, his Mystical Body, is again scourged by division and threatened by error. Those children who are faithful are called to bear great sufferings and to endure insult and outrage on the part of those who do not listen to me.

j   Humanity, in rebellion against the Lord, is rushing inexorably along the road of rejection of God, and this brings it to fall into the abyss of death and desolation. How many there are who are lost each day, swept along by this widespread and dangerous confusion!

k   Share in my motherly sorrow! Judge no one; condemn no one. Pray; love; carry the cross of this great suffering with me for the salvation of all.

l   *I am your heavenly Leader.*

m   I am the Woman Clothed with the Sun. I have gathered you together again in this cenacle, extraordinary for its graces, to obtain for you from the Father, through Jesus, the fullness of the Holy Spirit.

n   He will complete in you the work begun by me. He will mold your hearts to the perfection of love. He will bring you to understand everything. He will strengthen you and give you courage for the supreme witness for which I, as Mother, have formed you.

o   The times of the great trial have come. Go down from this mountain, and spread throughout every part of the earth the light from the merciful love of Jesus, which today is being poured out upon all humanity, by means of the love and the sorrow of my Immaculate Heart, in which I have enfolded you all forever. I bless you in the name of the Father, and of the Son, and of the Holy Spirit."

249

Instruments of My Mercy

a   "Beloved children, I am turning my merciful eyes upon you. I am the Mother of Mercy, of Fair Love and of Holy Hope, and my Immaculate Heart trembles with preoccupation for you. How many dangers are menacing you; how many snares my Adversary is setting for you!

b   In this hour of his rule and his triumph, numerous indeed are my children who are exposed to the danger of being eternally lost.

c   You see in what a grave situation you find yourselves today: humanity has rebelled against the God of love and is walking along the road of hatred and of sin, which is put forward as something good through the means of social communication.

d   You are living in a corrupted and unhealthy atmosphere, and you succeed with great difficulty in remaining faithful to the commandments of God, which lead you to walk along the road of love, flee sin and live in grace and holiness.

e   Thus each day the number of my poor children who allow themselves to be seduced by unbridled egoism, envy and impurity grows greater and greater. The easiest victims, and those who are less guilty, are the young people whose unhappy lot it is to be living at this time when the world has become worse than at the time of the flood.

f   That is why I feel that I am a gentle and merciful Mother especially to my young children, and I am sowing in their lives words of confidence and salvation. I am opening up their souls to a great thirst for good; I am opening up their hearts to the joyous experience of true love and self-giving; I am healing their numerous wounds, while I encourage all those who are good to come to their help through prayer, good example and penance.

g   If you, my beloved children, suffer and pray with me, you will succeed in leading many souls each day along the road which leads to paradise. You then, O children consecrated to my Immaculate Heart, must be today the instruments of my maternal mercy.

h   'How many souls go to hell because there is no one to pray and sacrifice for them!,' I said to Jacinta, Francisco and Lucia when I appeared to them at Fatima.

i   Today I say: how many souls you can save from the fire of hell and lead to paradise if, together with me, you pray and sacrifice each day for them!... It is above all in this, my merciful work of salvation and yours, that the triumph of my Heart is being brought about."

250
Nijmegen (Holland); September 8, 1982
Feast of the Nativity of the Blessed Virgin Mary

It Will Be Saved

a   "My chosen ones, remain about the crib of your infant Mother. I will lead you to understand the secret of littleness and of spiritual childhood.

b   I will teach you to walk along the way of humility and of trust. I will obtain for you the gift of wisdom of heart and of purity. Great joy fills heaven and earth today in the recalling of the birth of your heavenly Mother.

c   You too must share in this interior and profound joy. Today I bless each one of you who, about my crib, form a crown of fragrant flowers of love, of purity and of trust. You are living through tempestuous and difficult days: men are withdrawing further and further from God, and their hearts are being closed, in the chill of egoism and hatred.

d   The world in which you are living has become a cold and arid desert, but over this world of yours, there throbs my motherly and Immaculate Heart, which beats with love for all and is ever causing the dew of grace and of mercy to descend upon the earth. Thus am I able to cause the parched hearts of so many of my children to open up to love...

e   It is through you that I will be able to bring to fulfillment the loving plan of salvation which has been entrusted to me by the Most Holy Trinity. You will see a new birth of this poor humanity in its complete return to the God of salvation.

f   ...You are here, today, holding a cenacle with my chosen ones in this land where the great contestation on the part of my Adversary had its beginning. Here, you see the Church deeply humiliated and wounded, while an immense number of my poor children are confused and wandering. Satan may seem to be singing his song of victory, especially in this country. But from this place, I have also begun my irresistible action.

g   For this, I am making use of all my little children who have said yes to me: through littleness, I will conquer the power of the great; with humility, I will defeat pride; with docility, all rebellion will be overpowered. You will be increasingly aware of my presence..."

251

Paris (France); September 15, 1982
Feast of Our Lady of Sorrows

A Great Force of Reparation

a   "Today, I bend with love over the sores and wounds of all my children. I am your sorrowful Mother. My duty as Mother binds me to you in a strong and personal way. As your joys increase my happiness, so too each of your sufferings brings new sorrow to my motherly Heart. Today I see you all under the weight of an unspeakable suffering. See if there is any sorrow as great as my motherly sorrow.

b   In a world where egoism and pride have taken the field, the most numerous victims are the innocent. Today they are killed by the millions while still in their mother's womb, through the crime of abortion which is now legalized everywhere.

c   Why such cruelty? Why is such inhuman impiety so widespread in the world today? The blood of these innocent ones

328

cries out daily for vengeance in the sight of God and causes wounds of deep sorrow in my motherly Heart.

d   Little children who are just opening out to life are being presented with absolute transgressions of God's Law as values to be sought after; young people are disoriented and deceived; families bewail the destruction of their home-life; the immense multitude of my poor children are hastening along the road of sin and perdition: see if there is any sorrow as great as mine!

e   Above all, I look today with sorrowful apprehension at the Church, especially entrusted by Jesus to my motherly action. I see how it is violated by sin, its unity shattered, profaned by sacrileges, its truth obscured.

f   How many pastors there are today who no longer defend the flock which has been entrusted to them by Jesus! Some remain silent when they should speak courageously to defend the truth and to condemn error and sin. They tolerate to avoid risk; they descend to compromise simply to maintain their privileges. Thus error is spread under the form of ambiguous formulas, and reparation is no longer made for sin, in a progressive apostasy from Jesus and from his Gospel.

g   Today there is need for a great force of prayer. There is need for a great chain of suffering, raised up to God in reparation! I call upon you, my chosen ones, and upon all the children who are consecrated to my Immaculate Heart to unite yourselves to the sorrow of your heavenly Mother, that what is lacking in the passion of Jesus be completed in each one of you..."

252

Fatima (Portugal); October 13, 1982
Anniversary of the Last Apparition at Fatima

I Am the Dawn

a   "In the stormy sea in which you are sailing, hasten all to my Immaculate Heart. I came down from heaven to give you this anchor of salvation. Cling to the anchor which has been prepared for you by my merciful love.

b   Come to me, children, never before so menaced by the cold of sin, by the torment of hatred, by the tempest of rebellion against God and his Law, by the earthquake of moral disorder, by the danger of war, destruction and famine.

c   In this world, which has become worse than at the time of the flood, you are truly running the danger of being lost, along the wicked roads of sin and infidelity, in this life, and the threat of perdition for all eternity, in the next.

d   How many souls there are, in fact, who go each day to hell, because the request I made of you in this very place, to return to God along the road of prayer, of penance and of interior conversion, has not yet been acted on.

e   These then are times of chastisement and of salvation, of justice and of mercy. In view of these times, I have prepared a secure refuge for you where you must gather together to be comforted and saved.

f   *This refuge is my Immaculate Heart!*

g   From my Heart there issue in ever increasing reflected strength, the rays which come forth from the Heart of Jesus, so that you may walk along the way of grace and of holiness, of love and of mercy, of truth and of fidelity.

h   If the world is filled with the darkness of sin, these rays descend like a dew, and they urge it to open itself to the radiant noonday of its renewal. All creation will know the new and long-awaited time of its perfect glorification of God.

i   If the Church is, in its human reality, darkened and wounded, these rays will open it to the light of the Gospel of Jesus, to the custody of the deposit of faith which has been entrusted to it alone, and to the full witness of its unity and holiness.

j   *I am the dawn which precedes the day.*

k   My light, which shines out in the night which still enwraps the world, is you who are consecrated to my Immaculate Heart, you who are totally entrusted to me that you may listen to me and follow me. Increase in prayer, in humility, in suffering and in confidence.

l   Soon you will see the great day of the Lord, prepared for by so much sorrow and so many tears, by so much love and so much hope, by many prayers and by unceasing suffering. From the

Cova da Iria, on the sixty-fifth anniversary of my final apparition which was confirmed by the miracle of the sun, I bless you all in the name of the Father, and of the Son, and of the Holy Spirit."

253 *Rome (Italy); November 20, 1982*

Obedient, Chaste and Poor

a   "Live in my maternal predilection, responding to my call for prayer and trust. Allow yourselves, beloved sons, to be formed by me each day.

b   *I want you docile* and obedient to the Will of the Father, in perfect imitation of my Son Jesus: for this, you must always be obedient to the Church.

c   The virtue which I love most in my priest-sons is that of obedience. Today, you must be an example to everyone, by obeying with joy your superiors, especially the Pope.

d   How is it possible that, when he speaks today, he is no longer listened to by many, and when he gives directives, he is no longer obeyed? And it is sometimes some of my bishop-sons and priest-sons who are the first to disobey him! In this way the Church becomes truly threatened in its interior unity...

e   *I want you chaste* in mind, heart and body.

f   Through purity of mind, you will see the truth with greater clarity, and you will be always faithful to it; the Gospel of Jesus will appear to you in all its divine splendor.

g   Through purity of heart, you will attain perfect communion of love with Jesus, and you will be led by Him to understand the mystery of his burning love. You will become truly able to love everyone, and the flame of his love will set you afire and transform you.

h   Through purity of body, you will experience the joy of meeting me and of being increasingly in communion with the heavenly spirits and with the souls of your deceased brothers; the power of the Spirit will transform you, freeing you of the many limitations of the flesh. And thus, you will spread about you the light of divine grace and of holiness.

i Let celibacy, willed by Jesus and ardently sought by the Church, be loved, esteemed and lived by you: you will become the source of life for an immense number of souls, even of your own brother-priests.

j Take courage, O dearly beloved sons of mine! Follow me along the way of hiddenness and humility.

k *I want you poor* in material goods and in spirit.

l Only thus will you be able to understand the anxieties and the sorrows of many people and share in the concerns and the sufferings of your poorest brothers; of those who have no work or means of livelihood; of those who are pushed aside and persecuted; of those who are considered as nothings, while they are, for me, most precious treasures.

m Whoever meets you must be aware of the presence of their heavenly Mother who, through you, again caresses and consoles, who again helps, even materially, who encourages and saves and who embraces and defends everyone."

254

My Plan

a "I am your immaculate Mother: allow yourselves to be led by me, beloved sons, for the perfect fulfillment of my motherly plan.

b *It is a plan of enmity.*

c 'I will put enmity between you and the Woman, between your offspring and hers.' (Gen 3:15) Thus did the Lord speak of me, addressing Himself to the serpent when, by means of him, sin entered in at the beginning of the history of the human race: enmity between me and Satan, between the Woman and the serpent, between my cohort and his, between good and evil, between grace and sin.

d To walk along my way, there can be no descending to compromise with evil, because this road winds its way only over [the terrain] of enmity between these two opposed realities. My Son Jesus becomes the sign of this contradiction and has been given to you by the Father for the salvation and the ruin of many.

e   You are now living in obscure times, because in all kinds of ways an attempt is being made to reach a compromise between God and Satan, between good and evil, between the spirit of Jesus and the spirit of the world. Many are running the danger of becoming victims of this general confusion, and even in my Church a false spirit, which is not that of Jesus the Son of God, is seeking to spread itself about. Like a cloud of invisible poison gas, a spirit which jumbles the things of God with those of the world is expanding and succeeding in depriving the word of God of its vigor and in despoiling the announcement of the Gospel of its force.

f   *It is a plan of struggle.*

g   Assisted by me and following along the road which Jesus has traced out for you, you must fight against the Evil One, against sin, against error and infidelity.

h   If, by divine privilege, I have been exempt from all sin, even original sin, it is because I have been appointed by the Most Holy Trinity as Leader of this terrible battle, which involves heaven and earth, heavenly and earthly spirits. It is a great and continuous struggle, often invisible, and at this time it has become general.

i   In the Apocalypse, I have been announced as the Woman Clothed with the Sun who will conduct the battle against the Red Dragon and all his followers. If you want to second my plan, you must do battle, my little ones, children of a Mother who is Leader. Fight against sin and against compromise with the weapon of prayer and of suffering. In hiddenness and confidence, in the humble fulfillment of your daily duties, in the perfect imitation of Jesus and in poverty and contempt for the world and for your own selves, join me in waging this battle each day.

j   *It is a plan of victory.*

k   After the present triumph of evil, which has succeeded in subduing the world, in the end the victory will be solely that of my Son Jesus. He alone is the victor. The outcome of the great struggle, through which we are living, will be his glorious reign of peace and of goodness, of justice and of holiness, which will be established in the world and will shine forth resplendently in the hearts of all. Thus will be brought to completion the plan of enmity, of struggle and of victory in the triumph of my Immaculate Heart."

255

God Is with You

a   "A great silence enwraps the world. Darkness covers everything. Hearts keep vigil in prayer and expectation. A sense of confident hope opens the doors which have been closed by hatred and egoism.

b   The powers of hell feel themselves unexpectedly overpowered by a new force of love and of life.

c   In the darkness a brightness is enkindled. In the silence the harmonies of celestial hymns are heard. And in the heavens a great light suddenly appears.

d   *This is the holy night.*

e   This light now enwraps the poor shelter, where the greatest event in history is about to take place. The Virgin Mother gives you her Child, who is born poor and defenseless, trembling and in need of everything, weeping and tender as a lamb, who is to make visible, already in his little body, the great mystery of meekness and of mercy.

f   The life of every man takes on a new meaning from this night, because the little Child who is born is also his God. He is man like you, and He is God with you. He is Emmanuel, prophesied for centuries.

g   He is your Brother. He is the heart of the world. He is the heart-beat of an immortal life. He is the caress laid upon every human suffering. He is the victory which covers over every defeat.

h   He is the balm for the wound of egoism, of hatred, of sin. He is the light which shines resplendently forever for all who walk in the darkness. He is the only hope of this bewildered world.

i   With the concerned voice of a Mother, who hears a thousand voices which still reject Him and who listens with dismay to the sound of a thousand doors which are again closed, I say to you: Do not be afraid; God is with you. Today there is born to you a Savior for all!

j   With a Heart wounded by the great coldness which still permeates the roads of the world and with a soul made desolate because of this great rejection of God which has turned the earth into a great desert, in the face of such vast hopelessness, I say to you again: *Do not be afraid; God is with you!*

k   This is especially so today, when you are being called to live through the painful moments when it appears that my Adversary reigns in the world, as he spreads his deadly poison in the hearts of men.

l   In the face of such suffering which cannot be assuaged, of such great slavery which cannot be shaken off, of situations of injustice which cannot be successfully healed, of dangers of war which cannot be checked, of fierce threats which grow more and more ominous, on this holy night, here is the message which springs from my Immaculate Heart as a source of hope and comfort for all: *Do not be afraid; God is with you!*

m   Just as the Word of the Father made use of my humble assent for his first coming into your midst, in the frailness of human nature, so now does my Son Jesus make use of my prophetic announcement to prepare his second coming into your midst in glory.

n   Do not be afraid, O children so exposed to dangers. With the triumph of my Immaculate Heart, Jesus will manifest Himself to you in his glorious reign of love and of peace!"

256

December 31, 1982
Last Night of the Year

Watch in Prayer

a   "On this night, while the greater part of my children spend the last hours of the year in amusement and dissipation, watch with me, my beloved ones, in silence and more intense prayer.

b   *Prayer of thanksgiving*: for all the graces which, in this period of time, have been granted you by the Father, in the Holy Spirit, by means of my Son Jesus and through the unceasing intercession of my Immaculate Heart.

c   This world is at the mercy of my Adversary, who is ruling it with his spirit of pride and rebellion, and who is leading an immense number of children of God along the road of pleasure, of sin, of disobedience to the laws of God, and of contempt for his Will.

d   It is immersed in the deepest of nights, and no beginning of a year can dissipate the great darkness in which it is walking. Indeed, it has been created for the glory of the Father; it has been redeemed and saved by the Son, and it continues to be transformed by the action of the Holy Spirit.

e   Nothing can resist the power of the merciful love of God, which wants to transform this poor world into a new creation. And so, the interventions of my Immaculate Heart will become steadily more numerous, extraordinary and miraculous.

f   For this, give thanks with me to the Most Holy Trinity which is making use of me — its little handmaid — to lead all creation to the perfect glorification of God.

g   *Prayer of supplication*: to obtain from the merciful Heart of Jesus days of peace and not of affliction, days of serenity and not misfortune. There is a real danger of another war. Under the appearance of fragile promises of agreements, the most refined means of dealing death are being prepared, and humanity is being led along the road of hatred and of self-destruction. May your prayer obtain for all the grace which leads to the defeat of sin and that concord which causes violence and terror to cease so that universal peace, in truth and justice, may finally be yours. There is need of a great miracle; there is need to wrest through the power of prayer, this miracle from the mercy of God. Only thus can salvation come to you.

h   *Prayer of reparation*: because the cup of divine justice is full, very full; it is overflowing! See how hatred and sin burst all bounds. Today the majority of mankind no longer observes the Ten Commandments of the Lord. Your God is publicly ignored, denied, offended and blasphemed. The day of the Lord is more and more profaned.

336

i   Daily an attack is being made upon life. Each year, through-out the world, by the tens of millions, innocent children are be-ing slaughtered in their mother's womb and the number of mur-ders, robberies and acts of violence and kidnappings are increas-ing.

j   Immorality is spreading like a flood of filth and is being propa-gated by the means of social communication, especially the cin-ema, the press and television. By means of this last-mentioned, a subtle and diabolical tactic of seduction and corruption has found its way into every family. The most defenseless victims are chil-dren and youth, whom I look upon with the tender preoccupa-tion of a mother.

k   Only the powerful force of prayer and reparative penance will be able to save the world from what the justice of God has pre-pared because of its obstinate refusal to accept every demand for repentance.

l   Listen at least now to the voice of your heavenly Mother! I need much prayer of reparation and suffering, offered with faith. Pray your rosary always. Live, together with me, in trust and trepidation, because there are in preparation decisive hours which can determine the destiny of all humanity.

m   I bless you in the name of the Father, and of the Son, and of the Holy Spirit."

1983

OPEN WIDE THE GATES TO CHRIST
(Extraordinary Holy Year of the Redemption)

257

Mother of Hope

a "At the beginning of this year, the Church looks to me with confidence and venerates me in the mystery of my divine and universal motherhood.

b And in the midst of the innumerable sufferings of the present moment, of the great uneasiness, of the threats which hang over your future, raise your eyes to your heavenly Mother, as to the fount of divine mercy and as a great sign of hope for you.

c *I am the Mother of Hope.*

d This is the theological virtue which must be especially lived in the bloody hours of the purification.

e In how many ways my Adversary seeks to bring you to discouragement, in order to make you harmless and to weaken the power of my victorious cohort! Do not be afraid, because Satan has already been defeated by Jesus, and every apparent victory of his prepares a great new and real defeat for him.

f If hatred still causes blood to flow in your streets, if sin chills the souls and hearts of many, if humanity is not returning along the way of love, if rebellion against God becomes greater every day, your trust in the mercy of your Heavenly Father must be all the greater, and you must look to me as the sign of your hope.

g I am the Mother of love and of grace, of pardon and of mercy, and therefore, at the beginning of this year, marked by important events in the plan of Providence, I am going along the deserted roads of the world to scatter in the hearts of my children seeds of repentance, of goodness and of hope. There is such need today of light and of comfort; there is such need at this time for consolation and motherly encouragement for all my children! I look, with sorrowful compassion, at the innumerable crowds of my sinful children, at the young people who have been seduced and betrayed by the society in which they live, at the adults who remain slaves of unbridled egoism and hatred, at the sons of the Church who have become slothful through indifference and lack of faith. To all, I repeat today: *I am the Mother of your hope.*

h   The great coldness which covers the world must not discourage you, because each day I am spreading everywhere seeds of life and of resurrection.

i   I am the daybreak which precedes the sun; I am the dawn which begins the new day. I am the Mother of Holy Joy.

j   Live in the joy of knowing you are loved by God, who is a Father to you, you who are carried by the Spirit as children, and sustained by Jesus as his little brothers.

k   In the joy of living in the Heart of the Most Holy Trinity and of being safe in the garden of my Immaculate Heart, begin this new year so that all of you may live it with me."

258

I Am Asking You for a Spiritual Childhood

a   "If you consider with love the mystery the Church commemorates today, beloved sons, you will learn how the consecration you have made to me should be lived.

b   The Child Jesus whom, in company with Joseph, my most chaste spouse, after forty days I presented in the temple of the Lord, is truly God, our Savior, the Messiah so long awaited.

c   As a mother I brought Him into this earthly life, yet He is the Author of Life, for He is the Creator.

d   With my *yes* I permitted Him to enter into time, yet He is outside of time, for He is eternal.

e   I hold Him in my arms and support Him, yet it is He who upholds all things, for He is omnipotent.

f   In fulfillment of the divine Scripture, I carry Him into the temple of Jerusalem, yet He is the Fountain of Revelation, for He is the Eternal Word.

g   The Word of the Father, Creator, omnipotent and omniscient God, willed to clothe Himself in weakness and subjected Himself to the limitations of time, took upon Himself the frailty of human nature and was born of me; like every infant, He experienced all sorts of needs.

h　How often, while kissing Him with the tenderness of a mother, I said to Him: 'And yet You are the eternal kiss of the Father'; and while I caressed Him, I thought: 'You are the divine caress conferring beatitude upon souls'; while I clothed Him in his little garments, I whispered: 'It is You who clothe the earth with flowers and the immense universe with stars'; and while nourishing Him, I sang to Him: 'It is You who provide food for all living creatures.' When with maternal love I called Him 'My Son!', adoring Him in my soul, I prayed to Him: 'You are the Son of the Father, his eternal Only-begotten, his living Word…'

i　Oh! Penetrate today into the ineffable mystery of the infancy of my Son Jesus, whom I carried in my arms to the temple of the Lord, if you wish to journey along the road of spiritual childhood I have traced out for you.

j　All must travel along this road, even those who are further advanced in age, and who occupy important posts; even those who are learned, formed by years of study and experience; even those who are rich in culture and who have been called to perform tasks of great responsibility.

k　Allied with your human growth, which unfolds itself over the years, I am asking you for a spiritual childhood, an interior littleness leading you to robe yourselves in the humility and in the very fragility itself of my Child Jesus.

l　I want to see in you the candid hearts of children, knowing nothing of egoism and sin, open to love and to giving, expecting everything from the Heavenly Father so as to be able to give everything.

m　I want to see in you the virginal hearts of children, still firmly shut to the snares of deceit and duplicity, opening like flowers to receive the rays of knowledge, truth and wisdom.

n　I want to see in you the docile wills of little ones, like fragile clay ready to let themselves be formed with trust and abandonment; wills which must be molded by the good and the true, strengthening themselves by pursuing what is good and what is beautiful.

o　Oh! This way of spiritual childhood must of necessity be traversed by you, beloved sons, if you wish to live in a perfect manner the consecration to my Immaculate Heart.

p　It is only in this way that I can carry you, like my Infant Jesus,

342

and offer you in the temple of the Lord for the realization of the designs of love and mercy He has upon you, for the salvation of all my children, scattered throughout the world."

259

Love One Another

a   " 'Come in procession!' — I told the simple child Bernadette, when I appeared to her in the humble grotto at Massabielle.

b   Why did I make this request?

c   Because I want all my children to walk together, united in prayer and in love.

d   Today my Adversary is trying in every way to divide you, to isolate you, to set you against one another. He, who from the beginning was the father of lies and the sower of hatred, seeks more and more to break up your fraternal unity.

e   Thus it is that often — even under the specious appearance of good — one rises against another, this group struggles with that group in an endless quest for self assertion that leaves so many good efforts fruitless.

f   I want you to walk together toward me, because I am the Mother of all and because I want to form all of you together in prayer, in penance, and in your reciprocal love.

g   In these times it is more than ever necessary to live the new commandment given you by Jesus on Holy Thursday evening during the Last Supper: 'Love one another, as I have loved you.' (Jn 15:12)   I want to form you in a mutual and reciprocal love. It is necessary to give this testimony of ecclesial charity, that unites you all in the perfection of love, in order to combat the tactics of division and isolation used by my Adversary.

h   Come to me, all of you, making your way along the difficult paths of your times, praying together, giving praise together, and loving one another.

i   Come to me, therefore, not in isolation or in division, but in procession, strengthening those who are weak, leading on those who have come to a standstill.

j   Come to me, because I wish to lead all of you in unity to my

Son, present in the Eucharist.

k   Jesus is present in the sacrament of the Eucharist to help you build this unity of yours, to give you an example of how one must love, in total giving to all one's brothers.

l   Come to me together, therefore, that I may bring you to Jesus in the sacrament of the Eucharist, awaiting you in his silent immolation, really present among you in all the tabernacles of the world.

m   Then you will be able to accomplish what I am asking of you, for the realization of my maternal designs of salvation."

260

March 5, 1983
First Saturday of the Month and of Lent

The Path of Penance

a   "Beloved sons, follow me along the path of penance.

b   The weapons with which you are to fight my battle are those of prayer and penance. Today I want to show you the path of penance which is to be traversed by each of you.

c   The first stage is that of renunciation and self-denial.

d   It is necessary to renounce oneself, as well as all disordered attachments, passions, immoderate desires, ambitions. Even in your apostolic labors, you are never to seek success and human approval. Rather have a love for being hidden, for an apostolate carried out in silence, in humility, and the daily and faithful fulfillment of your duties.

e   In this way you will mortify egoism which constitutes your greatest peril, the easiest and most customary of the snares by which my Adversary attempts to impede your journey.

f   Then you will become free interiorly; it will be easy for you to discern in the light the Will of God, and you will find yourselves more suitably disposed to carry it to perfection.

g   The second stage is that of carrying one's cross properly.

h   This cross is made up of the difficulties one encounters when one desires to fulfill solely the Will of God, because this involves the task of daily fidelity to the duties of one's state in life. It is a

344

fidelity in which even the very smallest tasks are performed with perfection. Everything is done in the fullness of love; every moment of the day is lived in fulfilling the divine Will.

i   How precious, above all for you, my beloved sons, is this second stage of suffering!

j   In this you are shaped into the likeness of Jesus Crucified.

k   This interior crucifixion will take place each day and in every moment of your priestly day: in moments of prayer, which is so greatly necessary and which must be the center of your life; in that most precious moment of the celebration of Holy Mass, when with Jesus you too are interiorly immolated for the life of the world; in your fidelity to the priestly duties proper to the ministry of each one; in evangelization, in catechizing, in teaching, in the apostolate of charity; with each person you meet, especially the very poor, the lonely and forsaken, those who feel themselves despised and rejected by all.

l   In your priestly apostolate never seek to please yourselves or to procure some personal advantage; give yourselves always with all the inexhaustible force of love, and do not let ingratitude stop you or misunderstandings stand in your way; indifference should not make you hesitate, nor should lack of cooperation cause you to become weary. It is above all in your priestly suffering that souls can be begotten by you to the life of grace and to salvation.

m   The third stage is that of following my Son Jesus toward Calvary.

n   During his life, how often I found Him turning his glance with desire toward Jerusalem, where He would one day go to be betrayed, arrested, judged by his own, condemned, scourged, crowned with thorns and crucified. How greatly Jesus longed for this moment. He was always journeying toward the consummation of his Pasch [1] of love and immolation for you.

o   Therefore, you, my beloved, who are his priests, you too are called to follow him each day toward the consummation of your paschal immolation for the salvation of all.

p   Never lose courage. Today the voices of condemnation are for you the shouts of those who reject and challenge you. Sins,

---

[1] (n) (P)asch in Hebrew means: Immolation of a lamb, sacrificed and consumed as in the Passover meal. In the case of Jesus, He is the Lamb of God sacrificed and consumed. Used in the lower case, (p)asch is meant to signify the priests being the lambs of God sacrificed and consumed for the salvation of others.

committed but then justified and no longer atoned for, are for you the painful strokes of the scourge. The errors, which threaten to estrange great numbers of souls from the faith, are for you the crown of thorns. Today, to remain faithful to your calling is to follow the stern path that leads to Calvary.

q The obstacles found today in staying united and obedient in all things to the Pope, and to the hierarchy united with him, the lack of understanding on the part even of your brothers, the sense of being pushed aside with which you are often overwhelmed, are for you the painful falls.

r But, the entrusting of yourselves to my Immaculate Heart by means of your consecration, is today for you the meeting with your Mother, so full of sorrows.

s Together, from now on, let us go forward in the perfect imitation of Jesus, who invites us to follow Him on the way of the Cross.

t Some of you will even have to shed your own blood in the decisive moment of this bloody purification.

u Beloved sons, you see now described for you the road you must travel to reach a genuine experience of conversion.

v It is the simple and evangelical road, pointed out to you by my Son Jesus when He told you: 'He who wishes to come after Me, let him renounce himself, take up his cross each day, and follow Me.' (cf. Mt 16:24)

w Along this path, evangelical and sacerdotal, your heavenly Mother wishes to lead you."

261

March 25, 1983
Solemnity of the Annunciation of the Lord
Opening of the Holy Year of the Redemption

Open Wide the Gates to Christ

a "Beloved sons, today live this moment of grace which the Heart of Jesus has prepared for you.

b It is his feast day!

c Today adore the mystery of his coming among you. In my

346

virginal womb, the Eternal Word of the Father assumed his human nature, permitting Him to become a man like you, your true Brother.

d   At that same moment, humanity was redeemed, weakness found its support, poverty was ennobled, and for every human being the gate of his true, supernatural and divine greatness was thrown open.

e   But it is also my feast day!

f   The feast of the Son, conceived in me by the work of the Holy Spirit, is also that of the Mother who gave Him life, preserving forever the ineffable charm of perpetual virginity.

g   His *yes* of the Son to the Father, my *yes* of the Mother to the Son, united us wholly and forever after, in the perfect realization of the divine Will.

h   'Since neither holocausts nor sacrifices were acceptable, then I said: I come, O God, to do your Will.' (cf. Heb 10:5-7)

i   But today, O sons, is also your feast day.

j   At that same instant in which the Word became incarnate in my virginal womb, there sprang into being the real and practical possibility that each of you might become true sons of God, brothers of Jesus, recipients of the great gift of his redemption.

k   At that very moment of the Incarnation, I too become for all of you true Mother — in the supernatural order — of your divine life.

l   For these reasons, today, following an inspiration of the Holy Spirit experienced in a moment of intense prayer, my Pope is opening the holy door and beginning the Jubilee Year of the Redemption.

m   The redemption had its beginning at the moment of the incarnation of Jesus. It continued throughout his life and culminated in the sacrifice of his body, offered for you, and that of his blood, shed for you, a sacrifice consummated on the summit of Calvary and still renewed mystically upon the altar.

n   Let all correspond to this extraordinary period of grace which the merciful love of Jesus has prepared for this generation, so remote and perverse, so rebellious and endangered, so dominated by Satan and the spirits of evil, and consequently in immense need of being saved.

o   This HolyYear becomes the final effort of the divine Heart of
Jesus and of my Immaculate Heart to make all of you walk the
road of a return to God, in sincere repentance for your sins and
with a serious commitment to conversion, such as will lead you
to active works of justice and charity, of goodness and giving, for
the good of all.

p   Today my maternal summons becomes urgent. Through you,
my beloved sons, I wish to address it to all my children.

q   To those of my poor children who are straying, because they
have been seduced by the atheism that is prevailing everywhere,
and who live in a continual and obstinate rejection of God, I
appeal beseechingly: 'Return to the God of your salvation and of
your peace!'

r   To those of my poor children who are sinners, seduced by
evil, by hatred and violence, I repeat with the heartfelt lament of
the Mother: 'Return to God, who awaits you with the love of a
Father; let yourselves be washed in the precious blood and purified by the infinite mercy of my Son, Jesus.'

s   To the children of the Church, today living the hour of its
agony and its redemptive passion, I repeat my maternal invitation to walk the road of love and unity, of fidelity and holiness, of
prayer and penance.

t   To all of humanity, with the strength of an anguished Mother,
who sees the mortal dangers threatening it, I want to cry out:
'Open wide the gates to Christ who is coming! He alone is
God with you! He alone is your Redeemer! He alone is your
Savior!'

u   If you welcome my invitation, there will soon come upon
you the new era of justice and peace, and my Immaculate Heart
will experience its triumph, beholding all of you advancing along
the road of the glorification of the Father, the imitation of the
Son, and full communion with the Holy Spirit."

All Is Accomplished

a   " 'All is accomplished!' (Jn 19:30)

b   These were the last words before the loud cry with which my Son Jesus gave up his spirit.

c   Linger today with me beneath the Cross, beloved sons, to understand the meaning of these words of his.

d   It is Good Friday. It is the day of his passion and of his death upon the Cross. It is the precious moment of your redemption.

e   Let us enter into the recesses of the Heart of Jesus to taste the bitterness of his soul and to penetrate the profound mystery of his immolation.

f   Everything was accomplished at the moment his body was immolated and his blood was shed for you.

g   In his life, everything has been ordered toward this supreme moment: on each day of his earthly life, how greatly he had desired to consummate this, his Pasch of passion and death on your behalf!

h   Today I am to be found beneath the Cross on which my Son Jesus lived his tremendous agony, with John, who represents all of you, close by. In union of soul with Jesus, with whom I am intimately associated in his redemptive work, let us together retrace the moments that led Him to its perfect accomplishment:

i   — the joyous moment of the Annunciation when the Word of the Father became incarnate in my virginal womb, assumed the body prepared for Him enabling Him to begin immediately his precious work of redemption;

j   — the radiant day of his birth in the poor little shed in Bethlehem, when I could already see the signs, in his infant's tender frame, of the true Lamb of God, called to offer Himself in a perfect sacrifice for the salvation of the world;

k   — after returning from the exile endured in Egypt, the serene years of his childhood, when each day I watched Him open Himself up, like a flower, to the sun of beauty, of grace and of divine wisdom;

l   — the long years of his adolescence, during which I saw his body grow, that body in which was reflected the synthesis of every human perfection, intent on daily labor, marked by perspiration and fatigue;

m — Oh! Frequently in spirit I could already see his hands and feet pierced by wounds and his body covered with blood ... and then I would bend over Him with the renewed tenderness of a mother;

n — the short years of his public life, when He announced to all the Gospel of salvation, curing and pardoning, healing wounds and dispelling illnesses, pardoning sins and performing innumerable miracles; how many times, near to me, his Mother, to whom He confided everything, He went in spirit to the summit of Calvary, and together with me lived the moment of his sorrowful departure!

o 'All is accomplished.'

p And Jesus seeks to prepare his disciples for the scandal of this moment. 'The Son of Man must go up to Jerusalem, where He will be handed over to the pagans, and will be spat upon, scourged, condemned and crucified, but on the third day He will rise again.'

(cf. Mk 10:33)

q Now I see Him hanging on the Cross, and I behold his hands and feet torn by horrible wounds, the crown of thorns opening fissures of blood that stream down and disfigure his countenance. And while his body is shaken with tremendous spasms of fever and agony, his lips open once again for his last words: 'All is accomplished.'

r The Will of the Father has now been done. Every circumstance of his life has been oriented towards this perfect fulfillment... His work is here summed up in the deed toward which it was ever directed: in the divine gift, the ineffable and precious gift of the redemption.

s Like Him, you too, beloved sons, have been prepared by me for this supreme moment, so that the Father's design may be accomplished in this new hour of redemptive passion for the Church. Everything in your life has had this profound meaning. Read with me, the Mother of Sorrows, in the sealed book of your existence.

t In it everything has been prepared by God and arranged by me with love, as I did with my Son, Jesus.

u In a like manner, I can help you too, to accomplish today the Father's Will.

350

v   Love all with a heart that is open and generous; bring health to the sick; close the gaping wounds; bestow grace and peace; forgive sins.

w   And prepare yourselves to ascend, with me, your own Calvary..."

263

Let Nothing Disturb Your Peace!

a   "Jesus has risen, alleluia!

b   Today I communicate to you and to all your brother-priests, and to all my beloved children, the joy experienced by my Heart when Jesus came into the little room in which I was staying, and, in the divine splendor of his glorified body, leaned down to implant a kiss upon the face of his Mother, while in profound adoration I bathed the marks of his luminous wounds with tears of joy. 'Peace to you, peace to all!' With my risen Son, I repeat it again to you. Let nothing disturb your peace!

c   — Not the world in which you are living, rebelling against God, perverted and in the hands of the Evil One. Jesus has already overcome the world.

d   — Not the darkened and divided Church, into which have come idolatry and apostasy. Jesus loves his Spouse with a divine love, and in these moments of its purification He is closer to it than ever.

e   — Not the disconcerting succession of events, not the persecutions and fratricidal struggles, not the fire and the red scourge that is already spilling out over the world.

f   Jesus, risen and alive, is among you!

g   He is guiding the vicissitudes of the world and of history, according to the designs of his merciful love, for the salvation of all of his redeemed brothers.

h   Therefore, in Jesus, Life and Resurrection, peace to you in a joy that is pure and supernatural. Peace to all in the paschal joy of Christ. To the Pope and to all, my blessing in the name of the glorified Father, the risen Son, and the Holy Spirit, bestowed upon you as gift."

This Month of May

a   "During this month of May, try to live more intensely the consecration you have made to my Immaculate Heart, beloved sons, for it is only in this way that I can be venerated by each of you.

b   Bring me little flowers of mortification, to console my great sorrow in seeing all the appeals addressed to humanity, for a return to God, going unheeded.

c   How greatly saddened is Jesus by the great numbers who are traveling the road of sin, of impurity, of corruption and of unbridled egoism! For these poor diseased children of mine, offer the assistance of your penance and your mortification.

d   On each day of the month consecrated to me, give me little flowers of silence and docility, of complete availability, of humility and patience, of meekness, of your renunciation of comforts and the gratification of the senses.

e   In this way you will walk the road of self-contempt, effecting in yourselves that renunciation of the world and its seductions that constitutes the most important daily obligation assumed on the day of your baptismal and sacerdotal consecration.

f   Give me the garlands of your rosaries, recited more frequently and with a greater intensity.

g   Gather the religious and the faithful around you in cenacles of unceasing and fervent prayer, offered with me.

h   At this time above all, I am asking you to pray with fervor and joy by means of the holy rosary. It is the weapon which is to be used by you today in fighting and winning this bloody battle; it is the golden chain that binds you to my Heart; it is the lightning rod that will keep far from you, and from those who are dear to you, the fire of the chastisement; it is the sure means of having me always close to you.

i   Finally, I ask you to renew often and to live fully the consecration to my Immaculate and Sorrowful Heart.

j   Enter at once into this refuge to be protected by me.

k   My protection should become ever more manifest to all, because the days in which you are living are marked by great sufferings, and for so many of my poor children, who are so menaced today, the danger of being lost is increasing.

l   Let this month of May, especially consecrated to me, be a precious occasion for you to entrust yourselves to me with the offering of your little flowers of mortification, the frequent recitation of the holy rosary, and a more intense living of the consecration to my Heart."

265

May 22, 1983
Solemnity of Pentecost

New Heavens and a New Earth

a   "Everything is about to be fulfilled, beloved sons, whom for so long I have called to enter into my refuge, in order to second my plan of salvation and mercy.

b   For this reason I gather you into the cenacle of my Heart, to form you to a life of prayer with me, to a life of mutual love, of giving, and of holiness.

c   In this new cenacle, let us together invoke the gift of the Holy Spirit who, coming from the Father and the Son, through my maternal intercession again today wishes to pour out his fullness on the suffering Church, on all humanity shrouded in darkness.

d   Under the influence of his mighty work of love, the desert of this world can be entirely renewed by an immense profusion of the dew of grace, and thus transformed into a garden of life and beauty, wherein it may please God once again to display his reflection.

e   Give us, O Spirit of Love, new heavens and a new earth, where the Most Holy Trinity will be loved and glorified; where men can live together as in a single large family; where the wounds of egoism and of hatred, of impurity and injustice, may be entirely healed.

f   Give us, O Spirit of Love, a Church renewed by the irresistible force of your divine action, straightening what is contorted, bending what is inflexible, healing what is wounded, bringing water to what is parched, throwing open what is closed.

g   Give us, O Spirit of Love, a Church faithful to the Gospel, a herald of truth, resplendent in great sanctity.

h   Give us, O Spirit of Love, a humble Church, evangelical, poor, chaste and merciful.

i   By your divine fire, burn away whatever in it is imperfect; despoil it of so many human means of power; free it from compromise with the world in which it lives and which it should save; cause it to come forth from its purification completely renewed, ever more beautiful, without stain or wrinkle, in imitation of Mary, its immaculate Mother and your most loving Spouse.

j   It is only in the triumph of my Immaculate Heart that the task I have entrusted to my Movement of priests will be fully accomplished."

266

The Gate of Heaven

a   "My Immaculate Heart is the Gate of Heaven through which passes the Spirit of Love of the Father and of the Son, to come to you and to renew the whole world.

b   For this reason I am inviting you today to enter even further into the depths of this, my heavenly garden; you will then be covered with the light of the Most Holy Trinity.

c   In my Immaculate Heart, the Father gazes upon you with complacency, seeing that you have been formed by me to glorify Him in a most perfect manner.

d   My maternal task is to help each of you realize in all its fullness the design of the Father, who created you to participate in his being, his love and his glory.

e   Accordingly I help you to open yourselves to the sunshine of God's love which makes you grow in what is beautiful and good and true. The glory of God manifests itself, in all its divine harmony, through the ordered rhythm of your existence.

f   How many mysterious modulations vibrate through the melody of your prayer, your suffering, your silence, of all the virtues that should comprise the poem of your existence.

g   In your life you are opening your hearts to the chant of the glory of the Father, who would have his complacency reflected in you, while, by the mystery of his paternity, you are being generated to a new fullness of life and joy.

h   In my Immaculate Heart the Son assimilates you to make you more completely resemble Himself and to associate you with his own life. It is in my heavenly garden that the wonder of your transformation takes place.

i   It is above all through me that this happens; through me because Jesus, finding me to be as it were the purest and most supple clay, molded me so perfectly in his image that no other creature will ever be able to produce that image as did your heavenly Mother.

j   And so it is that I, though Mother, became the Daughter of my Son; and so it is that I became the first and most perfect of his disciples; and so too it is that, while I am leading you to Jesus, I am able to manifest myself to you as a model for imitation, if you want to succeed in reliving his life in your own.

k   I form you in his likeness in your minds, and I obtain the Spirit of Wisdom for you, to lead you to seek and receive, to meditate upon and to preserve, his divine word.

l   In this way it is possible for you to live the Gospel with the simplicity of little children, with the fidelity of the martyrs, and with the heroism of the saints.

m   I form you in your hearts and bring you to the plenitude of love for God, so that you may love all your brothers with the same divine charity. For this I make you always more sensitive, purer, more understanding and merciful, more compassionate and meek, more humble and strong.

n   And every day Jesus enters through the gate of this, my heavenly garden, to experience the great joy of seeing Himself imitated and relived by all of you, my sons and his little brothers.

o   In my Immaculate Heart the Holy Spirit communicates Himself to you in an ever more munificent manner, to produce in your souls that union of life and of love which He achieved in your heavenly Mother.

p   And seeing you in my maternal arms, He breathes upon you with the vehemence of love, transforming you into sparks of fire, flames of grace, stars of sanctity and zeal for renewing the firmament of the Church.

q   He communicates Himself to you with his seven holy gifts and makes you suitable instruments for converting the world to the God of Mercy and Salvation, preparing the kingdom in which Jesus will rule with his divine power and the Father will be everlastingly glorified by all creation.

r   Enter, therefore, through the heavenly gate of my Immaculate Heart, if you wish to participate in the divine prodigy, the new Pentecost for the Church and the complete renewal of the world."

267
Valdragone (San Marino); June 29, 1983
Solemnity of Sts. Peter and Paul
Spiritual Exercises with the Directors of the M.M.P.

Why I Wanted You Here

a   "This year I have again summoned you here, and from all over Europe, you have come to spend these days in a continuing cenacle with me.

b   Here my Heart is being consoled by you in these times of so much tribulation. How greatly glorified in you is your heavenly Mother! I reflect my light in your hearts and pour out the fullness of grace upon your souls.

c   I am always close to you; I associate myself with your prayer; I increase your love; I strengthen the bonds that unite you; I rejoice to see you so little and so docile, so prompt to understand and help one another, to walk together along the difficult road of the consecration you have made to me.

d   Why have I wanted you here this year?

e   To make you understand that now you must walk together, united in love, so that you form but a single entity. During these days in the cenacle of my Immaculate Heart, I want to form all of you into a single heart and a single soul.

f   The tactic of my Adversary is one of hatred and division. Where he penetrates, by his deceitful and malignant action, he succeeds in bringing rupture, misunderstandings and antagonism. Even within the Church he is making ever greater efforts to wound its interior unity. Therefore I am assembling you from every part of the world, to help you to love one another, to unite with one another, to grow in the perfection of love.

g   I have also summoned you here to make you understand that your public mission is now about to be consummated by your personal and precious immolation.

h   This is the Holy Year of the Redemption accomplished by my Son Jesus upon the Cross.

i   And now for you too, my Immaculate Heart, once a cradle, has become an altar upon which I must fix each of you on the cross the Father has prepared for you for the salvation of the world.

j   For this reason, my beloved sons, ready yourselves to live with trust and abandonment the bloody hours now awaiting you, while each day I make you more conformed to Jesus Crucified.

k   The errors spreading through the Church and obscuring her faith are the crown of thorns. Sins committed and not atoned for are the painful lashes. The deluge of impurity is reducing your sacerdotal body to a single wound. The hatred of the world, the lack of understanding, and even the ostracism that surround you, these are the nails that transfix you. You have been called to ascend Calvary with me, and there you are to be immolated for the salvation of the world.

l   I have also called you here to obtain for you the Holy Spirit, given to you in superabundance by the Father and the Son, through your unceasing prayer united to my maternal intercession. He will transform you into ardent flames of zeal for the glory of God and into courageous witnesses of Jesus, in these times which have become so evil.

m   The struggle between your heavenly Mother and her Adversary has now entered its decisive phase.

n   The Woman Clothed with the Sun is, with her cohorts, openly waging war against the cohorts submissive to the Red Dragon, at whose service is placed the Black Beast come up from the sea.

o   The Red Dragon is Marxist atheism, which has now conquered the whole world, and which has induced humanity to build a new civilization of its own, without God. In consequence, the world has become a cold and barren desert, immersed in the ice of hatred and in the darkness of sin and impurity.

p The Black Beast is also Masonry which has infiltrated the Church and attacks it, wounds it, and seeks by its subtle tactics to demolish it. Like a poisonous cloud, its spirit seeps in everywhere, to paralyze faith, extinguish apostolic ardor and produce an ever greater alienation from Jesus and his Gospel.

q Apostles of these last times, the time has come to fight with courage under the command of your heavenly Leader.

r To discord and division I wish to respond through you, strengthening your communion and the love that unites you, so that you will become a single entity. To the flood of sin and iniquity, I respond with your priestly immolation, and to achieve this I help you to ascend Calvary, and I place you upon the cross upon which each must be immolated. To the attack of the Red Dragon and the Black Beast, I respond by summoning all to the battle, so that God may be ever more glorified and the Church, in its children, healed from the wounds of infidelity and apostasy.

s Pray; love; do penance! Walk the road of humility and littleness, of contempt for the world and for yourselves, following Jesus who loves you and is leading you.

t Soon victory will be resplendent everywhere. Through the triumph of my Immaculate Heart, there will come upon you the glorious reign of Jesus who, in his Spirit of Love, will bring all of creation to the glorification of the Father, and at last the face of the earth will be renewed.

u Therefore, before you go down from this mountain, I look upon you one by one with maternal tenderness and fill your hearts with graces that you will understand only later on. I bless you in the name of the Father, and of the Son, and of the Holy Spirit."

268

July 16, 1983
Feast of Our Lady of Mount Carmel

The Holy Mountain

a "Ascend with me, beloved sons, the holy mountain of your perfect conformity to Jesus Crucified.

b   How many times my Son Jesus lovingly ascended the mountains, impelled by an ardent desire for solitude and silence, to live with greater intensity his union with the Father!

c   From the time of his adolescence, He often sought refuge in the hills surrounding Nazareth; it was on a mountain that He promulgated the evangelical Law of the Beatitudes; it was on Mount Tabor that He experienced the ecstasy of his transfiguration; in Jerusalem, a city on a mountain, He gathered his own together for the Last Supper and endured the sorrowful hours of his interior agony; on Mount Calvary He consummated his Sacrifice; on the Mount of Olives his final separation from his disciples took place, in the glorious Ascension into heaven.

d   Today ascend with me the holy mountain which is Jesus Christ, so that you can enter into a life of intimacy with Him. In these times of my decisive battle, each of you has been called to combat, armed with the very light of Christ, because you must be his own presence in the world.

e   For this reason, ascend the holy mountain of his wisdom, which is revealed to you if you remain little, humble and poor. Your minds will be drawn towards his divine mind, and you will penetrate into the secret of truth revealed in Holy Scripture; you will be captivated by the beauty of his Gospel, and with courage you will pronounce the word of Jesus to the men of today, that word which alone illumines and can lead to the fullness of the truth.

f   Ascend the holy mountain of his Heart, so that you may be transformed by the burning bush of his divine charity.

g   Then your hearts will be dilated and molded after his, and in the world you will be the very pulsations themselves of the Heart of Jesus, which seeks above all those who are furthest away, and wishes to envelop all in the flames of his infinite mercy.

h   You will become meek and humble of heart; you will be truly able to love; you will pour balm on the grievous wounds of the suffering and of those most in need; you will give your priestly help especially to those who have lost themselves along the road of iniquity and sin. In this way with your love, you will bring an immense number of my children to the path of salvation.

i   Ascend the holy mountain of his divine humanity, in order to become reflections of his perennial immolation for you: his eyes in your eyes, his hands in your hands, his Heart in your hearts, his sufferings in your sufferings, his wounds in your wounds, his Cross in your cross.

j   In this way you will become the potent presence of Jesus who, by means of you, can still today work mightily to bring all to salvation. In this salvation is the triumph of my Immaculate Heart; in it is to be found the conclusion of the battle to which I have summoned you and the realization of my heralded victory.

k   Therefore, beloved sons, it now becomes more urgent than ever to follow me, your heavenly Leader. Ascend with me, then, the holy mountain that is Christ, to become perfectly assimilated to Him, so that He may live again in each of you, in order to bring all men to salvation."

269

August 15, 1983
Solemnity of the Assumption
of the Blessed Virgin Mary into Heaven

In the Light of Paradise

a   "Today, beloved sons, I want you to be spiritually here above in paradise that I may fill you with trust and hope in the spectacle of your heavenly Mother assumed, even with her body, into the glory of heaven.

b   With heart and soul behold the paradise that awaits you. Paradise is your true goal. You have not been made for this earthly life that now so greatly absorbs, wearies and consumes you.

c   Life on earth is a long and sorrowful antechamber through which one must pass before entering the kingdom prepared for you by the Heavenly Father.

d   In this kingdom my Son Jesus is already arranging a place for each of you. The angels joyfully await your arrival, and all the saints pray and burn with love in expectation that all of these places will one day be forever occupied, and occupied by you.

e   Today you should look more intently at the paradise awaiting you, if you wish to walk in serenity, in hope and in trust.

f   In the light of paradise you will better understand the times in which you are living. It is a time of suffering. It is the time described in the Apocalypse in which Satan has established in the world his reign of hatred and death.

g   Those who are the very poorest, the weakest, the most defenseless, my little ones, are so often overwhelmed by sufferings, sufferings which become greater day by day.

h   Oh, the Lord will shorten the time of trial, mindful too of the sorrow and fidelity He sees in you.

i   But that you may be consoled, today you should look up at the paradise prepared for you.

j   In the light of the paradise awaiting you, you will be better able to read the signs of your times.

k   The days in which you live are evil, for the hearts of men have become cold and barren, closed tight by so much egoism, no longer capable of love.

l   Humanity is traveling the road of rebellion against God and of obstinate perversity. And so it is that the fruits you are harvesting today are themselves evil: hatred and violence, corruption, impiety, impurity and idolatry. The body is lifted aloft as an idol, and pleasure is sought after as if it were the supreme good.

m   How many signs the Lord sends you, to call you to repentance and change of heart: sickness, misfortune, a virtual flood of incurable ills, ever widening wars, threats of imminent harm! Lest you despair in these times and to keep you ever astride the path of secure and unshakeable faith, it has become urgent for you to live with your gaze upon paradise where, with Jesus, your heavenly Mother loves you, and in her glorious body she even follows you.

n   In the light of the paradise awaiting you, above all you will know how to fulfill to perfection the design I have for each of you, in these times of the great struggle between the Woman Clothed with the Sun and her Adversary, the Red Dragon.

o   In profound detachment from the world and from creatures, you will become truly little, trustful, humble and good; you will walk along the road of contempt for the world and for yourselves; you will be capable of mortifying your senses, and once again you will offer me the gift of your penitence.

p   It is my desire that you also return to the practice of fasting, recommended so much by Jesus in the Gospel. Thus you will become true disciples of Jesus, and in this time of pervasive darkness, you will shed his light around about you.

q   For these reasons I invite you today to look up to paradise, which exults in the mystery of the bodily assumption of your heavenly Mother who encourages all and blesses all."

270

Mother of the Purification

a   "Beloved children, look with my most merciful eyes at the evils afflicting humanity and the Church today, and you too will shed tears of sorrow and deep compassion.

b   With my Heart love all your brothers, and you will feel the immense sufferings of my poor children as if they were your own. I am the Queen of all nations, and my regency is one of love. I wish to convey the hearts of all to the greatest possible life of union with Jesus, in a way that will glorify the Father in the triumph of his Spirit of Love.

c   In your lives carry the sufferings of the peoples reduced to slavery by those who reject God and use every means to spread atheism.

d   Poland, of whom I have been officially proclaimed Queen, is a symbol of this unending and bloody persecution.

e   In these nations how many are prevented from professing their faith; how many are pushed aside by reason of their fidelity to Jesus and to the Church!

f   For so many years the Red Dragon has extended his dominion over these peoples and persecuted my children by the most subtle and refined means.

g   Feel in your hearts the deep wounds caused me by the millions of infants slaughtered in the wombs of their mothers; by sin which overabounds and seduces souls; by immorality which, like a terrible cancer, corrupts consciences; by the disorientation of the youthful victims of vice, drugs and violence; by the breakdown of so many households.

h Participate too in the sufferings of the Church as she lives through the hour of her greatest abandonment. How ailing she is, this my most beloved Daughter!

i In your hearts carry the sufferings of Jesus, and my sufferings as well, for the agonizing condition in which the Church now finds herself in every part of the world. Error is being taught and propagated beneath the ambiguous formulas of a new cultural interpretation of truth; the spirit of the world finds welcome; it spreads its malignant influence and leads so many souls to accept sin, to justify it and to live in it; loss of faith is becoming a deluge, and in many places of worship the images of the saints have been removed, even those of your heavenly Mother.

j The apostasy has now been spread into every part of a Church betrayed even by some of her bishops, abandoned by many of her priests, deserted by so very many of her children, and violated by my Adversary.

k You, my little child, are to go again into every part of the world and to announce with power my message to all.

l These are the terrible and painful times of your purification. Never so much as now must you look to me, in order to be consoled, to be defended, and to be saved.

m I am the Mother for these, your times. I am Mother for you in the present hour of purification."

271 *Vancouver (British Columbia, Canada); September 3, 1983*
First Saturday

Ministers of the Redemption

a "Beloved sons, respond to my maternal invitation to become the faithful ministers of the redemption accomplished by my Son, Jesus.

b To you has been entrusted the precious task of baptizing and of pardoning, of announcing the Gospel, of renewing, in the celebration of Holy Mass, the Sacrifice consummated upon Calvary, of communicating grace by means of the sacraments instituted by Jesus.

363

c   Cause his blood to flow down once again and wash away all the sins of the world. Each day with love and with sorrow, with the intimate participation of your own lives, celebrate the Holy Sacrifice of the Mass. It has the power to make reparation and to destroy so much evil in the world.

d   With the Heart of Jesus, have love for all your brothers and my children. How many of them are walking the roads of this world like sheep without a shepherd, exposed to every kind of danger! How many have been wounded by sin, made into slaves of evil, victims of hate! How many there are who are poor, who are exploited, weak, suffering… All the sufferings of my children are like a desperate cry for help reaching up to me, and deeply wounding my motherly Heart.

e   I am with you on all the by-ways of the world.

f   With maternal mercy I help those of my little ones who find themselves in greater need; I save the perishing, restore health to the sick, console the afflicted, encourage the down-hearted, raise up those who have fallen, find those who have lost the way.

g   This is the hour of the triumph of the Immaculate Heart of your heavenly Mother; it is the hour of the great miracle of divine mercy.

h   But I wish to act through you, my beloved sons. For this I invite all of you to consecrate yourselves to my Immaculate Heart. I can then make you perfect ministers of the redemption accomplished by Jesus.

i   From this city on the Pacific Ocean, the dividing line, as it were, between East and West, I call all of you to respond to my design, a design that from day to day will make itself more apparent. The Church and the world are to see wrought the greatest of the miracles of the divine mercy."

272   *Montreal (Quebec, Canada); September 8, 1983*
Feast of the Nativity of the Blessed Virgin Mary

The Smallest of My Children

a   "From every part of the world, I am gathering the smallest of

364

my children, to assemble them in my cohort and to place them in the depths of my Immaculate Heart.

b   Beloved sons, listen to their voices as they cry for your help. Go forward to meet them, take them into your arms, and carry them all to your heavenly Mother.

c   To me, little ones are all those infants who, already conceived, are to be put to death purposely while still in the wombs of their mothers. The love and the anxiety of your heavenly Mother, and of the Church, for their salvation, with the innocent blood being spilled by those who despise and disobey the Law of God, are a baptism of blood and desire saving all of them.

d   To me, little and defenseless ones are also the children who live and grow up, yet are educated in errors and taught values which are really transgressions of God's Law.

e   To me, little ones are those who are young and just beginning to venture out into life, but in a world reduced to a desert because of its want of love. These are being initiated into lives of most bitter experience with every sort of evil.

f   To me, little ones are the poor, those who lack means for getting along in life, who have neither shelter nor work, who are often exploited.

g   To me, little ones are all of my persecuted children, those who are rejected, oppressed.

h   They are those who suffer, who weep, who are alone, who have neither help nor comfort.

i   Little ones are all those of my children who are victims of sin and hatred, who travel along the roads of life without hope or trust. Who can help to save these poor sinful children of mine?

j   Today, around my crib, beloved sons, bring me a wreath of all these my infant children, that I may gather them together as a bouquet of flowers which you are pleased to offer me on the glorious feast of the birth of your heavenly Mother."

I Am Beneath the Cross

a   "Look upon your sorrowful Mother, beloved sons, beneath the Cross upon which Jesus is hanging, upon which He is in agony and upon which He dies. From that moment, this has been my place: to remain beneath the cross of each of my sons.

b   I am beneath the cross of the first of my beloved sons, Pope John Paul II, who loves and prays and suffers because of the agony now being lived by the Church and because of the fate that awaits poor humanity. Do you not recognize that the scourge of war has already come upon you? How many innocent victims will be called upon to endure unspeakable sufferings!

c   I am beneath the cross being carried today by the bishops who remain faithful, while the number of those who prefer to go their own way grows ever greater, heedless of and refusing to follow the Holy Father, whom Jesus has placed at the very foundation of his Church. They are preparing another Church, one separated from the Pope, and this will cause a further scandal, that of a sorrowful division.

d   I am beneath the cross carried today by my beloved sons, the priests, who have been called to live in absolute fidelity to Jesus, to his Gospel and to his Church. Often they must endure the interior martyrdom of feeling themselves misunderstood, ridiculed and even rejected by their own confreres.

e   I am beneath the cross of consecrated souls who wish to live their consecration in fidelity, in opposition to the spirit of the world which has now entered into so many religious houses, bringing into them tepidity, impurity, laxity and the pursuit of every kind of worldly satisfaction.

f   I am beneath the cross of so many of the faithful who have received my invitation courageously and with generosity. Amid enormous difficulties, they hope and have trust in me; in the thick of great trials, they pray with faith and perseverance; amid countless sufferings, in the spirit of reparation, they offer whatever the Lord orders in their lives.

g   I am beneath the cross of my poor sinful children, to lead them back to the road of repentance and reconciliation; beneath the cross of the sick, to bring them comfort and resignation; of those who have wandered away, to bring them back to the way of salvation; of those who are soon to die, to help them do so in the grace and love of God.

h Oh! In these times in which sufferings and tribulations are multiplying, more than ever before, I am your sorrowing and consoling Mother. I am here beneath your cross and that of all my children, to suffer with you, to pray with you.

i I offer the Father, together with you, the precious contribution of your personal collaboration in the redemption accomplished by my Son Jesus."

274   *Curaçao (Netherlands); September 29, 1983*
Feast of the Holy Archangels

The Role of the Angels

a "Today the Church is celebrating the feast of the Archangels Michael, Gabriel and Raphael.

b It is also your feast, beloved sons, because the angels of the Lord have a very important part to play in my victorious plan.

c See, now, what a role is theirs: under my command, they are fighting a terrible battle against Satan and all the wicked spirits. It is a struggle proceeding more particularly on the level of spirits, fought with intelligence and a perfect adhesion to the plans of the two great opposing leaders, the Woman Clothed with the Sun and the Red Dragon.

d To Saint Gabriel has been given the task of clothing you with the strength of God Himself.

e He fights against the most dangerous of the snares of Satan, which is that of weakening you, bringing you to discouragement and to weariness. How many of you have stopped along the way of the consecration you have made to me, because of this human weakness of yours!

f It is weakness that leads you to doubt, to uncertainty, to fear, to uneasiness. This is the temptation of my Adversary, to render you ineffective, locked up inside yourselves, hampered by your own problems, incapable of any real apostolic offensive.

g   The Archangel Gabriel has the task of helping you to grow in trust, by clothing you in the strength of God. And so it is that every day he leads you along the path of courage, of firmness, of a faith that is heroic and pure.

h   To Saint Raphael is given the task of pouring balm upon your wounds.

i   How often Satan succeeds in wounding you with sin, harming you by his deceitful allurements! He makes you feel the weight of your misery, of your incapacity and frailty, and stops your advance along the path of perfect giving.

j   Then also, to Saint Raphael is given the task of accompanying you along the road I have traced out for you, supplying you with the medicine that will heal all your spiritual ailments.

k   Each day he makes your footsteps more secure, your resolutions less uncertain, your acts of love and of the apostolate more courageous; he makes your response to my wishes more decisive and your minds more attentive to my maternal plan, and you fight your battle, strengthened by his heavenly balm.

l   To Saint Michael is given the task of defending you from the frightful attacks Satan unleashes against you.

m   In these times, my beloved ones, who have accepted my invitation and are consecrated to my Immaculate Heart and all my children who have come to be part of my victorious cohort, are targets assailed with particular fury and ferocity on the part of my Adversary and yours.

n   Satan attacks you on the spiritual field with every kind of temptation and suggestion, to bring you to evil, to disorientation, to doubt and to distrust. Often he uses his favorite weapon, which is that of diabolical suggestion and impure temptation.

o   He attacks you with terrible snares, frequently forcing you into a position of danger. Even physically he makes attempts upon your life and personal safety.

p   It is the Archangel Michael, Patron of the Universal Church, who, with his great power, intervenes and joins combat to liberate you from the Evil One and his dangerous snares.

q   For this reason I invite you to invoke his protection with the daily recital of that brief but so very efficacious prayer of exorcism composed by Pope Leo XIII.

r   You see now that the angels of the Lord have an important role in the battle plan for the present conflict: you should always live in their company.

s   Theirs is a function which is invaluable and irreplaceable: they are close to you, engaged in the same struggle; they give you force and courage, heal your many wounds, defend you from evil; and with you they form the mightiest part of the victorious cohort commanded by the heavenly Leader."

275 *Ft. Lauderdale (Florida, U.S.A.); October 7, 1983*
Feast of Our Lady of the Rosary
Anniversary of the Victory
of the Blessed Virgin Mary at Lepanto

The Dragon Will Be Shackled

a   "Beloved sons, in the battle in which you are daily engaged against Satan and his crafty and dangerous seductions, and against the mighty armies of evil, apart from the special help given you by the angels of the Lord, it is necessary for you to employ a weapon which is both secure and invincible. This weapon is your prayer.

b   With prayer you are always able to snatch back from the enemy whatever territory he has conquered, to make blossoms of goodness spring up on the desert of sin and evil, and especially you can free an immense number of souls whom Satan has succeeded in imprisoning. Prayer possesses a potent force and starts a chain reaction in good that is far more powerful than any atomic reaction.

c   The prayer of my predilection is the holy rosary.

d   For this reason, in my many apparitions I always ask that it be recited. I unite myself with those who say it; I request it from all with solicitude and maternal preoccupation.

e   Why is the holy rosary so efficacious?

f   Because it is a simple prayer, a humble one, and it forms you spiritually in littleness, in meekness, in simplicity of heart.

g   Today Satan is successfully conquering everything with the spirit of pride and of rebellion against God, and he is terrified by those who follow your heavenly Mother along the road of little-ness and humility. While this prayer is despised by the great and the proud, it is recited with so much love and so much joy by my little ones, by the poor, by children, by the humble, the suf-fering, by the many, many faithful souls who have welcomed my invitation.

h   Satan's pride will again be conquered by the humility of little ones, and the Red Dragon will find himself decisively humili-ated and defeated when I bind him not by a great chain but by a very frail cord: the holy rosary.

i   It is a prayer that you say together with me.

j   When you invite me to pray for you, I accede to your request and mingle my voice with yours, and I unite my prayer to yours.

k   Consequently it becomes more and more efficacious, because your heavenly Mother is suppliant omnipotence.

l   What I ask for I always obtain, because Jesus can never say *no* to what his Mother requests of Him.

m   It is a prayer that unites the voices of the Church and of hu-manity, because it is said in the name of all, and never exclusively on behalf of a single person.

n   By contemplating its mysteries, you are led to understand the plan of Jesus, as spelled out in all of his life, from the Incarnation to the consummation of his glorious Pasch, and thus you pen-etrate ever more profoundly into the mystery of the redemp-tion.

o   And you begin to understand this mystery of love through your heavenly Mother; moving through the passageway of her Heart, you gain possession of the immense treasure of the divine and burning charity of the Heart of Christ.

p   In the rosary you become formed for the perfect glory of the Father with the frequent repetition of the prayer Jesus taught you: 'Our Father who art in heaven; hallowed be thy name, thy kingdom come.' (Mt 6:9-10)

q   You are also formed for the everlasting adoration of the Most Holy Trinity with the recital of the 'Glory be to the Father, and to the Son, and to the Holy Spirit.'

r   Today your heavenly Mother asks you to make use of the holy rosary as the most efficacious weapon for fighting in the great battle, under the command of the Woman Clothed with the Sun.

370

s Give your support to my invitation; multiply your cenacles of prayer and fraternity; consecrate yourselves to my Immaculate Heart; frequently recite the holy rosary! Then the powerful Red Dragon will be shackled by this chain, and his margin of action will become ever more restricted. In the end he will be left impotent and harmless.

t The miracle of the triumph of my Immaculate Heart will be made manifest to all."

276

Leader of a Single Cohort

a "Beloved sons, an invaluable help for fulfilling the task I have entrusted to you is bestowed upon you by those of your brothers who have already arrived here above in paradise, and now participate in its beatitude without end.

b Today is the feast of All Saints, and you should look up at them with joy, with trust and with great hope.

c How many of these brothers of yours have lived through difficulties identical to your own, endured the same sufferings, shared in your sorrows. They responded to my maternal invitation and consecrated themselves to my Immaculate Heart.

d Here above they form a great crown of light, which together with your Mother, opens in an everlasting chant of praise to the Most Holy Trinity.

e Those who while on earth lived as my children, listened to me with docility, and followed me along the road I myself pointed out, now are components of a most luminous crown around my Immaculate Heart, a crown of love, of joy and of glory. How many of these my children have you known during these years! Now they are closer than ever to you, fighting the same battle under the command of the heavenly Leader.

f My motherly Heart today unites you in an extraordinary communion of life with all your brothers who are in paradise, and with those who now possess certitude as to their salvation but are still suffering the moment of their personal purification in purgatory.

g   This is an immense part, invisible but most valuable, of my cohort, because my holy children are now clothed with the very power of God and with the strength that is my own, while the souls in purgatory can give me the contribution of their suffering and their unceasing prayer.

h   For this reason you need never feel alone. Strengthen your bonds with the saints in heaven and with those still being purified in purgatory. They are very near to you. They see all your difficulties. They are aware of the terrible snares being laid for you by my Adversary, and they help you always in a very efficacious way. Look up today at all who have already preceded you into eternal life in the seal of faith and are now awaiting you with love and with joy.

i   I am the Mother and the Queen of all the saints.

j   I am the Leader of a single cohort!

k   I am the Mother of the entire Church: the militant, the suffering, and the triumphant Church, and my Immaculate Heart vibrates with joy to see you so united in the fraternal bonds of a single communion of life and of love.

l   From paradise, together with your brothers, these my beloved sons who are already here above, and with all the souls still praying and suffering in purgatory, I bless you today in the name of the Father, and of the Son, and of the Holy Spirit."

277   *Enugu (Nigeria, West Africa); November 21, 1983*
Feast of the Presentation of the Blessed Virgin Mary

Along the Roads of Africa

a   "Enter into the temple of my Immaculate Heart, beloved sons, if you wish to contemplate the wonders of my merciful love.

b   In these times your Mother is exerting her action of solicitous admonition in all parts of the world, to bring you to walk along the good road, that of love, of a return to God, your Redeemer. Everywhere I am revealing myself to little ones, to the simple, to the poor, to the pure of heart.

c   Even in this part of the African continent, you see how my invitation is being received by them with gratitude and great appreciation.

d   How much love for me you are finding along the roads of Africa! Here, amid such great poverty, where houses are still made of mud and my children often have neither food nor clothing, I receive from them more than what is given me in other more advanced parts of the world.

e   I receive a love that is open and sincere, a generous response, a correspondence that is enthusiastic and contented, prayer that is ardent and persevering.

f   You have seen with what great fervor they recite the holy rosary and with what veneration they surround my images, how they place me in every room of their poor homes.

g   To these I will manifest myself even more, by apparitions and by means of my maternal presence, aiding them and soliciting Providence so that they may not lack food and clothing.

h   In these days, my little son, you have been able to see with your own eyes how the heavenly Mother is working along the roads of this immense continent.

i   The hour of my greatest wonders has come. These are the times of the triumph of my maternal love.

j   For this reason I invite all, from the five continents, to enter the temple of my Immaculate Heart, that you may thus further my design."

278   *Grand Bassam (Ivory Coast, West Africa); December 8, 1983*
Solemnity of the Immaculate Conception

The Medicine You Need

a   "I am the Immaculate Conception.

b   Participate, beloved sons, in the great joy of the whole Church as she contemplates today this singular privilege with which the Most Holy Trinity adorned me, in view of my divine maternity.

c   I am your Mother all beautiful, and as such I am invoked by you. I wish to clothe you with my own beauty, and I exhort you to follow after me on the road of grace and of holiness, of purity and virginity.

373

d   It is sin alone that offends your interior beauty. For this reason I invite all of you to fight every day against so great an evil.

e   Sin is a consequence of that original disorder by which you unfortunately have been prevented from being conceived and born as I was, wholly immaculate.

f   All of you were born burdened by the weight of this heavy and evil inheritance. You were released from it at the moment of your baptism, but its consequences have remained with you, leaving you so very fragile and still so easily attracted by sin, to which you fall victim often during the course of your lives.

g   The first thing you must do is to recognize sin as an evil and to repent immediately with an act of pure and supernatural love.

h   How many of my children today no longer recognize it as an evil. Often they welcome it as something good, and as such they let it penetrate into their souls, into their hearts and into their lives. They are then no longer capable of repentance and live habitually infected by this grave disease.

i   You should resort to the medicine which the mercy of Jesus has prepared for you: the sacrament of Reconciliation.

j   Never as in these times has the practice of frequent confession been so necessary. Today confession is disappearing from the lives and practices of so many of my children, and this is a sign of the crisis the Church is undergoing.

k   By means of you, beloved ones, I wish to have the sacrament of Reconciliation in the Church brought back to its splendor. I wish all of my children to hasten in great numbers to this fountain of grace and of divine mercy. And I invite you, my beloved ones, to confess frequently, and, if possible, every week.

l   I ask you to go to the confessional and be at the disposal of all those who need this sacrament.

m   Thoroughly educate all the faithful on the necessity of using this sacrament, above all when they find themselves in a state of mortal sin.

n   This is the medicine you need if you wish to walk along the road of divine grace and of holiness. In this way you will follow your heavenly Mother who, in the train of her heavenly perfume, would draw you after her.

o   Then you yourselves will be clothed in the splendor that is mine, and the life of Jesus can cast deep roots within your being.

p From the African continent, today I am addressing to all, with maternal solicitude, my invitation to walk on the road of love and holiness, fighting against Satan and all his seductions. Soon, by means of you, I will be able to obtain the victory, when I will crush the head of the infernal dragon who today is ensnaring you in such a treacherous way."

279

His New Birth

a "In the garden of my Immaculate Heart, beloved sons, live the beautiful and precious hours of this holy night. Spend it in prayer, in silence, in the sweet company of myself and my spouse, Joseph.

b Participate in the moments of ecstasy and of ineffable joy lived by your heavenly Mother as she prepared to give you her divine Child. Prayer enveloped me like a mantle; silence took ever greater possession of my life, for the moment had come, so long awaited, of his birth in time. Hence I did not remember the fatigue from the long journey we had completed, nor did I feel discouragement at the refusal to open a door to us; I was drawn by the secluded quiet of the grotto and not troubled by its dreariness and want of everything.

c Then, suddenly, Paradise bent down on my nothingness, and I entered into a rapture of love and of life with the Heavenly Father; when I realized that I was still on earth, I now had in my arms my God, miraculously become my Son.

d Relive the industrious silence of my most chaste spouse, Joseph, his fatigue from conducting us down the long road, his persistence in looking for a house, his repeated patience with each refusal to open a door, his confidence as he led the way to a safe and protected place, his loving efforts to make the miserable grotto more hospitable, his prayerful awaiting for what was about to take place, and finally, his incomparable bliss as he leaned down to kiss and to adore his God, now born from me on this holy night.

e Let the light that appeared to the shepherds in the darkness of the night be upon you, and also the chants of the angels, and the joy of hearing the glad tidings: 'I announce good news to you, of great joy for all; today a Savior is born for you, who is Christ the Lord!' (cf. Lk 2:10-11)

f   In the thickness of the night that today has fallen over the world, in the suffering now reaching the point of bloodshed that the Church has been called to experience, while the doors of men and of peoples are again shut to Jesus, who is returning in glory, imitate your heavenly Mother, her most loving spouse, Joseph, and the shepherds who immediately rose up at the invitation addressed them by heaven.

g   Pray and be silent, so that you can hear the voice of God and recognize the great signs He is sending you today, and by your personal collaboration further his merciful design.

h   Like Joseph, devote yourselves to the task of attentively preparing all for his near return. Enkindle in hearts the lights that have gone out; open souls to grace and to love; throw wide all the gates for Christ, who is coming!

i   And following the example of the shepherds, those simple little ones, so also you must not shut your ears to the voices still more than ever before being given you by heaven.

j   Among them know how to recognize and follow that of your heavenly Mother, who in so many ways and with such great signs repeats to you her prophetic admonition: 'Prepare yourselves for the return of Jesus in glory.'

k   His second birth is close at hand. Live with me the conclusive hours of this second coming: in trust, in prayer, in suffering that is accepted and enlightened, in the expectation that the great day of the Lord will soon come.

l   The desert of the world will open to receive the heavenly dew of his glorious reign of love and of peace."

280

Return to Your Redeemer

a   "Spend the last hours of the year in silence, in recollection, and in prayer.

b   Beloved sons, I am your heavenly Mother, and I am presently arranging a great plan of love, to hasten the advent of the triumph of my Immaculate Heart. For never as in these moments has the world been in such need of my maternal presence.

c   The world is walking along the roads of hatred and obstinate rejection of God, of violence and immorality. Despite all the continuing invitations sent by the Divine Mercy, humanity persists in remaining deaf to every summons.

d   The signs the Lord sends are neither understood nor accepted; the dangers, pointed out by 'my Pope' who courageously and anxiously is predicting the storm awaiting you, are not believed.

e   The messages which I give, through simple and little souls chosen by me in every part of the world, are not taken into consideration.

f   The appearances which I am still making, often in faraway and dangerous places, are ignored. And yet you are only inches from your ruin. When all will be shouting for peace, a new world war could suddenly fall upon you, spreading death and destruction everywhere.

g   When they will say: 'Tranquillity and security,' then could begin the very greatest overthrow of peoples and individuals. (cf. 1 Thes 5:3) How much blood I see flowing in all the streets of the world!

h   How many of my poor children I see weeping because of the scourge of fire, famine and terrible destruction!

i   The Lord is at the doors of this generation, and during the Holy Year of his Redemption, He still knocks on the hearts of all, with insistence and love.

j   Return to your God, who wishes to save you and to lead you to peace! Return to your Redeemer! Open your hearts to Christ who is coming!

k   The moments you are living are of grave urgency. For this reason I would ask you to spend the last hours of the year on your knees, in confident and unceasing prayer. Unite your voices with the powerful supplication of your heavenly Mother, who is imploring for all the great miracle of divine mercy."

1984

I ASK THE CONSECRATION OF ALL

Have Courage

a   "Begin this new year in the light of my divine maternity. Beloved sons, this feast should be a sign of confidence and of hope for all of you.

b   Have courage; I am the Mother of Grace and of Mercy. If the new year is opening amid clouds that menacingly thicken on the horizon, if humanity is incapable of finding its way back to God, if the disintegrating forces of evil and death in the world are increasing, if insecurity and fear mark the passage of your days, look to me as to the Mother of Divine Mercy.

c   Today I bend down over this generation, so ailing and so threatened, with the love a mother has for the neediest of her children and for those exposed to danger. With my immaculate hands I gather up all the sufferings and immense miseries of humanity and present them to the Heart of my Son, Jesus, that He may cause the river of his merciful love to flow down upon the world.

d   Have courage, because Jesus loves you with his divine tenderness, and your heavenly Mother is always among you to share your difficulties and dangers.

e   Have courage; I am the Mother of the Savior and of your Redeemer.

f   On the Cross Jesus redeemed you forever, suffering and dying for you. His Sacrifice has an infinite value, transcending time. His blood, his wounds, his painful agony, his atrocious death upon the Cross, possess the value of salvation even for this generation of yours, which without Him would have gone to perdition.

g   His Sacrifice is mystically consummated in every Holy Mass which is celebrated.

h   To the general and renewed rejection of God, the answer is still that of his renewed and sorrowful prayer, with its infinite capacity for reparation: 'Father, forgive them, for they know not what they say or what they do.' (cf. Lk 23:34)

i   If sin and evil are overflowing, today there is offered anew to the divine justice the innocent blood of the true Lamb of God, who takes away all the sins of the world.

j   To the threat of war and of destruction, the answer is the certainty of having the real presence among you of Jesus in the Eucharist, he who is Life and who has conquered sin and death forever.

k   At the beginning of this new year, look to Jesus your Redeemer and to your heavenly Mother, who console you and lead you to penetrate into the wonderful plan of your salvation.

l   Have courage: I am the Mother and the Queen of Peace. Through me peace will come to you. Listen to my voice, and let yourselves be led by me with docility.

m   On the eve of the great trials awaiting you, in the threat, now feared by all, of a new and frightful war, know that my presence among you, confirmed today in so many ways and with such great prodigies, is a sign which tells you how, at the end of the great suffering, my Immaculate Heart alone will triumph.

n   This will be the great victory of love and of peace throughout the whole world!"

282   Shrine of Castelmonte (Udine, Italy); January 21, 1984
Feast of St. Agnes
(After the Gospel during the concelebration)

My Book

a   "I accept the homage from you, who have come up here to my Shrine, to give thanks to your heavenly Mother for the book. How many difficulties 'my book' has encountered, but how much good has it already done in every part of the world, translated now into so many languages!

b   It has been the instrument for carrying to the hearts and souls of so many beloved children the voice of the heavenly Mother, the manifestation of my maternal plan, my invitation to receive you all within the refuge of my Immaculate Heart.

c   How should this book be read?

d   With the simplicity of a child who is listening to his mother. He doesn't ask why she speaks, or how she speaks, or where her words are going to lead him. He loves her, and he listens to her. He does what she says. And then the child is happy, because he feels that in this way he is guided and illumined by his mother. Led by her and formed by her words, each day he continues to grow in life.

e   So should it be for you. Read it with simplicity, without minding about such problems as how I speak, why I speak, where I am speaking. My only concern is that you live everything I have told you. Then your hearts will be inflamed with love, your souls will be illumined by my light, and I will transform you interiorly to lead you to do each day what pleases the Heart of Jesus.

f   If you are consecrated to me, I take you just as you are, with your limitations, your defects and sins, your frailty, but then each day I transform you to bring you to be in accordance with the plan which God has entrusted to my Immaculate Heart.

g   What do I say in this book of mine?

h   I trace out a simple and beautiful road, but a difficult one, oh how difficult! It is necessary to travel it, if you wish to live the consecration.

i   I teach you how to live; I form you in a practical way to live with me.

j   I tell you the things which I have most on my Heart, because they are the very things which Jesus has told you in the Gospel, which today should be lived with the simplicity of little ones, with the ardor of martyrs, and with the fidelity of courageous witnesses: it should be lived to the letter!

k   Accordingly I am calling you to prayer, to penitence, to mortification, to the practice of virtue, to trust, to hope, to the exercise of an ever more perfect charity.

l   This is what I want to tell you. Don't be delayed, therefore, by the predictions I give you in the effort to make you comprehend the times in which you are living.

m   Like a mother, I am telling you the dangers through which you are going, the imminent threats, the extent of the evils that could happen to you, only because these evils can yet be avoided by you, the dangers can be evaded, the plan of God's justice always can be changed by the force of his merciful love. Also when I predict chastisements to you, remember that everything, at any moment, may be changed by the force of your prayer and your reparative penance.

n   Do not say therefore:'How much of what you predicted to us has not come true!' Instead, give thanks with me to the Heavenly Father because at the response of your prayer and consecration, your suffering, and on account of the immense suffering of so many of my poor children, again He alters the period of justice, to permit that of the great mercy to come to flower..."

283   *Zompita (Udine, Italy); January 24, 1984*

My Signs

a   "Beloved children, I welcome this rosary you are reciting together with such great love and fervor.

b   As Mother I want to tell you that I am here with you, represented by the statue you have here. Each of my statues is a sign of a presence of mine and reminds you of your heavenly Mother. Therefore it must be honored and put in places of greater veneration.

c   Just as you look with love at a photograph of a cherished person because it transmits to you a reminder and a likeness, so too you should look with love at every image of your heavenly Mother, because it transmits to you a reminder of her, and still more, it becomes a particular sign of her presence among you.

d   How deeply saddened I am by the fact that I am, so frequently today, ousted from the churches. Sometimes I am placed outside, in a corridor, like some trinket; sometimes I am put in the back of the church, so that none of my children can venerate me.

e   A sign of how much I am pleased with the fitting veneration given to my images is also what I am doing through this little statue. It is a triple sign I give you: that of my eyes, which suddenly come alive; that of the color of my countenance, which changes its hue; and that of my Heart, which exudes a fragrance, now a delicate one, now one of greater strength.

f   By the sign I give you in the eyes, I want to show you that your heavenly Mother, never so much as in these times, is watching you with her merciful eyes. She is not far from you; she takes cognizance of you in all the difficulties in which you find yourselves, in the difficult moments you are living through, with all the sufferings which are awaiting you, with the great cross you must carry.

g   And with these eyes I look at all, at those far away, at the atheists, at the drug addicts, at my poor sinful children, to know them just as they are, to help them, to guide them along the path of goodness, of a return to God, of conversion, prayer, fasting and penance.

h   In a particular way I look at you, my beloved, objects of my maternal complacency. Especially you, beloved of my sacerdotal Movement, who form for me an object of great gratification.

i   I look at you, and I illumine you with my own beauty. In you I reflect the candor of heaven that is mine. You should be lilies in your purity, roses in your fragrance, cyclamens in your littleness. In this way you compose this beautiful crown of love that makes the thorny crown of my sorrow break into blossom.

j   By the sign I give you in the color of my visage, I want to show you that I am Mother for all, and today I share in all your needs, and I rejoice in your joys. But I also suffer in all your numerous sufferings.

k   When a mother is happy and jumps for joy, you see the color of her face become rosy; when she is worried about the fate of her children, you see her face turn completely pale. If this happens to an earthly mother, it also happens to me, and the sign I give you, so human and maternal, is to tell you that as Mother I truly share in all the moments of your life.

l   When you suffer, I suffer. When you rejoice, I rejoice. When you are good, I jump for joy. When you love me, my face is all aflame because of the joy you give me.

m   By the sign I give you with the fragrance I exude, sometimes of lesser, sometimes of greater strength, I wish to show you that I am always among you, but especially when you are more in need of me.

n   If you do not recognize the perfume, or you notice it in a very faint way, it is not because I do not love you, or because you are

384

wicked. The Mother loves with merciful predilection even those who have the greater need for her!

o   Understand then why my maternal compassion goes out to sinners, all, but especially those who are furthest away, those most in need of divine mercy. Appearing at Fatima, I taught you to pray to Jesus in this way: 'Bring all souls to heaven, especially those most in need of thy mercy.'

p   I love all, beginning with the furthest away, those of my children who are sinners, for whom I am a secure and maternal refuge.

q   Look at my merciful eyes which shed tears of sorrow and compassion. In so many parts of the world I give this sign, causing copious tears to stream from my eyes, even tears of blood.

r   To give a sign of my presence and to accord to your lives a secure support, and amid the tribulations you are living, to call you to joy and to trust, in so many parts of the world, I am still giving my maternal messages. They announce to you the certitude that I am following you and am with you. I live with you; I prepare everything for you; I lead you by the hand along the difficult road of this time of purification.

s   A fragrant sign of my maternal presence is to be found in the apparitions I am still making in many regions of the world. Yes, in these times I am appearing in Europe, in Asia, in Africa, in America, and in distant Oceania. The whole world is wrapped in my mantle.

t   In the struggle, now conclusive, between me and my Adversary, my extraordinary presence tells you that my victory has already begun. My beloved children, how much I love you!

u   From you, to whom I have given so much, this I ask: that you increase your love for me!..."

284

San Marco (Udine, Italy); January 28, 1984
Feast of St. Thomas Aquinas

My Gift to You

a   "...Everything in life has been arranged for you, in every particular, by the providence of God the Father and of your heavenly Mother: the moments of suffering, those of spiritual trial and interior difficulties, the moments of joy and of consolation, the moments of special fervor and of union with me.

b   Everything is the gift of God to you, which Jesus gives you through the Immaculate Heart of your heavenly Mother. For this reason it is also a gift from me.

c   When my Heart, which is replete with grace and with love, opens and pours out upon you my maternal predilection, encouraging and consoling you, what is this unfolding of my maternal tenderness, of the fullness of my immaculate love, if not a gift I am giving you?

d   The task of the Mother is to prepare this gift each day for her children, for all; for the furthest away, it is a gift of mercy and pardon; for sinners, it is a sorrowful gift, one recalling them to the road of goodness; for the many who suffer, it is a gift of compassion and comfort; for those soon to die, it is a gift of support, helping them to close their lives here below in a good way and opening the golden gate of the life awaiting them after death.

e   And for you, my beloved ones, the gift is one of most particular predilection, expressing itself by the ordering of all things, the arranging of every circumstance of your day like an embroidery of perfect beauty woven by the fingers of your heavenly Mother.

f   Your being together among yourselves, your gathering together in prayer, the frequent recitation of my prayer, the holy rosary, your mutual love, and this even with your weaknesses and human miseries, all is a gift of my Immaculate Heart.

g   Walk forward always united, hand in hand like so many little brothers, praying together, loving together, rejoicing and suffering together, because I have now revealed to you my plan, which should be realized in a most perfect unity.

h   Also a gift of my Immaculate Heart — O yes, a most particular gift! — is the book containing my messages.

i   In my book what you should know has already been revealed. If you know how to read it, therein is my total plan, in its preparation, in its sorrowful actualization, and in its luminous and victorious completion.

j   Read it, my beloved sons; meditate on it; live it! Have no doubt; I am speaking to you. Through these words I am present in it and manifest myself. Only tomorrow will you understand the importance of this maternal message of mine.

k   A gift of my Immaculate Heart is the plan I have revealed to you. When I speak to you, I use your human words, but whereas you speak in virtue of the experience you have from your earthly life, I speak to you in virtue of the light of paradise. In the Heart of my Son Jesus and in the profound mystery of the Most Holy Trinity, a single reality is comprised, binding together in a true communion of life the present, the past and the future, the Church that is triumphant and rejoicing in heaven, that which is suffering and being purified in purgatory, and that which, as a pilgrim on your poor earth, is still struggling.

l   In the vision of this divine communion that now unites you, I speak to you always in the vision of eternity, so that for me there is no difference between my children living here in paradise, between those still in purgatory, and those yet walking upon earth...

m   For this reason I see close to you, still members as valuable as ever of my Movement, your brothers and my beloved ones who have arrived here above and compose so beautiful a harmony... You should feel them close to you, these brother-priests of yours who have arrived here above, because they are forever a part of my Movement. Perceive them as members who are living and working, and as valuable fighters in my victorious cohort, which battles at my command!

n   A gift of my Immaculate Heart to the Church is this, my Movement. It is my work alone.

o   For eleven years I have been diffusing it in every part of the world; I call my sons, and they respond. For eleven years I have been achieving a masterpiece of love and mercy for the triumph of my Immaculate Heart. Everything that I have told you will be fulfilled to the letter. The Church will come to an ever greater realization of how the Marian Movement of Priests is a gift of my Immaculate Heart, because with it too I wish to give the Church the certainty of my perennial presence and my maternal protection...

p   But above all, the gift of my Immaculate Heart will be the new Pentecost. Just as in the Cenacle of Jerusalem the Apostles, reunited with me in prayer, prepared for the moment of the first Pentecost, so also, in the cenacle of my Immaculate Heart — and consequently in the cenacles where you are gathered in prayer — you apostles of these last times can, with your heavenly Mother, obtain a new effusion of the Holy Spirit.

q   It will be the Spirit of Love, with his powerful action of fire and of grace renewing the very foundations of the whole world.

r   It will be He, the Spirit of Love, with his great force of holiness and of light, bringing my Church to new splendor, making it therefore humble and poor, evangelical and chaste, merciful and holy.

s   It will be the Spirit of Love, through the fire of innumerable sufferings renewing all creation, that it may become that garden of God, that terrestrial paradise in which Jesus will always be with you, like a sun of light reflecting its rays everywhere."

285

February 2, 1984
Feast of the Presentation of the Child Jesus

The Soul Transpierced

a   "At the moment I presented my Son Jesus in the temple and my Heart was overwhelmed by maternal bliss in seeing how the Spirit had revealed the secret plan of the Father to two simple and elderly creatures, my soul was transpierced by the prophetic words addressed to me: 'He is to be as a sign of contradiction, for the salvation and the downfall of many...and a sword will transpierce your soul!' (cf. Lk 2:34-35)

b   See now how the profound mystery of my divine and universal maternity was also revealed.

c   It is a mystery of love.

d   My motherly Heart opens itself to love in a perfect manner. No other creature can ever possess such a profound a capacity for love.

e   If the extent of maternal love can be measured by the number of the children, consider how great must be the love of your heavenly Mother, to whom Jesus has confided all mankind as her children.

f How great is my motherly love! It embraces all and each one in particular; it follows each one along his road; it participates in difficulties, shares in your sufferings, helps you in all your necessities; it assists you in dangers, keeps vigil in decisive moments. No one is ever abandoned or forgotten.

g Penetrate into the secret of my maternal love, and you will always be consoled.

h It is also a mystery of sorrow.

i At the moment my Infant Jesus was put back into my arms by the priest and I contemplated Him, then forty days old, in all his beauty with the freshness of a flower that has just begun to bloom, the prophetic voice of the aged Simeon caused me to behold Him mentally already stretched out on the Cross, and then my soul was truly transpierced by a sword.

j I am the Mother of the Transpierced Soul! Therefore all your wounds are now mine, O sons, just as those of my Son Jesus were mine!

k You are living days of great sufferings that are ever increasing, especially for you, my beloved ones. The time in which you are living is marked by wounds of every kind, caused by a persistent and general rejection of God, by a great neglect of your duties, by the widespread habit of ignoring and no longer obeying the commandments of God's Law.

l Within the Church the confusion grows; too few are those who accept my invitation to let themselves be formed and led by me, with the humble docility of my Infant Jesus; and consequently, the darkness deepens in minds, in hearts and in souls.

m I am your Mother of the Transpierced Soul. I am close by you to close your wounds.

n Do not lose heart! Pray; do penance; be little and docile; let yourselves be formed by me; let yourselves be carried in my Heart over the stormy waters. Courage!

o Above all, my transpierced soul today wishes to pour down upon you the fullness of its light and grace.

p I hold you in my Heart; each day I carry you to the temple of the Lord, and from my maternal arms I place you upon his altar, victims prepared by me and pleasing to Him, for the salvation of the world."

Look at My Spouse Joseph

a   "My beloved sons, today look at my most chaste spouse, Joseph, who is an example for all of you in furthering God's plan with love, with purity, with faith, and with perseverance.

b   During his life he was a chaste and faithful spouse for me, a valuable collaborator in the loving care of the Child Jesus, a silent and provident worker, careful to see that none of the things necessary for our human existence were lacking, just and firm in daily fulfilling the tasks entrusted to him by the Heavenly Father.

c   How much he loved and followed each day the wonderful growth of our divine Son Jesus! And Jesus repaid him with an affection that was filial and profound; how He listened to him and obeyed him; how He comforted him and helped him!

d   So also in you, beloved sons, I wish those virtues to flourish which made him so perfect in the fulfillment of the providential design for him.

e   May his silence and self-effacement, which are necessary in these times to enable you to carry out the plan I have entrusted to you, be in you.

f   Live far from noise and commotion, from shouting and the din that to an ever greater degree surrounds you. Maintain your interior quiet in silent colloquy with Jesus and with your heavenly Mother.

g   Take no part in worldly shows, and shut your eyes to the loose seductions of the world. Know how to avoid the subtle tactics of moral perversion, today disseminated in so insidious and dangerous a way by the press and the television.

h   Do not waste time in front of the television, stealing precious moments from prayer and from listening to my word.

i   May his virginal purity also be in you, in a detachment — which I wish to be as great as possible — from yourselves, from creatures, from human affairs, so that you will be interiorly free, able to love and to fulfill with faithful perseverance whatever the Lord asks of you.

j   Imitate my most loving spouse, Joseph, in his humble and trusting prayer, his heavy labors, his patience and great goodness.

k   Entrust yourselves and my Movement to his powerful protection. Just as once he knew how to protect the menaced life of the Infant Jesus, so now he will protect this, my work of love, during those moments in which it will be attacked and furiously combatted by my Adversary.

l   With him, and together with our divine Infant Jesus, I encourage you today, and I bless you."

287

March 25, 1984
Solemnity of the Annunciation of the Lord

I Ask for the Consecration of All

a   "Consider the ineffable moment of the Annunciation made by the Archangel Gabriel, sent by God to receive my *yes* for the realization of his eternal plan of redemption, and for the great mystery of the Incarnation of the Word in my virginal womb, and then you will understand why I ask you to consecrate yourselves to my Immaculate Heart.

b   Yes, I myself manifested my wish at Fatima, when I appeared in 1917; I have asked it many times of my daughter, Sister Lucy, who is still on earth for the accomplishment of this mission I have entrusted to her; during these years I have insistently requested it through the message entrusted to my sacerdotal Movement; today I renew my request that all be consecrated to my Immaculate Heart.

c   Before all I ask it of Pope John Paul II, the first of my beloved sons, who on the occasion of this feast, performed the consecration in a solemn manner, after writing to the bishops of the world and inviting them to do so in union with him.

d   Unfortunately the invitation was not welcomed by all the bishops; particular circumstances have not yet permitted the explicit consecration of Russia which I have requested many times. As I have already told you, this consecration will be made to me when the bloody events are well on the way to actuality.

e   I bless this courageous act of my Pope in his wish to entrust the world and all the nations to my Immaculate Heart; I receive it with love and gratitude, and because of it I promise to intervene to shorten greatly the hours of the purification and to lessen the gravity of the trial.

f   But I ask this consecration also from all the bishops, from all the priests, from all religious, and from all the faithful. This is the hour in which the whole Church must assemble in the secure refuge of my Immaculate Heart!

g   Why do I ask you for the consecration?

h   When a thing is consecrated, it is removed from all uses other than the sacred one to which it has been assigned, and so it is with an object designated for the divine worship.

i   But this can also be the case with a person, when such a one is called by God to render Him perfect worship. Understand then how your true act of consecration is that of baptism.

j   By this sacrament, instituted by Jesus, grace is communicated to you, placing you in an order of life higher than your own, namely the supernatural life. Through this you participate in the divine nature, you enter into a communion of love with God, and your actions, accordingly, have a new value exceeding that of your nature, because they have a value which is truly divine.

k   After baptism you are then destined for the perfect glorification of the Most Holy Trinity and consecrated to live in the love of the Father, in the imitation of the Son, and in full communion with the Holy Spirit.

l   The fact that characterizes the act of consecration is its totality: when you are consecrated you are then wholly so, and forever!

m   When I ask you for the consecration to my Immaculate Heart, it is to make you understand that you must completely entrust yourselves to me, in a total and everlasting way, that I may dispose of you according to the Will of God.

n   You must entrust yourselves in a manner that is complete, giving me everything; you should not give me one thing and hold on to another, for yourselves; you should truly be wholly mine.

o   And then you should entrust yourselves to me not on one day yes and on another day no, or for a period of time as you would have it, but forever.

p   It is to emphasize this important aspect of a complete and

392

lasting dedication to me, your heavenly Mother, that I ask for the consecration to my Immaculate Heart.

q   How should the consecration be lived by you?

r   If you consider the ineffable mystery the Church commemorates today, you will understand how the consecration I have asked of you should be lived.

s   The Word of the Father was entrusted completely to me, in love. After my *yes*, He came down into my virginal womb.

t   He was entrusted to me in his divinity.

u   The Eternal Word, Second Person of the Most Holy Trinity, after the incarnation, was received and hidden in the tiny dwelling, miraculously prepared by the Holy Spirit, of my virginal womb.

v   He was entrusted to me in his humanity, in a manner as profound as the way any son is entrusted to the mother, from whom everything is expected: blood, flesh, breath, food, love, to enable him to grow in her womb each day, and then — after birth — each year, always close to the mother.

w   For this reason, just as I am the Mother of the Incarnation, so also I am the Mother of the Redemption, which had on this occasion its wonderful beginning.

x   And so you see me intimately associated with my Son Jesus; I collaborate with Him in his work of salvation, during his infancy, his adolescence, his thirty years of hidden life at Nazareth, his public ministry, during his sorrowful passion and up to the Cross where I offer and suffer with Him, receiving his last words of love and sorrow, in which I am given to all humanity as true Mother.

y   Beloved sons, called to imitate Jesus in everything because you are his ministers, imitate Him also in this, his complete reliance on the heavenly Mother. For this reason I ask you to offer yourselves to me with your consecration.

z   I will be able to be an attentive Mother for you, concerned to make you grow in God's plan, to realize in your lives the great gift of the priesthood to which you have been called; I will bring you each day to an ever better imitation of Jesus, who must be your only model and your greatest love. You will be true instruments, faithful collaborators in his redemption.

A   Today this is necessary for the salvation of all humanity, so diseased and so far from God and from the Church.

B   By an extraordinary intervention of his merciful love, the Lord can save this humanity, and you, priests of Christ and my beloved sons, are called to be the instruments of the triumph of the merciful love of Jesus.

C   Today this is indispensable for my Church, which must be healed from its wounds of infidelity and apostasy in order to return to its splendor and to renewed holiness.

D   Your heavenly Mother wishes to heal the Church through you, my priests. I will do this soon, if you will allow me to work in you, if you entrust yourselves with docility and simplicity to my merciful maternal action.

E   Again today, with sorrowful supplication, I ask you all to consecrate yourselves to my Immaculate Heart."

288

April 20, 1984
Good Friday

Close to Every Altar

a   "I am your Mother, so very sorrowful. I am close to my Son Jesus at the moment He ascends Calvary, exhausted by immense suffering and by the weight of the Cross which He carries with meekness and with love.

b   His feet leave their bloody imprint on the ground; his hands grip the Cross, which weighs upon his wounded shoulders; his body is bruised and lacerated by the terrible scourging it has undergone; from his head fall streams of blood, flowing from the wounds opened by the crown of thorns...

c   What weariness the ascent costs Jesus; what suffering is imposed upon Him by each step He makes towards the summit of Calvary!

d   He staggers; He stops; He is shaken by spasms of fever and pain; He bends down as if to recoup new energies; this no longer avails Him, and He falls to the earth.

e   Behold the Man. Behold, O sons, your King.

f   With an outburst of my motherly Heart, I would help Him to his feet, to succor Him with the force of my sorrow, to comfort

Him with the strength of my presence; I caress Him with the moan of my prayer; I accompany Him with the anguish of a wounded mother; and upon my Immaculate Heart, now united with his in a single offering to the Will of the Father, I lead Him towards the summit of Golgotha.

g   I am close to Him when they strip Him of his garments, and with a mother's impulse, understood and accepted by the executioners, I give my white veil so that his modesty will be protected. I watch Him as they stretch Him out on the gibbet; I hear the hammer on the nails which pierce his hands and feet; the terrible thud of the Cross upon the ground penetrates my soul, and makes Him quiver with pain.

h   I am beneath the Cross on this Good Friday, to live together with my Son the long and terrible hours of his passion.

i   Like a mantle, the peace that comes from his immolated body envelops me; like a river of grace, it flows into me, and I feel myself opening to an immense capacity for love; a new and greater maternal vocation discloses itself to my soul, while my Immaculate Heart receives every precious drop of his sorrow during the hours of agony.

j   This Good Friday has truly illumined every day granted you by the Lord for your earthly pilgrimage, O my sons, because it was on this day that you were redeemed.

k   Let all behold Him whom today they have pierced!

l   Let yourselves be washed in his blood, penetrated by his love, be generated by his sorrow, hidden in his wounds, restored by his ransom, redeemed by his new and eternal Sacrifice.

m   This Good Friday is repeated when Jesus is again immolated for you, although in an unbloody manner, in the Sacrifice of Holy Mass. The supreme gift of this day is mystically renewed by you.

n   But, close to Jesus who is immolated, the sorrowful oblation of your heavenly Mother is also repeated. She is always present close to every altar upon which Holy Mass is celebrated, just as she was during the long and sorrowful Good Friday.

o   Let your confidence be great and irresistible!

p   Evil, every evil, and the spirit of Evil, Satan your Adversary from the beginning, has been vanquished and reduced henceforth to perpetual bondage.

q   His great commotion of today should not frighten you, should not disturb you. Live in the joy and in the peace of Jesus, the gentle and meek Victim, offered on the Cross to the Father as the price of your everlasting ransom.

r   Now that darkness has again fallen over the world, and the night envelops a straying humanity, on this, his Good Friday, behold Him whom they have pierced, so that you will understand how the victory over evil, over hatred, and over death, has now been forever obtained for you by the force of the merciful love of Jesus, your divine Redeemer."

289

May 13, 1984
Anniversary of the First Apparition at Fatima

Be Converted!

a   "These are my times. Today while you recall my first apparition which took place at Fatima in 1917, you are living the events I then predicted to you.

b   You are in the period in which the struggle between me, the Woman Clothed with the Sun, and my Adversary, the Red Dragon, is moving now toward its conclusion, and for this reason I am again appearing in a new and more extraordinary way to assure you that my presence in your midst is habitual.

c   I am communicating to all my maternal will with a message which today has become anguished and urgent:

d   Be converted, and repent of your sins!

e   Be converted, and return to the God who saves you!

f   Be converted, and walk along the road of goodness, of love, and of holiness!

g   This is still for you the precious time of conversion. Receive my invitation, which, in so many ways, I still wish to address to my children who are so endangered.

h   Pray more; pray with the holy rosary; pray among yourselves in the cenacles; above all, pray in the family.

i   I want Christian families to return to the practice of praying with me and by means of me, so that they will be saved from the great evils threatening them.

j   Mortify yourselves with penance and corporal fasting.

k   It is fasting from evil and from sin that I prefer, of renunciation of smoking, alcohol, motion pictures and television. Do not watch television shows which corrupt your interior chastity and bring so much dissipation into your souls, sowing the germs of evil in your hearts.

l   I am also asking for bodily fasting, at least every now and then, just as it has been requested of you by my Son Jesus, in the Gospel, when He said: 'Certain kinds of demons can be ejected only by prayer and fasting.' (cf. Mk 9:29)

m   Consecrate yourselves continually to my Immaculate Heart, and live in daily communion of life and of love with me.

n   I am the Mother of the Faith; I am the faithful virgin, and today you should ask me for help to remain in the true faith. For this reason I summon you to listen to and follow the Pope, who has from Jesus the promise of infallibility, and to recite the Creed often as a renewed profession of your faith.

o   If you do everything I ask you, you will be walking each day with me towards your conversion. Live well this space of time which the merciful love of Jesus still gives you.

p   You will live with trust and with joy the impending moment of the triumph of my Immaculate Heart."

290

June 30, 1984
Feast of the Immaculate Heart of Mary

The Mystery of My Immaculate Heart

a   "Venerate my Immaculate Heart, beloved children. Today the Church is inviting you to look at the mystery of love and of mercy enclosed in my Immaculate Heart.

b   *If you venerate* my Heart, you give praise to the Most Holy Trinity, which receives its greatest glory in it, because it has made of this, my heavenly garden, the place of its divine delight.

c   In it the Father is reflected with joy, the Word is placed therein as in a precious cradle, and the Holy Spirit burns with the purest light of his divine love.

d   If you venerate my Immaculate Heart, you also give praise to your heavenly Mother, because within it is enfolded the mystery of my predilection and of the privileges of grace with which I have been adorned by God. And thus you also venerate my singular privileges of the Immaculate Conception, of the divine motherhood, of the bodily assumption into heaven, of the fullness of grace and of perpetual virginity. Through the way of my Heart, enter in so that you may understand and delight in the divine masterpiece which is your heavenly Mother.

e *If you love* this Heart, you yourselves become clothed with my motherly love and my immaculate mercy. In the depths of my Immaculate Heart, there takes place the wonder which I accomplish every day with you in order to make you ever more like myself and to transform your soul into the image of my own soul.

f I also communicate my spirit to you in order that you may truly grow in my life and become, today, the expression of the presence of your heavenly Mother. I form you in purity of mind, of heart and of body; and thus, you will spread about you the brightness of my immaculate light. I communicate to you my capacity to love, and your hearts will open up as a refuge of salvation to all who have strayed along the path of error and of sin. I give gentleness to your way of acting, so that you may be good and merciful to all. I give comfort and balm to your actions, that you may heal the painful wounds of the sick and of all my poor sinful children.

g And thus, you yourselves become, today, the concrete expression of my motherly love.

h *If you offer reparation* to the sorrow of my Immaculate Heart, you become a source of great joy and consolation for me, because through you I am able to take action, in these years, in order to carry out my plan of salvation.

i It is a plan which I am still keeping secret; I reveal it only to my little ones, who accept my invitation to venerate, to love, and to offer reparation, as they are led by me to understand more and more the great mystery of love and of mercy of my Immaculate Heart."

291

Valdragone (San Marino); July 5, 1984
Spiritual Exercises in the Form of a Cenacle
with the Priests of the M.M.P. of the Italian Language

Mother of Jesus, the Priest

a   "Beloved children, how pleasing to my Heart is this continuous cenacle of fraternity and prayer which you are making together with me, your heavenly Mother!

b   *I am the Mother of Jesus, the Priest.*

c   My Immaculate Heart has always been the altar upon which Jesus has wished to present his priestly offering to the Father. From the ineffable moment of the incarnation, when the Word of the Father was placed in my virginal womb and divinity annihilated itself, assuming therein the beginnings of human nature, my Immaculate Heart became the altar upon which the first priestly action of my Son, Jesus, took place.

d   I always accompanied Him in every most perfect accomplishment of his continuous offering as Priest and Victim. From his birth in poverty to his infancy spent in exile, from his youth passed in humble labor and obedient service to his public life quickly expended amidst so many sufferings and misunderstandings until its painful completion in his bloody agony and death on the Cross, the whole life of Jesus was a continuous priestly action, offered with love to the Father for our salvation.

e   At every moment of this offering, Jesus willed to have his Mother with Him that she, too, might suffer and offer. In this, I became co-operator with Him in his work of redemption, truly Co-redemptrix, and I am, above all, the Mother of Jesus, the Priest.

f   And so you understand why I feel a particular predilection for you, my sons, to whom has been entrusted the great gift of the priesthood.

g   I am at your side in every moment of your day, so that it may be completely sacrificed and given to the Father in a continuous priestly offering. I am at your side at the time of prayer and of work, in the hours of joy and of suffering, of solitude and of abandonment.

h   I am always at your side when you celebrate the Holy Sacrifice of the Mass, which renews that accomplished by Jesus on the Cross. With Jesus who, by means of you, today carries out his Sacrifice, I am always at the side of each altar to offer with you to the Heavenly Father, on my Immaculate Heart, the precious Victim of our redemption.

i   Today it is necessary to shed greater light upon the value of Holy Mass as the Sacrifice which renews, in an unbloody but true manner, that accomplished by Jesus on Calvary.

j   These are my times, and I am at your side, sons, to receive your continuous priestly action. For this reason, allow yourselves to be formed by me with docility.

k   In these spiritual exercises in the form of continuous cenacles, which I wish to be multiplied more and more, I am gently preparing you for your offering.

l   As little lambs I have gathered you into my sheepfold to prepare you for the immolation which awaits you. And now I look upon you with pleasure because you are cooperating with my action which disposes you to be offered to the Lord, on the altar of my Immaculate Heart, for the salvation of the world."

292

August 15, 1984
Solemnity of the Assumption
of the Blessed Virgin Mary into Heaven

Walk in the Light

a   "From paradise, into which I have entered with my body as well, I look upon you today with my motherly and merciful eyes. I am shedding upon you the rays of my immaculate light, and, in the deep darkness in which you are more and more enveloped, I invite you to walk along the light-filled path which comes from my Heart. Little children, walk in the light of your heavenly Mother; allow yourselves to be carried upon the wave of her heavenly perfume.

b   *Walk in the light of faith.*

c   These are the times in which my children run the grave risk of straying from the true faith. Errors are being spread; they are listened to and followed; they are publicized and disseminated

400

especially through the press, even that which professes to be religious. How great a need there is today for a press which spreads the truth of the faith in all its clarity and integrity!

d   And so it is necessary to be vigilant, to pray and to remain strongly faithful to the authentic Magisterium of the Church. For this reason I invite you to listen to the teaching of the Pope and to recite often the Creed as a profession of your Catholic faith and also to meditate upon the complete profession of faith composed by my beloved son, Pope Paul VI, who is already up here. You will then remain in the true faith, beloved children of your Mother, who is for all the model of how you must believe, guard, love and live the one and only word of God.

e   *Walk in the light of grace.*

f   As a terrible cancer, sin is today infecting souls more and more and leading them to death. If you looked with my eyes, you would see how this real spiritual epidemic has spread, causing slaughter among so many of my children and making them victims of evil.

g   You must become instruments which I will make use of for the healing of all poor sinners. For this I invite you to walk along the way of love and of divine grace, of mortification and penance, of prayer and of holiness.

h   *Walk in the light of love.*

i   In these times, in an ever more dangerous way, hatred and unbridled egoism are spreading everywhere. My Adversary is bringing about division on all sides: in families, in religious communities, in the Church, in all human society. How difficult it is becoming to understand one another today; how hard it is to live together with understanding and in mutual agreement!

j   And so I ask of you to remain always in my peace, to become instruments of peace for all. For this reason I invite you, with gentle severity, to silence, to concrete gestures of charity and communion, to help whoever is in need, always to speak words of peace and reconciliation with everyone.

k   Thus you will diffuse my immaculate light in the darkness which has spread about, and you will contribute to the transformation of your earthly life according to the model which is lived here above in paradise, where your heavenly Mother has been assumed, even with her glorious body."

293

Altötting (Germany); August 30, 1984
Spiritual Exercises in the Form of a Cenacle
with the Priests of the M.M.P. of the German Language

Mother of Faith

a   "I am the Mother of Faith. I am the faithfulVirgin. Beloved sons of Germany, Switzerland, Austria, Holland and Hungary, how happy I am with these days of spiritual exercises which you are making with me, in the form of a continuous cenacle! How your fervent and persevering prayer consoles my Immaculate Heart, now more than ever surrounded by a great crown of thorns!

b   In these countries of yours, you are facing a great danger which causes concern to my motherly Heart, because errors are being spread much more, efforts are being made to weaken the bond which unites you to the Pope, and moreover many souls are being led away from devotion to your heavenly Mother.

c   And so, during these days of cenacle I am causing extraordinary graces to shower down from my Immaculate Heart upon you and upon all my consecrated children. I want to obtain for you from the Holy Spirit the gift of your spiritual transformation to lead you to be courageous witnesses today.

d   *Be witnesses of faith.*

e   Preserve in the true faith all those who have been entrusted to you. So therefore defend yourselves from the danger, so widespread today, of falling into error. Do not give acceptance to any error: unmask it when it presents itself hidden under the appearance of truth, because it is then even more dangerous. Do not be afraid if, because of this, you are judged as being backward and not up-to-date, because just as for Jesus, so also his Gospel is the same: yesterday, today and always.

f   Renew often with the faithful your profession of faith and ask of me, the Mother of Faith, the grace to remain always in the Truth which my divine Son, Jesus, has revealed to you.

g   *Be witnesses of unity.*

h   Above all you must be united with the Pope, whom Christ has placed as the foundation of his Church. Today only those who remain united to the Pope can be saved in the faith. Listen to him; follow him; spread his teaching with courage.

i   Be also united to your bishops with prayer, with good example and with effective collaboration. By the witness of your life, may they be assisted in rooting out error from the holy Church of God, and by your obedience and your filial love, may they receive encouragement in their difficult ministry.

j   Bring all the faithful to this unity of life with the bishops united to the Pope. And thus you will console my Heart, so sorrowful and wounded today because of the profound disunity which has entered into the interior of my Church.

k   *Be witnesses of true devotion to me.*

l   In your countries there is under way a strong attempt to remove me from the life and piety of many of my children. It is your duty to have me shine once again upon your path. For this reason, I invite you to multiply the cenacles of prayer and of life with me. Hold them everywhere. Gather the faithful about you to recite the holy rosary, to meditate on my word, to renew and to live the consecration to my Immaculate Heart.

m   The more I will begin again to shine within the life of the Church, the more the darkness of error and infidelity will recede from it.

n   Courage! Take leave of this cenacle with my motherly blessing. And in times of greater danger, I will be your defense and your protection. Many evils will be spared you because of your response, so generous and fervent, in consecrating yourselves to my Immaculate Heart and in walking with me.

o   With you, I bless all my priest-sons and faithful of the surrounding countries, who are especially suffering and who are praying in the hope of an early liberation."

294
Strasbourg (France); September 13, 1984
Anniversary of the Fifth Apparition at Fatima
Spiritual Exercises in the Form of a Cenacle
with the Priests of the M.M.P. of the French Language

In Cenacle with Me

a   "Beloved sons, how happy I am with your homage of prayer and brotherhood, which you are offering to my Immaculate

Heart during these days of continuous cenacle. These are the times in which I wish my beloved priests and all the children consecrated to me to gather together in cenacles of prayer and life with me.

b   *In cenacle with me*, I form you to prayer, which now becomes necessary to employ increasingly as the weapon with which you must fight and conquer in the battle against Satan and all the spirits of evil who, in these times, have been unleashed with great violence. It is above all a battle which is waged at the level of spirits, and so you must fight with the spiritual weapon of prayer.

c   How much power you bring to my motherly work of intercession and reparation when, together, you pray the Liturgy of the Hours, the holy rosary and above all when you offer the Sacrifice of the new and eternal Covenant, through your daily celebration of the Eucharist.

d   *In cenacle with me*, I encourage you to continue along the difficult road of your times, in order to respond with joy and immense hope to the gift of your vocation.

e   In these times, how many of my priest-sons there are who find themselves more and more isolated, surrounded by so much indifference and lack of response, with such a great burden of work to carry out, and thus they are often overcome with weariness and discouragement.

f   Courage, my beloved sons! Jesus is always at your side and gives vigor and strength to your weariness, makes your work efficacious and causes everything you do in the exercise of your priestly ministry to be fruitful in graces. These abundant and wonderful fruits you will see only in paradise, and they will be an important part of the reward which awaits you.

g   *In cenacle with me*, I teach you to look on the evils of today with my motherly and merciful eyes, and I form you, because I wish you yourselves to become the remedy for these evils.

h   Above all in your countries, you see how the Church is violated by my Adversary, who is seeking to obscure it with error which is being accepted and taught, to wound it with moral permissiveness which leads many to justify everything and to live in sin, to paralyze it with the spirit of the world which has entered its interior and has also rendered fruitless many consecrated and priestly lives.

i   There are especially three wounds which, in your countries, cause my Immaculate Heart to suffer:

j   — *Catechesis*, which is frequently no longer in conformity with the truth which Jesus taught you and which the authentic Magisterium of the Church still sets forth for all to believe.

k   — *Secularism,* which has entered into the lives of so many of the baptized and especially so many of the priests who, in their souls, and in their way of living, of acting and even of dressing, behave, not as disciples of Christ, but according to the spirit of the world in which they live. If you only saw with my eyes how great this desolation is which has struck the Church!

l   — *The emptiness, the abandonment and the neglect,* with which Jesus present in the Eucharist is surrounded. Too many sacrileges are committed by those who no longer believe in the real presence of Jesus in the Eucharist and by those who go to Holy Communion in the state of mortal sin without any longer going to confession.

m   Beloved sons, you must be the medicine for these ills by your greater adhesion to the Magisterium of the Church, and thus may your unity of thought and of life with the Pope become ever greater.

n   Give to everyone an example of a holy, austere, recollected and mortified life. Bear in your body the marks of the passion of Jesus and, outwardly also, the sign of your consecration to Him, by always wearing your ecclesiastical garb. In all things, be opposed to the secularism which surrounds you, and have no fear if, like Jesus, you also for this reason become a cause for contradiction.

o   Be burning flames of adoration and of reparation to Jesus present in the Eucharist. Celebrate Holy Mass with love and with intimate participation of life. Go to confession often, and help the faithful to make frequent confessions. Make frequent hours of Eucharistic adoration, and bring all souls to the Heart of Jesus, who is the fount of grace and of divine mercy.

p   And so, *in cenacle with me*, you are preparing the second Pentecost which is about to come so that, through the irresistible power of the Spirit of Love, the Church may be healed and the whole world renewed."

295

Fatima (Portugal); September 20, 1984
Spiritual Exercises in the Form of a Cenacle
with the Priests of the M.M.P.
of the Portuguese and Spanish Languages

Be My Apostles

a   "How my so sorrowful Heart is consoled by this continuous cenacle, which you, beloved sons of Portugal and Spain, are holding with me during these days!

b   Be united in prayer. In this way, you give power to my motherly work of intercession and reparation; implore from the Father and the Son the gift of the Holy Spirit who will gently transform your entire life; you are of great assistance to many of your brothers, my beloved sons, whom Satan, particularly at this time, is ensnaring, wounding and deceiving.

c   Be united in brotherhood. Grow increasingly in your love for one another. Overcome the snares of my Adversary who, especially in your countries, is seeking to lead you into division, putting obstacles in the way of your brotherly understanding and mutual love, which I want you to live in a perfect way.

d   For this reason, I invite you to littleness, to humility, to docility, to simplicity. Be little children who allow themselves to be carried in my motherly arms, so that my plan may be carried out through you.

e   Be also courageous witnesses of your heavenly Mother. I want to be glorified in you. Through you I want to be increasingly honored. You are called to be my apostles in these very difficult times of yours.

f   *Be my apostles*, in living and spreading what I have told you, during these years. I myself am leading forward my work of the

406

Marian Movement of Priests, by means of all that I have told you through the book of my messages and the little son whom I have chosen as my instrument to spread it in every part of the world. May you all be more and more united to this son of mine; only in this way are you sure of walking in the light which I give you. You must be vigilant because, in your countries, my Adversary is seeking to do all he can to break up this unity of yours.

g   *Be my apostles*, in spreading everywhere the one and only light of Christ. Proclaim with courage and without fear the truth of the Gospel, which the Pope and the Magisterium of the Church continue to set forth for all to believe. And then give the example of a life which is in all things in conformity with the Gospel. I want to bring you to a great summit of holiness, to repel the attack of my Adversary who — especially in your countries — is seeking to obscure the Church with the secularism which has entered deeply into the life of so many of my consecrated sons and into many religious houses.

h   *Be my apostles*, in spreading my light and in leading everyone into the refuge of my Immaculate Heart.

i   How great is the work of Masonry and Communism which, in a hidden way, is being carried out for the destruction of my Church, which has always shone forth and flourished in your countries. Respond to these dark attacks by spreading my light everywhere. Give to all the security which I have prepared for you in view of the bloody days which are awaiting you: the refuge of my Immaculate Heart. Fight with prayer and penance; let the rosary be your victorious weapon.

j   I am the Queen of the Holy Rosary.

k   I am the Mother of Faith.

l   I am the Queen of Peace.

m   From this place, where I appeared as the Woman Clothed with the Sun, I bless all of you in the name of the Father, and of the Son, and of the Holy Spirit."

296　　　　*London (England); October 24, 1984*
Spiritual Exercises in the Form of a Cenacle
with the Priests of the M.M.P. of the English Language

Do Battle, Beloved Sons!

a　　"I welcome with joy the prayer and fraternal sharing which, during these days, brings you together in a cenacle of life with me, dear sons of my Movement from England and Ireland, this land which is so threatened today by my Adversary, but so loved and protected by me.

b　　I unite myself to your unceasing prayer, to obtain for you from the Father and the Son the gift of the Holy Spirit, that He may confirm you in your vocation, give courage to your apostolic action, efficacy to your work and consolation to your souls.

c　　Take courage, beloved sons of mine, because these are my times, and I am calling you, who form my cohort, to do battle for the triumph of my Son Jesus, in the triumph of love and of good.

d　　You are being formed by me to spread the light of Christ, of his truth and of his Gospel in these days of obscurity and darkness. You are being called to be my apostles in the difficult times in which you are living.

e　　*Do battle, my beloved ones, by means of love,* which must become ever greater within you, until it reaches the very dimensions of the divine charity of the Heart of my Son Jesus.

f　　You see how, in your countries, my Adversary is fighting above all with hatred, which brings division and discord, unbridled egoism and violence everywhere. And thus many of my children often fall victims to terrorism, and blood flows in your streets.

g　　You must make love and goodness triumph. Quench the fire of hatred with the dew of your priestly love. Become my instruments for building up unity and brotherhood around you. For this, approach all, but especially those who are most in need and most alienated, with the tenderness of my motherly love.

h　　*Do battle, my beloved ones, by means of prayer,* which must be made in union with me and must be offered to God as your most precious contribution for the salvation of the world.

i　　In these countries of yours, the Church is seen as still divided, although the problem of its unity is keenly felt by many. I bless the efforts which are being made on the part of so many to bring about the restoration of the unity of the Church. But I confide to you, my children, that this can only take place through a special miracle on the part of the Holy Spirit and through a special intervention of my Immaculate Heart.

j   For this I need much prayer. More is obtained through one day of intense prayer than through years of continuous discussions. Pray with faith and trust, with recollection and perseverance. Recite well the Liturgy of the Hours and the holy rosary, and let Holy Mass be the center of your apostolic day. Multiply everywhere the cenacles of prayer and fraternal sharing. I promise you that, after the triumph of my Immaculate Heart, these countries of yours will have the joy of seeing once again a renewed and united Church, which will reflect everywhere the splendor of Christ.

k   *Do battle, my beloved ones, by means of your personal immolation.* Give me all your sufferings. They are precious to me because I can offer them to Jesus, that they may be united to his perennial and priestly intercession for you.

l   Above all in these countries of yours, my Adversary is seducing you with the venom of neo-paganism and with an immorality which is spreading more and more and claiming victims among many of my children. How many young people are seduced by vice in their quest for all kinds of pleasure and, allured by the great spread of impurity and of drugs, live like sick people in need of help that they might be healed!

m   Your priestly sufferings are the effective remedy for so many wounds which today, in ever-increasing numbers, are afflicting my poor children. Because of this, I am calling you each day to a greater immolation.

n   May the peace of Jesus and my peace be in you. Live in peace of heart. Spread peace around you. I am the Queen of Peace. I am the Mother of Consolation.

o   Through you I bless today all my beloved ones and all those children who are consecrated to me, both in these countries of yours and throughout the whole world."

My Messages

a   "Beloved sons, today you have once again come up here to my shrine before my image which is so venerated because it is a sign of my very special presence among you. You have come here to invoke my protection on the Church, on the world and on the whole Marian Movement of Priests scattered throughout the world.

b   How pleased I am with the Holy Mass which you are celebrating in my honor! I desire that all the beloved sons of my Movement from all the five continents be spiritually present with you because my times have at last come.

c   In these years, as Mother, I have formed you *through my messages*. They are so many words of wisdom, which I have caused to come down from my Immaculate Heart to form you according to my plan. *My messages* trace out, above all, a simple and luminous way which I have pointed out to you and upon which you should travel, each day, in order to live the consecration which you have made to me, to grow in my love and in life with me and to be ever more mature and prepared to carry out the task which I have shown you.

d   If any, after having consecrated themselves to me, have come to a halt, it is because they have no longer listened to, meditated upon, or lived my messages. Oh, after my triumph, these messages will be a light for the whole Church; then all that I have done for you during these years will be understood!

e   Meditate on my messages, and live them. If you live what I have shown you and travel the road which I have traced out for you, you will walk securely along the way of the consecration which you have made to me, and you will bring to fulfillment the great plan of the triumph of my Immaculate Heart.

f   Otherwise, you will be halted by doubts, discouragement, difficulties and the opposition which you will encounter. You will come to a halt and will not be ready to accomplish what I have arranged for you and which today is so necessary for the salvation of the world and the renewal of the Church, whose Mother I am.

410

g *In these messages,* I also reveal to you my plan in its silent preparation, in its painful realization and in its victorious fulfillment. You are already about to reach the most painful and bloody conclusion of the purification which will take place in these years, before the great triumph of my Immaculate Heart in the coming to you of the glorious reign of Jesus.

h This is a plan which embraces this century. In 1917 at Fatima, I anticipated it, as in a prophetic announcement, at the moment when the great struggle between the Woman Clothed with the Sun and the Red Dragon became evident, a struggle which was to last throughout the whole century, as a proud challenge to God on the part of my Adversary, who was certain that he would succeed in destroying the Church and in bringing all humanity to a universal rejection of God. The Lord has granted him this space of time, because in the end the pride of the Red Dragon will be broken and conquered by the humility, the littleness, and the power of your heavenly Mother, the Woman Clothed with the Sun, who is now gathering all her little children into her army, drawn up for battle.

i Now that you are coming to the most painful and bloody years of this great struggle, I have intervened personally in order to form for myself my cohort through the Marian Movement of Priests, which is my work. For this I have chosen as my instrument a son from among the weakest and, humanly speaking, least gifted, and I have brought him to every part of the world to show to all that what is to take place is due solely to my personal and extraordinary intervention.

j However do not be afraid, son, of the difficulties which you encounter when it seems to you that some instrument chosen by me, deceived by Satan, no longer wishes to respond to my plan. Have confidence in me; I alone am the Leader of my cohort; I alone am the Mother and Queen of my Movement. I make use of the instruments who respond to me; I choose others when those who have been chosen by me no longer respond.

k I myself am leading this work forward each day for the great battle which we are fighting..."

411

298

Zagreb (Yugoslavia); November 14, 1984
Spiritual Exercises in the Form of a Cenacle
with the Priests of the M.M.P.
of the Slovenian and Croatian Languages

My Urgent Invitation

a   "Beloved sons, I joyfully welcome this continuous cenacle of priestly fraternity and of prayer, which you are making together with me, your heavenly Mother.

b   You are in this land where my children are in pain and carrying the burden of innumerable sufferings, in this land which is so threatened by my Adversary and yours but which is so loved and protected by me. I spread over all of you my luminous mantle, and I enclose you in the sure refuge of my Immaculate Heart.

c   Through you, beloved sons, I want to spread everywhere in these countries of the East, my urgent and heartfelt message, so that it may reach all my children.

d   *I am the Queen of Peace.*

e   Never before as today has the human race been so threatened by the danger of war and of an immense destruction. Look to me as to her who has the task from God of bringing peace to the world.

f   For this, I invite you to beg for it through a prayer which is continuous, trusting and always made with me. Above all, recite the holy rosary. In this way you can obtain from the Lord the great grace of changing hearts, that all may open themselves to sentiments of love and of goodness. Thus peace can enter into the hearts of men and then be spread into families, nations and the whole world.

g   *I am the Mother of Consolation.*

h   In these so troubled times, I am taking my place at the side of each one of you, to share in the difficult moments of your life. I am at your side when you pray and work, when you walk and rest, when you rejoice and suffer.

i   It is to give you a sure sign of my motherly presence and to give you joy and comfort in the midst of your many sorrows, that I myself have chosen this land in which to appear in a new way, more prolonged and more extraordinary. The pure of heart know how to see me; the poor, the little, the simple know how to listen to me; the humble, the sick and the sinners know how to find me.

j   If there are difficulties or obstacles which make it impossible for you to come to the place of my apparitions, do not be saddened. When you pray and do penance and listen to my motherly invitation to walk along the way of conversion and of love, you come to meet spiritually with your heavenly Mother, who thus manifests herself, present in your midst.

k   *I am the Mother of Trust.*

l   In these times, how many of my poor children there are who have distanced themselves from God, because they become victims of the error of atheism, so widespread today, sustained and propagated through all the means of social communication! Innumerable is the company of those who walk in the darkness of the rejection of God, of the lack of faith, of immorality, of injustice, and of impiety. Evil is covering the whole earth like a thick coat of ice, and the cup of divine justice is already full and flowing over.

m   And now I am revealing myself to you to show you the road of salvation: it is the road of return to God. If humanity does not accept my motherly invitation to return to the Lord, it will be inevitably lost. And so I repeat again to you this, my heartfelt message: walk along the road of your return to the Lord. Be converted because, for yet a little while, this is the favorable time of conversion. Be converted, and return to your God.

n   From here, through you, I bless all my children who live in these countries, so loved and protected by me because they must bear great trials and sufferings: those of Yugoslavia, Albania, Bulgaria, Rumania, Hungary, Czechoslovakia, East Germany, Poland, Russia and the whole world, whom I want to enclose as soon as possible in the sure refuge of my Immaculate Heart."

The Will of God

a   "Today you are sharing, beloved sons, in the joy of Paradise, which exults in the contemplation of your heavenly Mother, so filled with privileges, with graces and with the fullness of holiness by her Lord, whose least servant she feels herself to be.

b   The exemption from every stain of sin, even from the original one, has made my life a pure reflection of the life of God. Thus my soul was filled with grace, and its powers were always directed to carrying out the divine plan in a perfect way. My mind was opened to seek and love the Will of God, and my Heart was impelled, with joy and complete abandonment, to fulfill only the divine Will.

c   This is the road which today I want to point out to you also, for you to journey along, if you wish to follow your heavenly Mother in her plan of immaculate purity and of sanctity.

d   *The Will of God*: this is where, even for you, sanctification is achieved! It is the Will of God that, in your lives, you walk along the road of an ever more perfect knowledge of Him. Let the word of God be the daily food with which you nourish your spirit. Seek this word in the sacred book of Divine Scripture; savor all its beauty in the Gospel of my Son Jesus. Through the wisdom which I am giving you, I am leading you to understand more profoundly the secret of Holy Scripture, so that you may fathom it, delight in it, guard it and live it.

e   The Word of God became Flesh and Life in Jesus Christ, who is the revelation of the Father, the Image of his substance, and the reflection of his glory. The Will of God is carried out through you only by your following, with love and complete trust, my Son Jesus. Jesus must be much more loved, listened to and followed by you, his brothers, his ministers, and my beloved sons.

f   The more you penetrate into the deep mystery of his divine love, as into a blazing furnace, the more you will be purified from sin, from frailty, from miseries, and from all your impurities. If you love and follow Jesus, you too will always walk along the road of an immaculate purity and of a great sanctity. When you happen to fall again into sin, his mercy will set you free and, in the sacrament of Reconciliation, will restore you to the life of grace and of intimate union with Him.

g   When discouragement takes hold of you, the bond with Him which is established in prayer and especially in the Eucharist will give you strength and infuse you with new energy for good. When aridity threatens you, communion with Him will open you up to new and profound experiences of love and joy. Then you too will carry out the divine Will, which is that of living to know, love and serve the Father, in a profound intimacy of life with the Son, whose mystery will become ever increasingly revealed to you in its fullness by the Holy Spirit.

h   Thus you will respond to the plan which I have for you for the triumph of my Immaculate Heart, which is carried out only in the reign of love, justice and peace of my Son Jesus. By his divine mercy all evil, sin and impurity will be washed away in such a way that the renewed world will be able to sing again the glory of the Lord."

300

Everything Has Already Been Revealed

a   "Beloved sons, be recollected with me in prayer during these hours which precede the birth of my Baby Jesus. Live in my Immaculate Heart the moments of the holy night. Follow me along the way of incessant prayer so that it may become a colloquy of love, of trust, and of filial abandonment to the plan of salvation of the Lord our God.

b   This abandonment carried me on the wave of a joyous experience of the presence of my Son, of which I was aware in a most powerful way, because the moment of his birth in time had come. My journey toward Bethlehem became nothing but a sweet and motherly bowing down to his divine wish to come and live among you as a brother. And I spoke with Him in a conversation made up of silence and listening, contemplation and love, adoration and expectation.

c   Thus unceasing prayer enwrapped the long journey, undertaken in order to reach the hospitable grotto, and there it became even more intense and more recollected, to the point of
lifting the veil which separated me from entering into a profound ecstasy with heaven, from which I emerged with my divine Baby already born.

d   Follow me along the road of a suffering understood, welcomed,
and lived by me, as a humble response to what, at this time, the
Lord was asking of me. An interior suffering, brought about by
unfolding circumstances, which presented themselves to me as a
claim on my motherly collaboration with his plan of love.

e   The necessity of abandoning the house in Nazareth, which
had been made ready with such care, the exhausting journey to
Bethlehem in my condition of motherhood already brought to
term, the uncertainty of that which we were to find there, the
refusal to put us up in any house, the squalid shelter in a freezing
cave: all these things were like so many thorns which pierced
my motherly Heart. But I understood that this suffering was
asked of me by the Father, in order to prepare a more precious
cradle for my Child who was about to be born.

f   Now I ask of you also, my beloved children, prayer and suffering, as your personal collaboration in preparing a fitting dwelling
place for Jesus who is about to return in glory.

g   Understand the meaning of my motherly interventions, which
today have become more frequent, extraordinary, and urgent.
On this holy night, my message, which I give you as heavenly
prophetess of the last times, appears clearer to you.

h   Prepare yourselves for the second birth of Jesus in glory: He is
about to come to reign in your midst. The ways by which He
will come are those of prayer and suffering. Already these are
the times in which you must all recollect yourselves in a continuous and trusting prayer, as was mine during the long journey
made to Bethlehem.

i   The time for projects and discussions is over.

j   *For those who wish to listen and understand, everything has now
already been revealed.*

k   The hearts of men have been dried up by hatred and sin; nations and people are rebelling against their God, and a great dark-

ness is surrounding them; humanity no longer wishes to throw open the doors for Christ, who is coming. So then let the poor caves of your hearts be opened which, in the deep night, must blaze in the light of an unshakable faith, of a sure hope and of a burning love.

l   And suffer with patience and with trust. As for me, so also for you, the sufferings which the Lord asks of you form part of a loving plan of his. The pangs must increase for everyone, the closer his new birth approaches. Accept them just as your heavenly Mother did.

m   Walk in the light of the star, which tells you that the time has already come in which the prophetic announcements that have already been given you during these years are coming to pass. And live each hour of your life in the greatest trust and in the joyous expectation of the glorious return of my Son Jesus."

301

The Signs of Your Time

a   "Beloved sons, pass the final hours of the year, which is about to close, in sweet intimacy with me.

b   How many of my children spend these moments in amusements and clamor and are inebriated with emptiness amidst so many frivolities and diversions which are often licentious and against the Law of the Lord!...

c   I invite you on the contrary to spend these hours in prayer, in recollection, and in interior silence, so that you may enter into a conversation with me, your heavenly Mother. Then, with the same familiarity that a mother has for her children, I will reveal to you the cares, the anxieties and the deep wounds of my Immaculate Heart, and, at the same time, *I will help you to understand and to interpret the signs of your times.*

d   Thus you can cooperate in the plan of salvation, which the Lord has for you and which He wishes to carry out in the course of the new days which await you.

e   —You are living under an urgent request made by your heavenly Mother, who is inviting you to walk along the road of conversion and of return to God. Beloved children, share in my anxious motherly concern as I see that this call of mine is neither welcomed nor followed. And yet I see that the only possibility of your salvation is bound up uniquely with the return of humanity to the Lord, with a strong commitment to follow his Law.

f   Be converted, and walk along the road of the grace of God and of love. Be converted, and build up days of serenity and peace. Be converted, and take part in the plan of divine mercy.

g   With how many signs has the Lord manifested to you his Will to at last put a fitting halt to the flood of impiety: incurable diseases which are spreading, violence and hatred which are exploding, misfortunes which are occurring, wars and threats which are spreading. Know how to read the signs which God is sending you through the events which are taking place and accept his strong admonitions to change your life and to return along the road which leads you to Him.

h   —You are living under your heavenly Mother's concerned and constant request to remain in the true faith. And yet I see, with anguish, that errors continue to be spread, taught, and propagated. The danger of losing the precious gift of faith in Jesus and in the truth which He revealed to you is thus becoming ever greater among my children. Even among my chosen ones, how great is the number of those who doubt or who no longer believe.

i   If you only saw with my eyes how vast this spiritual epidemic is which has struck the entire Church: it brings its apostolic action to a halt, wounds it and paralyzes its vitality, often even making its effort at evangelization empty and ineffective.

j   —You are living under my very painful anxiety as I see that you are still the victims of widespread sin. I observe how, by the means of social communications, experiences of life contrary to those indicated by God's holy Law are being proposed to my poor children everywhere. Every day you are being fed with the poisoned bread of evil and given to drink at the polluted spring of impurity. Evil is being proposed to you as something good, sin as a value, and transgression of the Law of God as a way of exercising your autonomy and your personal freedom.

k   And so you arrive at losing even the consciousness of sin as an evil, and injustice, hatred and impiety cover the earth and make of it an immense desert, deprived of life and love. The obstinate rejection of God and of return to Him, the loss of the true faith and the iniquity which is spreading and leading to the diffusion of evil and sin: *these are the signs of the evil time through which you are living.*

l   But at the same time see in how many ways I am intervening to lead you along the road of conversion, of goodness and of faith. With extraordinary signs which I am giving in every part of the world, through my messages and through my so frequent apparitions, I am pointing out to everyone the approaching of the great day of the Lord.

m   But how much sorrow my Immaculate Heart feels in seeing that these admonitions of mine are not heeded and are frequently and openly rejected and opposed, even by those who have the duty of being the first to accept them. For this reason, I am revealing myself today only to the little ones, to the poor, to the simple, to all my children who still know how to listen to me and follow me.

n   Now, as never before, I have need of a great force of supplication and reparation. For this reason, I am turning to you, beloved children, and inviting you to spend the hours of this last night of the year on your knees in a continuous prayer with me."

1985

I AM THE BEGINNING OF THE NEW TIMES

I Am the Beginning of the New Times

a   "Beloved children, you are united today with the whole Church in venerating me as true Mother of God and your Mother, in the order of the supernatural life of faith and of divine grace.

b   On this day, which for you marks the beginning of a new year, while all of you in the Church — bishops, priests, religious and faithful — look to me as to your Mother, I say to you if that is what I am and if you honor me as such, I must be loved, listened to, and followed by each one of you.

c   And so it is today, on the solemnity of my Divine Maternity, that I wish to give a message to the Church to be heard and welcomed by her.

d   *It is a message of trust and of hope.*

e   Notwithstanding the difficulties and the sufferings which the Church is called upon to bear, and the painful hours of agony and of passion which mark the time of her bloody purification, the moment of a renewed splendor and of a second Pentecost is in preparation for her.

f   My dearly beloved children, never lose confidence and hope. Beneath the great and vast clamor which evil is managing to spread everywhere, many sprouts of goodness and holiness are budding forth in silence and hiddenness. These precious sprouts of new life are being daily cultivated in the secret garden of my Immaculate Heart.

g   However be on your guard against three serious dangers which are threatening your growth in goodness and which have been pointed out to you by me many times: that of departing from the true faith by following the many errors which are being taught today; that of separating yourselves from the interior unity of the Church through contestation directed against the Pope and the hierarchy, which is still spreading within ecclesial life; and that of falling victims to secularism and moral permissiveness, which leads you to yield in the daily struggle against evil and sin.

h   If you allow yourselves to be led by me, you walk along the sure road of love and of holiness.

i *It is a message of comfort and of consolation.*

j Entrust yourselves, all of you, to your heavenly Mother that you may be consoled. In the great battle which you are fighting, find strength and comfort there, and never lose your courage in the face of the difficulties which you meet.

k During the new year, the trials and sufferings which await you will become even greater, because you have already entered into the final phase of what I have foretold to you. A great and bloody trial is about to shake the whole earth, to prepare it for its complete renewal in the triumph of my Immaculate Heart.

l But the more severe the trial will become, the greater will be my presence at the side of each one of you, that you may be comforted and encouraged by me. If you live in my Immaculate Heart, nothing that can happen will be able to disturb you; within this motherly refuge of mine, you are always safe, wrapped in the light and the presence of the Most Holy Trinity, who loves you and surrounds you with its divine protection.

m *It is a message of salvation and of mercy.*

n You must be my powerful help, which I wish to offer today to all humanity in order to lead it to return along the road of goodness and of love.

o I am the way of this, its return. I am the doorway of divine mercy. I desire that, through you, all my lost children may be able to come back to the Lord, who awaits them with the anxiety and the joy of a Father who loves them and wants to save them. Thus you become also instruments of divine mercy, in these times in which the greatest triumph of the merciful love of my Son Jesus is in preparation.

p It is in order to be your trust, your consolation, and your salvation in the last times through which you are living, that I am manifesting myself today in such a powerful way, through the messages which I am giving, by means of this little son of mine and the apparitions which I am carrying out in a continuous and extraordinary way in many parts of the world.

q Believe in my invitations; accept my messages; and look at my signs! I am the Queen of Peace; I am the beginning of the new times; I am the dawn of the new day.

r With the Pope, the first of my beloved sons, I bless you all today in the name of the Father, and of the Son, and of the Holy Spirit."

I See Your Littleness

a   "Beloved children, contemplate me in the mystery of the Presentation of my Child Jesus in the Temple. I want to reveal to you today what the sentiments were which filled my Heart as I passed my Child, forty days after his birth, from my arms into those of the priest.

b   *My Heart burned with gratitude* towards the Lord, who had at last fulfilled the plan of salvation for his people. For how many centuries had this moment been awaited! With my soul I saw the face of the Father, bending down with pleasure, while the Holy Spirit came down upon some of those present and revealed to their minds the hidden plan of the Lord.

c   *My Heart beat violently with ineffable motherly love,* in the contemplation of the whole of divinity enclosed in the members, so tiny, of my Baby, who was only forty days old.

d   *My Heart exulted with joy* at the moment when the Lord entered the temple, and I felt that the vast cohorts of angels and all the heavenly spirits were accompanying Him, as He was led to take possession of his dwelling place.

e   *My Heart was also wounded with sorrow* at the prophetic voice of old Simeon, who announced to me how my motherly mission was also a call to a profound suffering, to an intimate and personal participation in the sorrowful mission of my Son Jesus.

f   With these same sentiments I am leading you, dear children, each day to the altar of the Lord, to help you fulfill well his divine Will. 'Sacrifice and offering you did not desire, but a body you have prepared for me; I have come to do your Will, O God.' (cf. Heb 10:5-7)

g   I am filled with gratitude to my Son Jesus because, through you who have responded to me, I am able today to carry out my motherly plan of preparing the greatest triumph of his merciful love. I feel my Heart filled with love for you who, through your consecration, have offered yourselves to me as little children.

h   I see your littleness; I look upon your weakness and fragility and at the innumerable snares set for you by my Adversary. I see you as so small that you are not even able to take a single step without my motherly help. For this reason I stoop over you with the renewed tenderness of a mother.

i   I am happy too with the great degree of generosity with which you have responded to me. You have said *yes* to my request for consecration; you have offered me your entire life, that I might freely intervene to order it according to my plan, which is the Will of the Lord.

j   Finally, I am also sorrowful because, as for Jesus so also for you, the mission which awaits you is that of suffering and of immolation. It is above all by means of this that I am able to offer to the Father, to the Son and to the Holy Spirit a great force of imploration and of reparation, so that the golden door of divine mercy may be soon opened, and the greatest miracle of complete transformation of the world be accomplished.

k   For this reason, beloved children, each day, on my grateful Heart, happy and at the same time sorrowful, I carry you to the temple of the Lord and place you upon his altar, so that you may be offered to the perfect fulfillment of his divine Will."

304   *Shrine of Castelmonte (Udine, Italy); February 9, 1985*
(After the recitation of the holy rosary)

My Word

a   "Beloved children, you have come to my shrine in a spirit of prayer and of reparation. On pilgrimage, you have come up here, where I await you to fill you with graces, with comfort and with motherly consolation.

b   Each time you come to the feet of my image, so venerated, to bring me your filial homage of love, I cause many graces to come down from my Immaculate Heart upon you, upon all my beloved children throughout the world, upon the Church, upon my poor sinful children, and upon humanity which is so threatened by evil, by hatred, by violence, and by war and which is dried up by sin and by an ever more widespread immorality.

c   In this House, your heavenly Mother consoles and encourages you, molds and leads you, strengthens and confirms you by the word which she gives you to show you the way. Oh! How necessary is my motherly word for you today! For this reason I cause it to gush forth from my Heart in an ever more abundant manner. Feel a great desire for it; receive it with humility and docility; meditate upon it in your heart; put it into practice in your life.

d   *My word is above all a flower of wisdom*, which I cause to come down from heaven. It sets out from the eternal Wisdom, from the Word. It is He who is the uncreated Wisdom, who reveals the plan of the Father whose perfect image He is. This Wisdom, made flesh in my virginal womb, from Word became man, and has the task of always giving men the gift of eternal Truth. This divine word, contained in Holy Scripture and above all in the Gospel, is the only light which must guide you.

e   But today it is being surrounded by many doubts, because there is a desire to interpret it according to the human way of reasoning and of seeing things, and is often no longer presented in its integrity. Errors are spreading, and, when you come to the plan of God, you are impeded from understanding it in its fullness, because you are making use of an attitude which is too human and which seeks to understand only by means of reason. This is an attitude of pride, and it is the very least to be recommended for approaching the great mystery of God.

f   To understand his truth, it is necessary to be little; to see it in its proper light, it is necessary to be poor; to keep it in its integrity, one must be simple; to give it to others in the splendor of its authenticity, one must be humble. For this reason, with my word, I am forming you to humility, to simplicity and to littleness. I want to lead you to be like so many little children, because only then can I speak to you.

g   My word is a flower of wisdom, which forms you through the Holy Spirit, given to you by the Father and the Son and who leads you to an ever more complete and deep understanding of the Gospel. In the obscurity which today has fallen everywhere, my word of wisdom becomes a ray of purest light which points out to you the way you must follow and the road along which you must go in order to remain always in the truth.

h   Darkness, with a thick, cold fog, has entered the Church, obscuring it in the splendor of its truth. For this reason, every day, my word is forming you to the spirit of wisdom, that you may always see, in the light, the truth which my Son has taught you and proclaim it with courage to all in its integrity.

i The time has now come when only the little children, consecrated to my Immaculate Heart and entrusted completely to their heavenly Mother, will have the gift of keeping themselves intact in the faith and of bringing to the true faith the souls entrusted to them.

j *My word is also a drop of dew*, which I cause to fall upon the earth, which has become an immense desert, and upon human life, so dried up by sin and suffering. How many of my children are like dried up trees without life; and in the Church, how many among my beloved ones have allowed themselves to be seized by aridity and discouragement! They continue to exercise their ministry but without enthusiasm and without joy, because they have become hindered by difficulties and become crushed by the enormous weight of the purification which you are living through.

k You have need for my word to cause a rain of motherly tenderness to fall into your dried-up hearts, a rain of freshness, of filial abandonment and of hope for the beautiful days which await you, in the new era, which is even now about to blossom upon the desert of the last times. My word is therefore like a drop of dew which I cause to fall from my Immaculate Heart into your hearts, that they may be able to open up to the warmth of the new life which I am cultivating within you, to offer you as fragrant flowers, now finally opened, to the perfect homage of the Most Holy Trinity.

l *My word is lastly a spring of graces*, which I cause to flow over you, to open up your souls to a new splendor of beauty and holiness and to cleanse you also, once again, of every least stain of sin, because I want you to be beautiful, pure and luminous, opened to the divine gift of grace, so that the fullness of love and of the most perfect charity may blossom in your life. My graces come to you through the gift of my word, which becomes light to the mind, life to the heart, and support for your journey.

m In the fearful and bloody final period of the purification which awaits you and which, in these very years, will make itself felt in a particularly painful way, I am preparing you to receive, with

427

greater docility, the motherly gift of my word. Thus, in the midst of great darkness, you are able to walk in the light of wisdom; in aridity you can always be consoled by my tenderness, a balm which is placed on so many open and bleeding wounds. In every circumstance of your life, you can obtain the grace of responding to the love of Jesus and of singing today the glory of the Divine Trinity, walking along the road of a holiness which I want to be ever greater.

n   In these very years of the great purification, I want to offer you to the Church as an ever more visible sign of my motherly triumph."

305   *Shrine of Castelmonte (Udine, Italy); February 14, 1985*
(After the recitation of the holy rosary)

My Purity and Yours

a   "My beloved children, I have wanted you here today, on a brilliant day, with a blue sky, a warm sun and the snow which gives a tone of purity to the high mountains which form a crown for this place, from which rises the blessed house of your heavenly Mother. I enfold you with my motherly rays; I enlighten you with the light which comes from my Immaculate Heart; I cover you with my heavenly mantle to make you also ever purer.

b   *I am the Mother of Purity.* I am the ever Virgin Mother. I am Immaculate Whiteness, the Splendor of Heaven which reflects the light of the Most Holy Trinity upon the world, the dawn which puts an end to night, the Mother of Grace who drives away every sin from you, the Medicine of Paradise which, like soothing balm, closes up all your wounds.

c   *I am the all-beautiful Mother: tota pulchra, tota pulchra!*

d   *Mine is above all a purity of mind.* Oh, my reason was always directed to seeking, to meditating upon, to keeping and to living the Will of the Lord! His word was received by me with docility and with virginity; I was always diligent in understanding it and keeping it in its entirety. Throughout my whole life, not even the slightest shadow of a doubt or of an error ever grazed the virginal integrity of my mind, which was open only to receive the gift of divine wisdom.

e   This purity of mind was the road that led me to a *deeper purity of heart*. My Heart was completely formed to receive the love of God and to give it back to Him, with the virginal and motherly impulse of a creature cultivated in the garden of the Trinity, in the divine sun of a love received and exchanged in a perfect manner.

f   No human heart has ever loved nor will it ever be able to love, as has that of your heavenly Mother. It opened up like a flower which unfolds its petals to shed all about it the brightness, beauty, and fragrance of heaven. For this reason I was able to form the flesh and the blood for Him who is the Lily of the Valley and who loves, in a special way, the pure of heart.

g   I was also the purest in love of neighbor. After Jesus, no creature has been able to love humanity as has the Heart of your Mother; in this perfect love toward all is to be found the intimate source from which there springs the working of my divine and universal motherhood.

h   From purity of heart, enter yet further with me into the innermost depths of my life to discover *how I was pure in soul*.

i   The soul becomes impure when it is darkened or beclouded by even the least shadow of sin. The slightest stain of venial sin defiles its whiteness and causes the enchantment of its light to fade and be spoiled.

j   I, through a singular privilege, was preserved from original sin and was filled with grace. Throughout my whole life, my soul was never, not even for an instant, touched by sin, even venial sin; it has ever been all light, all beautiful, all pure.

k   If every soul created by God, being spiritual and raised to the state of sharing in his divine nature, reflects the light of the Trinity, you can understand how no soul will ever be able to reflect, as in a perfectly clear mirror, the splendor of the Father, of the Son, and of the Holy Spirit, as has the soul of your heavenly Mother.

l   The wrapping which was to enclose the precious treasure of a perfect purity of mind, of heart, and of soul was *to be this body of mine*. And so then my body too was completely wrapped by a light of inviolate purity.

_m_   *I have been pure in body*, not only through having always kept it intact from the slightest sin of impurity, but also because the Lord has willed to make his divine masterpiece shine forth in it in a marvelous way. My body, which, through its function of motherhood, had to be opened at the moment of the gift of the Son and to break the enchantment of its integrity, through a singular privilege remained intact. Thus I was able to give you my Son, while the virginal wrapping, by means of which even at the moment of my gift of motherhood I remained *ever a virgin*, remained intact:

_n_   Virgin before birth, because that which took place in me was solely the work of the Holy Spirit;

_o_   Virgin during birth, because that which was accomplished at that moment was the working of the Most Holy Trinity — enwrapped by the light of God and by his secret, before Him alone took place the miraculous birth of my divine Son;

_p_   Virgin after birth, because nothing ever disturbed the inviolate charm of my most pure body, called to guard my immaculate soul, so that in the person of your heavenly Mother there should be able to shine out, in a perfect way, the most holy splendor of the Divine Trinity.

_q_   Defend this privilege of mine, which is denied by many today in a facile and banal manner; defend it always.

_r_   And I ask all of you as well to be pure.

_s_   How great is my suffering when I see that, today, this virtue is no longer taught and cultivated in the hearts of the young and of adolescents, and even of those who are consecrated to God. In the name of a false freedom, they are led into experiences which take this delight of paradise from their souls.

_t_   How sorrowful is your heavenly Mother today as she sees so many priestly and consecrated lives dried up through impurity, which has spread everywhere like a terrible cancer! This is why you are no longer able to understand the plan of God and to be so simple and small as to listen with docility also to the voice of your heavenly Mother.

_u_   Only to the pure are the mysteries of the reign of God revealed:

_v_   —The pure of mind, because they know how to recognize

430

his plan and to accept it with humility,

w —The pure of heart, because they are detached from goods, from creatures and from their own way of seeing things, which impedes one from receiving my light because one wants to filter and judge it through one's own human and limited intelligence,

x —The pure of soul, who flee the least shadow of sin, because it obscures the light of God within you and makes you unable to accept his divine mystery,

y —The pure of body, because, consecrating it to God in celibacy and in the vow of chastity, it becomes more conformed to that of Jesus Crucified and enlightened by the immaculate light which clothes my glorious body.

z Beloved children, I want you all to be pure of mind, of heart, of soul, and of body in imitation of your all-beautiful heavenly Mother. Then, upon the world of today, so permeated with coldness and hatred, you will be the light of the sun, coming down to warm souls and open them up to the life of God. Amidst the threatening clouds which have appeared upon humanity's present moment, you open up a clear blue patch in the sky. Over the rotting and putrid swamp to which the world has been reduced, you will be a mirror of purity; in it the world will be reflected and will be helped to be slowly transformed into a new garden.

A Only in this way, beloved children of mine, will you be able to become the rays which shine down from my Immaculate Heart to light up the terrible time of purification through which you are living, and to give to everyone the sure sign of my presence and of my victory.

B I bless you in the name of the Father, and of the Son, and of the Holy Spirit."

306

Dongo (Como, Italy); March 16, 1985
A Saturday of Lent

The Fast Which I Ask of You

a "Walk along the road of penance and of mortification.

431

b *I am asking of you a bodily fast* as a means of mortifying your senses, in order to ward off the widespread deceit by which so many of my children are being seduced today, driven as they are to seek happiness only in the complete satisfaction of bodily and material pleasures.

c How many there are who are nourished with the poison food of impurity and drugs! How the putrid sore of immoral literature and pornography is spreading! The means of social communication are often becoming instruments for the moral corruption of consciences, for the diffusion of vice and obscenity, and for sin which is now proposed as a good and as something of value.

d For this reason I am asking you, my beloved ones and children consecrated to me, to provide me with a great force of reparation, with which I will form a dam against the flooding of so contagious and dangerous an evil. I am asking of you a bodily fast in order to mortify your senses, so as to witness today to the necessity of putting a limit to the mad quest for pleasure. By your good example you must teach that 'man does not live by bread alone, but by every word which comes from the mouth of God.' (Mt 4:4)

e *I am asking of you a spiritual fast* from every form of evil, so that you may be nourished only by what is good, by grace and by love. The food which is the word of God nourishes you spiritually and gives strength to your existence in the life of grace. I am requesting of you a fast of the mind, preserving it from every error as you welcome the truth which Jesus has revealed to you.

f Nourish yourselves — I tell you again — with the precious food of divine Scripture, above all with the Gospel of Jesus. Receive, meditate upon and live the messages which today, in so many ways, your heavenly Mother, as well, is giving you.

g For this, you must be careful to reject all ideologies which are contrary to your faith and which contain subtle and dangerous errors and so much damage your growth in fidelity to the commitments assumed at the time of baptism.

h *I am asking of you a fast of the heart,* closing it to disordinate attachment to yourselves, to goods, and to creatures.

i How many there are who can only think of themselves and

432

who allow themselves to be devoured by an unbridled egoism, which closes them up to any possibility of true communion with others! How many are slaves to a mad attachment to goods and to money, which they seek as the only object of their lives, and they become consumed with avarice, which is the source of many other vices and sins! And thus they close their hearts to the tremendous needs of the little people, of the poor and the marginalized; they are unable to see those who are in difficulties and are in need of being helped.

j   *I am asking of you a fast of the soul,* by keeping it far from any sin even the least, so that it may be nourished only by the life of grace and by the light of God. Flee mortal sin as the greatest of all evils; make your examination of conscience every day; allow yourselves to be led with docility by the Spirit. Let the custom, which is so very useful, of frequent confession, return.

k   Flee also from the easy occasions of sin. For this, I ask you to close your eyes and ears to television and to the cinema, in order to preserve your soul in the light of purity and of grace.

l   If you carry out this fast which I am asking of you, you will build about yourselves a strong barrier against the flood of evil and of sin, and you will offer to the Lord a holocaust of immolation and of reparation, to obtain the return to Him of many of my poor sinful children.

m   In this way you will become instruments of my peace; you will spread about you peace of heart, walking along the road which your heavenly Mother has traced out for you."

307

The Hour of a New Agony

a   "Beloved sons, live these hours in the depths of my Immaculate Heart, that you may be able to penetrate with me into the blazing furnace of the infinite and merciful love of my Son Jesus. During his life, how much He awaited this moment! 'I have greatly desired to eat this Passover with you before I suffer.' (Lk 22:15) It is Holy Thursday.

b   *It is the day of the institution of the Eucharist.* This great Sacrament allows Him to be really present in your midst, to renew mystically his Sacrifice of the new and eternal Covenant and to give Himself in a personal communion of life with you.

c   *It is also the day of the institution of the priesthood.* It is perpetuated through his commandment given to the Apostles and to those who succeed them in the exercise of the sacred ministry: 'Do this in memory of me.' (Lk 22:19)

d   *It is your day, beloved sons.* The heavenly Mother looks upon you with particular and sorrowful concern at the moment when, reunited in concelebration about your bishops, you renew the commitments assumed on the day of your priestly ordination.

e   How many are the dangers which surround you, the obstacles which my Adversary places in your way, the seductions of the world in which you live, the difficulties which weigh upon the faithful exercise of your ministry.

f   The institution of the Eucharist was immediately followed by the terrible and bloody agony of Gethsemane during which Jesus was left alone, at the moment when He had the greatest need of assistance and comfort, felt the bitter abandonment by his own, and was betrayed by Judas and denied by Peter.

g   Today, among my beloved ones, how many there are who flee from and abandon Jesus and the Church, seduced by the easy attractions of the world in which they live… How many of them betray Him, driven on by the desire to be more accepted and followed, in greater harmony with the tastes and ideologies of your time. How many repeat the gesture of Peter, who denied the Master out of cowardice and fear. This is for many the fear of not appearing up-to-date and in line with the cultural demands which are fashionable today.

h   On this Holy Thursday, allow your heavenly Mother to gather you into the sheepfold of her Immaculate Heart to form you to be ever more faithful to Jesus and to his Gospel. Be humble, strong, courageous. Do not allow yourselves to be seized either by fear or by discouragement. The night of error, of apostasy, and of infidelity has already descended upon the world and into the Church.

434

i   The Mystical Body of Jesus is living through the hour of a new painful agony. For this reason, there are repeated again today, in a much greater way, the same things that were done at that time: the abandonment, the denial, the betrayal.

j   You, O little sons formed in the Immaculate Heart of your heavenly Mother, must, like the Apostle John, keep watch in prayer and in trust during the painful hours of this new Holy Thursday."

308

Dongo (Como, Italy); April 5, 1985
Good Friday

Your Sorrowful Passion

a   "The cross for you, O son, is the Will of the Father, which you carry out well only if, at each moment, you second the plan of my Immaculate Heart.

b   Carry your cross each day, and never depart from the divine Will. Your wounds are the misunderstandings, the doubts, the perplexities and the numerous abandonments. These are the real wounds of the soul, which no one sees, more precious than gold, the blood from which I am always gathering up to water the garden of the dried up and thirsty souls of your brother-priests.

c   Your climb to Calvary is the journey you must undertake for me, advancing alone and full of trust, in the midst of your many fears and the proud skepticism of those who surround you and who do not believe. The immense weariness which you feel, that sense of exhaustion which so prostrates you, is your thirst. The scourges and the blows are the snares and the painful temptations of my Adversary.

d   The cries of condemnation are the venomous serpents which obstruct your way and the briars which pierce your frail body of a child, which has been struck so many times.

e   The abandonment to which I am calling you is the bitter taste of feeling yourself to be ever more alone, far from friends and disciples, rejected sometimes even by your most fervent followers.

f   But at your side is the sorrowful Mother; together with her, live out, with love and trust, *your sorrowful passion*, which no one is able to see, but which consumes you each day, as a victim immolated by me for all your brother-priests.

g   Your death is the very great silence, the hiddenness, the humiliation and rejection which I am always asking of you. The virginal bosom of your Mother is the new sepulchre for this, your pasch, which has now been perpetuated in the depths of my Immaculate Heart, my littlest and most loved from among the sons of predilection."

309
Pescara (Italy); May 2, 1985

Your Reparation

a   "Walk along the road which I have traced out for you, without allowing yourselves to be seized by lack of confidence or discouragement. This is the most dangerous snare with which my Adversary seeks today to check the force of my victorious cohort. And in this way he tries to bring misunderstanding and division into your midst; he makes you feel the burden of the difficulties which weigh upon the exercise of your priestly ministry; he emphasizes the sense of misunderstanding and rejection with which you are sometimes surrounded.

b   Do not stop before these snares which Satan places in your way, because he feels fear of my cohort, which I have formed for myself in every part of the world, with the little ones who have accepted my invitation to consecrate themselves to my Immaculate Heart.

c   Respond with the greatest confidence and with your filial abandonment to me. Offer me, with the simplicity of little children, everything that happens to you: joys and sorrows, interior trials and physical sufferings, the numerous wounds of your soul and everything which, in whatever manner, becomes a source of suffering to you.

d   Answer with that prayer which must become intensified and continual. Then you will have the strength from Jesus to resist all the subtle seductions of the Evil One; you will receive from the Holy Spirit the light of the wisdom which enlightens you and leads you to see every dangerous snare which is set along your path. From the Father there is given to you the joy of a tender and filial abandonment to his divine action which predisposes with love for each one of you every circumstance in your life.

e   In this month of May, consecrated to me, intensify as well your *filial reparation* for the sacrilegious and diabolical way in which the life of your heavenly Mother is being publicly presented. All Heaven trembles with indignation before the public and grave outrage tendered to the honor of your heavenly Mother, and Jesus is now personally taking up the defense of the Creature who is most loved and glorified by Him.

f   Not much time will go by before a great chastisement will strike the whole of your poor country, so loved and protected by me and which has publicly willed to permit this sacrilegious outrage tendered to your heavenly Mother.

g   My Heart bleeds to see how only the first of my beloved sons, my Pope, has willed to protest publicly and to make reparation and has raised his voice in a courageous act of condemnation. But no other member of the hierarchy has had the courage to do this; indeed some bishops and some priests have had the audacity to publicly justify this horrible sacrilege.

h   For this, there has now come for the Church the time of its greatest division, of the apostasy which has entered its interior, which will lead it to live through the moment of its gravest crisis, of its bloody and terrible persecution.

i   For this reason, I invite you to make reparation in a continual act of prayer and of penance, of trust and of filial abandonment. Then you, my beloved children, will pour the balm of love on the open and bleeding wounds of my Immaculate and so Sorrowful Heart."

310
Cagliari (Sardinia, Italy); May 26, 1985
Solemnity of Pentecost

Come, Spirit of Love

a   "Beloved children, who have entered into the cenacle of my Immaculate Heart to let yourselves be formed by me for the great task which the Lord has entrusted to you, pass this day in an unceasing prayer, addressed to the Father and to the Son, so that they may grant you the gift of the Holy Spirit.

b   For this reason alone have I invited you to enter into the cenacle of my motherly Heart. For this reason alone I invite today the whole Church to gather together in the cenacle of my Immaculate Heart in a continuous prayer made with me and through me. For this reason alone I recommend to you to gather together often in your cenacles, in order to give me a great force of prayer, with which I may be able to intervene before my Son Jesus, that He may quickly obtain for you from the Father the gift of a new and second Pentecost for the Church and for all humanity.

c   *Come, O Spirit of Love and renew the face of the earth*; grant that it may entirely become once again a new garden of grace and of sanctity, of justice and of love, of communion and of peace, so that the Most Holy Trinity may once again be reflected, pleased and glorified.

d   *Come, O Spirit of Love and renew the whole Church*; bring it to the perfection of love, of unity and of holiness, that it may become today the greatest of all lights which shines upon all in the great darkness which has spread everywhere.

e   *Come, O Spirit of Wisdom and Understanding,* and open the way for hearts to the understanding of the truth, whole and entire. With the burning force of your divine fire, root out every error; sweep away every heresy, so that the light of the truth which Jesus has revealed may shine forth for all in its integrity.

f   *Come, O Spirit of Counsel and Fortitude,* and make us courageous witnesses of the Gospel we have received. Sustain the persecuted; encourage the spurned; give strength to the imprisoned; grant perseverance to the downtrodden and tortured; obtain the palm of victory for those who, again today, are being led to martyrdom.

g   *Come, O Spirit of Knowledge, of Piety, and of Fear of God,* and renew, with the lymph of your divine love, the life of all those who have been consecrated in Baptism and signed with your seal in Confirmation, of those who have offered themselves in service to God, of the bishops, the priests and the deacons, that they may all be enabled to correspond to your plan which you are bringing about in these times of the second Pentecost, so long implored and awaited.

h   Only then will the task which I myself have entrusted to my Marian Movement of Priests be completed. Only then will there have taken place the triumph of my Immaculate Heart, at the beginning of a time in which the new heavens and the new earth will at last be able to be seen by all.'"

311   *Valdragone (San Marino); July 5, 1985*

Spiritual Exercises
(Message given orally at the end
of the evening procession)

Instruments of My Peace

a   "My beloved sons, how I have welcomed this evening the homage which you have offered to me, at the conclusion of a week in which you have all been gathered together here in the precious refuge of my Immaculate Heart. Never as in these present times has my Immaculate Heart been for each one of you the refuge and the sure way which leads you to God.

b   That which I predicted at Fatima to my daughter, Sister Lucy, is today becoming a reality. For humanity and for the Church there is great need of my motherly and immaculate refuge, because you are all living within my times. These are the painful times foretold by me, in which everything is moving towards its most painful and bloody fulfillment.

c   For this reason, I have again wanted you here on this mountain, on a week of Spiritual Exercises, so extraordinary in graces. These Exercises have a great and particular importance, which you will understand only later on.

d   During these days, I have formed you for prayer. I have taught you pray, to pray well, with me. In your prayer, which must come from the heart, your prayer of the heart, you must see and feel with your mind, your will, your heart and your soul the reality you address in prayer. Your heavenly Mother wants to form you ever more and more in the prayer of the heart, so that this prayer may be the way which leads you to peace of heart.

e   I want to obtain for each one of you the gift of peace of heart. You came with your hearts burdened with difficulties, with sorrows, with hopes, with cares and with expectations; I have taken everything into my Immaculate Heart, and I give you peace of heart. Go in the peace of your hearts, and to all about you, become *instruments of my peace.*

f   To this end, gather souls together ever more and more in cenacles of intense prayer, of deep prayer, so that I may be able to give them peace of heart. At a time when peace is departing ever further and further from men, from families, from nations, and from humanity, the sign of my motherly triumph is peace, which even now I want to bring into the hearts of all my children: of those who listen to me, follow me, and consecrate themselves to my Immaculate Heart. For this, I am again asking you to continue in your cenacles of prayer because, through the grace which springs from my Heart and which brings you to a fullness of love for my Son Jesus, I wish to give my children, today, the precious gift of peace of heart.

g   Here also I have taught you to love one another. How happy the Mother is when she sees you as so many little brothers who love one another and who want to grow in love, notwithstanding the difficulties which come from your limitations, from your numerous defects and from the subtle snares which are laid for you by my Adversary. He seeks only to rob your hearts of peace and to spread discord, misunderstandings, and divisions among you!

h   As with prayer I lead you to peace, so also with my motherly presence I bring you to brotherhood. You must increase more in your mutual love; you must know how to love one another more. The Mother rejoices when you love one another and when, after every least breach in this love, you know how to be reconciled with one another, to extend the hand to each other and to walk together, because I love each one of you individually and all of you together.

i   You cannot come to me alone. If you come alone, I ask you:

'And your brothers, where are they?' You must come to my Heart all together, joined by the divine bond of your ever increasingly perfect and reciprocal love.

j   Because my Adversary is laying many snares for you along this road, before you go down from this mountain, I want you to make me a promise: that of loving each other ever more and more, that of walking all together, taking each other by the hand because, in a world where my Adversary is succeeding in dominating through egoism, hatred, and division, the sign of my triumph is this mutual love of yours.

k   I want it to become even greater, as an anticipation of the new world which you are preparing and which awaits you, and which will be a world thrown open only to the perfect, immense, and true capacity of your loving one another.

l   But before you go down from this mountain, I am also accepting the gift of your personal suffering. As I foretold to you in the country where I am still appearing, as it were by way of anticipation and motherly preparation for that which was awaiting you, I have in the course of this year, profoundly purified my Movement. I have burdened it with a cross the weight of which you still feel, deep to be sure, very deep, so that this work of mine might be purified and might increasingly respond to my plan.

m   Do not be discouraged. Have strong faith in me. Something great and new is also about to open up for my work, because you have entered into the full phase of its fulfillment.

n   How much pain you will find along the roads of the world! As you go down from this cenacle in which I have gathered you, bring everywhere the motherly reflection of my merciful assistance. Pour balm on the many open and bleeding wounds; speak my sweet word to those who walk in aridity, in darkness, in discomfort, and in desperation.

o   You are the sign of my motherly presence, the rays of light which come forth from my Immaculate Heart to descend upon a devastated humanity and upon a darkened and divided Church.

p   Soon this division will become open, strong and widespread, and then you will have to be the bonds which unite those who want to remain in the unity of faith and of obedience to the hierarchy and, through innumerable trials, want to prepare the new times which are awaiting you. I have not let you go without speaking to you my motherly word and without giving you the comfort which comes down from my Immaculate Heart. I am always with you. You will always feel me close to you. I am your tender Mother who leads you to Jesus and brings you to peace.

q With joy and gratitude for whatever good you have done and for whatever comfort you have given to the deep sorrow of my Immaculate Heart, I, this evening, as your Mother, thank you all and bless you in the name of the Father, and of the Son, and of the Holy Spirit."

312

August 15, 1985
Solemnity of the Assumption
of the Blessed Virgin Mary into Heaven

Do Not Be Afraid

a "Today look at the paradise which awaits you, beloved children, if you want to walk in the light of joy and of hope. On this day the whole heavenly cohort of angels and saints, especially of your brothers who have preceded you here and who await you, forms a great crown of glory about the glorious body of your heavenly Mother, assumed into heaven.

b From my motherly and Immaculate Heart, I cause an extraordinary rain of graces to come down upon each one of you, to encourage you, to console you and to help you walk along the road which I have traced out for you.

c Never before as today has the world in which you live become such a desert which produces poisonous and rotten fruit. Never before as today has my Adversary attempted in every way to obstruct you, to seduce you, and to strike you. Never before as today has Satan, exercising the great power which has been conceded to him, done everything to ruin my project and to destroy my work of love, which I myself am carrying out in these last times of yours.

d For this, the Adversary is tormenting you in every way, is placing snares upon your path, is sowing misunderstandings and divisions to bring you to discouragement and is seducing you with temptations of all kinds, in order to intimidate you and cause you to halt. This is the time when his attacks against my Movement are becoming strong and continuous and when above all he is seeking to sow confusion and division among those whom I have chosen as directors in this work of mine.

e   *Do not be afraid*! I am covering you with my immaculate mantle and protecting you. I am always at your side, and I am leading you along the way which I have traced out for you. I allow his snares in order to purify you, but then I personally intervene in order to help you conquer them and to overcome them.

f   With my glorious body I often make myself present to give you signs of my motherly assistance. For this reason I am still appearing in a continuous, daily, and extraordinary manner. Even now the light of my motherly presence is uniting the heavenly world to the earthly one, in a perennial communion of love and of prayer, in the terrible moments which are awaiting you in this concluding period of the great purification."

313
Fulda (Germany); September 8, 1985
Feast of the Nativity of the Blessed Virgin Mary

The Hour of Public Witness

a   "Beloved sons, accept my invitation today to enter into my Immaculate Heart and to let yourselves be led by me. All those who accept this invitation of mine and consecrate themselves to my Immaculate Heart form part of my victorious cohort.

b   On this day, the feast of my birth, I want to have you all about my cradle as a fragrant crown of love and of prayer.

c   Today I am calling you all to a public and courageous witness. Look at your heavenly Mother who is born 'like the rising of the dawn, beautiful as the moon.' (Sg 6:10) What is it that is darkening the life of men today? It is the darkness of rebellion against God, of their obstinate and so very widespread denial. You must spread everywhere the powerful cry: 'God is! Who is like God?'

d   Only in return to God is the possibility of salvation opened up for humanity. And so you must spread with courage my motherly invitation to *conversion* and to return to the Lord, along the way of prayer and of penance, of charity and of fasting. For a little while yet, this is still the favorable time granted to humanity for its conversion.

e   Look at your heavenly Mother who is born 'bright as the sun.' (Sg 6:10) What is it that is obscuring the beauty and the brightness of the Church? It is the smoke of the errors which Satan has caused to enter into it. These are becoming constantly more and more disseminated and are bringing very many souls to the loss of the faith.

f   The cause of such a vast diffusion of errors and of this great apostasy rests with unfaithful pastors. They remain silent when they should speak with courage to condemn error and to defend the truth. They do not intervene when they should be unmasking the rapacious wolves who, hidden beneath the clothing of lambs, have insinuated themselves into the flock of Christ. They are mute dogs who allow their flocks to be torn to pieces. You, on the other hand, must speak out with force and with courage to condemn error and to spread only the truth. The time of your public and courageous witness has come.

g   The splendor of the Church is also darkened by the profound division which has entered into its interior and which is growing greater every day. And so you must bear witness to this unity, with a strong commitment of union with the Pope and with the bishops united to him. Do not follow those bishops who oppose the Pope. Make of yourselves courageous defenders of the Pope and denounce openly those who are opposed to his Magisterium and who teach in a manner contrary to it. Look to your heavenly Mother who is born 'terrible as an army in battle array.' (Sg 6:10)

h   What is it that makes your strength ineffectual and halts you with fear in the face of the great attack of my Adversary? It is the tolerance of sin which draws you away from the life of my Son Jesus. It is the great neglect of prayer, which gives you his very own strength.

i   So then be today courageous witnesses in fighting against sin. Through you, let the great gift which Jesus has made to you in the sacrament of Reconciliation shine forth once again in the Church. Return to the practice of going often to confession, and pray more. Pray with me; pray the holy rosary.

j   Everything that my Pope has said in this place corresponds with the truth.

k   You are close to the greatest chastisement, and so I say to you: entrust yourselves to me, and remember that the weapon to use in these terrible moments is that of the holy rosary. Then you will form my cohort which I am leading, in these times, to its greatest victory."

314
Fatima (Portugal); October 13, 1985
Anniversary of the Last Apparition at Fatima

The Two Cohorts

a   "From here, where I appeared as the Woman Clothed with the Sun, I am calling all of you to gather together about your heavenly Leader.

b   These are the times of the great battle between me and the powerful cohort which is under the orders of the Red Dragon and the Black Beast. Marxist atheism and Masonry are guiding this army, which has been mustered to lead all humanity to the denial of God and to rebellion against Him.

c   At its head is Lucifer himself, who is repeating today his act of defiance in placing himself against God to make himself adored as God. With him are fighting all the demons who are, in these times, being poured out from hell upon the earth, in order to lead the greatest possible number of souls to perdition.

d   United with them are all the souls of the damned and those who, in this life, are walking in rejection of God, whom they offend and blaspheme, as they walk along the road of egoism and hatred, of evil and impurity. They make their one and only aim the quest for pleasures; they satisfy all their passions; they fight for the triumph of hatred, of evil, and of impiety.

e   The cohort which I myself am leading is made up of all the angels and saints of paradise, guided by Saint Michael the Archangel, who is the head of all the heavenly militia.

f   This is a great battle which is being waged above all at the level of spirits.

g   On this earth, my cohort is made up of all those who live by

445

loving and glorifying God, according to the grace received in holy Baptism, and who are walking along the sure road of perfect observance of the commandments of the Lord. They are humble, docile, little and charitable; they flee from the snares of the demon and from the easy seductions of pleasure; they journey along the way of love, of purity, and of holiness. This cohort of mine is made up of all my little children who, in every part of the world, are answering me today with a *yes* and are following me along the road which, in these years, I have traced out for you.

h It is with my cohort that I am bringing on my victory in these times. It is with my cohort that I am building up, each day, the triumph of my Immaculate Heart. It is with my cohort that I am preparing the way along which the glorious reign of Jesus will come to you, and it will be a reign of love and of grace, of holiness, of justice, and of peace.

i From this place where I appeared, I repeat to you again today my motherly appeal: join together, all of you, as quickly as possible in this my cohort! The hour of the great battle has already arrived. Fight with the weapon of the holy rosary, and walk along the way of love for Jesus, of contempt for the world and for yourselves, of humility, of charity, of simplicity, of purity. Then you will be ready to bear the great trials which will soon begin for the Church and for humanity.

j From this blessed place, with my Pope and with my beloved ones and the children consecrated to me, I bless you all in the name of the Father, and of the Son, and of the Holy Spirit."

315　　　　　*Auckland (New Zealand); November 12, 1985*
Feast of St. Josaphat, Martyr

My Path

a "From this land of the Far East, where I have brought you to spread my motherly message and to gather together my children in the refuge of my Immaculate Heart, I am again calling the whole Church and all of humanity to follow the path traced out by your heavenly Mother. It is the sure path which brings you to the God of salvation and of peace.

446

b   Upon it you experience the love of the Father, who loves you very much and leads you, who prepares everything for you through his divine providence, and who calls you to an ever greater happiness. Allow yourselves to be carried at every moment by this fatherly love, like little children who entrust themselves completely to his divine Will.

c   Upon it you meet the divine Person of my Son Jesus, who, with his glorified body and his divinity, is ever close to each one of you. He wants to be your joy and your peace. He wants to be loved, followed and imitated by each one of you. The path upon which I am leading you is that of perfect imitation of my Son Jesus. In this way you live out the consecration of your baptism, and you renounce the world and its seductions, in order to walk along the way of divine grace, of love and of holiness.

d   Upon it you become transformed each day by the powerful action of the Holy Spirit, my most beloved Spouse, who is leading you to the perfection of your witness.

e   I have ordained that it is to be, for you, a painful witness. The times of the purification and of the bloody trial are drawing close. This is necessary for the salvation of my children and to purify the Church from the wound of apostasy and infidelity.

f   My motherly love constrains me to shorten the times. Within a short time, you will begin to understand all that I have been telling you for years.

g   Then all my little children, who, from every part of the world, have answered me with a *yes* and who have consecrated themselves to me and whom I am now cultivating in silence and in hiddenness, will open up like fragrant flowers to announce the new season of the triumph of my Immaculate Heart. I bless you all with love and with joy."

316
Melbourne (Australia); December 1, 1985
First Sunday of Advent

Blessed in Expectation

a   "My message has now reached every part of the world. Beloved children, sustain and support with generosity and trust the plan of your heavenly Mother.

b   Live in peace of heart. Love; pray; make reparation. With the simplicity of little children, live the present moment, which the Father is preparing for you as a gift of his divine providence.

c   Do not allow yourselves to be seduced by those who point to years and days, as though they wanted to impose a timetable on the infinite mercy of the divine Heart of my Son Jesus.

d   *Today, many are the false prophets* who are spreading lying messages in order to cast many of my children into anguish and fear.

e   I am the Mother of Hope and of Trust. Live with me through these times of your second Advent. As I was the virginal Mother of the first coming of Jesus, so also today I am the glorious Mother of his second coming.

f   Live in this expectation, and you will be blessed.

g   Blessed in the midst of trials and sufferings of every kind, because you have the certitude that the time of the present tribulation is preparing the time of the glorious return of my Son Jesus.

h   Blessed in the midst of misunderstandings and persecutions, because your names are written in my Immaculate Heart and because you are being guarded in my secure and motherly refuge.

i   Blessed also if you are living in a Church which is darkened, wounded, and divided because this, her hour of agony, is preparing for her the radiant dawn of a second Pentecost.

j   Live in my Immaculate Heart, blessed in the expectation of the blessed hope and the glorious coming of my Son Jesus."

317

Perth (Australia); December 8, 1985
Solemnity of the Immaculate Conception

Your Motherly Shepherdess

a   "I am the Immaculate Conception. I am your all-beautiful Mother.

b   Beloved children, walk along the road of love, of purity and of holiness.

c   Today I am happy to see how my motherly message has now spread to every part of the world.

d   Many priests, but especially the faithful in great numbers and with great enthusiasm, have responded to my invitation to consecrate themselves to my Immaculate Heart, to be united with the Pope, to walk along the way of divine grace, to flee sin, to pray the holy rosary and to gather together in cenacles of unceasing prayer, made with me and through me.

e And you, my little son, find yourself this day in a city, so very far away, set at the extreme south of this great continent to be the gentle shepherd's staff of your motherly Shepherdess, who wants to gather you all together as quickly as possible in the safe sheepfold of her Immaculate Heart.

f My times have now come. What I have foretold to you is now about to be accomplished. You are on the threshold of grave and painful events for the Church and for humanity.

g And so today, when heaven and earth are united with joy in venerating the singular privilege of my Immaculate Conception, I am inviting you all to gather together in the cohort, and at the orders of your heavenly Leader, who is leading you in the battle against the Evil One and sin, so that the most pure light of divine grace and of holiness may shine forth resplendently in you."

318   Dongo (Como, Italy); December 24, 1985
The Holy Night

A Great Silence

a "This is the holy night. Beloved children, spend it with me, in the joyous remembrance of the moments which I lived through, while the birth in time of the Word of the Father, of the true Son of God, was in preparation.

b *A mysterious silence* marked the unfolding of this great mystery of love. A sweet harmony of peace enwrapped my virginal person, called to open itself to the motherly gift of the Son.

c *A great silence* surrounded the accomplishment of this divine mystery. While silence enfolded everything, in the middle of the night, the Eternal Word of the Father came down as a dew upon the world, called to receive its divine bud. And upon this great silence, behold, the heavenly voices of the angels are opened up and also hearts of the shepherds, who are able to understand that which is hidden to the great ones.

d   And thus it must be for every encounter with the Word, who becomes flesh in the life of each one of you. Thus it must be in your daily encounter with my Son Jesus. Thus it must be for the Christmas which you are called to live out each day, as you welcome with love into your hearts and your souls the Lord who saves you and leads you to peace.

e   Thus too it must be for his second coming, when He will return in the splendor of his divinity and will come upon the clouds of heaven to establish his reign in glory.

f   There is need again today of a *great silence*, in order to understand the mysterious plan of God and to know how to read the signs of the times through which you are living and which announce to you his imminent return.

g   Open up your hearts to the humility, the simplicity, and the candor of little ones. Persevere in prayer and trust. Each day, in company with your heavenly Mother, live your perennial Christmas, which is already perpetuated in time, for the joy and salvation of all."

319

Dongo (Como, Italy); December 31, 1985
Last Night of the Year

Your Prayer with Me

a   "Beloved children, spend the hours of this last night of the year with me in prayer. So many of my children are spending these hours in amusements and in dissipation, in order to greet the new year with noise and diversion.

b   *You on the other hand, are to lift up to the Lord, with me, a powerful prayer of thanksgiving.*

c   His merciful love is continuing today to carry out a great plan of salvation and of mercy even for the people of these times of yours who are so lost and ill. Sin is your real illness, sin which is infecting my children more and more and leading them to live in egoism, in hatred, in impurity and in the obstinate rejection of the Lord your God, who has created you and is leading you along the road of true happiness.

d   The Lord is asking you to come back along the way of return to Him, and in many ways, even during this year, He has given you signs of his invitation to conversion.

e   *Lift up to the Lord, with me, a powerful prayer of reparation.*

f   Iniquity is covering the whole earth like a deep layer of ice and has dried up the hearts and the souls of many of my children. The cup of divine justice is full; it is flowing over; and it demands to be appeased.

g   While the greatest mystery of iniquity is about to be completed in the world, I am turning to you, my children, to invite you to form with me a great chain of reparation. Offer all your prayers and your sufferings of whatever kind, uniting them each day to the Sacrifice of my Son Jesus, which is everywhere being renewed in reparation and in remission for all the sins of the world.

h   Then you will be helping me to keep in suspension the chastisement, which this human race has even now drawn upon itself, because of its own impious way of life.

i   The new times are already at the gates. I am the Mother who is leading you along the way of salvation and of peace.

j   In prayer, in fasting, in mortification and in penance, dispose yourselves to live with me the new days which are awaiting you and which the mercy of the Father is preparing for you."

1986

QUEEN OF PEACE

Queen of Peace

a   "Look today at your heavenly Mother. This is the feast of my divine motherhood. It is also the first day of the new year, and the Church invites you today to pray in order to obtain the great gift of peace.

b   *I am the Queen of Peace.* On Christmas day, I gave you Him who is your peace, my Son Jesus. Jesus has brought you to peace with God, and thus He has opened up for you the way of your salvation and of true happiness. Jesus has brought you to peace with yourselves, and thus He has opened up for you the way to peace of heart.

c   This can be born only through living in divine grace, which He has merited for you by his birth in your midst, by his life and by his bloody immolation on the Cross. If you live in the grace of God, you live in peace of heart.

d   Egoism, hatred, impurity and any sin whatsoever take away your peace of heart.

e   Jesus has brought you to peace with all people and has traced out for you the way towards true brotherhood. Every human person must truly be looked upon by you as your brother.

f   I am asking you all to live in one true communion of brotherhood and of mutual love, without distinction of race, language or religion. You are all children of God, redeemed by Jesus, entrusted to my spiritual motherhood, and therefore you must all live with each other as true brothers. Only along the way of a brotherhood which is truly lived out will peace be able to come to you.

g   *But peace is, today, being ever increasingly threatened.* Men are walking in a vast and obstinate rejection of God; they are victims of sin and of impurity; they are incapable of understanding and loving each other, and thus human rights are trampled underfoot; the poor and the hungry are abandoned; oppression and injustices are increasing; acts of violence are exploding menacingly, and wars are constantly spreading more and more.

h   In this year, grave threats to peace and dangers of great evils are pressing in upon you. And so, today, on the feast of my divine motherhood, I invite you to entrust yourselves to me, who am the Queen of Peace.

i   Be converted, and return to the Lord along the way of prayer and of penance, of mortification of the senses, and of fasting. The space of time which God has yet granted to humanity for its conversion is almost over. For this reason, I address this message of mine to you, with heartfelt and motherly anxiety.

j   Listen to it, and you will be saved. Follow it, and you will find peace of heart. Spread it everywhere, and you will help to prepare, for all, days, not of misfortune and affliction, but of hope and peace."

321

February 2, 1986
Feast of the Presentation of the Child Jesus

The Way to the Divine Will

a   "Follow me, beloved sons, along the way which I am tracing out for you, in order to lead you all into the temple of the Lord, that you may sing today of his love and his glory.

b   While, with my most chaste spouse, Joseph, I walked along the road to the temple of Jerusalem, carrying in my arms my divine Infant and was absorbed with Him in a profound ecstasy of love and prayer, I was carrying out a prescription of the Law and fulfilling the Will of the Lord.

c   I am doing the same today with each one of you. I am leading you along the way of perfect fulfillment of the Will of the Lord.

d   *I am the way to the divine Will.*

e   *It is the Will of God* that you fulfill to perfection the obligations of your priestly state.

f   *It is the Will of God* that you give an important place to the life of prayer and of deep union with Him. For this reason, I am leading you to a scrupulous observance of your practices of piety: the Divine Office must never be neglected by you; your daily meditation must be made with calm and love; the rosary must be recited every day by you, with me; Holy Mass, celebrated and lived by you, must be the point of reference of your entire day.

g   *It is the Will of God* that also in your apostolic activity you should follow the norms set down for you by the Church. Never take part in profane shows: do not go to those places which are not suitable to your dignity as Ministers of God; know how to protect and defend the sacred character of your person.

h   You are in the world, but not of the world. Do not be ashamed of giving to all this public testimony. For this, I am asking you to always wear your ecclesiastical garb, so that it may be seen everywhere that you are priests of God and my sons of predilection. How it grieves my Immaculate Heart to see that many priests, and even some bishops, dress entirely in lay attire, openly disobeying the laws which the Church has set down for you.

i   *It is the Will of God* that you burn with great zeal for the salvation of souls and that you be always ready therefore for the serious task which has been entrusted to you as ministers of Reconciliation. In much of the Church, this sacrament, which is so necessary, is already in the process of disappearing, precisely because many priests no longer enter the confessional to be at the disposal of those souls who have extreme need of this sacrament of divine mercy.

j   *It is the Will of God* that you be always available for all the spiritual and material needs of your neighbor. Your priestly heart must be open, generous, sensitive and merciful. Only in this way do you fulfill the Will which the Lord has for each one of you and walk along the road which leads toward holiness.

k   For this I am leading you each day along the way of the perfect fulfillment of the divine Will so that, in the holy temple of your priestly life, the Most Holy Trinity may receive from you today its greatest glory."

322

Dongo (Como, Italy); March 27, 1986
Holy Thursday

A Divine Mystery

a   "This is your feast day, beloved sons, because it is your pasch. Remember the institution of the Eucharist and the Priesthood. Jesus so much desired to eat this Pasch with his disciples before He suffered! You should also desire to consummate with great love the mystery of your priestly pasch.

b   *It is a divine mystery of love.* You are called to the purity of love. For this I am working powerfully in you each day, to transform your hearts and make them conformable to that of my Son Jesus. I am leading you into the burning furnace of his divine and most pure love, because a priestly heart must be molded and transformed by the Heart of Jesus, the eternal High Priest.

c   A priestly heart must be meek and humble, merciful and sensitive, pure and compassionate, open like a chalice to loving God in an exclusive and total manner and then, filled with the fullness of divine love, to set all his brothers aflame with inextinguishable charity.

d   Today is also the day of the new commandment: 'Love one another as I have loved you.' (Jn 15:12) It is the day of his binding command: 'If I, as Teacher, have done this, you must do it also if you wish to be my true disciples.' (cf. Jn 15:14) Beloved sons, put yourselves ever at the service of all: you also must wash the feet of your brothers, by pouring balm on their wounds, by sharing with them in every way in their needs and in their poverty, and by taking upon yourselves the weight of the sin and evil in the world.

e   *It is a divine mystery of prayer.* Your priesthood is expressed in a perennial work of mediation between God and men. And this is exercised by your priestly prayer, above all with the offering to God of the daily Sacrifice of Holy Mass which, by means of you, makes the paschal gift of this Last Supper perennial and universal. The exercise of the priesthood in the gift, to the faithful, of the sacraments instituted by Jesus for your salvation is the perfection of prayer, that is to say, of deep union of life with God.

f   Above all, the perfection of prayer is to be found in your docile and obliging availability to the needs of souls, which often leads you to enter the confessional, as ministers of the sacrament of Penance, through which you can heal the deep wounds caused by many sins. Through your good example, may the practice of frequent confession return throughout the whole Church, thereby putting into effect that which, on this day, the first of my beloved sons, Pope John Paul II, has asked in his letter written to all priests.

g   *It is a divine mystery of suffering.* The institution of the Priesthood is above all ordered to a perpetual, even though unbloody, immolation of Jesus, which perpetuates that which was done by Him on Calvary. And so you too are called by me to suffer with Jesus, to immolate yourselves with Him for the salvation of souls. Climb the Calvary of this indifferent and cruel century, ready to die with Jesus, that the brothers may have life. To this purpose, I am asking of you, in these times, greater and more continuous sufferings.

h   Do not be discouraged; on the contrary, be happy. If you enter into the garden of my Immaculate Heart, you will experience ever more and more that which Jesus experienced in a perfect manner: the joy of being immolated for the sake of love and the salvation of all.

i   And so, each day, to the souls who have been entrusted to you, you can say with truth: 'How much I have desired to eat this Pasch of mine with you!'" (cf. Lk 22:15)

323
Dongo (Como, Italy); March 28, 1986
Good Friday

Why Have You Abandoned Me?

a   "I am today beneath the Cross upon which Jesus is living out the hours of his painful agony. In my motherly Immaculate Heart, weighed down by his suffering, I hear the cry of his final lament: 'My God, why have You abandoned Me?' (Mt 27:46)

b   Listen with me today, beloved sons, to this cry of his. It is, as it were, the summit of all his suffering, the supreme culmination of every pain. Oh, relive with me, the wounded and sorrowful Mother, these unspeakable moments of his sorrowful passion:

c   the agony of Gethsemane, the betrayal by Judas, the abandonment by the disciples, Peter's denial, the outrage and the condemnation on the part of the religious tribunal, the judgment before Pilate, the horrible flagellation and the crowning with thorns, his painful climb to Calvary, the spasm of the hands and the feet pierced by the nails, and those three interminable hours of atrocious agony, as He hung on the Cross.

d   Behold the Lamb who, silent, allows Himself to be led to the slaughter. Behold the true Lamb of God, who takes away the sins of the world. Upon the Heart of this meek body of an immolated and crucified victim, there weighs every sin of the world and all the iniquity redeemed by his Sacrifice.

e   'My God, why have You abandoned Me?'

f   Upon this divine Heart, so crushed and oppressed that He even feels abandonment by the Father, there weighs also all the lack of response and all the ingratitude of his Church, born, like a pure bride, from the womb of his great suffering.

g   Again today, in his Church, Jesus continues to be abandoned, denied, and betrayed.

h   He is denied by those who put Him in second place after their own comfort, their own self-seeking and their relish for being accepted and applauded. Pride leads many to deny Him in their words and in their life:'I do not know this man!' (Mt 26:74)

i   He is also betrayed on the part of those pastors who do not look after the flock entrusted to them, who remain silent out of fear or for the sake of convenience and do not defend the truth from the snares of errors, nor do they protect the sheep from the terrible scourge of rapacious wolves, who present themselves dressed as lambs.

j   He is abandoned by many priests and religious who leave the state of their lofty vocation or who do not live in faithfulness to their commitments and who allow themselves to be led completely by the spirit of the world in which they live.

k   He is rejected and spurned by many of the faithful who follow ideologies which are in style today but which propose values opposed to those of the Gospel, and they descend to compromises simply in order to always have everyone's approval.

l   Good Friday is truly being repeated today in a form immensely greater and more universal than that which took place at the time of the passion and death on the Cross. For one thing that was done at that time, a thousand such are being carried out at present. For this reason, in his Mystical Body which is the Church, Jesus continues to repeat his painful cry:'My God, why have You abandoned Me?'

m   This is the affliction of your heavenly Mother, which is being repeated today, as she sees the same sufferings which Jesus experienced being repeated in the Church on this day of its Good Friday.

n   See if there is any sorrow like mine! Share in my agony over the flood of sin, over the apostasy which is becoming ever greater because of the loss of faith on the part of many and over the unfaithfulness which is growing like a tide and submerging souls.

o   Never before as today, O Church, have you been so likened to your Crucified Spouse. For you too, this is the hour of your agony, of your abandonment, of your painful death on the cross.

p   But during your Good Friday, there stands at your side your sorrowful Mother, who is comforting you and watching in prayer and in the firm hope of your imminent and glorious resurrection."

324   *Dongo (Como, Italy); March 30, 1986*
Easter Sunday

Jesus Is Your Peace

a   "The peace of the divine Heart of your risen Brother, Jesus, and of the Immaculate Heart of your heavenly Mother which is filled with gladness at the sight of his glorious body, be always with you, my beloved children.

b   Peace be in your hearts and in your lives. May peace be the everlasting gift of your apostolate. Jesus, who was humiliated, despised, spat upon, scourged, condemned, crucified, slain on the Cross and buried, *is risen today!*

c   This is the Pasch of his resurrection! The risen Jesus is ever living and present among you.

d   *Jesus is your peace.* He alone is your life; He alone is your victory.

e   Share with me in this joy, which no one can ever disturb. Carry it in your soul so that hope may bloom therein.

f   I am the sorrowful Mother of the Passion.
I am the joyous Mother of the Resurrection.
I am the Mother of the Risen Christ.
I am the announcement of his victory.

g   To me has been entrusted the task of preparing his glorious return. In these painful times of purification, I say to you: 'Do not doubt; have great hope!' Jesus has conquered the world forever. Jesus alone is still today the true victor.

h   I am the Mother who is calling you from all sides to bring you all to Jesus and thus to prepare for you a new era of peace. I am the Queen of Peace who looks upon you with the tenderness of a mother and blesses you in the name of the glorified Father, of the risen Son, and of the Holy Spirit who is given to you as a gift."

325
Merine (Lecce, Italy); May 8, 1986

Mother of Grace and of Mercy

a   "I am the Mother of Divine Grace.
I am the Mother of Divine Love.
I am the Fount of Mercy.

b   Beloved sons, walk along the road which I have traced out for you during these years, if you wish to second my motherly plan for the salvation of all my children, especially my poor sinful children.

c   *You must be my hands*, which distribute copious graces to all who find themselves in any necessity. In these times, I want to manifest myself through you. I desire to distribute my graces through your priestly hands, which must always be opened as a help and comfort for all.

d   Pour balm upon the many painful wounds; bring help to those who are in poverty and neglect; assist the suffering, the marginalized, the little people, the oppressed and the persecuted to walk along the road of confidence and hope. You must be the hands of your heavenly Mother, which are always opened to pour the fullness of graces upon all her children!

e   *You must be my Heart*, which opens itself to give its motherly love. Love with the very beating of my Immaculate Heart. You are consecrated to me that I may be able to form you in the perfection of love. Be gentle and sensitive, pure and humble of heart. You must be the help which I want to give today to all who have need of love in order to be saved.

f   Love those who are far away and who are atheists; love even those who persecute you and reject you; love *all*, without any distinction of language, race or religion. In this way, each one of you becomes a beat of my Immaculate Heart, which comes down upon all, to give the comfort of my unwavering motherly love.

g *You must be the instruments of my mercy.* Today humanity has great need of divine mercy. Only through mercy can it be entirely renewed and saved. It is sick because of its obstinate rejection of God, which hinders it from walking along the road that has been pointed out by Him in order to lead it to salvation. It is gravely ill because it has become incapable of loving. The world has been reduced to an immense desert, devoid of love. In it there flourish the bad weeds of hatred, of division, of sin, of unbridled egoism, of impurity, of violence and of war. Only a great miracle of divine mercy will be able to save this straying and dying humanity, which has even now touched the depths of its extreme misery.

h This is the reason why, in these times, the entire world has been entrusted to the Immaculate Heart of your heavenly Mother. You, O priests consecrated to me, must be the instruments of my motherly mercy. In this way, you will cause new buds of life and holiness, of purity and love to sprout forth everywhere. And thus you will have a part in building, with me each day, new heavens and a new earth, as the most beautiful fruit of the fullness of grace and of mercy, which the Immaculate Heart of your heavenly Mother forever gives you."

326

June 7, 1986
Feast of the Immaculate Heart of Mary
First Saturday

Anchor of Salvation

a "Today I want to express my motherly gratitude to you for your having accepted my invitation to consecrate yourselves to my Immaculate Heart. You have responded in great numbers, from all parts of the world. Continue to respond to me with generosity, and allow yourselves to be led by me into the secure refuge which my motherly love has built for you.

b   *In these times, you all need to hasten to take shelter in the refuge of my Immaculate Heart,* because grave threats of evil are hanging over you.

c   *These are first of all evils of a spiritual order,* which can harm the supernatural life of your souls. Sin is spreading as the worst and most pernicious of epidemics, which is bringing sickness and death everywhere to many souls. If you live habitually in mortal sin, you are spiritually dead, and if you come to the end of life in this state, eternal death in hell awaits you. Hell exists; it is eternal, and today many are running the danger of going there, because they are being contaminated by this mortal disease.

d   *There are evils of a physical order,* such as infirmity, disasters, accidents, droughts, earthquakes, and incurable diseases which are spreading about. Even in that which happens to you in the natural order, see a warning sign for yourselves. You should see a sign of divine justice, which cannot allow the innumerable crimes which are committed every day to go unpunished.

e   *There are evils of a social order,* such as divisions and hatred, famine and poverty, exploitation and slavery, violence, terrorism and war.

f   *To be protected from all these evils, I invite you to place yourselves under shelter in the safe refuge of my Immaculate Heart.*

g   But, in these times, *you have need above all of being defended* from the terrible snares of my Adversary, who has succeeded in establishing his reign in the world. It is the reign which is opposed to Christ; it is the reign of the Antichrist. In this last part of your century, this reign of his will reach the peak of its strength, of its power, of its great seduction. The hour is in preparation when the man of iniquity, who wants to put himself in the place of God to have himself adored as God, is about to manifest himself in all his power.

h   Under the bloody scourge of this terrible trial, how are you to avoid being scattered and discouraged and to remain strong in the faith and faithful only to Jesus and to his Gospel? My Immaculate Heart will become your strongest defense, the shield of protection which will safeguard you from every attack of my Adversary.

i   *But today you have special need of being consoled.* To whom will you be able to turn in the painful moments which are awaiting you, when the great apostasy will reach its peak and humanity will arrive at the summit of denial of God and of rebellion, of iniquity and discord, of hatred and destruction, of wickedness and impiety?

j   In my Immaculate Heart you will be consoled! For this reason, I say again to each one of you today that which I said at Fatima to my daughter, Sister Lucy: 'My Immaculate Heart will be your refuge and the sure way which will lead you to God.' On this day, dedicated by the Church to its particular veneration, I desire that my Immaculate Heart appear as the anchor of salvation for all."

327   *Valdragone (San Marino); July 4, 1986*
 Spiritual Exercises in the Form of a Cenacle
 (Message given orally after the evening procession)

A Spirit of Joy and of Consolation

a   "Beloved sons, I do not want to let you go down from this mountain, where, for an entire week, you have remained united with me in an unceasing prayer and in a lived-out experience of brotherhood, willed and guided by me, without telling you of all the joy experienced, during these days, by the Immaculate Heart of your very sorrowful heavenly Mother.

b   Your love has been a gentle balm on all my wounds. Your prayer, made with me, has been a powerful force which you have given me to offer to the justice of the Father and in order to obtain for you, very soon, the rain of fire and of grace of the Holy Spirit, who will renew and transform the whole world, thus bringing to completion the greatest miracle of the merciful love of my Son Jesus.

c   I do not want to let you go down from this mountain, without telling each and every one of you of my motherly gratitude. During these days you have entered into the heavenly garden of my Immaculate Heart. Look at my Heart; enter into my Heart; live always in my Heart, and *a spirit of joy and of consolation will come upon you.*

464

d   You have come up here with many preoccupations, marked by many sufferings and also enveloped by an all-too-human discouragement. You have climbed up here, asking yourselves, in your heart, what new thing your Mother from heaven has to say to you this year.

e   *Beloved sons, look at my Immaculate Heart, and there will come down upon you a spirit of joy and of consolation.*

f   I am your Mother: I see the difficulties in which you are living, the heavy sorrow of these days of yours, the bloody hours which await you in the purification through which you are living. I see with what sadness your life is sometimes marked. I see also the moments in which you are oppressed by distress and discouragement, because today my Adversary is ensnaring you, above all with doubt and mistrust.

g   Look to my Immaculate Heart, and within you, like a gushing fount, *will flow forth a spirit of joy and consolation.*

h   Why do you doubt? Why are you sad? I am at your side at all times; I never leave you. I am Mother, and I am drawn close to you by the weight of the great difficulties in which you are living today.

i   From my Heart there comes a ray of light: it is the light of your Mother, faithful Virgin, which enlightens your mind and draws it gently to understand the mystery of the word of God and to penetrate deeply the secret of the Gospel.

j   In the darkness which has come down upon the world and is spreading throughout the Church, how many minds are becoming obscured by errors and dried up by the ever widening spread of doubts; how many intellects are being contaminated with error which leads many to become lost and to stray from the way of the true faith.

k   These are the times in which many in the Church are losing the faith, even from among my beloved sons.

l   If you look to my Immaculate Heart and allow yourselves to be penetrated by the ray of my light, your minds will obtain the gift of divine wisdom and will be drawn by the beauty of the truth which Jesus has revealed to you. The daily food of your mind will be only the word of God. Love it; seek it; guard it; defend it; live it. Thus, as the great apostasy spreads, you will walk in the joy and in the consolation of remaining ever in the truth of the Gospel.

m   *When you came up here, I looked at your souls,* the garden of my celestial and motherly domain, and I saw them to be still darkened by sins, which you often commit, because of your very human fragility. In you there are no grave sins, since you are seeking not to commit them any more. But even the little ones, which you call venial, displease my Heart. These can be egoism, attachment to yourselves, the inability to believe and to entrust yourselves to me with the docility of little children, the daily compromises with the world and attachment to creatures and to your way of thinking. These are little shadows which obscure the beauty of your soul. During these days, my motherly hand has passed along to wipe out all these shadows.

n   Walk in the joy and in the consolation of feeling that you are loved and led by me to become purer, better, more loving, holier, more beautiful. Your souls must return from this mountain more luminous and renewed by the grace of Jesus, while the Father bends down over them with a love of predilection and my divine Spouse, the Holy Spirit, transforms them into perfect copies of my Son.

o   *You came up here, and I saw your hearts, one by one:* they are consumed with great aridity, closed in upon themselves and hardened by the trials in which you are living. And so, as Mother, I have drawn close to each one of you; I have taken your heart in my hands; I have placed it into the burning furnace of my motherly Heart, and I have brought it into the depths of the divine Heart of my Son Jesus. Look at this Heart: it has been pierced for you! Enter into the wound of the Heart of Jesus, and allow yourselves to be transformed each day by the burning fire of his divine love. This Heart is a sea of infinite love, and it gathers in every human weakness, burns up every sin and calls to an ever greater charity, because Love must be loved, and every gift demands its own response. In here, as gold in the crucible, your hearts become continually transformed by the flame of an ardent charity, and thus you become ever more docile, humble, meek, merciful, good, little, pure.

p   *Behold, formed in the infinite sea of divine love, your new hearts and new spirits are born, that you may be witnesses of love, bringing love everywhere, and thus become, you yourselves, spirits of joy and of consolation for everyone.*

q   Do you still not understand that these are the years of the painful purification which is about to come to its most bloody finish? Why do you still ask questions? These are my years. This is the reason why I have wanted you here again, and, during these Spiritual Exercises which have been a continuous cenacle, I have given extraordinary graces to each one of you. For the present you do not understand, because they are like a seed placed in your soul, but later on you will understand; and then, you will look up here, to this mountain, and you will comprehend that which I have done for you during these days.

r   Here, this has been a true cenacle, like that of Jerusalem! Here, you my apostles have been united in prayer with me, because the new Pentecost is at the doors. Here, I have introduced you to an understanding of the secret of my Immaculate Heart so that, as you go down from this mountain, you yourselves may become my sign of joy and of consolation for all.

s   You cannot go back the way you came up. Go down with me. Look at this withered humanity. How many of my children are dead, because they have been slain by sin and hatred, by violence and impurity, victims of vice and of drugs. They are my children: desperate, afflicted, in need of help. With your love, speak my motherly word to them, and be, for them, my sign of joy and of consolation.

t   And then enter into the heart of my Church. Be signs of joy and of consolation for the Pope, the first of my beloved sons, who is suffering so much today, abandoned, criticized, and contradicted. You must be the support of love, which my motherly Heart wishes to give him. Because even he has need today of a spirit of joy and of consolation, and I want to give it to him through you, my priests and my beloved sons. Love the Pope; follow him; defend him.

u   Enter into an understanding of the mystery of the Church as the Mystical Body of Christ, which is divided and torn today and which you must restore in its unity. This Body is being mocked today; it is being scourged once again by sins which are spreading ever more and more. Make reparation for all sins, by helping many of my children to free themselves from them, through the use of the sacrament of Reconciliation which, by means of you, must once again shine throughout all the Church.

v   Bend down with me to kiss the wounds of this most beloved Daughter of mine, whose sons you also are, because the Church can

467

be renewed only through the power of your priestly love.

_w_   Thus you become signs of the new era which is beginning even now in the bitter winter of its most painful purification. In the agony through which she is still living, you are the chalice of comfort which the Immaculate Heart of your heavenly Mother is giving her to drink, that she may regain strength and walk with joy. And so you become today a spirit of joy and of consolation for the whole Church.

_x_   Do not allow yourselves to become discouraged. My triumph has already begun. In your hearts and in the silence of your priestly lives, consecrated to me and immolated by me, *the triumph of my Immaculate Heart has already begun.*

_y_   Thank you for the comfort which you have given me. I welcome the desires and the questions which you bring to me. I bless your apostolate, the souls entrusted to you and your difficult ministry. I bless your lives. They are precious to me.

_z_   You will go down from this mountain tomorrow, to return to your homes. I am accompanying you with my motherly blessing. Do not be afraid any more. I am always with you. In you and by means of you, I am the beginning of the new times. I am the Mother of Hope and of Consolation. I am the Queen of Peace.

_A_   I bless you in the name of the Father, and of the Son, and of the Holy Spirit."

328   *Rubbio (Vicenza, Italy); July 30, 1986*

Ark of the New Covenant

_a_   "Beloved children, I am leading you each day along the road of your perfect imitation of my Son Jesus. Only in this way can you become today a sign of joy and of consolation for all. These are the painful years of the trial. This has already been foretold to you by me, in many ways and with many signs.

_b_   But who believes me? Who listens to me? Who truly pledges himself to change his life? I am caught between two swords, which pierce my motherly Heart. On the one hand I see the great danger into which you are running, because of the chas-

468

tisement which is already at the doors, and on the other I see your inability to believe and to accept the invitations to conversion, which I am giving you, so that you may flee from it.

c   And so I turn again to you, my beloved ones and children consecrated to me, and I invite you to climb above the world, above your daily preoccupations, above your disordinate attachments to creatures and to yourselves, above mediocrity and tepidity, above an ever widening aridity.

d   Enter into the refuge which your heavenly Mother has prepared for you, for your salvation and that you may be able to pass in safety, in my Immaculate Heart, the terrible days of the great tempest which is already at hand.

e   *This is the moment for all to take refuge in me, because I am the Ark of the New Covenant.*

f   At the time of Noah, immediately before the flood, those whom the Lord had destined to survive his terrible chastisement entered into the ark. In these your times, I am inviting all my beloved children to enter into the Ark of the New Covenant which I have built in my Immaculate Heart for you, that they may be assisted by me to carry the bloody burden of the great trial, which precedes the coming of the day of the Lord.

g   Do not look anywhere else. There is happening today what happened in the days of the flood, and no one is giving a thought to what is awaiting them. Everyone is much occupied in thinking only of themselves, of their own earthly interests, of pleasures and of satisfying in every sort of way, their own disordinate passions.

h   Even in the Church, how few there are who concern themselves with my motherly and most sorrowful admonitions!

i   You at least, my beloved ones, must listen to me and follow me. And then, through you, I will be able to call everyone to enter as quickly as possible into the Ark of the New Covenant and of salvation, which my Immaculate Heart has prepared for you, in view of these times of chastisement.

j   Here you will be in peace, and you will be able to become signs of my peace and of my motherly consolation for all my poor children."

Climb the Mountain

a   "Climb today with me up the mountain of my peace, beloved children. Climb up the mountain of salvation and of prayer, of purity and of holiness, of docility and of meekness, of humility, of littleness and of your ever more perfect charity.

b   Climb up the holy mountain of your personal transfiguration, through an ever increasing conformation of yourselves to the divine humanity of my Son Jesus, through a filial abandonment to the love of the Heavenly Father and through a daily docility to the purifying action of the Holy Spirit. Thus you yourselves will be able to benefit from the gift of a complete transformation, in the glorious light of Christ who, in you and through you, wishes to manifest Himself in a greater way, in these times, in order to renew the whole world with the power of his merciful love.

c   On this holy mountain, you will also feel the extraordinary presence and the special action of your heavenly Mother, who wants every day to transfigure you into the very person of Jesus, so that you may become today a powerful witness of his love for you.

d   Here I am gently preparing you for the painful moments of the cross and of martyrdom. For you also, the days of abandonment, of agony and of immolation have already come. The great events which I have foretold to you during these years have arrived. Soon you will all be called to your most painful witnessing. And then you will be able to become, for all, the rays of light which come forth from my Immaculate Heart to reach every part of the world, in order to cast light upon the dark moments through which you are already about to live.

e   Thus you will assist my motherly plan, which is that of cooperating in the fulfillment of the greatest miracle of the merciful love of Jesus, who is even now about to pour out rivers of fire and of grace upon the world."

Mother of the Eucharist

a   "Beloved sons, how my Heart is filled with joy in seeing you here, on a priestly pilgrimage of adoration, of love, of reparation and of thanksgiving to Jesus, my Son and my God, present in the Eucharist, to console Him for the great emptiness, the great ingratitude and the great indifference, with which He is surrounded in his real and loving presence in all the tabernacles of the earth, on the part of so many of my children, and especially on the part of so many of my beloved sons, the priests.

b   Thank you for the joy which you are giving to the Heart of Jesus, who is smiling upon you with pleasure, as He is transported with tenderness for you. Thank you for the joy which you give to the deep sorrow of the Immaculate Heart of your heavenly Mother.

c   I am the Mother of the Most Blessed Sacrament. I became such by my *yes* because, at the moment of the incarnation, I made it possible for the Word of the Father to place Himself in my virginal womb, and, though I am also truly the Mother of God because Jesus is true God, my collaboration nevertheless took concrete form most of all in giving the Word his human nature. This made it possible for Him, who is the Second Person of the Most Holy Trinity and coeternal Son with the Father, to become also man in time, truly your Brother.

d   By his assuming human nature, it was possible for Him to carry out the work of redemption. Just as I am Mother of the Incarnation, so also am I Mother of the Redemption, a redemption which was carried out from the moment of the incarnation up to the moment of his death on the Cross, where, because of the humanity which He had assumed, Jesus was able to carry out that which, as God, it was not possible for Him to do: to suffer, to undergo his passion and to die, offering Himself as a perfect ransom to the Father and making a worthy and just reparation to his justice.

e   Truly, He has suffered for you all, redeeming you from sin and opening you up to the possibility of receiving that divine life which was lost for all, at the moment when the first sin was committed by your first parents.

f   Look at Jesus as He loves, works, prays, suffers and immolates Himself, from his descent into my virginal womb to his ascent upon the Cross, in this his unceasing priestly action, so that you may understand how I am above all Mother of Jesus, the Priest.

g   *I am therefore also true Mother of the Most Blessed Eucharist.* Not because I beget Him again to this mysterious reality upon the altar. *That task is reserved only to you, my beloved sons!* Nevertheless, it is a task which assimilates you very closely to my maternal function because you also, during Holy Mass and by means of the words of consecration, truly beget my Son. For me, the cold manger of a poor and bare cave received Him; for you, it is now the cold stone of an altar which welcomes Him. But you also, as I, give birth to my Son. This is why you cannot but be sons of a special, indeed a most special, predilection on the part of her who is Mother, true Mother of her Son Jesus.

h   But I am also true Mother of the Eucharist, because Jesus becomes truly present, at the moment of the consecration, through your priestly action. By your human *yes* to the powerful action of the Spirit, which transforms the matter of the bread and the wine into the body and the blood of Christ, you make possible for Him this new and real presence of his among you.

i   And He becomes present in order to continue the work of the incarnation and redemption and in order to accomplish, in mystery, the Sacrifice of Calvary, which He was able to offer to the Father because of his human nature, assumed with the body which I had given Him. Thus, in the Eucharist, Jesus becomes present with his divinity and with his glorious body, that body given to Him by your heavenly Mother, a true body, born of the Virgin Mary.

j   Sons, his is a glorious body, but it is not a different one; that is to say, there is no question of a new birth of his. In effect, it is the same body which I gave Him: born at Bethlehem, dead on Calvary, placed in the sepulchre and risen from there, taking on however a new form, his divine form, that of glory. In heaven, Jesus, with his glorious body, remains the Son of Mary. Thus, He whom, with his divinity, you beget at the moment of the Eucharistic consecration, is ever the Son of Mary.

k   *I am therefore the Mother of the Eucharist.*

472

l   And, as Mother, I am always at the side of my Son. I was there on this earth; I am there now in paradise, in virtue of the privilege of my bodily assumption into heaven; and I am still to be found wherever Jesus is present, in every tabernacle on earth.

m   Just as his glorious body, being beyond the limits of time and space, allows Him to be here before you, in the tabernacle of this little mountain church but at the same time allows Him to be present in all the tabernacles spread throughout every part of the world, so also your heavenly Mother, with her glorious body, which permits her to be both here and in every other place, is truly near every tabernacle in which Jesus is kept.

n   My Immaculate Heart becomes, for Him, a living, beating, motherly tabernacle of love, of adoration, of thanksgiving and of unceasing reparation.

o   *I am the joyful Mother of the Eucharist.*

p   You know, beloved sons, that wherever the Son is, there too the Father and the Holy Spirit are always present. Just as, in the glory of heaven, Jesus is seated at the right hand of the Father, in intimate union with the Holy Spirit, so also when, at your bidding, He becomes present in the Eucharist and is placed in the safekeeping of the tabernacle, surrounded by my motherly Heart, close to the Son there is always the real presence of the Father and the real presence of the Holy Spirit; there is always present the Divine and Most Holy Trinity.

q   But, as in heaven, so also at the side of every tabernacle, there is the enraptured and joyful presence of your heavenly Mother. Then, there are all the angels, arranged in their nine choirs of light, to sing, in diverse modulations of harmony and glory the omnipotence of the Most Holy Trinity, as if to make its great and divine power appear in different degrees. About the choirs of angels are all the saints and the blessed who, from the very light, the love, the unending joy, and the immense glory which issues forth from the Most Holy Trinity, receive a continuous increase of their eternal and ever greater beatitude.

r   To this summit of paradise, there also ascend the profound inspirations, the purifying sufferings and the unceasing prayer of all the souls in purgatory. Toward it they strain forward with a desire and a charity which becomes ever greater, the perfection of which is proportionate to their progressive release from every debt, owed because of their fragility and their sins, until the moment when, perfectly renewed by love, they can join in the heavenly song that arises about the Most Holy and Divine Trinity, that is found in heaven and in every tabernacle where Jesus is present, even in the most remote and isolated parts of the earth.

s   This is why, there at the side of Jesus, I am the joyful Mother of the Eucharist.

t   *I am the sorrowful Mother of the Eucharist.*

u   With the Church, Triumphant and Suffering, which palpitates around the center of love, which is the Eucharistic Jesus, the Church Militant should also be gathered together; you should all gather together, my beloved sons, religious and faithful, in order to form, with heaven and purgatory, an unceasing hymn of adoration and praise.

v   Instead, today, Jesus in the tabernacle is surrounded by much emptiness, much neglect and much ingratitude. These times were foretold by me at Fatima, through the voice of the Angel who appeared to the children to whom he taught this prayer: 'Most Holy Trinity, Father, Son and Holy Spirit, I adore You profoundly, and I offer You the most precious Body, Blood, Soul and Divinity of Our Lord Jesus Christ, present in all the tabernacles of the world, in reparation for the outrages, sacrileges and indifference with which He Himself is surrounded...'

w   This prayer was taught for these times of yours.

x   Jesus is surrounded today *by an emptiness*, which has been brought about especially by you priests who, in your apostolic activity, often go about uselessly and very much on the periphery, going after things which are less important and more secondary and forgetting that the center of your priestly day should be *here*, before the tabernacle, where Jesus is present and is kept especially for you.

y   He is also surrounded by the *indifference* of many of my children, who live as if He were not there and, when they enter church for liturgical functions, are not aware of his divine and real presence in your midst. Often Jesus in the Eucharist is placed in some isolated corner whereas He should be placed in the center of the church, and He should be placed at the center of your ecclesial gatherings, because the church is his temple which has been built first for Him and then for you.

474

z   What causes deep bitterness to my motherly Heart is the way in which Jesus, present in the tabernacle, is treated in many churches, where He is placed in a little corner, as though He were some object or other to be made use of, for your ecclesial gatherings.

A   But above all, it is the *sacrileges* which today form, around my Immaculate Heart, a painful crown of thorns. In these times, how many communions are made, and how many sacrileges perpetrated! It can be said that there is no longer any Eucharistic celebration where sacrilegious communions are not made. If you only saw with my eyes how great this wound is which has contaminated the whole Church and paralyzes it, halts it, and makes it impure and so very sick! If you only saw with my eyes, you too would shed copious tears with me.

B   And so, my beloved ones and children consecrated to my Heart, it is you who must be today *a clarion call* for the full return of the whole Church Militant to Jesus present in the Eucharist. Because there alone is to be found the spring of living water which will purify its aridity and renew the desert to which it has been reduced; there alone is to be found the secret of life which will open up for it a second Pentecost of grace and of light; there alone is to be found the fount of its renewed holiness: *Jesus in the Eucharist!*

C   It is not your pastoral plans and your discussions; it is not the human means on which you put reliance and so much assurance, but it is only Jesus in the Eucharist which will give to the whole Church the strength of a complete renewal, which will lead it to be poor, evangelical, chaste, stripped of all those supports on which it relies, holy, beautiful and without spot or wrinkle, in imitation of your heavenly Mother.

D   I desire that this message of mine be made public and be numbered among those contained in my book. I desire that it be spread throughout the whole world because I am calling you today from every part of the earth to be a crown of love, of adoration, of thanksgiving and of reparation, upon the Immaculate Heart of her who is true Mother — joyful Mother but also most sorrowful Mother — of the Most Holy Eucharist.

E   I bless you in the name of the Father, and of the Son, and of the Holy Spirit."

331   *Bagni di Tivoli (Rome, Italy); August 15, 1986*
Solemnity of the Assumption
of the Blessed Virgin Mary into Heaven

You Will Give Peace of Heart

a   "Look at your heavenly Mother, assumed into the glory of paradise, even with her body. Today I am causing a shower of graces to fall upon you all, my children.

b   The light from my glorious body is shining on you and pointing out to you the road you must follow. It is that of purity, of love, of prayer, of suffering, of holiness. It is that of a life united intimately to Jesus. Thus you also, even while living on this earth, can be illumined and surrounded by the light which is shining up here in paradise.

c   The light from my glorious body is shining for you with increasing strength, especially in these very difficult and painful times, in order to console you and encourage you in all your daily difficulties. Today you are being called to live through the bloody hours of the purification, because the great events which I have foretold to you during these years are already upon you.

d   And so you have need of my motherly consolation in order not to become discouraged. Look to paradise where your heavenly Mother has been assumed in body and soul, and you will be consoled by me. Live, with heart and soul, in paradise, where Jesus has already prepared a place for each one of you, and nothing will disturb your peace.

e   The light from my glorious body will draw you in the wake of my most exquisite fragrance. It is the fragrance of all the virtues which have adorned the garden of my earthly existence. It is the celestial aroma of all my immaculate beauty.

f   Today I want to sprinkle you all with the exquisite fragrance of purity, of humility, of simplicity, of silence, of prayer, of docility, of obedience, of contemplation.

g   Then you too will spread the heavenly fragrance of your immaculate Mother. And thus *you will give peace of heart* to all, and you will become today instruments of my peace. Because you are the beloved children of your Mother, assumed into the glory of heaven and who, in these times, desires to be invoked by all as Queen of Peace."

My Heart Is Bleeding

a   "I am your most sorrowful Mother. Again today, I am causing copious tears to fall from my merciful eyes. They want to make you understand how great the sorrow of the Immaculate Heart of your heavenly Mother is.

b   *My Heart is bleeding.*

c   My Heart is transfixed with deep wounds.

d   My Heart is immersed in a sea of sorrow.

e   You live unconscious of the fate which is awaiting you. You are spending your days in a state of unawareness, of indifference and of complete incredulity. How is this possible when I, in so many ways and with extraordinary signs, have warned you of the danger into which you are running and have foretold you of the bloody ordeal which is just about to take place?

f   — Because this humanity has not accepted my repeated call to conversion, to repentance, and to a return to God, there is about to fall upon it the greatest chastisement which the history of mankind has ever known. It is a chastisement much greater than that of the flood. Fire will fall from heaven, and a great part of humanity will be destroyed.

g   —The Church of Jesus is wounded with the pernicious plague of infidelity and apostasy. In appearance, everything remains calm, and it seems that all is going well. In reality, it is being pervaded with an ever widening lack of faith which is spreading the great apostasy everywhere. Many bishops, priests, religious and faithful no longer believe and have already lost the true faith in Jesus and in his Gospel. For this reason, the Church must be purified, with persecution and with blood.

h   —There has also entered into the Church disunity, division, strife and antagonism. The forces of atheism and Masonry, having infiltrated within it, are on the point of breaking up its interior unity and of darkening the splendor of its sanctity. These are the times, foretold by me, when cardinals will be set against cardinals, bishops against bishops and priests against priests, and the flock of Christ will be torn to pieces by rapacious wolves, who have found their way in under the clothing of defenseless and meek lambs. Among them there are even some who occupy posts of great responsibility, and by means of them, Satan has succeeded in entering and in operating at the very summit of the Church. Bishops and priests of the holy Church of God, how great today is your responsibility! The Lord is about to demand of you an account of how you have administered his vineyard. Repent; seek pardon; make amends; and, above all, be once again faithful to the task which has been entrusted to you.

i   — Sin is being committed more and more; it is no longer acknowledged as an evil; it is sought out; it is consciously willed; and it is no longer confessed. Impurity and lewdness cover the homes built by your rebellion.

j   *This is the reason why my Heart is bleeding*: because of the obstinate disbelief and the hardness of your hearts.

k   *My Heart is bleeding* to see you so closed and insensitive to my sorrowful, motherly admonition.

l   *My Heart is bleeding,* because I see your roads even now smeared with blood, while you live in an obstinate unconsciousness of that which awaits you."

333

Milan (Italy); September 8, 1986
Feast of the Nativity of the Blessed Virgin Mary

My Birth

a   "On the feast of my nativity, Paradise exults, and the Church Suffering and Militant look upon me as a sign of joy, of hope and of motherly consolation.

b   *My birth* is cause for your joy. At the moment your heavenly Mother is born, like the rising dawn, the radiant day of your salvation is already near at hand and certain for you. Close to my crib, Heaven leaps for joy, with the countless cohorts of angels, who have been forever awaiting this ineffable moment. Round

478

about my crib, there gather festively the spirits of the prophets and the just who have lived, prepared and hoped, in the expectation of this joyous event. Over my crib, with immense love of predilection, bend down the Father, as He contemplates his masterpiece of creation; the Word, in the expectation of placing Himself in my virginal and motherly womb; the Holy Spirit, who is already communicating Himself to my soul with the fullness of love.

For this reason, my birth is above all a cause of great joy for you all, who love to call upon me as the cause of your joy.

c   *My birth* is also cause for your hope. Even now the redemption, awaited, longed-for and predicted for hundreds of centuries, is about to become a real event of your history. I am born to give birth to Jesus, your Redeemer and Savior. There breaks a new dawn for all humanity. Sin is about to be conquered, and for the spirit of Evil, the moment of his complete defeat draws near, while all creation prepares itself to receive the gift of its total renewal. For this reason, my birth becomes also a cause of hope for all of you, who love to call upon me as Mother of Hope.

d   *My birth* is above all cause for your consolation. The little creature, scarcely born, whom you contemplate again today in her crib, is the object of a wondrous design by which she will become the Mother of Jesus and Mother of all humanity. And this gives you great comfort in the painful times in which you are living. Because you all have an immaculate Mother who knows you, understands you, helps you and defends you. Above all in the bloody hours of the great suffering to which you are being called, how much comfort you find in the sure knowledge that your heavenly Mother is always at your side, to share in your suffering, to strengthen your trust and to be a consolation to your many sorrows.

e   Do not be afraid. Have no fear. Feel at your side your heavenly Mother, whom you venerate today at the moment of her earthly birth, in order to become, especially in these your times, a cause of joy, of hope and of consolation for all."

I Am Forming You to Suffering

a   "Beloved children, learn from me always to say *yes* to the Heavenly Father, even when He asks of you the precious contribution of your suffering.

b   I am the sorrowful Virgin.

c   I am the Mother of Suffering.

d   My Son Jesus was born of me in order to immolate Himself, as a victim of love, for your ransom. Jesus is the docile and meek Lamb, who mutely allowed Himself to be led to the slaughter. Jesus is the true Lamb of God who takes away all the sins of the world. From the moment of his descent into my virginal womb, to the moment of his ascent upon the Cross, Jesus always gave Himself up to the Will of the Father, offering Him, with love and joy, the precious gift of all his suffering.

e   I am the sorrowful one because, as Mother, I formed, raised, followed, loved and offered my Son Jesus, as a gentle and meek victim, to the divine justice of the Father. And thus I became the greatest help and comfort in his immense suffering. In these most painful times, I am again, as Mother, at the side of each one of you, to form you, to help you and to give comfort in all your suffering.

f   *I am forming you to suffering*, by saying *yes* with you to the Heavenly Father, who is asking this of you, as your personal collaboration in the redemption carried out by my Son Jesus. In this I, your heavenly Mother, was an example and model for you, by my perfect cooperation in all the suffering of the Son, so that I became the first to collaborate in his work, through my motherly suffering.

g   I became true Co-redemptrix, and now I am able to offer myself as an example to each one of you in the giving of your own personal sufferings to the Lord, to assist everyone in walking along the way of good and of salvation. It is for this reason that, in these bloody times of purification, my motherly task is that of forming you, above all, to suffering.

h   I am also helping you to suffer, by my motherly presence, which is urging you to transform all your suffering into a perfect gift of love. For this, I am training you in docility, in gentleness, in humility of heart. I am helping you to suffer, with the joy of giving yourselves to your brothers, as Jesus gave Himself. Then you will carry your cross with joy; your suffering will become sweet, and it will be the sure road which will lead you to true peace of heart.

i   I comfort you in all sufferings, with the assurance that I am at your side, just as I was beneath the Cross of Jesus. Today, when sufferings are increasing from all sides, everyone will become aware, in an ever stronger way, of the presence of your heavenly Mother. Because this is my mission, as Mother and Co-redemptrix: to gather every drop of your suffering, to transform it into a precious gift of love and of reparation and to offer it, each day, to the justice of God.

j   Only in this way can we break open together the golden door of the divine Heart of my Son Jesus, so that He may be able to cause to descend soon, upon the Church and upon humanity, the river of grace and of fire of his merciful love, which will make all things new."

335

Naples (Italy); September 29, 1986
Feast of the Holy Archangels

With You in the Combat

a   "Fight, dearest children, my apostles, in these last times of yours. This is the hour of my battle. This is the hour of my great victory.

b   *With you in the combat* are also the angels of the Lord who, at my orders, are carrying out the task which I have entrusted to them. All the heavenly spirits are luminous and powerful beings, and they are very close to God whom they love, serve, defend and glorify. In the light of the Most Holy Trinity, they see all the dangerous and subtle snares, set for you by the wicked spirits who struggle against God and against his royal dominion.

c   This is a terrible battle, which is being waged above all at the level of spirits: those who are good against the wicked, the angels against the demons.

d   You are involved in this great struggle, and it is for this reason that you must always entrust yourselves to their sure protection and, through prayer, often invoke their powerful assistance.

e   All the heavenly spirits know my plan; they know the hour of my triumph, and they see how the attack of hell, in these times of yours, is becoming powerful, continuous and universal. Satan has succeeded in establishing his reign in the world, and he already feels that he is the sure victor. But the moment of his great and definitive defeat is close. For this reason, the battle is becoming more fierce and terrible, and you too, with the angels of the Lord, are being called to battle. The weapons used by the demons are those of evil, of sin, of hatred, of impurity, of pride and of rebellion against God. The weapons used by the heavenly spirits, who are at your side to do battle, are those of goodness, of divine grace, of love, of purity, of humility and of docile submission to the Will of the Lord.

f   The heavenly spirits have also the task of strengthening you, of healing you from your wounds, of defending you from the snares of my Adversary, of protecting you from evil and of leading you along the luminous way of my will.

g   The Archangel Gabriel was sent by God to accept the *yes* of your heavenly Mother; now, he has the duty of accepting your *yes* to the Will of the Father. He strengthens you and sustains you; he leads you along the way of courage and of a heroic witness to Jesus and to his Gospel.

h   The Archangel Raphael gives refreshment to your weakness, pours balm on every painful wound and lifts you up from the weight of your weariness and discouragement, in order to continue the struggle, with the shield of faith and with the armor of love and of holiness.

i   The Archangel Michael defends you from all the terrible attacks of Satan, who is particularly raging against you who form part of my cohort and are allowing yourselves to be led with docility by your heavenly Leader. How many times would you have become victims of the attacks of Satan, had not the Archangel Michael intervened in your defense and for your protection! Invoke him often with that so very efficacious prayer of exorcism against Satan and the rebellious angels, because he is guiding you in this battle in such a way that each one of you may be able to fulfill the task which has been entrusted to him by the heavenly Mother.

482

_j And so, be united in an affectionate and fraternal communion of life, of prayer and of action with all the heavenly spirits, who are engaged, together with you, in fighting the same battle and preparing God's great victory in the glorious reign of Christ, which will come to you with the triumph of my Immaculate Heart in the world."

336

October 7, 1986
Feast of Our Lady of the Rosary
Anniversary of the Victory
of the Blessed Virgin Mary at Lepanto

The Rosary Brings You to Peace

_a "I am the Queen of the Holy Rosary. I am your Leader who is guiding you in the terrible battle against Satan and all the spirits of evil. If you allow yourselves to be led with docility by me, you will always feel at your side the precious help which is given to you by the angels of the Lord, the blessed and the saints of paradise, and all the souls who are still being purified in purgatory.

_b I am, in fact, the Leader of one single cohort.

_c Today, as you recall the date of one of my great victories, I want to call upon you to fight, with courage and confidence, without allowing yourselves to become alarmed at the subtle and dangerous tactics made use of by my Adversary to bring you to discouragement.

_d For this reason, I want to uncover for you three traps which form part of a particular strategy employed by my Adversary, in this great battle.

_e — *The first* is that of spreading about the certainty that he has already succeeded in conquering the whole world, that he has established his reign in it and that he fully exercises his power there. His great conquest is this human race, which has rebelled against God and which is repeating his proud act of defiance: 'I will not serve the Lord!' A most dangerous means, made use of by Satan in these times, is that of giving the impression that there is no longer anything more to be done, that one will no

483

longer succeed in changing anything, and that it has already become useless to make any kind of an effort to lead humanity along the road of return to God and to good.

f   And so your heavenly Mother is assuring you that even this humanity forms a precious part of the people of God, won by Jesus at the price of his blood, shed to the last drop for its salvation. God, especially today, is alone the victor; and He loves all the poor sick humanity which has been snatched from Him; and He is preparing the moment when, by the greatest miracle of his merciful love, He will lead it along the road of return to Himself, that at last it may be able to know a new era of peace, of love, of holiness and of joy. For this reason, I am inviting you always to make use of the powerful weapon of trust, of filial abandonment, of a great and boundless charity, of a complete availability for all the spiritual and material needs of your neighbor and of a motherly and unlimited mercy.

g   — *The second* is that of having succeeded in putting the Church in a state of grave difficulty, shaking it to its foundation, by the wind of contestation, of division, of infidelity and of apostasy. Many are losing courage, as they see how numerous today are those pastors who are allowing themselves to be deceived by his subtle and dangerous action.

h   The means which you must use to fight back against this ambush of his is that of your consecration to my Immaculate Heart, because the Church, even though it appears wounded, darkened and routed today, has been entrusted by Jesus to the loving protection of your heavenly Mother. I want to help it, console it and heal it through you, beloved children consecrated to my Heart and docile instruments of my motherly will. Through you, I am pouring balm upon its painful wounds, comforting the hours of its desolate passion and preparing the moment of its greatest renewal.

i   I am doing this, in these times, in a very special way, through my Pope, John Paul II, who is bringing the sign of my motherly presence everywhere. He is giving you the battle sign; he is guiding you in the struggle; he is teaching you courage and confidence; he is already announcing to you my sure victory. Follow him along the road which he points out, if you wish to prepare, with me, a new and radiant Pentecost for the whole Church.

j — *The third* is that of succeeding in spreading everywhere, through all the means of social communication, his wicked works of destruction and death. Thus, divisions are multiplying; impurity is being exalted; corruption is extensive; violence is becoming more and more widespread; hatred is flooding the land, and wars are expanding menacingly.

k To fight and conquer all this evil, which is attempting to submerge the entire human race, you must have recourse to the powerful weapon of prayer. In fact, the new era will be able to come to you only as a gift of the Spirit of the Lord, not as the fruit of the work of man. And so it is necessary to ask for this gift through a continual, incessant, and trusting prayer.

l Pray with me. All the Church must enter into the cenacle of my Immaculate Heart, to invoke, with the heavenly Mother, a very special outpouring of the Holy Spirit, which will lead it to live the experience of a second and radiant Pentecost.

m Pray above all with the prayer of the holy rosary. Let the rosary be, for everyone, the powerful weapon to be made use of in these times.

n *The rosary brings you to peace.* With this prayer, you are able to obtain from the Lord the great grace of a change of hearts, of the conversion of souls, and of the return of all humanity to God, along the road of repentance, of love, of divine grace and of holiness.

o Then you will no longer say: 'But, always and everywhere, everything remains just as it was. Nothing ever changes!' — This is not true, my beloved children. Each day, in silence and in hiddenness, the heavenly Mother is waging her battle against the Adversary and is working, by means of most extraordinary signs and manifestations, to change the heart of the world."

337 Sant' Omero (Teramo, Italy); October 27, 1986
World Day of Prayer for Peace

The Task Entrusted to the Church

a "Today you are imploring peace, through a day which is bringing together representatives of all religions in a communion of prayer and of fasting. This is the road that I have pointed out to you. Peace can come to you only as a gift of God. The more you want to build peace through human discussions and reciprocal agreements, the more it will remove itself from you. For this reason, it is necessary for humanity to return to God along the road of conversion and of a change of heart.

b Jesus Christ alone has shown you the way to reach the Father in his Spirit of Love. It is necessary that all men come to a knowledge of the truth and to accept and to follow the Gospel of Jesus.

c *This is the task entrusted to the Church.*

d This is what her ministers, her consecrated ones, and all her faithful must do today: with the courage of martyrs and the strength of confessors of the faith, there is need to announce to the whole world the good news that Jesus Christ alone is your Savior and your Redeemer! Only Jesus Christ can bring you to peace. It is necessary to preach Him to all, without fear and without compromise, carrying out his divine mandate:'Go into the whole world, and proclaim my Gospel to all creation; whoever believes and is baptized will be saved.' (Mk 16:15-16)

e The attempt to bring together all religions, even those which adore false and lying gods, with the prospect of forming a worldwide religious union for the defense of human values, is vain, dangerous and not in conformity with the desire of my Immaculate Heart. It can on the contrary lead to an increase of confusion, to religious indifference and even make the attainment of true peace more difficult.

f For this reason, I say to you today: announce Christ to everyone; be faithful only to Christ and to his Gospel, and you will become true builders of peace."

338 Dongo (Como, Italy); November 1, 1986
Solemnity of All Saints
First Saturday

Your Place in Paradise

a "Today, look at those who have already gone before you into glory. Round about my Immaculate Heart, they form a luminous crown of love, of joy and of glory.

b   *This is also your place in paradise.* It is being prepared for all of you who listen to my voice, who consecrate yourselves to my Immaculate Heart, live in filial dependence upon me and offer yourselves completely for the perfect fulfillment of my plan. You are, here below, my dearly beloved children. You are my apostles, called to spread everywhere the light of my motherly presence and to point out to all the road that they have need to follow in order to reach Christ, from whom alone can come the new era of holiness, of justice and of peace.

c   For this reason, feel at your side, each day, the saints and the blessed of heaven; call upon them for help and protection. Feel also at your side the souls of the just, who are still suffering and praying in purgatory, awaiting the moment of their full beatitude in the perfect contemplation of the Lord. With you they form one single cohort, under my orders. For all, I am the Mother and the Queen. Each one has an irreplaceable part to play in my victorious plan.

d   In these times, I want to make deeper, stronger and more extraordinary your communion with those who have preceded you in the earthly life and now enjoy eternal salvation. As a motherly gift of my Immaculate Heart, I offer you, as a precious help, the souls of the saints in paradise and of the just in purgatory. You are being exposed to grave dangers, and they can assist you in overcoming them. You are victims of the subtle snares of my Adversary, and they can give you light that you may be able to see them and strength that you may flee from them. You are fragile and weak and often happen to fall again into sins; they can always lend you a hand to walk along the road of good and of holiness.

e   Travel therefore, together with them, along the road which I have traced out for you. Together, I am leading you to peace.

f   Peace will come to you from my Immaculate Heart when this, your communion of life, of love and of joy will have then been perfectly accomplished."

The Way Which Leads You to His Kingdom

a   "Today, in the glory of paradise and in the purifying light of purgatory, I am accepting the homage of the whole pilgrim Church on earth, in order to offer, together with you all, the crown of his royalty to Jesus Christ, our God, our Savior and our King.

b   *Jesus must reign above all in the hearts and in the souls of all*, because his is a royalty of grace, of holiness and of love. When Jesus reigns in the soul of a creature, it becomes transformed by a divine light, which renders it increasingly beautiful, luminous, holy and beloved of God.

c   For this, my motherly task is that of driving away from the souls of my children every shadow of sin, any snare whatsoever of egoism, any predominance of the passions, in order to lead everyone along the road of great sanctity. Then Jesus will truly be able to establish his reign in your hearts and in your souls, and you will become the precious domain of his divine royalty.

d   *Jesus must reign in families*, which must open themselves like buds to the sun of his royalty. For this reason, I am working in these times, in order that there may increase, in families, harmony and peace, understanding and concord, unity and faithfulness.

e   *Jesus must reign in all humanity*, that it may become again a new garden where the Most Holy Trinity may receive charm and beauty, love and fragrance from every creature and thus be glorified and establish its habitual dwelling place in your midst. For this, I am working powerfully today to lead all humanity along the road of return to God, by way of conversion, of prayer and of penance. And I myself am leading the cohort, called to fight against the army of evil so that the power of those who deny and blaspheme God and who work tirelessly to build a civilization without Him may be defeated as quickly as possible.

f *Jesus must reign in the Church,* the privileged portion of his divine and loving domain. The Church is all his because she is born of his rent Heart, brought up in his love, washed with his blood, espoused to Him by an inviolable pact of eternal fidelity. For this reason, I am working as Mother, in these painful moments of her purification, to cleanse the Church once again from every stain, to set her free from every human compromise, to defend her from the subtle attacks of her Adversary and to lead her along the road of perfection, that she may reflect everywhere the very splendor of her divine Spouse, Jesus.

g My motherly action is preparing, in this time of yours, the coming of the glorious reign of my Son, Jesus.

h *My Immaculate Heart is the way which leads you to his reign.* In fact, the triumph of my Immaculate Heart will coincide with the triumph of my Son, Jesus, in his glorious reign of holiness and of grace, of love and of justice, of mercy and of peace, which will be established in the whole world.

i For this reason I am inviting you today to prayer and to trust; I am calling you to peace of heart and to joy because the glorious reign of the Lord Jesus is already at the gates."

340

Dallas (Texas, U.S.A.); December 3, 1986
Spiritual Exercises in the Form of a Cenacle
with the Priests of the M.M.P.
from the United States and Canada

My Remedy for Your Illnesses

a "How happy I am with these days of continuous cenacle which you, the priests of my Movement, are making, coming as you do from even the most distant states of this great country, in order to live together in brotherhood and in prayer with me, your heavenly Mother. Your love, your docility and your generosity give much joy to my Sorrowful and Immaculate Heart.

b Today I want to give you my motherly word, that it may be a source of comfort in your sufferings and of confidence in the midst of the many difficulties you encounter.

c Be the smallest of my little children; be my courageous apostles;

489

be the rays of light that come forth from my Heart and spread about everywhere, to bear witness to my motherly presence.

d   There are three wounds, in this country of yours, which are causing pain to my motherly Heart and making it bleed.

e   *The first wound is caused by the apostasy*, which is spreading, because of the errors that are being taught and promoted more and more even in Catholic schools, and which are leading an immense number of my poor children to separate themselves from the true faith.

f   The responsibility for this grave situation rests above all with those who have consecrated themselves to God because, having been seduced by the spirit of pride, they continue on their way, despite my motherly admonitions and the directives given by the Magisterium of the Church.

g   You, my beloved sons, are to be my remedy for this illness, by preaching more and more the truth which Jesus has taught you and which the Pope and the bishops united with him are still presenting today to everyone with clarity and courage.

h   You must oppose anyone who teaches doctrines which are different, and, above all, you must speak openly to all the faithful of the grave danger, which they are encountering today, of swerving from the true faith in Jesus and in his Gospel. Recite often the profession of faith, composed by the first of my beloved sons, Pope Paul VI, now up here with me, as he foresaw these difficult moments.

i   *The second wound is caused by the disunity* that has entered into the Church which exists in your countries. How it makes the Heart of Jesus and my motherly Heart suffer to see that many bishops, priests, religious and faithful are no longer united with — and are even openly opposing — the Pope, whom Jesus has set up as the foundation of his Church.

j   This division is becoming daily more extensive and deeper, and soon it will become even open and proclaimed. How much pain I feel in seeing that often the greatest supporters of this rebellion are those who have consecrated themselves to God and have vowed to follow Jesus along the road of humility, of poverty, of chastity and of obedience.

k   You, my beloved sons, are to be my remedy for this deep wound

490

by being ever more united with the Pope, by helping your bishops to be united with him, through prayer, love and your good example, and by leading all the faithful to this unity.

l   *The third wound is caused by the infidelity* that has entered into the life of many children of the Church, who no longer follow the commandments of God and the teachings given by Jesus in his Gospel. Thus they walk along the wrong road of evil and of sin. Sin is no longer recognized as an evil. Often justification is made for even the gravest sins against nature, such as abortion and homosexuality. Sins are no longer confessed. To what a grave state of sickness have you now come!

m   You, my beloved sons, are to be my remedy for such a grave and so extensive an evil, by helping my children to walk along the road of purity and of holiness. Return again to teaching everyone true Catholic morality. Give a helping hand to my poor sinful children, to lead them to the observance of the Law of God. Make them understand the necessity of frequent confession, which becomes indispensable before one who is in the state of mortal sin may receive Holy Communion. The Church here is all wounded because of communions received sacrilegiously.

n   If you accept this motherly invitation of mine, you will then be the gift of love which my Immaculate Heart is offering today to the Church and to all of humanity which is living in this great country of yours.

o   *You will thus become my remedy for your illnesses.*

p   You are the instruments of my peace.

q   Together with all the members of my Movement, I bless you in the name of the Father, and of the Son, and of the Holy Spirit."

341   Santiago (Dominican Republic); December 8, 1986
Solemnity of the Immaculate Conception

My Candor of Heaven

a   "My candor of grace and of light, of holiness and of purity seeks to cover the whole earth like a mantle.

b   For this reason, my little child, I have brought you here today, to this island from which the evangelization of all the great continent of America began, in order to lead as quickly as possible my beloved ones and all my children into the safe refuge of my Immaculate Heart.

c   I am the dawn which precedes the great day of the Lord. I am the longed-for luminous cloud which will cause the heavenly dew of grace and of holiness to descend upon the desert of the world, wasted by evil and by sin.

d   Join my victorious cohort, all you who wish to fight the great battle for the triumph of good and of love. There, where the ray of my light reaches, the darkness of evil, of egoism, of hatred, of sin and of impurity vanishes. Bring my motherly announcement everywhere.

e   *Spread my candor of heaven throughout every part of the world.*

f   These are the times when I must gather all of you again under my immaculate mantle, at the orders of your heavenly Leader.

g   Through you, who have responded to me, my light will grow stronger from day to day, because the moment of the glorious triumph of my Son, Jesus, is already at hand.

h   From this land, I bless you today, together with all those who have accepted my invitation, listened to me and followed me."

342   Dongo (Como, Italy); December 24, 1986
The Holy Night

The Crib at His Glorious Return

a   "Accept my motherly invitation to pray, to meditate upon my word, to guard it in your heart, to keep vigil, remaining on the watch expectantly.

b   This is the holy night.

c   Spend it with me, beloved children; live it in the depths of my Immaculate Heart. You will then be able to penetrate the mystery of your salvation, which reveals itself to the poor, to the little, to the simple, to the pure of heart.

d   My soul is flooded by a divine light and my person becomes surrounded with a profound sense of peace and of blessedness, while my virginal womb opens itself to the divine gift of the Son.

492

e All about us, it is deep night: the doors, closed upon our plea for hospitality; the hearts of men, made hard through egoism and hatred; minds, blinded by error and a great coldness upon the world which has become incapable of love!

f But in the poor cave, a little light is enkindled, in the sign of expectation and of hope; two human hearts are beating with love, to prepare the crib in which to place the newborn child; my most chaste spouse, Joseph, is readying himself to make the squalor of the place more hospitable, while the heavenly Mother is absorbed in a profound and intense prayer with the Father.

g It is at this moment that heaven espouses itself to earth, that the shoot awaited for centuries comes to flower, that God is born among us, that the Savior enters his regal domain, that the Redeemer begins to pay the price of our ransom.

h And peace descends from heaven with the song of the angels; the earth opens to receive the dew of divine mercy, while the simple hearts of the shepherds open themselves to the voices which announce the wondrous event: 'Today there is born for you a Savior who is Christ the Lord.' (cf. Lk 2:11)

i Everything is again repeated for his second nativity. His return in glory is just as it was then. The night of the denial of God has descended upon the world; the coldness of rebellion against his Law of love has reduced humanity to an immense desert; error has closed minds to the understanding of the greatest mystery of love; hearts have become hardened by egoism and hatred which is spreading everywhere. Doors are still obstinately shut to the Lord as He comes.

j You, O beloved ones, throw open your hearts to blessedness and hope, and, in imitation of your heavenly Mother and of her most chaste spouse, Joseph, undertake to make yourselves attentive in preparing the roadways for Christ who is returning in glory.

k His second nativity is already at the doors. And so open your minds to the heavenly voices which, in many ways and through many signs, are telling you that his return is near. As the love of my motherly Heart was the most precious crib for his first nativity, so also *the triumph of my Immaculate Heart will be the crib at his glorious return*.

l On this holy night, I am gathering you all together to keep watch, with me, close to the little Child, who has such need of love. On this holy night, I am inviting you to open your hearts and your minds to receive the joyful announcement that his second nativity is near."

343 *Dongo (Como, Italy); December 31, 1986*
Last Night of the Year

And Peace Will Come to You

a   "During these last hours of the year, beloved children, I want all to gather close to me in an unceasing prayer.

b   *Pray* in order to give thanks to the Heavenly Father, who is guiding human events toward the fulfillment of his great plan of love and of glory.

c   *Pray* in order to console the divine Heart of the Son, wounded by so many sins and surrounded by an immense sea of human ingratitude. Jesus loves you. His Heart is a furnace of most ardent love for you. But this Heart is being continually pierced by offenses and sins. It is you who must be the consolers of the Heart of Jesus. My beloved ones, I am asking you to fill up, with your priestly love, all the emptiness, the negligence and the indifference with which He is surrounded.

d   *Pray* in order to invoke the Holy Spirit, that He may be able to accomplish as quickly as possible the prodigy of a second Pentecost of holiness and of grace, which may truly change the face of the earth. Pray, and do penance. Recite the holy rosary with love and with confidence. With this prayer, made by you together with me, you are able to influence all human events, and even the future events which are awaiting you. With this prayer, you can possess the grace of a change of hearts, and you can obtain the much-desired gift of peace.

e   *Peace will come*, after the great suffering to which the Church and all humanity are already being called, through their interior and bloody purification.

f   *Peace will come*, after the event of the terrible chastisement, which I have already announced to you beforehand, at the dawn of this century of yours.

Peace will come, as a gift of the merciful love of Jesus, who is about to pour forth upon the world torrents of fire and of grace, which will make all things new.

h *Peace will come*, as the fruit of a special outpouring of the Holy Spirit, who will be given by the Father and by the Son, in order to transform the world into the heavenly Jerusalem and to lead the Church to the summit of its sanctity and of its divine splendor.

i *And peace will come to you* from the triumph of my Immaculate Heart, as that space of time, which has been granted by the Lord to humanity for repentance and for its conversion, is about to come to an end.

j Even now the great events are coming about, and all will be accomplished at a faster pace, so that there may appear over the world, as quickly as possible, the new rainbow of peace which, at Fatima and for so many years, I have already been announcing to you in advance."

1987

THE RISING DAWN
(Marian Year)

I Am the Rising Dawn

a   "I am the Mother of God.

b   The Word placed Himself in my virginal womb, after the *yes* which, with such love and such joy, I had said to the Will of the Father. At that moment, the Holy Spirit enwrapped me with his spousal love and made of me a precious cradle for the incarnation of the Word.

c   My virginal womb opened itself to receive this gift of God. My Immaculate Heart unfolded itself to a motherly love towards the fruit of my most pure womb. And I became true Mother of God.

d   But I am also the Mother of all humanity. Jesus has willed to give his Mother to humanity, redeemed by his immense and bloody suffering.

e   I recall even today the scene of his ineffable gift of love: on the Cross, where He has been hanged as immolated victim, Jesus is on the point of living through the final moments of his heartrending agony. His Heart, which had begun to beat in my virginal womb, is now about to stop in the silence of death, when He feels an immeasurable love for each one of you and desires that not one of his brothers, redeemed with such pain, be abandoned. So then, in an impulse of extreme largesse, He opens Himself out to his final gesture: 'Behold your Mother.' (Jn 19:27) And thus I have become the Mother of all.

f   Today I want to cover the whole world with the immaculate mantle of my virginal motherhood. You are entering into a period when the events which have been foretold to you are being fulfilled. You are entering into the time of chastisement and of salvation, of suffering and of great mercy.

g   Already in the course of this year some important events will reach their fulfillment. At the beginning of this year, how much suffering and how many sorrows I see along your paths! And so, cooperate with the request of my Pope, John Paul II, who wants to entrust the Church and all humanity to the motherly love of my Immaculate Heart.

h   *These are my times.*

i   The mission which has been entrusted to me by the Most Holy Trinity should now be acknowledged by the whole Church. During this year, you are beginning an extraordinary jubilee in honor of your heavenly Mother, as my Pope is preparing to distribute throughout the Church an encyclical letter concerning the post which the Lord has assigned to me and the important mission which has been entrusted to me in these times.

j   This will again provoke the strongest reaction on the part of my Adversary, who perceives that the end of his universal dominion is now close at hand.

k   For this reason I ask you to begin the new year with me. Pray; love; make reparation. I am the heavenly Mother who is leading you to your God and bringing you to peace. I am the Queen of Peace and the rainbow of the new covenant.

l   *I am the dawn which is arising to announce the great day of the Lord.*

m   During these years, the Church and all of humanity will be left stupefied before the great events of grace and salvation which the Immaculate Heart of your heavenly Mother will bring to you.

n   With my Pope, with all my especially loved ones and the children who are consecrated to me, I bless you in the name of the Father, and of the Son, and of the Holy Spirit."

345   *Dongo (Como, Italy); February 2, 1987*
Feast of the Presentation of the Child Jesus

The Way to Divine Revelation

a   "Beloved sons, if you walk with me and with my most chaste spouse, Joseph, as I journey along the road which leads to the temple of Jerusalem, carrying in my arms with ineffable love the Child Jesus, forty days after his birth, you are then able to understand how my function as Mother is exercised above all in being the way along which the Lord comes to you.

b   From my *yes* at the annunciation to the birth at Bethlehem, from the presentation in the temple to the flight into Egypt, from the days of infancy to the years of his youth spent at Nazareth, from the beginning of the public life to his immolation on the Cross, the presence of the Mother was always the way for a new and greater manifestation of the life and the mission of my Son Jesus.

c   Indeed my *yes* gives consent to the Word of the Father to assume, in my womb, his human nature; my motherly and virginal collaboration makes possible his birth into earthly life; my arms present Him in the temple of his glory and manifest Him as revelation to all nations; my motherly love becomes a precious help during the days of his infancy, threatened with snares; my presence is a daily support to his human adolescence; the warmth of my affection is a sweet repose to his weariness; my silence is a garden at the blossoming of his word; my act of faith solicits the divine intervention and anticipates the time of his mission; my Immaculate Heart pours balm upon the wounds of every official rejection; my sorrowing closeness is strength for his climb up Calvary; my total offering is an interior participation in his immense suffering; the presence of my person beneath the Cross is a profound act of cooperation with Him in his plan of redemption.

d   Carried in my arms, Jesus is revealed to all nations; held aloft by me, my Son fulfills his divine mission; along the road which I am preparing for Him, Jesus is carrying out his work and manifesting Himself as Savior of the world.

e   I am carrying out the same motherly plan in respect to each one of you, my dearly loved ones, called to relive in your priestly lives the plan and the mission of my Son Jesus. And so understand why I ask you to entrust yourselves completely to me, by your act of consecration to my Immaculate Heart. This act allows me to intervene in your life in order to direct it to the perfect fulfillment of the Will of the Father.

f   Thus I am situated at your side at each moment of your day. With my silence I help you to speak; with my voice I teach you to pray; with my hands I lead you on the right way; with my presence I bring comfort to your weariness; with my motherly love I console your suffering; with my powerful intercession I make fruitful your apostolic work; with my Immaculate Heart I give you joy and peace in moments of discouragement and aridity.

g   I am above all always close to you in climbing Calvary with you, in gathering up every drop of your suffering, in helping you to say *yes* to the Will of the Father, who is preparing you for the perfect immolation for the salvation of the world.

h I am also always present during the earthly journey of the Church, the Mystical Body of Jesus, entrusted by Him to the zealous care of my universal motherhood. In every epoch of her history, I have helped the Church to give a luminous witness to my Son, so that, in her and by means of her, Jesus may be able to reveal Himself ever more fully to all nations.

i *I am the way to divine Revelation.*

j I am particularly close to the Church in these times of her painful trial and her bloody purification. You understand then the significance of my present and so concerned interventions. Today I am intervening in a new, strong and extraordinary way, such as has never hitherto been done, as the Mother who wants to help all her children and as the heavenly Prophetess of these last times of yours. My light which is spreading more and more in hearts and souls — as a rising dawn in the long dark night in which you are still living — is announcing to you that the great day of the Lord is near.

k For this reason I invite you to look to me, the Mother who is journeying along carrying in her arms the Child Jesus towards the temple of Jerusalem, towards the place of his manifestation. For this reason I invite you to look again to me, the Woman Clothed with the Sun, who is journeying along all the roads of the world, to be the way for his luminous and glorious revelation."

346 *Rubbio (Vicenza, Italy); February 24, 1987*

My Rays of Light

a "My beloved ones, remain in peace. I am near you at every moment: I am forming you, strengthening you, guiding you, defending you. Guard in your heart the precious pearl of a personal call to live in profound intimacy of life with your heavenly Mother.

b Do not allow yourselves to be brought to a halt by the snares of my Adversary. In these times he is exerting his great power, because he senses that the moment of his defeat is even now close at hand.

c   *Become therefore, you yourselves, my rays of light* which spread everywhere the announcement of my new dawn. Lighten up the dense darkness of your days with the light of faith and of holiness. Upon the arid desert of the world, let your rays descend to open it up to a new springtime of life and of beauty. Into the emptiness of many hearts, let your rays enter to fill them with love and with trust. Midst the dense darkness of many souls, let your rays arise to open them out to the life of grace and of intimate union with God. To the gloomy desperation of many of my poor children, let your rays bring the sweet balm of comfort and of hope, of love and of mercy.

d   You are the rays of light from my Immaculate Heart. You are the light of the Mother who wants to bring all to Jesus, that they may be saved by his divine and merciful love.

e   In these times I am calling you to illuminate all the earth. Thus, by means of you, I am able to bring about the painful passage to the new era which awaits you and which, each day, I am building in the depths of my Immaculate Heart."

347

Dongo (Como, Italy); March 4, 1987
Ash Wednesday

On This Luminous Pathway

a   "Follow me along the way which I have traced out for you, my children, so dearly loved and so protected and defended by me. It is the way *of conversion and of penance.*

b   *The conversion* which I ask of you is that which Jesus requested of you in his Gospel. Separate yourselves from the wicked way of evil, of pride, of egoism and of sin.

c   In the world in which you live, where rebellion against God and his Law of love is welcomed, propagated, exalted and set up as a new model of life, how many of my poor children there are who daily become victims of sin and of hatred, of violence and of corruption, of egoism and of impurity. Grave sin separates you from God, takes the precious gift of his life and his grace from your souls, makes you slaves of passions and of vices, weakens you in your resistance to temptations, opens up great spaces for the action of Satan, who thus takes greater and greater possession of your life and makes of it an instrument for the spread of unbridled egoism and of pride, of hatred and of division, of licentiousness and of impiety.

d   You bring about in yourselves a true pledge of conversion if you oppose, with courage and with strength, the world in which you live, to walk along the way of good and of divine grace, of love and of holiness. It is necessary today that all my children be converted and come back to a belief in the Gospel, to live according to the Gospel and to allow themselves to be guided solely by the wisdom of the Gospel. These are the propitious days for your conversion. They are the days of grace and of mercy, of hope and of expectation.

e   These are the *days of preparation* for what is now in store for you, for the great events which have been foretold to you. And so I am asking you again for daily works of mortification and of penance.

f   *Penance* is to be offered by you to my Heart in three different ways:

g   In the first place, offer me *interior penance*, which you must exercise in order to attain dominion over yourselves, over your passions and to become truly docile, humble, little and available for my designs. Sometimes my Heart is pained to see how you offer resistance to my motherly invitations, and thus you do not succeed in attaining that measure of docility, of humility, of true annihilation of yourselves, which I am asking of you, because it is indispensable for me in order to make use of you in the carrying out of my plan of salvation and of mercy.

h   Then offer me the *silent and daily penance*, which arises from your doing well, in every circumstance of your life, solely the Will of the Lord, by the humble, faithful and perfect carrying out of all your duties. If you act thus, how many precious occasions of suffering and of making offerings will present themselves to you in the course of one entire day! Your smile, serenity, calm, patience, acceptance and offering are true silent penances, which give greater value and light to every circumstance of your life.

i   I am asking you also for *exterior penance*, which is always exercised in controlling the passions, in mortifying your senses, especially those of the eyes, of the tongue, of hearing and of taste.

j   Do not look at the great evil which surrounds you and at so much impurity which infects your streets. Renounce watching television, in order to conserve the light in your soul and in order to give, in your life, greater space for recollection, for meditation and for prayer.

k   Know how to hold the tongue in check and to keep silence within you and about you, so that you may be able to speak only for the spread of good, in a spirit of love and humble service to all. Flee criticism and grumbling, gossip and malicious speech. Do not give in to the easy temptation of judgment and condemnation.

l   Close the ears and the mind to the uproar of voices, which today is becoming more and more deafening and is bringing you to live in the midst of clamor, of confusion and of aridity.

m   Mortify the appetite by refraining from that which gives you greater pleasure and also through the practice of bodily fasting, requested by Jesus in his Gospel and which I again ask of you today.

n   If you walk along this road which I am tracing out for you, the days of your life will then be blessed by the Lord and will bring you to peace of heart and purity of soul. You yourselves will become my lived word, and you will bring everywhere the light of my presence in the great darkness which has become heavier upon the world.

o   *On this luminous pathway* of conversion and of penance, I am ever leading you, especially during these days, preparatory to the great miracle of divine mercy, which as of now is about to be accomplished."

348 Dongo (Como, Italy); April 16, 1987
Holy Thursday

Enter with Jesus into Gethsemane

a   "Live, in the virginal cloister of my Immaculate Heart intimately associated with Jesus, these painful hours of his redemptive passion. This is his Pasch. This is your pasch.

b   Today, call to mind the institution of the new Sacrifice and of the new Priesthood. In his loving plan, with the twelve Apostles, you were also all present, my beloved sons. It is the great feast of the Priesthood. You are again gathered about your bishops, to renew the promises you made on the day of your priestly ordination.

c   Today I invite you all to renew with me the pledge of your greatest fidelity. Be faithful to Jesus and to his Gospel; be faithful to the Pope and to the Church united with him; be faithful to the lived-out celebration of the Eucharist and to the administration of the sacraments, above all the sacrament of Reconciliation; be faithful to the obligation of holy celibacy, which you have assumed; be faithful to prayer, to the apostolate, to the exercise of an ever more perfect charity. Then you will be able to console the divine and priestly Heart of your Brother Jesus, for such great abandonment and for such an enormous treason, which is again being renewed today.

d   *Enter with Jesus into Gethsemane.* Allow yourselves to be clasped in his arms, that you may savor all the agony of a Heart which has loved most, which has given of itself most, and which is crushed by all the evil, the hatred and the sin of the world. This Heart has now so much need of comfort and does not find it. It seeks out the three dearest Apostles, and they are asleep; the beloved disciples and they are far away; a gesture of a friend and it receives the kiss of a traitor; the confirmation of a special love and it receives in reply a denial. Kiss his lips to savor all the bitterness of his chalice.

e   Then you will understand why, under the enormous weight which crushes and oppresses Him, a copious sweat and drops of blood begin to cover his divine body, stricken under the weight of the justice of the Father.

f   For this interior and most painful agony of his, may your prayer be a gentle caress; your priestly love, a compassionate hand which wipes away his blood; your fidelity, the awaited comfort; the perfect exercise of your ministry, the requested companionship; the giving of yourselves to souls, the clear water which quenches his thirst; and your purity, your humility, your littleness, solace to his deep wounds.

g   *Enter with Jesus into Gethsemane,* which is always being perpetuated in time. Only in this way do you purify and sanctify yourselves at the very source of your priesthood. Only in this way do you become the precious salt to make wholesome so many poisoned foods. Only in this way can you be lights enkindled on a lampstand, in the midst of the dense night of agony which enwraps the Church and all humanity.

h   And in the Immaculate Heart of your heavenly Mother, the dawn which announces the radiant day of Christ, you can become today witnesses of his shining triumph."

349
Dongo (Como, Italy); April 17, 1987
Good Friday

On the Calvary of This Century

a   "Climb with me, beloved sons, the Calvary of this century, and live, with your sorrowful Mother, the bloody moments of the passion, of the crucifixion and of the death of my Son Jesus. Take part, you also, in his suffering.

b   Relive in your soul all his sufferings: the betrayal, the denial, the judgment and the condemnation on the part of the religious tribunal. Here his continual ostracization reaches its most painful peak in his official rejection, in very fact in his condemnation to death.

c   Follow Jesus as He is led to the trial before Pilate and is abused, insulted, scourged, crowned with thorns, led to the gibbet and crucified. Relive with me these moments, which are now beyond time, as they pertain to a divine and eternal plan of love. Climb with me the Calvary of this century of yours, in order to understand how again today his passion is being repeated.

d   *On the Calvary of this century*, Jesus is again abandoned by all those who rebel against God and who repeat the wicked words of his rejection: 'We do not want that man to rule over us!' (Lk 19:14) How great today is the sea of denial of God! How innumerable is the throng of those who wish to live without having anything to do with Him!

e   *On the Calvary of this century*, Jesus is again betrayed by those who are not faithful to the promises of their baptism. They al-

506

low themselves to be guided by Satan and become victims of all his facile seductions. Thus they walk along the roads of evil, of pleasure, of egoism, of pride, of hatred and of impiety. Jesus is also betrayed in the Church by those pastors who separate themselves from the true faith and from the truth of the Gospel and who drag a great number of souls along the road of infidelity.

f   *On the Calvary of this century,* Jesus is again denied by many of his disciples, who do not have the courage to witness to Him before all and who, through fear of not being considered or esteemed and in their dread of being derided or ostracized, repeat continually: 'I do not know this man!' (Mt 26:74)

g   Jesus is scourged in his body by the spread of sins of impurity, by this flood of filth which is submerging everything and by so many offenses which are committed against the dignity of the human person.

h   Jesus is again crowned with thorns by the errors which are propagated and by the loss of the true faith on the part of many.

i   *On the Calvary of this century,* Jesus is continually crucified and put to death in the millions of innocent babies, who are snatched from life while they are still in the wombs of their mothers, and in all the victims of hatred, of violence and of war. Jesus is crucified in the poor, in the exploited, in the weak, in the oppressed and in the persecuted. Jesus is struck again in the little ones, in the marginalized, in the abandoned, in the sick and in the dying.

j   *On the Calvary of this century of yours,* indifferent and cruel, Jesus repeats again his bloody passion.

k   But beneath the cross of this century, there is always your sorrowful Mother. Like John, you too remain with me, all of you, my beloved sons. Let us receive into our arms Jesus who, on Calvary, is taken down from the Cross, and let us surround Him with love and with tender pity. Let us place Him in the empty sepulchre, hewn from the hard and cold rock of this century of yours, which is marked by the triumph of Satan and of his dark reign of hatred and of death.

l   And let us keep watch in prayer, in hope and in expectation. Keep watch ever with me, your sorrowful Mother who, in the profound night of this century, still keeps burning the light of confidence and of the certainty of his glorious return."

The Sabbath of My Great Sorrow

a   "My beloved sons, remain today close to me, who am your so
sorrowful Mother. This is the day of my great sorrow. It is the
only day that I lived with Jesus dead.

b   After having devoutly placed Him in the sepulchre with the
help of John and the holy women, after a great stone had been
rolled before the entrance of his tomb, for the first time I remained without my Son. Time, for me, came to a halt at that
moment.

c   Then began my continual vigil, in an unceasing prayer which
gave rhythm to the passing of the hours, in a firm hope which
succeeded in penetrating the door of heaven, in a profound
and intense suffering, until I was finally able to give free expression to my motherly sorrow, and continuous tears flowed
down from my eyes, as though to form a cradle of weeping, in
which to place all of you, who had been entrusted to me by
Jesus on the Cross.

d   It is the Sabbath of the great repose.
It is the Sabbath of the great silence.
It is the Sabbath of my great sorrow.
It is the one and only day on which the Mother remains alone,
crucified and imploring, confident and faithful, crushed under
the weight of her suffering.

e   It is the day when your Mother too has such need of comfort.
It is the day when the Mother has need of the love of all her
children.

f   I gather you today in my motherly arms and am consoled to
feel that you truly love me as children. It seems to me that I
again hear his voice, reaching out in his extreme and most precious offering: 'Woman, behold your son!' (Jn 19:26)

g   Today, in the cradle of this sorrow of mine, all of you open
yourselves to receive the divine fruit of this, his ultimate gift.
This is my day, and yours. Enter into the new sabbatical repose
of my spiritual motherhood. The Church has received this gift
as the first fruit of the passion and the death of my Son Jesus.
This is the reason why — from most ancient times — the tradition has spread of dedicating Saturday to a special veneration in

my respect.

h   I am asking you again today to consecrate this day to me. It is the day that marks the passing of time between the death and resurrection of Jesus. It is a day of passage for all: from death to life, from passion to glory, from egoism to love, from slavery to freedom, from deepest darkness to the light which knows no decline. Enter into this luminous repose.

i   This is why I invite you again to dedicate Saturday in my honor, so that I can help you to enter into your repose, by living each day your pasch together with me, the sorrowful Mother of the Passion and the joyful Mother of the Resurrection."

351

Milan (Italy); May 13, 1987
Anniversary of the First Apparition at Fatima
Vigil of my Departure for the United States and Canada

Into What an Abyss You Have Fallen!

a   "Today you are calling to mind the seventy years since my first apparition in the poor Cova da Iria in Fatima, where I came from heaven to give you my message of conversion and of salvation. Since that time, the succession of these years has been a continual confirmation of what I had foretold to you:

b   —The refusal to return to God through conversion has brought all humanity along the arid and cold road of hatred, of violence, of sin and of an ever increasingly widespread impurity. Wars have continually succeeded, one upon another, and despite so many efforts you have not succeeded in building peace. On the contrary, today as never before, the world is being more and more threatened with its very own destruction.

c   — There is an unwillingness to respond to my demand for prayer, which I had made to you then, especially with the frequent recitation of the holy rosary, to obtain the conversion of sinners and the salvation of many souls, exposed to the grave danger of being eternally lost.

d   Thus the night of sin has enveloped the world, and evil has spread everywhere like a terrible cancer. There is an unwillingness to recognize sin as an evil; on the contrary it is openly justified and exalted as a good. People no longer go to confession.

They live and die habitually in mortal sin, and every day how many souls go to hell, because there is no one to pray and sacrifice for their salvation.

e   — My request that Russia be consecrated to me, by the Pope together with all the bishops, has not been accepted, and thus she has spread her errors in every part of the world.

f   You are living in a humanity which has built a new civilization, atheistic and anti-human. People no longer love one another; they no longer respect the life and the good of their neighbor; the flames of egoism and hatred are extinguishing those seeds of goodness which are still springing up in the hearts of men. The poor are being abandoned; the little ones are being ensnared and nourished with the poisoned food of scandal; the youth are being betrayed and led into precocious experiences of evil; homes are being profaned and destroyed...

g   How great is your desolation! How dense is the darkness which surrounds you! *Into what an abyss you have fallen!*

h   Satan has succeeded in extending everywhere his reign of darkness and of death, and he rules as an assured victor.

i   But you are now beginning to live through that which I had foretold to you at Fatima for the last years of this century of yours and which is still guarded under the veil of secrecy. These are my times. After the painful years of Satan's triumph, the years of the triumph of my Immaculate Heart are now beginning.

j   For this reason I invite you all today to second this plan of mine and to accept this loving work of mine, which I myself am carrying out in every part of the world through my Marian Movement of Priests. And I am still making use of you, the littlest of my children, and I am bringing you everywhere, to even the most distant places, for a new and ultimate call to action.

k   As of now, the great events are coming about. For this my Pope has called an extraordinary Marian Year. And so, enter, all of you, into the refuge of my Immaculate Heart which I have prepared for you.

l   These are the years when, from the profound abyss of darkness and of desolation, I will lead you to the highest summit of light, of grace and of love because, by means of the triumph of my Immaculate Heart, the glorious reign of my Son Jesus will shine resplendently upon all the world."

510

Your Light Will Return

a   "You find yourself here today in the National Shrine, dedicated to my Immaculate Conception, to hold a cenacle of prayer and of brotherly sharing with the priests and the faithful, who will be coming from even very far, and you are beginning a long and tiring journey which will bring you throughout all the United States and Canada.

b   I welcome into my Immaculate Heart this great nation, exposed to grave dangers. I welcome into my Immaculate Heart my Church, which is going through hours of agony and of painful crucifixion here, because of the loss of the true faith on the part of many, of an ever deeper division, and of an obstinate opposition to the Pope. This is concretized in the ignoring of his Magisterium and even in the spreading of doctrine opposed to it and openly contrary to Catholic faith.

c   The cause of this grave situation is the pastors. Bishops of the holy Church of God, return along the road pointed out by the Good Shepherd, be faithful to the Gospel, and guard, with strength and courage, the deposit of the faith which has been entrusted to you. Bishops of the holy Church of God, return to a full, humble and total unity with the Pope, because today you are running the danger of a most grave schism and because of this how great is your responsibility before God!

d   Bishops and priests of the holy Church of God, return once more to interesting yourselves in souls, the supreme good which has been entrusted to you. Defend them against the assaults of the rapacious wolves, who frequently disguise themselves today as harmless and gentle lambs. See how confusion is increasing, the darkness becoming deep, errors spreading and sin flooding everywhere. Take care of the flock which has been entrusted to you; lead it to sure pastures; nourish it with the word of God; strengthen it by prayer; heal it by the sacrament of Reconciliation; feed it with the bread of the Eucharist.

e   My motherly Heart wants to save all of this so great nation. I welcome you today, O America, into the refuge of my Immaculate Heart. I put myself at your side to help you to recover. I myself am traveling your roads in search of all my poor children, wandering, sick, marginalized, wounded, stricken, abandoned and betrayed. I welcome you into my Heart today, O Church of my Jesus, who are living and suffering here, O Church, one, holy, catholic, apostolic, united to my Pope of Rome.

f   The times of your suffering are now counted. Soon you will flower again, when my Immaculate Heart will have its triumph, *and your light will return* to shine with such intensity that it will draw all those who live in this great continent.

g   From my shrine, I encourage you all, and I bless you in the name of the Father, and of the Son, and of the Holy Spirit."

353   *Denver (Colorado, U.S.A.); May 23, 1987*

The Deep Wounds

a   "I am your immaculate Mother. I am the consoler of the afflicted. How many sufferings you find, O son, along this route of yours. While you receive from all sides such a generous response to my call, on the part of my priests and above all on the part of so many of my faithful, you see everywhere *the deep wounds* and the great sufferings, which are the signs of the wicked times in which you are living.

b   They are suffering, those who reject God and are walking along the road of an empty and hopeless life.

They are suffering, the little ones who are opening up to life upon a world which has become an immense desert, for lack of love.

They are suffering, the youth to whom are proposed all the experiences of evil and who are being betrayed by such a vast diffusion of impurity and of drugs.

They are suffering, the adults, because of the division which has entered into families and because of the tremendous wound of divorce.

They are suffering, the old people who have been abandoned to themselves and who are looked upon as an insupportable burden.

Your days of chastisement through which you are living are marked by profound sufferings.

c   Do not be discouraged. Enter into the refuge of my Immaculate Heart. Allow yourselves to be led by my light, which will shine out more and more, because these are my times. I am the dew upon all of your wounds; I am the consolation for all your sufferings.

d I am your tender Mother, who is at your side to conduct you to the Lord of salvation and of joy."

354   *Seattle (Washington, U.S.A.); June 2, 1987*

How It Makes His Divine Heart Suffer!

a "How I receive with joy the cenacle which you are holding here today, in the cathedral, with my beloved sons and with a great number of my children, come from even the most distant parts of this state. I accept the homage of your love and of your reparation.

b Jesus is today again despised, scourged and wounded in his Mystical Body. *How* the permissive attitude of many priests and of some bishops who justify even the gravest acts of impurity *makes his divine Heart suffer!*

c Precisely here, in this very place, the Heart of Jesus has been despised, wounded and outraged by the welcoming of so many of my poor children, consumed by this terrible vice and by the public encouragement given to them to continue along the road of impure sin against nature. Impure acts against nature are sins which cry for vengeance in the sight of God. These sins draw down upon you and upon your nations the flames of the justice of God.

d The time has come to proclaim to all, with clarity and with courage, that the sixth commandment given by God to Moses: 'Do not commit impure acts,' (cf. Ex 20:14) still has its full force and must be observed even by this corrupted and perverted generation.

e Every pastor who, in any manner whatsoever, would justify these sins, draws down upon his person and upon his life the fierce fire of divine justice. The cup of iniquity is now full, is more than full and is flowing over everywhere.

f And so I invite you to multiply your cenacles of prayer and to offer me your lives, made fragrant by the virtue of purity, as a powerful force of supplication and of reparation.

g   I promise you that even now the heavens are on the point of opening upon this poor corrupt world, to cause the fiery dew of divine justice and of mercy to descend so that it may again become a new garden of light, of purity and of holiness."

355

Detroit (Michigan, U.S.A.); June 7, 1987
Solemnity of Pentecost
Solemn Opening of the Marian Year

Come, Lord Jesus

a   "My dearly beloved ones and sons consecrated to me, today come all to the safe refuge of my Immaculate Heart. This is the cenacle which the Mother has prepared in these times for the Church, her beloved Daughter.

b   The whole Church must now enter into the cenacle of my Immaculate Heart: all the bishops, the priests, the religious and the faithful must enter. In the Cenacle of Jerusalem, upon the Apostles gathered in prayer with me, there descended the Holy Spirit, and there took place the miracle of the first Pentecost. Thus, only in the cenacle of my Immaculate Heart, when the whole Church will have entered in, will the great prodigy of the second Pentecost take place. It will be a divine fire of purification and of sanctification which will renew all the face of the earth.

c   My times have come. This is why the Pope, the first of my beloved sons, is today opening an extraordinary Marian Year in my honor. I am asking that the whole Church gather together in prayer with me, Mother of Intercession and of Reparation. I want that all who belong to my Movement increase in the personal commitment of their consecration, because in you my Immaculate Heart must be more and more glorified.

d   For this I am asking you to multiply everywhere your cenacles of prayer and of brotherly sharing and to lead the greatest number possible of my children to the consecration to my Immaculate Heart.

e   In this year there will already begin to take place some of the events of which I have foretold you, as signs of my proximate

514

triumph. Prepare yourselves in a spirit of humility, of confidence and of great hope. Open the doors of your hearts to receive the great Gift which the Father and the Son will cause to come down upon you.

f   The Spirit of the Lord will fill the earth and change the world.

The Spirit of the Lord will renew, with his divine fire, all the Church and will lead her to the perfection of holiness and of her splendor.

The Spirit of the Lord will transform the hearts and the souls of men and make of them courageous witnesses of his divine love.

The Spirit of the Lord will prepare humanity to receive the glorious reign of Christ, that the Father may be loved and glorified by everyone.

g   This is why I invite you today to begin with love and with prayer, this extraordinary year, dedicated to your heavenly Mother.

h   I will obtain for you the gift of the Holy Spirit.

I will lead you along the road of piety and of love.

I will gather you together in the cenacle of my Heart in an act of unceasing prayer.

I will bring you together from every part of the earth, because the hour of my triumph has come.

The hour that for years I have foretold you has arrived.

i   For this reason, my action will be, from now on, stronger, more extraordinary and more noticed by all.

j   Gather together in my Immaculate Heart, so that your voices can be joined with mine in a continuous prayer.

k   *I am the dawn which is arising to announce the arrival of the brilliant sun of Christ.* Welcome my message with joy, and in this Marian Year, unite yourselves all to your heavenly Mother in repeating her perennial invocation which she pronounces together with her divine Spouse:'*Come, Lord Jesus.*'" (Rev 22:20)

356   *Ottawa (Ontario, Canada); June 10, 1987*

This Marian Year

a   "Walk in trust. Join in my plan. *This Marian Year* which, under my interior inspiration, my Pope has promulgated for all the Church *is an extraordinary event of grace and of mercy.*

b During this year I am calling all the children of the Church to gather together with me in cenacles of unceasing prayer. Most of all I desire that the holy rosary be recited often, particularly by the little ones, by the sick, by the poor and by sinners.

c Surround the world with the chain of the rosary in order to obtain grace and mercy for all. Multiply your cenacles of prayer. During this year I am urging all to respond to my request to consecrate themselves to my Immaculate Heart.

d This request of mine finds its practical actualization in my Marian Movement of Priests which I myself am forming and spreading throughout every part of the world in order to call everyone to that consecration willed and demanded by me. It is my ardent motherly desire that during the Marian Year the work of my priestly Movement be officially welcomed with joy and recognized by the Church.

e It will moreover be particularly important for the development of the great events which have been foretold to you by me if, during this year, there be at last carried out my request, made to my daughter, Sister Lucia of Fatima, that Russia be consecrated to me by the Pope together with all the bishops of the world.

f During this year, I am calling all my children to gather together at my many shrines, spread throughout every part of the earth, in order to make a general appeal for my motherly assistance. This should also be accompanied by personal and communal works of penance and of reparation for the grave individual and social sins which are constantly being committed more and more.

g I then promise you that, in the course of this Marian Year, I myself will intervene to carry out part of what I have foretold to you and which for the present is still being guarded in secrecy and in silence.

h *During this year I will manifest my great power to the Church and to the world.* My light will become stronger, and the great events will begin to be accomplished.

i And so I beg everyone not to let pass uselessly such an extraordinary occasion of grace which, with this Marian Year, the mercy of the Lord has again granted to the Church and to all humanity."

516

357

Valdragone (San Marino); July 3, 1987
Spiritual Exercises in the Form of a Continuous Cenacle
(Message given orally after the evening procession)

My Times Have Arrived

a   "My beloved sons, how consoled I am by you this evening, and how many thorns you have drawn from my sorrowful Heart! You have wanted to carry me in procession, and you have wanted to honor me; I have smiled upon you. I have been so consoled by you; your love is the balm which my Son Jesus places on the many wounds of my Immaculate Heart. As Mother, I want to express to you my gratitude this evening.

b   Many of you have come from distant countries after a long journey. You have come up here, and you have offered me the homage of your prayer, of your filial love, of your priestly fraternal sharing, of your penance. You have wanted to offer up, in a spirit of penance and mortification, this heat, which has made the spiritual exercises a bit more burdensome.

c   My beloved sons, you have consoled me. My Heart leaps with joy and with tenderness. I am grateful to each one of you for the filial balm which you have wanted to pour on the many wounds of my immaculate and so sorrowful Heart.

d   Why have I called you up here once again? Why, during this Marian Year consecrated to me, have I wanted you about my person as the Mother who gathers her children together to make a recommendation which she has so very much at heart, a very last recommendation that keeps you company on your difficult journey?

e   *My times have arrived, my beloved sons*; these are my times.

f   And so I have called you here, in a cenacle which has never been so extraordinary for its graces. They have come down from my Immaculate Heart to enter into your hearts and into the hearts of all your brothers, scattered throughout every part of the world; they have come down upon the Church and upon all humanity.

g   Why has my Pope desired to consecrate this year to me by declaring an extraordinary Marian Year, in order to invite the whole Church to look to me, to listen to me, to honor me, to follow me, to enter into the refuge of my Immaculate Heart?

h   *Because my times have come.* As of this year, in a strong and official way, the times of your heavenly Mother will begin.

i   *These are the times of my strong admonition.* Come back, O humanity so far away and depraved; come back along the road of conversion and of a return to the Lord of your salvation! These are the times of my great admonition, and you are here because I want to make you instruments of this appeal of mine.

j   As you go down from this mountain, to all whom you will meet in all the countries to which you will return, you must proclaim and spread this motherly, anxious and urgent message of mine: Come back immediately to the God of salvation and of peace! The time that is granted to you for your conversion is almost over; the days are counted. Walk along the road of return to the Lord if you want to be saved.

k   Beloved sons, I have need of voices that will spread my word, of hands that will help, of feet that will walk along all the roads of the world. I have need that this urgent message of mine immediately reach every part of the earth. You must be my messengers; announce everywhere this concerned call of mine for return to the Lord.

l   *These are the times of the great chastisement.* The cup of divine justice is full, is more than full, is flowing over.

m   Iniquity covers the whole earth; the Church is darkened by the spread of apostasy and of sin. The Lord, for the triumph of his mercy, must as of now purify with his strong action of justice and of love. The most painful, most bloody hours are in preparation for you. These times are closer than you think. Already during this Marian Year, certain great events will take place, concerning what I predicted at Fatima and have told, under secrecy, to the children to whom I am appearing at Medjugorje.

n   And so bring all my children into the refuge of my Immaculate Heart; call them; take them by the hand; do not forget anyone. Beloved sons, see along your roads those who are far away, the little ones, the poor, those cast aside, the persecuted, the sinners, the drug addicts, those who are victims of the reign of Satan. I want to save all my children. I have need of you because I want to save them through you. In the time of the chastisement, they must be protected and defended; they must be helped and consoled. Why do you not want to heed my voice which is

518

imploring you this evening to go everywhere so as to gather the weakest, the littlest, the most fragile, those who are suffering most, those who are furthest away, those who are lost. Bring them all to me because I want them all in the secure refuge of my Immaculate Heart.

o   *These are the times of the great return.* Yes, after the time of the great suffering, there will be the time of the great rebirth, and all will blossom again. Humanity will again be a new garden of life and of beauty and the Church, a family enlightened by truth, nourished by grace, consoled by the presence of the Holy Spirit. Jesus will restore his glorious reign. He will dwell with you, and you will know the new times, the new era. You will at last see a new earth and new heavens.

p   *These are the times of the great mercy.* The Father thrills with ardor and wills to pour out upon this poor humanity the torrents of his infinite love. The Father wants to mold with his hands a new creation where his divine imprint will be more visible, welcomed and received and his fatherhood exalted and glorified by all. The breath of this new creation will be the breath of the love of the Father who will be glorified by all, while the fullness of his divine love will spread everywhere in an increasingly fuller way, like water which gushes from a living and inexhaustible fount.

q   And Jesus will reign: Jesus for whom all has been created, Jesus who became incarnate, who became your Brother, who lived with you, who suffered and died on the Cross to redeem humanity and bring it to a new creation and so that his reign might gradually be disseminated in hearts, in souls, in individuals, in families and in all society.

r   Jesus, who has taught you the prayer to invoke the coming of the reign of God upon earth, will at last see fulfilled this prayer of his, because He will restore his reign. And creation will again be a new garden where Christ will be glorified by all, and his divine kingship will be welcomed and exalted. It will be a universal reign of grace, of beauty, of harmony, of communion, of holiness, of justice and of peace.

s   The great mercy will come to you as a burning fire of love and will be brought by the Holy Spirit, who is given to you by the Father and the Son, so that the Father may see Himself glorified and the Lord Jesus may feel Himself loved by all his brothers.

t The Holy Spirit will come down as fire, but in a manner different from his first coming: it will be a fire which will burn and transform everything, which will sanctify and renew the earth from its foundations. It will open hearts to a new reality of life and lead all souls to a fullness of holiness and of grace. You will know a love that is so great and a sanctity that is so perfect that it will be such as you had never known before. It is in this that the Spirit will be glorified: in bringing everyone to the greatest love for the Father and for the Son.

u *These are the times of the great mercy*: they are therefore the times of the triumph of my Immaculate Heart. It is for this that I have again wanted you up here. Now you must go down to be the apostles of my message. Bring to every part of the earth my pressing request to gather together, all of you, in the cenacle of my Immaculate Heart, to prepare yourselves to live the awaited vigil of the new times which are now at the doors.

v Do not become discouraged by the difficulties which you encounter. I am your comfort. I am the Mother of Consolation. One by one, I welcome you and with you the souls who are entrusted to you, your dear ones, the persons whom you love, your brothers who are furthest away.

w Do not forget anyone; come to me together, because I am the Mother of all, and you are only the instruments, chosen by me, to bring all my children to my Immaculate Heart.

x With your dear ones, with those who have been entrusted to you, I bless you in the name of the Father, and of the Son, and of the Holy Spirit."

358   *San Quirino (Pordenone, Italy); July 23, 1987*
(After the recitation of the holy rosary)

The Families Consecrated to Me

a "How consoled I am by this day spent in prayer, in a simple and cordial fraternal gathering, with this family, consecrated to me and which belongs to me! I want now to give you my word of consolation, that it may be a comfort for you in the midst of the daily difficulties of your life. I love you; I am present in your midst; I am speaking to you and leading you because you are the instruments of my motherly will.

b   *I look with love on the families consecrated to me.* In these times, I am gathering the families and leading them into the depths of my Immaculate Heart, that they may be able to find refuge and security, comfort and defense. Just as I love to be invoked as Mother and Queen of my priests, so also I love to be invoked as Mother and Queen of the families consecrated to me.

c   *I am the Mother and the Queen of families.* I watch over their life; I take their problems to heart; I interest myself not only in their spiritual good but also in the material good of all their members. When you consecrate a family to my Immaculate Heart, it is as though you open the door of your house to your heavenly Mother, invite her to come in, and give her the opportunity to exercise her motherly function in an ever stronger way.

d   This is why I desire that all Christian families consecrate themselves to my Immaculate Heart. I ask that they open the doors of all their homes to me so that I may come in and take up my motherly dwelling among you. I then come in as your Mother, I dwell with you, and I take a part in all your life.

e   *Above all I see to the care of your spiritual life.* I seek to bring the souls of those who compose the family to live always in the grace of God. There where I enter in, sin goes out; there where I stay, grace and divine light are always present; there where I dwell, purity and holiness dwell with me. That is why my first motherly task is that of making the members of the family live in the state of grace and of making them grow in the life of holiness, through the exercise of all the Christian virtues.

f   And because the sacrament of Matrimony confers on you a particular grace to make you grow together, my task is that of cementing deeply the unity of the family, to bring the husband and wife to an ever deeper and more spiritual communion, to perfect their human love, to make it more perfect, to bring it into the Heart of Jesus, so that it may assume the new form of a greater perfection, which expresses itself in a pure and supernatural charity. I strengthen more and more unity within families. I bring them to a greater and reciprocal understanding; I make them feel the new exigencies of a more delicate and profound communion.

g   I lead their members along the road of sanctity and of joy, which must be built up and traveled through together, that they may be able to attain the perfection of love and thus enjoy the precious gift of peace. Thus I form the souls of my children, and through the way of the family, I lead them to the summit of holiness.

h   I want to enter families to make you saints, to bring you to the perfection of love, to stay with you, to make your family unity more fruitful and strong.

i   *And then I see also to the material good of the families consecrated to me.*

j   The most precious good of a family is its children. The children are a sign of a particular predilection on the part of Jesus and of me. The children must be wanted, welcomed and cultivated like the most precious gems of a family estate. When I enter into a family, I immediately look after the children; they become also mine. I take them by the hand; I lead them to walk along the road of the realization of a plan of God, which has from all eternity already been clearly traced out for each one of them. I love them. I never abandon them. They become a precious part of my maternal estate.

k   *I see to your work in a special way.* I never allow you to be lacking in the assistance of divine providence. I take your hands, and I open them upon the plan which the Lord is carrying out each day, by means of your human collaboration.

l   As my humble, faithful and daily motherly action in the little and poor house of Nazareth made possible the fulfillment of the Father's plan, which was realized in the human growth of the Son, called to carry out the work of redemption for your salvation, so too I am calling you to second the plan of the Father, which is being realized through your human collaboration and by means of your daily work.

m   You must do your part, as the Heavenly Father does his. Your action must be espoused to that of divine providence, that the

522

work may produce its fruit in those goods which are useful for the sustaining of your life, for the enrichment of the family itself, in such a way that its members can always enjoy spiritual and material well-being.

n   And then I will help you to carry out the plan of the Will of God. Thus I make the work more fruitful spiritually, because I make of it a source of merit for you and an occasion of salvation for many of my poor lost children. Then, in your person, action is united to love, work to prayer, fatigue to the burning thirst of an ever greater charity. In this way, by your collaboration with the Will of the Father, you form the masterpiece of a providence which, by means of you, becomes a day-to-day reality.

o   Do not be afraid; there where I enter in, security enters in with me. Nothing will ever be lacking to you. I make your activity more perfect; I purify your very work.

p   *I share also in all your preoccupations.* I know that the preoccupations of a family today are many. They are yours, and they become mine. I share with you your sufferings. That is why, in such difficult times as those of the present purification, I am present in the families consecrated to me, as a concerned and suffering Mother, who really takes part in all your suffering. Be therefore consoled.

q   *These are my times.* 'These,' that is to say the days in which you are living, are 'mine,' because they are times marked by my great and strong presence. These times will become even more mine, the more my victory will broaden out and become stronger, surpassing the victory which at present is that of my Adversary. This presence of mine will become very strong and extraordinary, above all in the families consecrated to my Immaculate Heart. It will become apparent to all and will become for you a source of a special consolation.

r   So then go forward in confidence, in hope, in silence, in your daily work, in prayer and in humility. Go forward more and more in purity and with an upright intention; advance with me along the difficult road of peace of heart and of peace in your families.

s   If you all walk along the road which I have traced out for you, if you listen to and put into practice what I have said to you today, your families will be the first buds of my triumph: small, hidden, quiet buds, which are already sprouting in every part of the earth, as though to anticipate the new era and the new times which are even now at your doors.

t   I encourage you all, and I bless you."

359

The Pope of My Light

a   "Beloved sons, I am calling you all today to form a strong barrier of prayer and of defense about my Pope. Pope John Paul II is the greatest gift which my Immaculate Heart has obtained from the Heart of Jesus for these times of yours, times of the painful purification.

b   He is my Pope. He has been formed by me. At every moment, he is led by me along the road of his personal consecration to your heavenly Mother, a road which he has followed with docility, with filial abandonment and with great trust. He is an important part of my plan.

c   *He is the Pope of my light* which, in these years, he has succeeded in spreading in the Church and in every part of this humanity which is so very threatened. I myself am leading him along all the roads of the world. He follows me with the docility of a little child, with the courage of an apostle, with the sacrifice of a martyr, with the abandonment of a son. This Pope is the masterpiece of my predilection and has the great task of giving to all the charism of my motherly tenderness.

d   I look on him at this time with the anxious concern of a mother, while my Immaculate Heart is filled with profound anguish. How many dangers surround him; how strong are the snares which my Adversary sets for him along his way! Those who are making attempts upon his life are on the point of carrying out their dark design. At this time, the hour of Calvary and of his personal immolation is close.

e   And so, my beloved ones and children consecrated to my Heart, you be his great crown of joy, by your filial affection, by your unceasing prayer, by your suffering which is accepted and offered up, by your unity which is lived out and witnessed to. Help him, by your priestly fidelity, to carry a very heavy cross. Sustain him by your loving presence in the painful journey towards Calvary. And be, all of you, beneath his cross, by your filial affection, like John, together with your heavenly Mother, to live with him the hour of his sacrifice."

360
Rubbio (Vicenza, Italy); August 21, 1987
Feast of St. Pius X
(Message given orally during the recitation of the holy rosary)

Mother of Adoration and of Reparation

a   "Beloved sons, I am happy that you have come up here, as little children who let themselves be carried in my motherly arms. Become ever littler, more docile, purer, simpler, more abandoned and faithful. How great is the joy which my motherly Heart experiences when I am able to carry you all, as a precious and fragrant homage to offer to my Son Jesus, truly present in the sacrament of the Eucharist!

b   *I am the Mother of Adoration and of Reparation.* Beside every tabernacle of the earth, there is always my motherly presence. It forms a new and loving tabernacle for the solitary presence of my Son Jesus; it builds a garden of love for his permanent residence among you; it forms a celestial harmony which surrounds Him with all the enchantment of paradise in the adoring choirs of angels, in the blessed prayer of the saints, in the painful aspiration of the many souls who are being purified in purgatory. In my Immaculate Heart all form a concert of perennial adoration, of unceasing prayer and of profound love for Jesus, really present in every tabernacle on earth.

c   Today my motherly Heart is saddened and is deeply wounded because I see that, about the divine presence of Jesus in the Eucharist, there is so much emptiness, so much abandonment, so much neglect, so much silence.

d   O Church, pilgrim and suffering, of which I am the Mother, Church, who are the family of all my children, ark of the new alliance, people of God, you must understand that the center of your life, the fount of your grace, the source of your light, the beginning of your apostolic action is found only here in the tabernacle where Jesus is truly kept. And Jesus is present to teach you how to grow, to help you to walk, to strengthen you in giving witness, to give you courage in evangelizing, to be a support for all your sufferings.

e   O pilgrim and suffering Church of these times, who are being called to live the agony of Gethsemane and the bloody hour of your Calvary, I want to bring you here today with me, prostrate before every tabernacle, in an act of perpetual adoration and reparation, so that you too may be able to repeat the action that is always being carried out by your heavenly Mother.

f   *I am the Mother of Adoration and of Reparation.* In the Eucharist Jesus is *really present* with his Body, with his Blood, with his Soul and with his Divinity. In the Eucharist, *there is really present Jesus Christ*, the Son of God, that God who, in Him, I saw at every moment of his earthly life, even if He was hidden under the veil of a fragile and feeble nature, which developed through the rhythm of time and of his human growth. By a continual act of faith in my Son Jesus, I always saw my God, and I adored Him with profound love.

g   *I adored Him* when He was still guarded within my virginal womb, as a little bud, and I loved Him, nourished Him, caused Him to grow, giving Him my own flesh and my own blood.

h   *I adored Him* after his birth, contemplating Him in the manger of a poor and bare cave.

i   *I adored my God* in the Child Jesus who was growing, in the adolescent who was maturing, in the young man who was bending over his daily work, in the Messiah who was carrying out his public mission.

j   *I adored Him* when He was rejected and repulsed, when He was betrayed, abandoned and denied by his own.

k   *I adored Him* when He was condemned and mocked, when He was scourged and crowned with thorns, when He was led to the gibbet and crucified.

l   *I adored Him* beneath the Cross, in an act of unspeakable suffering, and when He was brought to the sepulchre and placed in his tomb.

m   *I adored Him* after his resurrection when, firstly, He appeared

526

to me in the splendor of his glorified body and in the light of his divinity.

n   Beloved sons, by a miracle of love which you will be able to understand only in paradise, *Jesus has given you the gift of remaining always in your midst in the Eucharist.*

o   In the tabernacle, under the veil of the consecrated Bread, there is kept the same Jesus whom I was the first to see after the miracle of his resurrection, the same Jesus who, in the splendor of his divinity, appeared to the eleven Apostles, to many disciples, to the weeping Magdalen, to the holy women who had followed Him all the way to the sepulchre.

p   In the tabernacle, hidden beneath the Eucharistic veil, the same risen Jesus is present who appeared again to more than five hundred disciples and who struck with a bolt of light Saul, the persecutor, on the road to Damascus. He is the same Jesus who is sitting at the right hand of the Father, in the splendor of his glorified body and of his divinity, even though, for love of you, He hides Himself under the white appearance of the consecrated Bread.

q   Beloved sons, today you must believe more in his presence among you; you must spread, with courage and with force, your priestly invitation for a return of all to a strong and witnessed faith in the real presence of Jesus Christ in the Eucharist. You must orientate the whole Church so that she will find herself before the tabernacle, with your heavenly Mother, in an act of perennial reparation, of continual adoration and of unceasing prayer. Your priestly prayer must become wholly a Eucharistic prayer.

r   I ask that there be once again a return to the practice of making everywhere hours of adoration before Jesus, exposed in the Most Holy Sacrament. I desire that there be an increase in the homage of love towards the Eucharist and that this become manifest also through evident but most expressive signs of your piety. Surround the Eucharistic Jesus with flowers and with lights; encircle Him with delicate attention; draw close to Him with profound acts of genuflection and of adoration.

s   If you knew how the Eucharistic Jesus loves you, how a little gesture of your love fills Him with joy and with consolation! Jesus pardons so many sacrileges and forgets an infinity of ingratitude before one drop of pure priestly love which is placed in the chalice of his Eucharistic Heart.

t   Priests and faithful of my Movement, go often before the tabernacle; live before the tabernacle; pray before the tabernacle.

u   *Let yours be a continual prayer* of adoration and of intercession, of thanksgiving and of reparation. Let yours be a prayer which is united to the heavenly song of the angels and the saints, to the ardent supplications of the souls who are still being purified in purgatory. Let yours be a prayer which brings together the voices of all humanity which should prostrate itself before every tabernacle of the earth, in an act of continual gratitude and of daily thanksgiving.

v   Because, in the Eucharist, Jesus Christ is really present, He remains ever with you, and this presence of his will become increasingly stronger, will shine over the earth like a sun and will mark the beginning of a new era. The coming of the glorious reign of Christ will coincide with the greatest splendor of the Eucharist. Christ will restore his glorious reign in the universal triumph of his Eucharistic reign, which will unfold in all its power and will have the capacity to change hearts, souls, individuals, families, society and the very structure of the world.

w   When He will have restored his Eucharistic reign, Jesus will lead you to take joy in this habitual presence of his, which you will feel in a new and extraordinary way and which will lead you to the experience of a second, renewed and more beautiful earthly paradise.

x   But before the tabernacle, yours should be not only a presence of prayer, but also of *a communion of life with Jesus.* Jesus is really present in the Eucharist because He wants to enter into a continual communion of life with you. When you go before Him, He sees you; when you speak to Him, He hears you; when you confide something to Him, He welcomes into his Heart your every word; when you ask something of Him, He always hears your prayer.

y   Go before the tabernacle to establish with Jesus a simple and daily rapport of life. With the same naturalness with which you seek out a friend, or entrust yourself to persons who are dear to you, or feel the need of friends who assist you, in that same way

528

go before the tabernacle to seek out Jesus. Make of Jesus your dearest friend, the most trusted person, the most desired and the most loved.

z   Tell your love to Jesus; repeat it often because this is the one thing that makes Him immensely happy, that consoles Him for all the ingratitude, that compensates Him for all the betrayals: 'Jesus, You are our love; Jesus, You alone are our great friend; Jesus, we love You; Jesus, we are in love with You.'

A   Indeed the presence of Christ in the Eucharist has above all the function of making you grow in an experience of true communion of love with Him such that you never again feel yourself alone, because He has remained here below to be always with you.

B   And so then, you must go before the tabernacle to gather the fruit of the prayer and of the communion of life with Jesus which develops and matures *into your holiness*. Beloved sons, the more your life revolves wholly and entirely at the foot of the tabernacle, in intimate union with Jesus in the Eucharist, the more you will increase in holiness. The Eucharistic Jesus becomes the model and the form of your holiness. He brings you to purity of heart, to humility which is sought and desired, to a lived-out confidence, to loving and filial abandonment.

C   The Eucharistic Jesus becomes the new form of your priestly holiness which you attain by means of a daily and hidden immolation, of a continual presence of love toward your brothers, of a capacity to welcome in your own person the sufferings and the crosses of all, of a possibility to transform evil into good and to act profoundly that souls, who have been entrusted to you, may be led by you to salvation.

D   For this reason I say to you: The times have come when I want you all before the tabernacle, and above all I want you priests who are the beloved sons of a Mother who is ever in an act of perpetual adoration and of unceasing reparation. Through you, I desire that the cult of the Eucharist again flourish in all the Church in an ever more powerful way.

E   As for now there must be an end to this profound crisis in regard to devotion to the Eucharist, a crisis which has contaminated the entire Church and which has been at the root of so much infidelity and of the diffusion of such a widespread apostasy.

F   With all my beloved ones and the children consecrated to me, who form part of my Movement, I place you before every tabernacle of the earth, to give you in homage to Jesus, as most precious jewels and most beautiful and fragrant flowers.

G   As of now, the heavenly Mother wants to bring to Jesus, present in the Eucharist, an ever greater number of her sons, because these are the times when the Eucharistic Jesus must be adored, loved, thanked and glorified by all.

H   My most dearly beloved sons, together with Jesus who, in every tabernacle, is in a state of continual victimhood for you, I bless you in the name of the Father, and of the Son, and of the Holy Spirit."

361

Tokyo (Japan); September 8, 1987
Feast of the Nativity of the Blessed Virgin Mary
Spiritual Exercises in the Form of a Cenacle
with the Priests of the M.M.P. of Japan

The Great Marvels of the Lord

a   "In this year consecrated to me, beloved sons, I am inviting you to all gather about the cradle of your infant Mother. Learn from me humility and littleness, docility and meekness, obedience and silence.

b   The Lord works only by means of littleness and of weakness. He lifts up the poor from the dust and leads the little ones along the road of his glory.

c   The mercy of the Lord manifests itself only by means of poverty and of misery. He fills the hungry with good things, gives health to the sick, salvation to the lost, confidence to the despairing, grace to the sinners.

d   The power of the Lord acts only by means of humility and docility. He exalts the humble, gives strength to the weak, leads the oppressed and downtrodden along the road of his love, looks with eyes of special love upon the marginalized and the persecuted.

e   Sing today with me *the great marvels of the Lord*. Exalt the mystery of his divine mercy. The greatest miracle of the merciful love of Jesus is about to be accomplished by means of the triumph of my Immaculate Heart in the world.

f   As of this year, I will begin to realize this triumph in an ever stronger and more extraordinary way. The Church and humanity will look with joy at the accomplishment of my motherly plan.

g   For its actualization I will make use of you, priests and faithful consecrated to my Immaculate Heart. For this, my little child, I have again brought you to these far distant countries, in order that you might repeat my announcement even to the most distant frontiers of the earth.

h   I am the dawn which is arising.
I am your infant Mother.
I am the little slave of the Lord.

i   My time has come. As of now, you are being called to see *the great marvels of the Lord* in the triumph of my Immaculate Heart.

j   For this reason I am inviting you to all gather about the cradle where your newborn heavenly Mother has been placed, to offer yourselves to me as an homage of love, of humility, of purity and of prayer. I bless you with love and with joy."

362

Akita (Japan); September 15, 1987
Feast of Our Lady of Sorrows

Why Am I Still Weeping?

a   "I have wanted you here, O son so loved by me and so plotted against by my Adversary, at the liturgy which commemorates my sorrows and my motherly sharing in all the immense suffering of my Son Jesus.

b   In this journey of yours, so strewn with extraordinary graces which come from my Immaculate Heart and descend into the souls of my beloved ones and of all my children, I have led you today to this place blessed by me, before the statue which recalls the mystery of my co-redemption.

c   I stood beneath the Cross of Jesus. I am beneath the cross which each of my sons is carrying. I am beneath the cross which the Church and all this poor sinful humanity is carrying today. I am true Mother and true Co-redemptrix.

d   From the eyes of this image of myself, I have caused miraculous tears to fall more than a hundred times and over the course of several years.

e   *Why am I still weeping?*

f   *I am weeping* because humanity is not accepting my motherly invitation to conversion and to its return to the Lord. It is continuing to run with obstinacy along the road of rebellion against God and against his Law of love. The Lord is openly denied, outraged and blasphemed. Your heavenly Mother is publicly despised and held up for ridicule. My extraordinary requests are not being accepted; the signs of my immense sorrow which I am giving are not believed in.

g   Your neighbor is not loved: every day attacks are made upon his life and his goods. Man is becoming ever more corrupt, godless, wicked and cruel. A chastisement worse than the flood is about to come upon this poor and perverted humanity. Fire will descend from heaven, and this will be the sign that the justice of God has as of now fixed the hour of his great manifestation.

h   *I am weeping* because the Church is continuing along the road of division, of loss of the true faith, of apostasy and of errors which are being spread more and more without anyone offering opposition to them. Even now, that which I predicted at Fatima and that which I have revealed here in the third message confided to a little daughter of mine is in the process of being accomplished. And so, even for the Church the moment of its great trial has come, because the man of iniquity will establish himself within it and the abomination of desolation will enter into the holy temple of God.

i   *I am weeping* because, in great numbers, the souls of my children are being lost and going to hell.

j   *I am weeping* because too few are those who accede to my request to pray, to make reparation, to suffer and to offer.

k   *I am weeping* because I have spoken to you and have not been listened to; I have given you miraculous signs, and I have not been believed; I have manifested myself to you in a strong and continuous way, but you have not opened the doors of your hearts to me.

l   At least you, my beloved ones and children consecrated to my Immaculate Heart, little remnant which Jesus is guarding jealously in the secure enclosure of his divine love, harken to and accept this sorrowful request of mine which, from this place, I address again today to all the nations of the earth. Prepare yourselves to receive Christ in the splendor of his glory, because the great day of the Lord has even now arrived."

363 *Seoul (Korea); September 27, 1987*

To All the Peoples of the World

a   "I am much loved and venerated in this land. My children have recourse to me with a love which is born of simple, poor and humble hearts, and all are taking refuge under the mantle of my motherly protection. Here, my presence gives vigor and strength to the Church, which is growing and expanding upon the terrain made fertile by the blood of many martyrs.

b   Round about this little land, which is a privileged portion of my heavenly garden, extends a boundless region where there holds sway the Red Dragon, my Adversary, who has built up his kingdom upon rebellion against God, constraining by force into atheism an immense number of my children, who are walking in the deepest of darkness. But from here my light and my victory will spread and will cover all the nations of this great continent of Asia.

c   I am the dawn which is rising in an ever stronger and more luminous way. I am the Virgin Mother who brings help and salvation *to all the peoples of the world.* I am the way opened to the glorious triumph of Christ. I am the Woman Clothed with the Sun, who is about to intervene in an extraordinary way to bind the Red Dragon, in order to cast him down in his reign of fire and of death. From what is taking place here, all the Church should now understand that the Mother's presence is indispensable for its universal renewal.

d   This is the year consecrated to me. I bid you all to second my victorious plan. Pray, suffer and offer with me.

e   Through you, my littlest and poorest son, chosen by me that I may be glorified before the Church and the world, I want to bless Korea, land beloved of my Immaculate Heart, and all the nations of this continent of Asia and of the entire world."

Inchon (Korea); September 29, 1987
Feast of the Holy Archangels
Spiritual Exercises in the Form of a Cenacle
with the Priests of the M.M.P. of Korea

Heaven and Earth Are Uniting

a   "Beloved sons, I am calling you from every part of the earth. The angels of light of my Immaculate Heart are now actually gathering from everywhere the elect, called to form part of my victorious cohort.

b   They are signing you with my seal.
They are reclothing you with sturdy armor for the battle.
They are covering you again with my shield.
They are giving you the crucifix and the rosary as the weapons to be used for the great victory.

c   The time for the decisive struggle has come. For this, the angels of the Lord are intervening in an extraordinary way and placing themselves, each day, at the side of each one of you to guide you, to protect you and to comfort you.

d   As great freedom for their diabolical manifestations has in these times been granted to the demons and all the spirits of evil, so also these are the days when the angels of the Lord are being called to carry out the most important part of my plan. *Heaven and earth are uniting,* in this hour of the great conclusive struggle.

e   And so I bid you to all form one single entity with the angels and with the saints of paradise. Above all, I bid you to pray more to your guardian angels, because they, in these times, are being called to carry out a particular task, which I have assigned to them, in respect to each one of you my beloved sons. It is the desire of my Heart that, in the daily recitation of the Angelus, the prayer to the angel of God be again inserted.

f   I bid you to live always in intimacy and familiarity with your guardian angels. Call upon them in necessities; invoke them in dangers; associate them in your work; confide to them your difficulties; seek them in moments of temptation. They must now form one single entity with you.

g   Above all, feel close at hand the Archangels, whose feast the Church is celebrating today: Saint Gabriel, that he may give you the very strength of God; Saint Raphael, that he may be the remedy for all your wounds; Saint Michael, that he may defend you from the terrible snares which, in these times, Satan is setting for you. With them, walk in the light of my plan, and fight, joined together at my orders.

h   You are as of now being called to see my greatest prodigies, because you have entered into the time of my triumph."

365
Taipei (Taiwan); October 9, 1987

The Children Most Loved by Me

a   "I am gazing today with eyes of mercy on this great nation of China, where my Adversary is reigning, the Red Dragon who has set up his kingdom here, enjoining all, by force, to repeat the satanic act of denial and of rebellion against God.

b   I see the innumerable and profound sufferings of these poor children of mine, who are walking in the deepest darkness. *They are the children most loved by me.* I am at their side, as a mother who wants to console them, to help them and to encourage them.

c   And so, from this land, I want to give my motherly message to all my children who live in the regions where atheistic communism holds sway and where any external manifestation whatsoever of the worship due to the Lord our God is prohibited and punished.

d   — Above all, I am giving you the certitude that I am always with you, as a true mother, who is closer in moments of trial and suffering. I am attentive to your needs. I comfort you in pain, and I take all your sufferings into my Immaculate Heart.

e   I place in souls seeds of love and of goodness, so that you may be able to walk along the road of good, observing the commandments carved by the Lord in your hearts, by means of his Law which is engraved in the very depths of human nature.

f   — Then, with my motherly action, I open your hearts to receive the life of God, which acts within you in a special way, so that there be given Him in secret the adoration and the love which you are prohibited from giving Him with public and external worship. It is in this way that, in silence and in hiddenness, the true religion is again spreading in your midst and sending down roots in the life of many of my children.

g — Finally I am preparing the day, by now close at hand, of your liberation, with the definitive defeat of the Red Dragon of theoretical and practical atheism, which has conquered the entire world. The time of your slavery is about to end. All you nations of the earth, come out from slavery and darkness, and go to meet Christ who is coming to establish in your midst his glorious reign of love.

h At last the moment has come when I, the Woman Clothed with the Sun, will conquer the Red Dragon; I will bind him with a chain and cast him into hell so that he will no longer be able to harm the earth. It will in fact be entirely transformed into a new terrestrial paradise for the perfect glorification of the Most Holy Trinity."

366

I Will Put an End to Your Slavery

a "On this day, beloved sons, you are observing the seventieth anniversary of the last of my apparitions which took place at Fatima and which was confirmed by the miracle of the sun. Today, my little son, you find yourself here to conclude a wonderful journey in these nations of the Far East where, with particular intensity, my Immaculate Heart has been everywhere loved, implored, consoled and glorified.

b These are seventy years during which I have descended from heaven into your midst as the Woman Clothed with the Sun. These are seventy years during which my Adversary, Satan, has come up from the abyss into your midst, to manifest himself as the Red Dragon in all his terrible power. In fact, he has succeeded in extending his reign in many nations and in spreading his action of denial and of rebellion against God to every part of the earth. Thus, during the period of these seventy years, the Red Dragon has bound men with the chain of his slavery.

c — *He has made you slaves of pride and of haughtiness,* with the deceptive illusion of bringing you to getting along without God, of putting your own selves in the place of God, so that in you he may be able to renew his act of rebellion and of defiance against

536

the Lord. Thus he has spread everywhere the error of atheism and has driven humanity to build a new civilization without God.

d — *He has made you slaves of pleasure and of impurity*, to replace the true God with new idols, followed and adored today by many: sex, amusement, money, comfort. Thus sin has stretched out its tenebrous veil of coldness and of death over the world.

e — *He has made you slaves of egoism and of avarice*, by leading you on in the consuming quest for your own affirmation, for superiority over others, and you have become insensible to the great needs of the poor, the little ones, the sick, the needy. Thus the world has become a real desert for lack of love, and in this immense desert, how many of my children there are who, each day, become swept away, stricken down and defeated.

f You have lived seventy years as slaves of my Adversary, who has succeeded in transforming the world into the city of Babylon, perverse and sinful, which, with the cup of pleasure and of luxury, has seduced all the nations of the earth. But now the period of this babylonian slavery is about to end. *I will put an end to your slavery*. In this Marian Year, the heavenly Mother is opening the door upon the new era of your liberation.

g For this, you will see very soon the extraordinary signs which I will give, in order that you may prepare yourselves for the very great miracle which is at this time about to be accomplished. The miracle of the sun, which took place during my last apparition, was only a prophetic sign to indicate to you that you should all look at the Book which is still sealed. Today I am being sent by God to open this Book, in order that the secrets may be revealed to you.

h Thus everyone will at last be able to understand to what incomparable depth and universality of renewal the victory of the merciful love of Jesus will bring you, a victory which will be brought about by means of the triumph of my Immaculate Heart in the world."

Prepare Yourselves with Me

a "Begin this period of Advent with me, beloved sons. Surrounded by my immaculate light, which spreads itself everywhere like the dawn to announce the coming of Christ, prepare yourselves all to receive with joy the Lord who is coming. Prepare yourselves well for the holy Nativity.

b *Prepare yourselves with me* to live, in peace, in silence and in trembling expectation, the liturgical remembrance of his birth. In this time of preparation, let faith increase, hope be illumined, charity be strengthened and your prayer become more intense.

c *Prepare yourselves with me* for the coming of Jesus, which is realized each day in the mystery of his real Eucharistic presence and under the human clothing of every person whom you meet. This daily encounter with Jesus must become for you a joyous and perennial Nativity.

d Open your souls to receive the gifts of his grace and of his love. Throw open the doors of your hearts, to offer Him a warm dwelling place of love, when He comes to give Himself personally to each one of you, at the moment of Eucharistic Communion. Let your minds be illumined to know how to always recognize Him under the fragile and painful features of the little ones, the poor, the sick, the needy, the sinners, those far away, the marginalized, the oppressed, the persecuted, the dying.

e *Prepare yourselves with me* for his return in glory. In these times I must prepare the Church and all humanity for his proximate and glorious return. For this, my presence among you will become stronger, and my light will become even greater, like the dawn which attains its culmination in the rising of the sun, which removes every shadow of night from the world.

f Let the dark night of the proclaimed denial of God and of obstinate rebellion against his Law depart, to dispose you to receive the radiant sun of Emmanuel, of God with you.

g Let the night of sin and of impurity depart, to prepare you to receive the God of grace and of holiness.

h Let the night of hatred, of egoism and of injustice depart, that you may run towards the God of love and of peace.

i   Let the night of incredulity and of pride depart, to prepare you for the coming of Jesus in faith and in humility.

j   From this time on, you will see my light become stronger, until it reaches the vertex of its splendor, which will be reflected in every part of the earth. The more the immaculate light of your heavenly Mother will spread everywhere, the more will humanity and the Church be prepared to receive the Lord who is coming."

368   *Rubbio (Vicenza, Italy); December 8, 1987*
Solemnity of the Immaculate Conception

Do Not Allow Yourselves to Be Deluded

a   "My heavenly candor descends today upon you and wants to enwrap all the world. Walk in my light if you want to arrive at peace. The light of divine grace, of purity, of holiness, of prayer, of an ever more perfect charity must penetrate your life, O sons consecrated to my Immaculate Heart.

b   You are living the painful times of the chastisement. You are living the dark hour of the victory of my Adversary, who is the Prince of the Night. You are living the most difficult moments of the purification. And so I urge you to take refuge in the secure dwelling place of my Immaculate Heart and to let yourselves be enwrapped in the heavenly mantle of my most pure light. Walk along the road which I have traced out for you in these years, in order to become today the instruments of my peace.

c   *Do not allow yourselves to be deluded.* Peace will not come to the world from the meetings of those whom you call the great ones of this earth, nor from their reciprocal agreements. Peace can only come to you from the return of humanity to its God by means of conversion, to which I am again calling you in this my day, and by means of prayer, of fasting and of penance.

d   Otherwise, at the moment when all will be shouting 'peace and security,' (1Thes 5:3) suddenly calamity will fall.

e   For this reason I am asking you to second my urgent requests to walk along the road of goodness, of love, of prayer, of mortification of the senses, of contempt for the world and for yourselves.

f   Today I welcome with joy your homage of love, I join it to the song of glory of paradise, to the invocations of the souls who are being purified, to the chorus of praise of the Church Militant and Pilgrim, and I urge you to live in confidence and in a great hope in my imminent and extraordinary intervention."

369 *Dongo (Como, Italy); December 24, 1987*
The Holy Night

An Announcement of Joy

a   "In this year consecrated to me, beloved sons, I am inviting you to keep watch with me, your heavenly Mother, and with my most chaste spouse, Joseph, in prayer, in trust and in expectation.

b   This is the holy night.

c   How much fatigue during the long journey to Bethlehem; how much suffering in the face of each refusal to open a door to us; how much trust in the Father who is leading us by the hand to the fulfillment of his great plan of love! A plan which is carried out by the concourse of unexpected circumstances which prepare for the occurrence of this extraordinary prodigy.

d   The merciful action of a shepherd who points out a nearby cave; the opening of one single door upon a poor and bare shelter; the human bustling about to make the place more hospitable; above all our perfect acceptance of the Will of the Heavenly Father, who has prepared a crib of poverty and of cold for his only-begotten Son who is being born.

e   But sweet to his Heart, the heart of a newborn child, is the warmth of my love; and a soft cradle, my arms which entwine Him with boundless tenderness; and my motherly kisses become precious pearls; and a regal mantle for Him, the poor cloths with which I enfold Him.

f   All at once, the darkness is penetrated by a most lively light which comes pouring down from heaven; the silence resounds with the sweetest of songs and of heavenly harmonies; the solitude becomes populated with innumerable cohorts of angels, while the night opens up to the birth of a day which knows no setting.

g   This is the holy night. This is the night which has conquered all darkness for ever. This is the night which opens upon *an announcement of joy* which comes from heaven: 'I bring you an announcement of joy for all: a Savior is born to you who is Christ the Lord.' (Lk 2:10-11)

h   Today the night again enwraps the whole world, and the darkness becomes dense over the life of men and of peoples. It is the darkness of the lack of faith, of obstinate rebellion, of a very great rejection of God. It is the coldness of sin which kills every bud of life and of love in the hearts of men. It is the poverty of a man betrayed in his dignity, despised and reduced to an interior slavery. It is the silence of God which weighs upon the din of voices and of clamor, upon the continual diffusion of words and of images.

i   But, in the deep night of this century of yours, behold my motherly light which arises like the dawn and spreads itself to every part of the earth. With my voice which I cause you to hear in many places, with my presence which is becoming stronger and more extraordinary, with my messages which are now becoming urgent, in the holy night of this Marian Year, I want again to repeat to all: I am the dawn which is preparing the birth of the brilliant sun of Christ.

j   Today I want to give *an announcement of joy* to all my children: the time of his glorious return is now near!"

370

Dongo (Como, Italy); December 31, 1987
Last Night of the Year

The Great Tribulation

a   "In my Immaculate Heart, in an act of unceasing prayer, spend with me the last hours of this year, which is now about to end. It is an important year and one particularly blessed by my Immaculate Heart, because it has been solemnly and officially consecrated to me by my Pope.

b   You are now at the midpoint of this Marian Year. You have entered into my time. You are beneath the sign of the great events which have been foretold to you.

c   Know how to read and to meditate upon that which, in Sacred Scripture, has been clearly described for you to help you understand the time in which you are living. With my motherly voice I am leading you all to understand *the signs of the great tribulation*. From the Gospels, from the Letters of the Apostles and from the book of the Apocalypse, sure signs have been clearly described for you to make you understand what the period of the great tribulation is. All these signs are in the act of being realized in this time of yours.

d   — First of all, *a great apostasy* is spreading in every part of the Church, through the lack of faith which is flooding even among its very pastors. Satan has succeeded in spreading everywhere the great apostasy, by means of his subtle work of seduction, which has brought many to be alienated from the truth of the Gospel to follow the fables of the new theological theories and to take delight in evil and in sin, sought after as an actual good.

e   — Then, in your time, *overturnings of the order of nature* are multiplying, such as earthquakes, droughts, floods, and disasters which cause the unforeseen death of thousands of persons, followed by epidemics and incurable diseases which are spreading everywhere.

f   — Moreover, your days are marked by *continual rumors of wars* which are multiplying and are reaping, each day, innumerable victims. Conflicts and dissensions within countries are increasing; revolts and struggles between various peoples are propagating; bloody wars are continuing to extend themselves, notwithstanding all the efforts which are being made to attain peace.

g   — Finally, in your time, there are occurring *great signs in the sun, on the moon and in the stars*. The miracle of the sun which took place at Fatima was a sign which I gave you to warn you that the times of these extraordinary phenomena which are taking place in the heavens have now arrived. And how many times during my present apparitions have you yourselves been able to contemplate the great prodigies that are taking place in the sun.

h   Just as the buds which sprout forth on the trees tell you that spring has now arrived, so also these great signs which are taking place in your time are telling you that even now *there has come to you the great tribulation*, which is preparing you for the new era which I have promised you with the triumph of my Immaculate Heart in the world.

i   This is the reason why your time has been consecrated to me with a special Marian Year in my honor. Because the Most Holy Trinity has entrusted to the Immaculate Heart of your heavenly Mother the task of preparing the Church and all humanity to live with confidence *the hour of the great tribulation*, which prepares you for the glorious return of Christ."

1988

SHED LIGHT UPON THE EARTH
(Marian Year)

Shed Light Upon the Earth

a   "Today you are looking to your heavenly Mother and are all invoking her in order to obtain the great gift of peace. With the solemnity of my Divine Maternity, you are beginning this new year which is dedicated to a special veneration of me because it has been consecrated to me. There is a profound desire of my Immaculate Heart which today I want to make known to you, my little children, who, with your consecration, have completely entrusted yourselves to me.

b   *— First of all I confide to you my profound grief* at seeing how up to now this Marian Year has been passed, by many of the children of the Church, in the greatest aridity. While I am profoundly grateful to my Pope, John Paul II, for the way in which he reminds everyone of the gift of this year consecrated to me, I must also give expression to my interior suffering in the face of the attitude of complete indifference evidenced by so many bishops, priests, religious and faithful. In how many dioceses nothing has thus far been done with respect to what has been determined, in order to live out well this year consecrated to me: the fostering of practices of piety towards me and the gathering together in my shrines, where it is also possible to gain the special jubilee indulgence.

c   My Adversary who, in these days, has broken loose with particular violence, is doing everything to prevent this year from leading to a general renewal of devotion and prayer in respect to me. The forces of atheism and of Masonry, which have been brought in as far as the summit of the Church, have joined together to boycott, in a subtle and hidden way, this Marian Year. A veil of darkness has been spread over the Church, and the word of my Pope falls increasingly upon an immense desert.

d   *— And then I entrust my motherly will to you,* who are my docile and obedient children, because you listen to my voice and form a part of my victorious cohort. I ask you to make reparation for the indifference and for such a great lack of response on the part of many of my children, by living with greater generosity and with particular diligence the second half of this Marian Year.

e   I ask you to respond to my renewed request for consecration. Make it often, and above all live the consecration to my Immaculate Heart. Bring the greatest number possible of priests, religious and faithful to make this consecration willed by me and repeatedly requested, even up to your days.

f   Multiply your cenacles of prayer. Pray more; pray with me; pray, with the recitation of the holy rosary. I desire that Christian families consecrate themselves to my Immaculate Heart and become cenacles of prayer, of love and of life with me. Let the priests of my Movement gather the faithful entrusted to them in cenacles of prayer because, during this year, I have need of a great force of intercession and of reparation to bring to fulfillment the plan which the Most Holy Trinity has entrusted to my Immaculate Heart.

g   *— And lastly I promise you to welcome your filial homage* and to bless this time which has been entrusted to me. During this year, you will feel my presence becoming stronger and more extraordinary. The great events for which I have prepared you will begin to take place. For this reason I call upon you today to allow yourselves to be penetrated by the mystery of my divine and universal motherhood. Go forward with confidence and with hope.

h   The heavenly Mother is bringing you to live within the heart of the life of God and is making of you instruments of his peace. Thus you are ready for the task which I am entrusting to you: go, and *shed light upon the earth* in these days of dense darkness. Then, by means of you, the great rainbow of the reconciliation of humanity with God will be able to arise and enfold the whole world in new light."

372

Porto Alegre (Brazil); February 2, 1988
Feast of the Presentation of the Child Jesus

In You I Am Glorified

a   "Walk with me, beloved sons, as I carry the Child Jesus in my arms, to the temple of his light and of his glory. Allow yourselves also to be carried in my motherly arms, with humility, with docility and with meekness. I am leading you to the temple of the Lord. I am bringing you to the full manifestation of his light and of his glory.

b   These are the times of your full manifestation. The days of your public testimony have arrived. Show yourselves to all as little children consecrated to me and as great apostles of your heavenly Mother, in these last times. *The hour has come when I want to be glorified in you before all the Church and the world.*

c   — *I glorify myself in you, if you walk with me in the light of the faith.* Accept with humility the word of God; meditate upon it in your mind; keep it in your heart; live it in your daily life. Let Holy Scripture, above all the Gospel of Jesus, be the only light which illumines you in these times of darkness. Believe in the Gospel; live the Gospel; proclaim the Gospel in its fullness.

d   You, my beloved ones, must, today, be the Gospel alone, lived out and preached to the letter, against the errors which are being spread about and against the great betrayal being perpetrated by so many of my sons who have torn to pieces the Gospel of Jesus by means of human, rationalistic and natural interpretations. Thus, by means of you, the light of the faith shines forth once again, *and in you I am glorified.*

e   — *I glorify myself in you, if you walk with me in the light of love.* Love, with the beating of my Immaculate Heart, the Most Holy and Divine Trinity. Love the Father who surrounds you with his tenderness, carries you in his arms and ever assists you through his providence. Love the Son who has become your Brother and has given you a new heart and a new spirit so that you yourselves might become a lived out expression of his divine love. Jesus awaits only love from you. Love the Holy Spirit who dwells within you to bring you to the perfection of charity and who communicates Himself to you with his seven holy gifts, that you may become today a strong witness of love.

f   And then love, with the very Heart of Jesus, all your brothers, especially the poorest, the sinners, those furthest away, the sick, the wounded, the stricken, the marginalized, the weak, the littlest. Then, in these days of violence and hatred, of unbridled egoism

548

and of aridity, you cause the heavenly dew of divine mercy to descend upon the immense desert of the world. Thus, by means of you, the light of love shines forth once again, *and in you I am glorified.*

g   — *I glorify myself in you, if you walk with me in the light of holiness.* Walk along the road of disdain for the world and for yourselves, of unceasing prayer, of the mortification of the senses, of penance. Be opposed to the spirit of the world which spreads about everywhere tolerance in matters of morality, the satisfaction of all the passions, pleasure which is sought after and desired, and sin which is carried out with full awareness and in open disdain for the holy Law of the Lord.

h   Then, in these days of impiety and of a so great immorality, you spread about the perfume of sanctity. Thus, by means of you, the light of purity and of divine grace shines forth once again, *and in you I am glorified.*

i   I am glorified in you when you are humble, poor, little, pure and merciful. I glorify myself in you when you walk in the light of faith, of love and of holiness. And thus you spread my glory; you anticipate my triumph; you become the rays of light which come down from my Immaculate Heart to enlighten the earth in these days of intense darkness.

j   Today I am carrying you all with joy into the holy temple of the new era which is about to come upon the world."

373   Manaus (Amazonas, Brazil); February 11, 1988
Feast of Our Lady of Lourdes

The Lord Is Sending Me to You

a   "Today you are calling to mind my apparition, in the poor grotto of Massabielle, to my little daughter, Bernadette. Since then I have multiplied the times and the places of my extraordinary apparitions. This century has been marked by my strong presence in your midst, and, in order to make it perceptible to all, I have everywhere multiplied my miraculous manifestations.

b   Why am I, in these times, making myself present to you in a new, continuous and extraordinary way? Because these are the times of the reign of my Adversary, the Red Dragon, Satan, the old serpent, whose head I shall crush. Under the weight of his reign, there is an increase for you of trials and sufferings, of wounds and of falls, and thus the danger of being lost is much greater for all.

c   And so I am manifesting myself to you in an extraordinary way to urge you to confidence, to trust, to take refuge in me through your act of consecration to my Immaculate Heart. As of now, my presence is becoming all the stronger, as my victory draws nearer to the definitive defeat of Satan.

d   For this I urge you all to look to me with confidence and with great hope.

e   *The Lord is sending me to you* to bring you his salvation. Thank Him for this gift, and accept it with humility and gratitude. I am coming as an announcement of his victory. I am being sent to prepare the way for the glorious return of Jesus.

f   Walk in my light, and become the apostles of your heavenly Mother in these last times. Spread everywhere the perfume of my presence and of my motherly tenderness. With joy I bless you all."

374
Recife (Pernambuco, Brazil); February 17, 1988
Ash Wednesday

Be Converted and Return to the Lord

a   "From this land, so ensnared by my Adversary, where, especially in these last days, many of my children have become instruments of the reign of Satan, who is seducing all the nations of the earth with the cup of impurity and of lust, I direct to you my repeated and concerned *invitation to conversion.*

b   *Be converted, and return to the Lord* along the road of sincere repentance and of personal confession of your sins to the priests.

c   *Be converted, and return to the Lord* along the road of a conscious and serious resolve to flee sin and to keep far away from every occasion that can lead you to fall into sin.

d   *Be converted, and return to the Lord* along the road of mortification of the senses, of penance and of fasting.

e   There begins today the season of Lent of this Marian Year: a period when the Church entreats everyone to carry out works of charity and of penance. I, your heavenly Mother, am calling upon you to live well the time of Lent of this year which is consecrated to me.

f   The period of time granted by the Lord to humanity for its conversion is about to come to its end, and so, respond to my anxious call which is urging you to do what I am now asking of you for the salvation of all humanity.

g   — First of all I desire that each one of you take upon himself, with greater force, the obligation of living in the grace of God, renouncing Satan and all evil works and the world and all its numerous seductions. Walk always along the road of purity, of love and of a greater holiness.

h   — And then I am asking of you personal works of mortification and of penance. Offer to my Immaculate Heart each day a crown made up of many little and hidden mortifications, accomplished for the salvation of many of your brothers, who are habitually living in sin and are bound slavishly to Satan.

i   — Lastly, I ask you to remove yourselves far from anything that can contaminate the purity of your heart and the chastity of your life. Do not take part in profane shows. Do not waste time before the television set, which is the most powerful instrument in the hands of my Adversary in spreading everywhere the darkness of sin and of impurity. Television is the idol spoken of in the book of Revelation, built to be adored by all the nations of the earth, and to which the Evil One gives shape and movement so that it might become, in his hands, a terrible means of seduction and perversion.

j   If you do what I am asking of you today, you put in my hands a powerful force of intercession and of reparation. And thus I am able to present myself before the throne of the Lord, great and terrible, just and holy, to implore for you his divine mercy:'Pardon, O Lord, the iniquity of your people, whom You have acquired at the price of your most precious blood.'

k   And before that time which has been conceded to you for your conversion has come to an end, you will already be able to see the signs of the triumph of the merciful love of Jesus in the first extraordinary interventions of the Immaculate Heart of your heavenly Mother."

551

375

São Paulo (Brazil); February 25, 1988
Spiritual Exercises in the Form of a Cenacle
with the Priests and Faithful of the M.M.P. from all Brazil

My Motherly Message

a   "How my greatly sorrowing Heart is being consoled, during these days, by you my dearly beloved ones and children consecrated to me, coming from every part of this very great nation! I am always present in your midst, as I was with the Apostles and the disciples in the Cenacle of Jerusalem. I am uniting myself to your prayer. I am joining in, during the moments of your fraternal sharing.

b   From this cenacle today, I want to address *my motherly message* to all Brazil, this land which is so ensnared by my Adversary but so loved and protected by your heavenly Mother.

c   — My Heart is afflicted with great pain by the situation in which the Church here finds itself. It is interiorly divided; it is threatened with the loss of the true faith; many errors are being spread about within it.

d   The cause of this situation is the pastors who are no longer united with the Pope. Their only concern is exclusively directed toward social problems, and they forget that Jesus died on the Cross and rose again to obtain for you the great gift of redemption and to save souls. And thus the teaching of the theology of liberation, which is a true betrayal of Christ and of his Gospel, is becoming more and more widespread. Bishops and priests of the holy Church of God, return to full union with the Pope. Return to the teaching of the truth, which Jesus has revealed to you, with courage and fidelity. Preach the Gospel in its integrity, and take care of the flock which has been entrusted to you. Schism and apostasy are menacing today the Church which lives in this nation of yours.

e   — My Heart is pained by the great danger into which your homeland is running, because of the spread of violence and hatred, of evil and of immorality. In the name of a false way of understanding liberty, even the gravest moral disorders are today being permitted and justified. Impurity is exalted and spread about through the social means of communication, and thus a veil of darkness has descended to blind the souls of many of my children.

f   If there is not a general return to the Lord, along the road of conversion and repentance, a great chastisement can quickly strike this country of yours.

g   — I want to tell you that my Immaculate Heart has been consoled today by your response of consecration and of prayer. Bring the greater number of my children to the consecration to my Immaculate Heart, desired and requested by me. You who have taken part in this cenacle, become the apostles of the consecration to my Immaculate Heart throughout all Brazil. Multiply the cenacles of prayer. Above all, spread family cenacles, like a great net of salvation.

h   Thus you become the rays of light which come down from my Heart, to enlighten all Brazil in these days of dense darkness. You become the signs of my motherly triumph. You are the instruments of my victory. And by means of you who have responded to me, the heavenly Mother will bring to your Church and to your country the gift of salvation and of peace."

376   San Marco (Udine, Italy); March 22, 1988

The Glory of Mary

a   "With what joy I have received the act of consecration to my Immaculate Heart, on this your birthday. I have taken your heart and have brought it deeper yet into my motherly garden, and I have placed it in the burning furnace of the love of the divine Heart of my Son Jesus. This heart of yours now belongs entirely to us, and we want to make of it a perfect instrument of our most pure love. I am asking you to love ever more and more.

b   *Love* each day, and at every moment of your life. Let nothing disturb the purity and the intensity of your love.

c   *Love* the Most Holy and Divine Trinity, glorifying the Father, imitating the Son, receiving the gift of the Spirit.

d   *Love*, with the divine Heart of Jesus, all your brothers, especially the smallest, the poorest, and least, the desperate, the marginalized, the sinners. You must be the luminous ray of my motherly and merciful love.

e   *Love* your brother-priests, especially the weakest, the most fragile, those who fall, those who are imprisoned by the chains of the passions, especially of pride and of impurity. For them, immolate yourself, each day, in silence, in hiddenness, in humility, in docility. Become the sweet and meek victim, immolated by me, for the good and the salvation of all priests.

f   *Love always, without ever becoming weary.*
Everything must be done by you only out of love:
The journey you must undertake for me — out of love;
The cross which you must carry — out of love;
The heavy work which is your lot to accomplish — out of love;
The cenacles which you lead — out of love;
The countries you journey through — out of love;
The distant continents you reach — out of love;
The intense prayer that I ask of you — out of love;
The sufferings I ask of you each day — out of love;
The weariness which takes hold of you — out of love;
The exhaustion which prostrates you — out of love;
Your limitations which mortify you — out of love;
Your defects which accompany you — out of love;
All your life which you give me — out of love.

g   Only then will you be, here below, *the glory of Mary*. Only then will you be able to carry out the mission which I have entrusted to you and make blossom in your person, in your life and in your work, the garden of my greatest and most extraordinary wonders.

h   With my Pope, with all my beloved priests, with the children consecrated to me, I bless you with love and with joy."

377   *Dongo (Como, Italy); March 31, 1988*
                                                      Holy Thursday

The Johns of the Eucharistic Jesus

a   "My beloved priests, today is your feast. It is the day that recalls the Last Supper, the institution of the Eucharist and of the new Priesthood, in the Cenacle of Jerusalem. It is your feast because you, to whom it has been given to share in the ministerial priesthood of Jesus, were also spiritually present in the Cenacle.

b   I am the Mother of you priests, because you were entrusted to me by Jesus, in a special way, in the person of your brother, John. Enter today into the cenacle of my Immaculate Heart. Open for me the door of your priestly home that I may enter there as the Mother who loves you, who forms you and leads you, seconding also the desire which today, through his letter, my Pope, the first of the sons of my maternal predilection, has communicated to you. This is the most beautiful way to live this Holy Thursday of the Marian Year, consecrated to me.

c   I then lead you to realize fully the mystery of love of your priesthood; I help you to be faithful to the obligations which you have assumed, in particular that of celibacy; I point out to you the road you must travel, in order to respond to such a great gift as that which has been given you by my Son Jesus.

d   *I bring you to be priests according to his divine and merciful Heart.*

e   — For this, I cause you to increase in a profound intimacy of life with me, in a simple and spontaneous way, in such a way that I am able to live with you, in the dwelling place of your priestly life, just as I lived in his home with the apostle, John.

f   See how little children allow themselves to be led by their mother, follow her directions, listen to her teachings and expect everything from her. You also must do the same. You must accustom yourselves to doing everything with me: when you get up, pray, celebrate Holy Mass, recite the Liturgy of the Hours or are absorbed in your apostolic activity. Even when you are beautifying the church, when you want to undertake something new, do it with me, in a spirit of filial confidence and of habitual dependence. Then nothing will ever disturb the peace of your heart. If my Adversary does everything to cause you to be perturbed, he will find you covered with impenetrable armor, and you will always be immersed in an inalterable peace, and you will be led to the highest summit of interior quiet and of contemplation.

g   — I lead you also to a habitual intimacy of life, of love, of adoration, of thanksgiving and of reparation to Jesus present in the Eucharist. With the impetus of the faith which illumines you, with the flame of the love which consumes you, with the strength of those who are sincerely in love, like watchful sentinels, you must go beyond appearances to experience in the soul the presence of *Jesus in the Eucharist* because, under the white veil of each consecrated Host, Jesus is really present among you.

h   You cannot see Him; it is as if you were here, and He were on the other side of a closed door. There is only this thin partition, which impedes you from seeing Him with your eyes, from hearing Him with your ears, from communicating with Him through the external senses of the body. But you must go beyond the appearances, to commune with Him through the powers of the soul.

i   *The power of your intellect* causes you to see Jesus in the splendor of his glorious body, as He appeared to me after his resurrection, all light, with his enchanting face, with his hair of gold, with his eyes of an intense blue, with his feet which had walked so much for you, still shining from the wounds which had transfixed Him, with a smile of infinite goodness and with his wounded Heart, from which there gushed a luminous fount of love and of grace. See Him, with the light of the intellect, in the splendor of his divinity. Jesus will reveal Himself even more to you, will communicate Himself in a greater way to you, and thus you will contemplate Him in a way that will be more beautiful than if you were to see Him with the senses of the body.

j   *The power of the will* sets you on the way of always doing his divine Will. As a compass points toward the north pole, so also your will becomes irresistibly attracted to his Will. When sometimes you turn from it, almost without you noticing it, there is some force within you which turns you in the right direction, because your will becomes absorbed by his divine Will. Thus your mind becomes ever more and more enlightened, because you are thinking as He thinks, you want what He wants, and thus you live in an intimacy of life with Jesus who, in your priestly life, fulfills again today his divine mission of doing the Will of the Father: 'I have come, O God, to do your Will. Not my Will but yours be done.' (cf. Lk 22:42)

k   *Through the power of love* you are irresistibly attracted by his divine and merciful Heart. My dearest little children, let your heart be completely immersed in his Eucharistic Heart, that you may enter into a personal intimacy of life with Him. Jesus then takes your little heart, opens it, expands it and fills it with his love. He loves in you, and you love in Him; and thus, you become more and more immersed in the stupendous vortex of his divine and perfect charity. Then, just as John was the beloved apostle, called to a profound intimacy of life with Jesus, living in his human body, so too, you become *a new John*, called to have a profound intimacy of life with Jesus in his glorified body, really present in the condition of a victim and hidden under the appearance of consecrated Bread, which is kept in every tabernacle of the earth. Beloved sons, seek Jesus in order to quench your thirst for blessedness; go to Him to satisfy your great need for love; you too, place your head upon his Heart to feel its beating; live ever with Him, you who are called to be *other Johns of the Eucharistic Jesus.*

l — I confide to you now my maternal will that the Eucharistic Jesus find, in your churches, his royal palace, where He is honored and adored by the faithful, there where He is also continually surrounded by innumerable bands of angels, of saints and of souls who are being purified. See to it that the Most Holy Sacrament is again surrounded by flowers and by lights, as signs indicative of your love and of your tender piety. Expose Him frequently for the veneration of the faithful; multiply the hours of public adoration to repair for the indifference, the outrages, the numerous sacrileges and the terrible profanation, to which He is subjected during the black masses, a diabolical and sacrilegious rite which is becoming more and more widespread and which has, as its culmination, unspeakable and obscene acts directed toward the Most Holy Eucharist.

m Because of this, the world is immersed in the deepest night, in the darkness of sin and of impurity, of egoism and of hatred, of avarice and of impiety, and it now appears that there is no longer anything that can restrain it from falling into an endless abyss.

n But the great hour of justice and of divine mercy has as of now arrived. For you, my beloved priests, who are called to be the light of the world, there now falls the duty of illuminating the earth in these days of dense darkness. And so today I am asking you to allow me to enter the home of your priestly life, because the hour has also come for the triumph, in you, of the Immaculate Heart of your heavenly Mother."

Behold Your Mother

a   "Beloved sons, welcome today the supreme gift of my Son Jesus, who is about to die on the Cross.

b   *'Behold your Mother.'* (Jn 19:27) At this moment I am at the foot of his Cross, transfixed by a sword of sorrow.

c   *I have seen* my Son climb the hill of Calvary, crushed beneath the weight of the Cross, his head wounded by the crown of thorns, his entire body reduced to one single wound by the flagellation, his face disfigured by blood and by pain, his eyes glazed from weeping, his Heart overwhelmed by the weight of ingratitude and the lack of love.

d   *I have felt* the blows of the nails, which have pierced his hands and his feet; the heavy thump of the Cross in the earth, which causes Him to heave with pain; the moans that come from his crucified body in the last hours of his bloody agony. I am now beneath the Cross, and I am crushed beneath the weight of the blasphemies and the shrieks of hatred and of inhuman wickedness on the part of those who are assisting at his execution.

e   *I gather, in the motherly chalice* of my Immaculate Heart, every drop of his suffering, his great thirst, the pardoning of the repentant thief, the prayer for those who are crucifying Him, the feeling of being abandoned even by God, his act of filial entrustment to the Will of the Father. But a few moments before his divine Heart closes itself to earthly life, it opens itself to his last gift: *'Behold your Mother.'*

f   Thus I became the Mother of all humanity redeemed by my Son. I am the true Mother of all. The new sepulchre which receives Him, now dead, is transformed into the cradle in which you are all born into life. Receive with love this last gift of his, beloved sons, because, at the side of the cradle in which you have been reborn, there is the presence of the Mother whom Jesus has given to you.

g   *Accept me into your life*, that I may be able to help you walk along the same road upon which Jesus has preceded you.

h   *Open for me the doors* of your priestly home that I may be able to beautify it and adorn it with sanctity and purity.

i   *Live together with me* each day, to be comforted in the carrying of your cross and in following Jesus all the way to Calvary.

j   *Let yourselves be formed by me*, if you want your priestly life to be made fragrant by the blossoming of all the virtues.

k   On Good Friday of this Marian Year, understand all the preciousness of the gift which Jesus has given you when He disclosed his hidden thoughts to speak to you those words which you must never again forget: *'Behold your Mother.'*

l   And live ever in deep gratitude to Jesus for having given you this last gift of his."

379

Dongo (Como, Italy); April 2, 1988
Holy Saturday
First Saturday

Into the Sorrow of My Desolation

a   "This is the Holy Saturday. It is the day of my great sorrow. It is the day of my incessant prayer.

b   During this Marian Year, consecrated to me, this day coincides with the first Saturday of the month. I came from heaven to ask you to offer me the five first Saturdays of the month. I asked this of my daughter, Sister Lucia, when she was in the convent of Pontevedra, on the 10th of December, 1925. I asked that this day be spent in a spirit of reparation for the offenses which are directed at your heavenly Mother.

c   Why, among all the days of the week, have I asked you to offer Saturday to me? To recall the painful hours, spent by me, during the only day when I remained without my Son. The body of Jesus lies dead, placed in his new sepulchre, and I am keeping vigil, continually recollected in my virginal sorrow, in intimate union of faith, of love and of hope with the Heavenly Father, who bows down over the wounds of my inexpressible longing, with a kiss of his divine comfort.

d   Today I want all of you near me, the sorrowful Mother, to be consoled by you and to teach you to pray with confidence, to suffer with docility, to love with purity of heart, to believe with unshakeable certitude, to hope with heroism, even against the evidence of things.

559

e   This is the day when I receive you *into the sorrow of my desolation*, and I open the door to you so that all may be able to enter into the secure dwelling place of my spiritual motherhood. This is the day which sprouted forth like a flower, upon the heroism of my love, of my sorrow, of my faith and of my firm hope. It is the day of your new repose.

f   For this reason I am asking you to offer it to me, with the recitation of the holy rosary, with the meditation upon its mysteries, with sacramental Confession and a Communion of reparation, and with the renewal of your act of consecration to my Immaculate Heart. In this way you can make reparation for the offenses which are directed at me and which cause my Heart to suffer so much.

g   Among the errors which are being diffused today, there are even those which touch the person and the honor of your heavenly Mother. My Immaculate Conception and my fullness of grace is denied by some; others no longer believe in the great privilege of my perpetual virginity and of my divine and universal motherhood. And those children who have particular need of me, such as tiny babes, the little ones, the poor, the simple and the sinners are kept far away from me. Moreover, even my images are often removed from places of worship.

h   To make amends for these offenses which are being committed against the Immaculate Heart of your heavenly Mother, I am asking you to propagate again today the devotion of the five first Saturdays of the month. I had asked for this during the first part of this century of yours; I am returning today to ask for it as this century turns towards its most painful close.

i   If you do what I ask of you, devotion to me will spread more and more, and then I will be able to exercise the great power which the Most Holy Trinity has granted to me. Thus I will be able to prepare for all humanity the new era of its complete renovation, in the glorious triumph of my Son Jesus."

Rejoice with Me

a   "*Rejoice with me,* beloved children. Jesus, whom I carried with ineffable love in my virginal womb and to whom during nine months gave flesh and blood, to prepare Him for his human birth, *is risen.*

b   *Rejoice with me.* Jesus, whom as a child I clasped in my arms, whom I taught to take his first steps and whom I formed and raised, as a loving and attentive mother, *is risen.*

c   *Rejoice with me.* Jesus, whom I contemplated in his infancy and watched develop according to the rhythm of his human growth and become a young man in the course of his adolescence, *is risen.*

d   *Rejoice with me.* Jesus, who suffered misunderstanding, marginalization, and persistent rejection by the religious authorities, while He became more and more accepted and followed by the little, the poor, the sick and the sinners, *is risen.*

e   *Rejoice with me.* Jesus, who was abandoned by his disciples, denied, betrayed, condemned to death by the religious tribunal, brought before Pilate, scourged, crowned with thorns, led to the gibbet and crucified, *is risen.*

f   *Rejoice with me.* Jesus, who was slain on the Cross and laid in the tomb, *is risen.*

g   Beloved children, on this Easter Day, rejoice with me. Share in the ineffable joy which my Immaculate Heart experienced, when I saw for myself, before my eyes which were still filled with tears, my Son Jesus in the divine splendor of his glorified body.

h   In that moment, for all humanity, sorrow was transformed into joy, darkness into light, wickedness into goodness, sin into grace, hatred into love, death into life, justice into the triumph of divine mercy.

i   *Rejoice with me,* beloved children, in living together the joyful mystery of this Easter of the Marian Year consecrated to me.

j   Today even this poor humanity, which is still closed up in the cold sepulchre of sin, of the rejection of God, of hatred, of violence, of war, of impurity and of iniquity, is being called to come out from its tomb of darkness and of death.

k   *Rejoice with me, all of you,* because, on this day of his Pasch, I am announcing to you that the risen Jesus will return in the divine splendor of his majesty and of his glory.''

381   *Dongo (Como, Italy); May 1, 1988*
Feast of St. Joseph the Worker

Offer Me Fragrant Flowers

a   "You are beginning today the month of May of this Marian Year, consecrated to me. I invite you to spend it with me, in a more intense communion of life with your heavenly Mother.

b   My times have come, and now I am about to leave the desert, where I am, to accomplish my greatest prodigies and to obtain my foretold victory. For this I have need of you today, beloved sons.

c   I want to let shine upon the whole world the light of my Immaculate Heart, through you who have entrusted yourselves completely to me, with the act of your perfect consecration.

I want to act by means of you.

I want to love and to save by means of you.

I want to manifest myself to all and to complete the triumph of my Immaculate Heart by means of you.

d   I am asking you to spend this month in a profound intimacy of life with me.

e   *Offer me the fragrant flowers of your prayer.* Pray more; pray with love and with perseverance; pray with the prayer of the heart. Begin anew to gather about you the faithful who are entrusted to you, to form with your heavenly Mother a true cenacle of unceasing prayer, which can draw down upon the Church and upon the world the gift of a second Pentecost.

f   *Offer me the fragrant flowers of your trust.* My Adversary is trying you with the temptation of doubt and of discouragement. This is the subtle snare which he always employs to bring you to a halt along the road of total trust in me. How many of you have come to a halt because of doubt, of uncertainty and of incredulity.

Begin anew to listen to me with the purity of little children.

Begin anew to believe me with the simplicity of the poor.

562

Begin anew to follow me with the abandonment of children.

g *Offer me the fragrant flowers of your love.*
Love more. Love with greater intensity.

Be examples to all of the living out of the new commandment of my Son Jesus: 'Love one another as I have loved you.'
(Jn 15:12)

Do not judge; do not criticize; do not condemn. Be kind,
gentle and merciful to everyone.

Be the dew of my motherly tenderness which falls upon the
desert of egoism and of hatred, of unlovingness and of aridity.

h In these times Satan is ensnaring very much even this work
of love of mine, seeking to sow division among you. Therefore
I am urging you all to be more docile and more humble, more
obedient and more united with this little son of mine, whom I
have chosen as the instrument for the spread of the Marian
Movement of Priests in every part of the world.

i Then the fragrant flowers of prayer, of trust and of love, which
you offer me during the month of May of this Marian Year, will
be accepted by me as a most welcome homage offered on your
part, my little sons and courageous apostles whom I have chosen for the triumph of my Immaculate Heart."

382

Marienfried (Germany); May 13, 1988
Anniversary of the First Apparition at Fatima

These Are the Times

a "Beloved sons, live in my peace. Today you are calling to
mind my first apparition which took place in the poor Cova da
Iria in Fatima. I came down from heaven as your Mother and
Queen. I manifested myself to you in the splendor of my immaculate light. I appeared as the Woman Clothed with the Sun,
who has the task of forming for herself her cohort, for the decisive moments of battle.

b *These are the times of my great light.*

c *These are the times of prayer and of penance.* I call upon you again
today to pray especially for the conversion of poor sinners, of
the atheists and of those who are far away. Recite always the
holy rosary. Offer prayers and sacrifices for the salvation of

souls, because I repeat to you again today that many are going to hell because there is no one to pray and to sacrifice for them.

d   *These are the times of conversion and of return to the Lord.* As Mother, I am taking you by the hand and leading you along the road of goodness, of love and of holiness. I am obtaining for you the grace of repentance, that you may be able to live far removed from sin, from evil and from egoism. Each day, let the number of my children, who are renouncing sin to walk along the path of the grace of God, grow greater. Let the Law of the Lord become more and more observed and practiced. And in this way many of your brothers will follow you along the road of return to the Lord and of salvation.

e   *These are the times of my peace.* To those children who listen to me and consecrate themselves to my Immaculate Heart I give the gift of my peace. I lead you to live in peace of heart and of soul. I cause you to remain in serenity, even in the midst of great turmoil. You experience my motherly presence, especially in times of danger and of trial. I mark you with my seal that you may spread everywhere the light of the faith, of holiness and of love in these days of dense darkness.

f   *These are the times of the great mercy.* The Heart of Jesus is about to pour out torrents of his divine and merciful love. The hour of the great mercy for the world has come. It will come down as dew upon every wound; it will open the hardest hearts; it will purify souls immersed in sin; it will lead sinners to conversion and will grant to everyone the grace of a complete renewal.

g   In this day of the Marian Year, consecrated to me, I invite you to let yourselves — one and all — be penetrated by my immaculate light, that you yourselves may become my rays of light which brighten up the earth, immersed in the deepest darkness, with the sun of purity and of love."

383   *Heede (Germany); May 22, 1988*
Solemnity of Pentecost

The Holy Spirit Will Come

a   "Beloved sons, gather together from every part of the earth to live this feast day in the cenacle of my Immaculate Heart.

564

This is the day which recalls the descent of the Holy Spirit upon the Apostles, gathered together in prayer with me in the Cenacle of Jerusalem. On this day of Pentecost of the Marian Year, consecrated to me, I am calling upon you to unite your prayer to that of your heavenly Mother, to obtain the great gift of the second Pentecost. The time of the second Pentecost has come.

b   *The Holy Spirit will come*, as a heavenly dew of grace and of fire, which will renew all the world. Under his irresistible action of love, the Church will open itself to live the new era of its greatest holiness and will shine resplendently with so strong a light that it will attract to itself all the nations of the earth.

c   *The Holy Spirit will come*, that the Will of the Heavenly Father be accomplished and the created universe once again reflect his great glory.

d   *The Holy Spirit will come*, to establish the glorious reign of Christ, and it will be a reign of grace, of holiness, of love, of justice and of peace. With his divine love, He will open the doors of hearts and illuminate all consciences. Every person will see himself in the burning fire of divine truth. It will be like a judgment in miniature. And then Jesus Christ will bring his glorious reign in the world.

e   *The Holy Spirit will come*, by means of the triumph of my Immaculate Heart. For this, I am calling upon you all today to enter into the cenacle of my Heart. Thus you will be prepared to receive the gift of the Holy Spirit which will transform you and make you the instruments with which Jesus will establish his reign."

384

Monastery of Le Bouveret (Vallese, Switzerland)
June 11, 1988
Feast of the Immaculate Heart of Mary

The Great Apostasy

a   "On the feast of my Immaculate Heart of this Marian Year, consecrated to me, beloved sons, I am calling all of you to enter into the heavenly garden which I have built for you, during these painful and bloody moments of the purification.

b   *The hour of the great apostasy has come*. What has been foretold in Holy Scripture, in the Second Letter of Saint Paul to the Thessalonians, is now on the point of coming to pass.

c   Satan, my Adversary, with snares and by means of his subtle seduction, has succeeded in spreading errors everywhere, under the form of new and more updated interpretations of the truth, and he has led many to choose with full knowledge — and to live in — sin, in the deceiving conviction that this is no longer an evil, and even that it is a value and a good.

d   *The times of the general confusion and of the greatest agitation of spirits has come.* Confusion has entered into the souls and the lives of many of my children.

e   This great apostasy is spreading more and more, even through the interior of the Catholic Church. Errors are being taught and spread about, while the fundamental truths of the faith, which the authentic Magisterium of the Church has always taught and energetically defended against any heretical deviation whatsoever, are being denied with impunity.

f   The episcopates are maintaining a strange silence and are no longer reacting. When my Pope speaks with courage and reaffirms with force the truths of the Catholic faith, he is no longer listened to and is even publicly criticized and derided. There is a subtle and diabolical tactic, woven in secrecy by Masonry, which is used today against the Holy Father in order to bring ridicule upon his person and his work and to neutralize his Magisterium.

g   *Victims of the great apostasy* are those children of mine who, often unknowingly, allow themselves to be carried along by this wave of errors and of evil.

h   *Victims of the great apostasy* are many bishops, priests, religious and faithful.

i   In these times, in the Catholic Church, there will remain *a little remnant* who will be faithful to Christ, to the Gospel, and to its entire truth. The little remnant will form a *little flock*, all guarded in the depths of my Immaculate Heart. This little flock will be made up of those bishops, priests, religious and faithful who will remain strongly united to the Pope, all gathered together in the cenacle of my Immaculate Heart, in an act of unceasing prayer, of continual immolation, of total offering to prepare the painful way for the second and glorious coming of my Son Jesus.

j   On this feast of mine in this Marian Year, I address to all those who wish to become part of the little flock the motherly invitation to consecrate themselves to my Heart, to live in intimacy of life with me, to become my courageous apostles in these last times, because the moment when *my Immaculate Heart* must be glorified before all the Church and before all humanity has come."

385
Shrine of Knock (Ireland); June 29, 1988
Solemnity of Sts. Peter and Paul

With the Faith of Peter

a   "Beloved sons, enlighten the earth with the light of Christ. Beloved sons, bring all people to Christ *with the faith of Peter.*

b   It was upon Peter alone that Christ founded his Church. It was for Peter alone that Jesus prayed that his faith remain ever intact. It was to Peter alone that the Lord entrusted the task of confirming his brothers in the faith.

c   Today you are celebrating the solemnity of the Holy Apostles, Peter and Paul, during this Marian Year, consecrated to me.

d   As a sorrowful and concerned Mother, I urge you all to look today to the successor of Peter, Pope John Paul II. He is my Pope. He is the Pope who has been formed by me in the depths of my Immaculate Heart. He is the Pope of my great light, in these times of greatest darkness.

e   *With the faith of Peter,* he is enlightening the earth and confirming all the Church in the truth. The Pope today, as a new Peter, is reaffirming the total faith in Christ the Son of God and, as a new Paul, is going to every part of the world to proclaim with courage his Gospel of salvation.

f   Support the Pope by your filial unity. Pray for him; suffer with him; love him; surround him with a powerful force of humble and courageous obedience.

g   The heart of the Pope is bleeding today because of one bishop of the holy Church of God who, through an arbitrary episcopal ordination carried out against his [the Pope's] will, is opening up a painful schism in the Catholic Church.

h   But this is only the beginning. In fact many bishops are, as of

567

the present time, no longer united with the Pope and are moving along a road which is opposed to that which he is pointing out. This is a greater and more dangerous deviation, even if it is not yet visible, and one which gives pain to my motherly Heart and causes it to bleed and, as it were, causes my Pope to fall under the weight of a cross which is too heavy.

i   I have prepared you so that you may help him to carry his great cross. For this, the hour has come when there must appear, in all its force and its splendor, the great army which, in silence and in hiddenness, I have been forming for myself during these years in every part of the world, through my Marian Movement of Priests, for the defense and the strong support of the Pope.

j   Thus there is beginning to be delineated clearly the plan of the little flock, which will remain faithful to Christ and to his Church, guarded whole and entire in the garden of my Immaculate Heart."

386

Rubbio (Vicenza, Italy); August 15, 1988
Solemnity of the Assumption
of the Blessed Virgin Mary into Heaven
Solemn Closing of the Marian Year

I Have Intervened Forcefully

a   "Beloved sons, live in my peace. Today you are looking to me, the Woman Clothed with the Sun, on this day when the whole Church venerates the privilege of my bodily assumption into heaven.

b   My Pope has chosen this solemnity to officially bring to a close that space of time which has been consecrated to me, by a special Marian Year in my honor, begun on the day of Pentecost of last year. Even though it has not been lived out according to the expectations and the desires of my Immaculate Heart, I have nevertheless welcomed this special offering which my Pope has wished to make to me, in the name of the whole Church.

c   During this Marian Year, which today is living through its concluding moments, *I have intervened forcefully* in the life of the Church and of humanity.

d During this Marian Year, I have been able to exercise my motherly action in the heart, the soul and the life of many of my children who have opened the door of their life to me. Above all, I have been able to exercise my great power in the life of all those children who have entrusted themselves completely to me, by their act of consecration to my Immaculate Heart. In this heavenly garden of mine, I have prepared numerous buds of great sanctity for the new era which is at the doors.

e During this Marian Year, *I have intervened forcefully* as well in the life of the Church. At the present time, the tenebrous forces of evil are laying snares for her on all sides. The dark conspiracies woven by Masonry, by means of its many followers who have insinuated themselves at the summit of the Church, have succeeded in paralyzing her activity and in extinguishing her apostolic ardor.

f Many, even from among the Church's own pastors, are languishing in aridity and tepidity, while this most beloved Daughter of mine is living through the hour of her agony. I am placing myself at the side of my Daughter, the Church, to live with her through the painful moments of her agony and of her great abandonment, to savor the bitterness of her chalice, to bear her sufferings with her, and to share all her deep wounds.

g During this Marian Year, *I have intervened forcefully* to save this poor lost humanity. Alas, my call to conversion has not been accepted. People continue along the road of apostasy, of rebellion against God, of sin, of social evil, of blasphemy, of hatred and of impurity. And so I have urged all my children, who have listened to me and followed me, to gather together in cenacles of prayer and of penance, in order to obtain from Jesus the great gift of his divine mercy.

h What comfort my sorrowful Heart has felt in seeing that these cenacles have spread everywhere and that, during this Marian Year, they have multiplied in number and in generosity. And it is through the great response of prayer and penance, on the part of so many of my children, that I have been able to obtain from Divine Justice the setting aside once again of a great chastisement which ought to have struck all humanity.

i But now, with the close of this Marian Year, the space of time granted by the Lord to humanity for its conversion is also on the point of coming to a close. And now you are on the threshold of the events that I foretold to you.

j   For this reason I am calling upon you to walk, one and all, along the road of divine grace and of holiness, of purity and of prayer, of filial abandonment and of trust. Believe in what I am telling you, and you will remain in my peace and in my light. Only in this way will you be able to light up the earth in these days of dense darkness.

k   From this holy mountain I look upon you all with eyes of mercy, and I bless you."

387
Vienna (Austria); August 31, 1988
Spiritual Exercises in the Form of a Cenacle
with the Priests of the M.M.P.
from Austria, Germany, Yugoslavia and Hungary

The Eyes Raised to Mary

a   "Beloved sons, how it comforts my sorrowful Heart to see you here, all together, for a week of continuous cenacle! I am uniting myself always with your prayer, which you are making with me and by means of me.

b   I am taking part with joy in your fraternal gathering and am building up increasingly your love for each other; I am helping you to understand each other and to walk in greater unity along the difficult road of this time of yours. I accept with joy the act of consecration to my Immaculate Heart which you are renewing each day, during the concelebration of Holy Mass. I am obtaining for you, in superabundance, the gift of the Holy Spirit, which is communicated to you by the Father and the Son, through the powerful intercession of your heavenly Mother.

c   You have entered into my times. You are being called to be my apostles in these last times.

d   The Marian Year, which was officially concluded in the course of this month, has been willed by me as *the beginning of a period of time* during which your heavenly Mother will carry out her work, in an ever increasingly powerful way, in the hearts, in the souls and in the lives of her children, in order to bring to realization the triumph of my Immaculate Heart in the world.

e   *The time of the eyes raised to Mary is now beginning,* as my Pope,

John Paul II, has said to you.

f   *The eyes raised to Mary*: thus you are being enlightened with the virginal light of my faith, which is bringing you to accept the word of God with humility, to keep it with love, to live it with consistency, to preach it with fidelity. I am lighting up for you the way along which you must travel in order to remain ever in the true faith and in order that you yourselves may become courageous witnesses of the faith.

g   How many errors are being spread in your countries, frequently caused by the attitude of pride on the part of many theologians, who no longer accept the Magisterium of the Church. And thus many of my children draw away, each day, from the true faith and tumble into the deep darkness of apostasy.

h   You must be today strong witnesses of the faith, by accepting with docility whatever the Pope and the authentic Magisterium of the Church are still teaching, and by preaching all the truths of the Catholic faith, especially those which are no longer being talked about. And thus you become light for many of your brothers, who are walking in the deepest darkness.

i   *The eyes raised to Mary*: thus you are being enlightened with the virginal light of my purity and of my holiness. How many live surrounded by the darkness of sin, of evil, of impurity, of pride, of blasphemy, of idolatry and of impiety! You must follow me along the road of holiness, which is joined with a strong commitment to fight sin, in all its subtle manifestations, to live in the grace of God, in love, in purity, in charity and in the exercise of all the virtues.

j   And thus you contribute to the healing of the great wound of materialism, which has brought to your countries the malady of immorality, of the devastating search for pleasures, of comfort, of unbridled egoism, of avarice, of insensitiveness to the needs of the little, the poor and the most marginalized.

k   *The eyes raised to Mary*: thus you are being enlightened with the virginal light of my prayer and of my motherly love. Multiply your cenacles of prayer. Always recite the holy rosary. Spread throughout your countries family cenacles, as a remedy for the great evils which are menacing your families with division, divorce, the legitimizing of abortion and all the various means of impeding life.

l   Your prayer must always be oriented to Jesus in the Eucharist. Let it be a prayer of continual adoration, of reparation, of praise and of thanksgiving to the Eucharistic Jesus. May the love and adoration of Jesus present in the Eucharist begin anew to flourish everywhere.

m   The coming of the glorious reign of Christ will coincide with the triumph of the Eucharistic reign of Jesus. Love Jesus; imitate Him; walk along the road of disdain for the world and for yourselves. Let the light of Christ be the only light which illumines you, under the gaze of my motherly and merciful eyes, at the moment when you live through the great tribulation.

n   My light, as a dawn which is arising, is spreading from the East and becoming ever stronger, until it covers the whole world.

o   *Leave this cenacle with the light of Christ and of your immaculate Mother, and go to lighten up the earth in these days of profound darkness.*

p   With Austria and Germany, from here I bless the surrounding countries which are still under the yoke of a great slavery, and today I announce that the moment of their liberation is close."

388   *Basilica of the Sacred Heart of Montmartre (Paris, France)*
September 11, 1988
Cenacle with the Priests and Faithful of the M.M.P.

Love Is Not Loved

a   "Beloved children, how Jesus loves you! His divine Heart is a furnace of most ardent love for you.

b   For love of you, the Word descended from the bosom of the Father to my virginal motherly womb and was made Man.

c   For love of you, Jesus lived a life which was humble, poor, hidden and spent in prayer and in work.

d   For love of you, Jesus took upon Himself suffering, humiliation and marginalization.

e   For love of you, Jesus became the Man of Sorrows and offered Himself as a victim on the Cross.

f   For love of you, He allowed Himself to be condemned, mocked, tortured, crucified and killed.

g   For love of you, He rose again and ascended into heaven, where He is seated at the right hand of the Father.

h   For love of you, Jesus remains ever present in your midst in the state of a victim in the sacrament of the Eucharist.

i   For love of you, He has even given you his Mother.

j   O my poor children, so tried in this time of the great tribulation, if you knew how the Heart of Jesus loves you! Jesus loves you and in return receives from you ingratitude, indifference and lack of response. Jesus loves you, and you live as though He did not exist. Jesus loves you and, in the Eucharist, throbs with love for you, and you leave Him alone, abandoned, surrounded by a great void and so much unbelief.

k   Never before as in these stormy times is it so true that *Love is not loved.*

l   And so, allow your heavenly Mother to form you to love, to make you grow in love, to lead you each day along the road of perfect love. Only in this way will my Immaculate Heart be able to triumph. Only in this way will you be able to illuminate the earth, with the Sun of divine love, who will in the end succeed in driving away all darkness, so that the new era of the civilization of love will at last be able to shine forth resplendently upon the world."

389

Lourdes (France); September 18, 1988
Cenacle with the Priests and Faithful of the M.M.P.

A Period of Ten Years

a   "Today you are coming from every part of France to the foot of this rock upon which I appeared as the Immaculate Conception, to hold your great cenacle of prayer and fraternal sharing and to renew together the act of consecration to my Immaculate Heart.

b   From here I bless my Movement; from here I bless each one of you; from here I bless the Church and all humanity. You have entered into my times. On this day, I am asking you to consecrate to me all the time that still separates you from the end of this century of yours.

c   *It is a period of ten years.* These are ten very important years. These are ten decisive years. I am asking you to spend them with me because you are entering into the final period of the second Advent, which will lead you to the triumph of my Immaculate Heart in the glorious coming of my Son Jesus.

d   *In this period of ten years,* there will come to completion that fullness of time which was pointed out to you by me, beginning with La Salette all the way to my most recent and present apparitions.

e   *In this period of ten years,* there will come to its culmination that purification which, for a number of years now, you have been living through, and therefore the sufferings will become greater for all.

f   *In this period of ten years,* there will come to completion the time of the great tribulation, which has been foretold to you in Holy Scripture, before the second coming of Jesus.

g   *In this period of ten years,* the mystery of iniquity, prepared for by the ever increasing spread of apostasy, will become manifest.

h   *In this period of ten years,* all the secrets which I have revealed to some of my children will come to pass, and all the events which have been foretold to you by me will take place.

i   Therefore I am asking you today to consecrate to me all this period of time, as though it were a more extended and continuous Marian Year. Open to me the doors of your hearts, and let me work in you. Open to me the doors of your families, of your parishes, of your religious houses, and let the immaculate light of my presence enter in.

j   Multiply your cenacles of prayer, and live in the greatest trust and filial abandonment to me, without allowing yourselves to be seized by vain curiosity to know what is awaiting you.

k   May the water of divine mercy purify you of every sin and make of you new buds for the era of grace and of holiness which, in my Immaculate Heart, I am preparing for you each day.

l   From this most venerated shrine of mine, I bless you all."

390

Madrid (Spain); September 29, 1988
Feast of the Holy Archangels
Spiritual Exercises in the Form of a Continuous Cenacle
with the Priests of the M.M.P. from Spain

To the Angels of the Churches

a "Beloved sons, you have completed the spiritual exercises which, under the form of a continuous cenacle, you have carried out during these days, and you have come from every part of Spain, this land so much loved by me and so particularly ensnared and stricken by my Adversary. I have accepted gratefully the homage of your prayer, your fraternal sharing and your love. I have caused a copious rain of grace to come down from my Immaculate Heart upon you, upon the faithful entrusted to you, upon the Church and upon your native land.

b There are three snares with which Satan is trying today to seduce you in order to draw you away from Jesus and from me.

c — *The first is in regard to your native land*, which has officially departed from the road of its time-honored fidelity to Christian tradition to welcome atheistic and materialistic ideologies. Thus the error of indifferentism has been accepted into political and social life, and in the name of a false freedom, divorce, abortion and all the methods of preventing life have been legitimized. What is left that is Christian today in this country of yours, which has, however, been a light to all the world, thanks to the example given by many of its saints and many of its martyrs? Return, O Spain, along the road of conversion and of your greater fidelity to Christ!

d — *The second is in regard to the Church*, which is living in this country of yours. It is penetrated with a secularism which has particularly stricken the life of many priests and many religious. It has been lacerated by a deep interior division. It has been stricken in its pastors who, for fear of exposing themselves to criticisms, are remaining silent and are no longer defending the flock which Christ has entrusted to them.

e To you, who are *the Angels of the Churches*, I address today the sorrowful reproach of my motherly Heart, for your lack of faith, of zeal, of prayer and of holiness. The Lord is about to ask you for an account of how you have managed his vineyard and why you

575

have permitted rapacious wolves to enter into it, disguised as lambs, in order to devour a downtrodden and dispersed flock.

f   *The third is in regard to the life of my children,* especially youth, menaced with such a great spread of immorality. I beg you to return along the road of a general conversion to the Lord, through the observance of the laws of God and through the practice of the Christian virtues, especially of penance and of charity. Let the perfume of your purity once again bring serenity to your surroundings, so thick with threats and with dangers.

g   Entrust yourselves to the protection of your guardian angels, and especially of the Archangels, Saints Gabriel, Raphael and Michael, whose feast you celebrate today. Thus you will be clothed again in the virtue of fortitude, so needed today. You will be healed of the deep wounds which you have been dealt, and especially you will always be protected by Saint Michael in the terrible battle which, during these last times, is being waged between heaven and earth.

h   And in the end you will all be able to form part of the victorious army, guided by your heavenly Leader, the Woman Clothed with the Sun, for the soon-to-come triumph of her Immaculate Heart in the world."

391
Fatima (Portugal); October 13, 1988
Anniversary of the Last Apparition at Fatima

I Am Opening for You the Sealed Book

a   "Today you are bringing to a close, here in Fatima, the cenacles which, during this Marian Year, you have been holding in every country of Europe, with the priests and faithful of my Movement. My great net of love and of salvation has, as of now, been spread out in every part of the earth.

b   From this place, where I have appeared as the Woman Clothed with the Sun, I announce to you that the time of the purification has now reached its culmination and that you are therefore called to live through the most painful moments which have been foretold to you. The Lord is sending me to you that I might bring to fulfillment the task which the Most Holy Trinity has entrusted to me in these times of yours.

c   *I am opening for you the sealed Book,* that the secrets contained in it may be revealed. I have gathered you from all sides, and you have been formed by me in order to be ready for the great events which are awaiting you. Only in this way are you able to carry out your important mission.

d   *In the great apostasy,* which is spreading everywhere, you must remain strongly rooted in the true faith and be courageous witnesses of faith.

e   *In the great tribulation,* in which you are living, you must become the signs of my peace and of my motherly protection.

f   *In the great chastisement,* through which this world is, as of now, living, you must be of assistance to all to walk along the road of trust, of prayer, of hope and of a filial abandonment to the love of your Heavenly Father. My light will become continuously stronger in order to announce the coming of Jesus, King of justice and of peace, who will renew all things.

g   From this, my venerated shrine, I am asking you to accept my word and to believe in my messages.

h   Open for me the doors of your hearts, and live in the peace and in the grace of the Lord.

i   I am the Queen of the Holy Rosary, and I bless you all with this sign of my sure victory."

392

Zagreb (Yugoslavia); October 27, 1988
Spiritual Exercises in the Form of a Cenacle
with the Priests of the M.M.P.
of the Slovenian and Croatian Languages

This Is Your Hour

a   "Beloved sons, how happy I am to see you here, gathered together as so many brothers who love each other, to pray with me, in a cenacle which renews the marvelous reality of that of Jerusalem. You too, in this house, are gathered together with me to love each other, to pray together and to meditate on your life of consecration to my Immaculate Heart.

b   How many graces, during these days, I cause to come down upon the Church and the world! How many graces I cause to flow out from my Immaculate Heart for you, for all my Movement and for your homeland, which is living through moments of suffering and of difficulty and has, therefore, the need to be helped by your heavenly Mother.

c I am the Mother and Queen of your homeland. I love you with particular motherly tenderness. I want to bring comfort and consolation today to all those who live in this land, so loved by me. For this reason I am making use of you, priests and children consecrated to my Immaculate Heart.

d *This is your hour.* It is the hour of your public witness.

e — *Be witnesses of love.* Love your brothers with the Heart of Jesus and with my motherly Heart. Love everyone, especially those furthest away, the poorest, the most needy, those who are suffering most. Love with my Heart the sinners, those who are walking along the road of rejection of God, of atheism, of hatred, of violence and of impurity. Let your love now come down, as my motherly medicine, upon the many open and bleeding wounds, and thus become builders of peace, of communion and of great brotherliness.

f — *Be witnesses of prayer.* Pray always; pray more; pray with the holy rosary. Multiply cenacles of prayer, amongst you priests and with the faithful. Above all, spread all about you family cenacles, which are desired by me as a remedy for the great evils which are today threatening the life of Christian families, through the legitimizing of abortion, of divorce, and of all the methods which prevent life.

g With your prayer you can obtain everything from the Lord. With your prayer made together with me, your heavenly Mother, you can obtain the great gift of bringing about a change of hearts and conversion. Each day, through prayer, you can drive away from yourselves and from your homeland many dangers and many evils.

h — *Be witnesses of mercy.* Today you must be above all *a great and extraordinary sign* of divine mercy. Let your heart be similar to that of Jesus: good, patient, meek, humble and merciful. You will always then give the light of divine love, and you will lead all along the road of salvation.

i Never judge. Condemn no one. Your duty is only that of saving, with the supernatural force of your prayer, of your suffering and of your immolation.

578

j   The miracle of the merciful love of Jesus is about to be accomplished in your time. In this consists the triumph of my Immaculate Heart: in the greatest triumph of the merciful love of Jesus, which will change the whole world and bring you to a new era of love, of holiness and of peace.

k   From this cenacle I bless you all: my Movement, your homeland, the Church and all humanity."

393

Dongo (Como, Italy); November 12, 1988
Feast of St. Josaphat, Martyr

You Will Be Persecuted

a   "Beloved sons, because this is your hour, you are being called more and more to suffer. Jesus is inviting you to follow Him along the way of Calvary. I see how great the cross is which you must carry today, and I am close to each one of you, with my motherly tenderness!

b   — *Do not allow yourselves to be seized with distress.* My Adversary often wounds you, making use of good persons and persons whom you have also helped in many ways. Sometimes he makes use of your very own confreres. The times which I have foretold to you have come, when those priests who venerate me, listen to me and follow me are being derided, scorned and opposed by other priests, who are nonetheless sons of my maternal predilection.

c   You are therefore being called to enter into the Garden of Gethsemane, with Jesus your Brother, who wants to relive in you the sorrowful hours of his interior agony. You too, then, taste the bitterness of his chalice and repeat, together with Him, with filial abandonment: 'Father, not our but your Will be done.' (Lk 22:42)

d   Prepare yourselves to experience the indescribable suffering of being abandoned by the most trustworthy, mocked by confreres, set aside by superiors, opposed by friends, persecuted by those who have accepted a compromise with the world and have associated themselves with the secret cohort of Masonry.

e   — *Do not allow yourselves to be seized with discouragement.* These are the times for courage and witness. Your voice must proclaim, in an ever more powerful manner, the word of the Gospel and all the truths of the Catholic faith. You must unmask every error whatsoever, overcome subtle snares, reject every compromise with the spirit of the world and give to all an example of your fidelity to Christ and to his Church.

f   The times have come when Jesus Crucified must be loved and glorified by you. Bring Him always with you, and show Him to all as the only Savior and Redeemer. For this perverse generation of yours as well, there is no other possibility of salvation except in Christ Jesus Crucified.

g   — *Do not allow yourselves to be seized with fear.* The time of your immolation has now come. *You will be persecuted.* It will even be that those who oppose you, who calumniate you, who despise you, who push you aside and who persecute you will believe that they are doing something pleasing to the Heavenly Father and even to me, your immaculate Mother.

h   This forms part of the tenebrous time in which you are living. Because you are now entering into the most painful and dark phase of the purification, and soon the Church will be shaken by a terrible persecution, a new persecution, such as has hitherto been unknown.

i   Live in prayer. Live in trust. Live the precious hour of your priestly immolation with me, your tender Mother, who has received you all into the garden of her Immaculate Heart, to offer you to the Heavenly Father as victims, pleasing to Him, for the salvation of the world."

394   Rubbio (Vicenza, Italy); December 8, 1988
Solemnity of the Immaculate Conception

A Sign of Hope and of Consolation

a   "Today look, one and all, at me, your immaculate Mother. Join yourselves to the bands of angels and of saints in heaven, to all the souls who are suffering and praying in purgatory, to the pilgrim Church on earth, which is journeying through the desert of this world and time, in order to contemplate me as *a sign of hope and of consolation.*

b   The exemption from every stain of sin, even the original one, has made it possible for my soul to be completely filled with the life of God, for my mind to be filled to overflowing with the Spirit of Wisdom who has opened me to a comprehension of the divine word, for my Heart to be molded into the most perfect form of love, for my body to be enwrapped in the immaculate light of a virginal purity.

c   Gaze upon me, your heavenly Mother, in the splendor of my superhuman beauty, and hasten along, one and all, in the wake of the exquisite wave of this fragrance of mine from paradise. It is in my beauty that the profound reason for your hope and your consolation is found.

d   Because I am 'all beautiful' — tota pulchra — I am for you *a sign of hope* in the days in which you are living, when my Adversary has succeeded in making everything ugly, through the stain of sin and of impurity. You are living under the sign of his great bondage, which is depriving you of the reflection of all spiritual beauty. Souls are being darkened by sins, which prevent the glory of life and of union with God from reaching them. Bodies are being brutalized by the takeover of the passions and of impurity. Man is being crushed under the weight of a civilization without God, which disfigures in him the image of his original dignity. The world is being darkened by a persistent rejection of God. A dense darkness has now descended to obscure everything.

e   And so it is then that the immaculate Mother, at this time, is presenting herself as the sign of your sure hope. Because it is my motherly duty to bring souls back to grace, hearts back to love, bodies back to purity, people back to the great dignity of children of God, the world back to the perfect glorification of the Most Holy Trinity.

f   Because I am 'all beautiful' — tota pulchra — I am for you also *a sign of consolation.* You are living in the time of the great tribulation, and sufferings and trials are increasing for everyone. The wicked are continuing with obstinacy along the road of evil and of sin, without accepting my repeated urgings to conversion and to a return to the Lord.

g   The good are becoming tepid and, as it were, paralyzed by the unhealthy surroundings in which they live. Consecrated persons are given to the search for pleasure and are being attracted by the spirit of the world which, by their vocation, they had rejected. Priests are languishing; many are wicked and unfaithful and are squandering the treasures of the holy Church of God.

h   The hour of the chastisement as of now has arrived. And so, you have more need than ever of entrusting yourselves to me, your heavenly Mother, because I have the task from the Lord of leading you all along the road of goodness, of salvation and of peace.

i   Today I call upon you all to look at me, your immaculate Mother, as a sign of sure hope and of consolation, and to allow yourselves to be enfolded in my light, in these days of profound darkness and universal obscurity so that, led and guided by me, you may go to all places in order to illumine the earth."

395   *Dongo (Como, Italy); December 24, 1988*
The Holy Night

In the Night of Your Time

a   "Keep watch with me, beloved sons, during these hours of waiting. This is the holy night. Share, you also, in the joy of my motherly Heart. My divine Child, the Awaited of the ages, the Only-begotten of the Father, the Emmanuel, the God-with-us, is about to be born.

b   I want to bring you into the depths of my Immaculate Heart, to share with you also, my little children, the feelings which I experienced, during the hours which preceded the birth of my Son Jesus.

c   *My soul* was immersed in an ocean of peace and of blessedness. The presence of the Word who, for nine months, had been pulsating in his human body which was formed in my virginal womb, had filled my soul with the light and happiness of all paradise. There the Most Holy Trinity had made its habitual dwelling; the choirs of angels were prostrating themselves in perpetual adoration and interweaving sweetest harmonies of heavenly songs. The very light of God was transfiguring my soul, which became a most pure reflection of his divine beauty.

582

Thus I was preparing a precious and holy crib in which to place the Light which was about to rise in the midst of an immense darkness.

d   My Heart was opening itself to an experience of a love so great such as has not been granted to any other creature. What sentiments of ineffable love my Heart was experiencing in feeling that the awaited moment of the birth of my divine Child had now come! My motherly love was made even more perfect by my virginal state and the consciousness that the Child who was about to be born of me was the Son of God.

e   Thus, in the moment which preceded his birth, my Heart was filled to overflowing with the love of all those who had awaited Him for centuries. The love of Adam, of Abraham, of Moses, of all the prophets and the just ones of Israel, of the little ones and of the poor of Yahweh was becoming present in my virginal Heart, which was opening itself to love the Child, who was about to be born, with the heartbeat of all humanity redeemed and saved by Him.

f   My body was enwrapped in a light which was becoming stronger and stronger and more intense, the more I entered into an ecstasy of prayer and of profound union with the Heavenly Father.

g   On this night, paradise was completely contained within a poor and cold cave. As a ray of light passes through a crystal without even grazing it, so too the divine Child passed through the veil of my virginal womb without grazing the charm of my perfect virginity. In this wonderful manner there took place the birth of my Son. The greatest of all prodigies is accomplished in the fullness of time.

h   Beloved children, the Lord who has come in his first birth is about to return to you in glory. His second and glorious birth is close at hand. And so, in the night of your time, it is my maternal duty to prepare you to receive Him, as I received Him in his first coming.

i   Let your soul be illuminated by the light of divine grace and by his continual presence within you.

j   Let your heart be opened to a new and greater capacity for love. Love must burn within you as a fire so powerful that it envelops the whole world and burns away whatever there is in it of sin, of evil, of egoism, of hatred, of impurity.

k   *Let your body* be enwrapped in the mantle of holiness and of purity. Shine once again with the whiteness of lilies. Spread about you once again my virginal and immaculate fragrance.

l   And so, *in the night of your time*, enwrapped in the light of my Immaculate Heart, you too prepare a precious crib for his glorious return."

396   *Dongo (Como, Italy); December 31, 1988*
Last Night of the Year

Mother of Intercession and of Reparation

a   "Gather together in prayer with me, beloved children, at the end of this year which has been particularly dedicated to me. I am your heavenly Mother.

b   *I am the Mother of Intercession and of Reparation.*

c   — My maternal task is *that of interceding* each day for you, before my Son Jesus. As an attentive and concerned Mother, I am asking for all the graces that you have need of in order to walk along the road of goodness, of love and of holiness.

d   For my sinful children, I obtain the grace of repentance, of a change of heart, of return to the Lord. For my sick children, I grant the grace of understanding the meaning of every suffering, of accepting it with docility, of offering it with love, of carrying one's own cross with trust and with filial obedience to the Will of the Lord. For my good children, I obtain the gift of perseverance in good. For my priest-sons, I intercede that they may be holy ministers and faithful to Jesus and to his Gospel.

e   Each new day that opens out corresponds to a new act of prayer on the part of your heavenly Mother, to help you to walk forward, in the desert of your time, along the road of love and of the faithful fulfillment of the Will of God, which must be accomplished by you with filial docility.

f   — My maternal task is also *that of offering reparation* for the great evil which, still today, is being committed in the world. I unite myself with each Holy Mass which is celebrated, to offer to the Heavenly Father the precious blood of his Son Jesus, who is still immolating and sacrificing Himself for you on every altar of the earth. It is only his divine blood, shed for you, that can wash away all the evil, the sin, the hatred, the impurity, the iniquity that covers the world. Thus, in a spirit of maternal reparation, I unite to the blood of Christ all the sufferings which I gather together, each day, along your pathway.

g   I unite to the blood of Jesus, the blood poured out by millions of babies still being killed in their mothers' wombs and of all the victims of hatred, of violence and of wars.

h   I unite to the blood of Jesus, all the sufferings of the sick, especially those who are stricken with grave, humiliating and incurable maladies.

i   I unite to the blood of Jesus, the agonies of the dying, the sufferings of the poor, of the marginalized, of the little, of the exploited, of the persecuted.

j   I unite to the blood of Jesus, each suffering of the good, of those consecrated, of the priests.

k   I unite to the blood of Jesus, the great cross which the Church must carry today for the salvation of all humanity.

l   At the close of this year, which has been particularly entrusted to me, I want to associate you also in my maternal task of interceding and of making reparation for all my children.

m   And even so, in the darkness and the coldness which still surrounds the world, I urge you to live in hope and in great trust, because I am ever praying and making reparation in order to obtain, for all, new days of peace and salvation."

1989

COME, LORD JESUS

397

Dongo (Como, Italy); January 1, 1989
Solemnity of Mary, Mother of God

Come, Lord Jesus

a "I am your immaculate Mother, who is leading you to Jesus and bringing you to peace. Today the whole Church rejoices, as it contemplates the ineffable mystery of my divine and universal motherhood.

b At the beginning of this new year, which will be marked by a succession of grave and significant events, you are looking in a special way to me as the Mother of Hope and Queen of Peace.

c In the time of the great tribulation, through which you are living, my motherly presence will become continually stronger and more extraordinary. The greater and more universal the reign of my Adversary, the Red Dragon, will become, the greater and more universal the victorious presence of the Woman Clothed with the Sun will likewise become.

d For this reason you have, as of now, entered into a period of time marked by a strong presence of mine in your midst, and this will become manifest to all by means of extraordinary events.

e I am your tender Mother who has the duty of leading you to Jesus, your Lord and your Savior. In these years, which still separate you from the end of this century, I will take action in all manner of ways in order that the reign of Jesus be restored among you and that the Lord Jesus may be loved and glorified by all.

f *Come, Lord Jesus,* in the life of each one, by means of divine grace, of love and of sanctity. I will act in a very powerful way to bring all of you, who have consecrated yourselves to my Immaculate Heart, to a great sanctity, so that Jesus may live, work and shine forth more and more in your life.

g *Come, Lord Jesus,* in families, to help them to rediscover the life of communion, of mutual and reciprocal love, of perfect unity and of a complete availability to the gift of life.

h *Come, Lord Jesus,* in nations, which have need of becoming once again communities open to the spiritual and material needs of all, especially of the little, the needy, the sick, the poor and the marginalized.

i There is in preparation for you the coming of the reign of Jesus, which will bring you into a new era of great brotherhood and of peace. For this reason, at the beginning of a period of time which is very important — because during it a plan prepared and completed by myself will be carried out — I am today urging you all to band together in the prayer which your heavenly Mother, united with the Holy Spirit her divine Spouse, directs each day to the Father: 'Come, Lord Jesus!' (Rev 22:20)

j Only when Jesus will have brought his reign into your midst will all humanity at last be able to enjoy the great gift of peace."

398
Milan (Italy); February 2, 1989
Feast of the Presentation of the Child Jesus

I Am Bringing You to Jesus

a "Beloved sons, live with joy the mystery of the Presentation of the Child Jesus in the Temple of Jerusalem, and with docility let yourselves also be carried in my motherly arms.

b Forty days after his birth, in fulfillment of the prescriptions of the Law, together with my most chaste spouse, Joseph, I go up to the temple both to offer to the Lord my first-born Son and to carry out the sacrifice prescribed for his ransom. With what love I clasp the Child Jesus in my motherly arms! And with what docility and filial abandonment the little Babe allows Himself to be carried by me, as I press Him with boundless tenderness to my Heart.

c And carried, presented and offered by the Mother, Jesus enters into the glory of his temple.

d Jesus enters into the temple of Jerusalem, because for Him, the Messiah, Lord and Redeemer, it was built and sanctified.

e Jesus comes, in the splendor of his glory, and takes possession of his divine dwelling place.

f Jesus is manifested in the splendor of his light for revelation to all the gentiles.

g Jesus is announced in advance as a sign of contradiction, for the salvation and ruin of many in Israel.

h Jesus is received into the arms of old Simeon as the Messiah awaited for centuries and as Savior of his people.

i And within the mystery of his mission, there is intimately engrafted the unfolding of my motherly function: 'As for you, O Mother, a sword shall pierce your soul.' (cf. Lk 2:35) Because my

589

duty as Mother is that of bringing Jesus to you and of bringing you all to Jesus. I am the way along which you must travel if you want to reach your Lord and Savior.

j   *I am bringing you to Jesus.*

k   *I am bringing you to Jesus, your Truth.* This is why in these times, when many are leaving the faith to follow errors, I am intervening with my numerous and extraordinary manifestations, in order to lead you all to the full truth of the Gospel. You must be only the lived-out Gospel so that you too may be able to give the light of the truth.

l   *I am bringing you to Jesus, your Life.* This is why today, when many are falling into the darkness of sin and of death, I am helping you through my strong presence in your midst, to live in the grace of God, so that you also can share in the very life of the Lord Jesus.

m   In these dark times of the great tribulation, if you do not allow yourselves to be carried in my arms, with filial abandonment and with great docility, it is difficult for you to succeed in escaping the subtle snares which my Adversary sets for you. His seductions have become so dangerous and subtle that hardly anyone any longer succeeds in escaping them. You are running the great danger of falling into the seduction, which my Adversary is setting for you in order to draw you away from Jesus and from me.

n   All can fall into his trap. Priests and even bishops can fall into it. The faithful and even those consecrated can fall into it. The simple and even the learned can fall into it. The disciples and even the masters can fall into it.

o   Those will never fall into it who — as little children — consecrate themselves to my Immaculate Heart and allow themselves to be carried in my motherly arms. As of now, it will become ever clearer and clearer to the Church and to the world that *the little flock* which, in these years of the great apostasy, will remain faithful to Jesus and to his Gospel, will be entirely protected in the motherly enclosure of my Immaculate Heart.

p   *I am bringing you to Jesus, your Way.* You are thus led by Him to your Heavenly Father. Jesus is the perfect Image of the Father;

He is his only-begotten Son; He is the Word consubstantial with Him; He is the reflection of his beauty; He is the revelation of his love.

q Jesus and the Father are one single being. From the Father, through the Son, there is given to you as gift the Spirit of Love, in order that you too may be able to penetrate into the stupendous mystery of this divine Unity.

r If Jesus becomes your way, you come into the arms of his, and your, Heavenly Father. If you walk with Jesus, you carry out the divine Will in your life, with that love and that docility with which Jesus has always done the Will of the Father. And thus you live with the confidence and the abandonment of little children who expect and receive everything as a gift of love from their Father who is in heaven.

s And then I, your heavenly Mother, am able to carry you each day, upon the altar of my Immaculate Heart, to the temple of the glory and the light of the Lord. Thus I am able to offer you, in life, to the perfect glorification of the Most Holy Trinity, and by means of you, I am able to spread everywhere the light of its divine splendor.

t When this light will have illumined and transformed the whole world, Jesus will come to you in glory to restore his kingdom."

399 — Dongo (Como, Italy); March 23, 1989 — Holy Thursday

Dongo (Como, Italy); March 23, 1989
Holy Thursday

Jesus Comes

a "Beloved sons, today is your pasch. Live it in intimacy of life with Jesus, your Brother, who has personally associated you in the exercise of his high and eternal Priesthood. Live in love for Him.

b How Jesus has loved you! 'Having loved his own who were in the world, He loved them to the end.' (Jn 13:1) 'I have earnestly desired to eat this Pasch with you before I suffer.' (Lk 22:15)

c How Jesus loves you! Each day He renews again the gift of this, his Last Supper, of his Sacrifice accomplished on Calvary. You are an important part of this, his plan of love.

d Today you find yourselves gathered about your bishops, to renew the promises which you made at the moment of your priestly ordination. Renew them with joy and with confidence. Renew them with love, as a sign of profound gratitude to Him who has chosen you.

e *Each day Jesus comes by means of you,* his priests and sons of my maternal predilection.

f *Jesus comes,* by means of your word, which repeats the words of his Gospel of salvation in every language and to all men: 'Go into the whole world, and preach the Gospel to every creature.' (Mk 16:15)

g *Jesus comes,* by means of your priestly action, which is exercised in bringing all to Him, your Redeemer and Savior. 'He who believes and is baptized will be saved.' (Mk 16:16)

h *Jesus comes,* by means of the Eucharistic Sacrifice, which renews that accomplished by Him on Calvary, to wash again today, with his divine blood, all the sin and the evil of the world. 'Do this in memory of Me.' (Lk 22:19)

i *Jesus comes,* by means of the sacrament of Reconciliation, which brings back all sinners to the house of his merciful love. 'Whose sins you shall forgive, they are forgiven.' (Jn 20:23)

j *Jesus comes,* by means of the sacraments of which you are the ministers and of your person which must reflect the light of his perennial presence. 'I am with you all days, until the end of the world.' (cf. Mt 28:20)

k In this your day of Holy Thursday, I ask of each one of you to give to all the joy of his divine presence in your midst.

l Then, in the immense darkness which still surrounds everything, you brighten up the earth with the light of Jesus Christ, who comes again today by means of you."

400

Dongo (Como, Italy); March 24, 1989
Good Friday

Remain with Jesus on the Cross

a "I am here with the Apostle John who represents all of you, my beloved sons, beneath the Cross on which my Son Jesus is living out the bloody hours of his atrocious agony. Every moan of his agony pierces, as a sword, my sorrowful soul. Every drop of his suffering is gathered in the open chalice of my Immaculate Heart.

b   I am here to seek a little love and compassion to offer, in order to alleviate the great thirst of Jesus who is in agony. I am asking for a little love, but about us there is inhuman wickedness, deep hatred, shrieks and blasphemies which go up from the hearts and the lips of those who are assisting at his execution. And, among these, there is a cry which pierces my Heart, wounds it and causes it to bleed with indescribable pain. 'Come down from the Cross. If you are the Son of God, save yourself. Come down from the Cross, and then we will believe in you.' (cf. Mt 27:40, 42)

c   But indeed it was to mount this Cross that my Son was born, that He grew up, that He lived: to become the docile lamb who, meek, is led to the slaughter. He is the true Lamb of God, who takes away all the sins of the world.

d   I, through my motherly presence, must today help Him to remain on the Cross, that the Will of the Father be accomplished and that you might be redeemed and saved by Him. Remain, O my Son, on the Cross. I am here to help You stretch Yourself on your scaffold, to suffer, to die. Remain, O my Son, on the Cross: only thus do You save us; only thus do You draw the whole world to Yourself.

e   For this You came down from the bosom of the Father into my virginal motherly womb.

f   For this, for nine months, I carried You in my womb and gave You flesh and blood for your human birth.

g   For this You were born of me in Bethlehem, and You grew up, like every man, through the rhythm of your human development.

h   For this You opened up like a flower, during your infancy, and You were formed in the vigor of your adolescence.

i   For this You bore the weight of daily labor in the poor home of Nazareth; You were assisted each day by me, your tender Mother, with the precious help of your legal father, Joseph.

j   For this You have spent the three fatiguing years of your public life, announcing the Gospel of salvation, healing the sick, pardoning sinners, opening the gates of the kingdom to the poor, the little, the humble and the oppressed.

k   For this You have undergone the judgment and the condemnation of the religious tribunal, ratified by Pilate, who has delivered You over to the Cross. And today, behold, You are stretched upon the throne of your glory, prepared by the Heavenly Father for You, his only-begotten Son, gentle and divine Lamb who take away from the world all sin, evil, hatred, impurity and death. O precious and fruitful Cross who carry in your arms the Savior of the world!

l   O sweet and saving wood, upon which is hung the price of our ransom! O Cross, blessed and sanctified by the Paschal Victim who today is immolating Himself upon you in the one and only Sacrifice which redeems and saves all!

m   Beloved sons, on this day of Good Friday, permit that I might repeat also to you: *Remain with Jesus, on the Cross.* Do not give in to the subtle temptations of my Adversary, to the facile seductions of the world, to the voices of those who again today repeat to you: 'Come down from the cross!'

n   No! You also, like Jesus, must understand the divine plan of your personal priestly offering. You too must say yes to the Will of the Father and be open to words of prayer and of pardon. Because today, you also, like Jesus, must be immolated for the salvation of the world."

401

Dongo (Como, Italy); March 25, 1989
Solemnity of the Annunciation of the Lord
Holy Saturday

In the New Sepulchre

a   "*In the new sepulchre*, the body of my Son Jesus rests in the sleep of death.

b   Upon my virginal bosom, where the Word of the Father placed Himself after the *yes* which I gave at the moment of the Annunciation, his Spirit is placed. And I feel myself to be a sorrowful and contented Mother, wounded and soothed, submersed in an ocean of sorrow and enwrapped in a mantle of peace, racked by tears and composed in an interior and divine blessedness.

c   All has now been accomplished.

d   Now I am keeping vigil in an act of incessant prayer, as my

Heart opens itself to the certainty of the resurrection of my Son Jesus, my mind is illumined by the light of his prophecy, and my person is all straining forward in the expectation of this, his glorious moment.

e   This is the day of my motherly solitude.
This is the day of my immense sorrow.
This is the fruitful day of my sure hope.
This is the first day of my new and spiritual motherhood.

f   Enter, beloved sons, into the cradle of my Immaculate Heart, and prepare yourselves as well for the moment of your new birth.

g   *In the new sepulchre*, where the lifeless body of my Son Jesus lies for this one day, place the man who, in you, must die. Place the man of sin and of vice, of hatred and of egoism, of avarice and of lust, of pride and of haughtiness, of discord and of disbelief.

h   Let there die in you today all that you have inherited from the first man. And let there emerge at last into the light the new man, who is born *in the new sepulchre*, where Christ is risen in the glorious splendor of his divinity:

i   The new man of grace and of holiness,
The new man of love and of communion,
The new man of mercy and of purity,
The new man of humility and of charity,
The new man of docility and of obedience,
The new man of light and of sanctity,
The new man formed *in the new sepulchre* and who comes to life at the joyous moment of the resurrection of Christ.

j   This new birth of yours comes to pass in the cradle of my Immaculate Heart, beside me, your tender Mother, who thus initiates the new task of her spiritual and universal motherhood.

k   Only this new man, who is born in the paschal mystery of Christ, can throw open wide the door of the sepulchre, in which there lies today the whole of humanity, at this point dead, to cause it to arise to a new era of grace and of holiness, which the risen Christ brought you at the moment of his victory over sin and over death."

Dongo (Como, Italy); March 26, 1989
Easter Sunday

In Expectation of His Glorious Return

a   "Beloved sons, live in the joy of Easter. Jesus Christ, scourged, crowned with thorns, reviled, led to the Cross, crucified and put to death as a malefactor, is risen. With the power which comes to Him from his Person and from his divine nature, He has summoned from death his human nature, and in the splendor of his glory, He comes forth victorious from the sepulchre.

b   Christ Risen is alive in your midst. Do not fear: He is guiding the events of human history to the realization of the Will of the Heavenly Father and of his great plan of salvation. Christ Risen is now seated in heaven upon his throne of glory, at the right hand of the Father.

c   To Him all things are subjected. Beneath his footstool all his enemies will be humbled and defeated. As of today, human history is opened up to the full glorification of the risen Christ. The risen Christ will come again to you on the clouds of heaven, in the full splendor of his glory.

d   *Live today in expectation of his glorious return.*

e   Do not allow yourselves to be discouraged by the momentary triumph of evil and of sin. Do not let the present victory in the world — the victory of the obstinate rejection of God, of rebellion against his Law of love and of a so universal impiety — sadden you. Nor should you allow yourselves to be seized by doubt or lack of confidence in seeing the Church so wounded and stricken, ensnared and betrayed. Let the paschal joy be greater than every human reason for apprehension and sadness.

f   Christ Risen is alive in your midst. Christ Risen marks with his victory the events of the world and of history. Christ Risen wills to restore his kingdom in your midst, that He may be glorified by the whole created universe.

g   Live always in joy and in a firm hope, *in expectation of his glorious return.*"

The Two Wings of the Great Eagle

a   "My beloved sons, today you are venerating me in a special way, on the first Saturday of this month of May, which is specially dedicated to me by you. You are gathered in cenacles of brotherly sharing and of prayer with your heavenly Mother.

b   How much comfort you give to my deep sorrow; how much joy you bring to my Immaculate Heart! Because, by means of you who have responded to me, devotion to me is now flourishing again in all the Church.

c   Thus I am able to exercise, in these times of yours, the great power which has been given to me by the Most Holy Trinity, to render harmless the attack which my Adversary, the Red Dragon, has unleashed against me, vomiting from his mouth a river of water to submerge me. The river of water is made up of the collection of all the new theological doctrines, which have sought to obscure the image of your heavenly Mother, to deny her privileges, to restructure devotion to her, and to cast ridicule upon all those who are devoted to her. Because of these attacks of the Dragon, in these years, piety toward me has steadily diminished among many of the faithful and, in some places, has even disappeared.

d   But to the help of your heavenly Mother, there have come *the two wings of the great eagle.* The great eagle is the word of God, above all the word contained in the Gospel of my Son Jesus.

e   Of the four Gospels, the eagle indicates that of Saint John, because he flies higher than all, enters into the very Heart of the Most Holy Trinity, affirming with forcefulness the divinity, the eternity and the consubstantiality of the Word and the divinity of Jesus Christ.

f   *The two wings* of the eagle are the word of God, *received*, loved and kept with *faith* and the word of God *lived* with *grace and charity.* The two wings of faith and of charity — that is to say, of the word of God received and lived by me — permitted me to fly above the river of water of all the attacks made upon me, because they have manifested to the world my true greatness.

g   And then I sought a refuge for myself in the desert. The desert, in which I have made my habitual dwelling place, is made up of the hearts and the souls of all those children who receive me, who listen to me, who entrust themselves completely to me, who consecrate themselves to my Immaculate Heart. In the desert in which I find myself, I am working today my greatest prodigies. I am working them in the heart and in the soul, that is to say, in the life of all my littlest children. Thus I am leading them to follow me along the road of faith and of charity, bringing them to receive, to love and to keep the word of God and helping them to live each day with consistency and courage.

h   In silence and in hiddenness, that is to say, in the desert in which I find myself, I am working forcefully that my children consecrated to me believe today in the Gospel, let themselves be guided only by the wisdom of the Gospel, be ever the Gospel lived out.

i   This is the task which I have prepared for the army which I have formed for myself in every part of the world, with my Marian Movement of Priests: to let themselves be carried with me on the *two wings of the great eagle,* namely of faith and of charity, receiving with love and living solely, in these times of yours, the word of God.

j   The great prodigies which I am accomplishing today, in the desert in which I find myself, are those of transforming completely the life of my little children, that they may become courageous witnesses of faith and luminous examples of holiness.

k   In this way, in silence and in hiddenness, each day I am preparing my great victory over the Dragon, in the triumph of my Immaculate Heart in the world."

404

Shrine of Tindari (Sicily, Italy); May 14, 1989
Solemnity of Pentecost

The Huge Red Dragon

a   "Beloved sons, today you adore and call upon the Holy Spirit, descended at Pentecost upon the Apostles and the disciples, gathered together with me in the Cenacle of Jerusalem. You are calling upon Him again in these times of yours, with confidence and perseverance, gathered together with me in cenacles of prayer, which are now spread in every part of the earth.

b   With my Marian Movement of Priests, I am today inviting all the children of the Church to gather together in a continuous cenacle of prayer with me, your heavenly Mother. I am inviting all the bishops, the priests, the religious and the faithful.

c   My Immaculate Heart is the place of this new, spiritual and universal cenacle. You must enter into it through your act of consecration, which commits you to me forever, so that I may unite my voice to yours in calling down upon the Church and upon all humanity the gift of a second Pentecost.

d   Only the Spirit of the Lord can bring back humanity to the perfect glorification of God. Only the Spirit of the Lord can renew the Church with the splendor of its unity and its sanctity. Only the Spirit of the Lord can overcome the power and the victorious force of *the huge Red Dragon*, which, in this century of yours, has broken loose everywhere, in a formidable way, to seduce and ensnare all humanity.

e   *The huge Red Dragon* is atheistic communism which has spread everywhere the error of the denial and of the obstinate rejection of God. *The huge Red Dragon* is Marxist atheism, which appears with ten horns, namely with the power of its means of communication, in order to lead humanity to disobey the Ten Commandments of God, and with seven heads, upon each of which there is a crown, signs of authority and royalty. The crowned heads indicate the nations in which atheistic communism is established and rules with the force of its ideological, political and military power.

f   The hugeness of the Dragon clearly manifests the vastness of the territory occupied by the uncontested reign of atheistic communism. Its color is red because it uses wars and blood as instruments of its numerous conquests.

g   *The huge Red Dragon* has succeeded during these years in conquering humanity with the error of theoretical and practical atheism, which has now seduced all the nations of the earth. It has thus succeeded in building up for itself a new civilization without God, materialistic, egoistic, hedonistic, arid and cold, which carries within itself the seeds of corruption and of death.

h   *The huge Red Dragon* has the diabolical task of taking all humanity away from the dominion of God, from the glorification of the Most Holy Trinity, from the full actualization of the plan of the Father who, by means of the Son, has created it for his glory.

i   The Lord has reclothed me with his light and the Holy Spirit with his divine power, and thus I appear as a great sign in heaven, a Woman Clothed with the Sun, because I have the task of taking humanity away from the dominion of the huge Red Dragon and of bringing it all back to the perfect glorification of the Most Holy Trinity.

j   For this I have formed for myself the army of my littlest children, in every part of the world, and I am asking of them that they consecrate themselves to my Immaculate Heart. Thus I am leading them to live only for the glory of God, by means of faith and charity, and I myself am jealously cultivating them in my heavenly garden.

k   Then each day I present myself before the throne of my Lord in an act of profound adoration; I open the golden door of my Immaculate Heart; and I offer in my arms all these little children of mine, as I say: 'Most Holy and Divine Trinity, at the moment when You are being universally denied, I present to You the homage of my motherly reparation, by means of all these little ones of mine whom I am forming each day to your greater glorification.'

l   Thus again today, from the mouths of infants and sucklings, the Lord receives his perfect praise."

405

Milan (Italy); June 3, 1989
Feast of the Immaculate Heart of Mary
First Saturday

The Beast Like a Leopard

a   "Beloved sons, today you are gathered in cenacles of prayer to celebrate the feast of the Immaculate Heart of your heavenly Mother. From every part of the world, I have called you to consecrate yourselves to my Immaculate Heart, and you have responded with filial love and generosity. I have now formed for myself my army, with those children who have accepted my request and have listened to my voice.

b   The time has come when my Immaculate Heart must be glorified by the Church and by all humanity because, in these times of the apostasy, of the purification and of the great tribulation, my Immaculate Heart is the only refuge and the way which leads you to the God of salvation and of peace. Above all, my Immaculate Heart becomes today the sign of my sure victory, in the great struggle which is being fought out between the followers of the huge Red Dragon and the followers of the Woman Clothed with the Sun.

c   In this terrible struggle, there comes up from the sea, to the aid of the Dragon, *a beast like a leopard.*

d   If the Red Dragon is Marxist atheism, the Black Beast is *Freemasonry*. The Dragon manifests himself in the force of his power; the Black Beast, on the other hand, acts in the shadow, keeps out of sight and hides himself in such a way as to enter in everywhere. He has the claws of a bear and the mouth of a lion, because he works everywhere with cunning and with the means of social communication, that is to say, through propaganda. The seven heads indicate the various masonic lodges, which act everywhere in a subtle and dangerous way.

e   This Black Beast has ten horns and, on the horns, ten crowns, which are signs of dominion and royalty. Masonry rules and governs throughout the whole world by means of the ten horns. The horn, in the biblical world, has always been an instrument of amplification, a way of making one's voice better heard, a strong means of communication.

f   For this reason, God communicated his Will to his people by means of ten horns which made his Law known: the Ten Commandments. The one who accepts them and observes them walks in life along the road of the divine Will, of joy and of peace. The one who does the Will of the Father accepts the word of his Son and shares in the redemption accomplished by Him. Jesus gives to souls the very divine life, through grace, that He won for us through his Sacrifice carried out on Calvary.

g   The grace of the redemption is communicated by means of the seven sacraments. With grace there becomes implanted in the soul the seeds of supernatural life which are the virtues. Among these, the most important are the three theological and the four cardinal virtues: faith, hope, charity; prudence, fortitude, justice and temperance. In the divine sun of the seven gifts of the Holy Spirit, these virtues germinate, grow, become more and more developed and thus lead the soul along the luminous way of love and of sanctity.

h   The task of the Black Beast, namely of Masonry, is that of fighting, in a subtle way, but tenaciously, to obstruct souls from traveling along this way, pointed out by the Father and the Son and lighted up by the gifts of the Spirit. In fact if the Red Dragon works to bring all humanity to do without God, to the denial of God, and therefore spreads the error of atheism, the aim of Masonry is not to deny God, but *to blaspheme Him.* The Beast opens his mouth to utter blasphemies against God, to blaspheme his name and his dwelling place, and against all those who dwell in heaven. The greatest blasphemy is that of denying the worship due to God alone by giving it to creatures and to Satan himself. This is why in these times, behind the perverse action of Freemasonry, there are being spread everywhere black masses and the satanic cult. Moreover Masonry acts, by every means, to prevent souls from being saved, and thus it endeavors to bring to nothing the redemption accomplished by Christ.

i   If the Lord has communicated his Law with the Ten Commandments, Freemasonry spreads everywhere, through the power of its ten horns, a law which is completely opposed to that of God.

j   To the commandment of the Lord: 'You shall not have any other gods but me,' (cf. Ex 20:3) it builds other false idols, before which many today prostrate themselves in adoration.

k   To the commandment: 'You shall not take the name of God in vain,' (Ex 20:7) it sets itself up in opposition by blaspheming God and his Christ, in many subtle and diabolical ways, even to reducing his Name indecorously to the level of a brand-name of an object of sale and of producing sacrilegious films concerning his life and his divine Person.

l   To the commandment: 'Remember to keep holy the Sabbath Day,' (Ex 20:8) it transforms the Sunday into a weekend, into a day of sports, of competitions and of entertainments.

m   To the commandment:'Honor your father and your mother,' (Ex 20:12) it opposes a new model of family based on cohabitation, even between homosexuals.

n   To the commandment:'You shall not kill,' (Ex 20:13) it has succeeded in making abortion legal everywhere, in making euthanasia acceptable, and in causing respect due to the value of human life all but disappear.

o   To the commandment:'You shall not commit impure acts,' (cf. Ex 20:14) it justifies, exalts and propagates every form of impurity, even to the justification of acts against nature.

p   To the commandment:'You shall not steal,' (Ex 20:15) it works to the end that theft, violence, kidnapping and robbery spread more and more.

q   To the commandment: 'You shall not bear false witness,' (Ex 20:16) it acts in such a way that the law of deceit, lying and duplicity becomes more and more propagated.

r   To the commandment:'You shall not covet the goods and the wife of another,' (cf. Ex 20:17) it works to corrupt in the depths of the conscience, betraying the mind and the heart of man.

s   In this way souls become driven along the perverse and wicked road of disobedience to the laws of the Lord, become submerged in sin and are thus prevented from receiving the gift of grace and of the life of God.

t   *To the seven theological and cardinal virtues*, which are the fruit of living in the grace of God, Freemasonry counters with the diffusion of *the seven capital vices*, which are the fruit of living habitually in the state of sin. To faith it opposes pride; to hope, lust; to charity, avarice; to prudence, anger; to fortitude, sloth; to justice, envy; to temperance, gluttony.

u   Whoever becomes a victim of the seven capital vices is gradually led to take away the worship that is due to God alone, in order to give it to false divinities, who are the very personification of all these vices. And in this consists the greatest and most horrible blasphemy. This is why on every head of the Beast there is written a blasphemous name. Each masonic lodge has the task of making a different divinity adored.

v   The first head bears the blasphemous name of pride, which opposes itself to the virtue of faith and leads one to offer worship

603

to the god of human reason and haughtiness, of technology and progress.

w   The second head bears the blasphemous name of lust, which opposes itself to the virtue of hope and brings one to offer worship to the god of sexuality and of impurity.

x   The third head bears the blasphemous name of avarice, which opposes itself to the virtue of charity and spreads everywhere the worship of the god of money.

y   The fourth head bears the blasphemous name of anger, which opposes itself to the virtue of prudence and leads one to offer worship to the god of discord and division.

z   The fifth head bears the blasphemous name of sloth, which opposes itself to the virtue of fortitude and disseminates the worship of the idol of fear, of public opinion and of exploitation.

A   The sixth head bears the blasphemous name of envy, which opposes itself to the virtue of justice and leads one to offer worship to the idol of violence and of war.

B   The seventh head bears the blasphemous name of gluttony, which opposes itself to the virtue of temperance and leads one to offer worship to the so highly extolled idol of hedonism, of materialism and of pleasure.

C   The task of the masonic lodges is that of working today, with great astuteness, to bring humanity everywhere to disdain the holy Law of God, to work in open opposition to the Ten Commandments, and to take away the worship due to God alone in order to offer it to certain false idols which become extolled and adored by an ever increasing number of people: reason, flesh, money, discord, domination, violence, pleasure. Thus souls are precipitated into the dark slavery of evil, of vice and of sin and, at the moment of death and of the judgment of God, into the pool of eternal fire which is hell.

D   Now you understand how, in these times, against the terrible and insidious attack of the Black Beast, namely of Masonry, my Immaculate Heart becomes your refuge and the sure road which brings you to God. In my Immaculate Heart there is delineated the tactic made use of by your heavenly Mother, to fight back against and to defeat the subtle plot made use of by the Black Beast.

E   For this reason I am training all my children to observe the

Ten Commandments of God; to live the Gospel to the letter; to make frequent use of the sacraments, especially those of Penance and Eucharistic Communion, as necessary helps in order to remain in the grace of God; to practice the virtues vigorously; to walk always along the path of goodness, of love, of purity and of holiness.

F   Thus I am making use of you, my little children who have consecrated yourselves to me, to unmask all these subtle snares which the Black Beast sets for you and to make futile in the end the great attack which Masonry has launched today against Christ and his Church. And in the end, especially in his greatest defeat, there will appear in all its splendor, the triumph of my Immaculate Heart in the world."

406

The Beast Like a Lamb

a   "Beloved sons, today you are calling to mind my second apparition, which took place in the humble Cova da Iria in Fatima, on June 13, 1917. Even as of then I foretold to you that which you are living through in these times. I announced to you the great struggle between me, the Woman Clothed with the Sun, and the huge Red Dragon, which has brought humanity to live without God.

b   I also foretold to you the subtle and dark work, carried out by Freemasonry with the purpose of separating you from the observance of the Law of God and thus making you victims of sins and of vices.

c   Above all, as Mother, I have wanted to warn you of the grave dangers which threaten the Church today, because of the many and diabolical attacks which are being carried out against it to destroy it.

d   To attain this end, there comes out of the earth, by way of aid to the Black Beast which arises out of the sea, *a beast which has two horns like those of a lamb.*

e   The lamb, in Holy Scripture, has always been a symbol of

605

sacrifice. On the night of the exodus, the lamb is sacrificed, and, with its blood, the doorposts of the houses of the Hebrews are sprinkled, in order to remove them from the punishment which on the contrary strikes all the Egyptians. The Hebrew Pasch recalls this fact each year, through the immolation of a lamb, which is sacrificed and consumed. On Calvary, Jesus Christ sacrifices Himself for the redemption of humanity; He Himself becomes our Pasch and becomes the true Lamb of God who takes away all the sins of the world.

f   *The beast has on its head two horns like those of a lamb.* To the symbol of the sacrifice, there is intimately connected that of the priesthood: the two horns. The high priest of the Old Testament wore a headpiece with two horns. The bishops of the Church wear the mitre with two horns to indicate the fullness of their priesthood.

g   The black beast like a leopard indicates Freemasonry; the beast with the two horns like a lamb indicates Freemasonry infiltrated into the interior of the Church, that is to say, *ecclesiastical Masonry*, which has spread especially among the members of the hierarchy. This masonic infiltration, in the interior of the Church, was already foretold to you by me at Fatima, when I announced to you that Satan would enter in even to the summit of the Church. If the task of Masonry is to lead souls to perdition, bringing them to the worship of false divinities, the task of ecclesiastical Masonry on the other hand is that of *destroying Christ and his Church*, building a new idol, namely a false christ and a false church.

h   Jesus Christ is the Son of the living God; He is the Word incarnate; He is true God and true Man because He unites in his divine Person human nature and divine nature. Jesus, in the Gospel, has given his most complete definition of Himself, saying that He is the Truth, the Way and the Life.

i   *Jesus is the Truth*, because He reveals the Father to us, speaks his definitive word to us, and brings all divine revelation to its perfect fulfillment.

j   *Jesus is the Life*, because He gives us divine life itself, with the grace merited by Him through redemption, and He institutes the sacraments as efficacious means which communicate grace.

k   *Jesus is the Way* which leads to the Father, by means of the

606

Gospel which He has given us, as the way to follow to attain salvation.

l   Jesus is the Truth because it is He — the living Word — who is the font and seal of all divine revelation. And so ecclesiastical Masonry works to obscure his divine word, by means of natural and rational interpretations and, in the attempt to make it more understandable and acceptable, empties it of all its supernatural content. Thus errors are spread in every part of the Catholic Church itself. Because of the spread of these errors, many are moving away today from the true faith, bringing to fulfillment the prophecy which was given to you by me at Fatima: 'The times will come when many will lose the true faith.' The loss of the faith is apostasy. Ecclesiastical Masonry works, in a subtle and diabolical way, to lead all into apostasy.

m   Jesus is the Life because He gives grace. The aim of ecclesiastical Masonry is that of justifying sin, of presenting it no longer as an evil but as something good and of value. Thus one is advised to do this as a way of satisfying the exigencies of one's own nature, destroying the root from which repentance could be born, and is told that it is no longer necessary to confess it. The pernicious fruit of this accursed cancer, which has spread throughout the whole Church, is the disappearance everywhere of individual confession. Souls are led to live in sin, rejecting the gift of life which Jesus has offered us.

n   Jesus is the Way which leads to the Father, by means of the Gospel. Ecclesiastical Masonry favors those forms of exegesis which give it a rationalistic and natural interpretation, by means of the application of the various literary genres, in such a way that it becomes torn to pieces in all its parts. In the end, one arrives at denying the historical reality of miracles and of the resurrection and places in doubt the very divinity of Jesus and his salvific mission.

o   After having destroyed the historical Christ, *the beast with the two horns like a lamb* seeks to destroy the mystical Christ which is the Church. The Church instituted by Christ is one, and one alone: it is *the* one, holy, catholic and apostolic Church, founded on Peter. As is Jesus, so too is the Church founded by Him which forms his Mystical Body, truth, life and way.

p   *The Church is truth*, because Jesus has entrusted to it alone the

607

task of guarding, in its integrity, all the deposit of faith. He has entrusted it to the hierarchical Church, that is to say, to the Pope and to the bishops united with him. Ecclesiastical Masonry seeks to destroy this reality through *false ecumenism*, which leads to the acceptance of all Christian Churches, asserting that each one of them has some part of the truth. It develops the plan of founding a universal ecumenical Church, formed by the fusion of all the Christian confessions, among which, the Catholic Church.

q   *The Church is life* because it gives grace, and it alone possesses the efficacious means of grace, which are the seven sacraments. Especially it is life because to it alone is given the power to beget the Eucharist, by means of the hierarchical and ministerial priesthood. In the Eucharist, Jesus Christ is truly present with his glorified Body and his Divinity. And so ecclesiastical Masonry, in many and subtle ways, seeks to attack the ecclesial devotion towards the sacrament of the Eucharist. It gives value only to the meal aspect, tends to minimize its sacrificial value, seeks to deny the real and personal presence of Jesus in the consecrated Host. In this way there are gradually suppressed all the external signs which are indicative of faith in the real presence of Jesus in the Eucharist, such as genuflections, hours of public adoration and the holy custom of surrounding the tabernacle with lights and flowers.

r   *The Church is way* because it leads to the Father, through the Son, in the Holy Spirit, along the way of perfect unity. As the Father and the Son are one, so too must you be one among yourselves. Jesus has willed that his Church be a sign and an instrument of the unity of the whole human race. The Church succeeds in being united because it has been founded on the cornerstone of its unity: Peter, and the Pope who succeeds to the charism of Peter. And so ecclesiastical Masonry seeks to destroy the foundation of the unity of the Church, through a subtle and insidious attack on the Pope. It weaves plots of dissension and of contestation against the Pope; it supports and rewards those who vilify and disobey him; it disseminates the criticisms and the contentions of bishops and theologians. In this way the very foundation of its unity is demolished, and thus the Church becomes more and more torn and divided.

s   Beloved children, I have urged you to consecrate yourselves to my Immaculate Heart and to enter into this, my motherly refuge, above all in order to be preserved and defended against this terrible snare. In this way, through the act of consecration of my Movement, I have urged you to renounce every aspiration of building up a career. Thus you will be able to remove yourselves from the strongest and most dangerous snare, made use of by Masonry in order to associate in its secret sects so many of my beloved children. I bring you to a great love for Jesus–Truth, making you courageous witnesses of the faith; to Jesus–Life, leading you to great holiness; to Jesus–Way, asking you to be in life the Gospel alone, lived out and proclaimed to the letter.

t   Then I lead you to the greatest love for the Church.

u   *I bring you to love the Church–truth,* making of you strong proclaimers of all the truths of the Catholic faith, as you set yourself in opposition, with strength and courage, to all errors.

v   *I make of you ministers of the Church–life,* helping you to be faithful and holy priests. Be always available for the needs of souls, lend yourselves, with generous abnegation, to the ministry of Reconciliation, and be burning flames of love and of zeal for Jesus present in the Eucharist. In your churches may you once again hold frequent hours of public adoration and reparation to the Most Holy Sacrament of the altar.

w   *I transform you into witnesses of the Church–way,* and I make of you precious instruments of its unity. For this reason, I have given you, as a second pledge of my Movement, a special unity with the Pope. By means of your love and of your fidelity, the divine plan of perfect unity in the Church will once again shine forth in all its splendor.

x   Thus to the dark force which ecclesiastical Masonry is today exercising to destroy Christ and his Church, I am opposing the powerful splendor of my priestly and faithful army, so that Christ may be loved, listened to and followed by all, and that his Church may be more and more loved, defended and sanctified.

y   In this there shines forth above all the victory of the Woman Clothed with the Sun, and my Immaculate Heart attains its most luminous triumph."

The Number of the Beast: 666

a   "Beloved sons, you now understand the plan of your heavenly Mother, the Woman Clothed with the Sun, who, with her army, is engaged in the great struggle against all the forces of evil, in order to attain her great victory in the perfect glorification of the Most Holy Trinity.

b   Join me in battle, little children, against the Dragon, who seeks to lead all humanity against God.

c   Join me in battle, little children, against the Black Beast, Masonry, which seeks to lead souls to perdition.

d   Join me in battle, little children, against the beast like a lamb, Masonry, infiltrated into the interior of ecclesial life in order to destroy Christ and his Church. To attain this end, it seeks to build a new idol, namely a false christ and a false church.

e   — Ecclesiastical Masonry receives orders and power from the various masonic lodges and works to lead everyone secretly to become part of these secret sects. Thus it stimulates the ambitious with the prospect of easy careers; it heaps up with goods those who are starved for money; it assists its members to exceed others and to occupy the most important positions while it sets aside, in a subtle but decisive way, all those who refuse to take part in its designs. Indeed the beast like a lamb exercises all its power from the first beast, in its presence, and it forces the earth and all its inhabitants to adore the first beast.

f   Ecclesiastical Masonry goes as far as even building a statue in honor of the beast and forces all to adore this statue.

g   — But, according to the first commandment of the holy Law of the Lord, only God is to be adored and to Him alone must every form of worship be rendered. And so they substitute for God a strong, powerful and dominating idol. An idol so powerful that it puts to death all who do not adore the statue of the beast. An idol so strong and dominating as to cause all, small and great, rich and poor, freemen and slaves, to receive a mark on the right hand and on the forehead, and that no one can buy or sell without having this mark, that is to say, the name of the beast or the number of its name. This great idol, built to be served and adored by all, as I have already revealed to you in the preceding message, is a false christ and a false church.

h   But what is its name?

i   — In the thirteenth chapter of the Apocalypse, it is written, 'This calls for wisdom. Let him who has understanding reckon the number of the beast: it represents a human name. And the number in question is 666 (six hundred and sixty-six).' (cf. Rev 13:18) With intelligence, illumined by the light of divine wisdom, one can succeed in deciphering from the number, 666, the name of a man and this name, indicated by such a number, is that of the *Antichrist*.

j   Lucifer, the ancient serpent, the devil or Satan, the Red Dragon, becomes, in these last times, the *Antichrist*. The Apostle John already affirmed that whoever denies that Jesus Christ is God, that person is the Antichrist. The statue or idol, built in honor of the Beast to be adored by all men, is the Antichrist.

k   Calculate now its number, 666, to understand how it indicates the name of a man. The number, 333, indicates the divinity. Lucifer rebels against God through pride, because he wants to put himself above God. 333 is the number which indicates the mystery of God. He who wants to put himself above God bears the sign, 666, and consequently this number indicates the name of Lucifer, Satan, that is to say, of him who sets himself against Christ, of the Antichrist.

l   333 indicated once, that is to say, for the first time, expresses the mystery of the unity of God. 333 indicated twice, that is to say, for the second time, indicates the two natures, that of the divine and the human, united in the divine Person of Jesus Christ. 333 indicated thrice, that is to say, for the third time, indicates the mystery of the Three Divine Persons, that is to say, it expresses the mystery of the Most Holy Trinity. Thus the number, 333, expressed one, two and three times, expresses the principal mysteries of the Catholic faith, which are: (1) the Unity and the Trinity of God, (2) the incarnation, the passion and death, and the resurrection of our Lord Jesus Christ.

m   If 333 is the number which indicates the divinity, he who wants to put himself above God Himself is referred to by the number 666.

n   *666 indicated once,* that is to say, for the first time, *expresses the year 666, six hundred and sixty-six.* In this period of history, the Antichrist is manifested through the phenomenon of Islam, *which directly denies the mystery of the Divine Trinity and the divinity of our Lord Jesus Christ.* Islamism, with its military force, breaks loose everywhere, destroying all the ancient Christian communities, and invades Europe, and it is only through my extraordinary motherly intervention, begged for powerfully by the Holy Father, that it does not succeed in destroying Christianity completely.

o   *666 indicated twice,* that is to say, for the second time, *expresses the year 1332, thirteen hundred and thirty-two.* In this period of history, the Antichrist *is manifested through a radical attack on the faith in the word of God.* Through the philosophers who begin to give exclusive value to science and then to reason, there is a gradual tendency to constitute human intelligence alone as the sole criterion of truth. There come to birth the great philosophical errors which continue through the centuries down to your days. The exaggerated importance given to reason, as an exclusive criterion of truth, necessarily leads to the destruction of the faith in the word of God. Indeed, with the Protestant Reformation, Tradition is rejected as a source of divine revelation, and only Sacred Scripture is accepted. But even this must be interpreted by means of the reason, and the authentic Magisterium of the hierarchical Church, to which Christ has entrusted the guardianship of the deposit of the faith, is obstinately rejected. Each one is free to read and to understand Sacred Scripture according to one's personal interpretation. In this way, faith in the word of God is destroyed. The work of the Antichrist, in this period of history, is the division of the Church and the consequent formation of new and numerous Christian confessions which gradually become driven to a more and more extensive loss of the true faith in the word of God.

p   *666 indicated thrice,* that is to say, for the third time, *expresses the year 1998, nineteen hundred and ninety-eight.* In this period of history, Freemasonry, assisted by its ecclesiastical form, will succeed in its great design: that of setting up an idol to put in the place of Christ and of his Church. A false christ and a false church. Consequently, the statue built in honor of the first beast, to be adored by all the inhabitants of the earth and which will seal with its mark all those who want to buy or sell, is that of the

612

Antichrist. You have thus arrived at the peak of the purification, of the great tribulation and of the apostasy. The apostasy will be, as of then, generalized because almost all will follow the false christ and the false church. Then the door will be open for the appearance of the man or of the very person *of the Antichrist!*

q   This is why, beloved children, I have wanted to enlighten you concerning the pages of the Apocalypse which refer to the times you are living through. This is to prepare you with me, for the most painful and decisive part of the great struggle which is on the point of being fought out between your heavenly Mother and all the forces of evil which have been let loose.

r   Take courage! Be strong, my little children. To you befalls the duty, in these difficult years, of remaining faithful to Christ and to his Church, putting up with hostility, struggle and persecution. But you are a precious part of the little flock, which has the task of fighting against, and in the end of conquering, the powerful force of the Antichrist.

s   I am forming you all, defending you and blessing you."

408
Valdragone (San Marino); June 28, 1989
Spiritual Exercises in the Form of a Cenacle
with the Priests of the M.M.P. from America and Europe

Bear Within Yourselves the Witness of Jesus

a   "Beloved sons, with what love I look at you, and how my sorrowful Heart is consoled by this continuous cenacle of yours, which renews here the reality of that of Jerusalem! You are gathering together in prayer which is continuous, intense and made with me. How pleasing to me is the prayer of the Liturgy of the Hours, the entire rosary which you recite, the Eucharistic adoration and the solemn concelebration of Mass, which forms the heart of the entire cenacle!

b   You are united as brothers who love each other and who help each other to carry together the burden of the difficulties which you encounter. You renew each day your act of consecration to my Immaculate Heart in diverse languages, and thus you truly unite yourselves to all your brothers of my Movement who are spread throughout every part of the world. You are part of my army. You are a precious portion of my maternal heritage.

c   *You bear within yourselves the witness of Jesus,* and you observe the commandments of God.

d   Satan unleashes himself against you, because you form my heel, that is, the weakest and most fragile part of me, and because you are my offspring. Thus today he lies in ambush for you in a powerful manner, and he unleashes himself against you with every sort of temptation and persecution. Remain serene. Have confidence in me. These are the times of the battle, and you must fight for my victory. Because of this, I invite you all to bear within yourselves the witness of Jesus.

e   *Bear within yourselves the witness of Jesus* in these times of the purification in order to walk along the road of fidelity to Christ and to his Church, and of an ever greater holiness. Thus you will remain in security and peace, in trust and in filial abandonment to me.

f   *Bear within yourselves the witness of Jesus* in these times of the apostasy in order to be strong and courageous witnesses of faith. For this, I invite you to be ever more united to the Pope, to sustain him with your prayer and with your love, to accept and spread his teaching: in this way you will indicate to souls the secure way to follow in order to remain in the true faith.

g   *Maintain the witness of Jesus* in these times of the great tribulation. The days foretold by the Gospel and the Apocalypse have arrived. The forces of evil, united by the power of the one who opposes himself to Christ, will perform great prodigies in heaven and on the earth in order to thus seduce a great part of humanity. You must remain solid in your heroic witness to Jesus and fight with me against the powerful force of him who manifests himself as the enemy of Christ. In the end you will be able to contemplate with joy my great victory in the glorious triumph of Christ.

h   I bless you all with your dear ones, the souls confided to your care, your priestly ministry, and I gather in my hands all the good intentions you carry in your heart."

Rubbio (Vicenza, Italy); August 15, 1989
Solemnity of the Assumption
of the Blessed Virgin Mary into Heaven

Here Must Appear the Constancy of the Saints

a   "Today, look to me, your heavenly Mother, in the splendor of my glorified body assumed, with my soul, into the glory of paradise.

I am the Woman Clothed with the Sun.

I am your heavenly Leader.

I am the Queen of all the saints.

b   Look to me as a sign of sure hope and of consolation, in these times of the purification, of the apostasy and of the great tribulation. The times of the struggle and the greatest conquest on the part of the Dragon, of the beast which comes up from the earth and of the beast which comes up from the sea have come.

c   These are therefore the times when a civilization without God is being constructed and all humanity is being led to live without Him.

d   These are the times when Satan and the diabolic forces are making themselves adored by an ever increasing number of men, and thus the spread of the satanic cult, of the sects and of the black masses is becoming vaster.

e   These are the times when an idol is being built to be put in the place of the true God and of the true Church, and this idol is a false christ and a false church.

f   These are the times when all those who will follow this idol will be signed with its mark on the forehead and on the hand.

g   These are the times when the faithful followers of the Lamb will be subjected to marginalization, to persecutions, to prison and to death.

h   These are therefore the times of your constancy.

i   *Here must appear the constancy of the saints.*

j   *Here must appear the constancy* of those who belong to the Lord, who put into practice the commandments of God and who remain faithful to Jesus.

k   *Here must appear the constancy* of those who will be persecuted and led to martyrdom, because blessed are they who die in the Lord, who find rest from their labors, and the good that they have done accompanies them.

l   *Here must appear the constancy* of those who do not adore the beast and who will not allow themselves to be signed with his diabolical mark. Those, on the other hand who will adore the beast and its statue and will receive its mark on the forehead and on the hand, will drink the wine of the wrath of God, poured out from the chalice of his terrible chastisement and will be tortured, in the presence of the Lamb and of the holy angels, with fire and sulfur.

m   *Here must appear the constancy* of those who bear, written upon their foreheads, the name of the Lamb and the name of his Father, because they have not betrayed their God, there has never been a lie in their speech, and they follow the Lamb wherever He goes.

n   *Here must appear the constancy* of all my little children, whom I am calling to consecrate themselves to my Immaculate Heart, to live out with me the conclusive moments of the battle and of the fall of Babylon, when the vintage of the earth will be harvested, and the grapes will be cast into the wine press, which represents the *great chastisement of God*.

o   For this reason I invite you all today to look to me, your heavenly Mother, in the splendor of my glorified body, that my light may illumine you, my Immaculate Heart enfold you, and my motherly love support you to be, in these times, *courageous witnesses of constancy* before the Church and before all humanity."

410

Dongo (Como, Italy); September 8, 1989
Feast of the Nativity of the Blessed Virgin Mary

The Mark on the Forehead and on the Hand

a   "Today is the feast of the birth of your heavenly Mother, my dear beloved ones and children consecrated to my Immaculate Heart. Live it in joy and in peace, in silence and in prayer, in confidence and in filial abandonment.

b   You are the little infants of your infant Mother. You are part of my progeny and a strong point of my victorious plan. You form a precious crown of purity, of love and of humility about

616

the cradle in which I am placed.

c   Allow yourselves to be nourished and formed by me; allow yourselves to be led by me with docility; allow yourselves to be signed by me with my motherly seal.

d   These are the times when the followers of him who opposes himself to Christ are being signed with his mark on the forehead and on the hand.

e   *The mark on the forehead and on the hand* is an expression of a total dependency on the part of those who are designated by this sign. The sign indicates him who is an enemy of Christ, that is to say, the sign of the Antichrist. And his mark, which is stamped, signifies the complete belonging of the person thus marked to the army of him who is opposed to Christ and who fights against his divine and royal dominion.

f   *The mark is imprinted on the forehead and on the hand.*

g   *The forehead* indicates the intellect, because the mind is the seat of the human reason.

h   *The hand* expresses human activity, because it is with his hands that man acts and works.

i   Nevertheless it is the person who is marked with the mark of the Antichrist in his intellect and in his will.

j   He who allows himself to be signed *with the mark on his forehead* is led to accept the doctrine of the denial of God, of the rejection of his Law, and of atheism which, in these times, is more and more diffused and advertised. And thus he is driven to follow the ideologies in mode today and to make of himself a propagator of all the errors.

k   He who allows himself to be signed *with the mark on his hand* is obliged to act in an autonomous manner and independently of God, ordering his own activities to the quest of a purely material and terrestrial good. Thus he withdraws his action from the design of the Father, who wants to illumine it and sustain it by his divine providence, from the love of the Son who makes human toil a precious means for one's own redemption and sanctification, from the power of the Spirit who acts everywhere to renew interiorly every creature.

l   *He who is signed with the mark on his hand* works for himself alone, to accumulate material goods, to make money his god, and he becomes a victim *of materialism.*

m   *He who is signed with the mark on his hand* works solely for the gratification of his own senses, for the quest of well-being and pleasure, for the granting of full satisfaction to all his passions, especially that of impurity, and he becomes a victim *of hedonism.*

n   *He who is signed with the mark on his hand* makes of his own self the center of all his actions, looks upon others as objects to be used and to be exploited for his own advantage, and he becomes a victim *of unbridled egoism and of lovelessness.*

o   If my Adversary is signing, with his mark, all his followers, the time has come when I also, your heavenly Leader, am signing, with my motherly seal, all those who have consecrated themselves to my Immaculate Heart and have formed part of my army.

p   I am imprinting *my seal on your foreheads* with the most holy sign of the Cross of my Son Jesus. Thus I am opening the human intellect to receive his divine word, to love it, and to live it. I am leading you to entrust yourselves completely to Jesus who has revealed it to you. And I am making of you today courageous witnesses of faith. Against those signed on the forehead with the blasphemous mark, I am opposing my children signed with the Cross of Jesus Christ.

q   And then I am directing all your activity to the perfect glorification of the Most Holy Trinity. For this, I am imprinting *upon your hands* my seal which is the sign of the Father, of the Son and of the Holy Spirit. With the sign of the Father, your human activity becomes directed towards a perfect cooperation with the plans of his divine providence, which still today arranges all things for your good. With the sign of the Son, all your actions become profoundly inserted into the mystery of his divine redemption. With the sign of the Holy Spirit, everything you do becomes open to his powerful force for sanctification, which breathes everywhere like a powerful fire, to renew from its foundations the whole world.

r   My beloved children, allow yourselves all to be signed on the forehead and on the hand with my motherly seal, on this day when, gathered with love about my cradle, you celebrate the feast of the earthly birth of your heavenly Mother."

618

Great Is My Sorrow

a   "Share, beloved sons, in my sorrow. I am your sorrowful Mother. My Immaculate Heart is being pierced with numerous and painful thorns.

b   The dominion of my Adversary is becoming daily greater and greater, and his power is expanding in hearts and in souls.

A dense darkness has now descended upon the world.

It is the darkness of the obstinate rejection of God.

It is the darkness of sin, committed, justified and no longer confessed.

It is the darkness of lust and of impurity.

It is the darkness of unbridled egoism and of hatred, of division and of war.

It is the darkness of the loss of faith and of apostasy.

c   In the chalice of my Immaculate Heart, I am gathering, again today, all the pain of my Son Jesus, who is mystically again living through the bloody hours of his agony. A new Gethsemane for Jesus is to see today his Church so violated and deserted, where the greater part of its pastors are sleeping in indifference and in tepidity, while others repeat the act of Judas and betray it out of thirst for power and for money.

d   The Dragon is exulting at the vastness of his conquest, with the help of the Black Beast and the beast like a lamb, in these days of yours, when the devil has unleashed himself upon you, knowing that there is little time left him. For this reason, the days of my greatest sorrow have also arrived.

e   *Great is my sorrow* in seeing my Son Jesus again despised and scourged in his word, rejected because of pride and lacerated through human and rationalistic interpretations.

f   *Great is my sorrow* in contemplating Jesus, really present in the Eucharist, more and more forgotten, abandoned, offended and trampled upon.

g   *Great is my sorrow* in seeing my Church divided, betrayed, stripped and crucified.

h   *Great is my sorrow* in seeing my Pope who is succumbing under the weight of a most heavy cross, as he is being surrounded with complete indifference on the part of bishops, priests and faithful.

i   *Great is my sorrow* for an ever vaster number of my poor children, who are running along the road of evil and of sin, of vice and of impurity, of egoism and of hatred, with the great danger of being eternally lost in hell.

j   And so I am asking you today, children consecrated to my Immaculate Heart, that which, in this very place in May 1917, I asked of my three little children, Lucia, Jacinta and Francisco, to whom I appeared.

k   *Do you also want to offer yourselves as victims to the Lord*, on the altar of my Immaculate Heart, for the salvation of all my poor sinful children? If you accept this request of mine, you must do what I now ask of you:
— Pray ever more and more, especially with the holy rosary.
— Make frequent hours of adoration and of Eucharistic reparation.
— Accept with love all the sufferings which the Lord sends you.
— Spread without fear the message which I am giving you, as heavenly Prophetess of these last times of yours.

l   If you only knew the chastisement which awaits you if you again close the door of your hearts to the anguished voice of your heavenly Mother! Because the divine Heart of my Son Jesus has entrusted to my Immaculate Heart the last and extreme attempt to lead you all to salvation."

412
Dongo (Como, Italy); October 13, 1989
Anniversary of the Last Apparition at Fatima

The Angel of the First Plague

a   "You are recalling today my last apparition, which took place at Fatima on the 13th of October, 1917, confirmed by the miracle of the sun. Look more and more to the Woman Clothed with the Sun, who has the task of preparing the Church and humanity for the coming of the great Day of the Lord.

b   The times of the decisive battle have come. The hour of the great tribulation has now descended upon the world, because the angels of the Lord are being sent, with their plagues, to chastise the earth.

c   How many times have I urged you to walk along the road of mortification of the senses, of mastery over the passions, of modesty, of good example, of purity and of holiness! But humanity has not accepted my urging and has continued to disobey the sixth commandment of the Law of the Lord which prescribes that one shall not commit impure acts.

d   On the contrary, it has sought to exalt such a transgression and to put it forward as the acquisition of a human value and a new way of exercising one's own personal freedom. Thus today it has reached the point of legitimating as good all the sins of impurity. It has begun to corrupt the consciences of little children and of youth, bringing them to the conviction that impure acts committed by oneself are no longer sins; that relations before marriage between those engaged is licit and good; that families may behave as they please and may also make use of the various means of birth control. And they have come to the justification and the exaltation of impure acts against nature and even to the proposing of laws which put homosexual cohabitation on a par with marriage.

e   Never as today have immorality, impurity and obscenity been so continually propagandized, through the press and all the means of social communication. Above all, television has become the perverse instrument of a daily bombardment with obscene images, directed to corrupt the purity of the mind and the heart of all. The places of entertainment — in particular the cinema and the discotheques — have become places of public profanation of one's human and Christian dignity.

f   This is the time when the Lord our God is being continually and publicly offended by sins of the flesh. Holy Scripture has already warned you that those who sin by means of the flesh find their just punishment in that same flesh. And so the time has come when *the Angel of the first plague* is passing over the world, that it might be chastised according to the Will of God.

g   *The Angel of the first plague* cuts — into the flesh of those who have allowed themselves to be signed with the mark of the monster on the forehead and on the hand and have adored his image

621

— with a painful and malignant wound, which causes those who have been stricken by it to cry out in desperation. This wound represents the physical pain which strikes the body by means of grave and incurable maladies. The painful and malignant wound is a plague for all humanity, today so perverted, which has built up an atheistic and materialistic civilization and has made the quest for pleasure the supreme aim of human life. Some of my poor children have been stricken by it because of their sins of impurity and their disordered morals, and they carry within their own selves the weight of the evil they have done. Others, on the other hand, have been stricken, even though they are good and innocent; and so, their suffering serves for the salvation of many of the wicked, in virtue of the solidarity which unites you all.

h   *The first plague is that of malignant tumors* and every kind of cancer, against which science can do nothing notwithstanding its progress in every field, maladies which spread more and more and strike the human body, devastating it with most painful and malignant wounds. Beloved children, think of the spread of these incurable maladies, throughout every part of the world, and of the millions of deaths which they are bringing about.

i   *The first plague is the new malady of AIDS,* which strikes, above all, my poor children who are victims of drugs, of vices and of impure sins against nature.

j   Your heavenly Mother wants to be a help, a support, a comfort and a source of hope for all, in these times when humanity is being stricken by this first plague. For this, I urge you all to walk along the road of fasting, of mortification and of penance.

k   *Of little children* I ask that they grow in the virtue of purity and, in this difficult journey, let them be assisted by their parents and teachers.

l   *Of the youth* I ask that they form themselves in the control of the passions through prayer and a life of union with me, and that they renounce going to the cinema and the discotheques, where there exists the grave and continuous danger of offending this virtue which is so dear to my Immaculate Heart.

m   *Of engaged couples* I ask that they abstain from all relations before marriage.

n   *Of Christian husbands and wives* I ask that they form themselves in the exercise of conjugal chastity and never make use of artificial means of birth control, as they follow the teaching of Christ, which the Church still puts forth today with enlightened wisdom.

o   How very much I ask *of priests* the scrupulous observance of celibacy and, *of religious*, the faithful and austere practice of their vow of chastity!

p   To my poor children, stricken by the first plague of the painful and malignant wound, I present myself as a merciful mother, who assuages and comforts, who brings to hope and to peace. Of these I ask that they offer their sufferings in a spirit of reparation, of purification and of sanctification. Above all, for them my Immaculate Heart becomes the most welcome refuge and the sure road that leads them to the God of salvation and of joy.

q   In this, my heavenly garden, all will be consoled and encouraged, while I myself personally and lovingly take care to give consolation in suffering and, if it be in the Will of the Lord, to offer the gift of healing.

r   Consequently, in this time when humanity is being stricken by the first plague, I urge you all to look to me, your heavenly Mother, that you may be comforted and assisted."

413

The New Jerusalem

a   "Today is the feast of All Saints, and tomorrow you remember those who are saved, but who are still immersed in the purifying suffering of purgatory. In these times of the great tribulation, the communion of saints must be lived vigorously by you. I am the Queen of All Saints. I am the Leader of one single army.

b   To all the snares which the dragon, the black beast, the beast like a lamb and the evil spirits set for you every day, the angels of the Lord have from me the task of responding, with force and power.

c   How great today is their heavenly power, because they are being sent by me to fight back the tactic of my Adversary, which is that of leading many of my poor children away from the adoration that is due to our God, by the ever greater spread of the satanic cult and of the black masses! To this perverse and blasphemous action of the demons, the angels respond with their perennial, profound and incessant act of adoration and of glorification of the Lord.

d   To the dangers which, in these times, the wicked set for you, seeking to strew with obstacles, with difficulties, and with subtle opposition, the road along which you must walk, the saints in paradise respond with their powerful assistance and intercession. The hidden and obscure plots which Masonry sets against you, to make you fall into its net, are revealed and destroyed by the saints, who cause to come down from paradise a strong light which surrounds you to make your whole life fragrant with the perfume of faith, of hope, of love, of purity and of holiness.

e   The communion of life with the saints of paradise is the remedy which I am giving you against the subtle and very insidious dangers which today the black beast of Masonry is setting for you.

f   Against the difficulties, the acts of derision, and the marginalization which the beast like a lamb uses against you, my beloved children, have recourse to a perpetual communion of prayer with the holy souls in purgatory. This communion of prayer, with the souls who are being purified, gives *to them* the light and the comfort of shortening the time of their purification and grants *to you* the security and the courage to carry out my plan in your life, which is that of helping you to fulfill at each moment the divine Will of the Lord.

g   Today I am contemplating you with joy, gathered together in the heavenly garden of my Immaculate Heart, to live this stupendous reality of the communion of saints, which unites you, helps you and pledges you all to fight for the full triumph of Christ, in the coming upon the world of his glorious reign of love, of holiness, of justice and of peace.

h   Thus you are already contributing to the forming of *the new Jerusalem*, the holy city, which must come down from heaven, as a bride adorned for her husband. And you are forming the dwelling place of God among men, that all may become his people, where every tear will be wiped from their eyes, and there will no longer be any death, or strife, or mourning, or anguish, because the former things have passed away."

624

A Crown of Twelve Stars

a   "Beloved sons, today you are gazing upon the immaculate splendor of your heavenly Mother. I am the Immaculate Conception. I am the only creature free from every stain of sin, even the original one. I am 'all beautiful' — *tota pulchra.*

b   Let yourselves be enfolded by my mantle of beauty, that you too may be illumined by my heavenly splendor, by my immaculate light. I am all beautiful, because I am called to be the Mother of the Son of God and to form the virginal shoot, from which the divine Flower shall blossom. For this reason, my purpose is included in the very mystery of your salvation.

c   At the beginning, I am announced as the enemy of Satan; she who will obtain the complete victory over him. 'I will put enmity between you and the Woman, between your offspring and hers; she will crush your head, as you will attempt to bite her heel.' (Gen 3:15)

d   At the end, I am seen as the Woman Clothed with the Sun, who has the task of fighting against the Red Dragon and his powerful army, to conquer him, to bind him and to drive him away into his kingdom of death, that Christ alone may reign over the world.

e   Behold me, then, presented by Sacred Scripture in the splendor of my maternal royalty: 'And another sign appeared in the heavens: a Woman Clothed with the Sun, with the moon beneath her feet, and on her head a crown of twelve stars.' (Rev 12:1)

f   About my head there is therefore a *crown of twelve stars.* The crown is the sign of royalty. It is composed of twelve stars because it becomes the symbol of my maternal and royal presence in the very heart of the people of God.

g   *The twelve stars* represent the twelve tribes of Israel, which compose the Chosen People, selected and called by the Lord to prepare for the coming into the world of the Son of God, the Redeemer. Because I am called to become the Mother of the Messiah, my purpose is that of being the fulfillment of the promises, the virginal shoot, the honor and the glory of all the people of Israel. In fact, the Church exalts me with these words: 'You are the glory of Jerusalem; you are the joy of Israel; you are the honor of our people.' (cf. Jdt 15:9) For this, the tribes of Israel form twelve precious gems of the crown which surrounds my head, to indicate the function of my maternal royalty.

h   *The twelve stars* also signify the twelve Apostles, who are the foundation upon which Christ has founded his Church. I was often with them, to encourage them to follow and to believe in Jesus, during the three years of his public mission. In their place, together with John, I stood beneath the Cross at the moment of the crucifixion, of the agony and of the death of my Son Jesus. With them, I took part in the joy of his resurrection. At their side, recollected in prayer, I assisted at the glorious moment of Pentecost. During my earthly life, I remained at their side, with my prayer and my motherly presence, to help them, to form them, to encourage them and to urge them on to drink the chalice which had been prepared for them by the Heavenly Father. I am thus Mother and Queen of the Apostles who, about my head, form twelve luminous stars of my maternal royalty.

i   I am Mother and Queen of all the Church.

j   *The twelve stars* also signify a new reality. Indeed the Apocalypse sees me as a great sign in heaven: the Woman Clothed with the Sun who does battle with the Dragon and his powerful army of evil. And so the stars about my head indicate those who consecrate themselves to my Immaculate Heart, who form part of my victorious army, and who allow themselves to be guided by me in order to fight this battle and to attain in the end our greatest victory. Thus all my beloved ones and children consecrated to my Immaculate Heart, called to be today the apostles of the last times, are *the most luminous stars* of my royal crown.

k   *The twelve stars*, which form the luminous crown of my maternal royalty, are made up of the tribes of Israel, of the Apostles and of the apostles of these last times of yours.

l   And so, on the feast of my Immaculate Conception, I am calling you all to form a precious part of my crown and to become the brilliant stars which spread the light, the grace, the holiness, the beauty and the glory of your heavenly Mother throughout every part of the world."

The Time Has Reached Its Fullness

a   "Beloved sons, live these hours of the holy night with me in an act of unceasing prayer and of profound recollection.

b   *The time has reached its fullness.* For hundreds of years, this event had been awaited: the voices of prophets and of envoys from God had kept the torch of hope and of expectation burning. The course of time and of history all flowed toward this extraordinary moment.

c   On this holy night everything has its fulfillment. I, Virgin and Mother, bring forth my divine Son. My most chaste spouse, Joseph, is at my side and brings, in his person, the presence of all the poor of Israel. The barren cave becomes a royal palace for the Son of David, called to sit upon his royal throne. The shepherds hasten to offer the homage of the simple and of the poor in spirit. The choir of angels sings and brings the innocent light of infants, of little ones, of the pure of heart.

d   With how much ineffable love and delicate tenderness I place my divine Son in the poor manger, the First-born of the new people of Israel, the only-begotten Son of the Father, the Messiah, promised and expected for centuries!

e   On this holy night the prophecies are realized, and everything attains its perfect fulfillment.

f   *The time has reached its fullness.*

g   Live this Christmas with love, with confidence and with great hope. It is the Christmas of 1989. It is the Christmas of a year that has been very important.

h   Live it with me, the Mother who each day brings you forth to that life which my Child has given you, through his coming into your midst.

i   Live it with my spouse, Joseph, in an act of humble and docile collaboration with the plan of your Heavenly Father.

j   Live it with the shepherds who hasten jubilantly, in the joy that you too are witnesses to the announcement, which again today proclaims peace and salvation to all men.

k   Live it with the little, the simple, the poor, who form a royal throne for the reign of my Son Jesus.

l   Live it with the angels who chant divine harmonies and offer love to this poor earth, never before so threatened and stricken.

m   Live this Christmas of yours in a spirit of profound joy, *because the time has reached its fullness.*

n   Enter as of now into the events which are preparing you for his second Christmas. You are drawing close to the moment of the glorious return of Christ. And so, do not allow yourselves to be seized with fear, or with sadness, or with vain curiosity, or with useless anxiety.

o   Live, in my Immaculate Heart, with the simplicity of little ones, each moment of this new advent, and make yourselves eagerly ready to throw open the doors of men and of nations to Christ who is coming. And open your heart to hopefulness, to welcome with joy the announcement which I am making to you today: the time of his glorious return is in the very act of reaching its fullness."

416

Rubbio (Vicenza, Italy); December 31, 1989
Last Night of the Year

Open Your Hearts

a   "From every part of the world, gather together in the cenacle of my Immaculate Heart, in an act of intense and continual prayer, to live together with me the last hours of this year which is about to end. It has been a very important year.

b   I have held in my motherly hands the prayers and the sufferings of all my children, and I have deposited them in the open chalice of the divine and merciful Heart of my Son Jesus. Thus I have been able to carry out, in a powerful way, my work of mediation between you and my Son, and, as your sorrowful and merciful Mother, I have interceded before Him for all.

c   — I have obtained many graces for my priest-sons, to help them to walk along the road of an ever more perfect witness of life, which would be in conformity with the plan of Jesus and with the great needs of the Church of today.

d   — I have placed myself at the side of my children, consecrated, by virtue of their religious profession, to give them the courage and the enthusiasm to follow Jesus, chaste, poor and

628

obedient even to Calvary.

e   — I have prayed for all my poor sinful children, victims of passions, of vices, of sins, of impurity, of egoism, of hatred and of rejection of God. In my Immaculate Heart, I have prepared for them the help of which they have need, that they may be able to return into the arms of their Heavenly Father, who is awaiting them all that He may bind them to Himself with the chain of his divine and merciful love.

f   — I have prayed for the sick that they may obtain the gift to accept with docility and meekness the cross of their illness. I have prayed for divided families, for the scattered youth, for the nations oppressed under the yoke of slavery, for all the peoples of the earth. I have prayed to obtain for all humanity the great gift of peace.

g   In this, my work of intercession before my Son Jesus, you, my little children, through your prayer, have given a great power to your heavenly Mother.

h   I thank you for your generous response to my wishes and my repeated requests. By means of my Marian Movement of Priests, from every part of the world, I have been able to obtain, on the part of priests and of faithful, a great response to my request for consecration and for prayer. The cenacles, which I had asked of you in my message of January 17, 1974, have spread everywhere.

i   Now your heavenly Mother can exercise her great power. As of now, I have in my hands the precious key, with which to open the golden door of the divine Heart of Jesus, so that He can pour out upon the world the ocean of his mercy. The water, which flows from the Most Sacred Heart of Jesus, will wash and purify the entire world and will prepare it to live the new era of grace and of holiness which all are awaiting.

j   In these years you will see come to fulfillment the great miracle of divine mercy.

k   *Open your hearts.* Open the hearts of all men, so that they can welcome Christ who is coming in the splendor of his light, to make all things new."

1990
MOTHER OF THE SECOND ADVENT

Mother of the Second Advent

a   "Beloved children, begin this new year in the immaculate light of my divine maternity. I am your Mother as well, by the Will of my Son Jesus.

b   And, as Mother, I want to take you by the hand and accompany you on the threshold of this decade, which you are beginning precisely on this day. It is a very important decade. It is a period of time particularly marked by a strong presence of the Lord among you. During the last decade of your century, the events which I have foretold to you will have reached their completion. Therefore, it is necessary that you allow yourselves to be formed, one and all, by my motherly action.

c   — I am forming you in your hearts, in order to bring you to conversion and to open you to a new capacity for love. In this way, I heal you of the malady of egoism and of aridity.

d   — I am forming you in your souls, helping you to cultivate in them the great gift of divine grace, of purity and of charity. And, as in a heavenly garden, I am bringing to blossom the flowers of all the virtues which cause you to grow in holiness. Thus I remove from you the shadow of evil, the coldness of sin, the wilderness of impurity.

e   — I am forming you in your bodies, causing to shine forth in them the light of the Spirit who is dwelling there as in a living temple of his. Thus I lead you along the way of purity, of beauty, of harmony, of joy, of peace, of communion with all Paradise.

f   During these years I am preparing you, by my motherly action, to receive the Lord who is coming. This is why I have asked you for the consecration to my Immaculate Heart: to form all of you in that interior docility which is necessary for me in order that I may be able to work in each one of you, bringing you to a profound transformation which should prepare you to receive the Lord worthily.

g   *I am the Mother of the Second Advent.*

h   I am preparing you for his new coming. I am opening the way to Jesus who is returning to you in glory. Make level the high hills of pride, of hatred, of violence. Fill in the valleys dug by vices, by passions, by impurity. Clear away the barren soil of sin and of the rejection of God.

i   As a sweet and merciful Mother, today I urge my children; I urge all humanity to prepare the way for the Lord who is coming. At the beginning of this last decade of your century, the task which the Lord has entrusted to me is that of preparing his coming among you. For this reason, I ask all to return to the Lord along the road of conversion of heart and of life, because this is still the favorable time which the Lord has granted you.

j   I urge you all to consecrate yourselves to my Immaculate Heart, entrusting yourselves to me as little children, so that I may be able to lead you along the road of holiness, in the joyous practice of all the virtues: of faith, of hope, of charity, of prudence, of fortitude, of justice, of temperance, of silence, of humility, of purity, of mercy.

k   I am forming you to prayer, which must always be carried out by you in union with me. Multiply, in every part of the world, the cenacles of prayer which I have asked of you, like torches lit in the night, like sure points of reference, like shelters needed and sought for. Above all, I ask that family cenacles be multiplied more and more, in order to provide you with a safe dwelling place in the great trial which is now awaiting you.

l   *I am the Mother of the Second Advent.* Allow yourselves therefore to be formed and prepared by me, during these years, so that you can be ready to receive Jesus, who will come in glory to restore among you his reign of love, of holiness, of justice and of peace."

418
Jauru (Mato Grosso, Brazil); February 2, 1990
Feast of the Presentation of the Child Jesus

Only in the Hearts of Little Ones

a   "Look at all these children of mine: they are simple; they are little; they are so tried by suffering and by poverty. And yet, see how they have responded with generosity to my request for consecration and for prayer.

b   — *This response has been made to me by little children,* who love me and who surround me with filial tenderness, who gather together in cenacles of prayer, made with me, and who renew together their act of consecration to my Immaculate Heart. The generous response on the part of little children gives such joy to my Immaculate Heart and forms a great force of intercession and of reparation before the Eucharistic Heart of Jesus. I ask that children's cenacles be multiplied, in every part of the world, because I am calling them to a crusade of prayer and of consecration for the salvation of the world.

c   — *This response has been made to me by the youth*, who in great numbers have accepted in their life the commitment deriving from their consecration to my Immaculate Heart and who are seeking to live it in the effort to flee sin, to keep in the state of sanctifying grace, and to exercise the Christian virtues, especially that of purity. They come together in cenacles to pray with me and to meditate on my word, which gently leads them to live the Gospel of Jesus. The number of young people who are following the way traced out by your heavenly Mother will become greater and greater.

d   — *This response has been made to me by the families* who consecrate themselves to my Heart and who gather together in family cenacles, desired by me and which I have asked of you several times. Thus families consecrated to me resist the grave malady of division and of divorce and are preserved from the contagion of the terrible cancer of abortion and of recourse to all the means of impeding life. For this reason, nowhere else as here do you see so many children who are welcomed as the most beautiful and precious gift, granted by the Lord to the families who are still faithful.

e   — *This response has been made to me by the parish*, in all its components: the pastor and the flock entrusted to him. The parish community has consecrated itself to my Immaculate Heart and, each day, gathers together in a cenacle of prayer with me, with the recitation of the holy rosary and prostrating itself in adoration before the Eucharistic Jesus, solemnly exposed on the altar. Thus Jesus is able to release within souls his great power of love and, in this poor and out-of-the-way place, is already bringing about the triumph of his merciful love in the coming of his Eucharistic reign in your midst.

f   Today, as you are venerating me at the moment when I am carrying in my arms the Child Jesus to the temple of Jerusalem, I announce to you that here my triumph has already begun. Each day, *only in the hearts of little ones*, am I forging the greatest triumph of my Immaculate Heart."

419

Brasilia (Brazil); February 8, 1990
Spiritual Exercises in the Form of a Cenacle
with the Priests Responsible for the M.M.P. in Brazil

Mother and Queen of Brazil

a   "How happy I am, beloved sons, with this cenacle of prayer and brotherly sharing of yours, which you are holding, together with your heavenly Mother.

b   — *You are gathering together in prayer:* you pray thus as one, with the Liturgy of the Hours and with the recitation of the holy rosary. In the evening, you all gather together about the Eucharistic Jesus, solemnly exposed on the altar, for an hour of adoration and reparation. During the concelebration of Holy Mass, you always renew your act of consecration to my Immaculate Heart.

c   — *You are gathering together in brotherly sharing*: as it was in the Cenacle of Jerusalem, so also in this cenacle of yours, I am helping you to grow in mutual love. You get to know each other, to understand each other, to share difficulties and problems, and as so many brothers, you help each other to grow in the exercise of an ever more perfect charity. Thus you live the new commandment which Jesus has given you, that of loving each other as He has loved you. And by means of you who have responded to me, the plan of my Immaculate Heart is now being accomplished for your country too and for the Church which lives here in Brazil.

d   *I am the Mother and Queen of Brazil.* As I have told you in my preceding message, I confirm to you that the Church here is running into a grave danger, that of becoming a victim of apostasy and loss of the true faith. The dangers which are threatening her are those of contestation, division, and numerous and public criticisms which are directed at the Pope and his Magisterium on the part of some bishops, priests, religious and faithful. Return, all of you, along the road of a full, docile and obedient unity with the Pope if you want to remain in the true faith and in fidelity to Christ and to his Gospel.

e   Your country, too, is more and more threatened with materialism and hedonism, while the gap between those who enjoy many material goods and those who are deprived of even the necessities of life grows wider. It is menaced with the wounds of divorce, of abortion, of recourse to all the means of impeding life, of immorality, of impurity, spread through the means of social communication, particularly that of television. But, as I have promised you, I have intervened and am intervening every day to lead your country and your Church along the road of unity, of salvation and of peace.

f   *I am the Mother and Queen of Brazil.* Today I declare to you my motherly satisfaction for your having accepted the request, which I have made to you, that family cenacles be spread everywhere, as a great network of salvation. You have responded to my request, and I have kept my promise.

g   Now that you are entering into the last decade of this century, during which the decisive events that will bring you to the triumph of my Immaculate Heart will be completed, I am asking you that cenacles among priests, cenacles among the faithful and especially family cenacles be multiplied even more. I am asking in particular that there be formed everywhere children's cenacles, as a crusade of innocent prayer, in order to form a great barrier against the spread of evil and sin, and allow God and your heavenly Mother to bring about the victory of goodness and of love. Go back to your homes in peace, and become the apostles of this Movement of mine throughout all Brazil.

h   I am accompanying you with my motherly love, assuring you that I am always at the side of each one of you, and I bless you."

420

São Paulo (Brazil); March 13, 1990

When the Son of Man Returns

a   "You read in the Gospel: 'When the Son of Man returns, will He still find faith on earth?' (cf. Lk 18:8)

b   Today I want to invite you to meditate on these words, uttered by my Son Jesus. They are grave words, which cause one to reflect and which succeed in making you understand the times through which you are living. First of all, you can ask why Jesus has uttered them: to prepare you for his second coming and to describe for you a circumstance which will be indicative of the proximity of his glorious return.

c   This circumstance is the loss of faith.

d   Also, in another part of Holy Scripture, in the letter of Saint Paul to the Thessalonians, it is clearly announced that, before the glorious return of Christ, a great apostasy must take place. The loss of the faith is a true apostasy. The spread of the apostasy is therefore the sign which indicates that the second coming of Christ is, as of now, close at hand.

e   At Fatima, I have foretold to you that a time would come when the true faith would be lost. These are the times. Your days are marked by this painful and significant situation, which was foretold to you in Holy Scripture: the true faith is in the process of disappearing in an ever increasingly greater number of my children.

f   The causes of the loss of faith are: (1) the spread of errors which are being propagated and are often taught by professors of theology in seminaries and in Catholic schools and which thus acquire a certain character of credibility and legitimacy; (2) the open and public rebellion against the authentic Magisterium of the Church, especially against that of the Pope, who has from Christ the duty of preserving the whole Church in the truth of the Catholic faith; (3) the bad example given by those pastors, who have allowed themselves to be completely possessed by the spirit of the world and who become propagators of political and sociological ideologies, rather than messengers of Christ and of his Gospel, thus forgetting the mandate received from Him: 'Go into the whole world and preach the Gospel to every creature.' (Mk 16:15)

g   Thus, in these days of yours, apostasy on the part of many of my poor children is inundating you more and more.

h   *'When the Son of Man returns...'*

i   If indeed his return is close at hand, then my motherly action becomes more concerned and vigorous, in order to assist all my children to remain ever in the truth of the faith. This is why I have asked you to consecrate yourselves to my Immaculate Heart. This is why, in these times of yours, I have spread everywhere my Marian Movement of Priests: to form the little flock, reunited in the prayer of the cenacles and watchful in expectation — the flock gathered together and formed by me to ever preserve the true faith.

j   Thus, *when the Son of Man returns,* He will still find the faith on earth in all those who will have consecrated themselves to me, allowing themselves to be gathered together in the heavenly garden of my Immaculate Heart."

421

Rubbio (Vicenza, Italy); April 12, 1990
Holy Thursday

He Loved Them to the End

a   "Beloved sons, live with me this day of Holy Thursday, gathered together in the cenacle of my Immaculate Heart. This is the day of your pasch. This is the day of your priesthood.

b   You are recalling it today, gathered about your bishops, in the concelebration of the Eucharist, during which you renew the promises which you made on the day of your priestly ordination. They are the promises of your fidelity to Christ and to his Church. They are the promises of your availability and of your obedience. They are the promises of your total and exclusive love which pledges you to love Jesus and the souls which are entrusted to you by Him. These are all promises for life; they are all pledges of love.

c   'Jesus, having loved his own who were in the world, loved them to the end.' (cf. Jn 13:1) — Thus John, the beloved Apostle, introduces in his Gospel the account of the institution of the Eucharist, of the new Sacrifice and of the new Priesthood.

d   *Jesus loved them to the end.*

e   *He loved them to the end,* that is to say, to the end of his life, because the Last Supper corresponds also with the last night of his human life lived among you: 'I have eagerly desired to eat this, my Pasch, with you before I suffer.' (Lk 22:15)

f   *He loved them to the end*, that is to say, to the summit of every possibility of love, because Jesus renders perpetual, today, the Sacrifice accomplished one single time on Calvary for the salvation of all: 'No one has greater love than He who lays down his life for those whom He loves.' (cf. Jn 15:13)

g   *He loved them to the end*, that is to say, to the ultimate demand imposed by love, which desires the presence of the person who is loved, because in the Eucharist Jesus remains always with you, truly present with his glorified body and his divinity, as He is in paradise, even though He is hidden under the veil of the Eucharistic species: 'I am with you always, to the end of the ages.' (Mt 28:20)

h   *He loved them to the end*, that is to say, to the limit of your misery and your poverty, because in the sacrament of the Eucharist Jesus makes Himself one with you and becomes flesh of your very own flesh, blood of your very own blood, to communicate to you, earthly creature that you are, the precious gift of his divine life: 'I am the living bread come down from heaven. Whoever eats of this bread will have life, and I will raise him up on the last day.' (cf. Jn 6:40, 51)

i   *He loved them to the end*, that is to say, until the end of time, because the presence among you of Christ in the state of a victim, in every tabernacle of the earth, gives you security and confidence, joy and hope in his glorious return: 'We declare your death, O Lord, we proclaim your resurrection, in the expectation of your coming.' [1]

j   Today is the day of the new Sacrifice and of the new Priesthood. Today is the great day of love. His divine Heart opens itself to give you his new commandment: 'I give you a new commandment: love one another as I have loved you.' (cf. Jn 15:12)

k   On this day, beloved sons, I am asking you to renew your pledge of love for Jesus present in the Eucharist. Make Holy Mass the center of all your piety, the summit of your priestly day, the heart of your apostolic action. Celebrate it with love, with the scrupulous observance of the liturgical laws; live it, participating personally in the Sacrifice which Jesus renews by means of you.

l   Surround with lights and flowers the tabernacle where the Eucharistic Jesus is kept. Go often before the tabernacle for

---

[1] (i) cf. *Dominicae Cenae* by Pope John Paul II, Chapter 1, #3.

your personal encounter of love with Jesus who is awaiting you; let Him become for you the one and only treasure, the precious treasure which, like a magnet, draws your priestly heart. Expose once again the Eucharistic Jesus on the altar for hours of solemn and public adoration and reparation, because the rise of the new era will lead to a general reflowering of the Eucharistic cult in all the Church.

m   In fact, the coming of the glorious reign of Christ will coincide with the greatest splendor of his Eucharistic reign among you. The Eucharistic Jesus will release all his power of love, which will transform souls, the Church and all humanity.

n   Thus the Eucharist becomes a sign of Jesus who, *still today, loves you to the end*, because He is leading you to the end of these times of yours, to introduce you into the new era of holiness and of grace, toward which you are all journeying and which will begin at the moment when Jesus will have restored his glorious reign in your midst."

422

Rubbio (Vicenza, Italy); April 13, 1990
Good Friday

The Son and the Mother

a   "This day, close to me, your sorrowful Mother, live the painful hours of the passion and the death of my Son Jesus.

b   Enter into the depths of his divine Heart, to share in the intensity of all his suffering: during the trial of the religious tribunal, when Jesus is insulted, abused and in the end condemned for having borne witness to the truth and for having proclaimed Himself the Son of God; during the trial undergone before the civil tribunal where, after having been acknowledged as innocent of all the accusations that were brought against Him, He is made to undergo the terrible punishment of the scourging and the crowning with thorns; and in the end as He is condemned to the death of the Cross.

c   Like a gentle lamb who is led to the slaughter, without a word of bitterness, without any complaint, crushed under the weight of the Cross which the Heavenly Father gives Him, as He climbs Calvary, thus today I meet my Son. His face has no longer the semblance of a man, so disfigured is it by the blood and from the blows; because of the flagellation, his body is reduced to one entire living wound, from which flow rivulets of blood. His strength no longer sustains Him, and He totters; fever consumes Him; life slips from Him; He falls under the weight of his gibbet; and there He lies stretched out on the ground, crushed like a worm and no longer able to raise Himself.

d   It is at this moment that the Heavenly Father gives Him the comfort of his Mother. From this moment we live together the mystery of his redemptive passion.

e   *The Son and the Mother.* Together we make our way along the final distance of this terrible journey. He with the immeasurable weight of his suffering which crushes Him; I with the painful sword which penetrates into my Immaculate Heart and wounds it and makes it bleed.

f   *The Son and the Mother* together toward Calvary, carrying the Cross of one and the same affliction. The drops of blood which descend from his head are mingled with the copious tears which flow from my motherly eyes. The crown of thorns which surrounds his head forms a sharp sword which pierces my Heart. His wounded body is a mirror of my transfixed and lacerated soul.

g   *The Son and the Mother.* Together we arrive at the summit of Golgotha; together we are hung on the gibbet; together we are pierced with the nails; together we live out the painful hours of the agony; together we hear the wicked shrieks of those who insult and blaspheme; together we pardon the executioners; together we pray and love; together we feel the abandonment of the Father; together we trust and commit ourselves to Him; together, in the end, we die. Jesus dies in his body; I, his Mother, in my Heart. Miraculously I remain still alive because, as Mother, I must help my Son to die.

h   Now you understand the profound significance of his last gift: 'Behold your Mother.' (Jn 19:27) I am Mother for Him and for you.

i   *The Son and the Mother. The children and the Mother.*

j   Here beneath the Cross I am, miraculously, still alive because, as Mother, I must help you all to be born and to live in Him and for Him.

k   All persons redeemed by Jesus are, as of today, my children as well. I am the Mother of the people of all times, even to the end of times, when Jesus will return in glory, and then my spiritual motherhood will be finally completed."

423   Rubbio (Vicenza, Italy); April 14, 1990
                                              Holy Saturday

Keep Watch with Me in Expectation

a   "Beloved children, today *keep watch with me in expectation*. This is the Holy Saturday. This is the day of my firm hope. This is the day of my unshakeable faith and of my immaculate sorrow. Jesus now lies dead in his new sepulchre.

b   From the moment when, with John and the holy women, I withdrew after it had been closed, a large stone having been rolled before it, time as it were came to a halt for me, the sorrowful and crucified Mother. I recollected myself in an incessant prayer, while the tears fell from my eyes in a continuous lament, and my motherly Heart formed, as it were, a cradle of love and of expectation for the new and glorious birth of my Son Jesus.

c   Faith in his divine word, which had always sustained me during his human life and which, in the hours of his painful passion, had become the sole and steady support of my unspeakable pain, now changes to the absolute certitude of his imminent resurrection.

d   And I live, wounded and soothed, mourning and consoled, sorrowing and joyous, because I know that Jesus, torn and killed in such a cruel way, is now about to rise.

e   And at the dawn of the first day after the Sabbath, Jesus Christ, in the splendor of his glorified body, with such great love and filial tenderness, draws close to me, enfolds me in his arms, enwraps me in his most powerful light and speaks to me divine words of comfort.

f   Beloved children, *keep watch with me in expectation*, in the long and painful Holy Saturday which leads to his resurrection and his glorious return.

642

g   *Keep watch with me in expectation,* and be strong in your faith in Him, during these times when acts of betrayal and abandonment on the part of his own are being renewed, when the faith of true disciples is being put to severe test by the spread of the most subtle and insidious errors.

h   *Keep watch with me in expectation,* and be firm in the hope that Jesus will return on the clouds of heaven, in the splendor of his glorified body, as He predicted before the tribunal of Caiaphas, wanting to give a sure sign of his divinity, for these times when doubts are being spread about, concerning his divine nature and the fulfillment of his promises.

i   *Keep watch with me in expectation,* and be ardent in love, in these times when it has become cool in the hearts of men, and humanity has become a desert for want of life and of love and is more and more consumed and threatened with egoism, with violence, with hunger and with war.

j   *Keep watch with me in expectation* in these last times of your so lengthy Holy Saturday because the moment is close at hand when my Son Jesus will return on the clouds of heaven, in the splendor of his divine glory."

424   Rubbio (Vicenza, Italy); April 15, 1990
Easter Sunday

The Second Pasch in Glory

a   "May your hearts be filled with joy and with peace, beloved children, on this Easter Day.

b   My Son Jesus, despised, insulted, scourged, condemned and put to death on the Cross, today rises from the dead through the power of his divinity and in the splendor of his glorified body.

c   By the divine power of this, his new and glorious birth, the shadow of the sepulchre is changed into most powerful light; the heavy sealed stone is removed by a sudden earthquake; the guards who were sent to keep watch are struck down unconscious by a limitless power; the angels bow down in adoration at his luminous passage; surrounding nature sings for joy, quivering through and through with a renewed life. Christ Risen comes forth from the grave in the divine splendor of his glorified body.

d   This is his Pasch of resurrection.
This is the beginning of the new humanity, redeemed and taken in conquest by Him.
This is the dawn of his new reign.
This is the first day of his royal triumph.

e   Let your hearts be filled with joy, beloved children, because *the second Pasch in glory* is being prepared for you. A dark and cold sepulchre molds this poor humanity, which is walking in the darkness of the rejection of God, is worn out by the impetuous wind of the passions, and is slain by sin, by egoism, by hatred and by impurity. It appears that now death alone triumphs in the world. But have confidence and hope. Christ Risen is alive among you. The living Christ is your great victory.

f   *Close at hand is the second Pasch in glory.*

g   A little while yet and the door of this immense sepulchre, in which lies all humanity, will be opened. Jesus Christ — surrounded by the choir of angels on the clouds of heaven, prostrate at his feet to form a royal throne — in the splendor of his divinity, will return to bring humanity to a new life, souls to grace and love, the Church to its highest summit of sanctity; and He will thus restore in the world his reign of glory."

425

Fatima (Portugal); May 13, 1990
Anniversary of the First Apparition at Fatima

I Am Coming Down from Heaven

a   "I came down from heaven, seventy-three years ago, in this Cova da Iria, to point out for you the path you should tread in the course of this difficult century of yours. The very painful events which followed have, through their occurrence, given complete fulfillment to the words of my prophecy.

b   — Humanity has not accepted my motherly request to return to the Lord along the road of conversion of heart and of life, of prayer and of penance. Thus it has known the terrible years of the second world war, which brought about tens of millions of deaths and vast destruction of populaces and of nations.

c   — Russia has not been consecrated to me by the Pope together with all the bishops, and thus she has not received the grace of conversion and has spread her errors throughout all parts of the world, provoking wars, violence, bloody revolutions and persecutions of the Church and of the Holy Father.

d — Satan has been the uncontested dominator of the events of this century of yours, bringing all humanity to the rejection of God and of his Law of love, spreading far and wide division and hatred, immorality and wickedness and legitimating everywhere divorce, abortion, obscenity, homosexuality and recourse to any and all means of obstructing life.

e Now you are beginning the last decade of this century of yours.

f *I am coming down from heaven,* so that the final secrets may be revealed to you and that I may be able thus to prepare you for what, as of now, you must live through, for the purification of the earth.

g My third secret, which I revealed here to three little children to whom I appeared and which up to the present has not yet been revealed to you, will be made manifest to all by the very occurrence of the events.

h The Church will know the hour of its greatest apostasy. The man of iniquity will penetrate into its interior and will sit in the very temple of God, while the little remnant which will remain faithful will be subjected to the greatest trials and persecutions.

i Humanity will live through the moment of its great chastisement and thus will be made ready to receive the Lord Jesus who will return to you in glory.

j For this reason, *especially today, I am coming down again from heaven*: through my numerous apparitions; through the messages which I give; and through this extraordinary work of my Marian Movement of Priests, to prepare you to live through the events which are even now in the process of being fulfilled, in order to lead you by the hand to walk along the most difficult and painful segment of this, your second Advent, and to prepare the minds and the hearts of all to receive Jesus at the closely approaching moment of his glorious return."

The Time of the Holy Spirit

_a   "In the cenacle of my Immaculate Heart, beloved children, invoke today, together with your heavenly Mother, the gift of the Holy Spirit. — 'Come, Holy Spirit, come by means of the powerful intercession of the Immaculate Heart of Mary, your well-beloved Spouse.' — Repeat this invocation frequently. Let it become your habitual prayer during these years which still separate you from the great jubilee of the year two thousand, as you live through the concluding times of this second Advent.

_b   You are drawing close to the moment when the great prodigy of the second Pentecost will come to pass.

_c   Only the Spirit of Love can renew the whole world. Only the Spirit of Love can form the new heavens and the new earth. Only the Spirit of Love can prepare hearts, souls, the Church and all humanity to receive Jesus who will return to you in glory.

_d   For this, you are entering into times when the divine action of the Holy Spirit will become stronger and stronger.

_e   In these times, the Holy Spirit has the task of bringing you to the realization of the plan of the Heavenly Father, in the perfect and universal glorification of his Son, Jesus Christ. Thus the Holy Spirit is fulfilling his divine mission of giving full witness to the Son and will lead you to the understanding of the truth, whole and entire.

_f   *The Holy Spirit* has the task of making you today courageous witnesses of the truth and of bringing you to the heroic witness of faith in Jesus.

_g   *The Holy Spirit* has the task of enlightening your souls with the light of divine grace and of leading you along the way of holiness. For this, He is pouring out upon you his seven holy gifts, thus giving strength and an increase in the theological and moral virtues which transform your life into that blossoming garden where the Most Holy Trinity makes its dwelling place.

_h   *The Holy Spirit* has the task of forming your hearts to the perfection of love and thus burns away, within you, every form of egoism and purifies you in the crucible of innumerable sufferings.

_i   *The Holy Spirit* has the task of bringing the Church to its greatest

splendor, that it may thus become all beautiful, without stain or wrinkle, in imitation of your heavenly Mother, and be able to spread the light of Christ to all the nations of the earth.

j   *The Holy Spirit* has the task of transforming all humanity and of renewing the face of the earth, that it may become a new terrestrial paradise in which God may be possessed, loved and glorified by all.

k   *The Holy Spirit* opens and closes the doors of the second Advent. This is why the entire period of the second Advent, in which you are living, *is the time of the Holy Spirit.* You are living in his time.

l   I urge you to multiply everywhere cenacles of prayer with me. The whole Church must enter into the spiritual cenacle of my Immaculate Heart and recollect itself in incessant prayer with your heavenly Mother, because my Immaculate Heart is the golden door through which the Holy Spirit passes to come to you and to bring you to the second Pentecost."

427

Rubbio (Vicenza, Italy); June 23, 1990
Feast of the Immaculate Heart of Mary

My Immaculate Heart Is Glorified

a   "Beloved children, today the Church is celebrating the liturgical memorial of my Immaculate Heart. This feast is being lived with particular solemnity by all who belong to my Marian Movement of Priests.

b   You are entering into my times. The mysterious and powerful events of which I have foretold you are in the process of unfolding. For this, the time has come when my Immaculate Heart must be glorified before the Church and all humanity.

c   You are being chosen to be the smallest of children consecrated to me and completely entrusted to me. You are being formed in order to prepare for, and to bring about, my motherly triumph in the glorious triumph of my Son Jesus. You are being called to be apostles of these last times.

d   To you therefore falls the duty of proclaiming, in every part of the earth, the love and the glory of your heavenly Mother.

e   *For this, my Immaculate Heart is being glorified in you.*

f   *My Immaculate Heart is glorified by you,* when you allow yourselves to be led with docility along the road of purity, of love and of holiness.

g   *My Immaculate Heart is glorified by you,* when you give to all a daily witness of heroic fidelity to Christ and to his Gospel, becoming today courageous witnesses of faith.

h   *My Immaculate Heart is glorified by you,* when you give an example of strong unity with the Pope and of perfect obedience to his Magisterium.

i   *My Immaculate Heart is glorified by you,* when you put yourselves at the total disposal of the spiritual needs of souls, especially by the assiduous exercise of your priestly ministry in the sacrament of Reconciliation.

j   *My Immaculate Heart is glorified by you,* when you become burning flames of love and of zeal for Jesus present in the Eucharist; when you bring to Him all the souls who are entrusted to you; when you multiply the hours of solemn adoration and reparation, exposing the Most Holy Sacrament on the altar, surrounded by lights and flowers, as signs indicative of your piety.

k   *My Immaculate Heart is glorified by you,* when you multiply everywhere cenacles of prayer made with me, which I have asked of you: among priests, faithful, youth, children and in families.

l   In this way you are preparing the time of the second Pentecost for the Church and for all the world. With the second Pentecost, the Holy Spirit will render his perfect witness to the Son and will bring upon the earth his glorious reign of love, that Jesus Christ may be loved, adored and glorified by a completely renewed humanity.

m   Only then will my Immaculate Heart have its triumph."

428   *Valdragone (San Marino); June 28, 1990*
Spiritual Exercises in the Form of a Cenacle
with the Directors of the M.M.P. from America and Europe

The Second Pentecost

a   "Beloved sons, again this year I have called you up here on this mountain, to live days of brotherly sharing and of prayer with me, in a continual cenacle as was that of Jerusalem.

b   You are entering into the last decade of this century of yours, when the events which I have foretold to you will come to completion and when my secrets will be revealed to you. You are entering into the time of the triumph of my Immaculate Heart. You are now close to the second Pentecost.

c   *The second Pentecost* will come because, even now, there are spread about in every part of the world the cenacles of prayer which I have asked of you many times and with greater and greater insistence. You are here so that you yourselves may undergo the sweet and powerful experience of the cenacle, where I make myself particularly present among you, in order that you can become apostles of cenacles in every part of the world. My Immaculate Heart is the new and spiritual cenacle, into which all the Church must enter in order to obtain the gift of the new Pentecost.

d   *The second Pentecost* will come like a river of grace and of mercy which will purify the Church and make her poor and chaste, humble and strong, without spot or wrinkle, all beautiful, in imitation of your heavenly Mother. You are here to be molded by me in order to become the new heart of this Church, completely renewed by the Spirit.

e   For this reason, you must allow yourselves to be formed by me in order to arrive at a complete change of heart. Let your heart become meek and humble, gentle and merciful, sensitive and pure. Let your heart be a chalice filled with smooth balm which runs over and flows down to close open and bleeding wounds; to comfort innumerable sufferings and sorrows; to give hope to the desperate, grace to sinners, comfort to the ailing, help to the needy, peace to the distressed, courage to the disheartened.

f   *The second Pentecost* will come like a dew upon the world and will transform the desert into a garden, in which all humanity will run, like a spouse, to meet her Lord, in a renewed covenant of love with Him. Thus the Most Holy Trinity will receive its great glory, and Jesus will restore his glorious reign of love among you.

g   For this reason, you must become the silent and courageous artisans of this general renewal. Take into your priestly arms this poor ailing humanity and bring it to the maternal clinic of my

Immaculate Heart, that it may be healed by your heavenly Mother. You do this when you bring everyone — priests, faithful, children, youth and families — to the consecration to my Immaculate Heart.

h   Take courage, my beloved ones. During these extraordinary days of cenacle, I have given you comfort and consolation, grace and love, purity and holiness. You are leaving this cenacle completely renewed, because the Holy Spirit, invoked by means of me, has communicated Himself to you with his seven holy gifts, which give vigor and strength to the development within you of all the virtues.

i   Leave now as courageous apostles of these last times, and go into every part of the world, to carry the light of Christ in these times of darkness and the dew of his divine love in these days of great aridity. In this way you are preparing hearts and souls to receive with joy the Christ who is coming.

j   Together with your dear ones and with the souls who are entrusted to you, I bless you with the joy of a Mother who has been so consoled by you."

429

Rubbio (Vicenza, Italy); August 15, 1990
Solemnity of the Assumption
of the Blessed Virgin Mary into Heaven

The Way of Light

a   "Look today at the splendor of your heavenly Mother, beloved children, to be consoled in the painful moments through which you are living and to walk along my way, in the final portion of your second Advent.

b   *It is the way of light.* It is the way which I have traced out for you during these years, to lead you all to the Church of light.

c   Jesus is now forming this Church of his, by means of the powerful action of the Holy Spirit and in the garden of the Immaculate Heart of your heavenly Mother. It is the new Church of light, which has a splendor greater than a thousand suns put together.

d   It is being formed in the hearts of the simple, of the little, of the pure, of the poor, of those who know how to receive and follow Jesus with perfect docility, without any compromise with the spirit of the world. Jesus is building this, his new Church, in a way which is invisible and utterly mysterious: in silence, in hiddenness, in prayer, in simplicity.

e   For this reason, today I urge all my beloved ones and children consecrated to my Immaculate Heart to journey along the way of light, in order to reach the goal of the second Advent which you are now living.

f   — *On this way of light,* you are being encircled by the powerful splendor of *your Heavenly Father,* who reflects his love in you, takes you into his arms and leads you, more and more, to understand the mystery of his divine paternity. Thus you yourselves become the reflection of the glory of the Father.

g   — *On this way of light,* you are becoming intimately penetrated by the very light of *Christ,* who leads you to set yourselves strongly against the darkness of sin, of error and of evil. Thus you walk in the splendor of his divine word, which causes to come down upon your life the radiant beams of joy, of purity, of love, of beauty and of holiness. Thus you yourselves become the reflection of the splendor of the Son.

h   — *On this way of light,* you are intimately transformed by the most powerful fire *of the Holy Spirit* who, as a cauterizing flame, consumes you and purifies you of everything which, within you, is of uncleanliness or imperfection. Thus He makes you fit to penetrate into the intimate relationship of love which exists between the Father and the Son, in such a way that in you the Father may be perfectly glorified and the Son may come to be more and more loved and imitated by you. Thus you yourselves become the reflection of the love of the Holy Spirit.

i   Today, as you gaze at the splendor of my glorified body assumed into heaven, I urge you to walk, each and all, along the way of light which I have traced out for you, to offer your life to the perfect glory of the Most Holy Trinity, to live well the last times of this second Advent, in such a way as to be ready and with lamps burning to receive the Lord who is coming."

Budapest (Hungary); August 22, 1990
Feast of the Queenship of Mary
Spiritual Exercises in the Form of a Cenacle
with the Priests of the M.M.P. from Hungary

Queen of Love

a   "I am your Mother and Queen. Today you are observing the liturgical memorial of my maternal Queenship. And you are here, beloved sons of Hungary, to make your retreat, in the form of a continuous cenacle, as was that of Jerusalem.

b   I am uniting myself to your unceasing prayer, to obtain the gift of the Holy Spirit, in order to confirm you in your vocation.

c   I am building up a greater brotherliness among you, and as a mother, I am bringing you to know each other, to understand each other, to help each other and to love each other, so that the new commandment which my Son Jesus has given you may be lived by you more and more.

d   I am pointing out to you the way along which you must walk, to live each day the consecration to my Immaculate Heart, which you have made to me, so that you can become the rays of light which come down into the midst of such great darkness, to announce the proximate triumph of my Immaculate Heart in the world.

e   *I am the Queen of Love.*

f   You have emerged from a difficult and painful period of time, during which my Adversary has exercised, in a strong way, his dominion over you. Thus, you have known moments of great affliction; the rejection of God and of his Law of love has been spread among you; you have savored the bitterness of egoism, of hatred, of division, of fear and of a great aridity. But I have come to your aid, as your Mother and Queen, because this country has been consecrated to me by your patron, King Saint Stephen. And in these years I want to exercise, in an increasingly stronger way, my maternal Queenship.

g   *I am the Queen of Love.* For this reason I am calling today you priests and, by means of you, all the faithful to consecrate themselves to my Immaculate Heart. In this way I can truly take possession of your lives and make you instruments of the triumph of my Immaculate Heart in the world. You are the rays of light, which come down from my Immaculate Heart, upon this land of Hungary which has been so tested. Spread everywhere the light from my Heart, because dense yet is the darkness which surrounds you and great are the dangers through which you are passing. Open up the hearts of all to receive the gift of my maternal Queenship.

h   *I am the Queen of Love,* and the hearts of my sons are the privileged portion of my reign.

i   If you walk along the road which I have traced out for you, you succeed in overcoming all the obstacles which my Adversary is still setting for you; you prepare new days of peace; and you help many of my wandering children to be converted and to return to the Lord, who is waiting for them with great fatherly love.

j   I bless you, together with all the souls who are entrusted to you; I assure you of my maternal protection; and I ask you to bring everywhere in this country of the east my word of hope, of consolation and of peace."

431

Milan (Italy); September 8, 1990
Feast of the Nativity of the Blessed Virgin Mary

The Task Which I Have Entrusted to You

a   "Beloved children, you are sharing today in the joy of the whole celestial and terrestrial Church, which is contemplating your heavenly Mother at the moment of her birth. I am the dawn which is arising to announce the birth of the eternal sun of my Son Jesus, our Redeemer and Savior. For this, the Lord has made me immaculate from the moment of my human conception. He has wanted me all beautiful, full of grace and clothed in holiness.

b   Thus today, on the feast of my birth, you are contemplating me as the rising dawn, beautiful as the moon, brilliant as the sun, terrible as an army set in battle array.

c   — I am the dawn which announces the stupendous event of your salvation and which prepares you all for the coming of the great day of the Lord.

d   — I am beautiful as the moon, which shines with the reflected light of the sun, because mine is the very beauty of the Most Holy Trinity which enfolds me, mine the fullness of the grace of God which transforms me, mine his divine holiness which covers me.

e   — I am brilliant as the sun, because I am called to become the Mother of Jesus Christ, who is the eternal splendor of the Father.

f   — I am terrible as an army drawn up in battle array, because the task which has been entrusted to me by the Lord is that of conquering Satan; of crushing the head of the ancient serpent; of enchaining the huge Red Dragon and of casting him into his abyss of fire; of struggling with and of defeating the one who opposes himself to Christ, namely the Antichrist, in order to prepare the second coming of Jesus, who will restore his glorious reign among you.

g   This is my plan.

h   The stronger my presence becomes among you, the more will the darkness of evil, of sin, of hatred and of impurity withdraw themselves from you, because Satan is becoming more and more imprisoned and destroyed.

i   In these last times of yours, the task of your heavenly Mother, beautiful as the moon, brilliant as the sun, terrible as an army set in battle array, is to announce that the great day of the Lord is in the very act of coming upon you.

j   On this day of my nativity, little son so loved by me, you are on the vigil of a long and tiring journey, which I am again asking you to undertake for me, to many countries of another continent. *This is the task which I have entrusted to you*: to bring my motherly announcement to every part of the world, and to call all my children to enter, through their act of consecration, into the bright and safe refuge of my Immaculate Heart, because the trial which is about to come upon you is very great, and you are all being called to suffer with me.

k   But yours is like the suffering of a mother who must bring her child to the light. In fact, the immense pain of these last times prepares the birth of a new era, the new times, when Jesus will come in the splendor of his glory and will restore his reign in the world.

l   Then all creation, set free from the slavery of sin and of death, will know the splendor of a second terrestrial paradise, in which God will dwell with you, will wipe away every tear, and there will no longer be day or night, because the former things have passed away and your light will be that of the Lamb and of the new Jerusalem come down from heaven upon the earth, ready as a bride for her Spouse."

432

St. David (Maine, U.S.A.); September 15, 1990
Feast of Our Lady of Sorrows

The Travail of the New Birth

a "Beloved children, today I am associating you in the great suffering of your immaculate Mother. You are the children of my motherly predilection. You have been chosen by me to form part of my victorious cohort. You are an important part of my plan as Mediatrix and Co-redemptrix.

b My Son Jesus wanted me beneath the Cross, to associate my immaculate suffering with all his divine suffering. He wanted to unite my human suffering to his, and He associated me intimately in the mystery of his redemption. Thus He called me to be true Co-redemptrix.

c The fruit of my co-redemption is my spiritual motherhood. Beneath the Cross, through the Will of my Son Jesus, in the cradle of a very great suffering, I became your Mother, Mother of all the redeemed, Mother of the Church and of the entire human race. And I have carried out this maternal function by standing, as a true mother, at the side of all my children, during the earthly course of human history.

d I have not left anyone alone or abandoned; no one has ever been rejected or sent away from me. I have always been close to everyone, as a loving and sorrowful Mother. I have carried in my Heart the sufferings of all. I have carried in my Heart the sufferings of the whole Church. I have shared in the immense pain of the poor and the outcast, of the sinners and the despairing, of those far away and of the atheists, of the good and of the wicked, of the great and of the small, of the priests and of the faithful, of the suffering and of the sick, of the agonizing and of the dying. I have become the Mother of all sorrows.

e   Above all, it is my motherly task to share in the great sufferings of the Church and of all humanity, in these days of the purification and of the great tribulation. It is these sufferings which are preparing the new times, the rise of the new era.

f   *This is therefore the travail of the new birth.* And, as Mother, I am called to the task of begetting today, in suffering, the new humanity, ready for the meeting with its Lord, who is returning to you in glory.

g   For this reason, my little son, I have wanted you here again in the United States of America, to begin a long and wearying journey through many countries, to hold the cenacles of my Movement and to lead all into the safe refuge of my Immaculate Heart. I want you thus to be associated in my motherly work of co-redemption, and I am making you more and more a participant in my great sorrows.

h   Become therefore the sign of my motherly presence, and give to everyone the charism of my soothing balm. Give assistance to those who are far away, comfort to the sick, courage to the weak, support to the little ones, grace to the sinners, love to the priests, light to the faithful, hope to the discouraged and great confidence to all.

i   You will see the greatest marvels everywhere, because the times of my maternal co-redemption have arrived."

433   St. Albert (Alberta, Canada); September 29, 1990
Feast of the Holy Archangels

The Hour of the Angelic Powers

a   "You are celebrating today the feast of the Archangels, Gabriel, Raphael and Michael, and you are invoking their protection. In these times of the great tribulation, I urge you to live in a union of life with the angels of the Lord. Today they have an important task to carry out on your behalf.

b   —They light up for you the path along which you must journey, in order to be faithful to the consecration which you have made to me. It is a difficult and painful path, marked by many obstacles and threatened by the many snares of my Adversary.

The angels take you by the hand and lead you along the path of light, of love and of holiness.

c   —They give you courage and comfort in the many difficulties which you must put up with, and they support you in your human weakness. They are at your side as true brothers, who take to heart your person and your life.

d   —They defend you against the continuous attacks of Satan, against his numerous snares, against the obstacles which he puts along your path.

e   The great battle which is now being waged is above all at the level of the spirits: the wicked spirits against the angelic spirits. You are being involved in this struggle which is being waged between heaven and earth, between the angels and the demons, between Saint Michael the Archangel and Lucifer. To the angels of the Lord is entrusted the task of defending your person, the life of the Church and the good of all humanity.

f   In this great country where you find yourself holding cenacles, you see how humanity, deceived by the false spirits, is going along the way of evil and of a great immorality and how the Church itself is becoming more and more undermined by errors and by sins and is running the danger of losing the true faith, as a result of its division from the Pope and its opposition to his Magisterium.

g   In these evil times, you must pray much to the angels of the Lord.

h   *This is the hour of the angelic Powers.* It is the angelic Powers who are guiding all my children in the decisive battle for the final defeat of Satan and the coming of the glorious reign of Christ, in the triumph of my Immaculate Heart in the world."

434   Quebec (Quebec, Canada); October 7, 1990
                         Feast of Our Lady of the Rosary
                         Anniversary of the Victory
                         of the Blessed Virgin Mary at Lepanto

My Greatest Victory

a   "On this day, when the anniversary of one of my victories, obtained through the powerful weapon of the holy rosary, is being celebrated, you find yourself journeying through the provinces of Canada — this land so loved by me and so threatened and wounded by my Adversary — to gather together, in cenacles of prayer and fraternal sharing, the priests and faithful who are consecrated to me.

b   Today, by means of you, I want to give a word of assurance and of hope to many of my children who live in this great country.

c   — My Adversary has violated, in a very grievous way, this land, leading many of my poor children along the road of materialism, of a frantic search for pleasure and money, of egoism, of pride and of impurity. Obscenity and immorality are flooding everywhere, especially through the press and television, and thus the souls of the little ones and the simple are being corrupted.

d   — Even the Church here is being particularly threatened by the spread of errors, which bring one to the loss of the true faith. The pastors are responsible for this painful situation, because many of them are not defending the truth with courage and often remain silent and tolerate abuses of every kind, and thus the integrity of the Catholic faith is becoming more and more threatened.

e   It is necessary that all the bishops and the priests return to a greater unity with the Pope, he whom Christ has set as the foundation of the Church and as the infallible guardian of his truth.

f   But my great sorrow is appeased by an ever increasing number of my children, who are accepting my motherly urging to conversion, to the consecration to my Immaculate Heart, to the spreading everywhere of cenacles of prayer made with me, through the recitation of the holy rosary. Spread these cenacles everywhere, like rays of light which come down to lighten up the earth, in these days of great darkness.

g   Above all, multiply family cenacles, as a strong defense against all those evils which today are threatening to destroy the family, such as division, divorce, the recourse to the means of birth control, and the abortions which are increasing more and more and crying for vengeance in the sight of God.

h   The spiritual cenacle of my Immaculate Heart is the refuge into which all of you must enter in order to receive the gift of the second Pentecost. Thus, with the powerful weapon of the holy rosary, you will be able to attain again today *my greatest victory* in the history of the Church and of all humanity."

435
Mexico City (Mexico); October 13, 1990
Anniversary of the Last Apparition at Fatima

I Reveal My Secret

a   "Today you are recalling my final apparition, which took place in Fatima on this very day in 1917, and which was confirmed by the miracle of the sun.

b   Today I announce to you that there is about to be born the new Church of light, which my Son Jesus is forming for Himself in every part of the earth, so that it will be ready to receive Him, with faith and with joy, in the proximate moment of his second coming.

c   The glorious reign of Christ, which will be established in your midst, with the second coming of Jesus in the world, is close at hand. This is his return in glory. This is his glorious return, to establish his reign in your midst and to bring all humanity, redeemed by his most precious blood, back to the state of his new terrestrial paradise.

d   That which is being prepared is so great that its equal has never existed since the creation of the world. Prepare yourselves with humility, with faith, with intense prayer. Prepare yourselves by gathering together, each and all, in the spiritual cenacle of my Immaculate Heart. Prepare yourselves in silence and in expectation.

e   *I reveal my secret* only to the hearts of the little, the simple and the poor, because it is being accepted and believed by them. For this, Jesus is working powerfully in these times, to prepare his coming in the lives of the simple, the poor, the pure, the little.

f   With a small number of these children, the Lord will soon restore on earth his glorious reign of love, of holiness and of peace."

Paradise Will Be Joined to Earth

a　"Look today to paradise, where many of your brothers and sisters have arrived, to participate in the endless joy of a blessed eternity. This feast should be for you a reason for joy, for hope and for comfort.

b　— *Let yourselves be filled with joy* at the certainty that the saints in paradise shed upon you the light of their blessedness, to help you live on earth for the perfect glorification of the Most Holy Trinity. In this way, while yet still here below, you share in the same experience as do the saints, and you live, with the heart and the soul, in paradise, enjoying in a small degree the same happiness as they do.

c　— *A cause of hope* should be, for you, the fact that many have preceded you to the heavenly kingdom, after having journeyed along the same road as you, after having endured the same sufferings as you, after having experienced the very same difficulties as you. And so go forward with fortitude and without ever allowing yourselves to be discouraged, along the road of the perfect observance of the Law of God, of the practice of all the Christian virtues, of a daily communion of life with the Eucharistic Jesus, who leads you along the road of sanctity.

d　— *A great comfort* for you all should be the certainty that the saints are assisting you with their prayers, are at your side to console you in your afflictions, to give you strength in difficulties, to remove the obstacles which you find along your road, and to make you overcome the snares which my Adversary and yours sets for you.

e　In the hour of the great trial, *paradise will be joined to earth*, until the moment when the luminous door will be opened, to cause to descend upon the world the glorious presence of Christ, who will restore his reign in which the divine Will shall be accomplished in a perfect manner, as in heaven, so also on earth."

437   *Malvern (Pennsylvania, U.S.A.); November 15, 1990*
Spiritual Exercises in the Form of a Cenacle
with 3 Bishops and 250 Priests of the M.M.P.
from the United States, Canada and Latin America

The Hour of the Great Trial

a   "Beloved sons, today I want to tell you of the joy and the comfort that my Immaculate Heart feels in seeing you gathered together in such great numbers in these, your spiritual exercises, which you are carrying out in the form of a continuous cenacle. You have come from almost all the states of this country of yours, from Canada and from other countries of Latin America.

b   You are gathered in prayer, offered together with me, by the recitation of the entire rosary, by your listening to my word, by a solemn holy hour of Eucharistic adoration, and by the concelebration of Holy Mass, always presided over by a bishop, during which you renew your act of consecration to my Immaculate Heart.

c   You have also wished to make more intense your act of love and reparation to Jesus present in the Most Holy Eucharist, by your nocturnal adoration, so pleasing to me and blessed by me, because it has given great comfort and joy to the Eucharistic and priestly Heart of Jesus.

d   And now, I announce to you that *the hour of the great trial* is on the point of arriving.

e   — *The great trial has arrived for your country.* How many times, as a concerned and sorrowing Mother, have I endeavored to urge my children to follow the path of conversion and of return to the Lord.

f   I have not been listened to. You have continued to walk along the way of rejection of God and of his Law of love. Sins of impurity have become ever more widespread, and immorality has spread like a sea which has submerged all things. Homosexuality, a sin of impurity which is against nature, has been justified; recourse to the means of preventing life have become commonplace, while abortions — these killings of innocent children, that cry for vengeance before the face of God — have spread and are performed in every part of your homeland.

g   The moment of divine justice and of great mercy has now arrived. You will know the hour of weakness and of poverty, the hour of suffering and defeat, the purifying hour of the great chastisement.

h   — *The great trial has arrived for your Church.* Those errors which have brought people to the loss of the true faith have continued to spread. Many pastors have been neither attentive nor vigilant and have allowed many rapacious wolves, clothed as lambs, to insinuate themselves into the flock in order to bring disorder and destruction.

i   How great is your responsibility, O pastors of the holy Church of God! You continue along the path of division from the Pope and of the rejection of his Magisterium; indeed, in a hidden way, there is in preparation a true schism which could soon become open and proclaimed.

j   And then, there will remain only a small faithful remnant, over which I will keep watch in the garden of my Immaculate Heart.

k   — *The great trial has arrived for all humanity.* The chastisement, predicted by me at Fatima and contained in that part of the secret which has not yet been revealed, is about to take place. The great moment of divine justice and of mercy has come upon the world.

l   For this reason I have wanted you here. You must be the apostles of these last times. Go out everywhere, and proclaim with strength and courage the Gospel of Jesus. Walk along the path of contempt for the world and for yourselves. Illuminate the earth in these times of great darkness. Cause the rays of the light of your faith, of your holiness and of your love to come down upon the world.

m   You have been chosen to combat courageously against the power of him who places himself in opposition to Christ, in order to obtain, in the end, my greatest victory.

n   Leave this cenacle in confidence; leave in joy and in great hope. I am with you. I am manifesting myself by means of you. I will work prodigies in you, so that all will be able to see my light and feel my maternal presence.

o   Together with your dear ones, together with the souls which are entrusted to you, I bless you all in the name of the Father, and of the Son, and of the Holy Spirit."

Open Your Hearts to Hope

a   "Contemplate me today in the splendor of my Immaculate Conception. Allow yourselves to be enfolded in my light of grace, of holiness and of virginal beauty.

b   My dearly beloved ones and children consecrated to me, second my plan, and enter, all of you, as quickly as possible into the spiritual cenacle of my Immaculate Heart.

c   — My Immaculate Heart is the heavenly garden in which I want to gather you together, to offer you to the perfect glory of the Most Holy Trinity, in these times of the apostasy.

d   — My Immaculate Heart is the safe refuge which I have prepared for you, so that you may live in serenity through the painful moments of the great tribulation.

e   — My Immaculate Heart is the luminous path which leads you to the joyous meeting with Jesus, who is about to return to you in glory. And so, cooperate with my pressing request, which I am presenting to you by means of my work of the Marian Movement of Priests and of this little son of mine, whom I am still leading to every part of the world, to bring everyone to the consecration to my Immaculate Heart. Thus you take part in my motherly plan, which is that of preparing hearts and souls to receive the Lord who is coming.

f   — I was chosen by the Most Holy Trinity to become the Mother of the Word, who became incarnate in my virginal womb, and thus I have given you my Son Jesus. His first coming among you took place in poverty, in humility and in suffering, because Jesus wanted to assume the limitations, the misery and the weakness of our human nature. And so my motherly action was carried out in silence, in prayer, in hiddenness and in humility.

g   — I was chosen by the Most Holy Trinity to become the Mother of the Second Advent, and thus my motherly task is that of preparing the Church and all humanity to receive Jesus, who is returning to you in glory. His second coming will take place in the light of his divinity, because Jesus will return to you on the clouds of heaven, in the splendor of his royalty and will make subject to Himself the peoples and the nations of the earth, and all his enemies will be crushed under the throne of his universal dominion.

h   Thus my maternal action, in these last times, is being exercised in a manner which is open and always more powerful, and my light is becoming bright in every part of the earth. For this reason, I am manifesting myself today everywhere by means of my numerous apparitions and of my extraordinary manifestations.

i   My reign of love, which I am establishing in hearts and souls, is the way which prepares the glorious reign of Christ. The triumph of my Immaculate Heart will coincide with the second coming of Jesus in glory, to make all things new.

j   And so, listen, one and all, to my voice, and hasten after the immaculate light of my virginal beauty, to the encounter with the divine splendor of Christ.

k   *Open your hearts to hope.* The second coming of Christ is near at hand. The signs that He Himself has given you, to prepare yourselves to receive Him, in these times of yours, are all on the point of being realized.

l   *Open your hearts to hope.*
Live in peace of heart and in prayer.
Live in faith and in joy.
Live in grace and in purity.
Live in love and in holiness.
Because Jesus Christ, our Redeemer, our Savior and our King, is about to come to you in the splendor of his glorified body."

439

Receive the Prophetic Announcements

a   "Live with me, beloved children, through the precious hours which precede the birth of my divine Child. This is the holy night. Spend it with me: in silence, in contemplation, in prayer, in peace. Share in the joy of my Immaculate Heart, which is opening itself to give the Redeemer and the Savior to the world.

b   For how many centuries this event was awaited! The promise of his coming came down like a torch to lighten up the dark unfolding of time and of history. The prophets had foretold of this moment; the just were awaiting it with faith; the poor were hoping for it with ardent expectation; the Spirit was preparing hearts and souls for his coming. In the invocation of this ineffable moment, all the saints and the just ones of Israel fell asleep.

c   On this holy night, the expectation of centuries comes to an end, because the Eternal Word of the Father, while silence enwraps all things, is born in his human life and becomes your Brother. He is born in a cave, amidst great poverty, rejected by all, received with love and tenderness by me his virginal Mother and by my most chaste spouse, Joseph, and made joyous by the heavenly voices of the angels and by the presence of the little, the poor, the simple, the pure of heart.

d   Beloved children, you too, live with me the joyous mystery of this Christmas. Surround the bare crib with your priestly love; make amends, in the face of the rejection of many, with the fullness of holiness and of faithful witness; kiss with me his tender limbs, and let us thank together the Heavenly Father for his only-begotten Son who today is given to us all.

e   And prepare yourselves, all, for his second birth. Again the coldness of sin covers the life of men and of peoples; the darkness of errors pervades the whole world; the rejection of God and of his Law of love is set up as a norm of human life. Hatred, impurity, egoism and division are spreading, and the threat of a new and terrible war is becoming, on this very day, more concrete and close at hand.

f   You have entered into the times that have been foretold to you. You have entered into the last times.

g   *And so, receive the prophetic announcements* which, in so many ways, have pointed out to you that this, his second birth, is close at hand.

h   While the deep night has once again fallen upon the world and such coldness dries up the hearts of men, open your souls to confidence and to hope, and listen with joy to my prophetic announcement.

i   As Mother of the Second Advent, I am preparing you for his new birth. For this reason, in every part of the world, I am on the point of forming the cohort of the little ones, of the poor, of the humble, and the pure in heart to prepare thus a precious cradle for Jesus who is returning to you in glory."

440

Rubbio (Vicenza, Italy); December 31, 1990
Last Night of the Year

My Tear Drops

a   "Gather together with me in prayer of adoration and reparation, to spend the last hours of this year, which is about to end, in an act of profound intercession.

b   Pray in order to ask for the salvation of this world, which has now touched the depths of impiety and of impurity, of injustice and of egoism, of hatred and of violence, of sin and of evil.

c   How many times and in how many ways have I personally intervened to urge you to conversion and to a return to the Lord of your peace and of your joy. This is the reason for my numerous apparitions, for the messages which I give by means of this little son of mine and of my work of the Marian Movement of Priests, which I myself have spread in every part of the world. As Mother I have repeatedly pointed out the path along which you must walk to attain your salvation.

d   But I have not been listened to. They have continued to walk along the way of rejection of God and of his Law of love. The Ten Commandments of the Lord are continually and publicly violated. The day of the Lord is no longer respected, and his most holy Name is becoming more and more despised. The precept of love of one's neighbor is daily violated through egoism, hatred, violence and division which have entered into families and into society, and by violent and bloody wars between the nations of the earth. The dignity of man, as a free creature of God, is crushed by the chains of an interior slavery which makes him a victim of disordinate passions, of sin and of impurity.

e   For this world, the moment of its chastisement has now arrived. You have entered the grievous times of the purification and sufferings must increase for all.

f   Even my Church has need of being purified of the evils which have stricken her and which are causing her to live through moments of agony and of her sorrowful passion. How apostasy has spread, because of the errors which are at this time being disseminated and being accepted by the majority, without any further reaction! The faith of many has died out. Sin, committed, justified and no longer confessed, renders souls slaves of evil and of Satan. To what a miserable state has this, my most beloved Daughter, been reduced!

g   Pray with me during these last hours of the year which is about to end. During its course, I have again intervened many times, to obtain from the Lord the gift of his divine mercy. But the time which awaits you is that time when mercy will be espoused to divine justice, for the purification of the earth.

h   Do not await the new year with noise, with cries and with songs of joy. Await it with the intense prayer of one who wants to again make reparation for all the evil and the sin in the world.

i   The hours through which you are about to live are among the gravest and the most painful. Pray, suffer, offer, make reparation together with me, who am the Mother of Intercession and of Reparation.

j   Thus you — my beloved ones and children consecrated to my Heart — you become, in these last hours of the year, *my tear drops*, which are falling upon the immense pain of the Church and of all humanity, as you enter into the grievous times of the purification and the great tribulation."

1991

THE ANNOUNCEMENT OF THE NEW ERA

The Announcement of the New Era

a   "In the light of my divine maternity, begin this new year in prayer and in confidence. I am true Mother of God. He who is born of me, in the holy night of Christmas, and is placed in the manger with great love, surrounded by such squalor and with such immense poverty, is the true Son of God, the Word of the Father, made flesh in my virginal womb, the Image of his substance, the Splendor of his glory.

b   By the Will of my Son Jesus, I have become your Mother also.

c   —As Mother, I am close to each one of you to help you carry out, in the time which has been granted you, the plan of your Heavenly Father. This plan is that his divine Will be accomplished by you. And the divine Will is that you become holy. I, therefore, help you to walk along the road of holiness, so that the divine Will may be accomplished by you in a perfect way, and thus you may give, in your life, the greatest glory to the Most Holy Trinity.

d   — As Mother, I am close to the Church, my most beloved Daughter. In these times, the Church is being called to live the hours of agony and of Gethsemane, the hours of the redemptive passion, the hours of her bloody immolation on Calvary.

e   At the beginning of this new year, on the road of Calvary, I am meeting all my children: the Pope, especially loved, guided and defended by me, the bishops, the priests, the religious and the faithful. How heavy a cross they must carry today, these most beloved children of mine: the cross of apostasy and of the lack of faith; the cross of sins and of innumerable sacrileges; the cross of abandonment and of rejection; the cross of condemnation and of crucifixion!

f   For my Church, the moment of the shedding of blood and of her bloody immolation is close at hand. Especially in these times, I am ever close to this suffering and agonizing Daughter of mine, as I was beneath the Cross, upon which Jesus was immolated for our redemption.

g — As Mother, I am close to this poor humanity, sick and oppressed under the weight of its obstinate rejection of God and of his Law of love. How greatly has it turned away from the Lord! It has wanted to build for itself an atheistic and materialistic civilization; new values have been proposed, values founded on the satisfaction of all the passions, on the search for all pleasures, on the legitimization of all moral disorders. Thus, love has been replaced by egoism and hatred; faith, by pride and unbelief; hope, by avarice and lust; honesty, by fraud and deception; goodness, by malice and hardness of heart.

h Satan has sung his victory because he has brought sin into souls and division into families, into society, into nations themselves and between nations. Thus peace has never been so threatened as in your days. You are beginning this new year under the grave threat of a conflict which could become the spark for the outbreak of the terrible third world war.

i Pray, beloved children, and do penance, because you have now entered into the time of the great chastisement which the Lord will send for the purification of the earth. Multiply everywhere the cenacles of prayer which I have been asking of you for so long, and do not let yourselves be seized by fear or discouragement. Have great confidence in the powerful work of intercession and of mediation of your heavenly Mother.

j The great suffering which awaits you is to prepare you for the birth of the new era, which is coming upon the world. Live this new year in my Immaculate Heart: it is the refuge which I have prepared for you for these times, burdened with sufferings for individuals and for nations. And so, you will not be afraid. Your suffering will increase with the increase of the trial which has already begun.

k *I am the announcement of the new era.* In the deep darkness of this, your time, if you live with me, you can already glimpse the glimmer of the new times which are awaiting you. Look to this light, and live in peace of heart and in hope. If you remain always in my Immaculate Heart, my beloved ones and children consecrated to me, even as of these moments you can begin the new era of holiness and of grace, of light and of purity, of love and of peace.

l Thus, in the hour of the great trial, you will give to all the charism of my motherly presence, and you will be a soothing and longed-for balm for so many open and bleeding wounds.

m   At the beginning of this new year, which opens the door on the last decade of this century and which will be marked by grave and decisive events, I enclose you in the depths of my Immaculate Heart, and I bless you in the name of the Father, and of the Son, and of the Holy Spirit."

442

Milan (Italy); February 2, 1991
Feast of the Presentation of the Child Jesus
First Satuday

The Road Which Leads to the New Era

a   "Contemplate me today in the mystery of the presentation of my divine Child in the temple. With how much docility and filial abandonment does Jesus allow Himself to be carried in my motherly arms as, with my most chaste spouse, Joseph, I go up to the temple of Jerusalem, to satisfy the precept of the holy Law of the Lord. I entrust the Child to the hands of the priest, and thus He is offered to the Father as Victim and Sacrifice for our ransom.

b   Jesus enters into the glory of his temple, as Light which illumines every man, for the salvation of all the nations.

c   The mystery, hidden from the eternal centuries in the secret of the Father, is manifested at this moment. Not to the great and the wise, not to the powerful and the clever, not to those who are first and to those who are more important. It is revealed to the little, to the poor, to the simple, to the least of all, to the pure of heart. And thus a simple woman and a poor old man, open to receive the gift of the Spirit, come to be the first to enter into the understanding of this great mystery.

d   'Now, O Lord, you let your servant depart in peace, because my eyes have beheld the Savior, a light for revelation to the gentiles and glory of your people Israel.' (cf. Lk 2:29-32)

e   This is a mystery of love and of sorrow, of light and of darkness, of joy and of suffering, of death and of life. —'He will be set up as a sign of contradiction, for the salvation and the ruin of many.' (cf. Lk 2:34)

672

f And I become intimately associated in the unfolding of this, his divine mission. — 'And as for you, O Mother, a sword will pierce your soul.' (cf. Lk 2:35)

g You too, my beloved ones and children consecrated to my Heart, you too must allow yourselves to be carried in my motherly arms. The time of your light and your witness has come. For this reason, I invite you all to enter into the temple of my Immaculate Heart. Here, you are offered to the glory of the Father; here, you become molded in imitation of the Son; here, you are transformed by the powerful work of the Holy Spirit. Your priestly immolation is necessary for the salvation of all peoples.

h You have entered into the conclusive period of the great tribulation, and the hour of the great trial, which I have been foretelling to you for so many years, has now arrived for you. It is a trial so great and painful, that you cannot even imagine it, but it is necessary for the Church and for all humanity, in order that the new era, the new world, and the reconciliation of humanity with their Lord may come upon you.

i In these days, Jesus is working in a very powerful way in every part of the world, to carry out the plan of his merciful love. For the present, this plan is hidden and enclosed in the secret of his divine Heart. Today it is again being revealed only to the little, to the simple, to the poor, to the pure of heart. With these little ones, whom He is gathering from every part of the earth, Jesus will soon restore his reign of glory.

j *This is the road which leads to the new era.*

k Thus today, as you venerate me at the moment when I present the Child Jesus in the temple of Jerusalem, I invite you to enter, each and all, into the spiritual temple of my Immaculate Heart, so that I can offer you to the glory of the Lord, and I can form you in simplicity and littleness, in poverty and purity. Only thus can you yourselves become the road which leads to his reign and be a most powerful light which points out to all poor humanity the way which leads to the new times which await you."

443   *Brasilia (Brazil); February 26, 1991*
Spiritual Exercises in the Form of a Cenacle
with Bishops and Priests of the M.M.P. from all Brazil

Not by Bread Alone

a   "During these days, my Immaculate Heart is consoled in seeing you in such great numbers at this continuous cenacle of prayer
and of brotherhood. You have come from all Brazil, this land so
loved by me and increasingly ensnared by my Adversary.

b   Today I welcome into the garden of my Immaculate Heart
the Church which lives and suffers here, and your fatherland
which is again passing through moments of great difficulty and
of danger. I invite all my children to consecrate themselves to
my Immaculate Heart, and to enter as quickly as possible into
the safe refuge, which I have prepared for you, for these times of
the purification and of the great tribulation.

c   I am a tender and understanding Mother for all of you. I want
to lead you along the way of peace, of prayer, of holiness, of your
more profound union with Jesus, our Redeemer and our Savior.

d   I see your zeal in the apostolate; I know of your great difficulties; I carry with you the burden of your daily sufferings. Above
all, I look with love upon your diligent care for the poorest, the
marginalized, and those in the last places, in your effort to set
them free from the slavery of poverty and misery. But, as your
Mother, I take you by the hand and lead you to the understanding of the truth, whole and entire.

e   *'Not by bread alone does man live.'* (Dt 8:3)

f   Man lives also by every word that comes from the mouth of
God, to nourish the hunger of his mind. Besides the poverty of
material goods, there exists a greater poverty of spiritual goods.

g   How many there are of these children of mine who live under the yoke of this spiritual slavery! They are those who become victims of false ideologies, founded on the denial of God.
How great is the spreading of the error of theoretical and practical atheism, which brings many to pass their life, getting along
without God! They are those who withdraw from the Church
to join the various sects, which are spreading here, more and
more. This has come about because the hungering minds of so
many of my children are no longer nourished with the bread of

the word of God.

h   I ask you to give with abundance this spiritual food, and above all, to you my beloved ones and sons consecrated to me, I ask a still greater effort in communicating to all the light of the Gospel. Preach the Gospel with courage and without fear; present it with the clarity of its completeness; announce it with the same vigor with which my Son Jesus preached it to you. Thus you will help all to walk along the way of the true faith, in the greatest obedience to the Magisterium of the Pope and of the bishops united with him.

i   *'Not by bread alone does man live.'*

j   Man lives also by divine grace, which Jesus has given him, to nourish the hunger of his soul. Besides the poverty of material goods, there exists a greater and more dangerous moral poverty, consisting in the heavy yoke which makes many of my children slaves of evil and of sin, of unruly passions, especially of impurity. How great is this wound among you!

k   How subtle is the snare of my Adversary, who often leads you to put all your priestly energy into healing the wounds of the poor and exploited, in order thus to make you forget to look above all at the deep wounds of the sinners and of the wicked. Give the food of the grace of God to these souls who are dying of hunger. For this, you must help sinners to return to the fount of divine mercy, by putting yourselves at their disposal in the sacrament of Reconciliation.

l   This is the favorable time for you. This is the time of conversion and of return to the Lord. Beloved sons, you yourselves must become solicitous ministers of reconciliation, for the salvation of many souls, who are running the danger of being lost.

m   *'Not by bread alone does man live.'*

n   Man lives also by the Living Bread come down from heaven, to nourish the hunger of his heart. How many there are today who live under the terrible slavery of pride, of unbridled egoism, of avarice, of hatred, of violence, of a great incapacity to love! The way which leads to salvation is solely that of communion and of love. For this reason, Jesus has made you the inestimable gift of the Most Holy Eucharist.

o   Jesus becomes present in the Eucharist to be the food of your spiritual life and to form you to a true capacity for love.

675

p   Jesus gives Himself to you in the Eucharist to love in you, with you and by means of you.

q   The Eucharistic Jesus is the Living Bread come down from heaven, the food to eat that one may hunger no longer, the water to drink that one may thirst no longer.

r   The Eucharistic Jesus wants to become today the Good Samaritan for your Church, so divided and suffering, and for your fatherland, so ill and threatened.

s   The Eucharistic Jesus wants to lead all of you along the road of love, of reconciliation, of communion, of peace, of mercy and of salvation. Learn of Him who is meek and humble of heart, and you will find rest for your souls.

t   This year, Brazil is celebrating its National Eucharistic Congress. May your Church and your fatherland prostrate themselves in an act of profound adoration directed to the Eucharistic Jesus.

u   *Today I ask all to throw open the doors to Jesus Christ who is coming.* I am the Mother of the Second Advent and the door which is being opened on the new era. This new era will coincide with the greatest triumph of the Eucharistic reign of Jesus.

v   For this, I invite you, in this extraordinary year, to make flourish everywhere the cult of adoration, of reparation and of love for the Most Holy Eucharist. In your churches, return to the exposition of the Most Holy Sacrament, through solemn hours of public adoration. Let the Eucharist become the center of your prayer, of your life, of your cult and of your ecclesial gatherings.

w   Thus, again today, the Eucharistic Jesus, with his word, will nourish the hunger of minds; with his grace, will nourish the hunger of souls; with his love, will nourish the hunger of your hearts.

x   And it will be the Eucharistic Jesus who will finally give you the great gift of the true liberation from every form of physical, spiritual and moral slavery. And thus, in all of you, there will shine forth the great dignity of sons of God, created by Him, loved, redeemed, sanctified and saved.

y   Go forth now, from this your cenacle, and become the apostles of this new evangelization in all of Brazil. I accompany you with my immaculate love, and I sustain you with my motherly blessing."

676

The Pasch of Love and of Sorrow

a   "Beloved sons, today is your feast, because it is the day of the birth of your priesthood. At the Last Supper, with the words — 'Take and eat of this, all of you, this is my body; drink of this, all of you, this is the chalice of my blood.' (cf. Mt 28:26-28) — Jesus institutes the new Sacrifice, the pact of the new and eternal Covenant. And with the words which He addresses to the Apostles — 'Do this in memory of me.' (Lk 22:19) — He institutes his new Priesthood.

b   To this new and eternal Priesthood of Christ, all of you also, my beloved sons, have been associated — you who have participated in the indelible sign of the priestly character, on the day of your presbyteral ordination. And today you are recalling this gift, renewing your complete availability in the service of Christ and of the brothers, gathered about your bishops during the concelebration of the Holy Mass of Chrism, which allows you to express, in such a profound and visible way, the unity which exists among yourselves, the bishop, and Christ.

c   On this day, I ask you to renew your act of complete and total love for Jesus. Live the moments of his such great suffering. Enter with Him into the Garden of Olives, to live his very agony of Gethsemane.

d   How Jesus has awaited this day! — 'I have ardently longed to eat this, my Passover, with you before I suffer.' (Lk 22:15)

e   *It is the Pasch of love.*

f   It is the Pasch of the institution of the Sacrifice of love; it is the Pasch of the sacrament of love, of the new commandment of love, of the service given as a perfect act of love, of the prayer for the unity of you all, as a fulfillment of love.

g   *It is the Pasch of sorrow.*

h   And lo, no sooner has Jesus entered into the Garden of Olives, than a profound anguish takes hold of Him and almost paralyzes Him. He feels Himself to be an innocent victim, an immaculate lamb, an immolated sacrificial victim upon whom has fallen the burden of all the sin of the world. In an instant He has the clear vision of every detail of his painful and opprobrious passion. And then, with a deep voice which comes forth from his whole divine Person, He entrusts Himself to the Father. — 'Father, if it is possible, let this cup pass me by.' (Mt 26:39)

i   He prostrates Himself on the ground; He prays; He moans; He weeps. Deep shudders shake his whole body which begins to sweat profusely, and the drops of sweat are changed into drops of blood.

j   He has need of comfort. He asks it of the three most beloved disciples: Peter, James and John. Three times He goes to them, crushed by such great suffering; three times He finds them asleep.

k   I am far away with my presence, but with my soul and my Heart, I am always close to my Son. And thus, the only earthly creature who assists Him even in these moments of sorrowful agony is his Mother. Comforted by this, my spiritual and motherly help, Jesus offers Himself in an act of perfect abandonment: 'Father, let not my Will but yours be done.' (cf. Mt 26:39)

l   And now, the angel is sent Him by the Father with the chalice of gentle comfort, of divine consolation, to give Him the courage to go forward to the encounter with his traitor, who has already come. — 'He who betrays me is at hand.' (cf. Mt 26:46)

m   Beloved sons, in your priestly life, there must be renewed the great mystery of love and of sorrow of your divine Brother, Jesus. You too are called to enter into the Gethsemane of these last times, which are making ready your priestly immolation, for the new era which awaits you.

n   How many times the weight of sorrows oppresses you; the powers of evil paralyze you; the misunderstandings leave their mark on you; the acts of opposition bring you to a halt; the sins of this humanity crush you; the betrayals weary you. — 'Father, if it is possible let this cup pass us by.'

o   Beloved sons, do not seek human consolations or superficial comforts. It is my motherly task to give you that chalice of comfort which the Heavenly Father has prepared for you. In this way, you are assisted by me to carry out today only the Will of the Father. Entrust yourselves, all, to my Immaculate Heart, that I may be able to lead you along the road of the divine Will.

p   And live with me, in the Gethsemane of these last times, *your pasch of love and of sorrow*, in expectation of the new era which now awaits you."

The Man of All Times

a   "Gather together in the garden of my Immaculate Heart, beloved sons, to live together with Jesus the terrible hours of his painful passion. It is Good Friday. It is the day of his condemnation and of his death on the Cross.

b   After having spent all the night, amidst the insults and the effronteries of the members and the servants of the Sanhedrin, as the day wears on, Jesus is led before Pilate. Here takes place a second and more humiliating trial. Before a great crowd, stirred up into a rage against Him, face-to-face with the religious leaders who accuse Him of blasphemy and sacrilege, Jesus, meek as a lamb which silently allows itself to be led to the slaughter, assists

c   in august silence throughout the entire unfolding of events: the initial honesty of Pilate, who finds no guilt on his part; 'If He were not guilty we would not have brought Him here before you!' (cf. Jn 18:30); the incipient fear of the crowd; the doubt over the reality of his word: 'Are You a King?' (cf. Jn 18:33); the attempt to save Him, proposing his liberation in the place of Barabbas; the fear caused by the cries of the people; the terror of the judgment of Rome: 'If you set this fellow free, you are an enemy of Caesar.' (cf. Jn 19:12) And thus, with cowardice, Pilate signs his condemnation to death.

d   He hands Jesus over to the soldiers to be scourged. His whole body becomes one deep, living wound, from the gashes which the terrible Roman scourges gouge in his immaculate flesh.

e   He is then crowned with thorns. The thorns open up on Him rivulets of blood, which run down from his head and disfigure his face, and they strike Him and cover Him with spittle and with insults. — 'We have looked upon Him, stricken and humiliated; his face no longer bore human semblance.' (cf. Is 52:14)

f   The final and most wicked and cruel contrivance: they cover Him with a scarlet scrap of cloth as his royal robe; they put a reed in his hands as scepter; and they lead Him to Pilate who presents Him to the crowd: '*Behold the Man!*' (cf. Jn 19:14)

g   *Behold the Man of all times.* Upon Him, in Gethsemane, have been placed all the sins of the world. In the praetorium, there have been heaped on Him the sufferings, the humiliations, the abuses, the acts of exploitation and enslavement of all men.

h *He is the Man of all times.* The men who went before Him have lived in the hope of seeing this, his day, and in Him they have found salvation. He is the One who, in Abel, was killed; in Isaac, was bound by the feet; in Jacob, walked as a pilgrim; in Joseph, was sold; in Moses, was exposed on the waters; in the lamb, was slaughtered; in David, was persecuted; and in the prophets, was dishonored.

i *He is the Man of all times.* By the gift of his redemption, all men who have lived after Him have been called to live in communion of life with God. He has borne on his body the sufferings of all the victims of hatred, of violence, of wars; He has enclosed within his wounds the blood shed by millions of innocent babies, slaughtered while still in their mothers' wombs. He has been scourged by all the sufferings and the sicknesses, especially the incurable diseases that are spreading about; He has been crowned with thorns in those who succumb to the false ideologies and to the errors which lead far from the faith, to pride and to human conceit. He has been despised in the little, in the poor, in the marginalized, in those who are the last of all, in the exploited. He has been spit upon in those who are rejected and have given up hope. He has been exposed to derision in those who display as merchandise the dignity of their own bodies.

j *Behold the Man.* Now He takes upon Himself the wood of the condemnation; He climbs toward Calvary; He meets me, his transfixed Mother; He is nailed to the gibbet; He is raised upon the Cross; the three anguishing hours of his agony, near me, his Mother, and John, the beloved apostle; and in the end, his act of complete abandonment to the Father and his death on the Cross, toward three o'clock of this day.

k *Behold truly the Man of all times.* In Him is every man — from the first, Adam, to the last who will find himself on the earth at the end of time — who has lived and has been redeemed and saved. With the help of John, of Joseph of Arimathea and of the holy women, I bring Him to the sepulchre, where He is laid until the dawn of the first day after the Sabbath. His divine resurrection is the greatest proof that He alone is the Man of all times.

680

l   *He is the Man of the new times.* Because only in Him will there rise all the men who have lived, have died, have been buried and have wasted away to dry dust. So then, even in the great desert of your time, live with me these hours of his passion and of his death on the Cross.

m   Live them in silence, in recollection, in prayer, in sweet intimacy of life with your divine Crucified Brother. Because only in Him will the new times which await you be accomplished, when He will return to you in glory, and all the powers of heaven, of earth and of hell will prostrate themselves before Him, to the perfect glory of God the Father.''

446   *Rubbio (Vicenza, Italy); March 30, 1991*
Holy Saturday

In the Long Holy Saturday

a   "Beloved children, let us live together this day of Holy Saturday. Jesus rests, lifeless, in the new sepulchre where He has been placed. I am keeping watch, in confidence, in prayer, in hope and in expectation. This is the day of your spiritual rest. This is the first day of my spiritual motherhood. In these last times, let your commitment to live in union of life with your sorrowful Mother become stronger.

b   *This is a long Holy Saturday,* which is now about to end. And so, let your prayer become more intense. Do not allow yourselves to become absorbed or taken up by activity and by excessive preoccupation. In the moment of suffering, in the sorrows of the last times through which you are living, I urge you to keep watch with me in assiduous prayer.

c   *In the long Holy Saturday* through which you are living, keep watch with me in confidence and in hope. In the sepulchre of your long Holy Saturday, iniquity and human misery are buried once and for all; evil and sin, pride and hatred, impurity and arrogance and every form of corruption and death are laid away.

d   *In the long Holy Saturday* of these last times of yours, you must above all keep watch with me in expectation. That which made lighter for me the great sorrow of this day was the certitude that Jesus was to be gloriously risen. The Saturday of the sepulchre was to be succeeded by the first day of the resurrection.

e   Even though you are still living the pain, the fatigue, the suffering and the death of *this long Holy Saturday*, live with me in expectation. Jesus will return on the clouds of heaven, to restore his reign of glory and to make all things new. Beloved children, live with me today, in the expectation of this, his return."

447

Mother of Joy

a   "Share with me in the joy of all the universe, beloved children. Jesus is risen! The dark hour of Gethsemane and Calvary has passed. In three days, the greatest mystery of history has been completed: the betrayal, the judgment, the condemnation, Calvary, the agony, the death and the new sepulchre. All has passed. Jesus is risen! Jesus is alive in our midst. Let your joy be great, together with me who am *the Mother of Joy*.

b   From the moment when Jesus appeared to me in the splendor of his glorified body, my Heart was filled with such a great fullness of joy that it has never again abandoned it. Let nothing now disturb the deep joy of your human existence: not the sin, which has been canceled out; not the sorrow, which has been ransomed; not death, which has been conquered for ever.

c   Your earthly journey is passing through the stages of the very journey of Christ. You are still in the moments of the purification and the suffering, of Gethsemane and of Calvary.

d   But today, open the doors of your heart only to the joy, with me who am the Mother of your joy. Christ, risen and living in our midst, arranges all events for the accomplishment of his divine plan and predisposes everything so that his reign of glory may quickly come upon you."

The Times of Your Witness

a   "With this first Saturday of the month of May, you begin the period of time which is set aside for my special veneration. In this month of May, I want you to be more completely united with me, so that I may cause you to grow in your life of consecration, to the point of full maturity. The times of your maturity have come.

b   *These are the times of your witness.*

c   *Give to all the witness of being consecrated to me.* Your life must be illumined by my motherly presence, and you must spread about you the charism of my holiness, of my purity, of my mercy, of my charity, of my tenderness. Whoever sees you must see the power of my light; whoever meets you must find the sweet balm of my mercy. Give my help to those who are far away, to the poor, to the sick, to the sinners, to the despairing. Come with me, your motherly shepherdess, in the search of the many little sheep who have lost their way and are running the danger of dying of hunger and of cold.

d   *Give to all the witness of walking with me along the road of faith.* In these times, errors are spreading in a way which is so vast and profound that it is not possible for you to so much as imagine it. Many are losing the faith, and apostasy is expanding more and more within the Church, like a terrible cancer which has spread through all its members. You are being called to follow me along the road of heroic and pure faith. I am making you the gift of preserving you in the integrity of the faith, so that you can illumine my children in these times of great darkness. For this reason, I ask you to be strongly united with the Pope who has, from Jesus, the great task of confirming all in the truth of the Catholic faith.

e   *Give to all the witness of walking with me along the road of prayer.* Prayer is the strength of the Church; prayer is necessary for your salvation. Prayer, made together with me, can obtain for you the gift of the second Pentecost. Only with prayer can you enter into the new era which awaits you. So then I invite you to call everyone to prayer. Multiply the cenacles of prayer which I have asked of you. I want you priests to be the first to give the example of taking part in these cenacles. And then, I ask that, in these decisive times, cenacles be spread among the children, among the youth and in the families. The time has come when all the Church must gather together with me in prayer, in the spiritual cenacle of my Immaculate Heart.

f   *Give to all the witness of walking with me along the road of holiness.* My Immaculate Heart must be honored and glorified by the Church and by all humanity. For this reason, I want to bring you to a great holiness. Thus, by means of you, little children consecrated to me, the whole Church can become illumined and transformed by the very holiness of your heavenly Mother. I am taking you along the road of perfect imitation of Jesus, of littleness and of humility, of disdain for the world and for your own selves, of the heroic exercise of all the virtues, and of a great love for the Most Holy Eucharist.

g   You are now in the decisive times, which are bringing you to the new era. You are in my times. In these days of great darkness, your light will shine forth with greater and greater strength, to the point of surrounding with its rays and illuminating souls, the Church, and all humanity."

449
Salzburg (Austria); May 13, 1991
Anniversary of the First Apparition at Fatima

The Pope of My Secret

a   "Today you are gathered here in this, my venerated shrine, in a cenacle made up of very many priests and faithful of my Marian Movement of Priests. You are observing in this way the anniversary of my first apparition, which took place in Fatima on the thirteenth of May 1917.

b   You are aware of being spiritually very much united with my Pope, John Paul II, this precious gift which my Immaculate Heart has made to you, who, in these very moments, is in prayer at the Cova da Iria, to thank me for the motherly and extraordinary

684

protection which I gave him, by saving his life, on the occasion of the bloody attempt made upon it, which took place ten years ago in Saint Peter's Square.

c   Today I confirm for you that *this is the Pope of my secret,* the Pope about whom I spoke to the children during the apparitions, the Pope of my love and of my sorrow. With great courage and with superhuman strength, he goes about every part of the world, heedless of the fatigue and the many dangers, in order to confirm all in the faith, and thus he carries out his apostolic ministry as successor of Peter, Vicar of Christ, universal Pastor of the holy Catholic Church, founded on the rock of my Son, Jesus.

d   The Pope gives to all the light of Christ, in these times of great darkness. With vigor, he confirms us in the truth of the faith, in these times of general apostasy. He invites us to walk along the road of love and of peace, in these times of violence, of hatred, of tumult and of war.

e   My Immaculate Heart is wounded in seeing how, all about him, there is an expanding emptiness and indifference; contestation on the part of some of my poor children — bishops, priests, religious and faithful; haughty opposition to his Magisterium. For this reason, my Church is today wounded by a deep division; it is threatened with the loss of the true faith; it is pervaded with an infidelity which is becoming greater and greater.

f   When this Pope will have completed the task which Jesus has entrusted to him and I will come down from heaven to receive his sacrifice, all of you will be cloaked in a dense darkness of apostasy, which will then become general.

g   There will remain faithful only that little remnant which, in these years, by accepting my motherly invitation, has let itself be enfolded in the secure refuge of my Immaculate Heart. And it will be this little faithful remnant, prepared and formed by me, that will have the task of receiving Christ, who will return to you in glory, bringing about in this way the beginning of the new era which awaits you."

The Understanding of the Whole and Entire Truth

a   "Today you are here to observe the liturgical solemnity of Pentecost, in a continual cenacle of brotherhood and of prayer, carried out with me and by means of me. Thus there is renewed the very same reality which took place in the Cenacle of Jerusalem when, under the form of tongues of fire, the Holy Spirit came down upon the Apostles, gathered together in prayer with your heavenly Mother. That was the first Pentecost. That was the beginning of the earthly journey of the Church in the history of humanity.

b   With the extraordinary abundance of his charisms, the Spirit of the Lord has completely transformed the Apostles, from being timid and fearful to being courageous witnesses of Jesus and of his Gospel. With the powerful force of his divine action, He has brought them to *the understanding of the whole and entire truth*, and He has made them into perfect witnesses of Jesus, even to the shedding of blood.

c   You have now entered into the times of the second Pentecost. For this reason, it is necessary that these cenacles be multiplied in every part of the world. I ask that all the Church be gathered together in the spiritual cenacle of my Immaculate Heart. Then the Holy Spirit will bring you *to the understanding of the whole and entire truth*.

d   He will bring you into the secret of the word of God and will give you the light of wisdom to understand all the Gospel and whatever is described in it concerning the times through which you are living. The Holy Spirit will make you understand the signs of your time. They are the times foretold by Holy Scripture as those of the great apostasy and of the coming of the Antichrist. They are times of great tribulation and of innumerable sufferings for all, which will bring you to live through these final events in preparation for the second coming of Jesus in glory.

e   The Holy Spirit gives his perfect witness to Jesus and proclaims Him as the only-begotten Son, coeternal and consubstantial with the Father, He through whom all things have been made, the Incarnate Word, the King of all the universe, who must come again in glory to restore his reign in the world.

f   The Holy Spirit prepares hearts and souls for the second coming of Jesus. For this reason, He is today pouring out his charisms in a manner which is even stronger and more extraordinary than at the time of the beginning of the Church, because you have now entered into the last times, which will lead you to the new era.

g   The task of the Spirit is to prepare humanity for its complete change, to renew the face of creation, to form the new heavens and the new earth. For this reason, I ask you to persevere with

h   fidelity in the cenacles which I have requested of you, and allow the Holy Spirit to mold you with his sweet and powerful action of love. Only thus can you be ready for the great plan which awaits you."

451

Dongo (Como, Italy); June 8, 1991
Feast of the Immaculate Heart of Mary

Apostles of the Last Times

a   "Today you are celebrating the liturgical memorial of my Immaculate Heart. This is your feast, my beloved ones and children consecrated to me.

b   You have been chosen by me and called to form part of my victorious cohort. You form part of my estate. I have a great design upon you. This design of mine has been revealed to you in every detail. It must now appear to the Church and to humanity in all its splendor, because these are the times of your maturity and of your public witness.

c   Show yourselves to all as my consecrated ones, as *the apostles of these last times.*

d   *As apostles of the last times,* you must announce with courage all the truths of the Catholic faith; proclaim the Gospel with force; and resolutely unmask the dangerous heresies which disguise themselves with truth in order to better deceive minds and thus lead astray from the true faith a great number of my children.

e   *As apostles of the last times*, you must withstand with the strength of little ones the proud force of the great and the learned, who, seduced by a false science and by vainglory, have torn to pieces the Gospel of Jesus, by propounding an interpretation of it which is rationalistic, humanistic, and entirely erroneous. The times foretold by Saint Paul have come, times when many announce false and strange doctrines, and thus they go running after these fables and stray away from the truth of the Gospel.

f   *As apostles of the last times*, you must follow Jesus along the road of disdain for the world and for yourselves, of humility, of prayer, of poverty, of silence, of mortification, of charity and of a more profound union with God. You are unknown and despised by the world and by those who surround you; you are often obstructed, marginalized and persecuted, because this suffering is necessary for the fecundity of your very mission.

g   *As apostles of the last times*, you must now illumine the earth with the light of Christ. Show yourselves to all as my children, because I am always with you. Let the faith be the light which illuminates you in these days of apostasy and of great darkness, and, in these times of such a vast infidelity, let it be zeal alone for the glory of my Son Jesus which consumes you.

h   *As apostles of the last times*, there befalls you the duty of carrying out the second evangelization, so much asked for by my Pope, John Paul II. Evangelize the Church, which has strayed from the spirit of Christ and has allowed itself to be seduced by the spirit of the world, which has penetrated it deeply and has pervaded it entirely. Evangelize humanity, which has again become pagan after almost two thousand years since the first announcement of the Gospel. Evangelize all men, who have become victims of errors, of evil, and of sin and who let themselves be swept away by the impetuous wind of all the false ideologies. Evangelize the peoples and the nations of the earth, immersed in the darkness of the practical denial of God, as they prostrate themselves in the worship of pleasure, of money, of power, of pride and of impurity.

i   Your times have come, and I have formed you during these years, so that you may be able to give now your strong witness as *faithful disciples of Jesus*, even to the shedding of your very own blood.

688

j   When, from every part of the earth, all of you, my little children, will give this witness as *apostles of the last times*, then my Immaculate Heart will have its greatest triumph."

452
Valdragone (San Marino); June 26, 1991
Spiritual Exercises in the Form of a Cenacle
with the Priests of the M.M.P. from America and Europe

In You I Manifest Myself

a   "Beloved sons, again this year I have called you up here on this mountain, to spend a week of continuous cenacle together with me. And you have responded in so generous a way. You have come from every part of Europe and from many countries of America, offering me the discomfort of long and tiring journeys.

b   I am with you always. I unite myself to your prayer; I am building up among you a more perfect brotherhood. I help you to know one another, to understand one another, to love one another, and to go forward together on the painful road of these last times.

c   Why have I again wanted you here? Because the times have arrived in which I wish to manifest myself through you to the Church and to the whole of humanity.

d   *In you I manifest myself as Leader* of my cohort, formed by me in every part of the world, to fight against the great army of the enemies of God under the orders of him who opposes himself to Christ, that is, of the Antichrist. My cohort is made up of the little ones, of the poor, of the humble servants of the Lord whom I call to enter into the cenacle of my Immaculate Heart, so that they may receive in fullness the gift of the Holy Spirit. It is in the hearts and the souls of the littlest ones that I am working my greatest prodigies in these years. For this reason I have wanted you here again: to form you all to littleness, to spiritual childhood, to poverty, to humility, because it is with the weakness of the little ones that I will conquer the proud power of the great.

e   *In you I manifest myself as Queen*, because it is by means of you that each day I am bringing about the triumph of my Immaculate Heart in the world. Open the doors of your lives, so that I can reign in you and prepare the way for the glorious reign of Christ.

f   I am the dawn that announces the arrival of the great day of the Lord.

g   *In you I manifest myself as Prophetess* of these last times. This is why I speak to you. Because I know that I am listened to, obeyed and followed by you, my sons. So, I still continue to manifest myself through the messages which I am giving to the heart of this, my littlest son. Believe in my word. Receive with docility these messages of mine because, in them, everything has already been said to you about that which awaits you.

h   *In you I manifest myself as a tender and merciful Mother,* in these painful hours of the purification and of the great tribulation. You are called to be the instruments of my motherly tenderness. Love everyone with my motherly Heart. For this, I want to manifest myself in you more and more. Because, in you, I want to console those who suffer, to support those who are weak, to lift up those who have fallen, to lead back to the Lord those who have strayed, to convert sinners, to heal the sick, and to give hope to all who have lost their confidence. Be my sweet balm which comes down to soothe the great sufferings of so many of my children.

i   Walk along the road which I have traced out for you in these years. Show yourselves to everyone as my children, as those who are consecrated to me, because I am always with you. Live in contempt for the world and for yourselves. Let the faith be the only light which enlightens you in these times of great darkness. Let zeal for the glory of God be the only thing which consumes you, in these days of such widespread aridity. You are called to be the new heart of the new Church which Jesus is forming, in a wholly mysterious way, in the heavenly garden of my Immaculate Heart.

j   I thank you for the comfort which you give, in these days, to the great sorrow of my Immaculate Heart. With those dear to you, and with the souls who are entrusted to you, I bless you in the name of the Father, and of the Son, and of the Holy Spirit."

690

Rubbio (Vicenza, Italy);August 15, 1991
Solemnity of the Assumption
of the Blessed Virgin Mary into Heaven

The New Era

a   "Today, beloved sons, contemplate me in the splendor of my glorified body, assumed into the glory of paradise. Live in joy and confidence the last times of this, your second Advent, by looking to me as to the sign of sure hope and of consolation.

b   *The new era,* which awaits you, corresponds to a particular encounter of love, of light and of life between paradise, where I am in perfect blessedness with the angels and the saints, and earth, where you, my children, live in the midst of many dangers and innumerable tribulations. This is the heavenly Jerusalem, which comes down from heaven upon earth, to transform it completely and to thus shape the new heavens and the new earth.

c   *The new era,* toward which you are journeying, is bringing all creation to the perfect glorification of the Most Holy Trinity. The Father receives his greatest glory from every creature which reflects his light, his love and his divine splendor. The Son restores his reign of grace and of holiness, setting free every creature from the slavery of evil and of sin. The Holy Spirit pours out in fullness his holy gifts, leads to the understanding of the whole truth, and renews the face of the earth.

d   *The new era,* which I announce to you, coincides with the complete fulfillment of the divine Will, so that at last there is coming about that which Jesus taught you to ask for, from the Heavenly Father:'Your Will be done, on earth as it is in heaven.' (Mt 6:10) This is the time when the divine Will of the Father, of the Son and of the Holy Spirit is being accomplished by the creatures. From the perfect fulfillment of the divine Will, the whole world is becoming renewed, because God finds there, as it were, his new garden of Eden, where He can dwell in loving companionship with his creatures.

e   *The new era,* which is just now beginning, brings you to a full communion of life with those who have preceded you and who, here in paradise, enjoy perfect happiness. You see the splendor of the heavenly hierarchy; you communicate with the saints of paradise; you relieve the purifying sufferings of the souls who are still in purgatory. You experience, in a strong and visible way, the consoling truth of the communion of saints.

f   *The new era,* which I am preparing for you, coincides with the defeat of Satan and of his universal reign. All his power is destroyed. He is bound, with all the wicked spirits, and shut up in hell from which he will not be able to get out to do harm in the world. Herein, Christ reigns in the splendor of his glorified body, and the Immaculate Heart of your heavenly Mother triumphs in the light of her body, assumed into the glory of paradise.

g   This feast of mine, which bids you to look to your heavenly Mother, assumed into heaven, thus becomes for you a reason for deep joy and great confidence.

h   In the midst of the innumerable sufferings of the times through which you are living, you look upon me as a sign of sure hope and of consolation, because I am the luminous door which opens upon the new era that has been prepared for you by the Most Holy Trinity."

454   *Olomouc (Moravia, Czechoslovakia); September 3, 1991*
Spiritual Exercises in the Form of a Cenacle
with the Priests of the M.M.P. from Czechoslovakia

Apostles of the New Era

a   "How happy I am, my beloved sons, to see you in such great numbers at this retreat, which you are making in the form of a continuous cenacle. You have come from Moravia, Bohemia, and Slovakia to live days of intense prayer and of great brotherhood, in the company of your heavenly Mother. I am always with you.

b   As it was in the Cenacle of Jerusalem, so also in this cenacle of yours, I am uniting myself with your prayer; I am building up among you a greater capacity for understanding; I am helping you to walk along the way of your mutual love, so that the new commandment which my Son Jesus has given you —'Love one another as I have loved you.' (Jn 15:12) — may be more and more lived by you.

692

c   You have emerged from a painful and very burdensome trial. After many years of harsh communist slavery, I have obtained for you the grace of your liberation, as I had already foretold to you.

d   Now I am asking you to become *the apostles of the new era*, which is awaiting you. For this, I am forming a new heart in you, so that you may know how to love everyone with my maternal and merciful love. Do not be looking at some of those among you who, through weakness, have descended to compromise with my Adversary, who has now been defeated. Do not bear any resentment toward them. The past is now canceled out. You are now called to live this new time, and new tasks are awaiting you.

e   — *There awaits you the task of rebuilding the Church*, here where it has been so persecuted and violated by my Adversary. For this, I urge you to be ever faithful priests, witnesses of unity and of love for the Pope and for your bishops. Exercise your ministry with joy and with enthusiasm; give to all the light of Christ and of his Gospel; be ministers of grace and of holiness. Thus, by means of you, the Church will begin again to shine forth with great light for all those who live in this country of yours.

f   — *There awaits you the task of evangelizing this poor humanity*, which has been so deceived and seduced by the spirit of Evil. Think of the great number of my children — above all, the young — who have been formed for years in the school of the denial of God and of the rejection of his Law of love. They are little sheep snatched from the flock of your divine Shepherd and led astray along the way of evil, of sin and of unhappiness. Take them up in your priestly arms, these straying children of mine, and carry them all into the safe sheepfold of my Immaculate Heart. Be therefore persevering in your ministry of catechesis, giving the light of the truth which Christ has revealed to you, in order to help all to remain in the true faith. In this way, you accomplish the task of this second evangelization, so very much demanded by the first of my beloved sons, Pope John Paul II.

g   *There awaits you the task of causing the sweet balm of my motherly tenderness to come down* upon so many open and bleeding wounds. See how numerous are the poor, those far away, the sinners, the unhappy, the stricken, the downtrodden, the discouraged, the abandoned, the lonely, the desperate. You must be an expression of my love and my motherly concern. Love all with the strength of your priestly heart and with the light which is given you by your heavenly Mother.

h If you carry out this task which I am entrusting to you today, you become truly *the apostles of the new era*, which I have already initiated here.

i Leave this cenacle with joy, with confidence and with great hope. I am always with you. You are a precious part of my motherly property. With your dear ones and with the souls entrusted to you, I bless you in the name of the Father, and of the Son, and of the Holy Spirit."

455 *Velehrad (Bohemia, Czechoslovakia); September 8, 1991*
Feast of the Nativity of the Blessed Virgin Mary

The Crown of the Slavic Peoples

a "Today I have wanted you here to celebrate the day of my nativity, with a cenacle which you are holding in this important shrine, where I am venerated, along with the memory of the two great Slavic apostles, Saint Cyril and Saint Methodius. You are meeting many priests and faithful, who have also come from afar, to spend this day in continuous prayer with the heavenly Mother and to renew together your consecration to my Immaculate Heart.

b Bring to me, as a filial gift, about the crib where I am placed on the day of my birth, *the crown of the Slavic peoples*. With it, adorn and make fragrant, with love and with trust, this day of my birth. From this, my venerated shrine, I bless you today, O Slavic peoples, who are particularly loved and protected by me, especially in these times, during which I have been close to you.

c — *I have always been close to you*, in the long years of your harsh and bloody slavery. The Red Dragon had been exerting all his power over you, setting everywhere, in blood and in tears, the seal of his cruel reign. But I have obtained from the Lord the great grace of your liberation.

d — *I have always been close to you*, in the decisive moments when communism was forever defeated by you, and I have personally intervened in order that this changeover take place without fratricidal struggles, without the shedding of blood and without further acts of destruction.

e   — *I am now particularly close to you,* to help you walk along the road of true liberty, in the faithful fulfillment of your baptismal promises, and in a daily commitment to follow Jesus along the way of the grace of God, of love, of purity, of communion and of brotherhood.

f   Let the wounds of the past be closed forever and open yourselves upon the new times which await you. All Europe must become one great single family, faithful to Christ and to his Church, in one effort of conversion and of return to the Lord, so that the most dangerous enemy of practical atheism, of hedonism, of impurity and of impiety be defeated by you. As your great teachers and patrons, Cyril and Methodius, have brought you the first evangelization, so also all of you, my beloved ones and children consecrated to me, are now being called to be the apostles of this second evangelization.

g   Be in peace and in joy; live in confidence and in great hope. I am always with you.

h   From this place, together with Saints Cyril and Methodius, I bless today all the Slavic peoples and this new Europe, completely renewed, which I am forming each day in the heavenly garden of my Immaculate Heart."

456   Sastin (Slovakia, Czechoslovakia); September 12, 1991
Cenacle held at the National Shrine of Slovakia

In the Name of Mary

a   "Today, my dearest son, on the feast of the venerated name of your heavenly Mother, you are bringing to a close your journey, so extraordinary for its graces, with a great cenacle which you are holding for the priests and the faithful, in this great national shrine, dedicated to the memory of my sorrows.

b   You have seen everywhere a most generous response, on the part of all, to my request for prayer and for consecration. Especially, you have been astounded, because you have come here for the first time and have found my Marian Movement of Priests so widely spread, received and followed. This is my work alone, and I myself am furthering it in every part of the world, because these are the times of my triumph, of my victory and of your salvation.

c   — In the name of your heavenly Mother, yes, *in the name of Mary*, the Turks were defeated, when they laid siege to the city of Vienna and threatened to invade and destroy the whole Christian world. They were far superior in strength, in numbers and in weapons, and they felt that their victory was assured. But I was publicly invoked and called upon; my name was inscribed upon their banners and shouted out by the soldiers, and thus through my intercession, there took place the miracle of this victory which saved the Christian world from its destruction. It is for this reason that the Pope instituted, on this day, the feast of the Name of Mary.

d   — *In the name of Mary*, Marxist communism, which for decades had been exercising its rule and holding so many of my poor children in oppressive and bloody slavery, has been defeated in these countries. Not because of political movements or persons, but through my personal intervention, has your liberation finally come about.

e   It will again be *in the name of Mary* that I will bring to completion my work with the defeat of Masonry, of every diabolical force, of materialism, and of practical atheism, so that all humanity will be able to attain its encounter with the Lord and be thus purified and completely renewed, with the triumph of my Immaculate Heart in the world.

f   It is for this reason that I desire that the feast in honor of the name of Mary be restored, now that you are entering into the fiercest moments of the struggle and the most painful stage of the great tribulation.

g   From this, my shrine, I look with love upon those countries which have still preserved the feast of the name of your heavenly Mother, and I promise them my special and motherly protection. In particular, I bless this land of Slovakia, where I am so loved, venerated and more and more glorified."

457

Budapest (Hungary); September 15, 1991
Feast of Our Lady of Sorrows

Great Is My Sorrow

a   "Today you find yourself here in order to hold two great cenacles with the priests and the faithful of my Movement in Hungary.

b   You see the deep wounds left by so many years of harsh communist oppression. But with joy you are able to contemplate the new buds which have sprouted from so much suffering, and today you are gathering them up in the heavenly garden of my Immaculate Heart.

c   Give to all the balm of my motherly tenderness. Make it felt how great my motherly love is for them.

d   Here, I have personally intervened to bring these children of mine along the road of their liberation from a great slavery.

e   But *great is my sorrow* in seeing that all humanity is still a slave to materialism, to practical atheism, to hedonism, to rebellion, to hatred and to impurity.

f   *Great is my sorrow* because my motherly and anguished calls for conversion and for a return to the Lord are not being listened to or followed.

g   For this reason, I turn again to you, my beloved ones and children consecrated to me, and I ask you to offer to the Lord your life of prayer and of suffering, in a spirit of love and of reparation, for the salvation of this poor humanity, which is rushing along the road of its own destruction.

h   Thus, by means of you, I am able to continue my motherly work of mercy, which I have begun in these countries, but which I must still bring to completion in every part of the world, for the triumph of my Immaculate Heart."

458
Birkenhead (England); October 13, 1991
Anniversary of the Last Apparition at Fatima

The Great Sign in Heaven

a   "Look to me, beloved sons and you who are consecrated to me, in the great battle which you are fighting, under the orders of your heavenly Leader. I am the Woman Clothed with the Sun.

b   *I am the great sign which appears in heaven.*

c   Today you are calling to mind my last apparition, which took place in Fatima in the Cova da Iria and which was confirmed by the miracle of the sun. This miracle shows you, in an extraordinary way, that I am the Woman Clothed with the Sun. This miracle invites you to look to me as to the great sign which appears in heaven.

d   *I am a great sign of battle* between me and my Adversary, between the Woman and the Dragon, between my army and the army guided by the enemy of God. You are entering into the decisive times of the battle.

e   You are preparing to live through the most difficult hours and the greatest of sufferings. It is necessary that all of you come as quickly as possible to form part of my army. For this, I again invite my children to consecrate themselves to my Immaculate Heart and to entrust themselves to me as little children.

f   Today, I am extending this invitation of mine, above all, to the little ones, to the poor, to those who are least, to the sick and to the sinners. Come, all of you, to fight beneath the sign of your immaculate Mother, because it is with the weakness of the little ones, with the trust of the poor and with the suffering of the sick that I am today fighting my great battle.

g   *I am a great sign of victory.*

h   I am the victorious Woman. In the end, the power of Satan will be destroyed; and I myself will bind him with my chain; and I will shut him up within his kingdom of death and of eternal torment, from which he will not be able to get out.

i   In the world, there will reign the one and only Conqueror of sin and of death, the King of the entire created universe, Jesus Christ.

j   Let yourselves be now signed with my seal.

k   In these times, the angels of light are going about the world to mark, with the sign of the Cross, all those who form part of my victorious army. Against these, the Star of the Abyss will have no power, even if they will be called to great sufferings and some to shed their own blood.

l   But it will be with the great sufferings of these children of mine that I will obtain my greatest victory.

m   Today, I am inviting you to look to me, *as to the great sign which is appearing in heaven,* in order to live in trust and in serenity, as you are enlightened by my own light and signed by my motherly seal."

698

459 Birmingham (England); October 16, 1991
Spiritual Exercises in the Form of a Cenacle
with the Priests of the M.M.P. from Ireland and Great Britain

The Gift Which I Am Making to the Church

a   "I look upon you with motherly tenderness, my beloved sons, priests of my Movement, who have come from every part of Ireland and Great Britain in order to live these days of retreat, in the form of a continuous cenacle.

b   The great sorrow of my Immaculate Heart is consoled by you, and many of its wounds are closed by the sweet balm of your filial love. I am always with you. I unite myself to your prayer; I am building up amongst you a greater capacity for communion and mutual love; I am giving you peace of heart and the joy of being, today, priests of my Son Jesus. I want to make you into instruments of my motherly tenderness; the apostles of my triumph; *the gift which I am making to the Church,* in these times of her purification and her great tribulation.

c   *It is above all a gift of love and of mercy.*

d   You see, my beloved sons, how great is her abandonment, how deep her desolation!

e   The Church is today climbing Calvary, bearing a heavy cross. The spirit of the world has penetrated into her interior and has spread everywhere. How many are the priestly and religious lives dried up by secularism, which has possessed them completely.

f   The faith, in many of them, has been extinguished, because of the errors which are increasingly taught and followed; the life of grace has been buried by sins which are committed, justified and no longer confessed. Their hearts have become enslaved by many disordered passions and no longer have the capacity to feel joy and peace.

g   You, O priests consecrated to my Immaculate Heart, be the expression of my motherly love and my great mercy. Love these brothers of yours by good example, by prayer, by advice and by welcoming with love, for them, all the sufferings which the Heavenly Father sends you.

h   Then the whole Church will feel the comfort which the heavenly Mother is giving her through you, and in this way she will be helped to carry her great cross towards Calvary.

i *It is also a gift of consolation and of hope.*

j Through you, the Church will feel, in an increasingly power-ful way, the presence of the heavenly Mother. And the presence of the Mother will bring to the Church the grace of her total renewal, causing her finally to emerge from the long night in which she finds herself, towards the bright day of the new times which are about to come. Thus the Church will be consoled at seeing the faith again flourishing everywhere, hope being re-newed, charity expanding and a great holiness spreading.

k You, O beloved sons, be the flowers which come to maturity on the tree of your life of consecration to my Immaculate Heart, in order to cause the heavenly dew of hope and of my motherly consolation to come down upon the immense desert of today.

l *It is above all a gift of salvation.*

m How many are my children today who run the risk of being lost! How numerous are those far off, the atheists, the sinners, the victims of evil, of egoism, of violence and of hatred!

n Look at the millions of innocent babies who are being killed in the wombs of their mothers; at the young people set upon the evil experience of impurity and drugs; at the families which have been destroyed; at the sick, the poor, the abandoned and those in desperation.

o Through you, my beloved ones, my tender and anxious moth-erly help must come to all of them, to bring them to salvation. Gather up with your priestly hands these fallen, lost and scat-tered children of mine, and bring them all into the motherly sheepfold of my Immaculate Heart.

p Be light and security for all those who form part of other Christian confessions, and point out the harbor into which they must enter in order to fulfill the Will of my Son Jesus: the holy and Catholic Church, which has the Pope as its foundation and sure guide.

q I confirm to you that, after the triumph of my Immaculate Heart, there will remain, in these countries of yours, solely this one and only true Church.

r Leave this cenacle with joy. I am with you. Bear everywhere the charism of my presence and the light of my glory.

s With those who are dear to you, with all the souls who are entrusted to you, I bless you in the name of the Father, and of the Son, and of the Holy Spirit."

460

In the Temple of My Immaculate Heart

a "Beloved children, live on this day the joyful mystery of my presentation in the temple of the Lord. This is a mystery of silence, of offering, of prayer and of personal immolation. As a sweet and immaculate victim of love, I am offered to the worship of my Lord. I now belong to Him forever, rejoicing to put myself at his service, in prayer and in silence, for his greatest glory.

b For all of you also, O children who have consecrated yourselves to me, the hour has now arrived to enter *into the temple of my Immaculate Heart.*

c — *In the temple of my Immaculate Heart,* I am forming you more and more to a deep silence. In these times, when my Adversary is succeeding in seducing humanity with words, and the din of voices and of images is turning the world into a new Tower of Babel, you are being called to give a witness of deep silence: silence in order to receive only the word of God, silence to meditate on it in the heart and to keep it with love, silence to live it and give it to all in the light of its integrity. And thus you speak with life. Life becomes your word. And thirsting souls receive it like a heavenly dew, which comes down to give light and life on the immense desert of such a great aridity.

d — *In the temple of my Immaculate Heart,* I am preparing you for your priestly offering. In these times of the great tribulation, you are being called to carry the burden of a very heavy cross. How many sufferings await you! So then, you must prepare yourselves for your priestly offering, as a token of reparation and expiation for the salvation of many of my poor lost children. Offer your whole life to the Lord: your body, your heart, your soul, your mind, your will, your freedom. In this way, you become the chosen victims, precious and pleasing to God, which I can offer to Him, so that the times of the great trial may be shortened.

e — *In the temple of my Immaculate Heart,* I am calling you to a continuous prayer. Pray, my beloved children. I want so much prayer of you! Transform your day into an act of unceasing prayer. Be a good example of prayer to all. Pray with the prayer of the heart. Pray with abandonment, with confidence, with perseverance. Such difficult and dangerous moments are drawing close that only those can be saved who accept my invitation to pray always with me.

f — *In the temple of my Immaculate Heart,* I am preparing you for your priestly immolation. There is a spiritual immolation which I am asking of everyone. It is made up of the acceptance, with love, of every circumstance of your life as a fulfillment of the Will of the Heavenly Father. Do always and at every moment only the divine Will. Then the Father will be pleased with you, who are giving to the Son the joy of doing, in you, only the Will of the Father. There is also a physical immolation for which I am preparing you gently, as Mother, who is making of her Immaculate Heart, in which you are enclosed, the altar upon which you will be immolated for the salvation of the world.

g Do not be troubled. The powerful times of the purification, of the great tribulation and of the apostasy have arrived. For this reason, I invite you all today to enter into the temple of my Immaculate Heart, so that I may offer you to the perfect glorification of the Most Holy Trinity."

461

Milan (Italy); December 8, 1991
Solemnity of the Immaculate Conception

The Gate Which Opens

a "Rejoice, beloved children, with all Paradise which today contemplates, in the divine light of the Most Holy Trinity, the splendor of your heavenly Mother. I am the Immaculate Conception. I am the most pure reflection of the light, the love and the holiness of God. I am all beautiful: tota pulchra. Only thus have I been able to be ready to fulfill my virginal and maternal purpose of being the Gate of Heaven: Janua Coeli.

b — *I am the Gate which opens to hope.* At the very moment when all humanity, in the sin committed by the first parents, knows the hour of defeat and of death because of the victory of the serpent, I am prophesied as *Gate* which opens to allow hope to descend upon the world. — 'I will put enmity between you and the Woman, between your offspring and hers. She will crush your head, while you strike at her heel.' (Gen 3:15)

c — *I am the Gate which opens to my greatest gift,* when, with my maternal collaboration, the Redeemer, your Savior, comes to you at the moment of the birth of my Son Jesus. It is He, my victorious offspring, who will crush forever the head of the serpent and bring about his definitive victory over Satan, over evil and over death. I am the Mother of the First Advent, because I am the Gate of Heaven, through which Jesus passes to come to you in the fragility and the humility of human nature.

d — *I am the Gate which opens upon your salvation* because, through it, every one of you must pass to arrive at your personal encounter with the Lord. For this, my Son Jesus has constituted me true Mother of all humanity. Only if you pass through this, my Gate, can you gain entrance into the heavenly garden of mortification and penance, of faith and prayer, of humility and purity, of charity and sanctity. And in this, my maternal estate, Jesus has, each day, the great joy of meeting you. Jesus communicates Himself to you with his grace; He enlightens you with his word; He assimilates you through his real Eucharistic presence; He fills your soul with his divine splendor; He brings your hearts to the fullness of joy and peace.

e — *I am the Gate which opens upon the new era,* which awaits you and which is just now coming upon the world. For this reason, in your times, I am called to be the Mother of the Second Advent. Just as, by means of me, Jesus has come to you in the fragility and humility of his human nature, so too, again by means of me, Jesus will return to you in the splendor of his glory, to restore his kingdom in the world.

f My presence in your midst must now become more and more powerful, continuous and extraordinary. With it, I want to announce to you that you must lift up your heads from the heavy yoke of the great tribulation through which you are living, because your deliverance is at hand.

g I am the Gate which opens on the new times which await you. Enter, all of you, into my Immaculate Heart, with your consecration; in this time of your second Advent, keep watch in prayer and with confidence, and await with lighted torches, within the Gate of Heaven of your heavenly Mother, the approaching return of the Lord Jesus in glory."

462
Dongo (Como, Italy); December 24, 1991
The Holy Night

The Bright Cave

a "Live with me, beloved children, the mystery of love and light of this, your Christmas. I want to take you with me on the long journey which led us to Bethlehem.

b I was absorbed in a continuous ecstasy of love with the divine Child, whom I was carrying in my virginal womb, comforted by the precious assistance of my most chaste spouse, Joseph, who devoted himself so completely to making the wearying journey less burdensome. Thus an interior silence surrounded our presence in the midst of a noisy caravan. And the deep prayer of the heart marked the slow flow of our approach to our goal. And a tranquil peace of soul descended upon the calm unfolding of time, in a loving knowledge of the great mystery which was now about to take place.

c When we arrived in Bethlehem and every door was closed upon our request for hospitality for that night, there was pointed out to us by some shepherds a poor cave which, for all its squalor, was ready to welcome us.

d This is the holy night. This is the night which brings to an end the expectation of the centuries. This is the night which is opened to the Light and brings to an end forever the time of the first Advent. This is the night which brings to a beginning the new day which knows no setting.

e In this night, heaven is espoused to earth; the song of the angels blends with the voices of the little ones, of the poor, of the pure; to the shepherds is given the announcement which gives joy to all: 'Today is born for you a Savior.' (cf. Lk 2:11)

704

f Bow down, together with me, to cover the Child with kisses and tears, with warmth and love, with sweet and affectionate tenderness. He is so little; He is just born; He cries because of the sharpness of the cold; He wails because of the great coldness which enfolds the whole world. Like the shepherds, you too, bring Him simple gifts. Your priestly heart, filled with love, becomes for Him his one great comfort.

g And do you also welcome the great announcement of joy that is given to you today: his second birth in glory is close at hand. You too are traveling along the last stage of a long journey. You too are coming to the end of the time of the second Advent. So therefore, live with me and with my spouse, Joseph, the precious hours of this new vigil.

h Let a deep silence surround the great noise of words and of images, which today is filling the whole world. Let the prayer of the heart bring you to a continuous loving dialogue with the Lord Jesus who has come, who comes and who will come in glory. And let the tranquil peace of the soul mark the passing of your days, so threatening and thick with sorrows for all.

i Go forward safely on the tempestuous waves of these last times of the great tribulation, without becoming troubled at seeing that the doors are still closing to Jesus Christ, who is coming.

j My Immaculate Heart is the *bright cave*, which brings to an end this second Advent, because it is with its triumph that Jesus will return to you in glory."

463 *Rubbio (Vicenza, Italy); December 31, 1991*
Last Night of the Year

Prostrate Yourselves with Me

a "Beloved children, keep watch with me in prayer and in recollection. Spend thus the last hours of this year, which has been marked by grave and important events, for the destiny of all humanity.

b *Prostrate yourselves with me in an act of profound adoration* before the Eucharistic Jesus. His real presence among you in the Eucharist, kept with love in all the tabernacles of the earth, is a light upon your path; it is a comfort for all your weariness; it is a balm upon every wound; it is a joy in all your sorrows; it is peace which calms every anxiety; it is the dawn which marks the beginning of each new day of your human life.

c   *Prostrate yourselves with me in an act of fervent thanksgiving* for all the favors that have been given you, by the love and the providence of your Heavenly Father. It is the Father who arranges for you every minute of your life, as an expression of his love and of his divine mercy. You are living within time, in order to bring to realization a great loving plan of his. Even when you draw away from Him, He never abandons you, but prepares for, awaits and brings to completion your every return. His divine mercy is a heavenly dew which comes down to make fertile the great dryness of this world and to make the desert, in which you live, blossom with holiness and with life.

d   You are now entering into the times when the miracle of divine mercy will become manifest to all. See how humanity lies prostrate and wounded, lacerated and defeated, threatened and stricken, diseased and dying. Of itself it can no longer rise again, unless a great mercy lift it up.

e   The moment is at hand when the Heavenly Father will take it up in his arms, will relieve it of evil, will heal it and bring it with Him into his delightful garden.

f   *Prostate yourselves with me in an act of intense reparation* for the innumerable offenses committed against the Spirit of the Father and of the Son, who groans within you with unutterable groanings. How much evil is still committed each day in the world! The Law of God is openly violated; his name is blasphemed; his day is profaned. The value of life is no longer respected; the number of abortions grows greater and greater; homicides and crimes, hatred and violence, spread; cruel and bloody wars suddenly break out, threatening the peace of all humanity.

g   How numerous are the sins against the Holy Spirit, which are being committed today! Let us pray together, with humility and trust, to invoke the gift of the Holy Spirit that He come down, as a dew, to purify the earth and to renew the whole world.

h   Do not spend the last hours of this year in noise and dissipation. *Prostrate yourselves with me* in a prayer of adoration, of thanksgiving and of reparation, to obtain from the Father, from the Son and from the Holy Spirit that there may be a shortening of the time of the great tribulation in which you are now living, in order to enter into the new era which now awaits you."

1992

YOUR LIBERATION IS NEAR

Your Liberation Is Near

a   "Today I invite you to lift up your eyes to me, beloved sons, because *your liberation is near.* You are entering into the decisive times which are leading you to the triumph of my Immaculate Heart in the world.

b   Events are rapidly following one upon the other, and the new year, which you are beginning today, will bring to fulfillment that which I have revealed to you in some of my secrets.

c   The activity of my Adversary, to extend his reign over all humanity, will become stronger. Thus evil and sin, violence and hatred, perversion and unbelief will increase everywhere. Wars will spread, involving additional peoples and nations, and many of my poor children will have to carry the heavy burden of this bloody cross.

d   But have confidence. Lift up your eyes to me, Mother of God and your true Mother. *Today I announce to you that your liberation is near.*

e   Even in the Church, the darkness will descend more densely yet and will succeed in enveloping everything. Errors will spread much more, and many will wander away from the true faith. Apostasy will spread like an epidemic, and pastors will be stricken by it along with the flocks entrusted to them. In every part of the earth, the Church, this poor agonizing and crucified Daughter of mine, will have much to suffer.

f   The contestation directed against the Pope will become stronger: theologians, bishops, priests and laity will openly oppose his Magisterium. My Pope will feel himself more and more alone, as he is abandoned, criticized and ridiculed by many.

g   But have great confidence and patience. Be strong in faith and in hope. Lift up your eyes to me, Mother of God and your true Mother. *Today I announce to you that your liberation is near.*

h   Come out from your hiding, my beloved sons, and go everywhere to enlighten the earth with the sole light of Christ. Your times have arrived. Do not be afraid if you are unknown to the world, if you are despised, rejected and persecuted. I am always

with you. Show yourselves to all as my beloved sons, my consecrated ones, the apostles of these last times whom I, for twenty
years now, have been forming, with the messages which I give
by means of this littlest of my sons.

i   Walk along the road of contempt for the world and for yourselves, of humility and littleness, of love and purity. In this way
you become Good Samaritans for the Church of today which is
suffering so much. Love always; judge no one. Assist all with the
tenderness of your priestly love.

j   Be united to the Pope in order to support him in carrying his
great cross to Calvary.

k   Set out upon all the roads of the world, in search of my poor
straying children. Take up in your priestly arms the poor, the
sick, the desperate, the abandoned, the stricken, the oppressed,
and all the innumerable victims of violence, of hatred and of
wars. Carry them all into the safe refuge of my Immaculate
Heart.

l   Lift up your eyes from this dark epoch in which you are living,
and do not fear if, at present, Satan is the uncontested ruler of the
world and the master of all humanity. Soon his reign will be
reduced to a heap of ruins, and his power will be destroyed, because I myself will bind him with a chain and will shut him up
in his pool of eternal fire and death, from which he will no longer
be able to get out.

m   And it will be Jesus Christ, King of eternal glory, who will
reign over the whole renewed world and thus bring about the
beginning of the new times, which are on the point of arriving.

n   For this reason, I repeat to you at the beginning of this new
year: have confidence. Live each day in faith and in a great hope.
Lift up your eyes to me, Mother of God and your true Mother.

o   *Today I announce to you that your liberation is near.*"

465   *San Salvador (El Salvador); February 2, 1992*
Feast of the Presentation of the Child Jesus

To Meet the Lord Who Is Coming

a   "Beloved children, come with me, your heavenly Mother, *to
meet the Lord who is coming.*

b   Let yourselves be carried in my motherly arms as, with love and immense happiness, I carried the Child Jesus to the temple of Jerusalem. Today, in the liturgical celebration, you are reliving this mystery.

c   And you, my little child, find yourself this day carrying out your cenacles in this country which has been, for many years, divided, wounded and stricken by a bloody and cruel civil war. And precisely on this day, I have given it the precious possession of peace.

d   — *Come with me to meet the Lord who is coming in peace.* Jesus is your peace. He brings you to communion with the Heavenly Father in his Spirit of Love, and He gives you his very own divine life which He has merited for you on Calvary, by the Sacrifice of redemption.

e   This world does not know peace because it does not accept Jesus. And so my motherly task is that of opening the hearts of all my children, to receive the Lord who is coming, because only then can peace, so implored and awaited, come upon the world.

f   — *Come with me to meet the Lord who is coming in love.* This humanity lies prostrate beneath the heavy yoke of violence, hatred, unbridled egoism, division and war. How many people suffer; how many are trampled upon and are oppressed and killed each day, because of this so great incapacity to love! Thus the world has been reduced to an immense desert, and the hearts of men have become cold and cruel, insensitive and closed to the needs of the little ones, of the poor and of the destitute.

g   This world is not capable of loving because it does not accept Jesus. Jesus is Love. Jesus, who is coming, will bring all to the perfection of love. And then the world will become a new garden of life and of beauty and will form one single family, united by the sweet bonds of divine charity.

h   — *Come with me to meet the Lord who is coming in joy.* Only Jesus in your midst can open your hearts to the sweet experience of blessedness and joy.

i   Forget the bloody past. Let the deep wounds of this painful time of the purification and the great tribulation be closed, because your liberation is near.

j   For this reason, on this day, as you contemplate me in the mystery of the presentation of my Child Jesus in the temple, I invite you to let yourselves be carried in my arms, into the spiritual temple of my Immaculate Heart, that I may offer you to the glory of the Most Holy Trinity and thus lead you toward the new times which await you."

466

Managua (Nicaragua); February 11, 1992
Feast of Our Lady of Lourdes

I Set You Free from Slavery

a   "I am the Immaculate Conception. With these words I revealed myself to my little daughter, Bernadette, appearing to her in the Grotto of Lourdes. I am the cause of your joy.

b   Today, my little son, you find yourself here in this country of Central America, where I am especially loved, entreated and glorified by these children of mine. You have heard how they repeat often this cry which is an expression of their faith and of their love: 'Who is it that causes us such jubilation? It is Mary's virginal conception!'

c   During these last years, the Church here has been particularly tested and stricken, and also these little children of mine have had to carry the weight of a harsh slavery, imposed by an atheistic and communistic regime. But I have heard their prayers; I have taken heed of their profound sufferings, and I have personally intervened to set them free from this slavery.

d   I now promise to give to this people of mine who have been consecrated to me, and to this land which has been entrusted to me, the great gift of peace.

e   Hasten in the wake of the sweet fragrance of your immaculate Mother; thus, you are set free from the yoke of every slavery.

f   — *I set you free from the slavery of sin* which keeps you under the dominion of Satan, and I am leading you each day to live as free children of God.

g   — *I set you free from the slavery of disordinate passions,* especially that of impurity, to make you walk along the way of holiness

713

and of chastity.

h   — *I set you free from the slavery of egoism and hatred* to make you live in love and communion with all.

i   — *I set you free from the slavery of political regimes* which are founded on the denial of God and on atheism which is proclaimed and propagated, so that I may prepare you to live as a new people of God which is opening itself to the perfect worship of his glory.

j   — *I set you free from the slavery of these evil times of yours* to dispose you to enter into the new times which are now drawing near. For this, I am inviting you today to walk in the wake of the sweet fragrance of your immaculate Mother, in order to arrive quickly at the safe haven of your liberation.

k   I bless with love this land of Nicaragua and all my children who love me here, who honor me and who invoke me with such confidence and such hope."

467
Quito (Ecuador); February 27, 1992
Spiritual Exercises in the Form of a Cenacle
with the Priests of the M.M.P. from Latin America

Mother of the Second Evangelization

a   "How happy I am, beloved sons, with this cenacle of prayer and brotherly sharing which, during these days, you are carrying out with me, your heavenly Mother. I am always with you. I unite myself to your prayer, and I strengthen the bond of your brotherhood.

b   This year, you are celebrating the fifth centenary of the evangelization of Latin America. I have called you to this cenacle because I desire to communicate to you the love, the apprehensions and the designs which my Immaculate Heart has on this land, blessed by me and so ensnared and stricken by my Adversary.

c   — In the first place, I tell you of *my great joy* in feeling myself so loved here by my children, especially the little ones, the poor, the simple, the sick and the sinners. Because of this, I love you with a motherly and merciful love; I am always near you as a

714

tender and attentive Mother, and I am leading you along the way of peace, of holiness, of purity and of love.

d   — And then I share with you the *preoccupations and the sufferings of my Heart* in the face of the painful situation in which the countries here and my Church, called to spread the light of Christ and his Gospel, find themselves. Peace is threatened by violence which is spreading, by the social injustices which are still strong, by the divisions, by the prevalence of many personal interests over the common good, by the great number of my poor children who are living in conditions of subhuman misery. Moreover, there are spreading, more and more, those evils which threaten the moral integrity of the people, such as impurity, pornography, drugs, divorce, the recourse to all the means of birth control and these accursed abortions which cry for vengeance in the sight of God.

e   Even the Church, which lives and suffers in this continent, is threatened with an interior division caused by dissension from the Pope and by opposition to his Magisterium on the part of some bishops, theologians, priests and lay persons. Above all, my Adversary has sought to strike her with the subtle snare of liberation theology, which is a true betrayal of Christ and his Gospel. For this reason, my Heart is again pierced today by the sword of sorrow.

f   — Finally, I want to reveal to you *the designs of grace and mercy* which your heavenly Mother has upon you. I consider this land as a precious portion of my estate. For this reason, in the fifth centenary of its evangelization, I have wanted it to be totally consecrated to my Immaculate Heart. Thus I have sent this little son of mine everywhere in order to call bishops, priests, religious and faithful to make this consecration, willed and requested by me for your times.

g   *I will save Latin America.*
h   *I am the Mother of the Second Evangelization.* I am guiding you as a star along the bright way of fidelity to Christ and to his Gospel. You need to return to a belief in the Gospel of Jesus. You must announce it to all in the strength of its integrity. Preach it with the same clarity with which my Son Jesus announced it to you.

715

i   *My motherly task is that of forming you into apostles of the second evangelization.* I invite you, beloved sons, to consecrate yourselves, each and all, to my Immaculate Heart, in order to be formed and guided by me in this, your important mission. Moved by the power of the Holy Spirit, which your heavenly Mother is obtaining for you, go and preach to every creature: be converted; believe in the Gospel; the reign of God is at hand.

j   Go out from this cenacle in peace and in joy. I am with you always. With the souls which are entrusted to you, I bless you all in the name of the Father, and of the Son, and of the Holy Spirit."

468   *São Paulo (Brazil); March 27, 1992*
                       Spiritual Exercises in the Form of a Cenacle
                       with the Priests of the M.M.P. from all Brazil

Go and Evangelize

a   "My Immaculate Heart is today glorified by you in this continuous cenacle of prayer and brotherhood, in which you find yourselves, you the Directors of the M.M.P. who have come from every part of Brazil. I am with you. I am joining you in your prayer, to obtain for you the gift of the Holy Spirit, that He may transform you into apostles of these last times.

b   The moment of your public witness has come. Show yourselves to all as my little sons, as the apostles formed by me for the great task of the new evangelization which is awaiting you.

c   As in the Cenacle of Jerusalem I opened the door so that the Apostles could go out and preach the Gospel, initiating the first evangelization, so also, in this cenacle of yours, I am calling you all to be apostles of the second evangelization.

d   Therefore, at the end of this extraordinary cenacle, I am entrusting to each one of you my motherly mandate: *go and evangelize.*

e   — Go into every part of this great nation of yours.

f   Go into every place, even the most distant and out-of-the-way.

g   Go to all my children, especially those furthest away, to the sinners, to the poor, to those who are victims of evil, of vice, of

716

egoism, of hatred, of impurity.

h   *Go* to every creature, with the power which is given you by this, my motherly mission.

i   *Go* as apostles of the second evangelization, to which the first of my beloved sons, Pope John Paul II, is urgently calling you.

j   *Go and evangelize.*

k   — *Evangelize* this poor humanity which has again become pagan after nearly two thousand years since the first announcement of the Gospel. Evangelize it, preaching the urgent need of conversion and of its return to the Lord. Let the idols be destroyed, the idols it has built with its own hands: pleasure, money, pride, impurity, atheism, unbridled egoism, hatred and violence. And let it return to its God along the way of penance, of the rejection of Satan and his seductions, of the rejection of sin and of every form of evil. And then there will blossom along its way grace and holiness, purity and love, harmony and peace.

l   — *Evangelize* the suffering and divided Church, filled with the smoke of Satan and threatened with the loss of faith and with apostasy. Let the Church once again believe in the Gospel of Jesus. Let the Gospel of Jesus, preached and lived to the letter, become the only light which guides it along its earthly journey. Then will the Church once again be humble, holy, beautiful, poor, evangelical, without spot or wrinkle, in imitation of its heavenly Mother, who is leading it each day toward its greatest renewal.

m   — *Evangelize* all men, preaching that the reign of God is at hand. The moment of the second coming of Jesus is drawing close, the moment of the return of Christ in glory, to restore in your midst his reign of grace, of holiness, of justice, of love and of peace. Announce to everyone this, his glorious return, so that hope may blossom upon the world and the hearts of men be opened to receive Him. *Throw open the doors to Jesus Christ who is coming!*

n   To this end, preach the need for prayer and penance; for the courageous practice of all the virtues; for a return to the perfect cult of love, of adoration and of reparation, offered to Jesus present in the Eucharist. Spread everywhere the cenacles of prayer which

717

I have been asking of you: among children, youth, priests, the faithful. Above all, spread everywhere the family cenacles which I am requesting as a powerful means of saving the Christian family from the great evils which are threatening it.

o   Go out from this cenacle as the apostles of this second evangelization. Do not be afraid. I am with you always, and I am leading you along this bright path.

p   With your dear ones and with the souls which are entrusted to you, I bless you all in the name of the Father, and of the Son, and of the Holy Spirit."

469
Rubbio (Vicenza, Italy); April 16, 1992
Holy Thursday

You Will Be Faithful Priests

a   "Beloved sons, I am particularly close to you, on this day of Holy Thursday. It is your day. It is your pasch.

b   Jesus, having loved his own who were in the world, loved them to the end. You have been born in the cradle of love. Your priesthood has its origin in the mystery of the infinite love of the divine Heart of Jesus.

c   With the Apostles, in the Cenacle of Jerusalem, you also were present. All the bishops and priests to the end of the world were there, because this place and this day are outside of time and of history. This is the day of the new Priesthood and of the new Sacrifice which is being offered in every part of the earth, for the life of the world.

d   Enter into the Heart of Jesus, your Brother; enter with me into the Gethsemane of his love and his sorrow; let yourselves be immersed in the infinite ocean of his divine charity, and *you will be faithful priests*.

e   This is also the day of the betrayal: 'In all truth I tell you, one of you is going to betray me.' (Mt 26:21) Jesus is deeply moved; his Heart is pierced with deep wounds in feeling Himself betrayed by his own: 'One of you is going to betray me!'

f   It is also the moment of human weakness and desertion. Peter denies Jesus three times; the Apostles run away out of fear and forsake Jesus.

718

g   Young John remains, the apostle who loves, the faithful friend; the first of my beloved sons. And he remains with me, the sorrowful and crucified Mother.

h   This, his Pasch, is perpetuated in time; this mystery of divine love, and of the human lack of return for that love, is renewed every day.

i   How many are those today who participate in his priesthood, who share in his inheritance and who, in so many ways, betray Him!

j   *They betray Him* because they no longer believe in his divine word; the lack of faith is spreading; apostasy is diffused more and more within the Church.

k   *They betray Him* because they prefer the thirty pieces of silver to Him, the silver coins of convenience and pleasure, of impurity and pride, of the search for comfort and of self-affirmation. How many are the Judases who today betray the Son of Man!

l   How numerous are those from among his own who deny Him, repeating the words of the human weakness of Peter: 'I do not know this man.' (Mt 26:72)

m   *They deny Him* out of fear of not being thought well of and esteemed by the world in which they live, out of fear of being considered backward and old-fashioned, out of fear of being criticized and rejected.

n   Bishops and priests, beloved sons of mine, why do you repeat today, in such great numbers, by the way you live, the cruel gesture of Judas' betrayal and Peter's denial? The new passion which is being repeated by Jesus in this pasch of 1992 is that of *infidelity* on the part of many of his priests.

o   Like John, beloved sons, remain with me, your sorrowful and crucified Mother. Let us stay together, close to Jesus in Gethsemane; let us follow Him with love and compassion along the painful road to Calvary. I ask you to consecrate yourselves to my Immaculate Heart, to enter into my heavenly garden, so that I can form you to be, today, *faithful priests*, the new Johns who will never, not even for an instant, abandon my Son Jesus.

p   Thus, for Jesus, who is reliving tonight in an immensely greater way the painful agony of Gethsemane, your heavenly Mother is preparing the chalice of comfort which the Father gives Him and which Jesus drinks with infinite gratitude, in feeling Himself so loved, again today, by his faithful priests."

470
Rubbio (Vicenza, Italy);April 17, 1992
Good Friday

Let Us Adore Jesus Crucified

a   "Prostrate yourselves on this day, my beloved sons, and together with me, your sorrowful Mother, with love and immense gratitude, *let us adore Jesus Crucified.*

b   He is the true God. He is our King. Behold Him now, stretched out upon his royal throne:'When I shall be lifted up from the earth, I will draw all men to myself.' (Jn 12:32)

c   Draw close therefore to the throne of grace and mercy, to obtain salvation, in this propitious time of your redemption. Because He who is, today, judged, condemned to the scaffold of the Cross, and cruelly put to death on Calvary is *the true Son of God.* He is the consubstantialWord of the Father; He is his only-begotten Son; He is the perfect Image of his substance; He is the Splendor of his glory.

d   — 'You took no pleasure in burnt offering or sacrifice, butYou have prepared a body for me: I come, O Father, to do yourWill.' (cf. Heb 10:5-7)

e   — 'The Father has so loved the world that He has given his only-begotten Son.' (cf.Jn 3:16)Jesus is the precious gift of the love of the Father; He is the obedient and docile Servant; He is the meek and silent Lamb who is led to his death; He is the Redeemer and Savior of all humanity.

f   — 'God though He was, He did not consider remaining within divinity a treasure to be jealously guarded, but He emptied Himself, taking the form of a servant and, becoming man, became obedient even unto death, the death of the Cross.' (cf. Phil 2:6-8)

g   *We adoreYou, O Jesus Crucified*, because on your royal throne You free humanity from the slavery of Satan;You cancel out every stain of sin, andYou offer the precious gift of your redemption.

h   *It is my Son* Jesus who, today, dies on the Cross, conceived in

720

my virginal womb, formed for nine months in preparation for his human birth, nourished with my flesh and my very own blood, born in a cave, placed in a manger, nourished with my milk, brought up in my arms, cradled with my love, led by my hand, instructed by my words, guarded and defended in his threatened infancy, contemplated with motherly happiness in the rhythm of his human growth, helped by my presence in the fulfillment of his public mission, assisted by me on this day of his unjust and so inhuman execution.

i   Look, with me, at his body, completely reduced to one single wound by the terrible scourging; his face, disfigured with blood which runs down from his head, pierced by the crown of thorns; his wounded shoulders which support with great effort the wood of his gibbet. Feel in your heart, with me, the terrible blows of the nails, which pierce his hands and his feet; the thud of the Cross in the ground, which causes Him to start with renewed pain; the moans of his bloody agony; his last breath which He breathes forth at the moment of his death on the Cross.

j   *It is my Son* who dies, close to me, his afflicted Mother, who opens her Heart to receive you all into the sorrowful cradle of her new and universal motherhood.

k   *Jesus Crucified is your Redeemer and Savior.* Today the purpose of his entire life is fulfilled, and the Will of the Father is carried out to complete perfection, because He immolates Himself as a victim for your salvation.

l   Look, today, with love and with immense gratitude, in a spirit of joy and consolation, upon Him whom they have pierced. He is the true Lamb of God who takes away the sins of the world; He is the High Priest who enters once and for all into the sanctuary to obtain for you, with his blood, an eternal redemption.

m   He is your Pasch: the Bridge which makes it possible for you to pass from sin to grace, from death to life, from slavery to freedom. He is your Brother who takes you by the hand and leads you to be true sons of God.

n   Jesus will return on the royal throne of his glory, to bring to fulfillment that word of his, which was the cause of his condemnation; the clouds of heaven will prostrate themselves as a footstool at his feet, and He will come to restore his reign of grace, of holiness, of love, of justice, and of peace, bringing thus to perfect fulfillment the plan of his redemption.

721

o Live in the expectation of his glorious return and of your imminent liberation."

471

The Sepulchre of Your Slavery!

a "Stay close to me, beloved sons, on this day when I remained without my Son. His body is placed in the new sepulchre, in expectation of his resurrection.

b The Apostles have become terrified and have scattered; I remain on with the holy women, who are keeping me company, and I am keeping watch in prayer and expectation.

c This is the day of my immaculate sorrow. This is the first day of my spiritual motherhood. For this reason, from the very earliest times, there was established in the Church the custom of setting this day aside as one on which I was to be especially venerated.

d Today I want you with me, in a continuous vigil of prayer and love, close to the sepulchre in which there lies the lifeless body of Jesus. In his sepulchre, sin and evil, faithlessness and egoism, impurity and pride, corruption and death are laid away once and for all.

e And the new man, of grace and holiness, of faith and hope, of purity and love, is born. The Church is born; the new humanity, modeled on the glorious humanity of Jesus risen and ascended to the right hand of the Father, is born.

f Today I invite you to descend — you also — into the sepulchre with Christ, in order to die to the world and to yourselves and to live only for the Lord and for his glory.

g Let this new sepulchre be *the sepulchre of your slavery*.

h — *Let it be the sepulchre of your slavery*, where all the chains which hold you under the dominion of Satan are destroyed, and where the new man is born, called to be a free son of God.

i — *Let it be the sepulchre of your slavery*, where this humanity dies once and for all, this humanity distanced from God, rebellious to his Law, corrupt, slave of the spirit of Evil, and lying under the power of darkness; and where the new humanity is born, enlightened and sanctified by the glorious humanity of Jesus.

j — *Let it be the sepulchre of your slavery*, where the Church dies, the Church which is sick and divided, pervaded with the spirit of the world, darkened in its loyalty and holiness, assailed by the loss of faith and apostasy; and where the new Church is born, holy, faithful, enlightened, evangelical, poor and chaste, reflecting solely the light of its Christ upon the world.

k — In the new sepulchre of this day, may every form of slavery of this time of yours, which holds you under the power of Satan and of his universal seduction, be laid away once and for all, and may the new times be born, the new times of your liberation, which is given to you by Jesus Christ, risen and living in your midst."

472   *Rubbio (Vicenza, Italy); April 19, 1992*
 Easter Sunday

The Victory Which Conquers the World

a "Do not be afraid, beloved sons. Look at Jesus who, with the power of his divinity, rises from the dead and, with his glorified body, more resplendent than the sun, comes forth victorious from the tomb.

b Christ, risen and living in your midst, is the reason for your joy, for your confidence, and for your hope, in these last times. Satan has been conquered, and as of this moment, all his power has been taken away from him by Christ, who has accepted to die in order to become, Himself, the medicine which heals you from the sickness of sin and from death.

c Today let your heart exult and overflow with the same joy which I experienced when I saw my Son Jesus, in the splendor of his divinity, bowing over me to put an end to my motherly sorrow.

d Proclaim to all this extraordinary event so that they may live, in these painful times of the purification, the virtue of faith and hope.

e Announce his death; proclaim his resurrection. Do so today when this is so easily denied and when, even in the Church, many of my poor children speak of the resurrection of Jesus, as though it consisted merely in an act of faith and not in a historical event which truly took place.

f   The resurrection of Christ is the most historical, certain and proven fact of all the events which have ever taken place.

g   As your Mother, I admonish you to remain attentive and vigilant, because my Adversary is seducing you in your minds, with subtle and dangerous errors, in order to make you lose the faith and to bring you to apostasy.

h   You must preach to all, with courage, that Christ is the Son of God, dead and risen, ascended into heaven and now seated at the right hand of the Father.

i   *This is the victory which conquers the world*: your faith.

j   Christ Risen is now bringing the Will of the Father to perfect fulfillment, through his second coming in glory, to restore his reign, in which the divine Will may be accomplished by all on earth."

473
Bologna (Italy); May 13, 1992
Anniversary of the First Apparition at Fatima

The Sign of My Presence

a   "Beloved children, today you are observing the seventy-fifth anniversary of my first apparition, which took place at Fatima, in the Cova da Iria, on the 13th of May, 1917. I want to invite you to live this day in prayer and in filial intimacy of life with me, your heavenly Mother. You are the fruit of this apparition of mine. You are the actualization of this message of mine.

b   — At that time, I predicted the times of the loss of the true faith and of the apostasy, which would be spread throughout every part of the Church. You are living the times which I foretold to you.

c   You are *the sign of my presence* in the times of the purification and the great tribulation. Indeed, I am calling you to take part in my work of the Marian Movement of Priests, which I myself have spread throughout every part of the earth, in order to transform the children consecrated to me into strong witnesses of faith and courageous apostles of the truth.

d   For this, I am training you in the greatest fidelity to Christ, and I am inviting you to live and to preach the Gospel to the letter, in a great spirit of unity with the Pope, who has from Jesus the task of maintaining his Church in the truth of the faith. In this way, you become the powerful help which I am offering against the great evil of infidelity and apostasy.

e   — At that time, I predicted the times of the war, and of the persecution of the Church and the Holy Father, because of the spread of theoretical and practical atheism, and of the rebellion of humanity against God and his Law.

f   You are *the sign of my presence* in these times. Indeed, I am asking you to walk along the way which I myself, during these years, have traced out for you, with the messages given to the heart of this little son of mine, so that you may be able to live for the glory of the Heavenly Father, in the perfect imitation of my Son Jesus, docile to the sanctifying action of the Holy Spirit.

g   Thus you are able to give today a strong witness of love and hope, of faith and justice, of humility and purity. You become the powerful help which I am offering, against the great evil of materialism and hedonism, of egoism and pride, of avarice and impurity.

h   — At that time, I predicted the chastisement and that, in the end, my Immaculate Heart would have its triumph.

i   You are *the sign of my presence* in the times of the painful trial which is preparing the triumph of my Immaculate Heart in the world. Indeed, through my Marian Movement of Priests, I am calling all my children to consecrate themselves to my Heart, and to spread everywhere cenacles of prayer: among priests, the faithful, children, youth, and in families.

j   In this way I am able to obtain a great force of intercession and reparation, and I am able to intervene in order to change the hearts of my poor sinful children; in this way I am bringing about each day the triumph of my Immaculate Heart.

k   The more this motherly triumph of mine comes about in the hearts and souls of my children in ever increasing numbers, the more the chastisement is put off by you, and the more Jesus can

725

pour out upon the world the torrents of his divine mercy.

l   For this reason, I invite you all today to follow me as your heavenly Mother who am coming down from heaven in order that I myself may become, in these times, your salvation and your sure liberation."

474

Valdragone (San Marino); July 1, 1992
Spiritual Exercises in the Form of a Cenacle
with the Bishops and Priests of the M.M.P.
from America and Europe

Your Priestly Love

a   "How happy I am to see you in such great numbers, in this continuous cenacle of prayer and brotherhood, bishops and priests of my Movement, who have come from all the countries of America and Europe.

b   I am present among you. I am uniting myself with — and giving strength to — your prayer. I am building up among you a greater sense of brotherhood. I am helping you to grow in mutual love to the point where you become totally one.

c   You must keep in contact with each other; get to know each other; love each other, and help each other to walk together, with courage and confidence, along the difficult road of the painful times in which you are living.

d   The sorrow of my Heart is being consoled by you during these days. My Immaculate Heart is being glorified by you. You are being called to be the instruments of the triumph of my Immaculate Heart in the world.

e   For this, I have called you up here. For this, I have obtained for you a special outpouring of the Holy Spirit, and during these days, I have worked deeply in your hearts and in your souls, to make you fit to carry out my great plan of love and of mercy.

f   My times, and yours, have arrived. Show yourselves to all as my little children, as priests consecrated to me, as the apostles of these last times. Your light must shine ever more brightly in the great darkness which is covering humanity and which has pervaded the Church.

g   *Let your priestly love* be the sign of my motherly presence among you.

h   *Let your priestly love* come down, as a heavenly dew, upon this poor humanity, sick and wounded, far from God, victim of a materialistic and atheistic civilization which is living under the slavery of sin, hatred, unbridled egoism and impurity.

i   *Let your priestly love* be a soothing balm on the deep and bleeding wounds of these times of yours.

j   Go out from this cenacle, and go into every part of the world, in search of my poor children who have wandered astray, and carry them all into the safe sheepfold of my Immaculate Heart. Take by the hand the children, exposed to so many dangers and victims of the subtle snares of my Adversary; give strength and courage to the youth in order to lead them away from the facile seductions of pleasure and impurity; be a support to married couples so that they may live in holiness and love, ever open to the gift of life, and thus be preserved from the great evil of divorce and abortion; bring back to the house of the Heavenly Father my many sinful children; bring assistance to the weak, comfort to the sick, hope to the despairing.

k   *Let your priestly love* be the reflection of the love of the divine and merciful Heart of Jesus and of my Immaculate Heart, for this humanity which is so ailing.

l   *Let your priestly love* come down like a heavenly dew upon the suffering and divided Church, which is carrying the cross towards the Calvary of its purification and its martyrdom.

m   For this, I am asking you to be my very own motherly and merciful presence in the Church.

n   Be a strong support for the Pope, and help him to carry his cross, which has become so heavy today.

o   Help your bishops with prayer, with your love and with your good example.

p   Above all, let your priestly love be a dew which soothes the deep wounds of many of your brother-priests, who are succumbing under the weight of the great difficulties of these times of the purification and the great tribulation.

q   Judge no one. Love all with the tenderness of my motherly Heart.

r   In this way, you become the precious instruments of the triumph of my Immaculate Heart in the world. You form thus the new heart of the new Church which I am forming in the heavenly garden of my Immaculate Heart.

s   The task, which you are undertaking and the work which you are carrying out to spread more and more, in your countries, my work of the Marian Movement of Priests, gives great joy to my Heart. Be zealous in multiplying everywhere the cenacles of prayer which I have asked of you: among priests, among the faithful, and in families. In this way, you cooperate each day in the carrying out of my great plan of salvation and mercy.

t   Go out from this cenacle, renewed by the Holy Spirit, as the courageous apostles of the second evangelization to which I am calling you. I am always with you. I am guiding you with certainty along the road which you have yet to travel.

u   With those who are dear to you, and with all those who are entrusted to your care, I bless you in the name of the Father, and of the Son, and of the Holy Spirit."

475   *Rubbio (Vicenza, Italy); August 15, 1992*
                         Solemnity of the Assumption
                  of the Blessed Virgin Mary into Heaven

The Rays of My Splendor

a   "Look at the heavenly splendor of my body, assumed into the glory of paradise, beloved children, and walk with me towards the safe haven of your liberation, which is now close at hand.

b   You are my joy and my crown. You are the shining stars which cause my royal mantle to shine still more brilliantly.

c   And so I invite you to live with me, this day, together with the souls of the saints in paradise and with the blessed souls who are being purified in purgatory.

d   Today, as they contemplate, in the light of paradise, the glorious and glorified body of your heavenly Mother, the angels and all the angelic cohorts exult; the saints of heaven rejoice; the souls who are being purified jump for joy; and the pilgrim and suffering Church, which is journeying through the desert of the world and of history, is strengthened in its hope and consoled in the midst of its many tribulations.

e   Bring everywhere the balm of my motherly comfort. Spread my light in the deep darkness which surrounds you.

f   *You are the rays of my splendor.*

g   By means of you, I want these rays to be spread everywhere and to descend, as a heavenly dew, upon poor humanity, now in the possession of the Evil One, and upon my Church which is living the hour of its painful passion.

h   Spread the rays of faith, in these times of great apostasy; of hope, in a world pervaded by materialism and by the ever worsening search for pleasure; of love, in the midst of the egoism and hatred and of a great indifference toward the weak, the poor and the suffering; of purity, amidst such widespread foulness; of silence, in the deafening uproar of voices; of prayer, amidst general dissipation; of humility, in the midst of such great pride; and of obedience, amidst such a vast rebellion.

i   Cause the rays of my glory to descend everywhere, O you who are the shining stars of my bright and motherly mantle.

j   In this way, you are forming the new Church; you are bringing together from all sides my children, called to form part of the little faithful remnant; you shorten the times of your most cruel slavery; you prepare hearts and souls to receive the Lord who is coming.

k   On this day, when paradise is united to earth, I reaffirm you in my plan; I welcome you into the depths of my Immaculate Heart; I lead you with steadiness along the road of your liberation in order to attain, at last, the new heavens and the new earth."

476   *Milan (Italy); September 8, 1992*
Feast of the Nativity of the Blessed Virgin Mary

Your Priestly Fidelity

a   "Beloved sons, you exult with all the Church on earth and in heaven, in contemplating the joyous mystery of the birth of your Mother.

b   You gaze today upon your infant Mother, and around my crib, you lay down the precious crown of *your priestly fidelity*.

c   Be faithful priests.

d   Be faithful to your vocation, which binds you to be ministers of Christ and of his Gospel.

e   Just as I was, from my earliest childhood, faithful to the call of God, by entering into his plan, a plan which He had for me from all eternity, so also must you be faithful to your priestly call.

f   If you are little, you remain faithful.
       If you are poor, you remain faithful.
       If you are docile, you remain faithful.

g   It is the task of your heavenly Mother to lead you all along the road of *your priestly fidelity*.

h   — *Be faithful to the ministry of the word.*

i   How numerous today are those priests who become victims of many errors. These errors are taught, disseminated and propagated under the form of new cultural interpretations of the truth. And thus they are easily accepted, and they lead a great number of my children away from the true faith.

j   Yours are the times foretold by Holy Scripture. There are arising today many false teachers, who are teaching fables and leading the faithful away from the truth of the Gospel.

k   You must always preach the Gospel of Jesus with courage and in its full literal sense. It is in this way that you remain in the true faith, and you help the little remnant to remain firm in the security of the faith in these times of universal apostasy.

l   — *Be faithful to the ministry of grace.*

m   Jesus has associated you intimately in the exercise of his eternal High Priesthood, in order to cause the divine gift of grace to descend into the souls of all the redeemed. This you accomplish through the administration of the sacraments, instituted by Christ as an efficacious means of communicating grace.

n   Be faithful to the ministry of the sacraments, especially that of Reconciliation, which has the function of restoring grace to those who have lost it, because of mortal sins which have been committed. Today, this most precious and necessary sacrament is fading away within the Church.

o   Pastors of the Church, bishops placed in positions of leadership by Christ for the guidance of his flock, open your eyes to this evil which is spreading throughout the whole Church like a terrible cancer. Intervene with courage and zeal, so that the sacrament of Reconciliation may again flourish in all its fullness; and thus, souls may be helped to live in the state of grace, and the Church may be healed of the bleeding wounds caused by sins and sacrileges, which cover it completely as though covering a leper.

p — *Be faithful to the ministry of prayer.*

q Jesus is constantly offering Himself and interceding before the Father, by means of you.

r In these times, how greatly prayer is being neglected by so many of my priest-sons! If you saw with my eyes how widespread and deeply imbedded within the Church is this, its interior wound, you too would shed copious tears with me. People no longer pray. They are absorbed in action. All apostolic efficacy is made to rely on activity and on pastoral programming. You forget that you can do nothing by yourselves and that it is Jesus Christ alone who, by means of you, works and saves. You forget that you are useless servants, that you are poor, that you are sinners.

s Return to prayer. Make the Eucharistic Jesus the center of your prayer, the secret of your life, the soul of your apostolic action.

t Today, I ask you to offer me the homage *of your priestly fidelity*, as a crown which you place about the crib in which I am being placed, at the moment of my earthly birth. And always be little, as is today your infant Mother.

u It is only in remaining ever little children that you succeed in being, in these last times, faithful priests."

477 Sant' Omero (Teramo, Italy); September 15, 1992
Feast of Our Lady of Sorrows

The Hour of My Great Sorrow

a "Beloved children, remain today with me, your sorrowful Mother, who have begotten you beneath the Cross, upon which my Son Jesus died for your salvation. I am the Mother of Sorrows.

b   Enter today into the deep mystery of my desolation, in order to understand how my spiritual and universal motherhood is

c exercised, above all, in love and in sorrow: in love for all of you, my children; in sorrow for your sorrows, for the grave dangers which threaten you, for the many sufferings of these last times of the great tribulation.

d   For this reason, the days through which you are living mark also *the hour of my great sorrow.*

e   — *It is the hour of my great sorrow for the Church,* my dearly beloved Daughter.

f   How grievously the Church is suffering in these times, as she carries her great cross and climbs the bloodstained Calvary of her passion and her bloody immolation!

g   Never before, as today, has the Church been made so utterly like my Son Jesus. She is like Him in solitude and abandonment; she is like Him in denial and betrayal; she is like Him in contempt and condemnation; she is like Him in her crucifixion and in her agony.

h   This is the hour of my great sorrow for the Church, because the hour of her redemptive passion has come.

i   — *It is the hour of my great sorrow for humanity,* so ill and so reduced to slavery by the spirits of evil.

j   The diabolical powers are ruling the earth and producing everywhere the wicked fruits of their dark reign. And thus this humanity has again become pagan, after almost two thousand years of its redemption and of the first announcement of the Gospel of salvation.

k   Faithlessness and impiety again cover it; sins wound it; evil poisons it; pride rules it; impurity seduces it; egoism and hatred enchain it; Satan reduces it more and more to slavery and reigns over you with his diabolical power.

l   This is the hour of my great sorrow for all this poor humanity, under the control of the spirits of evil, because the hour of its great chastisement has now come.

m   — *It is the hour of my great sorrow for you, my children.*

732

n How heavy has the burden of your suffering become during these days! With tear-filled eyes, I look at the little children who have been led precociously into experiences of evil and sin; at the youth who have been ensnared and betrayed by the society in which they live, youth to whom false values have been proposed and who have now become victims of impurity and drugs; at the families who have become divided and destroyed; at the poor who are dying of hunger; at those who have been tortured and killed by wars; at the sick who are denied care and assistance; at the abandoned, the isolated, the despairing; at those who are in agony and those who are dying.

o As Mother, I am today at the side of each and every one who is groaning under the weight of their cross. Never do I abandon you; I am with you above all at the moment of your greatest need.

p This is the hour of my great sorrow for all of you, my poor children, because the time of your great suffering has come.

q Take refuge in me. Hasten to the sure refuge of my Immaculate Heart, because we must live together through the hour of the greatest trial, which has now come for you, for the Church and for all humanity."

478

Milan (Italy); October 2, 1992
Feast of the Holy Guardian Angels

The Announcement of the Three Angels

a "Today the angels of light of my Immaculate Heart are at your side, my beloved ones and children consecrated to me. This is their feast day. Honor them; call upon them; follow them; live always with them, they who have been given to you by the Heavenly Father as your guardians and protectors.

b Today is their time. This final period of the purification and the great tribulation corresponds with a particular and powerful manifestation of the angels of the Lord.

c You have entered into the most painful and difficult phase of the battle between the spirits of good and the spirits of evil, between the angels and the demons. It is a terrible struggle which is taking place around you and above you. You, poor earthly creatures, are caught up in it, and thus you experience the particularly powerful force of those snares which are set for you by the wicked spirits, in their attempt to lead you along the road of sin and evil.

d   And so these are the times when the action of your guardian angels must become still stronger and continuous. Pray to them often; listen to them with docility; follow them at every moment.

e   The cult of veneration and praise offered to the angels of the Lord must become more widespread and solemnly observed in the Church. For indeed, to them is reserved the task of making to you the much-awaited announcement of your proximate liberation.

f   *The announcement of the three angels* should be looked forward to by you with confidence, received with joy and followed with love.

g   —Your liberation will coincide with the termination of iniquity, with the complete liberation of all creation from the slavery of sin and evil.

h   What will come to pass is something so very great that it will exceed anything that has taken place since the beginning of the world. It will be like a judgment in miniature, and each one will see his own life and all he has done in the very light of God.

i   *To the first angel* there befalls the task of making this announcement to all: 'Give to God glory and obedience; praise Him because the moment has come when He will judge the world. Go down on your knees before Him who has made heaven and earth, the sea and the springs of water.' (cf. Rev 14:7)

j   —Your liberation will coincide with the defeat of Satan and of every diabolical spirit.

k   All the demons and the spirits of the damned who, during these years, have been poured out into every part of the world for the ruin and damnation of souls, will be cast into hell, from which they have come, and they will no longer be able to do harm.

l   All the power of Satan will be destroyed.

m   *To the second angel* there befalls the task of making this announcement: 'Fallen, fallen is Babylon the great, she who made

all the nations drink of the intoxicating wine of her prostitution.'
(cf. Rev 14:8)

n — Your liberation will coincide, above all, with the reward granted to all those who have remained faithful during the great trial, and with *the great chastisement* meted out to those who have allowed themselves to be drawn away by sin and evil, by faithlessness and godlessness, by money and pleasure, by egoism and impurity.

o *To the third angel* there befalls the task of announcing the great chastisement: 'Anyone who worships the beast and its image, and accepts its mark on forehead or hand, will drink the wine of God's wrath, poured full strength into the cup of his terrible judgment, and will be tormented with fire and sulfur, in the presence of the Lamb and of the holy angels. The smoke of the fire that torments them never ends. Anyone who worships the beast and its image and whoever accepts the mark of its name has no relief day or night.' (cf. Rev 14:9-11)

p At this final time of the great tribulation, announced as that of the end of the iniquity, of the defeat of Satan, and of the chastisement of the godless, the constancy of those who belong to the Lord, who put into practice the commandments of God and who remain faithful to Jesus, is put to a hard test.

q For this reason, I urge you today to be particularly united with your guardian angels, in prayer, in harkening to their voice, and in accepting with docility their sure guidance, along the road of goodness and holiness.

r In these stormy times, when Satan is ruling with all his dark power, the task of the angels of light of my Immaculate Heart is that of leading you all along the road of constancy and of fidelity to Jesus, in the observance of the commandments of God and in the practice of all the virtues.

s Today, together with your guardian angels, I bless you with the joy of a Mother who is consoled and ever more glorified by you."

Blumenfeld (Germany); October 7, 1992
Feast of Our Lady of the Rosary
Anniversary of the Victory
of the Blessed Virgin Mary at Lepanto

The Angel with the Key and the Chain

a   "Today, you find yourself here at the center for my Movement in Germany, in order to hold a cenacle with the priests and the faithful who are consecrated to my Immaculate Heart. You are venerating me as the Lady of the Holy Rosary.

b   The rosary is my prayer; it is the prayer which I came down from heaven to ask of you, because it is the weapon which you must make use of, in these times of the great battle, and it is the sign of my assured victory.

c   My victory will be won when Satan, with his powerful army made up of all the infernal spirits, will be shut up within his kingdom of darkness and death, from which he will no longer be able to escape in order to do harm in the world.

d   For this reason, there is to come down from heaven an angel to whom there is given the key of the abyss and a chain with which this angel will bind the great Dragon, the ancient serpent, Satan, with all his followers.

e   An '*angel*' is a spirit who is sent by God to carry out a particular mission.

f   I am the Queen of the Angels, because it is of the very nature of my role to be sent by the Lord to accomplish the very great and important mission of conquering Satan.

g   In fact, from the very beginning, I was announced as she who is the enemy of the serpent, she who does battle with him, she who in the end will crush his head: 'I will put enmity between you and the woman, between your offspring and hers. She will crush your head, as you attempt to bite at her heel.' (Gen 3:15)

h   My offspring is Christ. In Him, who has carried out the work of redemption and set you free from the slavery of Satan, my complete victory is accomplished.

i   And so, there has been entrusted to me the key with which it is possible to open and shut the door to the abyss.

j   *The key* is the sign of the power which belongs to him who is lord and master of a place which belongs to him.

k   In this sense, He who holds the key of the universe is the Incarnate Word alone, because all things have been made through Him, and therefore Jesus Christ is the Master and King of all the universe, namely, of heaven, of earth and of the abyss.

l   My Son Jesus alone possesses the key of the abyss, because He Himself is the Key of David, who opens and no one can shut, who shuts and no one can open.

m   Jesus consigns this key, which represents his divine power, into my hand because, as his Mother, Mediatrix between you and my Son, there is entrusted to me the task of conquering Satan and all his powerful army of evil. It is with this key that I am able to open and shut the door to the abyss.

n   *The chain*, with which the great Dragon is to be bound, is made up of prayer made with me and by means of me. This prayer is that of the holy rosary. A chain has in fact the function of first of all limiting action, then of imprisoning, and finally of making ineffective every activity of the one who has been bound by it.

o   —The chain of the holy rosary has first of all the function *of limiting the action* of my Adversary. Every rosary which you recite with me has the effect of restricting the action of the Evil One, of drawing souls away from his pernicious influence, and of giving greater impetus to the expansion of goodness in the life of many of my children.

p   —The chain of the holy rosary has also the effect *of imprisoning Satan*, that is, of making his action impotent, and of diminishing and weakening more and more the force of his diabolical power. And so, each rosary which is recited well deals a mighty blow to the power of evil, and it represents one part of his reign which is destroyed.

q   —The chain of the holy rosary brings about, in the end, the result *of making Satan completely harmless*. His great power is destroyed. All the evil spirits are cast into the pool of fire and sulfur; the door is shut by me with the key of the power of Christ, and thus they will no longer be able to go out into the world to do harm to souls.

r   You understand now, my beloved children, why, in these last times of the battle between me, the Woman Clothed with the

Sun, and the great Dragon, I am asking you to multiply every-where the cenacles of prayer, with the recitation of the holy rosary, meditation on my word, and your consecration to my Immaculate Heart.

s   With these, you make it possible for your heavenly Mother to take action in binding Satan, so that I may thus carry out my mission of crushing his head, that is to say, of defeating him once and for all, shutting him up in his abyss of fire and sulfur.

t   The humble and fragile cord of the holy rosary forms the strong chain with which I will take as my prisoner the dark ruler of the world, the enemy of God and of his faithful servants. Thus the pride of Satan will once again be defeated by the power of the little, the humble and the poor.

u   As I announce to you today that this, my great victory, is near at hand, the victory which will bring you to your assured libera-tion, I give you the comfort of my motherly presence among you, and I bless you."

480

Milan (Italy); October 13, 1992
Anniversary of the Last Apparition at Fatima

Lift Up Your Eyes to Heaven

a   " 'Lift up your eyes to heaven,' I said to little Lucy at the end of my last apparition, which took place on the 13th of October, 1917, at Fatima in the lowly Cova da Iria. And she, turning to an immense multitude, invited all to look toward the sun. Then began that extraordinary phenomenon, seen by all with pro-found emotion, and described as 'the miracle of the sun.'

b   This was the confirmation of the truth of my apparitions. It was the sign, intended to point out to all that your heavenly Mother had come down from heaven as the Woman Clothed with the Sun.

c   Lift up your eyes to heaven, I repeat to you today, as you live out the events which were foretold to you by me at Fatima.

d   — Lift up your eyes from the world in which you are living, so corrupt, so dried up with egoism, with hatred, with sin, and with such a vast impiety.

e — *Lift up your eyes* from this humanity, possessed by the spirit of Evil, which has built a civilization without God and which falls prostrate in adoration before the false gods of money and pleasure, of pride and haughtiness, of violence and impurity.

f — *Lift up your eyes* from the times in which you are living, from the painful purification and the great tribulation. These times of yours are wicked times, because the hearts of men have become wicked, closed, cold, hard and permeated with a great aridity.

g In these times, Satan has established his reign over your world and over this humanity, and he rules as sure master. The forces of evil, with the help of the dark powers of atheism and of Masonry, have attained their victory.

h What must you do, my poor children, exposed to such great dangers and so loved and protected by your heavenly Mother?

i *Lift up your eyes to heaven,* because your liberation is near. From heaven, there will come to you the new era of light and holiness. From heaven, there will come to you the definitive defeat of Satan and of his whole powerful army of evil. From heaven, there will come to you Christ, in the splendor of his glory, riding on the white horse of his divine power.

j Today, as you observe the anniversary of the apparition of your heavenly Mother as the Woman Clothed with the Sun, I invite you all to lift up your eyes to heaven, because 'in the opened heavens there appears a white horse. Its rider is called, "Faithful and True," because He judges and wages war in righteousness. His eyes are like a fiery flame, and on his head are many diadems. He has a name inscribed that no one knows except Himself. He wears a cloak that has been dipped in blood. His name is: "The Word of God." The armies of heaven follow Him, mounted on white horses, clothed in white of the finest pure linen. Out of his mouth there comes a sharp sword to strike the nations. He will rule them with an iron rod, and He will tread out the wine press, which represents the terrible chastisement of God, the Ruler of the universe. He has his name written on his cloak and on his thigh: "King of kings and Lord of lords." ' (cf. Rev 19:11-16)

k *Lift up therefore your eyes to heaven,* my beloved ones and children consecrated to me, because, on the bright clouds, my Son Jesus will come to you, in the splendor of his glory, to establish in your midst his reign of love, of holiness, of justice and of peace."

At the Hour of Your Death

a   "Beloved sons, today you are gathered together in prayer, as you call to mind your brothers who have gone before you in the sign of faith and are now sleeping the sleep of peace.

b   How great is the number of my beloved ones and children consecrated to my Immaculate Heart, who have now entered into the repose of the Lord!

c   Many of them are sharing in the fullness of joy, in the perfect possession of God and, together with the angelic cohorts, are lights which shine in the eternal blessedness of paradise.

d   Many are in purgatory, with the certainty of having been saved for ever, although still in the suffering of purification, because their possession of God is not yet full and perfect.

e   Today I want to tell you that these brothers of yours are especially close to you and form the most precious part of my victorious cohort. I have but one single cohort, just as my Church is one and one alone, united in the joyous experience of the communion of saints.

f   The saints intercede for you, light up your path, assist you with their most pure love, defend you from the subtle snares which my Adversary sets for you, and anxiously await the moment of your meeting.

g   The souls who are being purified pray for you, offer their sufferings for your well-being, and through your prayers, they are assisted in being set free from those human imperfections which prevent them from entering into the eternal joy of paradise.

h   Those saints who, while on earth, had lived the consecration to my Immaculate Heart, making up a crown of love to alleviate the sorrows of your heavenly Mother, form, here above, my most beautiful crown of glory. They are close to my throne and follow your heavenly Mother wherever she goes.

i   Those souls in purgatory, who, while on earth, had formed part of my cohort, now enjoy a special union with me, feel in a special way my presence which sweetens the bitterness of their suffering and shortens the time of their purification. And it is I myself who go to receive these souls into my arms, that I may lead them into the incomparable light of paradise.

740

j   Thus I am always close to all of you, my beloved ones and children consecrated to my Heart, during your painful earthly pilgrimage, but I am close to you in a most special way *at the hour of your death.*

k   How many times, as you recite the holy rosary, have you repeated this prayer to me:'Holy Mary, Mother of God, pray for us sinners, now and *at the hour of our death!*' This is an invocation which I listen to with great joy, and it is always heard by me. If, as Mother, I am close to each one of my children at the hour of death, I am especially close to you who, through your consecration, have always lived in the secure refuge of my Immaculate Heart.

l   *At the hour of your death,* I am close to you, with the splendor of my glorified body; I receive your souls into my motherly arms, and I bring them before my Son Jesus, for his particular judgment.

m   Think of how joyful must be the meeting of Jesus with those souls who are presented to Him by his very own Mother! This is because I cover them with my beauty; I give them the perfume of my holiness, the innocence of my purity, the white robe of my charity; and where there remains some stain, I run my motherly hand over it to wipe it away and to give you that brightness which makes it possible for you to enter into the eternal happiness of paradise.

n   Blessed are those who die close to your heavenly Mother. Yes, blessed, because they die in the Lord, they will find rest from their labors, and their good deeds will follow them.

o   My beloved ones and children consecrated to my Immaculate Heart, today I invite you to enter into a great intimacy with me during your life, if you wish to experience the great joy of seeing me close to you and of welcoming your souls into my motherly arms, *at the hour of your death.*"

482   *San Marco (Udine, Italy); November 22, 1992*
Solemnity of Christ the King

An Oracle of the Lord

a   "Beloved children, today you are participating in the great joy of the Church in heaven and on earth which, together with the choirs of the angelic hierarchy, prostrate themselves in an act of profound adoration before Jesus Christ, King of the universe.

b   — Jesus Christ is King, because He is the Eternal Word, the only-begotten Son of the Father, the Image of his substance, the Splendor of his glory. Through Him all things have been created, and thus everything which exists, apart from God, is subject to his royal and universal dominion.

c   '*An oracle of the Lord* to my Lord: sit at my right hand till I make your enemies your footstool. The scepter of your power the Lord stretches forth from Zion: rule in the midst of your enemies. Royal dignity is yours in the day of your strength, in sacred splendors; from the womb of the dawn, like dew, I have begotten you.' (cf. Ps 110:1-3)

d   — Jesus Christ is King, moreover, because of his conquest. Indeed, at the moment of the Incarnation, the Word assumes human nature into his divine Person, and in this hypostatic union, humanity is raised to a personal communion with divinity itself.

e   Through the work of redemption, accomplished on Calvary, Jesus frees the created universe from the slavery of Satan, to whom it has become subject because of the sin committed by the first man. This He Himself does, on the Cross, by paying the price due to divine Justice.

f   Thus the whole universe, redeemed from the Evil One and led back to a full communion of life with the Heavenly Father, belongs to the royal dominion of Christ and shares in his very plan as conqueror of sin and death, as Son of God, and as citizen of the heavenly Jerusalem.

g   'I am the First and the Last, the One who lives. Once I was dead but now I am alive forever and ever, and I have power over death and over the netherworld.' (Rev 1:17-18)

h   'To the victor who keeps my ways until the end, I will give authority over the nations. He will rule them with an iron rod, and he will smash them like clay vessels, with the same authority that was given Me by my Father. And to him I will give the morning star.' (Rev 2:26-28)

i   'I will never erase his name from the book of life, but will acknowledge him in the presence of my Father and of his angels.' (Rev 3:5)

j   'The victor I will make into a pillar in the temple of my God, and he will never leave it again. On him I will inscribe the name of my God, and the name of the holy city, the new Jerusalem, which comes down out of heaven from my God, as well as my new name.' (Rev 3:12)

k   — Jesus Christ is King, because it pertains to his divine mission to bring the created universe back to the perfect glorification of the Father, purifying it with the burning fire of the Holy Spirit, in such a way that it may become completely freed of every spirit of evil, of every shadow of sin, and thus be able to open itself to the enchantment of a new earthly paradise.

l   Then will the Father be glorified and his name be held holy by all creation.

m   In this creation, renewed by a perfect communion of life with the Father, Jesus Christ will restore his reign of glory, so that the work of his divine redemption may attain its perfect fulfillment.

n   The Holy Spirit will open hearts and minds, in such a way that all will be able to carry out the Will of the Father and the Son, so that, as in heaven so also on earth, the divine Will may be perfectly accomplished.

o   To attain these new heavens and this new earth, it is necessary to pass through the painful and bloody trial of the purification, of the great tribulation and of the chastisement.

p   My beloved ones and children consecrated to my Immaculate Heart, listen to the words of your heavenly Mother, who is gently preparing you and leading you to live through these events, because the times which were foretold to you by the prophet Zechariah have now come.

q   '*An oracle of the Lord*: I will strike the shepherd, and the sheep will be completely scattered; and then I will turn my hand against the little ones.

r   '*An oracle of the Lord*: In all the land, two thirds of them will be cut off and perish; and one third shall be left.

s   'I will pass this third through fire; I will refine it as silver is refined, test it as gold is tested.

t   'It will call upon my Name, and I will hear it; I will say: "This

743

is my people." And it will say:"The Lord is my God. " ' (cf. Zec 13:7-9)

u   Today, as you celebrate the liturgical solemnity of Jesus Christ, King of the universe, I urge you to render Him your homage, the homage of a heroic faith, of a sure hope, and of an ardent charity, in expectation of his glorious return, which will bring you to your approaching liberation.

v   Because, as Holy Scripture attests: 'Jesus Christ is the faithful witness, the firstborn from the dead, the ruler of the kings of the earth. Jesus Christ loves us and has set us free from our sins by the Sacrifice of his life. He has made us reign with Him, as priests at the service of God his Father. To Him be glory and power forever and ever. Amen.

w   'Look! Jesus Christ is coming amid the clouds, and everyone will see Him, even those who killed Him; and all the races of the earth will mourn over Him. Yes, amen.

x   'I am the First and the Last, says God, the Lord who is, who was and who is to come, the Ruler of all the universe.' (cf. Rev 1:5-8)

y   With the joy of a Mother, who sees herself more and more heeded and followed by her little children, along the road which has been pointed out by me, as Prophetess of these last times in which you are living, with my Son, Jesus Christ, today adored in the splendor of his divine royalty, I bless you in the name of the Father, and of the Son, and of the Holy Spirit."

483   *Sant' Omero (Teramo, Italy); December 8, 1992*
Solemnity of the Immaculate Conception

The Holy City

a   "Today, you are contemplating me with joy, in the splendor of my Immaculate Conception. My beloved children, allow yourselves to be drawn by the immaculate light of your heavenly Mother, and run in the sweet wake of my heavenly fragrance.

b   Because I am without sin, the Father has directed upon me his gaze of predilection; the Word has chosen me to become his Mother; and the Holy Spirit has united Himself to me with the bond of spousal love. I have thus entered into the very Heart of the Most Holy Trinity.

c   Because I am without sin, the Divine Trinity has chosen me as Leader and Conqueror, in the terrible struggle against Satan and all the evil spirits.

d   Because I am without sin, Jesus has associated me intimately, as Mother, in his plan of salvation and has made me the first collaborator in his work of redemption, entrusting to me, as Daughter, all humanity redeemed and saved by Him.

e   I am therefore the Mother of Humanity. It pertains to my function as the new Eve and to my task as Mother, to bring all humanity back to the full communion of life with God, helping it to come to birth and to grow in grace and holiness.

f   Therefore, it is my task above all to drive far away from you, from the Church and from humanity the dark shadow of sin and evil, in order to lead you all to the *Holy City* of purity and love.

g   The light of this *Holy City* is the very splendor of the Father; the sun which gives warmth is the Immolated Lamb, from whose Heart come forth burning rays of fire and of love; the breath is the exhalation of the Holy Spirit, who gives life and rouses all creatures to their hymn of glory and celestial harmony.

h   This is the task entrusted to your heavenly Mother.

i   — *The Holy City* must first of all be established in the hearts and the souls, that is to say in the life, of all my children.

j   This takes place when you turn away from all the seductions of evil and of the passions, and give place to the love of God, who brings you to live in perpetual communion of life with Him.

k   You are thus set free from the slavery of sin and brought back to that experience of grace, of purity and of joy, which was the habitual state of life of Adam before he succumbed to the snare of the serpent and to his first fall.

l   Then you will drink at the fountain, which springs forth from paradise; you will be conquerors over evil and over the Evil One; you will come into the possession of those blessings which the Lord has prepared for you; you yourselves will become children of the Most High.

m   'From his throne, God spoke: "Now I am making all things new. That which I say is trustworthy and true. I am the Beginning and the End, the First and the Last. I will give the water of life free to anyone who is thirsty. To the victors will befall this share of the gifts. I will be their God, and they will be my children.' ' (cf. Rev 21:5-7)

n — *The Holy City* must also shine forth in the Church, purified of all its human weaknesses, set free from the stains of infidelity and apostasy, sanctified by its painful passion and its bloody immolation. Then the Church will once again be all beautiful, without spot or wrinkle, in imitation of your immaculate Mother.

o In the Church, purified and completely renewed, there will shine forth in all its great power, the one and only light of Christ, which will be spread by it in every part of the earth, and thus all nations will run to it, for the perfect glorification of the Most Holy Trinity.

p 'The Spirit took me to the top of a great mountain which was very high, and the angel showed me Jerusalem, *the Holy City*, which is that of the Lord. It was coming down out of heaven from God. It gleamed with the splendor of God; its radiance was like that of a precious stone, like a gem, clear as crystal.

q 'The city has no need of sun or moon to shine on it, for the glory of God gives it light, and its lamp is the Lamb. The nations will walk by its light, and to it the kings of the earth will bring their treasure. During the day its gates will never be shut, and there will no longer be any night there.

r 'The treasures and the honor of the nations will be brought into it. Nothing unclean will be able to enter in, nor anyone who would do abominable things or commit sin. Only those will enter whose names are written in the Lamb's book of life.' (cf. Rev 21:10-11,23-27)

s — *The Holy City* shall, in the end, gather together that humanity which has been redeemed and saved, once it will have been set completely free from the slavery of Satan, sin and evil, by means of the purification, the great tribulation and the terrible chastisement.

t In these last times, the struggle against Satan and his powerful army, made up of all the wicked spirits, will become more bitter and bloody, because you are living under the heavy yoke of his universal reign.

746

u And so then, you understand how it pertains to my task as Woman Clothed with the Sun and as Conqueror of Satan, to bind the great Dragon and to cast him into his pool of fire, from which he will no longer be able to escape to harm the world.

v In this world, Christ will reign. Jesus will return in glory, to bring all creation back to the full splendor of his new earthly paradise.

w The sinful city will now have vanished, and thus all creation will open itself with joy to receive *the Holy City*, the new Jerusalem, come down out of heaven, the permanent dwelling place of God with men.

x 'I saw a new heaven and a new earth, because the former heaven and the former earth had passed away, and the sea was no more. I saw *the Holy City*, the new Jerusalem, coming down out of heaven from God, prepared as a bride adorned to meet her husband.

y 'A loud voice, which came from the throne, exclaimed: "Behold, the dwelling place of God with men; they will be his people, and He will be their God. God will wipe away every tear from their eyes. There shall be no more mourning, no more wailing, no more pain, because the old order has passed away."' (cf. Rev 21:1-4)

z Beloved children, today you are contemplating me in the splendor of my Immaculate Conception; allow yourselves to be drawn by the enchantment of your heavenly Mother, and follow me, in the wake of my sweet fragrance, in order to go with me to meet *the Holy City*, which will come down out of heaven, at the end of the painful purification and of the great tribulation in which you are living in these last times."

484 — Dongo (Como, Italy); December 24, 1992
The Holy Night

The Morning Star

a "Beloved children, enter with me into the deep mystery of this holy night. Live it close to your heavenly Mother and to my most chaste spouse, Joseph. Live it in silence, in prayer, in humility, in purity and in love.

b   I am opening for you the door of my Immaculate Heart, to have you enter and feel its beating, in these last instants which precede the birth of my heavenly Child.

c   Each beat of my motherly Heart, in this holy night, becomes a sigh of expectation, a moan of desire, a spark of love, a prayer of quiet, a word with the Father, a transport of the Spirit, who comforts me in a profound ecstasy of life with paradise, which I see all enclosed in this poor cave.

d   As night surrounds everything and deep darkness has come down upon the world, your heavenly Mother is penetrated with a most powerful light: my mind becomes absorbed in the splendor of eternal Wisdom; my Heart opens itself to the most ardent brightness of Love; my soul is penetrated by the ray of the fullness of grace and of holiness; my virginally inviolate body opens to the gift of my divine Son.

e   With my motherly arms, I place in the squalid manger my heavenly Child, born in this night of deep darkness.

f   But the stars shine brightly in the heavens, as the angels proclaim the song of celestial harmonies and the shepherds come to the cave to bring the homage of the simple, the poor, the pure of heart.

g   Thus is the Infant Jesus comforted by the love which He receives from the little ones, even amidst the vast rejection of the great.

h   And so, in the deep night which enfolds the world, *the Morning Star* opens to give you his light.

i   My divine Child is *the Morning Star*, who shines with the very light of the Father, who brings his life into the desert of the world and of history, who gives a beginning to the new day for a redeemed and rescued humanity.

j   'The true Light that enlightens every man was coming into the world. He was in the world, and the world was made through Him, yet the world did not know Him. He came into the world which is his own, but his own people did not accept Him. A few however have believed in Him, and to these God has given the gift of becoming children of God. The Word became man and made his dwelling among us. We have contemplated his divine splendor. It is the splendor of the only-begotten Son of God the Father, full of grace and truth.' (cf. Jn 1:9-14) *k*   Beloved children, on this holy night, allow yourselves to be penetrated by his divine splendor, and become, you yourselves, witnesses and apostles of his light. Because the darkness is now becoming deeper, as the moment of the return of Jesus in glory draws closer.

l   It is the darkness of the lack of faith and of apostasy, which has spread everywhere.

m   It is the darkness of evil and sin, which has now obscured hearts and souls.

n   It is the darkness of faithlessness and impiety, of egoism and pride, of hardness of heart and impurity.

o   In this great night, the second birth of Jesus in glory is about to take place, a glory which, *as morning star*, will brighten up the dawn of the new heavens and the new earth.

p   For this reason, I urge you today to fight and, together with me, to gain the victory in the great battle of these last times, to assure that you may ever remain faithful to Jesus.

q   'Do not seal up the prophetic words of this book, for the appointed time is near. Let the wicked still act wickedly and the filthy still be filthy. The righteous must still do right, and he who belongs to the Lord must consecrate himself more and more to Him. I am coming soon, and I will bring with me the recompense which I will give to each, according to his deeds.' (cf. Rev 22:10-12)

r   'To the victors, who carry out my Will until the end, I will give authority over the nations, as I myself have received it from my Father, and I will give them also *the morning star*.' (cf. Rev 2:26-28)

s   'I, Jesus, have sent my angel to give you this message for the Churches. I am the root and offspring of David, *the bright morning star*.

t   'The Spirit and the Bride of the Lamb say: "Come!" And whoever harkens to these things says: "Come!" ' " (cf. Rev 22:16-17)

The End of the Times

a   "With docility, allow yourselves to be taught by me, beloved children. On this last night of the year, gather together in prayer and in listening to the word of your heavenly Mother, the Prophetess of these last times.

b   Do not spend these hours noisily or in dissipation, but in silence, in recollection, and in contemplation.

c   I have announced to you many times that *the end of the times* and the coming of Jesus in glory is very near. Now, I want to help you understand the signs described in the Holy Scriptures, which indicate that his glorious return is now close.

d   These signs are clearly indicated in the Gospels, in the letters of Saint Peter and Saint Paul, and they are becoming a reality during these years.

e   — *The first sign is the spread of errors*, which lead to the loss of faith and to apostasy.

f   These errors are being propagated by false teachers, by renowned theologians who are no longer teaching the truths of the Gospel, but pernicious heresies based on errors and on human reasonings. It is because of the teaching of these errors that the true faith is being lost and that the great apostasy is spreading everywhere.

g   'See that no one deceives you. For many will attempt to deceive many people. False prophets will come and will deceive very many.' (cf. Mt 24:4-5, 11)

h   'The day of the Lord will not come unless the great apostasy comes first.' (cf. 2 Thes 2:3)

i   'There will be false teachers among you. These will seek to introduce disastrous heresies and will even set themselves against the Master who ransomed them. Many will listen to them and will follow their licentious ways. Through their offense, the Christian faith will be reviled. In their greed, they will exploit you with fabrications.' (cf. 2 Pt 2:1-3)

j   — *The second sign is the outbreak of wars and fratricidal struggles*, which lead to the prevalence of violence and hatred and a general slackening off of charity, while natural catastrophes, such as epidemics, famines, floods and earthquakes, become more and more frequent.

k   'When you hear of reports of wars, close at hand or far away, see that you are not alarmed, for these things must happen. Nation will rise against nation, and kingdom against kingdom. There will be famines and earthquakes in many places. All this will be only the beginning of greater sufferings to come. Evildoing will be so widespread that the love of many will grow cold. But God will save those who persevere until the end.' (cf. Mt 24:6-8,12-13)

l   — *The third sign is the bloody persecution* of those who remain faithful to Jesus and to his Gospel and who stand fast in the true faith. Throughout this all, the Gospel will be preached in every part of the world.

m   Think, beloved children, of the great persecutions to which the Church is being subjected; think of the apostolic zeal of the recent popes, above all of my Pope, John Paul II, as he brings to all the nations of the earth the announcement of the Gospel.

n   'They will hand you over to persecution, and they will kill you. You will be hated by all because of me. And then many will abandon the faith; they will betray and hate one another. Meanwhile, the message of the kingdom of God will be preached in all the world; all nations must hear it. And then the end will come.' (cf. Mt 24:9-10,14)

o   — *The fourth sign is the horrible sacrilege*, perpetrated by him who sets himself against Christ, that is, the Antichrist. He will enter into the holy temple of God and will sit on his throne and have himself adored as God.

p   'This one will oppose and exalt himself against everything that men adore and call God. The lawless one will come by the power of Satan, with all the force of false miracles and pretended wonders. He will make use of every kind of wicked deception, in order to work harm.' (cf. 2 Thes 2:4,9-10)

q   'One day, you will see in the holy place he who commits *the horrible sacrilege*. The prophet Daniel spoke of this. Let the reader seek to understand.' (cf. Mt 24:15)

r   Beloved children, in order to understand in what this *horrible sacrilege* consists, read what has been predicted by the prophet

Daniel:'Go, Daniel; these words are to remain secret and sealed until the end time. Many will be cleansed, made white and upright, but the wicked will persist in doing wrong. Not one of the wicked will understand these things, but the wise will comprehend.

s   'Now, from the moment that the daily Sacrifice is abolished and the horrible abomination is set up, there shall be one thousand two hundred and ninety days. Blessed is he who waits with patience and attains one thousand three hundred and thirty-five days.' (Dn 12:9-12)

t   The Holy Mass is the daily Sacrifice, the pure oblation which is offered to the Lord everywhere, from the rising of the sun to its going down.

u   The Sacrifice of the Mass renews that which was accomplished by Jesus on Calvary. By accepting the Protestant doctrine, people will hold that the Mass is not a sacrifice but only a sacred meal, that is to say, a remembrance of that which Jesus did at his Last Supper. And thus, the celebration of Holy Mass will be suppressed. In this abolition of the daily Sacrifice consists *the horrible sacrilege* accomplished by the Antichrist, which will last about three and a half years, namely, one thousand two hundred and ninety days.

v   — *The fifth sign consists in extraordinary phenomena,* which occur in the skies.

w   'The sun will be darkened, and the moon will not give its light; and the stars will fall from the sky; and the powers of the heavens will be shaken.' (Mt 24:29)

x   The miracle of the sun, which took place at Fatima during my last apparition, is intended to point out to you that you are now entering into the times when these events will take place, events which will prepare for the return of Jesus in glory.

y   'And then the sign of the Son of Man will appear in heaven. All the tribes of the earth will mourn, and men will see the Son of Man coming upon the clouds of heaven, with great power and splendor.' (Mt 24:30)

z   My beloved ones and children consecrated to my Immaculate Heart, I have wanted to teach you about these signs, which Jesus has pointed out to you in his Gospel, in order to prepare

752

you *for the end of the times, because these are about to take place in your days.*

A   The year which is coming to a close, and that which is beginning, form part of the great tribulation, during which the apostasy is spreading, the wars are multiplying, natural catastrophes are occurring in many places, persecutions are intensifying, the announcement of the Gospel is being brought to all nations, extraordinary phenomena are occurring in the sky, and the moment of the full manifestation of the Antichrist is drawing ever nearer.

B   And so I urge you to remain strong in the faith, secure in trust and ardent in charity. Allow yourselves to be led by me, and gather together, each and all, in the sure refuge of my Immaculate Heart, which I have prepared for you especially during these last times. Read, with me, the signs of your time, and live in peace of heart and in confidence.

C   I am always with you, to tell you that the coming about of these signs indicates to you with certainty that *the end of the times*, with the return of Jesus in glory, is close at hand.

D   'Learn a lesson from the fig tree: when its branches become tender and sprout the first leaves, you know that summer is near. In the same way, when you see these things taking place, know that your liberation is near.'" (cf. Mt 24:32-33)

753

1993

THE TIME OF THE GREAT TRIAL

The Time of the Great Trial

a   "My beloved ones and children consecrated to my Immaculate Heart, today you are living spiritually united in the solemn liturgical observance of my Divine Maternity.

b   I am the true Mother of God. The Word of the Father has assumed human nature in my virginal womb and has become your Brother. On the Cross, a few moments before He died, Jesus entrusted to me this humanity which had been redeemed and saved by Him.

c   I have thus become the Mother of all humanity. It is in virtue of my role as Mother of God and of humanity that I am intervening in your life, in the life of the Church and in the life of humanity, to assist you in carrying out the designs of the Heavenly Father, by responding to the gift which my Son Jesus made to you and by seconding with docility the action of the Holy Spirit.

d   As Mother, I am always close to you, to the Church and to humanity, in order to lead you along the way of the fulfillment of the Father's Will, of the imitation of the Son, and of communion with the Spirit of Love, in such a way that the Most Holy and Divine Trinity may be more and more glorified.

e   The fountain of your joy and your peace is to be found in the perfect glorification of the Most Holy Trinity. Peace is given you by the Father, shared with you by the Son, and becomes communicated to you by the Holy Spirit.

f   The Father has indeed so loved the world that He has given his only-begotten Son. The Son Himself is the peace which is communicated to the world. The Holy Spirit brings you to that love from which alone peace can spring.

g   The Evil One, Satan, the ancient serpent, the great Dragon, has always acted and works in all kinds of ways to take away the precious blessing of peace from you, from the Church and from humanity. It enters then into my function as Mother to bring you all to a great communion of life with God, so that you may have the sweet experience of love and of peace.

h   Never as in your days has peace been so threatened, because the struggle of my Adversary against God is becoming stronger and stronger, more insidious, continual and universal.

i   You have thus entered *into the time of the great trial.*

j   — *The great trial has come for all of you,* my poor children, so threatened by Satan and stricken by the evil spirits. The danger you are in is that of losing grace and the communion of life with God, which my Son Jesus obtained for you at the moment of redemption, when He delivered you from slavery to the Evil One and set you free from sin.

k   Now sin is no longer considered an evil; indeed, it is often exalted as a thing of value and as something good. Under the perfidious influence of the mass media, the awareness of sin as an evil has been gradually lost. Thus it is committed and justified more and more and is no longer confessed.

l   If you live in sin, you return again to slavery under Satan, subjected to his wicked power, and thus the gift of redemption which Jesus accomplished for you is made useless. Thus peace disappears from your hearts, from your souls and from your life.

m   O my children, so threatened and so ill, accept my motherly urging to return to the Lord along the way of conversion and of repentance. Recognize sin as the greatest of evils, as the source of all individual and social evils. Never live in sin. If you should happen to commit it out of human weakness, or through the subtle temptations of the Evil One, have recourse quickly to confession. Let frequent confession be the remedy which you make use of against the spread of sin and evil.

n   You then live in great communion of love and of life with the Most Holy Trinity, who takes up its dwelling in you and who is more and more glorified by you.

o   — *The great trial has come for the Church,* so violated by the evil spirits, so divided in its unity, so darkened in its holiness. See how error has flooded throughout it, error which leads to the loss of the true faith. Apostasy is spreading everywhere.

p   A special gift of my Immaculate Heart for these times of yours is the *Catechism of the Catholic Church,* which my Pope has wished to promulgate, to be as it were his shining last testament. But how many are those pastors who grope about in the mist, become speechless out of fear or compromise, and who no longer defend their flocks from the many rapacious wolves!

q   Many priestly and consecrated lives have become dried up by impurity, seduced by pleasures and the search for comfort and well-being. The faithful are being drawn in by the enticements of a world which has become pagan, or by the countless sects which are spreading more and more.

r   The hour of its great trial has above all come for the Church, because it will be shaken by the lack of faith, obscured by apostasy, wounded by betrayal, abandoned by its children, divided by schisms, possessed and dominated by Freemasonry, turned into fertile soil from which will spring up the wicked tree of the man of iniquity, the Antichrist, who will bring his kingdom into its interior.

s   — *The great trial has come for all humanity*, already lacerated by spreading violence, by destructive hatred, by wars which are expanding menacingly, by great ills which no one is able to heal.

t   At the dawn of this new year, the threat of a terrible third world war is becoming stronger and more worrisome. How many people will have to suffer the scourge of hunger, of famine, of discord, and of fratricidal struggles which will spill much blood on your roads.

u   *If the time of the great trial has come*, the time has come also for all to hasten into the safe refuge of my Immaculate Heart. Do not lose courage. Be strong in trust and confidence. I have told you beforehand of the times which await you, painful and difficult times, precisely in order to help you live in trust and in a great confidence in your heavenly Mother.

v   The further you enter into the time of the great trial, the more will you experience, in an extraordinary way, my motherly presence close to you, to help, defend, protect and console you, and to prepare for you new days of serenity and peace.

w   In the end, after the time of the great trial, there awaits you the time of great peace, great joy, great holiness, the time of the greatest triumph of God in your midst.

x   Pray with me on this, my feast day, and live in that expectation which sweetens the bitterness of your daily suffering. Today I am spreading my mantle over you to shelter you, as does a mother hen with her chicks, and I bless you all in the name of the Father, and of the Son, and of the Holy Spirit."

In the Temple of My Immaculate Heart

a   "Let yourselves be carried in my motherly arms, beloved children, as newborn babes, in the spiritual temple of my Immaculate Heart.

b   — *In the temple of my Immaculate Heart,* I offer you to the perfect glory of the Most Holy and Divine Trinity.

c   I offer you to the glory of the Father, who takes delight in you, and I lead you, at each moment of your life, to do his divine Will with love, docility and filial abandonment. Thus as in heaven, so also on this earth, the Heavenly Father is glorified, and his name is adored and sanctified.

d   I offer you to the glory of the Son, who pours out upon you the torrents of his divine mercy, to wipe away every shadow of evil and sin from your souls; who imprints there his image as the only-begotten Son of the Father; and who associates you in his divine splendor, so as to make of you yourselves light for revelation to all the gentiles. For this, I am leading you with gentle firmness, along the way of faith and purity, of hope and mortification, of love and an ever greater holiness.

e   I offer you to the glory of the Holy Spirit, who gives Himself to you in inexhaustible abundance, in order to lead you into the heart of his very own design of love for the Father and the Son, thus making of you burning witnesses of divine charity. For this, I am obtaining for you his seven holy gifts, which give you vigor and constancy, courage and strength, zeal and perseverance in the fulfillment of the mission which has been entrusted to you.

f   Thus, while in the temple of the created universe God is denied, scorned and blasphemed, in the temple of my Immaculate Heart, the Most Holy and Divine Trinity receives again today, from the mouths of my little children, the praise and perfect glory that is due It.

g   — *In the temple of my Immaculate Heart,* I am forming you for the greater splendor of the Church, the new Israel of God. In the time of the great trial for the Church, you become the help which it earnestly awaits, the help which my Immaculate Heart gives it, for these bloody moments of the great tribulation.

h And so I am bringing you to the heroic witness to Christ and to his Gospel, making of you courageous heralds of all the truths of the Catholic faith, in such a way that you illumine with your light the deep darkness of these times of great apostasy. By means of you, the Church will become more and more enlightened and will recover its confidence and strength, so that it may accomplish the task of the second evangelization, to which it is being strongly urged by the Spirit.

i — *In the temple of my Immaculate Heart,* I give to all humanity the refuge, so sought for and awaited, for these times of the great trial which is now upon you. During these years, how very many of my children will you see, starved and scattered, crushed and wounded, hastening in search of protection and salvation in the temple of my Immaculate Heart.

j I desire that the task entrusted to the Marian Movement of Priests be brought to its conclusion in the shortest time possible and that all make right away the consecration to my Immaculate Heart, which I have asked of you for these days of the great trial.

k It is for this reason, my little son, that you find yourself again today in a very distant place, where I am venerated and Jesus is adored by a great number of my little children, poor, humble, simple, but faithful and docile to the request of your heavenly Mother.

l In the hearts of all my little children, I take up my dwelling, where I myself find my refuge, to be consoled by your tender filial love and to obtain that great reparation which I have asked of you and of which I have need, in order to shorten the great sufferings of these, your days."

488
São Paulo (Brazil); February 11, 1993
Feast of Our Lady of Lourdes

The Dangers Which Threaten You

a "Look today at the splendor of your heavenly Mother, who

760

appeared in Lourdes as the Immaculate Conception.

b   I appeared in order to announce to you that you have entered into the time of my full manifestation. I appeared in order to point out to you the way along which you should travel in these final times of yours. I appeared in order to carry out my motherly task in your regard, my children, so ensnared by my Adversary and yours. In the time of the great trial, I am pointing out to you *the dangers which threaten you.*

c   —The gravest danger is that of succumbing to the seduction of the world in which you live, of becoming the victim of sin and evil, of returning to slavery under Satan and his diabolical power. And so I have manifested myself to you as the Immaculate Conception, that is, as the only creature who has never known the shadow of sin, not even original sin, which every person contracts at the moment of his human conception.

d   And I have directed to you my motherly invitation to walk along the way of goodness and grace, of purity and humility, of love and of an ever greater holiness. I have also asked you to make use of those means which are indispensable for walking along this difficult road: penance and the sacrament of Reconciliation.

e   — Another danger which threatens you is that of allowing yourself to be taken up with inordinate activity, and so forgetting the powerful force which prayer has in obtaining the grace of conversion for many of my poor sinful children. And so I have invited you to pray much for the conversion of sinners, by showing you, through my little daughter Bernadette, that the most efficacious prayer, the prayer which is most preferred by me, is that of the holy rosary.

f   — And lastly, there is the continual danger of falling ill, of allowing yourself to be seized by discouragement and lack of confidence, thus reducing you to a true spiritual impotence. And so, I have wished also to manifest myself as a medicine for your ills, a help in your needs, and a support in your human weakness. I have invited you to go and wash at the fountain, with that water which I have caused to spring up miraculously from the rock on which I appeared.

761

^g Today, now that the time of the great trial has already come, I again repeat to you my motherly invitation to follow me along the way of grace and purity, of penance and prayer, in order to obtain the gift of healing and salvation."

489 *Fatima (Portugal); March 15, 1993*

I Have Wanted You Here

^a "Today I invite you to come here in spirit, my beloved children, to the poor Cova da Iria in Fatima, where I appeared that I might be a light upon your path in this period of time in which you are living. And so *I have again wanted you here*, my little child, at my feet, in the very same place where I began this great work of love, my Marian Movement of Priests.

^b *I have wanted you here*, to receive from your hands this work of mine, which has now spread throughout the whole world, and by means of which there comes to me from all sides the homage of my beloved priests and children who have consecrated themselves to my Immaculate Heart. This generous response which I receive, especially from the little ones, the poor, the simple, and the humble, gives much joy to my motherly Heart and consoles me in my great sorrow.

^c *I have wanted you here*, to tell you that you must now all enter right away into the safe refuge of my Immaculate Heart. Just as Noah, in the name of the Lord, called into the ark those who were to be saved from the flood, so now must you, my littlest child, in the name of your heavenly Mother, call into the refuge of my Immaculate Heart those who must be protected, defended and saved from the great trial which has now come for the Church and for all humanity.

^d *I have wanted you here*, because you must communicate to all that as of now – as of this year – you have entered into the events which I foretold to you, and which are contained in the third part of the secret, which has not yet been revealed to you. This will now be made evident by the very events themselves which

762

are about to take place in the Church and in the world.

e   *My Church* will be shaken by the violent wind of apostasy and unbelief, as he who sets himself against Christ will enter into its interior, thus bringing to fulfillment the horrible abomination which has been prophesied to you in Holy Scripture.

f   *Humanity* will know the bloody hour of its chastisement: it will be stricken with the scourge of epidemics, of hunger and of fire; much blood will be spilt upon your roads; war will spread everywhere, bringing down upon the world incommensurable devastation.

g   You, my poor children, must all bear the weight of great sufferings and of unspeakable sorrows, so that the great miracle of divine justice and mercy may be manifest to all.

h   For this reason, from my shrine in Fatima, I renew today the pressing invitation for you to take refuge in me, through your consecration to my Immaculate Heart, and to multiply everywhere the cenacles of prayer, which I have asked of you, cenacles of priests, of little children, of youth, and cenacles within families.

i   Do not be afraid. Do not allow yourselves to be seized with discouragement. I am with you always.

j   *I have wanted you here,* because you must announce to each and all that the time has come when I will make myself manifest, in an extraordinary way, to all those who have consecrated themselves to me and have formed part of my victorious cohort.

k   From this place, where I appeared as the Woman Clothed with the Sun, to be your light in these dark years of the great tribulation, I bless you all in the name of the Father, and of the Son, and of the Holy Spirit."

490   *Rubbio (Vicenza, Italy); April 8, 1993*
Holy Thursday

A Service of Love

a   "Beloved sons, this is your feast day. This is your pasch. Today you are recalling the institution of the new Sacrifice and of the new Priesthood, which took place at the Last Supper. Gathered about your bishops in concelebration, you are renewing your promise of fidelity to Jesus and the Church.

b   You are his ministers; you are his servants. Let your priestly ministry be *a service of love*.

c   — *Love Jesus* who has chosen, called and consecrated you in order to perpetuate throughout time his Sacrifice, accomplished on the Cross for the salvation of the world.

d   Jesus asks of you, his priests, only to be loved. He asks this of you with the anxiety of a thirsty man who, moaning, waits for a drop of water; with the longing of a hungry man who stretches out his hand for a scrap of bread; with the ardor of a lover who longs to receive love from the one he loves.

e   My beloved sons, open your priestly hearts to the perfect love for my Son Jesus. Your love is balm upon his Heart which sweetens the bitterness of his feeling Himself so little loved, in these times when the hearts of men have become cold, frigid, closed by egoism and a great aridity.

f   Never before as today, has Love been so unloved. You who are his priests, love Jesus who is surrounded by great coldness and a general indifference. Let your priestly ministry be *a service of love for Him*.

g   Lay a caress upon his face, so often disfigured; bind up his head, pierced with deep thorns; kiss his lips to taste the bitterness of his chalice; anoint with balm his body, covered with sweat and blood; make reparation by your presence for the countless and repeated acts of abandonment; give your life to Him in loving compensation for the ongoing acts of betrayal. Enter with Jesus into Gethsemane, and live with Him the painful hours of his interior agony.

h   — *Love his brothers and yours*, with the infinite delicacy of his divine love. Learn of Jesus who is meek and humble of Heart. Learn from Jesus how to love. You too, gird yourself with the towel, to put yourself at the service of your neighbor. Let your priestly ministry be *a service of love for all*. Let it be Jesus Himself who loves in you.

i   To the poor give his richness; to the rich, his poverty; to the healthy, his weakness; to the sick, his strength; to sinners, his salvation; to the dying, his paradise; to the hungry, his body; to the thirsty, his blood; to the weak, his support; to the little, his defense; to all, his divine caress.

j On this Holy Thursday, beloved sons, learn from Jesus how to love. And so I invite you today to enter, each and all, into the Gethsemane of his divine love, never to leave it again."

491

Rubbio (Vicenza, Italy); April 9, 1993
Good Friday

His Sorrowful Passion Is Being Renewed

a "Beloved children, come with me to Calvary, to live the sorrowful hour of the passion and death of my Son Jesus. With what fatigue He makes his way towards Golgotha, carrying on his wounded shoulders the burden of his gibbet. How distant are the voices of his triumph: 'Hosanna to the Son of David! Blessed is He who comes in the name of the Lord.' (Mt 21:9)

b In place of the palm and olive branches, there are the lances of the Roman soldiers; in place of the *hosanna* cries of the crowd, there is the shouting and the insults of the executioners; in place of the joyful songs of the little children, there is the weeping of the faithful women; in place of the majestic and regal entrance, there is the slow advance carrying the Cross on his shoulders.

c The crowd fed by Jesus with his bread are not there, nor are the sick who had been healed, nor the sinners led back along the road of righteousness, nor the Apostles chosen to be his witnesses. But his Mother is there, and close to her, the beloved John, who represents all of you, my beloved sons.

d Together, let us kiss his wounds; let us collect his blood; close the deep gashes; arrange his blood-soaked hair; wipe away the bruises and spittle from his face; make clean again his martyred body, covered with injuries; drink the blood and water that flow from his pierced Heart.

e And let us ever live in spirit his sorrowful passion.

f *This, his sorrowful passion, is being renewed* in these last times when the great trial has come for all.

g   *His sorrowful passion is being renewed* by the Church, his Mystical Body. She too is called to enter into the Gethsemane of his agony. She too knows the kiss of betrayal, the denial and the abandonment on the part of her own. She too must taste all the bitterness of his chalice. She is likewise mocked, scourged and crowned with thorns. She likewise experiences the condemnation and abuse of many. Indeed, she is crucified and immolated so that the plan of the Heavenly Father may be fulfilled.

h   *His sorrowful passion is being renewed* by you, my beloved children. And so I have called you time and again to enter, by your consecration, into the Gethsemane of my Immaculate Heart. This is in order to form you for your priestly immolation and to give you the strength to go forward without fear to the Calvary of your martyrdom, close to me, the sorrowful Mother, who has begotten you beneath the Cross upon which my Son Jesus has been put to death.

i   The time of your painful passion has now arrived. You too will be persecuted and stricken, rejected and condemned, imprisoned and killed. But do not let yourselves be seized with apprehension or fear. I am as close to you, as I was beneath the Cross.

j   I am at your side at the hour of the painful passion which is being renewed by you, my beloved ones, because today also it is beneath the cross that I am fulfilling my role as Mother of the new times, which are coming to birth from your painful suffering."

492

Rubbio (Vicenza, Italy); April 10, 1993
Holy Saturday

Close to Every Sepulchre

a   "Live together with me in prayer, in silence and in expectation, close to the sepulchre where lies the lifeless body of my Son Jesus. Beloved children, live close to me on this day of my immaculate sorrow.

b   This is the day of my new and spiritual motherhood. This is the only day when I am left without my Son. This is the first day when I feel myself called to be a mother to you, to the Church and to all humanity.

c   From today on, as Mother, I am *close to every sepulchre* in which each of my new children is laid.

d   *I am close to the sepulchre,* where millions of innocent little babies repose, babies who have never been born into life, as they were killed in the wombs of their mothers. In the new sepulchre, where the body of my Son is laid, I see gathered together all these countless sepulchres, and copious tears flow down the cheeks of a Mother who is mourning for all her little babes who have been killed in such a cruel and inhuman way.

e   *I am close to the sepulchre,* where lie all the victims of hatred, violence and wars, and who have been put into common graves, without as much as a gesture of human pity.

f   *I am close to the sepulchre,* where there rest in the sleep of death all my sinful, poor, sick, marginalized, persecuted, oppressed and battered children.

g   *I am close to the sepulchre* which gathers together the mortal remains of my priest-sons, of the religious, and of those who have consecrated their lives to the service of my Son Jesus.

h   *Close to every sepulchre,* I want to keep watch today with you, my beloved ones, in sorrow and in prayer. As of this Holy Saturday, copious tears flow daily from my motherly and merciful eyes, as I mourn over each of my new children who is being carried to the sepulchre.

i   *But close to every sepulchre,* I keep watch above all in hope and expectation.

j   From the moment when my Son Jesus came forth from his sepulchre, alive once again and victorious over death and hell, I have been waiting with confidence for the moment when all my children too will come forth from their sepulchres, to share forever in the immortal life which Jesus has obtained for you by his death and resurrection."

The Pasch of the New Times

a   "Beloved children, rejoice with me, the joyful Mother of the Resurrection. Your hearts, hearts of newborn babes, like little white flowers blossoming from the bloody torment of Calvary, are exulting with purest paschal joy.

b   Jesus, scorned, scourged, crowned with thorns, condemned to the gibbet, crucified, put to death and buried, today comes forth victorious from his sepulchre in the splendor of his divine glory.

c   Jesus is alive; Jesus is holy; Jesus is immortal; Jesus is God! In the light of his risen body, Jesus Christ is spreading over the world and the entire universe the splendor of the Father, the reflection of his glory, the imprint of his divine substance.

d   And peace descends into your souls, set free from slavery to Satan and sin; into your hearts, purified by the fire of his love; into your minds, opened up to the gift of his word of life; into your spirits, upon whom his very own Spirit comes gently to rest; into your eyes, called upon to reflect his most ardent light; into your bodies, called to share in the new experience of divine immortality.

e   Yes, Jesus Christ has conquered death; has made Satan, the ancient Adversary, his slave; takes you by the hand and leads you into the stupendous kingdom of his freedom.

f   Do not let the hour of a new Gethsemane, through which humanity is now living, make you sad. Do not be discouraged if evil has the upper hand in the world today. Do not be alarmed if Satan has reached the summit of his diabolical reign.

g   Humanity is now lying in its sepulchre of death, of sin, of impurity, rent asunder by the impetuous wind of violence and hatred. Soon it too will come forth from this, its immense sepulchre, to live *the pasch of the new times*, when Jesus will return in glory to restore his kingdom of love and of life.

h   Prepare yourselves to live *the pasch of the new times*. It is the pasch prepared for you. It is the pasch which awaits you at the end of the gloomy period of the purification and the great tribulation, through which you are now living. It is with great hope

768

and in this certain expectation that you must live through the time of the great trial which has now arrived for all.

i In this pasch of 1993, I invite you all to look to 'Jesus Christ, the FaithfulWitness, the First-born of the dead, and the Ruler of the kings of the earth.

j 'To Jesus Christ who loves us and has freed us from our sins by his blood and who has made us into a kingdom, priests to his God and Father, to Him be glory and power for ever and ever!

k 'Behold! Jesus Christ is coming amid the clouds, and every eye will see Him, even those who pierced Him. The peoples of the earth will be confounded. Yes. Amen.' (cf. Rev 1:5-7)

l Beloved children, in the paschal joy of this announcement, which brings you to peace, with my risen Son, I bless you all today in the name of the Father, and of the Son, and of the Holy Spirit."

494 *Sant' Omero (Teramo, Italy); May 1, 1993*
Feast of St. Joseph the Worker
First Saturday

My Motherly Presence

a "Beloved children, today I invite you to live with particular diligence your consecration to my Immaculate Heart. It is the best way of offering me this month of May, which has been set aside by the Church for my particular veneration.

b I am especially close to you during this month, and I want *my motherly presence* to be felt by each one of you. You will succeed in feeling my presence as Mother close to you if, as little children, you accustom yourselves to do everything together with me. Pray with me; work with me; love with me; suffer with me; offer yourselves with me; keep silence with me. Silence must become for you the sign of *my motherly presence*.

c Let yours be an *exterior silence*, which protects you from the deafening roar of voices and images, which continually fill the course of your days. Remove yourselves from the easy seduction of the press and television, this terrible means made use of by my Adversary to draw you away from me and my Son Jesus.

d   Let yours be an *interior silence*, which leads you to listen, with love and faith, to the word of God alone. Penetrate into the deep mystery of truth and beauty, which is revealed to you in the Gospel. Let the Gospel of Jesus be the only word of life which you seek, welcome, love and live. Let yours be that interior silence which leads you to contemplation and prayer. Let your prayer become more intense. Let it be a true prayer of the heart, which you make with me and by means of me.

e   For this, let the cenacles of prayer which I have asked of you flourish everywhere, like fragrant flowers which blossom in the desert of a great aridity and general dissipation.

f   Mortify your senses. Let the tongue be loosened only for words of wisdom and goodness. Let your mouth be ever closed to judgments, criticisms, affronts, gossip, calumnies, duplicity and insincerity. Let the eyes be opened to see the deep wounds of the sick, the poor, the little ones, the abandoned, the stricken, the persecuted, the oppressed and the slain. Turn your gaze away from impurity and malice, from evil and wickedness, from seduction and impiety.

g   Open your hands to the aid of all. Go along the rough and blood-stained roads in search of my poor wandering children. Offer me your hearts so that I may love in you and by means of you, in such a way that all may receive the comfort *of my motherly presence.*

h   Beloved children, these are the flowers which I am asking you to give me, to make more pleasing to me this month of May which you are beginning today.

i   Only in this way do I feel myself ever close to you. Only in this way do you spread about you the charism *of my motherly presence.* Only in this way do you reflect my light of love and hope. Only in this way do you live the consecration which you have made to me.

j   Then, by means of you, the heavenly Mother becomes more and more invoked, listened to, followed and lived, and my Immaculate Heart attains its greatest triumph."

770

The Bloody Years of the Battle

a   "By a day-long cenacle at this venerated shrine, you, the priests and faithful of my Movement in the region of Lombardy, are today observing the anniversary of my first apparition which took place at Fatima, in the poor Cova da Iria.

b   You are still in the period described by me in my apparition. Above all, you are in the heart of my message. The struggle between the Woman Clothed with the Sun and the Red Dragon has, during these years, reached its highest peak. Satan has set up his kingdom in the world. He is now ruling over you as a sure victor.

c   The powers which are directing and arranging human events, according to their perverse plans, are the dark and diabolic powers of evil. They have succeeded in bringing all humanity to live without God. They have spread everywhere the error of theoretical and practical atheism. They have built the new idols before which humanity is bowing down in adoration: pleasure, money, pride, impurity, mastery over others, and impiety.

d   Thus, in these years of yours, violence is spreading more and more. Egoism has made the hearts of men hard and insensitive. Hatred has blazed up like a scorching fire. Wars have multiplied in every part of the world, and you are now living in the danger of a new terrible world war which will bring destruction to peoples and nations, a war from which no one will emerge victorious.

e   Satan has succeeded in entering into the Church, the new Israel of God. He has entered there with the smoke of error and sin, of the loss of faith and apostasy, of compromise with the world and the search for pleasure. During these years, he has succeeded in leading astray bishops and priests, religious and faithful.

f   The forces of Masonry have entered into the Church, in a subtle and hidden way, and have set up their stronghold in the very place where the Vicar of my Son Jesus lives and works.

g   You are living *the bloody years of the battle*, because the great trial has now arrived for all.

h   There is now taking place that which is contained in the third part of my message, which has not yet been revealed to you, but which has now become evident from the events themselves through which you are now living.

i   To prepare you for them, I have caused my Marian Movement of Priests to spring up in every part of the world. And thus I have chosen this littlest and poorest child of mine and have brought him everywhere, as an instrument of my motherly plan of salvation and mercy.

j   By means of him, I have called you from all sides to consecrate yourselves to my Immaculate Heart; to enter, each and all, into the safe refuge which your heavenly Mother has prepared for you; to multiply the cenacles of prayer as lightning rods which protect you from the fire of the chastisement. How many of you have responded to my call with filial love and with great generosity!

k   My plan is now on the point of being realized, and the task which I have entrusted to this little son of mine is about to be completed. And so today I am looking upon you with the special satisfaction of a Mother who is being consoled and exalted by you.

l   I urge you to live without fear, but rather with great confidence and trust, *these bloody years of the battle*. From the chalice of sufferings never experienced until now, there will come forth the divine sun of a new era, of a humanity heretofore unknown, of grace and holiness, of love and justice, of joy and peace."

496   *Notre Dame de Laus (Gap, France); May 30, 1993*
Solemnity of Pentecost

Comfort Amidst Mourning

a   "You are bringing to completion today, in this venerated shrine, the journey which you have undertaken all through France. In fifteen days, you have held a good twenty cenacles, in which bishops, priests and a great number of the faithful of my Movement have taken part.

b   Everywhere you have gathered together in prayer with me before the Eucharistic Jesus solemnly exposed on the altar, and you have renewed your consecration to my Immaculate Heart. Everywhere you have contemplated the marvels of love, of grace and of mercy of your heavenly Mother.

c   You are completing this extraordinary journey today, on the solemn feast of Pentecost. This is a sign which I am giving you, to make you understand that, in the garden of my Immaculate Heart, the new Church and the new humanity, purified, sanctified and completely renewed by the Holy Spirit, are even now ready to come to birth.

d   This decisive time of the purification and the great tribulation is the time of the Holy Spirit. And so I renew again today my invitation to multiply the cenacles of prayer, which I have asked for, with such motherly insistence.

e   Let these cenacles be spread among the priests, my beloved sons. Surrender to me your concerns and your many occupations. Do not give in to the easy seductions of the world. Return to the spirit of simplicity, of humility, of littleness. Recollect yourselves in prayer in the cenacle of my Immaculate Heart, and then you will be able to see, with your own eyes, the wonder of the second Pentecost.

f   Let children come together in cenacles, because their innocent prayer, united to mine, has today a great power of intercession and reparation. From how many evils you have already been spared, because of the prayer of these little children of mine!

g   I want to gather young people together in cenacles, so that they may experience my motherly presence, the presence of a Mother who loves them, protects them from the great dangers to which they are exposed, and who leads them with gentle firmness, along the road of goodness, of love, of purity and of holiness.

h   The cenacles which I have asked of families are a precious gift to them, so that in them they may experience the joy of my presence, the comfort of my assistance, and the help offered against the grave evils which threaten their very existence. In these cenacles, the Holy Spirit will come down to lead you to the second Pentecost.

i   It is necessary, above all in these last times, that the Church

773

and all humanity be transformed into a continuous cenacle of prayer, made with me and through me. Then the Holy Spirit will come down *as a comfort upon the mourning* of your days, in which the great trial has already come.

j *Amidst the mourning* of a humanity without God, there will come down *the comfort* of the Holy Spirit, who will lead the whole world to the perfect glorification of the Heavenly Father, bringing about a new marriage of love between a renewed humanity and its Lord who has created, redeemed and saved it.

k *Amidst the mourning* of a divided, darkened and wounded Church, there will be felt *the comfort* of the Holy Spirit, who will clothe it with fortitude and wisdom, with grace and holiness, and with love and light, in such a way that it may give its full witness to Jesus, living in it until the end of the world.

l *Amidst the mourning* of souls, made slaves of Satan, immersed in the shadow of sin and death, there will alight *the comfort* of the Holy Spirit, who will give the light of the presence of God, the life of divine grace, and the fire of love, so that in them the Most Holy and Divine Trinity will be able to take up its permanent dwelling.

m *Amidst the mourning* of the great trial, there will come down *the comfort* of the divine presence of the Spirit of the Lord, who will lead you to live — with confidence, courage, hope, serenity and love — through the events, which are awaiting you.

n Then, in the midst of fire, you will feel his refreshment; in the cold, his heat; in the darkness, his light; in mourning, his comfort; in fear, his courage; in weakness, his strength; in great suffering, his divine solace.

o And so today, I invite you to unite your prayer to mine, so that the Spirit of the Lord may come down upon you, with all his gifts.

p Come, O Holy Spirit.
Come, and change the face of the earth.
Come, quickly.
Come, in these last times.
Come, now that the great trial has arrived.
Come, and bring us your second Pentecost, so that our eyes may see your greatest miracle, that of the new heavens and new earth."

774

My Work

a   "With a great cenacle of priests and faithful of my Movement from French-speaking Switzerland, you are celebrating today the liturgical memorial of my Immaculate Heart. You are completing the journey which you have been making through all Switzerland, so ensnared and stricken by my Adversary, but so loved and defended by your heavenly Mother.

b   Here, where my Adversary is exercising his great power through hedonism, moral permissiveness and impurity, and is obscuring the splendor of my Church through division, through the spread of errors which are leading many away from the true faith, through disobedience and contestation directed against the Pope, I am taking action in a powerful way to spread everywhere *my great work of love and salvation.*

c   *It is my work*, which I am carrying out in every part of the world in these last times.

d   *It is my work*, which I am raising up everywhere for the triumph of my Immaculate Heart.

e   *It is my work*, which I myself am now carrying out, in order to gather from all sides the little remnant which will remain faithful to Jesus and to his Gospel, to the Pope and to the Church united with him.

f   *It is my work*, because I myself am accomplishing it and spreading it in a silent and hidden way.

g   Satan and all the diabolic spirits are able to do nothing against it. The Lord has prohibited them from harming it. The powers of evil, the dark forces of Satanism, and the secret rulers of Masonry can do nothing against it, because it is protected, preserved and defended by me.

h   *It is my work*, which I am carrying out in every part of the world in order to conquer Satan, in the great battle against all the wicked spirits, because in the end my Immaculate Heart will triumph.

i   *It is my work*, which I am accomplishing to spread the truth in these times of great apostasy, to bring you to greater unity with the Pope in these days of division and of widespread rebellion, to lead you along the way of grace and holiness amidst the general spread of sin and impurity.

j   *It is my work,* which I am carrying out by means of my Marian Movement of Priests. For this, I have chosen this little child of mine and made him an instrument of my greatest marvels in every part of the world.

k   Satan has sought in many ways to destroy it, by stirring up opposition and criticisms against it, persecutions and obstacles, subtle snares on the part of false visionaries and false messages, which have succeeded in misleading a great number of my poor children.

l   But I have personally intervened, in an extraordinary way, to prevent him from harming it, because I am jealous of this work of mine with the very jealousy of God. For it is through it that I will bring about the triumph of my Immaculate Heart in the world.

m   And so, now that the great trial is here, my work must shine forth with a light that becomes stronger and stronger, because the times have arrived when my Immaculate Heart must be exalted by all the Church and all humanity."

498

Valdragone (San Marino); July 1, 1993
Spiritual Exercises in the Form of a Cenacle
with the Bishops and Priests of the M.M.P.
from America and Europe

The Mission Which I Entrust to You

a   "During these days, beloved sons, how much joy you give to my Immaculate Heart, and in my sorrow, how greatly am I consoled by you! You have come from faraway countries of America and from all over Europe. And now, bishops and priests of my Movement, you find yourselves reunited in a continuous cenacle.

b   Your heavenly Mother is present in an extraordinary way, to pray with you, in order to make you grow in love and unity, to obtain for you the gift of the Holy Spirit so that He will confirm you in your vocation, and give you courage in your apostolate, and bring joy and peace to your hearts.

c   Your heavenly Mother is glorified in you. Through you the

776

triumph of my Immaculate Heart is accomplished. For this reason, I have once again called you up here, on this mountain, and you have responded with great generosity. And so I have exercised my motherly action in a powerful way in your hearts and your souls, because you must now be ready for the mission which I am entrusting to you.

d   — *The mission which I entrust to you* is that of going everywhere to bring *the light of the truth*, in these times when the darkness of error has spread everywhere. See how the lack of faith is spreading like a flood; see how the apostasy becomes greater and greater each day!

e   You must be the light lit in the night; you must be apostles faithful to the Gospel, which must be lived by you and proclaimed to the letter. Do not allow yourselves to be misled by false teachers, who have become so numerous today. Do not let yourselves be deceived by new doctrines, even if they are generally followed. Because, like Christ, his truth is ever the same: yesterday, today and always.

f   Then, in these days, your light will shine forth before men, who will glorify your Heavenly Father. You will point out the way they should go in this new evangelization, and you will become the apostles of these last times.

g   — *The mission which I entrust to you* is that of going everywhere to bring *the salvation of Christ*, to a humanity which has once again become pagan, after almost two thousand years since the Gospel was first announced. Give Jesus, the only Redeemer and the only Savior, to the world of today. Give Him through the faithful exercise of your priesthood, which puts you at the service of souls, by the ministry of the sacraments which have been entrusted to you.

h   Above all, be diligent in prayer, zealous in the apostolate, ardent in love in the celebration of the Eucharist, assiduous and available for the sacrament of Reconciliation, which is being much neglected today by a great number of my priest-sons. So then, help the faithful entrusted to your care to walk along the way of holiness, of the grace of God, of love, of purity and of the exercise of all the virtues.

i   — *The mission which I entrust to you* is that of going everywhere to bring *the fire of love* to a humanity dried up by egoism, darkened by hatred, wounded by violence, threatened with war. See how many poor children of mine give way every day under the weight of this general inability to love. Now that the great trial is at hand, go into every part of the world to seek out my children who have gone astray. Take them in your priestly arms, and carry them all into the safe refuge of my Immaculate Heart.

j Support the weak; restore strength to the timid; convert the sinners; bring those far away to the house of the Father; heal the sick; comfort the dying; give to all the heavenly dew of my motherly and merciful love.

k Even now, as of this year, events will worsen in the Church and in the world, because you are entering into the times which I foretold to you in the message which I have given you at Fatima and which up to now has not been revealed to you. But now it will become evident by the very events through which you are living.

l And so, *the mission which I entrust to you* is that of going everywhere to bring the light of the truth, the salvation of Jesus, and the tenderness of my motherly love. Thus you become instruments of the triumph of my Immaculate Heart in the world.

m Go from this cenacle in joy; may peace of heart be the sign of my daily presence near you. Live in confidence and in great hope, and become a sign of consolation for all those you meet along your way.

n With your dear ones and all those who have been entrusted to your care, I bless you in the name of the Father, and of the Son, and of the Holy Spirit."

499

Rubbio (Vicenza, Italy); August 15, 1993
Solemnity of the Assumption
of the Blessed Virgin Mary into Heaven

Close to All of You

a "Beloved children, look with joy at the splendor of my glorified body, assumed into the glory of paradise. The Most Holy and Divine Trinity is glorified today by your heavenly Mother.

b   The Father contemplates in me the masterpiece of his creation and is pleased at seeing me surrounded with the splendor of his glory and his divine power. The Son joyfully sees me at his side and shares with me his royal power over all the universe. The Holy Spirit is glorified in his Spouse who is exalted above all creatures in heaven and on earth.

c   On this day, I reflect upon you the rays of my splendor, and I ask you to walk in the light of my motherly presence *close to all of you*.

d   Precisely because of the privilege of my bodily assumption into heaven, I am always able to be *close to all of you,* my poor children, still pilgrims upon this earth.

e   I am close to my Church, suffering and divided, crucified and immolated, still living through the painful hours of its martyrdom and its Calvary.

f   I am close to all humanity, redeemed by Jesus, but now so far from its Lord, and walking along the wicked way of evil and sin, of hatred and iniquity.

g   I am close to my straying children, that I may lead them along the way of conversion and return to the Lord; to the sick, that I may give them comfort and healing; to all who are far away, that I may lead them to the house of the Heavenly Father who awaits them with great love; to the despairing, that I may give them hope and confidence; to the dying, that I may open up for them the gate of eternal happiness.

h   I am particularly close to my Pope, who is being guided, led and immolated by me; to the bishops and priests, that I may give them courage and strength to walk along the way of heroic witness to Jesus and his Gospel; to the religious, that I may help them follow Jesus, obedient, poor and chaste, all the way to Calvary; to all the faithful, that I may give them the grace of keeping their baptismal promises in all circumstances.

i   Now that the great trial has come, you will feel me in an extraordinary way, *close to all of you*, that I may be the great sign of consolation and certain hope in these last times of the purification and the great tribulation."

Along the Way of Humility

a   "Beloved children, look today at your infant Mother, and place a fragrant crown of love and humility about the crib in which you venerate me at the moment of my earthly birth. I am your Mother who am leading you along the way of humility and littleness, of docility and obedience, of mortification and purity.

b   Follow me each day *on the way of humility*, because you are being called to contemplate, in these last times, the greatest marvels of the Lord. As the Lord has looked upon the humility of his servant, so also today the Lord is looking upon the humility of all of you, my little children.

c   *Along the way of humility*, learn to be little. Today, when my Adversary is succeeding in deceiving all with the spirit of pride and arrogance, remain ever in the truth, and proclaim it with courage, in all its fullness. Thus, in these times of great darkness, you give to all the light of the Gospel.

d   You then become today the very voice of God, who speaks again by means of you and achieves, by means of the silence of my little children, his greatest victory over his strong and powerful adversaries.

e   *Along the way of humility*, learn to be docile. In these times when my Adversary is succeeding in misleading many, through the wicked spirit of self-affirmation and rebellion, give a good example of humble and courageous obedience.

f   Be obedient to the Pope and the bishops united with him. Obey all the norms which regulate your priestly life. Obey the Will of God, which becomes more and more manifest to you, so that your Father who is in heaven may be glorified in you, each day, in the perfect fulfillment of his divine Will.

g   *Along the way of humility*, learn to be pure. In these days in which you are living, when my Adversary is succeeding in misleading everyone through the darkness of sin and impurity, remain pure, and give the good example of a holy and spotless priestly life.

h Above all, give the witness of a joyful faithfulness to your promise of celibacy, because your priestly body should be a body crucified to the world and to all its seductions.

i For this, my little son, I have brought you once again to this great country, so very far away, on the day of my nativity. Look at the tens of millions of your brothers who are still living plunged in the darkness of paganism, and who are awaiting the moment when they will enter the one and only sheepfold, to know at last the consoling voice of the one Good Shepherd.

j Today I announce that this great miracle will take place soon. With the triumph of my Immaculate Heart in the world, this entire great nation, which is still pagan, will enter and become part of the flock of which Jesus Christ is the Good Shepherd. Prepare yourselves for this moment, with humility and confidence, listening with docility to the voice of your heavenly Mother.

k Today I bless you and take you by the hand, in order to lead you to live through the painful hours of the great trial, which is even now upon you, to prepare the world for the meeting with its Lord, who is about to return to you in the splendor of his reign of glory."

501

Tokyo (Japan); September 15, 1993
Feast of Our Lady of Sorrows
Spiritual Exercises in the Form of a Cenacle
with the Priests of the M.M.P. from Japan

A Cause of My Great Sorrow

a "Today I see you gathered here in this cenacle of prayer and brotherhood, beloved sons of my Marian Movement of Priests of Japan, and I am consoled by you in my great sorrow.

b *A cause of my great sorrow* is all of these poor children of mine, who are still living immersed in the darkness of paganism and who are unaware of the truth of the Gospel. In this great country, almost all are still far from faith in Jesus Christ, who has come into the world to be your only Savior, your only Redeemer.

c   I am the Mother of all these pagans as well, a Mother who is concerned and anxious for their salvation. I nurture seeds of life and goodness in their hearts. I help them to observe that Law which the Lord has engraved in the depths of each man. I stir up in their minds a desire for the truth, and thus lead them gently to the encounter with my Son Jesus. Their full and total adhesion to the Gospel will be an extraordinary work of my Immaculate Heart.

d   *A cause of my great sorrow* is my Church which, in every part of the world, is passing through the painful and bloody Gethsemane of its great tribulation. You have seen, my little son, how, even here in Japan, the Church is being threatened with the loss of faith and with the increasingly vast and subtle spread of errors. It is wounded in its unity by the contestation and opposition directed against the Pope and his universal Magisterium. Its holiness is being obscured by the spread of sins and sacrileges.

e   Thus it is becoming paralyzed, and its drive to evangelize has become greatly weakened.

f   *A cause of my great sorrow* is the hardness of your hearts and your incapacity to accept what your heavenly Mother is asking of you. How many times have I spoken to you, and you have not listened! I have given extraordinary signs of my motherly intervention, and you have not believed. How many have closed the door of their own hearts and have not wanted to receive me as a mother in their lives!

g   In this very country I have given you an extraordinary sign, causing copious tears to fall more than a hundred times from the eyes of one of my statues, in which I am represented as the sorrowful Mother beneath the Cross of my Son Jesus. And I have also given you three messages to warn you of the great dangers into which you are running.

h   I now announce to you that the time of the great trial has come, because during these years all that I have foretold to you will come to pass. The apostasy and the great schism in the Church is on the point of taking place, and the great chastisement, about which I foretold you in this place, is now at the very

782

doors. Fire will come down from heaven, and a great part of humanity will be destroyed. Those who will survive will envy the dead, because everywhere there will be desolation, death and ruin.

i And so, once again I have wanted you here, my little son. For you must tell all that the hour of the chastisement has come and that, in order to be protected and saved, they must all enter right away into the safe refuge of my Immaculate Heart.

j Return to your homes, my beloved children, and bring to all this message of mine, as a final call from your heavenly Mother, who is calling you all and gathering you under her mantle, that you may be consoled and defended by her, during the painful trial of these last times of yours."

502

Milan (Italy); October 2, 1993
Feast of the Holy Guardian Angels
First Saturday

The Task of the Guardian Angels

a "Beloved children, on this first Saturday of the month, you are gathering together in cenacles to renew your consecration to my Immaculate Heart and to observe the liturgical memorial of your guardian angels. In the times of the great trial, I invite you to strengthen the bond which unites you to your guardian angels. They have a special and important task to carry out with regard to you, especially in these last times.

b —The guardian angels have above all the task of being a *light upon your path*. The days in which you are living are marked with a great darkness which is becoming ever more profound and widespread. It is the darkness of errors which encompasses the minds of men and which makes them victims of the great apostasy. It is the darkness of sins which obscures the beauty and holiness of the soul. It is the darkness of impurity which degrades the splendor of your body, called to reflect the glory of the living God. Thus, how many of my poor children are today living like shadows, submerged in the darkness of error, of sin and of impurity!

c To your guardian angels has been entrusted the task of protecting you from the great darknesses which surround you, to make you walk always in the light of truth, of holiness, of purity, of humility, of trust and of love.

d — And secondly, the guardian angels have the task of being a *defense for your life.* How numerous and subtle are the snares which the wicked spirits set each day for you: these demons who have now been poured out over the world and who are working everywhere to lead souls to eternal damnation! Their activity has now become powerful, because it has become associated with the powers who have control of the mass media, such as the press and television. With subtle refinement, evil has been spread under the guise of good; sin, as an exercise of one's own freedom; and transgression of the Law of God, as a new conquest on the part of this poor and perverted humanity.

e How strong and continuous are the attacks of the wicked spirits in striking you even in your physical life, by accidents, misfortunes, assaults, sicknesses, calamities, explosions of violence, wars and revolutions! To the guardian angels has been entrusted the task of protecting you against all these evils, of defending you against these snares, and of making you walk through life under their secure and powerful protection.

f — And lastly, the guardian angels have the task of *waging together with you one and the same battle* to obtain the same victory. In the great trial which has now arrived, the fierce struggle between the Woman Clothed with the Sun and the Red Dragon, between the forces of good and evil, between Christ and the Antichrist, is becoming still stronger and more bloody.

g It is a battle which is being waged above all at the level of the spirits: the good spirits against the wicked spirits, the angels against the demons, Saint Michael the Archangel against Lucifer.

h You are involved in this great struggle, which is immensely above and beyond you. And so you must be particularly close to those who are close to you in the great encounter, who have great power in this struggle, who assist you in fighting, and who lead you to certain victory.

i   Littlest of my children, entrust to the particular protection of your guardian angels the long and wearisome journey which you must undertake in a few days to Malaysia, Indonesia, Australia, the Fiji Islands and New Zealand, in order to hold cenacles everywhere with the priests and faithful of my Movement.

j   I urge you all today to be more assiduous in prayer, stronger in your bond of unity and deeper in your affection in respect to these angels of light, who are being given to you by the Lord as your guardians and protectors.

k   Together with them all, I bless you in the name of the Father, and of the Son, and of the Holy Spirit."

503   *Jakarta (Cisarua, Indonesia); October 21, 1993*
Spiritual Exercises in the Form of a Cenacle
with the Priests of the M.M.P. from Indonesia

Have Confidence and Great Hope

a   "How happy I am to see you here, gathered together in a continuous cenacle of prayer and brotherhood, priests of my Movement who have come from every part of Indonesia. I am united with your prayer; I am helping you grow in brotherly love; I am obtaining for you from the Lord those graces which make your ministry fruitful and holy. And I want today to give you a message of confidence and hope, which will accompany you on your difficult journey.

b   — *Have confidence* in your heavenly Mother who is ever close to you, to be of assistance and comfort to you in your priesthood. I see your innumerable difficulties. I welcome all your entreaties. I am close to you to comfort you in your solitude. I give you joy and consolation amidst so much bitterness.

c   Do not feel yourselves alone. Even if the field of the apostolate is sometimes dry and difficult, even if the society which surrounds you places obstacles in the way of your priestly action, even if the weight of human weakness seems often to overwhelm you, never become discouraged!

d   I am always close to you, as a good and understanding mother, and I am supporting, leading, consoling and encouraging you. I am gathering up your tears like precious jewels, and I am treasuring your every fatigue in the secret of my Immaculate Heart.

e — *Have great hope* in the full triumph of God for this poor humanity, so ill and far from Him. You are living the painful years of the great tribulation, and the sufferings are becoming daily heavier for all. Spend the present hour in the Gethsemane of my Immaculate Heart, and set yourselves to carry out with love the Will of your Heavenly Father.

f Be witnesses of faith in these times of the great apostasy. Be witnesses of holiness in these days of great perversion. Be witnesses of love in a world which has become hard and insensitive, consumed and dried up by egoism, hatred, violence and wars. Bring everywhere the balm of my motherly love and mercy. Take into your priestly arms my children who have strayed, those far away, the poor, the weak, the sick and the sinners, and bring them all into the safe sheepfold of my Immaculate Heart.

g Go out from this cenacle with joy. Return to your homes in peace, and become apostles of this, my Movement, in every part of this great country.

h With you, and with your dear ones and the faithful who are entrusted to your care, I bless today all Indonesia and the Church which lives, suffers and works here, so that my Son Jesus may bring to all the gift of his love, of his life and of his peace."

504

Suva (Fiji Islands); November 12, 1993
Feast of St. Josaphat, Martyr

In the Heart of the Little Ones

a "You find yourself here today, my little child, in this great island of the Pacific, to hold cenacles with my beloved ones and with the faithful, come from even very distant islands. My voice has reached even here; even here have I received a generous response. You see how it is especially the littlest ones, the simple and the poorest who have responded to me. You see how they are able to understand my voice, to listen to my word, to obey my requests, to pray with perseverance, to consecrate themselves joyfully to my Immaculate Heart.

b — *In the heart of the little ones,* I experience my great comfort. How many from among the great ones, even from among my beloved ones, reject my invitation and close the door of their hearts to my motherly presence. This persistent rejection is a cause of deep pain to me. But I am consoled in receiving such a generous response from the little ones, because it is these who are the balm which the Heavenly Father gives me and which is placed upon every new wound which opens in my motherly Heart.

c — *In the heart of the little ones,* I find my greatest joy. In them I reflect my light, and I see my plan reproduced. Because little, I am pleasing to the Most High. Only in the hearts of the little ones does the Father take pleasure, is the Son glorified, and does the Holy Spirit find his permanent dwelling place. Thus, by means of them, the Immaculate Heart of your heavenly Mother can repeat her eternal Magnificat, her canticle of adoration and praise to the Divine and Most Holy Trinity.

d — *In the heart of the little ones,* I again set my delight, because I am able to exercise fully my function as Mother. Thus, I am able to nourish them, clothe them, form them, and lead them gently along the road of purity, love and holiness.

e — *In the heart of the little ones,* my Immaculate Heart already achieves its triumph. It is by means of these that I am able to carry out my great work of love and mercy for the salvation of the world and the greatest renewal of all the Church.

f — *In the heart of the little ones,* you too must find your repose. On such a burdensome journey, amidst such great fatigues which seem humanly impossible to bear, rest on the Heart of your heavenly Mother, and rejoice in the response which you receive everywhere from all my littlest children."

The Glorious Reign of Christ

a   "Beloved children, you are celebrating today the solemnity of Jesus Christ, King of the universe, and you are doing this by way of a great cenacle in which priests and faithful of my Movement, coming from other cities of this great nation as well, are taking part.

b   Your heavenly Mother wants to enfold each one of you in the secure refuge of her Immaculate Heart, to protect you in the time of the great trial and to prepare you to receive Jesus, who is about to return to establish his glorious reign among you.

c   — *The glorious reign of Christ* will be above all established in hearts and souls. This is the most precious part of the divine royalty of Jesus. In fact, for this the Word became man and came to dwell among us. For this, the Son made Himself obedient to the Father even to death, the death of the Cross.

d   Through the redemption, carried out by Jesus on Calvary, you were rescued from the reign of Satan, set free from sin which is the yoke of slavery under him, and you became children of God, because He has communicated his Love and his very own Life to you. Those hearts renewed by Love and those souls sanctified by grace form then the most precious part of the divine royalty of Jesus.

e   — *The glorious reign of Christ* will correspond to a general flowering of holiness and purity, of love and justice, of joy and peace. For the hearts of men will be transformed by the powerful force of the Holy Spirit, who will pour out Himself upon them through the miracle of his second Pentecost.

f   And souls will be enlightened by the presence of the Most Holy Trinity, who will produce in them an extraordinary unfolding of all the virtues.

g   — *The glorious reign of Christ* will also be reflected in a new form of life in everyone, because you will be drawn to live only for the glory of the Lord. And the Lord will be glorified when his divine Will will be perfectly accomplished by each one of you. The glorious reign of Christ will coincide, then, with the perfect accomplishment of the Will of God on the part of every one of his creatures, in such a way that, as it is in heaven, so it will also be on this earth.

h   But this is not possible unless there first takes place the defeat of Satan, the tempter, the lying spirit, who has ever intervened in the history of mankind in order to lead men to rebellion against the Lord and disobedience to his Law.

i   — *The glorious reign of Christ* will be established after the complete defeat of Satan and all the spirits of evil, and the destruction of Satan's diabolical power. Thus he will be bound and cast into hell, and the gates of the abyss will be shut so that he can no longer get out to harm the world. And Christ will reign in the world.

j   — *The glorious reign of Christ* will coincide with the triumph of the Eucharistic reign of Jesus, because in a purified and sanctified world, completely renewed by love, Jesus will be made manifest, above all, in the mystery of his Eucharistic presence.

k   The Eucharist will be the source from which will burst forth all his divine power, and it will become the new sun, which will shed its bright rays in hearts and souls and then in the life of individuals, families, and nations, making of all one single flock, docile and meek, whose sole shepherd will be Jesus.

l   Your heavenly Mother is leading you on toward these new heavens and this new earth, the Mother who is gathering you today from every part of the world to prepare you to receive the Lord who is coming."

506
Sydney (Australia); November 23, 1993
Spiritual Exercises in the Form of a Cenacle
with the Priests of the M.M.P. from Oceania

Your Light Will Shine

a   "How happy I am, dear priests of my Movement in Australia, to see you gathered together here in a continuous cenacle of prayer and brotherhood. Grow in love among yourselves. Live these days with the joy of brothers who meet together, who know each other, love each other, and help each other to walk together along the painful road of these times of the great tribulation.

b   Pray with perseverance and trust. I am uniting myself with your prayer. I am close to you to give strength and power to your prayer, so that the Holy Spirit can come down, with his gifts, upon this cenacle of yours and make you fit for the mission which awaits you.

c   Brighten up the earth in these days of great darkness, and be a source of comfort and consolation for all the Church in this time of its great desolation. Your light will shine more and more and will spread throughout all this vast continent of Oceania, so ensnared and possessed by my Adversary and yours.

d   — *Your light will shine* by way of your priestly witness of faith.

e   See how the apostasy has spread everywhere; how errors are taught and propagated; how the lack of discipline and confusion is increasing. How many pastors no longer keep watch over the flock entrusted to them, and thus many rapacious wolves, in lambs' clothing, are entering to wreak havoc in the sheepfold of my Son Jesus.

f   Be the light set on a lampstand, to draw along the road of truth many of my poor children who are walking in the darkness of error and of the loss of the true faith. Thus, you will be faithful ministers of the Gospel, and by means of you, the Church, after the painful trial through which it is now living, will once again shed, in all its splendor, the light of Christ and of his truth.

g   — *Your light will shine* by way of your priestly witness of holiness.

h   See how materialism and hedonism are threatening this great country. The search for pleasure, money, comfort, entertainment and impurity have become for many the only ideal in life. And thus the little ones are led astray along the path of evil. Youth are drawn into vice and drugs. Families are destroyed by divorce and by the selfish shutting off of the gift of life.

i   Bring back to the house of the Father these poor children of mine who have gone astray. For this, be faithful ministers of grace and holiness, through the ministry of the sacraments which

Jesus has entrusted to you, above all that of Reconciliation. Put yourselves at the disposal of the faithful to lead them along the way of good and love, of purity and grace, of peace and salvation.

j — *Your light will shine* by way of your priestly witness of love.
k Love everyone with the divine Heart of Jesus and with the tenderness of my motherly love. See how the world today has become a desert for want of love! Unbridled egoism rules; violence and hatred are spreading; indifference has the upper hand in many hearts, become cold and insensitive toward the most needy.

l Priests consecrated to my Immaculate Heart, you must be the soothing balm which is placed on every open and bleeding wound. Take the little ones by the hand; support the weak; lead the uncertain; comfort the sick; save the lost; convert the sinners; give confidence to the despairing; go out to meet those who are far away, and bring them, in your priestly arms, into the safe refuge of my Immaculate Heart.
m In this way, you become the instruments of the triumph of my Immaculate Heart in the world.
n Go out from this cenacle, and go to every part of this most vast continent to brighten up the earth with the light of your faith, of your holiness and of your love. I am always with you. As Mother, I follow you on your journey, and I am close to you, to give you help and comfort.
o With your dear ones, and with those persons who are entrusted to your care, I bless you all in the name of the Father, and of the Son, and of the Holy Spirit."

507

The Years of My Triumph

a "Today you are concluding a long journey which, in two months, you have undertaken in many countries of Asia and Oceania. You have been able to hold seventy-three cenacles, in which bishops, priests and faithful of my Movement have taken part. You have seen, my little son so loved and protected by me, the great marvels of my Immaculate Heart in every part of this vast continent.

b   These are the years during which I am forming for myself the new Church and the new humanity, in the heavenly garden of my Immaculate Heart.

c   *These are the years of my triumph.*

d   — Satan has deceived this entire poor humanity, bringing it so far away from God and building for it idols of his own perversion: pleasure, money, pride, egoism, amusement and impurity. And so humanity is today greatly threatened by violence, hatred, rebellion and war.

e   During these years, you will see the great chastisement, with which the justice of God will purify this world, which has become a thousand times worse than at the time of the flood and so very possessed by evil spirits.

f   And so I am gathering my little children from every part of the earth and enclosing them in the safe refuge of my Immaculate Heart, so that they may be defended and saved by me at the moment of the great trial which has now arrived for all.

g   Thus in the very years when Satan is triumphing, by leading humanity along the road of its own destruction, my motherly Heart is also triumphing, as I bring my little children along the way of salvation and peace.

h   — Satan has also entered into the interior of the Church and has succeeded in darkening her splendor. With the darkness of sin, he has obscured the splendor of her holiness; with the wound of division, he has made an attack upon the strength of her unity; with the spread of errors, he has stricken her in her proclamation of the truth. This poor gravely ill Daughter of mine!

i   And so I am calling my little children from all sides to consecrate themselves to my Immaculate Heart, in order to entrust themselves to me as babes. In this way, in the garden of my Immaculate Heart, I am forming for myself each day the new Church, holy, united, a faithful herald of the Gospel, who gives her perfect witness to Jesus.

j   These are the years when Satan is ruling as a sure victor; these are therefore also *the years of my triumph*. My light will become stronger and stronger, the more you enter into the decisive moments of the battle. In the end, the victory will be that of your immaculate Mother who, with her virginal foot, will crush the head of the serpent and, with her hands, will bind the great Dragon, that he may thus be rendered powerless and no longer be able to do harm in the world.

k   Both humanity and the Church will experience this new era, which you are now awaiting in confidence and in prayer, in suffering and in hope.

l   For this, as a breaking dawn, you will as of today see my light becoming stronger and stronger until it encircles the whole earth, ready now to open itself to the new day, which will begin with the triumph of my Immaculate Heart in the world."

508   *Dongo (Como, Italy); December 24, 1993*
The Holy Night

This Holy Night

a   "Recollect yourselves with me, in silence and expectation. Forget every other preoccupation, and enter into the quiet of prayer. Live together with me this precious moment which precedes the birth of my divine Child.

b   This is the night of love and of light.
This is the night of reconciliation and of peace.
This is the holy night.

c   Share in the joy of your heavenly Mother, who feels that the moment of her virginal motherhood has now come.

d   For me, it is as though everything that surrounds me is far away: the fatigue of the journey to Bethlehem; the noise of the crowded caravan; the anxious search to find a place to spend the night; the sad surprise before each door as it is closed; the trusting confidence before a poor little cave which opens itself to us.

e   The gentle and loving assistance of my most chaste spouse, Joseph, surrounds me like a caress. It is he who seeks to make the place more hospitable; who prepares the crib in a warmer manger; who looks about for a shield against the rigor of the cold; who stays close to me and joins in my great prayer; who sees the heavens open; who contemplates in wonder the prodigy, hears the song of the angels and is conscious of the peace which comes down from heaven; who opens the door to the poor and the little ones and graciously accepts the simple gifts of the shepherds.

f   As for myself, I am absorbed in a profound rapture: the face of the Father is revealed to me, and I contemplate the divine mystery of his merciful love; the Word, who has taken human form in my virginal womb, becomes present in my motherly arms as a newborn Babe, and I cover Him with kisses and tears; the Holy Spirit looks with pleasure on the fruit [of his overshadowing].

g   Beloved children, live with me in this profound rapture throughout *this holy night.*

h   It is Love which is born into a world consumed with hatred. It is Light which dawns upon the long season of deep darkness. It is the awaited Reconciliation between a lost humanity and its Lord who loves and redeems it. It is Peace which comes down from heaven upon all men of good will.

i   Enter with me into the mystery of *this holy night.* For the great trial has now arrived for all. Violence and the fire of hatred are bringing death to the world. A deep darkness enwraps this humanity, which no longer sees light. The pact of the Covenant is again broken by men who have openly rebelled against their God. And wars, rebellions and destruction fill your journey with tears and blood. For you, the time of the great trial has come.

j   And so, once again, I invite you to let yourselves be carried by me into the mystery of *this holy night.* And then, like Joseph, exert yourselves earnestly to open up the souls and hearts of men to receive Jesus in his second coming. And do not allow yourselves to be taken up with vain and useless preoccupations, but keep watch with me in prayer and in the expectation of his now closely approaching return in glory."

Great Is My Concern

a   "Beloved children, spend with me, in recollection and prayer, the last hours of this year which is about to end. Do not let yourselves be taken up with dissipation, clamor and amusements, in which the majority of my poor children spend these hours. Read, in silence, the signs of your time, and join in my great concern for what awaits you.

b   — *Great is my concern* because this humanity, so ailing, is continuing in its obstinate rejection of God and of his Law of love. In many ways and with numerous signs and extraordinary interventions, I have intervened in the course of this year, to urge it to conversion and to its return to the Lord.

c   But I have not been listened to. The name of the Lord is scorned, and his day is more and more profaned. Egoism is suffocating the hearts of men, become cold and closed due to a great incapacity to love. Life is considered of little value: violence and homicides are increasing; all kinds of means are being used to prevent the birth of more children; willful abortions, this terrible crime which day and night cries to your God for vengeance, are increasing everywhere; impurity is spreading like a great tide of filth which is sweeping everything before it.

d   The cup of divine justice is full to overflowing. I see the chastisement by which the mercy of God wishes to purify and save this poor sinful humanity. How numerous and great are the sufferings which await you, my poor children, so enticed and ensnared by Satan, the spirit of falsehood, who is seducing you and leading you to your death!

e   — *Great is my concern* because my Church is at the mercy of the forces of evil which are threatening it and attempting to destroy it from within. Masonry, with its diabolical power, has set up its center in the very heart of the Church, where the Vicar of my Son Jesus resides, and from there it is spreading its evil influence to every part of the world. And now the Church will once again be betrayed by its own; it will be cruelly persecuted and led to the gibbet.

f I see that the bloody persecution is now at the doors, and many of you will be scattered by the violent wind of this frightful hurricane.

g During these hours, share in my great concern, and unite yourselves, each and all, to my prayer of intercession and reparation. Multiply everywhere the cenacles of prayer which I have asked of you, as safe places, as refuges in which you take shelter in the tremendous storm which awaits you.

h In the cenacles, you will be aware of my extraordinary presence.

i In the cenacles, you will experience the security and peace which your heavenly Mother gives you.

j In the cenacles, you will be preserved from evil and defended from the great dangers which threaten you.

k In the cenacles, you will be formed by me in confidence and in a great hope because the cenacle is the place of your salvation, which the heavenly Mother has prepared for you, in these last times in which the great trial has now come for all."

1994

OPEN YOUR HEARTS TO HOPE

510

Open Your Hearts to Hope

a   "Beloved children, you are beginning this new year with the liturgical solemnity of my divine motherhood. I am true Mother of God. From eternity, the Heavenly Father has chosen me for this ineffable mission.

b   'Sacrifices and offerings You willed not, O God, but a body You have prepared for me.' (cf. Heb 10:5)

c   In order to form a body for the Son, in his eternal plan of wisdom, the Father also prepared a body for the Mother. Thus from eternity I have come forth from his divine thought.

d   From all eternity, the Word contemplated me at the moment when, through my maternal assent, He was to descend into my virginal womb, even to becoming man. And thus my God was to become my Son.

e   From eternity, the Holy Spirit contemplated the divine prodigy of his love, which was to miraculously make my virginal womb fruitful, making me Mother without any human intervention. Thus the Holy Spirit was to become my divine Spouse.

f   Contemplate me today in the light of my divine motherhood, my beloved children, and open your hearts to hope.

g   — *Open your hearts to hope,* because these are the years when the greatest triumph of God, with the return of Jesus Christ in glory, is in preparation.

h   My divine motherhood is exercised today in preparing the way for his glorious return. As I was the humble and poor Mother of his first coming, so too am I the glorious and powerful Mother of his second coming among you.

i   Mine is the task of opening the door of the new era, which is awaiting you. Mine is the task of leading you towards the new heavens and the new earth. Above all, the task entrusted to the Mother of God is that of conquering Satan and every evil force, in order that God may achieve his greatest triumph in the world.

j   — *Open your hearts to hope,* because I am also Mother of all humanity. And as Mother I have always followed my children with love, throughout the course of human history.

k   Above all, in these last times, I feel that I am Mother of a humanity which is very much ensnared and possessed by the evil spirits. Satan is triumphing today. He has led all humanity to the rejection of God and has thus made it subject to his evil reign.

l   Because of this, how much have you had to suffer! Because of this, tears and blood have become your daily nourishment. Because of this, the year which is opening today will also bring you the weight of an immense suffering.

m   As Mother of humanity, there has been entrusted to me the task of releasing you from the slavery to Satan. Therefore, it is necessary that you now follow me in the bloody struggle, in order to obtain in the end my greatest victory. Because, Satan will be made powerless by me, and the great force of evil will be completely destroyed by me.

n   Then all humanity will return to a new marriage of love with its Lord, who will take it in his arms and lead it into the terrestrial paradise of a full and perfect communion of life with Him.

o   — *Open your hearts to hope,* because I am true Mother of all the Church.

p   In the course of the years, I have always been close to this beloved Daughter of mine, with the anxious concern and the tenderness of my motherly love. I am especially close to the Church in these last times, when she must live through the bloody hour of her purification and of the great tribulation.

q   For her also, the plan of the Heavenly Father must be carried out, and thus she is being called to climb the Calvary of her immolation. This most beloved Daughter of mine will be stricken and wounded, betrayed and despoiled, abandoned and led to the gibbet, where she will be crucified. The man of iniquity will enter into her interior, and he will bring to its culmination the abomination of desolation, foretold in the Holy Scriptures.

r   Do not lose courage, beloved children. Let your trust be strong.

s   At the beginning of this new year, *open your hearts to hope,* because you will see the events of which I foretold you already taking place. You will understand that the final years of this, your century, form part of a divine and mysterious plan, which is about to be disclosed.

t   *Open your hearts to hope,* because the moment has come when your heavenly Mother will manifest herself in all her power.

u   I am the dawn which precedes the great day of the Lord. I am the voice which becomes strong in these times, in order to spread my prophetic announcement in every part of the earth: prepare yourselves, one and all, to receive my Son Jesus, who is even now about to return among you, on the clouds of heaven, in the splendor of his divine glory."

511   *Sant' Omero (Teramo, Italy); February 2, 1994*
Feast of the Presentation of the Child Jesus

The Gift of My Trust

a   "Beloved children, let yourselves be carried in my motherly arms into the temple of the Lord, to be offered by me to the perfect glory of the Most Holy Trinity.

b   For this I am gathering you from every part of the world. For this I ask you to consecrate yourselves to my Immaculate Heart. For this I am leading you each day along the road pointed out by me, and I am forming you, for many years now, with the gift of my motherly word.

c   In you, the Father must be glorified in the perfect fulfillment of his divine Will. In you, the Son wants to be relived in such a way that you become the instruments of his divine mercy. In you, the Holy Spirit is at work, with the force of his love, in order to make you capable of transforming hearts and souls.

d   Thus, in these last times, you must become light to whomever is walking in darkness, life to whomever is under the yoke of sin and death, love to whomever is consumed by violence and hatred, comfort to whomever is overwhelmed by suffering, balm upon the wounds of the poor and the sick, strength for the weakness of the little and the oppressed.

e   In this way you are able to communicate to all *the gift of my trust.*

f   — *Be the gift of my trust for the Church,* today so suffering and divided, crushed and oppressed, a Church which is climbing the Calvary of its painful passion.

g   Never as in these times of yours has the Church had such need of experiencing all the tenderness and merciful compassion of its heavenly Mother. I want to exercise through you my motherly duty toward the Church. Love the Church with the beating of my Immaculate Heart. Wipe away its sweat; heal its wounds; soothe its pain; share in its suffering; help it to carry its heavy cross toward the Calvary of its immolation.

h   Stay close to the Pope and to your bishops, with prayer and with your filial love. Support your brother-priests. Above all, run to meet the weakest, the most fragile, those who are yielding under the weight of the great difficulties of these last times. You must be the gentle and merciful hand of your heavenly Mother who bends over to place balm on the wounds of the sinners, of those who are estranged, of the poor, of those who are marginalized, of the oppressed, and of the abandoned. In this way, you yourselves become the gift of my trust for the Church of these, your times.

i   *— Be the gift of my trust for all this poor humanity.* Help it to return to God along the road of prayer and penance. The pathway of conversion is the only way along which it must journey in order to attain salvation and peace.

j   But now you are entering into the decisive times, times for which I have been preparing you for many years. How many will be swept away by the terrible hurricane which has already hurled itself upon humanity. This is the time of the great trial; this is my time, O children consecrated to my Immaculate Heart.

k   I want to manifest myself by means of you and to give to all *the gift of my trust,* above all when the days of the great desolation and of a general despair will have come.

l   For this reason, I ask you to let yourselves be carried in my motherly arms into the temple of the glory of the Lord, in order that you may become for all a light of hope, by spreading everywhere the gift of my trust in these, your final times."

I Am Consoled

a   "Today you are celebrating the anniversary of my apparition in Lourdes, to my little and poor daughter, Bernadette.

b   And you find yourself here, little child, in this country of Central America, where I am particularly loved and venerated by many of my children. Have you seen with what enthusiasm they have accepted the message of your heavenly Mother, and what filial and tender love they have for me?

c   In these years when my Heart is being deeply wounded by sins and infidelity, by pride and aridity, and by the obstinate rejection of my motherly interventions, *I am consoled* by my littlest children.

d   *I am consoled* by the poorest, who respond to me with the richness of their love, of their humility, of their docility. With what openness of soul and heart, they listen to my word, accept it and live it! Truly, for these who are poor in goods and in spirit, there is prepared the reign of God, which will very soon come to you in all its divine splendor.

e   *I am consoled* by the littlest, by those who live truly as little children, whom Jesus forms and guards within the heavenly garden of his divine love. With what tenderness I carry them in my motherly arms, that they may be consoled by me. To them alone do I reveal the secret of my Immaculate Heart, the light of my design, the battle plan and the moment of my victory.

f   *I am consoled* by the new hearts, formed within the bright recesses of my Immaculate Heart. Against hatred which is spreading, egoism which consumes, aridity which chills, hardness which paralyses the hearts of so many, become cold and insensitive, hard and closed to the needs of the poor and destitute, I form new hearts which know how to spread everywhere the beating of my motherly and merciful love. These hearts know how to love God with that love which alone glorifies Him, and to love your heavenly Mother with that love which alone consoles her.

g   *I am consoled* by this little country of Honduras, which has a big heart and one filled with love for me. Today you have been in the presidential house in order to make, with the President of the Republic, the consecration of the Republic to my Immaculate Heart.

h   I take this country under my special protection because, since you have done what I asked of you at Fatima, *I have been consoled by this nation in a special way."*

513   *Ilobasco (El Salvador); February 13, 1994*

I Fill the Poor with Good Things

a   "Here also you have seen my greatest triumph, and you are astounded, my littlest child, because you see how, in every part of the world, I am being received with love, with joy and with great enthusiasm by all the little, the simple and the poor.

b   By my personal and particular intervention, I am forming everywhere for myself this army of mine, to fight the final part of the battle and to attain my greatest victory. With what joy I see my little children running from all sides into the heavenly garden of my Immaculate Heart.

c   The hour has now arrived. Once again, through the mouths of infants and babes at the breast, the Lord will overcome the tumultuous uproar of his adversaries and reduce to nothing the power of all his enemies.

d   Therefore, as does the Lord, I too your heavenly Mother *fill the poor with good things.*

e   *I fill the poor with the precious good* of the grace of God and of full communion of life with Him. To these I grant the gift of humility of mind and of simplicity of heart, in such a way that they are able to receive his divine word with love. Today the Gospel of Jesus can be believed and lived, not by the great and the proud, but only by the little and the poor.

f   In these times of the great apostasy, the poor in spirit obtain from your heavenly Mother the inestimable good of remaining ever in the true faith and of following with docility the entire truth of the Gospel.

g   *I fill the poor with the good* of love and of generosity. What wickedness exists today among the rich! How great is the egoism which is spreading among those who seek only comfort and who want to build a society founded on the greatest possession of material goods.

h   The poor have from me the great gift of being detached from these things, of living in the entrustment of themselves to the goodness of Divine Providence, of knowing how to give to others part of the little they possess, of welcoming all with the generosity of servants of the Lord.

i   *I fill the poor with the good* of a particular predilection on the part of the Lord. The Lord looks upon the poor with the same satisfaction with which He surrounded me, as his littlest and poorest handmaid. To the poor, the Holy Spirit communicates Himself with inexhaustible abundance, because only from the poor can the Most Holy Trinity receive its praise and its perfect glory.

j   In this country, where my Adversary has succeeded in seducing very many of my children with the dangerous error of liberation theology, I am forming my cohort with all my poor and little children.

k   This is the reason why I am working here in a powerful way, to build up my triumph in hearts and in souls. It is for this reason that here I am especially loved and glorified. It is for this reason that I am spreading out upon this country the fullness of my motherly assistance and of my immaculate protection."

514

Bogotá (Columbia); February 22, 1994
Feast of the Chair of St. Peter
Spiritual Exercises in the Form of a Cenacle
with the Priests of the M.M.P. from Latin America

On the Rock of the Apostolic Faith

a   "Beloved sons, priests consecrated to my Immaculate Heart, how happy I am to see you gathered here, in a continuous cenacle of prayer and fraternity.

b   I am present in your midst. I give strength to your prayer. I deepen your unity. I help you to grow in mutual love, to the point of making you one single heart and one single soul. I obtain for you the gift of the Holy Spirit, who descends upon you to confirm you in your priestly ministry and make you apostles of the second evangelization.

c   Let your preaching be founded *on the rock of the apostolic faith*, that you may become courageous witnesses of faith, in these times of the great apostasy. Do not become troubled when you see that today errors are becoming openly taught, spread and followed. Never become discouraged.

d   Be faithful ministers of the Gospel of Christ, by proclaiming all the truths of the Catholic faith, and thus you will become lights lit upon a lamp stand, burning torches set upon the mountain tops, to throw light upon these times of great darkness.

e   Let your witness of unity and of ecclesial communion be based *on the rock of the apostolic faith*. Peter has received from Jesus the task of being the foundation of the Church and of confirming the entire Church in the truth of the Gospel. The Pope is the successor of Peter in this, his ministry of being the foundation of the unity of the Church and infallible guardian of her truth.

f   Be today witnesses of love for, and of unity with, the Pope. Bring the flock which has been entrusted to you to this unity, so that very soon there may be but one single flock under one single Shepherd. Love, support and assist your bishops in their difficult and wearying ministry.

g   Let your priestly holiness flourish *on the rock of the apostolic faith*. Be thus faithful ministers of the sacraments which have been entrusted to you. Above all, be assiduous in that ministry which is so precious and so neglected today, namely that of Reconciliation. Make the Eucharistic Jesus the center of your prayer, the sun of your life, the love of your entire priestly life. Begin once again to hold hours of public Eucharistic adoration, so that Jesus may bring his reign of holiness and life into hearts and souls.

h   In this way you become a soothing balm which is placed on the open and bleeding wounds of your holy Mother, the Church.

She will thus be made aware, by means of you, of my motherly comfort and will be assisted in continuing along the painful way of these last times, so that she may give her perfect witness to Jesus.

i   My light will shine forth more and more throughout all this great continent of Latin America, which loves me so very much and which enjoys a special protection on the part of your heavenly Mother.

j   With your dear ones, and with all those who have been entrusted to your ministry, I bless you in the name of the Father, and of the Son, and of the Holy Spirit."

515

Let Yourselves Be Possessed by His Love

a   "Beloved sons, today I look upon you with joy and with motherly predilection. This is your feast day. This is your pasch.

b   Gathered about the bishops, you are renewing the promises which you made on the day of your priestly ordination. They are the promises of your love and of your fidelity to Jesus, who has chosen you and has called you to share in his high and eternal Priesthood. By means of you, Jesus is still able to immolate Himself each day for your salvation.

c   *Let yourselves be possessed by his love.*

d   How much Jesus loves you! For love of you, the Word of the Father became incarnate in my virginal womb, submitted Himself to the limitations of time and place, was born into his human life, and grew up like a flower in the garden of my motherly love.

e   For love of you, Jesus knew exile during his infancy, poverty and fatigue during his adolescence, misunderstanding and rejection during the years of his public mission.

f   For love of you, He was subjected to betrayal and outrage, to judgment and condemnation, to crucifixion and death on the Cross. How much Jesus loves you!

g   *Let yourselves be possessed by his love.*

h   'Having loved his own who were in the world, He loved them to the end.' (Jn 13:1) Above all, for love of you, Jesus has instituted the new Sacrifice and the new Priesthood. Thus, in every part of the earth, from the east to the west, there may be presented to the Heavenly Father a pure offering, the perfect Sacrifice which appeases his divine justice, which makes reparation for all the sin of man, for the salvation and the life of the world.

i   And you, beloved sons, you are the priests chosen by Him, to renew everywhere this, his Sacrifice of the new and eternal Covenant.

j   *Let yourselves be possessed by his love.*

k   Do not look at your miseries; do not be discouraged by your weaknesses; do not count your sins; do not go back over your infidelities; but *let yourselves be possessed by his love,* because the divine charity of the Heart of Jesus surpasses infinitely every human ingratitude.

l   In these last times, how many are those priests who weep over their falls, who succumb under the forces of evil which has now been unleashed, who yield to the enticements of a world again become pagan, and who fall under the subtle snares of my Adversary and yours.

m   Beloved sons, even if there is being repeated the action of Peter who denies, or that of Judas who betrays, or that of the Apostles who flee and abandon Jesus, open your hearts today to hope, because Jesus loves you. His love overcomes your every human weakness.

n   On this, your day, let joy be great and peace profound.

o   With the voice of the Mother who ever assists you and leads you, consoles you and encourages you, I invite you today to let yourselves be possessed by his love, so that you too may be priests according to his divine and merciful Heart."

The Bright Cross

a   "Draw near to the Throne of Grace to obtain mercy on this day of the redemption. Look, with love and immense gratitude, upon Him whom today they have pierced.

b   He is the Eternal Word of the Father who has become Man. He is the Son of God offered for your ransom. He is the true Lamb of God who takes away the sins of the world.

c   He is my Son Jesus, born and brought up by me, assisted and accompanied, contemplated with the happiness of a mother, in the rhythm of his human growth.

d   He is my Son, comforted and encouraged by me in the face of every official rejection, followed by me and listened to in the desert of so much unbelief, consoled by the voices of the little ones, of the poor, the sick and the sinners.

e   He is my Son, whom I meet today, as He carries the heavy weight of his gibbet on his wounded shoulders. Live with me the indescribable moment of this encounter.

f   My motherly love is placed like a balm on each of his wounds. The immense pain of the Son falls upon the Heart of the Mother, pierced by his very suffering. And the Cross crushes Son and Mother, now united in this one single offering.

g   Stay with me, beloved sons, beneath the Cross, together with your brother, John.

h   There is such need for comfort. For Jesus, who is nailed to the gibbet, raised up from the earth and who is living through the bloody hours of his agony. And for me, his Mother, intimately associated in his redemptive passion.

i   There is such need for faith. Behold Jesus crushed like a worm. All the sins of the world weigh upon his immolated body. His Heart is overwhelmed by human ingratitude and by such a profound lack of faith. 'He saved others, and He cannot save Himself. Let Him come down from the Cross if He is the Son of God, and we will believe in Him.' (cf. Mt 27:42) With me, with John, with the devout and faithful women, with the penitent centurion, you too must say: 'Truly, this is the Son of God!' (Mt 27:54) *j*   There is such need for love. On Golgotha, love appears to be defeated. There is only hatred, bitterness, wickedness and inhuman savagery. Darkness descends and obscures the world. Love is all gathered together in Christ Crucified, who prays, pardons, bows to the Will of the Father and docilely abandons Himself to Him. Love descends from Him upon the Mother, called to open her Heart to a new and spiritual motherhood, and upon John, who represents all of you, in receiving this supreme gift of the divine Heart of the Son.

k   There is such need for hope. Now the lifeless body of Jesus, from the Cross, is placed in my motherly arms. I cover it with kisses and tears and, with the help of the faithful women, I wrap it in purest linen, and we place it in his new sepulchre. And a large stone closes it, but the door of hope opens, the hope that Jesus cannot remain in death, because He is the Son of God: the Son of God who will rise because He had foretold this many times; the Son of God who will meet his disciples again in the joyful and fertile land of Galilee.

l   In the sorrow of this Good Friday, your heavenly Mother asks you to open your hearts to hope. The bloodied Cross, which you contemplate today in tears, will be the cause of your greatest happiness, because it will be transformed into *a great bright cross.*

m   *The bright cross*, which will extend from east to west and will appear in the heavens, will be the sign of the return of Jesus in glory.

n   *The bright cross* will be transformed from a gibbet to a throne of his triumph, because Jesus will come upon it to establish his glorious reign in the world.

o   *The bright cross*, which will appear in the heavens at the end of the purification and the great tribulation, will be the door which opens the long and dark sepulchre in which humanity is lying, to lead it into the new reign of life which Jesus will bring with his glorious return."

517

The Sabbath Which Is About to End

a "Spend this day with me, my beloved children, and open your hearts to hope. My Son Jesus rests today in his new sepulchre.

b It is the only day when I remained without my Son.
It is the first day of my new and universal motherhood.
It is the day which precedes the greatest feast: Easter!

c On this day, we commemorate the departure of the Chosen People from the long slavery spent in Egypt. It is the passage of the Angel of the Lord, who strikes the first-born of the Egyptians and spares the houses of the Hebrews, marked with the blood of the lamb.

d The true Lamb of God has now been immolated on the Cross. His blood has descended upon the houses of all and has redeemed the entire human race. The Lamb immolated for you now lies in his new sepulchre.

e The Mother keeps watch in sorrow and in tears, in faith and in prayer, in love and in hope. This day has been dedicated by the Church to a special veneration of your heavenly Mother, because on it the tomb is transformed into a crib, in which humanity is placed, redeemed and now born to a new divine life.

f My Immaculate Heart is opened to receive here each of my new children. The tears unfold into a smile, the sorrow into joy, the hope into the greatest certitude.

g Within a few hours my Son Jesus will come forth triumphant from the sepulchre, Victor over sin and death.

h This is the Sabbath which prepares the radiant day of the resurrection.
This is the sorrow which leads to joy.
This is the death which opens upon life.
This is the Sabbath which is about to end.

i Humanity, corrupted by sin, slave to Satan, wounded by evil, oppressed under the yoke of a great slavery, still lies in its sepulchre. The hour is drawing close when Jesus, who has risen and ascended to the right hand of the Father, will return to you on the clouds of heaven, in the splendor of his divine glory, thus bringing to perfect fulfillment the work of his redemption."

It Is the Paschal Joy

a   "Share today in the joy of your heavenly Mother, who is living the blessed hour of the resurrection of the Son Jesus. Each of my sorrows is assuaged, and every wound is closed at the moment when Jesus, in the splendor of his glorious body, draws close to me, takes me in his arms, and presses me to his pierced Heart, from which flows a fount of most powerful light that surrounds me completely and plunges me in a sea of immense blessedness.

b   How beautiful is my Son in the splendor of his glorious and divine body! Gone now is the memory of his despised and stricken body, scourged and wounded, pierced with thorns and nails, crucified and put to death, taken down from the gibbet and placed in the sepulchre. Now his body is filled with energy and strength, shines brightly in its divine beauty, gives forth refulgence and power, emits rays of supernatural light, fashions a new harmony of life and of peace, opens like a gentle caress and closes every wound of my motherly sorrow. The Son and the Mother are again united in one single joy.

c   *It is the paschal joy*. It is the joy which takes hold of all humanity, made anew according to the designs of the Father.

d   *It is the paschal joy*, which comes down upon his entire creation, renewed and redeemed by his bloody Sacrifice.

e   *It is the paschal joy*, which reaches Hades to set free from the darkness of death the souls of all the just, awaiting in expectation.

f   *It is the paschal joy*, which permeates all men, who have returned as children into the arms of the Heavenly Father.

g   *It is the paschal joy*, which brings cheer to the painful journey of the Church, called to live today the hours of Gethsemane and Calvary.

h   *It is the paschal joy*, which penetrates into the hearts of all my children, comforted and encouraged to live through the painful time of the purification and the great tribulation.

i   *It is the paschal joy*, which brightens up your hope and gives a sure response to the great expectation of all.

j   *It is the paschal joy*, which enters into your epoch and prepares it for the greatest event of all history, because the Easter resurrection will attain its complete fulfillment only when Jesus will return in glory to establish his reign in your midst, in the fulfillment of the Will of the Father on the part of all, and in the perfect glorification of the Most Holy and Divine Trinity."

519

Rome (Italy); May 1, 1994
Feast of St. Joseph the Worker

The Hour of Calvary

a   "Begin with me this month, dedicated by the Church to my special veneration. As little children, offer each day the flowers of love and prayer to your heavenly Mother. I ask you to spread more and more the cenacles which I have requested of you so many times.

b   —The rosary which you recite has a very great power against evil and against the numerous enticements of my Adversary. To the reign of Satan which is spreading, to the slavery of sin which is subjugating many of my children, to evil which is instilling its venom in hearts, to the snares of the Evil One which have become subtle and dangerous, to the powerful force of Freemasonry which has succeeded in insinuating itself everywhere, to the cult of Satan which is spreading, *respond with the prayer of the holy rosary*. This is my prayer; it is your prayer.

c   — Renew each day your consecration to my Immaculate Heart. Through this act, you make it possible for me to enter, as Mother, into your life and to dispose it for the perfect fulfillment of the design which the Lord has on each one of you. Thus you become my very own presence in the world, and in these last times, you spread everywhere the light of my holiness, of my purity, of my humility, of my obedience, of my docility, of my motherly and merciful love.

d　　—Above all, I ask you to offer me the fragrant and precious flower of your suffering. On the altar of my Immaculate Heart, I want to offer all my children, in a perennial act of immolation and reparation. Only through the suffering of my littlest children can I hasten the time of the triumph of my Immaculate Heart in the world. Precisely in this month, I have again asked a greater suffering, even of my Pope, John Paul the Second.

e　　*The hour of Calvary has now arrived.*

f　　*The hour of Calvary* has arrived for the Church, called to offer herself in holocaust and to be immolated on the cross of her bloody martyrdom.

g　　*The hour of Calvary* has arrived for this poor humanity, which is already beginning to live the painful hours of its chastisement.

h　　*The hour of Calvary* has arrived for you, my beloved ones, because you have now entered into the conclusive time of the great tribulation. As Mother, I am leading you each day to the fulfillment of your priestly immolation.

i　　For this reason, I invite you to live with particular intensity this month consecrated to me, offering me the fragrant flowers of your prayer and your suffering.

j　　Open your hearts to hope. Just as the blossoming of flowers in this month tells you that spring has now arrived, so too the blossoming everywhere of this, my great work of love, tells you that my motherly triumph has now arrived."

520　　*Shrine of Caravaggio (Bergamo, Italy); May 13, 1994*
Anniversary of the First Apparition at Fatima

An Apocalyptic Message

a　　"Again this year you are observing, with a day-long cenacle in this venerated shrine, the anniversary of my first apparition in the Cova da Iria in Fatima.

b　　My Immaculate Heart opens and causes rays of my motherly and merciful love to descend upon you. It is within your time that the fulfillment of the message is taking place, the message which I have given you at Fatima and against which my Adversary has thrown himself in fury, but which will now appear in all its extraordinary importance for the Church and for all humanity.

c   *It is an apocalyptic message.*
It has regard to the end of the times.
It announces and prepares for the return of my Son Jesus in glory.

d   *— Upon this humanity which has again become pagan,* enveloped in the coldness of the denial of God and of rebellion against his Law of love, corrupted by sin and evil, and over whom Satan reigns as a sure victor, I am causing the rays of love and of light from my Immaculate Heart to come down.

e   They shed light for you upon the way along which you must travel, to return to God along the road of conversion, of prayer and of penance.

f   Thus my Immaculate Heart becomes today the sure means of salvation for all this humanity, because only in my Immaculate Heart will you find refuge in the moment of the chastisement, comfort in the hour of suffering, relief in the midst of unspeakable afflictions, light in the days of densest darkness, refreshment amidst the flames of the fire which consumes, confidence and hope in a now general despair.

g   *— Upon this Church, darkened and wounded, stricken and betrayed,* I am causing the rays of love and of light from my Immaculate Heart to come down. When there will have entered into her the man of iniquity, who will bring to fulfillment the abomination of desolation which will reach its climax in the horrible sacrilege, as the great apostasy will have spread everywhere, then my Immaculate Heart will gather together the little faithful remnant which, in suffering, in prayer and in hope, will await the return of my Son Jesus in glory.

h   For this reason I urge you today to look to the great light which has spread out from Fatima over the events of this, your century, and which is becoming particularly strong in these last times.

814

i *Mine is an apocalyptic message,* because you are in the heart of that which has been announced to you in the last and so very important book of Sacred Scripture.

j I entrust to the angels of light of my Immaculate Heart the task of bringing you to an understanding of these events, now that I have opened the sealed Book for you."

521

Berlin (Germany); May 22, 1994
Solemnity of Pentecost

Come, Holy Spirit

a "Today you find yourselves gathered together here, in a continuous cenacle of prayer with your heavenly Mother, in the liturgical celebration of the solemnity of Pentecost.

b And you are repeating, with the intensity of love, the prayer which I myself have taught you: 'Come, Holy Spirit, come by means of the powerful intercession of the Immaculate Heart of Mary, your well-beloved Spouse.'

c *Come, Holy Spirit.*

d A new and universal effusion of the Holy Spirit is necessary to arrive at the new times, so longed for. It is necessary that the second Pentecost come quickly. It can come to pass only in the spiritual cenacle of my Immaculate Heart. For this reason, I renew today the invitation to all the Church to enter into the cenacle which the heavenly Mother has prepared for you for the final times. You are able to enter through the act of consecration to my Immaculate Heart.

e I request that this consecration, asked by me with such anxious insistence, be made by the bishops, the priests, the religious and the faithful. And let it be made by all in order to shorten the time of the great trial which has now arrived.

f The Holy Spirit will then bring you to an understanding of the whole and entire truth.

The Holy Spirit will cause you to understand the times through which you are living.

The Holy Spirit will be light upon your way and will make you courageous witnesses of the Gospel in the dreadful hour of

815

the great apostasy.

The Holy Spirit will bring you to grasp that which I will make manifest to you concerning what is contained in the still sealed Book.

The Holy Spirit will give his perfect witness to the Son, by preparing hearts and souls to receive Jesus who will return to you in glory.

g   *Come, Holy Spirit.*

h   Come by means of the powerful intercession of my Immaculate Heart. My hour is the hour of the Holy Spirit. The triumph of my Immaculate Heart will coincide with the great prodigy of the second Pentecost.

i   A new fire will come down from heaven and will purify all humanity, which has again become pagan. It will be like a judgment in miniature, and each one will see himself in the light of the very truth of God.

j   Thus sinners will come back to grace and holiness; the straying, to the road of righteousness; those far away, to the house of the Father; the sick, to complete healing; and the proud, the impure, the wicked collaborators with Satan will be defeated and condemned for ever.

k   Then my motherly Heart will have its triumph over all humanity, which will return to a new marriage of love and of life with its Heavenly Father.

l   *Come, Holy Spirit.*

m   Come at the voice of your well-beloved Spouse who calls You. I am the heavenly Spouse of the Holy Spirit. As, through a singular design of the Father, I have become true Mother of the Son, so also have I become true Spouse of the Holy Spirit. The Holy Spirit has given Himself to my soul by an interior and true spousal union, and of this has been born the divine fruit of the virginal conception of the Word in my most pure womb.

n   The Spirit cannot resist the voice of the Spouse who calls to Him. And so unite yourselves, each and all, to me, my little children, in invoking today the gift of the Holy Spirit. Let your supplication become the prayer of these last times. Let your prayer be habitual, repeated frequently by you, because it has been taught to you and is being passionately demanded of you by your heavenly Mother: *'Come, Holy Spirit, come by means of the powerful intercession of the Immaculate Heart of Mary, your well-beloved Spouse.'*

o And open your hearts to hope, because there is about to come upon you the greatest prodigy of the second Pentecost."

522
San Leonardo (Sardinia, Italy); June 11, 1994
Feast of the Immaculate Heart of Mary
Spiritual Exercises in the Form of a Cenacle
with the Youth of the M.M.P. from Sardinia

Your Refuge

a "Today you find yourself here, my little son, in a continuous cenacle of prayer and fraternity, with many young people of my Movement, to celebrate the feast of the Immaculate Heart of your heavenly Mother. See how I am loved by all these young people! Their love, their enthusiasm, their prayer, and their consecration to my Immaculate Heart close the deep wounds of my great sorrow.

b I open the golden door of my motherly Heart in order to have enter there all my children, exposed to many dangers, stricken by many sorrows, wearied by many battles, wounded by many defeats. In these difficult and painful years, I open, especially to my young people, the refuge of my Immaculate Heart. My motherly Heart thus becomes for you your secure refuge.

c — *It is your refuge*, in which you take shelter from the grave and threatening dangers which surround you. The pagan society in which you live — a society which has denied its God, in order to build the idols of pleasure and money, of pride and egoism, of amusement and impurity — constitutes for you a grave danger of betraying your baptism and of violating the obligations which you have assumed before God and the Church.

d In my Immaculate Heart you will be formed to the perfect glory of the Lord, through your promise of a life offered to Him, in the fulfillment of the divine Will and in the observance of his Law.

e   — *It is your refuge,* in which you are defended against the wicked influence which this world — so materialistic and utterly bent on the mad search for pleasure — has over you.

f   In my Immaculate Heart, you will be trained in renunciation and mortification, in prayer and penance, in poverty and the perfection of love. In this way, you will experience the joy of walking along the road which Jesus has pointed out for you, in a spirit of freedom, and of correspondence with the great gift which He has given you.

g   — *It is your refuge,* which protects you from being contaminated by sin and impurity. How impregnated with immorality and evil are the surroundings in which you live! Sin is committed and justified. Disobedience to the Laws of God is extolled and publicized. The diabolical power of Satan spreads more and more over individuals and countries. How are you to protect yourselves from this flood of misery, of corruption and of godlessness?

h   — *My Immaculate Heart is your refuge.* It is given to you precisely for these times of yours. Enter in, my dearly beloved children, and thus you will journey along the road which brings you to the God of salvation and peace.

i   — *My Immaculate Heart is your refuge,* in which I gather you together, as in a new spiritual cenacle, to obtain for you the gift of the Holy Spirit, who would transform you into apostles of the second evangelization.

j   Be apostles of this, my work, in all Sardinia. Go out from this cenacle, and go everywhere in search of my children who have strayed along the roads of sin and evil, of unbelief and pleasure, of impurity and drugs. Bring them all into the same refuge which I have prepared for you.

k   I am with you and am lighting up for you the way along which you must go. Today I look upon you with motherly tenderness, and, with all those who are dear to you, I bless you and encourage you to walk along the way of holiness and love, of purity and joy."

Valdragone (San Marino); June 30, 1994
Spiritual Exercises in the Form of a Cenacle
with 25 Bishops and 250 Priests of the M.M.P.
from Europe, America, Asia and Oceania

My Immaculate Heart Will Triumph

a   "Never have you come in such great numbers from every part of the world, bishops and priests of my Movement, and you are up here on this mountain for a week of a continuous cenacle of prayer and fraternity. You have come, drawn by the voice of your heavenly Mother.

b   I have called you up here. During these days, I am constantly close to each one of you. I unite myself with your prayer. I deepen the bond of your fraternal relationship. I obtain for you the gift of the Holy Spirit, who works profoundly in your life and who brings you to a transformation of heart.

c   How much comfort you give to your heavenly Mother! In you my Heart is glorified because, by means of you, I am able to bring about the triumph of my Immaculate Heart in the world, as I have announced to you at Fatima.

d   — *My Immaculate Heart will triumph* over this ailing and materialistic humanity, bent on the mad search for pleasure and comfort, which has built a new civilization without God and has again become pagan, after almost two thousand years since the first announcing of the Gospel.

e   Go and preach the necessity of penance and conversion, of return to the Lord along the way of prayer and repentance, of renunciation of Satan and all his wiles, of evil and the tyranny of the passions.

f   Let this humanity return, like the prodigal son, into the arms of the Heavenly Father, who awaits it with love, so that a new, profound and universal reconciliation may be thus achieved between God and humanity.

g   It is you who must be the instruments of this general return. It is you who must be the apostles of this second evangelization, so strongly requested by my Pope. Thus, by means of you, my Immaculate Heart will triumph.

h   — *My Immaculate Heart will triumph* over this, my suffering and divided Church, torn by the evil spirits and possessed, in an increasingly powerful way, by the dark power of Freemasonry. Because of this, errors are being spread about in her, and these are often being taught, spread and accepted midst general apathy and indifference. The lack of faith is spreading. Sins are committed and justified. The ministers of the sanctuary languish in lukewarmness and indifference and are dissipating the treasures which the Lord has put into their hands.

i How this most beloved Daughter of mine is suffering! How few are those who listen to the voice of your heavenly Mother and follow it. And these encounter difficulty, misunderstanding, and persecution, often on the part of their own confreres.

j It is you who must be the instruments of the interior renewal of all the Church, you who are called to be the new heart of the new Church, purified, enlightened and sanctified.

k For this reason I invite you to be today courageous apostles of faith and unity, of holiness and love. Bend down with me to soothe her great pain, to place balm and comfort on her many open and bleeding wounds. In this way you become for her today expressions of my motherly tenderness, and by means of you, my Immaculate Heart will triumph.

l — *My Immaculate Heart will triumph* over all my poor children, who are carrying the cross of the unspeakable sufferings of these last times of the purification and the great tribulation. How many are those who are far away! How numerous are the victims of my Adversary, who has established in the world today the summit of his diabolical power.

m Take by the hand those children who have been set on the road to precocious experiences of evil. Support the youth who have been ensnared and seduced by false values which have been proposed to them and who are succumbing under the weight of sins, of impurity and of drugs. Help Christian families to live as little communities of grace and prayer, of communion and love, and snatch them away from the grave danger of division and divorce, of recourse to the means of impeding life, and of the abortions which are increasing in every part of the world.

n Go in search of the little sheep, straying along all the roadways of the world. Convert sinners; support the wavering; lead the wandering; heal the sick; comfort the dying. To all, give the

820

grace and the love, the salvation and the life which my Son Jesus has given to you through his passion and death on the Cross.

o   Thus you become instruments of salvation for all, in these last times, when everything which I foretold to you must be accomplished. In this way, by means of you, my Immaculate Heart will, in the end, triumph.

p   Go out from this cenacle with serenity and joy. I have granted to all the grace of a change of heart and a transformation of life. No one is leaving this cenacle the same as they entered.

q   I am the Mother of grace and of purity, of love and of hope, of joy and of peace. Leave in peace, and become, in every part of the world, the instruments of my peace. I am with you, and I will cause you to feel my motherly presence in an extraordinary way.

r   With your dear ones, and with the persons who are entrusted to you, I bless you all in the name of the Father, and of the Son, and of the Holy Spirit."

524

Rubbio (Vicenza, Italy); August 15, 1994
Solemnity of the Assumption
of the Blessed Virgin Mary into Heaven

The Feast of Joy

a   "Beloved children, contemplate me today in the light of my glorified body, assumed into the glory of paradise. The Most Holy and Divine Trinity reflects in me the splendor of its power and of its greatest glory.

b   All the heavenly spirits leap for joy as they celebrate with hymns of exultation and prostrate themselves in an act of profound veneration for her who has been constituted their Queen.

c   As they see me at the side of my Son with my glorified body, surrounded with splendor and beauty, the bands of saints experience an increase in blessedness, at the thought that one day their bodies also, at present decomposed, will follow on in glory to the bright destiny, reserved for now only to your heavenly Mother.

d   Special comfort descends upon all the souls who are suffering in purgatory, in prayer and in pain, because, in the vision of my glorified body, their purification becomes stronger and the desire to be united with me in the glory of paradise becomes more ardent.

e   It is a consolation and sure hope for all the Church, still on pilgrimage in the desert of this world, loaded down with sufferings and wounds, as it contemplates me today, prays to me and calls upon me with fervor, that my motherly presence might help it to journey with confidence toward the heavenly fatherland.

f   But above all it gives great joy to you, my dearly beloved children, who are living through the last times of the purification and the great tribulation. The world has become a desert for lack of love and life. Impurity is being spread everywhere through all the means of communication, and with its wicked influence, it is bringing about the corruption and the perversion of morals. Your body, a temple of the Spirit, is being degraded and profaned. Sin is reducing you to a new and greater slavery.

g   Your heavenly Mother takes you by the hand and leads you along the bright, beautiful, pure and holy roads which lead you to paradise.

h   Today is the feast of my Assumption, body and soul, into heaven. It is the feast of light and grace, of beauty and purity, of love and life.

i   *Today is the feast of joy.*

j   The angels and saints in heaven rejoice.

All the souls who are being cleansed in purgatory rejoice.

The Church on earth which looks on me as a sign of consolation and sure hope rejoices.

My poor, sinful, sick, wounded, wandering and despairing children rejoice.

k   *Today is the feast of your joy.*

l   You, above all, my children, who are exposed to the very great sufferings of these last times, you must rejoice and open your hearts to hope. The Woman Clothed with the Sun is now on the point of attaining her greatest victory with the triumph of her Immaculate Heart in the world."

Vigilant Sentinels

a "Let yourself be carried in my motherly arms, my little child, and you will see everywhere the marvels of grace and mercy of my Immaculate Heart.

b Do not be concerned over such a long and wearisome journey, which you are preparing yourself to undertake in order to hold cenacles with the priests and the faithful of my Movement in all Canada, the United States, Mexico and the Dominican Republic.

c Entrust to the angels of light of my Heart all that has to do with this new itinerary of yours. They will carry you on their wings and will keep watch lest you strike your foot against any obstacle.

d Oh, in your days, how beautiful are the feet of those who announce peace, of those who spread the good news of salvation and of the triumph of divine mercy! You must be these announcers of peace. You must be today *vigilant sentinels* upon the mountains of confidence and hope.

e — *Be vigilant sentinels* in the dark time of infidelity and apostasy. Thus you will spread about you the fiercely burning light of the Gospel; you will give to all the strength of the word of God and point out the road one must travel to remain ever in the truth.

f The whole world awaits your announcement with ardent hope. You are the apostles of this second evangelization. Preach to all peoples that Jesus Christ is the one and only Lord, your Savior and Redeemer, and that He is now about to return to you in the splendor of his glory.

g — *Be vigilant sentinels* in the hour of the greatest triumph of Satan and of all the evil spirits. Humanity is in their possession. The world is set in the hands of the Evil One. And so souls have become slaves to sin and are bearing the burden of separation from God, the only source of your happiness. Thus despair is spreading; violence and hatred are reigning supreme in the relationships between individuals and countries; and you are becoming more and more crushed in the bloody winepress of revolutions and wars, of dissensions and fratricidal struggles.

h   You have come to the culmination of the tribulation, and you are living the years of the great chastisement, which, in many ways, has already been announced to you.

i   — *Be vigilant sentinels* who mark out the way of return to the God of peace and life, of love and joy. And so, you must free yourselves from the yoke of sin in order to live always in grace and in communion with God, setting yourselves against the spirit of the world in which you live. You will then be ever faithful to the promises of your baptism.

j   By means of you, the light of goodness and love, of brotherhood and peace, of trust and joy will be able to return upon the world.

k   — *Be vigilant sentinels* who announce that the great day of the Lord is now imminent. Make this announcement to all that they may open their hearts to hope, in order for the second Advent to come about in your time and so that all may prepare to receive the heavenly dew of divine mercy, which is now on the point of being poured out upon the entire world.

l   Thus, even in the indescribable sufferings of the time in which you live, your hearts and your souls can be opened to the joy of this announcement and to the expectation of this prodigious event which you invoke with inexpressible groanings:'Return, Lord Jesus!'"
(cf. Rev 22:20)

526   Ottawa (Ontario, Canada); September 8, 1994
Feast of the Nativity of the Blessed Virgin Mary

With the Littlest Ones

a   "You find yourself here in this great country, my little son, to celebrate today the earthly birth of your heavenly Mother. You have seen the extraordinary participation of priests and especially of the faithful in the cenacles, which you are holding in every part of Canada. My hour has come, and the cohort of the children consecrated to my Immaculate Heart is now ready.

b   *With the littlest ones*, I attain the triumph of my Immaculate Heart, and Jesus will establish his glorious reign in the world.

c   *With the littlest ones*, I am able to form for myself the faithful Church, which is now ready for its birth in the motherly garden of my Immaculate Heart.

d   *With the littlest ones*, I am waging my battle against the powerful cohort of the great and proud, who have hurled their defiance at the Lord. Thus, once again, the Lord will assert his power and, through the mouths of infants and babes at the breast, will reduce to nothing the forces of all his adversaries.

e   *With the littlest ones*, I am attaining each day my victory over Satan and his powerful army of evil, over the satanic and masonic forces organized against God, because I am leading my children along the road of heroic faith, of sure hope and of perfect love. In them, the Heavenly Father is being glorified; by them, Jesus is loved and lived; through them, the Holy Spirit is pouring out the power of his divine love upon the world.

f   In this great country also, I am leading you to salvation and peace by means of these little children of mine. See how they are responding to me with generosity and enthusiasm! See how they are living, with love and gratitude, the consecration to my Immaculate Heart!

g   By means of them, my triumph has already begun. I am now carrying it forward in haste, because the time of my greatest manifestation has now arrived.

h   For this reason, my little son, I am bringing you again to distant places and asking of you such a very toilsome work and a very heavy task, which is humanly impossible. But I am carrying and leading you, sustaining and assisting you, consoling and encouraging you, because from every part of the earth you must bring all my little children into the refuge of my Immaculate Heart.

i   It is only with them that the heavenly Mother can attain her triumph. It is only with them that Jesus can establish his glorious reign in the world.

j   And so, on the day on which you contemplate me in the cradle, where I have been placed after my earthly birth, I bless you with the joy of being followed more and more by you along the way of littleness and humility."

527 *Saskatoon (Saskatchewan, Canada); September 15, 1994*
Feast of Our Lady of Sorrows

The Pierced Soul

a " 'A sword will pierce your soul.' (cf. Lk 2:35) These words, spoken by the aged Simeon at the moment when I was offering my little Child to the Lord, were proven true during the whole course of my Son Jesus' earthly life.

b From his infancy threatened by snares to his hidden youth; from his public life, filled with opposition, to his condemnation to the gibbet; from his ascent of Calvary to his death on the Cross: the entire life of Jesus was a continual fulfillment of this prophecy.

c It has been thus also for the Church, the Mystical Body of my Son Jesus. During its earthly journey, in the course of its history, interwoven with pain and blood, how many times my soul has been pierced by a sword!

d But above all, in these last times, is your heavenly Mother's soul pierced with immense pain.

e *My soul is pierced* by the pain of all this poor humanity, which has distanced itself from its Lord in order to follow the idols of pleasure and comfort, of pride and money, of hatred and impurity. How great is the danger into which it can fall, the danger of destroying itself by its own hands!

f And so, as an anxious Mother, I am intervening in order to lead it along the road of conversion and penance, of a return to the Lord and of its salvation. But my extraordinary interventions are not accepted; on the contrary, they are often opposed and openly rejected.

g *My soul is pierced* in seeing my Church prostrate beneath the weight of a most painful agony. Those errors which lead to a loss of faith are being spread more and more within it. Sin is

seducing the minds and hearts of many of my children. Many
are giving in to the allurements of pleasures and falling into slavery to Satan, who has succeeded in seducing the whole earth.

h   My Pope is becoming more and more isolated, mocked, criticized and abandoned. Many from among the bishops and the
priests are going along the road of disloyalty and are fading away
like lights which are now burnt out. Many voracious wolves, in
sheep's clothing, are entering in to inflict slaughter on the sheepfold of my Son Jesus.

i   The Church is now being called to live through the hours of
its passion and its bloody immolation.

j   *My soul is pierced* by many souls who are being lost and going
each day into hell. Help me to save them. Help me with prayer,
with suffering, with your love, with your faithfulness. For this
reason I am asking you to multiply your cenacles of prayer, in the
conclusive time of the great tribulation. In this way, you help
me to save many of my poor children, who are walking toward
their eternal perdition.

k   *My soul is pierced* in seeing into what a dire situation this great
country, in which you find yourself, has fallen. It has again become pagan, a victim of materialism and of the mad search for
pleasure. The Law of God is more and more violated, and the
gift of life is being daily attacked through the innumerable abortions which are being carried out.

l   Cry out to all with a resolute voice, *to tell them of my immense
sorrow*. Announce, without fear, that the great chastisement has
already begun and that, to be saved, you must enter as quickly as
possible into the safe refuge of my Immaculate Heart. Here, you
will be consoled by me, and you yourselves will give comfort to
my soul which, especially in these times, is again being pierced
by an immense sorrow."

The Angels of Your Time

a   "Today you are celebrating the feast of the Archangels, Gabriel, Raphael and Michael.

b   *They are the Angels of your time.* They are the Angels of the final time of the purification and the great tribulation.

c   *They are the Angels of your time.* To them is entrusted a special task during the period of the trial and the great chastisement. To them befalls the task of saving the people of God, of gathering, from every part of the earth, those who are being called to form part of the little remnant which will remain faithful, in the safe refuge of my Immaculate Heart.

d   *They are the Angels of your time.* Above all, they are the Angels who reveal to you the final events described in the sealed Book.

e   *To the Archangel Michael* is entrusted the task of leading the cohorts of the angels and of my faithful children into the battle against the trained and well equipped armies of Satan, of evil, of the satanic and masonic forces, now organized on a worldwide scale into a single great force, in order to set themselves against God and against his Christ.

f   Saint Michael will above all intervene to fight against the ancient enemy, Lucifer, who in the final hour will appear with all the dark power of the Antichrist. His is the task of fighting against him and of conquering him, of driving him out into his reign of darkness and fire, offering to your heavenly Mother the chain with which she will bind him, and the key with which to lock the door of the abyss, from which he will no longer be able to come out to harm the world.

g   *To the Archangel Raphael* is entrusted the mission of taking part as a heavenly physician in the great struggle, in order to help you and to heal those who are stricken and wounded.

h   As he restored sight to Tobit, so too will he give vision to millions of my poor children, who have been made blind by sins, by errors and by the great darkness of your days, so that they may once again believe and contemplate the divine splendor of the truth.

i   *To the Archangel Gabriel* is entrusted the great mission of announcing the return of Jesus in glory, to restore his reign in the world.

j   As the heavenly announcement of the first coming of my Son into the world came through him, so once again will he be the bright messenger of the second coming of Jesus in glory. This second coming will take place in the power and the light, with Jesus who will appear upon the clouds of heaven, in the splendor of his divinity, to subject all things to Himself. And thus the divine power of my Son Jesus will be made manifest to the entire created universe.

k   To the Archangel, who is called 'Power of God,' is given the task of announcing to all the closely approaching return of Christ, with the force of his divine power.

l   For this reason, I invite you today to honor, to pray, and to invoke the protection of these three Archangels, called to carry out such a great mission in the conclusive time of the great tribulation and to bring you into the heart of the final events, through which you are now being called to live with confidence and with great hope."

529

Effingham (Illinois, U.S.A.); October 13, 1994
Anniversary of the Last Apparition at Fatima
Spiritual Exercises in the Form of a Cenacle
with the Bishops and Priests of the M.M.P.
from the United States and Canada

My Times Have Arrived

a   "My beloved sons, great is the joy which, during these days, you give to your heavenly Mother. You have come from many parts of the United States and Canada, to live with me in a continuous cenacle of prayer and fraternity.

b   I join myself to your prayer; I help you to grow in mutual love, so as to become one heart and one soul. I pour balm on your wounds; I give comfort to your numerous sufferings; and I encourage you to walk with trust and with great hope along the painful road of these last times.

c   Bring my motherly message to everyone.

d   *My times have arrived.*

e   The times which I foretold in Fatima have come. Today, you are commemorating the anniversary of my last apparition, which was confirmed by the miracle of the sun. At that time I foretold to you everything you are now experiencing in these years of the purification and the great tribulation.

f   — I foretold to you the great chastisement which would strike this poor humanity which has become pagan and built a new civilization without God, and which is threatened by violence, by hatred, by war, and which is running the risk of destroying itself by its own hands.

g   My extraordinary interventions, which I have worked in order to bring humanity back onto the road of conversion and of its return to the Lord, have been neither accepted nor believed.

h   So it is now that you find yourselves at the vigil of the great trial which I foretold to you: it will be the supreme manifestation of the divine justice and mercy.

i   Fire will descend from heaven, and humanity will be purified and completely renewed, so as to be ready to receive the Lord Jesus who will return to you in glory.

j   — I also foretold to you the great crisis which would take place in the Church, because of the great apostasy which has entered into her, caused by an ever wider diffusion of errors, by her interior division, by opposition to the Pope and by the rejection of his Magisterium.

k   This most beloved Daughter of mine must live the hours of her agony and of her sorrowful passion. She will be abandoned by many of her children. The impetuous wind of persecution will blow against her, and much blood will be shed, even by my beloved sons.

l   *My times have arrived.*

m   And so I invite you to follow me along the road of prayer and penance, of purity and holiness.

n   See how your countries have become victims of materialism and of the unbridled search for pleasure! The Law of God is being more and more violated. Impurity is being advertised through all the means of social communication. Recourse is being had to every means of impeding life. Abortions are increasing everywhere and are being legitimized by unjust and immoral laws.

o   *My times have arrived.*

p   Tell everyone to enter into the ark of my Immaculate Heart, in order to be protected and saved by me. I request that you multiply your cenacles of prayer among priests, among children, among youth, and especially in families.

q   I have been consoled by the very great response which I received in Canada and in the United States during these cenacles. Never before have they seen a participation in such great numbers, on the part of both priests and faithful.

r   Because of the generous response which I am receiving everywhere from my littlest children, I promise to intervene to save you in the hour of the great trial.

s   My maternal presence among you is the sure sign of protection and of salvation.

t   Open your hearts therefore to hope, and live in the greatest trust and in complete abandonment to my Immaculate Heart.

u   With your dear ones, and with the persons entrusted to you, I bless you in the name of the Father, and of the Son, and of the Holy Spirit."

530   *St. Francis (Maine, U.S.A.); November 1, 1994*
Solemnity of All Saints

In the Splendor of the Saints

a   "You are celebrating today the feast of All Saints. How many of your brothers and sisters, who on earth below have formed part of my cohort, form in paradise the crown of glory about the Immaculate Heart of your Mother and Queen. I am the Queen of All Saints.

b   *In the splendor of the saints,* there is formed one single and unique family of the children of God, loved, redeemed and saved by Him, who possess one perfect and eternal happiness and who intone the new hymn of his glorious triumph.

c   *In the splendor of the saints*, you too are living these days of painful purification and of great tribulation. They are close to you; they are helping you; they are protecting you by their powerful intercession and are leading you to the complete fulfillment of my motherly plan.

d   *In the splendor of the saints*, you are consoled in your suffering, and you are comforted in the bloody moments of the struggle against the powerful forces of evil, which today appear to have gained the upper hand. Thus you are being called to live out the painful hours of your martyrdom.

e   *In the splendor of the saints*, you must live out the present moments and bear the weight of the great trial, which has now come down upon the world, to purify humanity and prepare it for its meeting with the Lord who is returning to you in glory.

f   *In the splendor of the saints*, the entire suffering pilgrim Church must now open its heart to hope, because much light is coming down from heaven to illumine and comfort its sorrowful journey toward the Calvary of its immolation.

g   *In the splendor of the saints*, continue this, your so wearisome and extraordinary journey, my littlest child, called to carry the light of Christ to so many souls darkened by sin and the love and the comfort of the Mother to many sick and wounded hearts. Thus upon each step which you take, your heavenly Mother will cause hope, confidence and joy to blossom forth."

531

Lago de Guadalupe (Mexico); November 23, 1994
Spiritual Exercises in the Form of a Cenacle
with the Priests of the M.M.P. from Mexico and El Salvador

Let Your Trust Be Great

a   "How happy I am to see you, priests of my Movement from Mexico and El Salvador, gathered here in a continuous cenacle of prayer and fraternity. I unite myself with your prayer. I help you to grow in your mutual love, because you must walk together along the painful road of the great tribulation.

b   Love each other as so many brothers bound together in the love of your heavenly Mother. Live in joy and hope.

c   *Let your trust be great.* Jesus loves you with a divine and merciful love. He sees your great difficulties and the abandonment in which you often find yourselves, because of the painful and difficult times in which you are living.

d   Your countries have again become pagan. They are being dominated by the forces of evil and Masonry. They have become victims of materialism and of the unbridled search for pleasure. The Law of the Lord is becoming more and more violated in respect to every one of his commandments. The gift of life is being attacked in a subtle and perverse way. Violence and hatred are disseminated, while impurity is spreading like a poison which brings death to hearts and souls.

e   You are being called to be the instruments of divine mercy for all this poor humanity, so far from God. For this reason, I ask you to be faithful to your ministry. Be strong witnesses of faith in the time of the great apostasy, of holiness in the moments of the great perversion, and of love in the hour of violence and hatred, which is becoming stronger and stronger from day to day.

f   *Let your trust be great.* I am Mother, and I want to spread the balm of my motherly love upon all my children. I have need of you.

g   And so I ask you to consecrate yourselves to my Immaculate Heart, because I want to make of you instruments of my motherly mercy. Take my most needy children in your priestly arms, and bring them into the heavenly refuge of my Immaculate Heart. Support the weak; lead the hesitant; convert the sinners; heal the sick; comfort the despairing; bring those far away into the house of the Father; give to all the balm of my motherly and merciful love.

h   In this way, you become the precious instruments of the triumph of my Immaculate Heart in the world.

i   *Let your trust be great.* The triumph of my Immaculate Heart is near.

j   I am consoled by the response of love and prayer which, in this country, I am receiving from the littlest, the poor, the weak, the humble, the simple. In the heart and the life of these, my little children, the triumph of my Immaculate Heart has already begun.

k   This triumph will continue in an increasingly stronger way, because Latin America is my possession and belongs to me. And I will manifest myself to all, as a powerful and merciful Mother.

l   For this reason, I invite you to leave this cenacle in peace, in joy and with a great hope. With your dear ones and with those who are entrusted to your ministry, I bless you all in the name of the Father, and of the Son, and of the Holy Spirit."

532   Shrine of Our Lady of Guadalupe (Mexico City, Mexico)
December 5, 1994
National Cenacle of the M.M.P.

The Apple of My Eye

a   "With what love I look upon you, priests and faithful of my Movement, who find yourselves here in this, my most venerated Shrine, in order to hold your great cenacle, which brings to conclusion those held in many cities of Mexico, this land particularly protected and blessed by me! I am causing torrents of love and of mercy to come down from my Immaculate Heart upon you all, upon the Church and upon this poor humanity.

b   As the image of little Juan Diego, to whom I appeared, is imprinted in my eyes, so also are you imprinted in the eyes and the Heart of your heavenly Mother.

c   *You are the apple of my eye*, because you are my littlest babes, completely consecrated to me, and thus I am able to pour out, upon you, all the tenderness of my motherly love.

d   *You are the apple of my eye*, because you let yourselves be led by me with great docility. You listen to me; you carry out my requests; you walk along the road which I have pointed out to you. And thus, by means of you, I am able to carry out the great plan of the triumph of my Immaculate Heart in the world.

e   *You are the apple of my eye*, because through you I am able to spread the light of the faith in the days of the great apostasy, the perfume of grace and of holiness in the time of the great perversion, and the victorious force of love in the hour of violence and hatred.

f *You are the apple of my eye,* because of the great love which you have for the Eucharistic Jesus. With what joy I look upon you when you go before the tabernacle to give your priestly homage of love, of adoration and of reparation to Jesus. At a time when the Eucharistic Jesus is surrounded by so much indifference and with such emptiness, you still spread the solemn hours of Eucharistic adoration, and you surround the Eucharistic Jesus with flowers and lights as signs indicative of your love and your tender devotion.

g *You are the apple of my eye,* because you are simple, poor and humble. And thus you love me with all the candor of your childlike hearts.

h You have seen, my little son, with what enthusiasm I am loved, besought and glorified by all these Mexican children of mine. For this reason, my great victory against all the masonic and satanic forces will begin from here, for the greatest triumph of my Son Jesus.

i I confirm to you that, by the great jubilee of the year two thousand, there will take place the triumph of my Immaculate Heart, which I foretold to you at Fatima, and this will come to pass with the return of Jesus in glory, to establish his reign in the world. Thus you will at last be able to see with your own eyes the new heavens and the new earth.

j With all my love of a Mother, consoled and glorified by you, I bless you in the name of the Father, and of the Son, and of the Holy Spirit."

533 Santiago (Dominican Republic); December 8, 1994
Solemnity of the Immaculate Conception

Apostles of the Last Times

a "You find yourself here, my little son, to hold a cenacle with the bishops, priests and faithful of my Movement, on this day when the Church celebrates the solemnity of my Immaculate Conception.

b   The Most Holy Trinity has filled my entire being with this singular privilege, because I was destined to be the Mother of the Word, become man in my most pure womb.

c   In view of my divine maternity, I have been preserved from original sin and from every shadow of personal sin, and I have been filled with grace and holiness.

d   Because I am the Mother of Jesus, I have been intimately associated in the mystery of his work of redemption, as Co-redemptrix, and have thus become true Mediatrix of Grace between you and my Son Jesus.

e   Beneath the Cross, through the Will of my Son, I have become Mother of all of you, and in the Cenacle with the Apostles, I have participated as Mother in the birth of the Church.

f   My motherly task is that of leading the Church along the way of its evangelization. And so I have always been at the side of each of my children who, through two thousand years, have brought the announcement of the Gospel to every part of the world.

g   Precisely on this day, you are celebrating here the five hundredth anniversary of the beginning of the evangelization of all this great continent of America.

h   After nearly two thousand years since the first announcing of the Gospel, humanity has again become pagan. I am the Mother of the Second Evangelization. Mine is the task of forming the apostles of the second evangelization. During these years, I have formed you with particular care and through the gift of my words, to be *the apostles of these last times.*

i   *Apostles of the last times,* because you must announce to all, to the very ends of the earth, the Gospel of Jesus, in these days of the great apostasy. In the great darkness which has descended upon the world, spread the light of Christ and of his divine truth.

j   *Apostles of the last times,* because you must give to all the very life of God, by means of grace which you communicate with the sacraments of which you are the ministers. And thus you spread the fragrance of purity and of holiness in these times of great perversion.

836

k   *Apostles of the last times,* because you are being called to bring down the dew of the merciful love of Jesus upon a world parched by the inability to love and menaced more and more with hatred, violence and war.

l   *Apostles of the last times,* because you must announce the closely approaching return of Jesus in glory, who will lead humanity into the new times, when at last there will be seen new heavens and a new earth.

m   Proclaim to all his forthcoming return: 'Maranatha! Come, Lord Jesus!' " (cf. Rev 22:20)

534

Dongo (Como, Italy); December 24, 1994
The Holy Night

The Mystery of This Night

a   "Live with me, in prayer and expectation, *the mystery of this night.* Beloved children, enter into the heavenly garden of my Immaculate Heart, to relish all the joy and the immense blessedness of this event.

b   '*When the fullness of time had come.*' (Gal 4:4) Time, in its unfolding, is directed to that moment from the beginning, from eternity, in the mind of the Father, from the time when the Lord created the universe, from the time when the earth became a privileged garden for the man, raised to a particular communion with God, from the time when, due to the fall of the first parents, even creation itself became subjected to frailty and the earth began to produce thorns and thistles for man, now subjected to bitter trials and continuous sufferings.

c   '*I will put enmity between you and the Woman; between your offspring and hers. She will crush your head.*' (Gen 3:15) My offspring is the divine Child who is born of me on this holy night. It is He who is the Conqueror of Satan, because He is the Incarnate Word of the Father, the sole Mediator between God and humanity, the one and only Savior and Redeemer.

d   By means of Him, the plan of the Father is reinstated as it was in the beginning. Man once again reflects the glory of the living God, and all the universe is wondrously ordained to proclaim the perfect glory of its Lord.

e   'God sent forth his Son.' (Gal 4:4) This holy night is a response to the profound aspirations of all those who have lived in the hope and the prayerful expectation of this moment. It is the fullness of time because it condenses within itself the ardent expectation of all history: of Adam, of Abraham, of the patriarchs and the prophets, of the kings and the priests, of the great and the small. For how many centuries these just ones of Israel have lived, invoking, hoping for and awaiting this moment.

f   'God sent forth his Son.' He is the Word consubstantial with the Father. He is the Image of his substance. He is the Splendor of his glory who, on this night, is born in his human life.

g   'Born of a Woman.' (Gal 4:4) He is born of me, his Virgin Mother. Live with me the ecstasy of these hours. Enter into my Immaculate Heart to savor all the intensity of this moment, when time reached its fullness. You are in the heart of history. Here you can understand all the events of the past. Here you can give sense and significance to all the events of the future.

h   This night becomes a fount of light for humanity of all times, because the Son who is born of me, on this holy night, is God-with-you, is Emmanuel, is your Redeemer, is your one and only Savior.

i   Enter then with joy *into the mystery of this night.* And open your hearts to the fullness of the blessedness which comes to you with the fullness of time:'I bring you good news of a great joy which will come to all the people; for to you is born this day a Savior, who is Christ the Lord.' (cf. Lk 2:10-11)

j   *In the mystery of this night,* understand also how the fullness of time is accomplished in the new time which awaits you, since this first coming of Jesus in the frailty of his human nature is directed toward his second coming, when He will appear in the splendor of his divine glory. In this first Christmas, his divinity is obscured and hidden by his humanity; in his second birth, the humanity will be veiled over by the splendor of his divinity.

k Enter then *into the mystery of this night, to open your hearts to hope.* Today I bring you good news of a great joy which will come to all the people. The Lord Jesus, whom you are contemplating this night in the manger, small and frail, weeping and totally destitute, is about to return in the splendor of his divine glory.

l This, his glorious return, will bring to fulfillment the fullness of time, when He will initiate the new time of the new heavens and the new earth."

535

Milan (Italy); December 31, 1994
Last Night of the Year

A Sorrowful and Concerned Mother

a "Beloved children, spend the last hours of this year with me, in prayer and recollection. How many spend these moments amidst a din of voices and images, which prevent you from understanding the gravity and the imminent dangers of the time in which you are living.

b *I am a sorrowful and concerned Mother.*

c — *I am a sorrowful Mother*, as I see this poor humanity, so far away from its Lord, a humanity which, with great irresponsibility and indifference, is walking along the road of sin and evil, of impurity and godlessness, of hatred and war.

d How great is the danger of humanity reaching the point of destroying itself by its own hands! I see your roads bathed with blood, while violence and hatred hurl themselves like a terrible hurricane upon the life of families and nations.

e — *I am a sorrowful Mother*, as I see the Church, my dearly beloved Daughter, prostrate beneath the cross of a most painful agony. How many deny and betray her! How many abandon and condemn her! How many revile and crucify her!

f Among these are even some of my beloved sons: bishops and priests who repeat and renew the deed of Judas who betrays, or that of Peter who denies, or of the Apostles who flee out of cowardice.

839

g   You are called to be the new Johns, who remain with me beneath the cross upon which the Church is again being crucified and immolated for the salvation of the world.

h   — *I am a concerned Mother,* because my extraordinary interventions, which I have carried out in order to lead you to conversion and salvation, have been neither accepted nor followed.

i   How can you now save yourselves from the great chastisement which is upon you, if you have refused what the heavenly Mother has offered you for your salvation?

j   — *I am a concerned Mother* because the time of the final events has now come. Until now, I have been able to put off the beginning of the great trial, through the response which I have received in every part of the world from my littlest children. But now you must enter into, and live out, the final time of the great tribulation.

k   For these moments, I have raised up everywhere my Marian Movement of Priests. For this, I have brought this littlest son of mine to every part of the world, to make you enter, each and all, into the safe refuge of my Immaculate Heart. Live within this refuge throughout the time of the great trial which has now come for all.

l   And *open your hearts to hope* because, as of this year, you will see my motherly presence among you becoming ever brighter, more powerful, more frequent and more strongly experienced."

840

1995

MOTHER OF MERCY

Mother of Mercy

a   "Beloved children, begin this new year by celebrating the liturgical solemnity of my divine motherhood. I am true Mother of God because Jesus, who is born of me and is being placed in the manger, is true Son of God.

b   He is the Eternal Word, consubstantial with the Father, and He assumes his human nature in my virginal womb. He is the gift of love of the Father:'God has so loved the world that He has given it his only-begotten Son.' (cf. Jn 3:16) He is the manifestation of his divine mercy.

c   Jesus is born of me to be your Redeemer and to set humanity free from slavery to Satan and to lead it back to a full communion of life and of love with God.

d   — *I am Mother of Mercy.* My motherly task has been that of giving you Jesus, who is the revelation of the merciful love of the Father. Thus, in order to come to you, divine mercy has passed through the way of my divine and immaculate motherhood.

e   But I am also your Mother. Beneath the Cross, through the Will of my Son Jesus, I have become true Mother of all humanity, redeemed and saved by Him. Thus the divine mercy of Jesus, in order to reach you, must pass through the motherly way of my Immaculate Heart. For this reason, the triumph of my Immaculate Heart coincides with the triumph of divine mercy upon the world.

f   — *I am Mother of Mercy.* To me was entrusted the task of preparing humanity to receive the heavenly dew of divine mercy.

g   You have now entered into the final years, which are preparing you for this new and second Advent. They are the most important and difficult years, the most painful and bloody, because during them there must take place the final events which have been foretold to you by me.

h   My motherly work of mercy is being made manifest during these years in this way:

i   *...in leading you along the way of conversion and of return to the Lord.* I desire to give you the grace of a change of heart and of life. I help you to free yourselves from sin, to fight against the passions, to conquer evil; and I lead you to full reconciliation with the Lord your God. It is necessary that this general reconciliation come about quickly, to prepare you thus for the great trial which awaits you, for the complete purification of all humanity.

j   *...in bringing you to a strong experience of prayer.* For this, I ask you to multiply and to spread everywhere the cenacles which I have asked of you: among priests, children, youth and in families. My Immaculate Heart must now become the new and spiritual cenacle, in which you must all gather together, to obtain the gift of the second Pentecost. The purification of the world will come about through the work of the Spirit of Love, who will pour out from heaven *his blazing fire* to renew the face of the earth.

k   *...in helping you to live through the hour of the great trial.* Sufferings never before experienced are awaiting you, because the moment of a universal renewal is drawing close. Satan will be defeated; the power of evil will be destroyed; Jesus will restore his glorious reign among you, and in this way the new heavens and the new earth will be formed. Without an extraordinary intervention of my motherly love, you would not be able to support the pain of the great trial which has now come for all.

l   — *I am Mother of Mercy.* The motherly task of assisting the Church in the hour of her greatest suffering has been entrusted to me, because she must climb the Calvary of her immolation and her martyrdom. This merciful action of mine will be exercised in helping her to carry the cross of betrayal and abandonment, when the apostasy becomes general and the man of iniquity foretold by Sacred Scripture enters her, he who will bring the abomination of desolation into her interior.

m   My merciful action will become still stronger when my children will be persecuted and imprisoned, tormented and led to martyrdom.

n   It is then that I will manifest myself to them in an extraordinary way, according to a mysterious design which my Immaculate Heart has, for a long time now, already outlined in all its particulars.

843

o — *I am Mother of Mercy.* All my children, from this year on, will see fulfilled the prodigy of the Woman Clothed with the Sun, and I will pour out upon the world the light and the merciful power of my Immaculate Heart.

p For this reason, at the beginning of the new year, I invite all to live in confidence and in prayer. Have no fear. I am with you, and I will manifest myself in an extraordinary way. The more you enter into the time of the purifying trial, the more you will feel, in a powerful way, my merciful and motherly presence.

q I bless you all in the name of the Father, and of the Son, and of the Holy Spirit."

537 Sale (Alessandria, Italy); February 2, 1995
Feast of the Presentation of the Child Jesus

The Hour of Your Immolation

a "With the lights of your hearts burning with love, beloved children, accompany me to the temple of the Lord, to offer with me in sacrifice my divine Child to the glory of the Heavenly Father. As I place my Child in the hands of the priest, the Most Holy Trinity bows with pleasure and with a blessing on the offering of your heavenly Mother.

b *The Father,* who has so loved the world that He has given it his only-begotten Son, takes pleasure in accepting the gift of the Son, become now the living image of his merciful Love.

c *The Son,* who from eternity lives in the bosom of the Father, rejoices in feeling Himself offered on the altar of his glory, in a Sacrifice of ransom and of redemption, for the salvation of all.

d *The Holy Spirit* comes to rest in the heart of a poor old man and opens it to an understanding of the divine mystery: 'He is set as a sign of contradiction, for the salvation and the ruin of many in Israel, and as for you, O Mother, a sword will pierce your soul.' (cf. Lk 2:34-35)

e Live with me the mystery of this offering, and let yourselves all be offered, my little children, to the glory of the Most Holy Trinity.

f *The hour of your immolation has come.*

844

g — On the altar of my Immaculate Heart, you are being immolated to the perfect glory of the Father. Your Heavenly Father must be glorified. For this, He has created all the universe, and in your life, He arranges with love every least circumstance for your good. For this, He has given you his Son for your salvation. In you, in your life, in your peace, in your joy, the Heavenly Father is glorified.

h — On the altar of my Immaculate Heart, you are being immolated to the perfect glory of the Son. The Son must be glorified. For this, He has come into the world. And the Son is glorified when the Will of the Father is accomplished by all in a perfect way. Thus, in you, the Son continues to render his testimony to the Father. This is his testimony: that his Will be accomplished by every creature. His Will is that you all be perfectly one in the Son, so as thus to be perfectly one with the Father. Thus you render your testimony to the truth, and the truth will set you free.

i — On the altar of my Immaculate Heart, you are being immolated to the perfect glory of the Holy Spirit. The Holy Spirit must be glorified. For this, He is constantly being given to you by the Father and the Son. And the Holy Spirit is glorified when, with his divine fire, He purifies you and transforms you, so that you may love, in Him and through Him, the Father and the Son.

j Thus you live in the Heart of the Most Holy Trinity, and you are offered to its perfect glory.

k *The hour of your immolation has come.*

l In these times, the Most Holy Trinity must be glorified. And for this reason, you are being called to be strong witnesses *of the truth*. The hour of the great apostasy has come, and yours is the task of giving to all the splendor of the divine truth.

m You are living the moments of the great perversion, during which humanity has become pagan and worse than in the times of the flood, and you are being called to spread the light *of holiness*. Be torches ablaze with holiness and purity in the deep darkness of sin which has descended upon the world.

n You are being called to become strong witnesses *of love*, in the hour of violence and hatred, of unbridled egoism and of war.

o Now the hurricane is at your doors, and the Church and hu-

845

manity will be called to live the tremendous hour of the great trial. For this, you are being immolated today on the altar of my Immaculate Heart.

p   *The hour of your immolation has come.*

q   I am ever close to you, and I am leading you by the hand at each moment, as a mother leads her little children. I will be at your side, in an extraordinary way, during the bloody moments of your priestly passion and of your martyrdom.

r   You will see me then and rejoice, because you will contemplate your heavenly Mother who offers you, as little lambs, on the altar of her Immaculate Heart, to the perfect glory of the Most Holy and Divine Trinity."

538   *San Marco (Udine, Italy); February 11, 1995*
Feast of Our Lady of Lourdes

Wash Yourselves at the Fountain

a   "Gaze today at the splendor of holiness and purity of your heavenly Mother, who has appeared at Lourdes as the Immaculate Conception. And hasten, one and all, my sick and sinful children, to the fountain of grace and of divine mercy.

b   *Wash yourselves at the fountain.* Wash yourselves at the fountain of living water, gushing from the Heart of Jesus, pierced by the lance of the Roman soldier. For this, with the hands of little Bernadette, I caused a fountain of purest water to gush forth from the rock. And so, I have asked you to go and wash yourselves at the fountain.

c   *Wash yourselves at the fountain.* A person who has dirtied himself has need to be washed. It is sin which darkens the beauty of your soul; it is sin which takes sanctifying grace away from you and separates you from the communion of life with the Lord your God; it is sin which causes you to return to slavery under Satan, who thus exercises his evil dominion over you; it is sin which leads you along the road of your eternal perdition.

d   *Wash yourselves at the fountain.* Immerse yourselves in the fountain of divine mercy. This fountain, which has gushed from the pierced Heart of Jesus, is given to you through the sacrament of Reconciliation. Jesus has instituted it as a precious fruit of his redemption and in order to meet your extreme weakness. On the day of his resurrection, He said to the Apostles: 'Receive the Holy Spirit. Whose sins you shall forgive they are forgiven.' (Jn 20:22-23) From that moment, there was given to you the possibility of washing yourselves, each and every time your souls become degraded by sin.

e   *Wash yourselves at the fountain.* During these years, the sacrament of Reconciliation has become more and more neglected; in fact, it is being attacked in a subtle and perverse way. Thus, there is spreading the wicked habit of committing sin with levity, of justifying it, of not regretting having committed it, and of no longer confessing it.

f   In many parts of the Church, sacramental confession has totally disappeared. Priests who are making themselves available for this indispensable sacrament are becoming more and more scarce. In this way, the Church is becoming utterly paralyzed in her apostolic action; she is wounded and covered with deep sores, like a leper.

g   *Wash yourselves at the fountain.* Today I am setting before you the ardent and impassioned request of your heavenly Mother that, in these last times of the great tribulation, the sacrament of Reconciliation be restored in all its splendor in my Church.

h   Because, it is only from this fountain that divine mercy can be poured out upon all humanity. It is in this sacrament that Jesus can form new hearts and a renewed life. It is only with this precious sacrament that the merciful love of Jesus can be communicated to the Church and to all humanity.

i   For this reason, I invite you today to let yourselves be immersed in the fountain of divine mercy and to look to me, your heavenly Mother, who have been conceived immaculate for the very purpose of becoming for you Mother of Mercy."

539

Fatima (Portugal); March 11, 1995
Cenacle with the Priests and Faithful
of the M.M.P. from Portugal

My Secret

a "In this my venerated shrine, I welcome you all, my beloved ones and children consecrated to me, that I may enclose you all within the safe refuge of my Immaculate Heart.

b — Here, I appeared as the Woman Clothed with the Sun, to point out to you the road along which you must journey in this century of yours, so ensnared and in the possession of the spirit of Evil.

c — Here, I came from heaven to offer you the refuge in which to take shelter at the moment of the great struggle between me and my Adversary and in the painful hours of the great tribulation and chastisement.

d — Here, I caused the Marian Movement of Priests to spring up, and by means of this little son whom I have brought to every part of the world during these years, I have formed for myself the cohort, now ready for the battle and for my greatest victory.

e — I want you here today, spiritually united with this son of mine, as a great cenacle of my Movement is being held before the image of your heavenly Mother, placed in the very spot where I appeared to the three children, Jacinta, Francisco and Lucia.

f — Here, I am gathering you all round about me and expressing to you my pleasure for the way in which you have accepted the invitation to become part of the Marian Movement of Priests, to consecrate yourselves to my Immaculate Heart and to spread everywhere cenacles of prayer among priests, children, youth, and in families.

g I want you spiritually here with me, because as of now you are entering into the last period of time of this century of yours, when the events which I have predicted to you will come to their complete fulfillment. For this reason, here in the very place where I appeared, I want today to reveal to you *my secret*.

h *My secret concerns the Church.*

i In the Church, the great apostasy, which will spread throughout the whole world, will be brought to its completion; the schism will take place through a general alienation from the Gospel and from the true faith. There will enter into the Church the man of iniquity, who opposes himself to Christ, and who will bring into her interior the abomination of desolation, thus bringing to fulfillment the horrible sacrilege, of which the prophet Daniel has spoken. (cf. Mt 24:15)

j *My secret concerns humanity.*

k Humanity will reach the summit of corruption and impiety, of rebellion against God and of open opposition to his Law of love. It will know the hour of its greatest chastisement, which has already been foretold to you by the prophet Zechariah. (cf. Zec 13:7-9)

l Then this place will appear to all as a bright sign of my motherly presence in the supreme hour of your great tribulation. From here my light will spread to every part of the world, and from this fount will gush the water of divine mercy, which will descend to irrigate the barrenness of a world, now reduced to an immense desert.

m And in this, my extraordinary work of love and of salvation, there will appear to all the triumph of the Immaculate Heart of her who is invoked as the Mother of Mercy."

540
Madrid (Spain); March 22, 1995
Spiritual Exercises in the Form of a Cenacle
with the Priests of the M.M.P. from Spain and Gibraltar

I Am Consoled by You

a "My sorrowful Heart is consoled by you, during these days of continuous cenacle, beloved children of my Movement who have come from many parts of Spain, this land so ensnared by my Adversary, but loved and protected by your heavenly Mother. You are pouring balm on my injuries and closing the wounds of my deep sorrow.

b *I am consoled by you.*

c — *I am consoled by you,* through your *continuous prayer,* made with recollection and love, and which you offer to the Lord with me and by means of me.

d   You give a great force of intercession and reparation to your heavenly Mother, and thus I am able to intervene in order to dispose the events of your time according to the design of mercy and salvation of my Immaculate Heart.

e   How great is my sorrow in seeing that prayer is being more and more neglected by many of my beloved children. They no longer pray. An immoderate and wasteful activity occupies the day of many priests, who get submerged in the spirit of the world and become tasteless salt and lights that have now burned out.

f   — *I am consoled by you* through your pledge to walk along the road *of holiness.* Today, how necessary for the salvation of the world is the holiness of priests!

g   In a world possessed by the Evil One, in a Church darkened by secularism and moral permissiveness, it is necessary that priests be holy, to point out to all the sure road which leads to salvation and peace.

h   Fight against sin as your greatest evil. Make yourselves always available for the sacrament of Reconciliation, which is today being so neglected. Give the grace of God to the souls darkened by evil. Walk with joy along the road strewn with flowers of all the virtues, and thus you will arrive at sanctity.

i   For this, I ask you to consecrate yourselves to my Immaculate Heart, because I want to communicate to you also, my little children, the very holiness of your heavenly Mother.

j   — *I am consoled by you* through your special pledge *of fidelity and unity.*

k   In this country of yours, how widespread and dangerous is the contestation directed against the Pope and the opposition to his Magisterium! And thus, fundamental truths of the Catholic faith are questioned and denied; errors are taught and followed; the loss of faith becomes diffused, and the great apostasy from Jesus and his Gospel spreads everywhere.

l   You must be strong witnesses of unity with the Pope and fidelity to the Gospel, whose ministers you are. Pay no attention to the bad example which superiors and confreres may give you in this matter. Look only at the profound sorrow and the bleeding wound which this increasing apostasy, spreading more and more in the Church, causes the Heart of your heavenly Mother.

m   And pour the balm of your faithfulness and your unity on the open and bleeding wounds of my Immaculate Heart.

n   — *I am consoled by you* because you are following the road which, in these years, I have traced out for you with the messages which I have given to the heart of this little son of mine. Be more and more united with him; accept the word which I give you by means of him.

o   Do not let yourselves become distracted or enticed along other roads, because today many are those who are spreading false messages and untrue visions. In this way, work together toward an ever increasing diffusion of this work of mine, the Marian Movement of Priests, throughout all your country. And become the precious instruments of my motherly action of salvation and mercy for all my poor wandering children. In this way above all, *I am consoled by you.*

p   With your dear ones, with all those who are entrusted to your priestly ministry, I bless you in the name of the Father, and of the Son, and of the Holy Spirit."

541

Capoliveri (Livorno, Italy); April 13, 1995
Holy Thursday

I Have Ardently Desired

a   "Beloved sons, live this Holy Thursday in the Gethsemane of my Immaculate Heart. It is your Passover. It is the day which recalls the institution of the new Sacrifice and of the new Priesthood.

b   You were present in the loving design of the Heart of Jesus, who was about to open Himself to his greatest offering. 'I have ardently desired to eat this Passover with you before I suffer.' (Lk 22:15)

c   'I have ardently desired.' All the life of Jesus has been directed to this supreme and ineffable moment. From the incarnation in my virginal womb to his birth, from the threatened childhood to youth, from early manhood spent in the poor house of Nazareth to his public life, each day Jesus was constantly impelled toward this moment.

d   *'I have ardently desired.'* When Jesus was crushed with weariness and fatigue; when He was surrounded by the Pharisees' snares and rejected by the mighty; when He was making his way along the roads of Galilee and Judea to announce the Good News; when He was healing the sick, pardoning sinners, and setting free the possessed; when He was awaited by the poor and consoled by the little ones… Jesus was constantly yearning to reach the fulfillment of this, his Passover. 'I have ardently desired to eat this Passover with you before I suffer.'

e   *It is the Passover of love.* On this day, Jesus gives his body as food and his blood as drink to those who are being redeemed and saved by Him. There is no greater love than this, that one lay down his life for those whom he loves.

f   In this, his gift, the new and eternal Covenant between God and humanity is established, and the rite of the *new Passover* in the true Lamb of God who takes away the sins of the world is instituted. Beloved sons, accept with gratitude this great gift of the love of Jesus, who has associated you intimately in his supreme and eternal Priesthood.

g   *It is the Passover of suffering.* Love is proven with suffering. So then, to this, his utmost gift of love, Judas responds with betrayal, Peter with denial, the Apostles with desertion, and the servants of the high priest with outrage and buffets.

h   *'I have ardently desired.'* The Heart of Jesus burns now forever with this, his ardent desire. Merciful Love flows forth with the blood and the water, from the wound in his pierced side. And it descends like a heavenly dew to wash away every stain, to cancel every sin, to heal every malady, to close every wound, to help every stricken person, to relieve all who have fallen, to set free every prisoner, to save whomever is lost.

i   In these last times of yours, the hour so longed for by Jesus has come, because his merciful love is preparing his greatest triumph. And so, I invite you today to enter, each and all, into the

Gethsemane of my Immaculate Heart.

j   Thus you will be formed by me, Mother of Mercy, to become the precious instruments of the triumph of the merciful love of Jesus upon all this poor humanity, which has extreme need of being saved.

k   Thus today, you too must earnestly desire to eat this Passover, before your suffering."

542   *Capoliveri (Livorno, Italy); April 14, 1995*
Good Friday

Tears and Blood

a   "You are looking today upon Him whom they have pierced. Beloved children, live this day with me, sorrowful Mother of the Passion.

b   How much blood have my weeping eyes seen this day! My Son Jesus is reduced, by the scourging, to one great wound. The terrible Roman scourges have cut into his body deep wounds from which there flows copiously the blood which covers Him with a mantle of purple. Piercing his head is the crown of thorns from which spurt rivulets of blood which run down, covering and disfiguring his face. 'So disfigured was He, that He was beyond human semblance.' (cf. Is 52:14) The nails pierce his hands and feet, and the blood spurts out and runs down upon the wood of the Cross.

c   During the three hours of excruciating agony, I remain beneath the Cross with John and the holy women, and together we are bathed in his precious blood.

d   Then, after He has emitted his last breath, the Roman centurion, with lance in hand, pierces his side, from which flow blood and water, symbols of the sacraments of your rebirth. From this fount the Church is born, born in the cradle formed by the blood of the Son and the tears of the Mother.

e   *Tears and blood.* They are the price of your ransom. They are the sign of an immense suffering. They are the gift of divine Mercy which has come down to renew the whole world.

f   Today you are living a new Good Friday. And how much

blood flows down again from the weeping eyes of your heavenly Mother! It is the blood of children killed in the wombs of their mothers. It is the blood poured out by all the victims of violence and hatred, of fratricidal struggles and wars. And again copious tears flow down from my motherly eyes in the face of a humanity which bears within itself the reason for its own condemnation.

g   *Tears and blood.* I want to help this poor humanity return to its Lord, along the road of conversion and of repentance, and so I am giving it evident signs of my motherly affliction and my sorrowful anxiety. This is why I am causing *tears and blood* to flow down from some of my images.

h   How can a child not be moved before its mother who is weeping? How can you, my beloved children, not be moved before your heavenly Mother who is weeping tears of blood? And yet, these very grave signs, which I am giving you today, are neither accepted nor given credence, but on the contrary are openly opposed and rejected. Thus the extreme action that I am undertaking, to lead you to salvation, is being obstructed by you.

i   So then, my poor children, I am no longer given the possibility of holding back the hand of the justice of God who, by his terrible chastisement, will purify this humanity which can not be helped, because of its obstinate refusal to accept all these extraordinary interventions of your heavenly Mother.

j   As of now, for the Church and for humanity, the painful and bloody trial has finally come. I see your roads smeared with tears and blood. Thus this world will be purified by divine Justice, this world which has touched the bottom of perversion and of rebellion against its God who, for your salvation, is today being immolated and put to death on the Cross.

k   At least you, my beloved ones, remain with me beneath the Cross, together with your brother John, to give comfort and consolation to your sorrowful Mother, pierced once again by the sword of such a vast rejection. And unite your sorrow with mine, to implore once again the miracle of divine mercy upon the world."

Keep Watch with Me

a　　"Beloved children, stay close to your heavenly Mother, on this day while the body of my Son Jesus rests lifeless in his new sepulchre.

b　　*Keep watch with me.*

c　　*In prayer,* which you should make with me and by means of me. During this day, your heavenly Mother was living in a constant communion of life with the Heavenly Father, who was bestowing on me all his love and, with his divine tenderness, was putting precious balm on all my wounds. The Father thus saw all the suffering of the Son and the Mother blossom into the joy which He experienced, because He could at last embrace, in his bond of love and life, all humanity, now redeemed and saved.

d　　During this day, I was living with my soul ever close to the body of my Son, laid in his new sepulchre. My prayers were covering Him like a fragrant ointment. My tears were washing Him clean of all his blood, and my hands were passing over his body to close, with motherly tenderness, each of the wounds. And thus was I preparing this lifeless body to receive its new and powerful breath of life.

e　　During this day, the Holy Spirit was bringing me into his spousal enclosure, giving me joy and peace and speaking to me his divine thanks for having received into my virginal womb and accompanied all the way to the sepulchre the only-begotten Son of the Father.

f　　*Keep watch with me.*

g　　*In hope* which, on this day, is about to become certainty. When my Son Jesus presented Himself to me in his glorious body, more resplendent than the sun, and tenderly pressed me to his divine Heart, for me all suffering came to an end. Now death had been conquered by life; sin, by grace; evil, by good; hatred, by love; Satan, by the Son of God, dead and risen.

h　　*Keep watch with me.*

i　　*In confidence* live with me this Sabbath day. In the sepulchre lies all this poor humanity, once again in the possession of the Evil One and reduced to the slavery of sin and evil. This is the Sabbath of its lengthy entombment.

j   Soon it will come forth from the tomb in which it lies, when Jesus returns in glory and leads it into the new garden of his resurrection. The great miracle of divine mercy is in preparation. It will repeat for all humanity that which happened to my Son Jesus. Because, this humanity will be completely renewed by the powerful breath of the Holy Spirit, who will be poured out upon the whole earth, and it will return into the arms of its Heavenly Father, who will be pleased to be reflected in it, as Jesus will have brought into a renewed world his reign of glory.

k   For this, beloved children, I invite you today to keep watch with me in prayer, in hope and in confidence, on this your long Sabbath, which is about to come to an end."

544 *Capoliveri (Livorno, Italy); April 16, 1995*
Easter Sunday

The Triumph of Divine Mercy

a   "Beloved children, rejoice with me, sorrowful Mother of the Passion, and consoled and joyous Mother of the Resurrection.

b   Your joy is united with that of all the angelic cohorts, who bow down to adore my Son Jesus, as He appears to them in the dazzling splendor of his divinity. It is united also with the joy of all Paradise, which welcomes the Son of God, risen and seated at the right hand of the Father, and in that of the just who, in the lower regions, salute the moment of their liberation. Today new quiverings of life are running throughout all creation. All humanity exults with greatest joy because, in Jesus Crucified, dead and risen, it contemplates the *triumph of divine mercy.*

c   — *The triumph of divine mercy* is accomplished in the debt paid to divine justice, because of the sin which was committed by our first parents and which has brought condemnation upon all their descendants. Today, in Christ who rises, there comes about this marvelous return of all humanity into the arms of its Heavenly Father. Jesus is offered as victim of expiation, so that the merciful love of the Father might be able to receive, into his communion of life, this humanity, now redeemed and saved.

d —*The triumph of divine mercy* is accomplished in the victory of good over evil, of grace over sin, of love over hatred, of life over death. In Christ who comes forth victorious from the grave, a way of light is traced out for all humanity, so that it may thus respond to the great gift which it has received from Him. It is the way of love. Now love is called to triumph over egoism and hatred, over violence and war, over misunderstanding and all divisions.

e —*The triumph of divine mercy* is accomplished over Satan and all his wicked spirits, because this day marks the moment of their greatest defeat. Satan can still act to lead to ruin and perdition this frail humanity, even though it is redeemed. But in the end the triumph will be totally God's, because Christ is the only Savior and your Redeemer.

f In these last times, the struggle between good and evil, between grace and sin, between God and Satan, is reaching the summit of its power.

g It seems that, in your days, Satan has attained his victory, as during the Sabbath when Jesus lay lifeless in the sepulchre. But the moment is close when Christ Risen will manifest Himself in all his power; evil will be destroyed; Satan will be defeated forever; and then will appear in all its splendor the triumph of divine mercy over the world."

545

Pray for the Pope

a "You are recalling today the first apparition, which took place in the Cova da Iria in Fatima, with the first of many cenacles of my Movement, which this little son of mine will again hold in all of France, a land so ensnared and possessed by my Adversary, but so defended and protected by your heavenly Mother.

b   And nowhere as here has the message which I gave at Fatima in 1917 been so pertinent and urgent. Look with the merciful eyes of your heavenly Mother on the suffering and divided Church, threatened with the loss of faith and with a great apostasy. See how the pastors are being stricken and becoming tepid and unfaithful, and thus the flock is being more and more scattered along the ways of evil and sin and is running the danger of arriving at eternal perdition.

c   Feel the profound sorrow of my Immaculate Heart in seeing the disunity which has entered deeply into the very heart of the Church, due to the disobedience and the opposition of bishops and priests to the Pope, who has been constituted by Jesus as the foundation of the Church and infallible guardian of its truth.

d   — *Pray for the Pope.* This Pope is the greatest gift which my Immaculate Heart has given you for the time of the purification and the great tribulation. An important part of my message and of my secret, that I revealed to the three children to whom I appeared, refers precisely to the person and the mission of Pope John Paul II.

e   How great is his suffering! Often it is as though he were being crushed beneath the weight of a cross which has become so very heavy. Humanity is hastening along the road of violence and hatred, of fratricidal struggle and war, despite his *anguished cry*, which he causes to go out to all in order to invoke peace.

f   This humanity has become more and more enslaved to comfort and pleasure, to materialism and hedonism, to hardness of heart toward the needs of the little, the poor, the marginalized, the oppressed and the exploited.

g   How great is the suffering of the Pope, in seeing humanity so threatened with running irresponsibly along the way of its own destruction.

h   — *Pray for the Pope.* How his heart is caused to bleed because of the division which is taking root in the Church, the loss of faith which is becoming more widespread, the errors which are being taught and propagated despite the courage and force with which he goes everywhere in the world to confirm all in faithfulness to Christ and to his Gospel.

858

i His encyclical letters are true beacons of light, which shine down from heaven upon the intense darkness which envelops all the world.

j — *Pray for the Pope.* He is living the hour of Gethsemane and Calvary, of crucifixion and of his immolation. The Lord looks upon him as the most precious victim, who must now be immolated on the altar of his priestly sacrifice.

k Beloved children, remain ever with me beneath the cross upon which my Pope, fashioned, led and so loved by me, is as of now consummating his great offering of love and sorrow.

l It is precisely through the sacrifice of this, the first of my beloved sons, that divine justice will be espoused to a great mercy. After the time of the trial, which will be one of purification for all the earth, there will spring up upon the world the new era foretold and announced by him; and thus, in these final times, he invites you all to cross the bright thresholds of hope."

546

Vacallo (Switzerland); June 4, 1995
Solemnity of Pentecost

Tongues of Fire

a "Gathered together in an extraordinary cenacle of prayer made with me, beloved children, you are celebrating today the solemnity of Pentecost.

b I found myself gathered together with the Apostles and disciples, in the Cenacle of Jerusalem, when the miracle of the descent of the Holy Spirit took place, under the form of tongues of fire. And I saw with joy the miracle of their complete transformation. Timid and fearful as they had been, they came forth from the Cenacle courageous and intrepid witnesses of Jesus and of his Gospel.

c In the spiritual cenacle of my Immaculate Heart, the miraculous event of the second Pentecost must now be accomplished, implored and expected by you. Again there will descend upon the Church and upon all humanity miraculous tongues of fire.

d   — *Tongues of divine fire* will bring heat and life to a humanity which has now become cold from egoism and hatred, from violence and wars. Thus the parched earth will be opened to the breath of the Spirit of God, which will transform it into a new and wondrous garden in which the Most Holy Trinity will make its permanent dwelling place among you.

e   — *Tongues of fire* will come down to enlighten and sanctify the Church, which is living through the dark hour of Calvary and being stricken in her pastors, wounded in the flock, abandoned and betrayed by her own, exposed to the impetuous wind of errors, pervaded with the loss of faith and with apostasy.

f   The divine fire of the Holy Spirit will heal her of every malady, will purify her of every stain and every infidelity, will clothe her again in new beauty, will cover her with his splendor, in such a way that she may be able to find again all her unity and holiness, and will thus give to the world her full, universal and perfect witness to Jesus.

g   — *Tongues of fire* will come down upon you all, my poor children, so ensnared and seduced by Satan and by all the evil spirits who, during these years, have attained their greatest triumph. And thus, you will be illuminated by this divine light, and you will see your own selves in the mirror of the truth and the holiness of God. It will be like a judgment in miniature, which will open the door of your heart to receive the great gift of divine mercy.

h   And then the Holy Spirit will work the new miracle of universal transformation in the heart and the life of all: sinners will be converted; the weak will find support; the sick will receive healing; those far away will return to the house of the Father; those separated and divided will attain full unity.

i   In this way, the miracle of the second Pentecost will take place. It will come with the triumph of my Immaculate Heart in the world.

j   Only then will you see how *the tongues of fire* of the Spirit of Love will renew the whole world, which will become completely transformed by the greatest manifestation of divine mercy.

860

k   And so, I invite you to spend this day in the cenacle, gathered together in prayer with me, Mother of Mercy, in the hope and the trembling expectation of the second Pentecost, now close at hand."

547
Valdragone (San Marino); June 28, 1995
Spiritual Exercises in the Form of a Cenacle
with 20 Bishops and 300 Priests of the M.M.P.
from Europe, America, Africa, Asia and Oceania

For the Salvation of the World

a   "During these days, my Immaculate Heart is being consoled and glorified by you, bishops and priests of my Movement who, never before as in this year, have come in such great numbers from every part of the world, to live with me a week of continuous cenacle, united in prayer and fraternity.

b   I unite myself with your prayer. In these times of yours, the prayer of my priests is necessary to me *for the salvation of the world*. I am building up among you a greater and deeper spirit of brotherhood. As Mother, I call you to meet with each other; I help you to get to know one another; I urge you to love one another.

c   My Heart rejoices in seeing you grow in your mutual love, so that you become more and more one heart and one single soul. It is thus that I am able to realize in each one of you the plan for the triumph of my Immaculate Heart, *for the salvation of the world*.

d   — *For the salvation of the world*, I am making you precious instruments of divine mercy.

e   See into what an abyss of misery and despair this humanity has fallen, this humanity which has withdrawn itself completely from God. Now of itself it can no longer find relief without a great act of mercy bringing it to salvation. May the merciful Lord be able to work through you, bishops and priests, who are the sons of my motherly predilection.

f   See with my motherly eyes all the sorrows, the sins, the acts of rebellion, and the perversions of this humanity, which bears the weight of the great tribulation through which you are living. And let tears of sorrow and profound compassion fall from your eyes too.

g With my hands, help all to return along the road of repentance and conversion: carry in your arms the little ones, the poor, the weak; give courage and strength to the youth; urge divided families to reconciliation; comfort those who are suffering; let no one be forgotten or abandoned by you.

h Walk with the feet of your heavenly Mother to seek out those who are farthest away, to help those who are marginalized and abandoned, to give hope to the despairing and oppressed, to pour balm on the deep wounds of the stricken, to collect the blood shed by the innumerable victims of hatred, of fratricidal violence and of wars.

i Love all with the beating of my Immaculate Heart, and then you will become the instruments of the triumph of divine mercy and of the triumph of my motherly Heart.

j — *For the salvation of the world*, I want to make of you the new heart of the new Church, which will be consoled by you, in these days when she is living through the hour of her agony and becoming more and more abandoned, betrayed, scourged and crucified by many of her children.

k Be, in the Church, my very presence, impassioned and faithful. Love with my Heart your holy Mother, the Church, who is suffering and carrying such a great and heavy cross on her shoulders.

l Be a strong support to the Pope, who is living through the hour of his immolation. Support your bishops with prayer and with your docility. Give every help to your brother-priests, who are succumbing under the weight of great difficulties and from the subtle snares of my Adversary.

m Judge no one. Love all with the tenderness of my motherly Heart, and thus you will form the new heart of the new Church, which will be born with the triumph of my Immaculate Heart.

n If you saw the splendor of holiness and the fullness of unity of the Church, after this period of great tribulation, you too, with me, would jump for joy! Because then all the nations will walk toward her, who will have become once again a light of truth and grace, of unity and holiness, *for the salvation of the world*.

o   Beloved sons, during these days I have poured out great graces upon each one of you. Truly I have obtained in abundance the gifts of the Holy Spirit, who has worked in you a transformation of heart and of life. You will soon come to understand how important these days have been for you. For now, I give you the grace of living in the Heart of the Most Holy Trinity, where your heavenly Mother has her habitual dwelling place.

p   *— For the salvation of the world*, be everywhere the faithful ministers of the merciful love of Jesus, and allow yourselves to be ever led by me, who am the Mother of Mercy, because only in the triumph of divine mercy can the triumph of my Immaculate Heart become realized in the world.

q   Leave this cenacle in joy and peace, and go forth to bring everywhere the comfort of my motherly presence among you. With your dear ones, and with those who are entrusted to your ministry, I bless you all in the name of the Father, and of the Son, and of the Holy Spirit."

548

Sant' Omero (Teramo, Italy); August 5, 1995
Feast of Our Lady of the Snows
First Saturday

White Flakes of Snow

a   "Follow me, beloved children, along the road which I have marked out for you through my messages, if you wish to live always and perfectly the consecration to my Immaculate Heart, which you have made to me.

b   — On the road of my messages, learn to abandon yourselves to me as little children and to let yourselves be guided with the simplicity, the confidence and the complete abandonment of children. This abandonment of yours is necessary to me, so that I can act in you and in your life.

c   My motherly task is to transform you each day, so that you may accomplish perfectly the Will of the Lord. Thus I assist you to set yourselves free from sin, in order to walk along the way of divine grace, of love, of purity and of holiness. In the great desert in which you are living, in the immense sea of impurity which is submerging this world possessed by the Evil One, *white flakes of snow* are falling from my Immaculate Heart upon you, children consecrated to me, so that you may spread everywhere my fragrance from heaven and become signs and instruments of divine mercy in the world.

d — On the road of my messages, you are being formed to proclaim the Gospel of Jesus with courage and zeal. How much my motherly Heart suffers because, in the face of a flood of errors and heresies, of scandals and bad examples, a heavy silence is maintained, charged with indifference and compromise, on the part of those who have the duty to speak.

e Never as in your days have so many pastors become 'mute dogs,' who do not defend the flock entrusted to them from being menaced, seduced and devoured by many rapacious wolves. It is because of this that the Gospel of my Son Jesus is being lacerated and torn to shreds in all its parts.

f So then, my motherly task is that of leading you to believe in the Gospel, to let yourselves be guided solely by the wisdom of the Gospel, and to live the Gospel to the letter. For this, I am guiding you, with gentleness and motherly firmness, by means of my messages.

g Thus, in the great apostasy which is spreading everywhere, *white flakes of snow* are coming down from my Immaculate Heart upon you, children consecrated to me, so that you may bring everywhere the light of the divine word and become instruments which make shine everywhere, in its greatest splendor, all the truth contained in the Gospel of my Son Jesus.

h —Along the road of my messages, I am bringing you to the understanding of that which is written in the Book which is yet sealed. Many pages of what is contained in the Apocalypse of Saint John have been already explained to you by me. Above all, I have pointed out to you the great battle which is taking place between the Woman Clothed with the Sun and the Red Dragon, assisted by the Black Beast, namely Masonry.

i I have also revealed to you the subtle and diabolical snares set for you by Masonry, which has entered into the interior of the Church and has established the center of its power there where

Jesus has established the center and the foundation of her unity. Do not be disturbed, because this forms part of the mystery of iniquity, which the Church has known from her very birth. In fact, Satan — who drove Judas, one of the twelve, to become the traitor — has entered even into the Apostolic College.

j   In these times of yours, the mystery of iniquity is on the point of manifesting itself in all its terrible power.

k   And so, at the present moment of the great tribulation, which has come for the Church and for humanity, *white flakes of snow* are coming down from my Immaculate Heart upon you, children consecrated to me, so that you may bring to all my motherly voice which leads you to hope and confidence.

l   Thus you can take by the hand many of my poor children, stricken and oppressed by the impetuous wind of the great tribulation, and cross together the bright thresholds of hope in the joyous expectation that there fall on the world, with the triumph of my Immaculate Heart, the *white snowflakes* of divine mercy."

549

Rubbio (Vicenza, Italy); August 15, 1995
Solemnity of the Assumption
of the Blessed Virgin Mary into Heaven

A Sign of Sure Hope

a   "Look today at your heavenly Mother, assumed to the glory of paradise, even with her body. Unite yourselves to the joy of all the angelic cohorts, of the saints, and of the souls who are still being purified in purgatory.

b   Share also in the joy of the Church, pilgrim in the desert of the world and of history, which contemplates your heavenly Mother as a sign of consolation and sure hope.

c   — *I am a sign of sure hope* for the Church, as she walks toward her perfect glorification, which she will know at the moment when Jesus Christ returns to you in glory.

d   In these last times of the great tribulation, in the conclusive hour of the second Advent through which you are living, what great hope is opened up in the life of the Church by the assurance of having always been assisted and protected by me with the beating of my motherly and merciful Heart! Thus my presence close to the Church is a comfort to her suffering, a consolation to her weariness, strength to her proclamation, support to her faith, aid to her journey toward holiness.

e — *I am a sign of sure hope* for humanity today, so possessed by the Evil One, so threatened in its very life, so lacerated by egoism and hatred, by fratricidal struggles and wars. As Mother, I help all humanity to return to its Lord, along the way of repentance and prayer, of conversion, and of a change of heart and life.

f And thus, I am preparing for it new days of peace and not affliction, of serenity and joy. Above all, in these last times, I am making myself present in a powerful way to prepare humanity to receive Jesus who is about to return in glory to bring about its total and perfect transformation.

g — *I am a sign of sure hope* for all of you, my poor children, who are carrying the weight of many sufferings and great sorrows. These sufferings must now increase for all, and the pains will increase more and more, because you are living through these last times of the great tribulation.

h Look today to your heavenly Mother, assumed into the glory of paradise, if you wish to cross the thresholds of hope. From my Immaculate Heart, I let fall the dew of divine mercy, a gentle balm which is placed on the open and bleeding wounds of all my children.

i — *I am a sign of sure hope* for you sinners and you who are far away, for you the sick and discouraged, for you the oppressed and persecuted, for you the stricken and crushed, for you who are smitten by violence and hatred, for you who are trampled underfoot and slaughtered by fratricidal struggles and wars.

j At the conclusive moment of the great trial, you will feel my motherly presence, which assists you to cross the threshold of hope, in order to enter into the new era of peace, which will come for the Church, for humanity and for all of you, with the triumph of my Immaculate Heart in the world."

Light, Love and Motherly Tenderness

a "Look today at your infant Mother. Exulting about my crib are the angels and saints of paradise, the souls who are being purified in purgatory, and the pilgrim Church which, in the desert of the world, is living out its painful pilgrimage toward the heavenly homeland.

b Today I want you all, my beloved ones and children consecrated to me, about the crib where I am being placed after my birth.

c — *I want to look at you with these eyes of mine*, which have just opened to the light. You are called to be the pupils of my eyes; you are destined to carry my light to the ends of the earth. The light which I give you is that of my Son Jesus. Bring everywhere the light of his word, to rout the great darkness of error, which has spread through the world. Bring the light of his life to overcome the coldness of sin and evil, which has made the hearts of many of my children hard and dry. Bring the light of his presence among you, so that the heavenly dew of divine mercy may descend in every part of the earth.

d — *I want to love you with this Heart of mine*, which has hardly begun to give its first beats, destined now never to cease. You are called to be the greatest love of my Immaculate Heart; you are destined to bring my love to every part of the world. The love which I give you is that of my Son Jesus. Bring everywhere the throbbing of his ardent and divine compassion; burn away with the fire of love every human misery, all egoism, all violence, all hatred, all division, all sin.

e As of this day, there begins, still hidden but certain, the conclusive victory of Love, because this life has been given to me that I may become the Mother of Life and give the Eternal Word of the Father his human nature, with which He will carry out the work of redemption, thus setting all humanity free from the Evil One and from sin.

f Bring, then, everywhere the fire of his divine love, because, with the triumph of my Immaculate Heart, the new civilization of love will begin.

g   — I want to caress you with these hands of mine, which have the task of gathering together all my children. You are called to feel my caresses; you are destined to bring everywhere the comfort of my motherly tenderness.

h   For this, I am leading you into the house of the Most Sacred Heart of Jesus, so that you may be transformed by his divine tenderness. Let your hearts become sensitive and open, humble and meek, tender and compassionate.

i   Then your priestly tenderness will descend upon every wound: it will be food to the hungry, drink to the thirsty, pardon to sinners, help to the needy, health to the sick, support to the tottering, a guide to the uncertain, comfort to the oppressed, salvation for all.

j   Only in this way can you hasten the triumph of my Immaculate Heart. Only if you spread everywhere the light, the love and the motherly tenderness of this, your infant Mother, can you become the precious instruments of the triumph of divine mercy upon the world."

551

Milan (Italy); September 14, 1995
Feast of the Exaltation of the Holy Cross
Eve of my Journey throughout Brazil

Jesus Crucified Is Your Salvation

a   "Once again, you are on the eve of a long and wearisome journey, in order to hold cenacles of my Movement in a good sixty dioceses throughout all Brazil, this land so powerfully ensnared by my Adversary, but especially loved and protected by your heavenly Mother. Offer me your prayer and suffering, your labor and your weariness, your littleness and your poverty, your trust and your filial abandonment.

b   This time you will feel more the weight of the cross which the Heavenly Father has prepared for you, but you will see, in an even greater way, the triumph of my Immaculate Heart in the hearts and souls of many of my children.

c   You are beginning this journey of yours on the feast of the Exaltation of the Holy Cross.

It is the Cross of Jesus, the sign of my sure victory.

It is only Jesus Crucified who must today be preached and exalted by you in every part of the world. Jesus Crucified is your Redeemer and Savior.

Jesus Crucified is your God, lifted up on the gibbet for your salvation.

Jesus Crucified, above all in your times, is foolishness for the wise and a scandal for the learned and proud, but it is in Him alone that your salvation resides.

d — *Jesus Crucified is the salvation* for this humanity, which has wandered so far away from God, has built a civilization without Him and has given itself a moral law opposed to the holy Law of the Lord. For this reason, it is carrying the weight of immense sufferings and walking in the deep darkness of hatred and division, of violence and wars. And Jesus is immolating Himself on the Cross for its salvation.

e It is necessary that the Cross of Christ be planted in the heart of this humanity, so that it may thus rediscover the way of its conversion and of its return to the Lord.

f Then will the dew of divine mercy descend to renew the desert in which it finds itself. Then will there blossom the new garden of the full reconciliation of all humanity with its Lord, who has created, redeemed and saved it.

g — *Jesus Crucified is the salvation* for the Church, his Mystical Body, which is now living the very events of his passion and his immolation. It is in his Church that Jesus renews the Sacrifice of redemption, communicates the gift of his grace and takes away, through his pardon, all the sin and the evil of the world. It is in his crucified Church that Jesus becomes salvation for the humanity of these last times of the purification and the great tribulation. For this, you will be called more and more to suffer, to climb with Jesus the Calvary of your priestly immolation, for the life of the world.

h — *Jesus Crucified is salvation for you all,* my children, exposed to such great dangers of being lost. His Sacrifice, which is renewed at every moment, from the rising to the setting of the sun, ever gives to the Father a just reparation, causes the dew of his divine grace to come down everywhere, communicates in his Spirit the fire of love, and renews the hearts and souls of all.

i   Jesus Crucified becomes, above all in these final times, a sign of hope and of certain victory. His bright Cross, which will stretch itself out in the heavens from the east to the west, will indicate to you all the return of Jesus in glory. And so today I invite you to look to the Cross, where Jesus is being raised up to draw all people to Himself.

j   My little child, go without fear on this new journey of yours. The angels of light of my Heart, at my orders, will arrange everything for you. As for you, walk once again along all the roads of the world to bring to all the announcement of the triumph of my Immaculate Heart."

552   *Manaus (Amazonas, Brazil); September 17, 1995*

Ever Farther

a   "You have seen, as never before, the triumph of my Immaculate Heart in the hearts and the lives of my little children. They have participated by the thousands in the cenacle with an intensity of prayer and with an enthusiasm which is so simple and spontaneous that they have moved my motherly Heart.

b   See how, from every part of the world, my children are responding to me with a *yes*. They are the littlest, the poorest, the humble, the simple. Their response fills my Heart with joy. The wounds of my sorrow are closing, and the thorns are being transformed into fragrant and precious flowers. My tears are being changed into a smile.

c   Even in this so vast state of Amazonia, you have been able to see the triumph of my Immaculate Heart in the world. This is now taking place everywhere, and you, my little child, are the instrument chosen by me for such a great mission.

d   For this, carried in my arms and led by me, you must go *ever farther.*

e   — *Ever farther*, as regards the place, because you must reach even the most remote and scattered parts of the earth, wherever

870

there are hearts of my little children which beat with love for me. And you must gather up these precious heartbeats and place them in the bright garden of my Immaculate Heart.

f   — *Ever farther* in extent, where you find, all united in one single and great family, my children who are rejoicing in paradise, being purified in purgatory, or who are still suffering and struggling in the arid desert of this world.

g   You are being called to contemplate this stupendous reality which forms, in one profound unity, the great family of the Church, fashioned in the Heart of the Most Holy Trinity and whose true Mother and Queen I have been constituted.

h   — *Ever farther* in time, because your mission is to unite, in my Immaculate Heart, the hours of suffering to those of joy; the hours of the great tribulation to those of the new heavens and the new earth; the painful hours of the trial to those of my motherly triumph.

i   For this reason, continue on your way with serenity because, carried and led by me, you must go *ever farther*.

j   Pay no regard to your weakness and poverty, to your great fragility, to the weariness and exhaustion which take hold of you. Look on the other hand at the joy which, through you, the heavenly Mother brings into hearts, to the grace which fills souls, to the life which flourishes anew, to the triumph of my Immaculate Heart which becomes greater each day.

k   Love and bless all those whom you meet along a journey which now, in place, in extent and in time, brings you *ever farther*."

553   *Rio de Janeiro (Brazil); September 29, 1995*
Feast of the Holy Archangels

The Times Will Be Shortened

a   "My plan is now being accomplished everywhere. My little son, you see how the triumph of my Immaculate Heart is taking place in the world.

b   What is happening here is a sign for you. By the tens of thousands, my children are responding to me with such a love and great enthusiasm that it moves my motherly Heart. Because of the response that I am receiving everywhere from these little children of mine, I am intervening in order to shorten the times of the great trial which is so painful for you.

c   *The times will be shortened*, because I am Mother of Mercy, and each day I offer, at the throne of divine Justice, my prayer united to that of the children who are responding to me with a *yes* and consecrating themselves to my Immaculate Heart.

d   I unite the sorrows of my Heart with all the sufferings of the good people, who are carrying with patience the cross of these times of the great tribulation.

e   The sufferings of the poor and the exploited, of the little ones and the marginalized, of the sinners and those far away, of the sick and the desperate, of the abandoned and the oppressed are gathered together in the garden of my motherly suffering and offered to the divine justice as a sign of reparation and perennial intercession.

f   *The times will be shortened*, because I am your Mother, and I want to help you, with my presence, to carry the cross of the painful events through which you are living.

g   How many times have I already intervened in order to set back further and further in time the beginning of the great trial, for the purification of this poor humanity, now possessed and dominated by the spirits of evil.

h   *The times will be shortened*, because the great struggle which is being waged between God and his Adversary is above all at the level of spirits and is taking place above you. This terrible battle is taking place between the heavenly spirits and the infernal spirits, between the angels of the Lord and the demons, between the powers of heaven and the powers of hell.

i   In this great struggle, a special task has been entrusted to the Archangel Gabriel, who clothes you in the very strength of God; to the Archangel Raphael, who pours a healing balm on each of your wounds; and to the Archangel Michael, who leads all the angelic cohorts to the complete victory over the infernal cohorts.

For this reason, I entrust you to the powerful protection of these archangels and of your guardian angels, so that you may be guided and defended in the struggle which is now being waged between heaven and earth, between paradise and hell, between Saint Michael the Archangel and Lucifer himself, who will appear very soon with all the power of the Antichrist.

k Thus you are being prepared for the great prodigy which will take place when, with the triumph of my Immaculate Heart, the heavenly dew of divine mercy will descend upon the world."

554

Uruacu (Goias, Brazil); October 7, 1995
Feast of Our Lady of the Rosary
Anniversary of the Victory
of the Blessed Virgin Mary at Lepanto
First Saturday

My Victory

a "I am the Queen of the Holy Rosary. I am the Queen of Victories. The task which has been entrusted to me by the Most Holy Trinity is that of directing the battle and leading to victory the cohort of the children of God who are fighting against the powerful army of the slaves of Satan and of the spirits of evil.

b 'I will put enmity between you and the woman, between your offspring and her offspring; she will crush your head, and you will lie in wait for her heel.' (Gen 3:15)

c Each day I am carrying forward this struggle and attaining my victory.

d — *My victory* takes place in the hearts of all my children who consecrate themselves to my Immaculate Heart and allow themselves to be formed and led by me as little children. I open up these hearts to the purity of love, and in this way I am able to achieve the victory over every form of egoism, of hatred and of violence, and to spread everywhere the sweet perfume of divine charity.

e — *My victory* is being achieved in the souls who are being assisted by me in fighting against and in conquering every form of sin. The souls of my children, enlightened by grace and in possession of divine life, sing with me the perennial *Magnificat* of perfect glory to the Most Holy Trinity.

f — *My victory* is being accomplished in the Church, which I enlighten with my faith, assist with my presence and comfort with my motherly tenderness. I myself am leading her by the hand, in this time of the purification, toward her greatest splendor which will reclothe her, making of her the greatest light for all the nations of the earth.

g — *My victory* takes place each day over this poor humanity, which is so sick and far from God and which has wanted to build a new civilization without Him. I am opening up new roads for its return to the Lord, who awaits it with the love of a Father. I am calling my little children to become instruments of salvation for all, and thus, in silence and hiddenness, I am preparing each day and spreading among you the reign of God.

h — *My complete victory* will come about with the triumph of my Immaculate Heart in the world. Then the miracle of divine mercy, in the power of the Holy Spirit, will renew the face of the earth, and it will again become a fragrant and precious garden in which the Most Holy Trinity will be pleased to be reflected and will receive from the whole created universe its greatest glory."

555   *Jauru (Mato Grosso, Brazil); October 12, 1995*
Feast of Our Lady of Aparecida, Patroness of Brazil

I Am Glorified

a "My little son, you find yourself again in this place where I am so loved and venerated, in order to hold wonderful cenacles with thousands of children and youth, who have come from even the most distant community. You have also conducted three days of spiritual exercises in the form of a continuous cenacle, with those faithful who are the apostles of my Movement in all of Brazil.

b Today you are celebrating, with joy and solemnity, the feast of your heavenly Mother, as Patroness of this great nation. You see how, here, *I am glorified* everywhere.

c — *I am glorified* by the response which I receive everywhere from many of my children, who have accepted my request to consecrate themselves to my Immaculate Heart. They are now living in my Immaculate Heart and are a gentle balm which is placed upon every wound of my great sorrow.

d See how they love and glorify me. They are the littlest, the poorest, the simplest, the ones whom the world ignores and despises.

e Oh! Bring me more and more of these little children of mine, because they are for me the greatest and most precious of treasures.

f — *I am glorified* by the powerful intensity of prayer which is offered to me here in these times of aridity and great dissipation. See how the cenacles have spread everywhere, above all among children and youth and in families.

g How many families are being saved from division or have become reunited after years of separation, as a result of the great spread of family cenacles.

h These are the powerful means which my Immaculate Heart gives you to defend the Christian family from the dangers which threaten it, such as infidelity, divisions, separations, recourse to the means of preventing life and those cursed abortions which are being permitted by civil laws but which cry for vengeance in the sight of God.

i — *I am glorified* because, while neglect, disregard, indifference and tepidity toward my Son Jesus truly present in the Eucharist is spreading more and more, here the Eucharistic Jesus receives an unending homage of love, adoration, thanksgiving and reparation.

j The Eucharistic Jesus is solemnly exposed upon the altar throughout the whole day, and my little children prostrate themselves in an act of loving adoration before the throne upon which reigns the Victim offered for your salvation.

k   How, in this place, the Heart of Jesus exults with joy, comfort, consolation and gratitude!

l   — *I am glorified*, because in this country my Marian Movement of Priests has spread everywhere, as in no other part of the world.

m   I bless all these children of mine, who have come from even the most distant places to take part in the three days of continuous cenacle. In them, *I am glorified!*

n   I repeat to you again today that Brazil belongs to me; it is my property. I am Mother and Queen of Brazil, and I want to bring to this great nation, where I am so much loved, implored and glorified, the gift of salvation and peace.

o   Thus what is taking place here becomes a sign for you which indicates to you how, in silence and hiddenness, each day I am bringing about the triumph of my Immaculate Heart in the greatest triumph of divine mercy upon the world.

p   It will soon be completely renewed by the powerful and extraordinary intervention of her whom you invoke as your Queen and Mother of Mercy."

556   *Pouso Alegre (Minas Gerais, Brazil); November 1, 1995*
Solemnity of All Saints

Paradise Is United with Earth

a   "Continue this marvelous journey of yours, my little son, and respond to the mission which I have entrusted to you. See everywhere the triumph of my Immaculate Heart which I am carrying forward, now in an increasingly powerful way, in hearts and souls.

b   — *Paradise is united with earth*. In my Immaculate Heart there takes place each day for you, the meeting with your brothers and sisters who have preceded you up here and are now enjoying the eternal happiness of the saints. In the light of the Most Holy Trinity, they contemplate my plan, and the vision of the full triumph of Christ, who will at last form new heavens and a new earth, causes their joy to increase.

c   — *Paradise is united with earth* in a great communion of prayer, which ascends from all my children, that Jesus might hasten his return in glory and all the world be transformed into that wonderful garden of grace and holiness, where the Most Holy Trinity may once again be pleased to be reflected.

d   — *Paradise is united with earth* in forming one single cohort, whose heavenly Leader I am, to wage the most important part of the battle against Satan and all the forces of evil and to achieve my greatest victory.

e   — *Paradise is united with earth*, now that you are living through the conclusive period of the purification and the great tribulation. Thus the saints of heaven are casting light on your lives, are coming to your assistance with their powerful aid, are defending you against the subtle snares of my Adversary, are leading you by the hand along the road of holiness, in the trembling expectation of associating you also one day in their eternal happiness.

f   For this reason, I invite you today to live the joyous experience of the communion of saints. In this way, you receive strength and courage to overcome the moments of the trial; and, from paradise, the painful road, along which all must journey to cross the bright threshold of hope, becomes brightened up for you.

g   — *Paradise is united with earth* in the heavenly garden of my Immaculate Heart because, with its triumph, there will descend from heaven the dew of divine mercy, which will bring all the world to a new life."

557   Barretos (City Of Mary, Brazil); November 15, 1995
Spiritual Exercises in the Form of a Cenacle
with the Bishops and Priests of the M.M.P. from all Brazil

Spread My Light

a   "The sorrow of my Heart is assuaged by you, and my tears are changed into a smile in seeing you gathered here in a continuous cenacle of prayer and fraternity, bishops and priests of my Movement, who have come from every part of Brazil.

b   I am always with you. I unite myself with — and give power
to — your prayer. I help you to walk together in mutual love,
until you become one single heart and one single soul.

c   I obtain for you the gift of the Holy Spirit, who descends
upon this, your cenacle, as He descended upon the Cenacle of
Jerusalem. It is the Holy Spirit who transforms you, who changes
your heart and gives wisdom to your mind, so that you may be
today a light burning on a mountaintop in these times of great
darkness.

d   — *Spread my light* in the deep darkness which has submerged
the world. It is the darkness of the denial of God; it is the darkness of the false ideologies, of materialism, of hedonism and of
impurity. See how the world has again become pagan and lives
under the yoke of a great slavery.

e   In your great nation, so ensnared by my Adversary but so loved
and protected by your heavenly Mother, how the sects, which
draw so many of my children away from the true Church, are
spreading more and more!

f   — *Spread my light*, by preaching the Gospel of Jesus with force
and fidelity. His divine word must be proclaimed by you with
the same clarity and simplicity with which Jesus has announced
it to you. If you are faithful ministers of the Gospel, set up the
strongest possible defense against the continual propagation of
the sects and every form of spiritism and superstition.

g   — *Spread my light* with your full priestly unity. One deep
wound which causes my Church in Brazil to suffer is caused by
bishops and priests who are no longer united with the Pope.
They ignore and refuse to accept his Magisterium, and thus errors are spread, are frequently taught, and many of my children
are running the danger of separating themselves from the true
faith.

h   You must be examples to all of strong unity with the Pope.
Love him; listen to him; help him to carry his great cross toward
the Calvary of his immolation.

i   Help your bishops with prayer, with your priestly zeal, and be
a comfort to them in their difficult and painful ministry. Let
your hearts be open in giving assistance to all your brother-priests,

especially toward those who are succumbing under the weight of the great tribulation through which you are living.

j   Judge no one. Love all with the beating of my Immaculate Heart.

k   — *Spread my light,* dispensing about you the balm of my motherly tenderness. Go out to meet, above all, the little, the poor, the sinners, those far away, the stricken, the innumerable victims of every injustice and every act of violence, and bring them all into the safe refuge of my Immaculate Heart.

l   In this way you become the apostles of the second evangelization, so much asked for by my Pope, and the precious instruments of my motherly triumph.

m   I express to you now my gratitude for the very generous response which I have received, in answer to my request that you be consecrated to my Immaculate Heart and to spread the cenacles among priests, children, youth and above all in families.

n   How much have I been loved, sought out in prayer, consoled and glorified by you, during these months in which this little son of mine has gone to every part of this great nation of yours!

o   I confirm to you once again that Brazil belongs to me; it is my property. Especially in the painful moments which are awaiting you, you will see the light of my Immaculate Heart surrounding your Church and your fatherland, and you will feel, in an extraordinary way, my motherly presence among you.

p   Go out from this cenacle in peace and joy. I am always with you. *Spread my light* everywhere so that the dew of divine mercy may reach all, and walk with confidence and a great hope toward the new times which are so very close.

q   With your dear ones and with all those who are entrusted to your priestly ministry, I bless you in the name of the Father, and of the Son, and of the Holy Spirit."

My Plan

a   "My little son, today you find yourself in the Canary Islands, to carry out many cenacles with priests and faithful of my Movement, and you are celebrating, with joy and exultation, the solemnity of my Immaculate Conception. Even here, you see the Marian Movement of Priests spread everywhere, and you see how my little children from all sides are responding to me with a *yes*.

b   My beloved ones and children consecrated to me, on this day look with confidence and immense trust at your immaculate Mother!

c   I have been conceived without original sin, and thus I have been able to realize in my life, in a perfect way, the plan of the Most Holy Trinity and to respond to the task which It entrusted to me on my becoming the Mother of the Incarnate Word.

d   *My plan* is that of leading in battle the cohort of the sons of God to fight and overcome the snares of those who have put themselves at the service of Satan and who are battling to spread in the world the reign of evil, error, sin, hatred and impurity.

e   *My plan* is to lead all creation back to its primal splendor, in such a way that the Heavenly Father may again be pleased to be reflected in it and to receive his greatest glory from all creation.

f   *My plan* is to lead all my children along the road of perfect imitation of Jesus, in such a way that He may live again in them and contemplate with joy the copious fruits which are born from his great gift of redemption.

g   *My plan* is to prepare hearts and souls to receive the Holy Spirit, who will pour Himself out in fullness to bring upon the world the second Pentecost of fire and of love.

h   *My plan* is to point out to all my children the way of faith and of hope, of love and of purity, of goodness and of holiness. Thus in the garden of my Immaculate Heart, I am preparing the little remnant who, in the midst of the tempestuous waves of the apostasy and the perversion, will remain faithful to Christ, to the Gospel and to the Church.

i   And it will be with this little flock, guarded in the Immaculate Heart of your heavenly Mother, that Jesus will bring about his glorious reign in the world."

559   *Dongo (Como, Italy); December 24, 1995*
The Holy Night

Merciful Love

a   "Beloved sons, live with me, in silence and in prayer, the anxious hours of the vigil.

b   Walk with my most chaste spouse, Joseph, and with your heavenly Mother on the long road which is bringing us from Nazareth to Bethlehem. Feel, you too, the fatigue of the journey, the weariness which takes hold of us, the assurance which leads us on, the prayer which accompanies each step, as a heavenly blessedness fills our hearts, now united in perfect communion with the Heart of the Heavenly Father which is about to open itself in the gift of his only-begotten Son.

c   The noise of the crowded caravan does not disturb us, nor does discouragement take hold of us before all the doors which are closed on our request to be taken in.

d   The compassionate hand of a shepherd points out to us a poor cave, which opens itself to the most sublime and divine prodigy. The only-begotten Son of the Father is about to be born to his human life. There is about to descend to the world that *Merciful Love* who becomes man in the Son born of me, his Virgin Mother. After long centuries of expectation and of prayerful supplication, your Savior and Redeemer at last comes to you.

e   This is the holy night.

This is the dawn which arises upon the new day of your salvation.

This is the light which shines forth in the deep darkness of all history.

f   My spouse Joseph seeks to make the frigid cave more hospitable and sets about transforming a poor manger into a crib.

g I am absorbed in an intense prayer and enter into ecstasy with the Heavenly Father, who surrounds me with his light and his love, and fills me with his fullness of life and blessedness, while paradise, with all its angelic cohorts, prostrates itself in an act of profound adoration. When I emerge from this ecstasy, I find in my arms the divine Child, miraculously born of me, his Virgin Mother.

h I press Him to my Heart, cover Him with tender kisses, warm Him with my motherly love, wrap Him in clean linens and place Him in the manger, which is now ready.

i My God is completely present in this Child of mine. The mercy of the Father is made visible in the newborn Infant who utters his first plaintive cries.

j Divine Mercy has given his Fruit to you: together let us prostrate ourselves and adore the *Merciful Love* who has been born for us.

k — Together let us look into his eyes, which open to bring upon the world the light of the truth and of divine wisdom.

l — Together let us wipe away his tears, which run down to bring compassion upon every suffering, to wash away every stain of sin and evil, to close every wound, to bring solace to each oppressed person, to cause the awaited dew to descend upon the frigid desert of the world.

m — Together let us clasp his hands, which open themselves to bring the caress of the Father upon human miseries, to bring help to the poor and the little, support to the weak, assurance to the discouraged, pardon to sinners, health to the sick, and to all the gift of redemption and salvation.

n — Together let us warm his feet which will follow the barren and insecure roads to search out the straying, to find the lost, to give hope to the despairing, to bring liberty to prisoners and the Good News to the poor.

o — Together let us kiss his little Heart, which has just begun to beat with love for us.

It is the very Heart of God.

It is the Heart of the only-begotten Son of the Father, who becomes man to bring back to God a humanity redeemed and saved by Him.

It is the Heart which beats to renew the heart of every creature.

It is the new heart of the world.

It is the *Merciful Love* which comes down from the bosom of the Father, to bring redemption, salvation and peace to all humanity.

p Receive Him with love, with joy and with immense blessedness. And let there come forth from your heart the hymn of perennial gratitude for this Child, virginally given to you by me who, on this holy night, have become for all the Mother of Divine Mercy."

560
Milan (Italy); December 31, 1995
Last Night of the Year

The Great Sign of Divine Mercy

a "Beloved sons, spend with me the last hours of this year which is now about to end.

b See how many spend these hours in dissipation and amusements and await the new year in a pagan atmosphere, often in an open transgression of the holy Law of the Lord!

c As for you, spend these hours with me, in prayer and in silence, in meditation on my word and with a great confidence in your Heavenly Father.

d It is Providence that prepares for you each new day and each new year, thus rhythmically arranging in the sequence of time what the Father arranges for the good of all his children. It is the Father who arranges for you new days of peace and not of affliction, of pardon and not of condemnation, so that the miracle of his divine mercy may shine forth upon the world.

e Together let us read, on this night, the signs of his merciful love which the Father gives us.

f   *I am the great sign of divine mercy.*

g   — For this, I am manifesting myself, in so powerful and extraordinary a way, through my apparitions, my numerous weepings, and the messages which I give to the heart of this little son of mine, whom I myself am leading along all the roads of the world, in search of sinners, of the sick, of those who have fallen, of the straying, of the despairing, of those who are succumbing to the seductions of sin and of evil.

h   — For this, I invite all to consecrate themselves to my Immaculate Heart, and I am extending this, my request, to the most extreme limits of the earth through my Marian Movement of Priests. In this way, I am offering you a safe refuge, which the Most Holy Trinity has prepared for you, for these stormy times of the great tribulation and of the painful trial which has come for the Church and for all humanity.

i   — For this, I am renewing my pressing request to return to the Lord, who awaits you with the love of a Father, on the road of conversion and of a change of heart and of life. Distance yourselves from sin and evil, from violence and hatred, from the cult which is increasingly being offered to Satan and to the idols of pleasure and money, of pride and arrogance, of amusement and impurity.

j   And walk along the renewed ways of love and goodness, of communion and prayer, of purity and holiness. In this way, you yourselves must become signs of divine mercy for a humanity swept away by the tempest of indescribable suffering, at the time when the great tribulation is on the point of reaching its apex.

k   —This is why I am calling you each day to follow me. I am the Mother of Fair Love and of Holy Hope. I am the Queen of Peace and the dawn which announces the new time which awaits you and which is drawing ever closer.

l   Multiply everywhere the cenacles of prayer which I have asked of you. Above all, spread the family cenacles which I am requesting as a means of saving the Christian family from the great dangers which threaten it. I am the Mother of Life. I am the

Queen of the Family.

m   Priests, my beloved sons, respond to my request to consecrate yourselves to my Immaculate Heart, because I am your understanding and merciful Mother.

n   Mine is the task of washing you from every stain, of consoling you in every sorrow, of bringing trust to you in your great discouragement, and strong hope to you in your loneliness. I assist you to be in the world without being of the world, because I desire that all of you belong solely and always to my Son Jesus.

o   Above all for you, my priest-sons, I am today *the great sign of divine mercy*.

p   As this year comes to an end, I bless you all in the name of the Father, and of the Son, and of the Holy Spirit."

1996

IN MY SAFE REFUGE

In My Safe Refuge

a   "Today you celebrate with joy the feast of my Divine Maternity, and you look to me with filial trust, imploring the great gift of peace for the Church and for all humanity. I am the Queen of Peace. I have been chosen by the Heavenly Father to become the Mother of his only-begotten Son, born to bring to all humanity the precious blessing of peace.

b   My divine Child, who is born in the poverty of a cave and placed in a manger, is Himself peace: peace between God and humanity, redeemed by Him and brought to a new communion of love and life with its Lord; peace among men, who have all become brothers because, being children of God, they share in his gifts and are members of the one same family.

c   My Son Jesus wanted me to be your Mother also. Thus I have become Mother of mankind, redeemed and saved by Him. My task is that of following, as a Mother, throughout the course of history, the lifelong events of all my children.

d   In a special way, I am the Mother of those who, through the sacrament of Baptism and the gift of faith and grace, become intimately engrafted into the very life of Jesus, making up his Mystical Body and forming part of his Church.

e   I am Mother of the Church. My maternal task is that of following, throughout the course of its history, all the earthly events of the Church. And, in every circumstance of its painful journey, I have always offered the Church *the safe refuge of my Immaculate Heart*.

f   My Immaculate Heart contains all my virginal and maternal love for you. My Immaculate Heart opens itself to give you assistance, comfort and protection. My Immaculate Heart becomes, for each one of you, the safest refuge and the road which brings you to the God of salvation and peace.

g   At the beginning of this new year, packed with significant and painful events for this poor humanity, already under the power of the forces of evil which have unleashed themselves, once again

888

I invite all to enter into the safe refuge of my Immaculate Heart.

h   — *Into my safe refuge* there enter those who are called to give a bloody witness to the Lord. From the first martyr, Stephen, whom I have gathered into my motherly arms after his slaying, to those who today are again giving their own lives, the great cohort of martyrs enters into the refuge of my Immaculate Heart, to receive new force and courage, in the hour of their immolation.

i   — *In my safe refuge* the countless cohort of confessors of the faith is gathered together, that they may obtain light and the Spirit of Wisdom which leads them to understand, to live and to proclaim the Gospel to all.

j   — *In my safe refuge* the white phalanx of virgins is being formed, that they may learn from my virginal motherhood to live only for Jesus, chosen as the one and only Spouse of their own life. Clothed in his immaculate light, they follow the Lamb wherever He goes.

k   — *In my safe refuge* there seek shelter and protection those who are called to offer themselves to the Lord by following Him along the way of the evangelical counsels. I myself cultivate these fragrant and precious flowers, which have sprung up in the garden of my Immaculate Heart.

l   — *In my safe refuge* I cultivate, with care and solicitude, all the priests who have been entrusted to me by Jesus and whom I cherish with a most special love. Here they are comforted, encouraged and formed by me to follow, to imitate and to relive Jesus in all his fullness.

m   — *In my safe refuge* Christian families take shelter, that they may be defended from many dangers and protected from the terrible evils which threaten them.

n   — *Into my safe refuge* I call the children, that they may breathe the atmosphere of purity and of prayer; the youth, that they may be helped to grow in grace, in love and in holiness; the sinners, that they may find mercy and pardon; the sick, that they may have health; the dying, that they may pass from earth to paradise through the heavenly gate of my Immaculate Heart.

o   — *Into my safe refuge*, above all, all of you, my children, must enter that you may be protected and defended by me, now that you are entering into the conclusive period of the purification and the great tribulation.

889

p   Now the events will follow one upon the other in rapid succession, toward their complete unfolding. My secrets will be revealed to you by the very events through which you have been called to live.

q   Because of this, seeing with motherly concern all that is now awaiting you, I once again invite the Church and all humanity to enter into the safe refuge of my Immaculate Heart. Only here will you be protected and consoled by my very own self. Only here will you find peace and will you cross with joy the bright threshold of hope.

r   Because, in the safe refuge of my Immaculate Heart, which the Most Holy Trinity is offering to you as an ark of salvation in these last times, you will await, in confidence and in prayer, the return in glory of Jesus, who will bring his kingdom into the world and make all things new.

s   In the expectation that the blessed hope will be fulfilled and in expectation of the glorious coming of my Son Jesus, I bless you all, as this new year begins, in the name of the Father, and of the Son, and of the Holy Spirit."

562

Milan (Italy); January 19, 1996
Eve of my Journey through
Thirteen Countries of Latin America

A Work of Love and of Mercy

a   "My most beloved son, you are again on the eve of a long, burdensome and wearying journey, which I am asking you to make through thirteen countries of Latin America, to bring a great number of my children into the safe refuge of my Immaculate Heart.

b   Do not be afraid for I am with you always. I lead you at every step of your journey, and I carry you in my arms where you will feel the comfort and the rest which the heavenly Mother has prepared for you. I am pressed for time, and I must complete as quickly as possible my great *work of love and of mercy*.

c   — *It is my great work of love* because, by means of it, I offer to all

890

the help which the heavenly Mother gives you to surmount the unspeakable sufferings of these last times. The help which I offer you, with my Marian Movement of Priests, is my Immaculate Heart.

d   My Immaculate Heart is the precious garden which encloses within it all the love which your heavenly Mother has for her children. You must all enter into my Immaculate Heart, so that you may feel the force and the tenderness of my maternal love. Through your consecration to my Immaculate Heart, you enter into the safe refuge, which the heavenly Mother has built for you in the painful hours of the great tribulation.

e   Through the voice of this, my little son, whom I am again leading to far distant places, I invite all the bishops, priests and faithful to consecrate themselves to my Immaculate Heart. In this way, you do what I have asked of you at Fatima for the salvation of this poor humanity, which is lying prostrate under the weight of its obstinate rejection of God and living in dark bondage to Satan, who has attained over it the summit of his power.

f   How can you take shelter in the painful hours of the great trial, which has now come for the Church and for humanity? Where can you find a refuge in the tremendous squall which is shaking heaven and earth because of the hatred which is spreading everywhere, of the violence which is exploding, of the evil which is being committed, of the sin which is being exalted, of the impurity which is submerging the whole world?

g   You are all being called to find assistance and protection in the heavenly garden of my motherly love. For this it will become ever clearer and clearer to the Church and to humanity how my Immaculate Heart is the sure refuge, which the Most Holy Trinity has prepared for your salvation, in the hour when justice will become manifest in all its divine power.

h   — *It is my great work of mercy* because the merciful love of Jesus wants to manifest itself to you, through the motherly means of my Immaculate Heart. To me has been entrusted by Jesus the task of going in search of my wandering children; of leading back the sinners along the road of righteousness; those who are far away, along the road of return to the Lord; the sick, along the way of healing; the despairing, along that of trust; the oppressed, along the road of relief; the lost, along that of salvation.

i   I am the Mother of Love and of Mercy.

j   At the moment when the world will be set free from the Evil One and the earth purified by the painful trial which, in many ways, has already been foretold to you, my Immaculate Heart will be the place where all will see fulfilled the greatest prodigy of divine mercy.

k   Thus the Holy Spirit will pour out upon the world his second Pentecost of grace and of fire, to prepare the Church and humanity for the return of Jesus in the splendor of his divine glory, to make all things new.

l   And so you understand now, my little son, the great design which I have upon you. Continue, with confidence and joy, your wearying journey, and second, at each moment, my great *work of love and of mercy.*

m   Even though you now feel more and more the weight and the fatigue of the journey, you will see as never before, the triumph of your heavenly Mother, who is always close to you and who leads you at each step. Extraordinary graces will descend upon my children who will take part in the cenacles, and all will have special signs of my love and of my motherly presence.

n   My angels of light are bearing you along at each moment and defending you from all the subtle snares which my Adversary sets for you. And everywhere you will contemplate, with emotion and joy, the triumph of my Immaculate Heart in the hearts and the lives of my little children who respond with a *yes* and are called by me to take part in this, my great *work of love and of mercy.*"

563

San Salvador (El Salvador); January 24, 1996
Spiritual Exercises in the Form of a Cenacle
with the Bishops and Priests of the M.M.P. from Latin America

Go in My Name

a   "With what love I welcome you to this cenacle, bishops and priests of my Movement, who have come from many countries of Latin America, this land so ensnared by my Adversary, but so loved and protected by your heavenly Mother. I unite myself always to your prayer; I help you to grow in mutual love; I console you in your numerous sufferings and carry with you the burden of your difficult ministry.

b   During these days, I am obtaining for you the gift of the Holy Spirit, who is coming upon this cenacle as He came down upon that of Jerusalem. And the Holy Spirit will open up hearts and souls to the understanding of the important and special mission which I entrust to you.

c   — *Go in my name* along the roads of this continent and bring to all the light of my motherly and merciful presence.

d   — *Go in my name* to search out my children who have strayed along the painful ways of sin and of evil. You see how your society has again become pagan, the victim of materialism, of the mad search for pleasure, of unbridled egoism, of violence, of injustice and of impurity. How many are my poor children who suffer and carry the weight of this hardness of heart, which turns the earth into an immense desert, devoid of love.

e   — *Go in my name,* and bring to all the tenderness of my motherly love. Seek out the lost; support the weak; lead the uncertain; pardon the sinners; reach out to those who are far away; heal the sick; give your priestly assistance to the poor and the little ones; bow down to pour balm on the open wounds of those stricken and those smitten by violence and hatred; take them into your arms, and carry them all into the safe refuge of my Immaculate Heart.

f   — *Go in my name,* and bring my motherly comfort to the Church which is suffering so much here and walking toward the Calvary of her immolation. My Adversary, during these years, has stricken her forcefully, in the shepherds and in the flock. How many sufferings the Church in your countries has endured; how many abandonments has she had to experience; how much bitterness has she drunk from the chalice of her daily faithfulness to Christ and to his Gospel!

g   I have always been close to her, as I was to Jesus beneath the Cross. And in this, her painful journey, the Church which lives in Latin America has felt the comfort and the assistance of your heavenly Mother. For this reason, in your countries, devotion to me has never weakened, but on the contrary it has everywhere become even stronger and greater, day by day. And thus it is that here I am particularly loved and glorified and that Latin America occupies a privileged place in the garden of my Immaculate Heart.

h — *Go in my name* to bring the light of my faith, my invitation to hope and the ardor of my charity to those who are entrusted to your priestly ministry. My beloved sons, go forward with courage along the painful roads of these last times. I am always with you. Do not feel that you are alone. Even if you must carry the cross of misunderstandings, of abandonments and of opposition, I am always close to you.

i I am with you at each moment, and I am helping you carry the cross which the Lord is asking of you for the salvation of those who have been entrusted to you. In the safe refuge of my Immaculate Heart, you will find your peace, and you will experience that joy which only Jesus knows how to give you.

j Leave this cenacle as apostles of my Movement in all Latin America. Spread everywhere the cenacles which I ask of you: among the priests, the children, the youth and especially in families, so that they may be protected and defended from the great dangers which threaten them.

k Then you become precious instruments of the triumph of my Immaculate Heart, as you feel with joy the comfort of my motherly presence.

l With those dear to you, with those who are entrusted to your ministry, I bless you in the name of the Father, and of the Son, and of the Holy Spirit."

564

Managua (Nicaragua); February 2, 1996
Feast of the Presentation of the Child Jesus

In the Spiritual Temple

a "My little son, you are here in this country, ensnared and stricken by my Adversary, but loved and guarded by your heavenly Mother in the safe refuge of her Immaculate Heart. I have obtained for it the gift of liberation from slavery to communism and that precious gift of peace.

b   The Church too, which lives and suffers here, has had to carry the cross of persecution and of betrayal on the part of some of her children. But I have intervened in her defense and for her protection, because she has been consecrated to my Immaculate Heart.

c   *Into the spiritual temple* of my Immaculate Heart, the Church and all humanity must now enter.

d   — *In this spiritual temple,* I lead the Church to the perfect glorification of the Most Holy Trinity. In her, the Heavenly Father is pleased to be reflected; in her, Jesus wants to live again in order to give the Father full assent to his Will; in her, the Holy Spirit pours Himself out that He may reflect his divine splendor upon you all.

e   For this reason, I am purifying the Church and leading her along the way of Calvary, where she will again give her full witness to my Son Jesus.

f   — *Into this spiritual temple,* I am leading all humanity, a humanity so far from God, now incapable of loving, seduced by errors and made into a slave of evil, of disordered passions and of sin. Over it Satan has now established his dominion.

g   In the spiritual temple of my Immaculate Heart, I am preparing for the complete return of humanity to the Lord along the road of conversion and penitence, of a change of heart and of life.

h   — *In this spiritual temple,* I am making all peoples into one single family. Thus I am preparing the new times of a universal pacification of all peoples, disposing them to receive the Lord Jesus, who is now returning in the splendor of his divine glory. Prepare yourselves to receive Him. For this, I invite all the nations of the earth to throw open the doors to Jesus Christ who is coming.

i — *Into this spiritual temple,* I am carrying in my arms all my little children, who have entrusted themselves completely to me through their act of consecration to my Immaculate Heart. They are experiencing the security of being carried in the arms of the Mother, and the Mother is experiencing the joy of seeing herself loved and glorified by these, her children.

j The hour of my triumph and yours has arrived. And so, I invite you to hasten, each and all, into the safe refuge which the heavenly Mother has prepared for you in the final times of the great tribulation.

k Here, in my arms, you will be consoled. As a mother caresses her son, you will be caressed by me. Because in the spiritual temple of my Immaculate Heart, I have already prepared for you the altar, upon which you too will be immolated for the salvation of the world."

565

Cuzco (Peru); February 22, 1996
Feast of the Chair of St. Peter

The Powers of Hell Will Not Prevail

a "My little son, how wearying is this journey, which I am asking you to make through thirteen countries and in fifty-two cities, in order to hold wonderful cenacles with the priests and faithful of my Movement. Today you find yourself here, in this city, situated at an altitude of almost four thousand meters, in the midst of the great Peruvian Andes range. And, with a great cenacle held in the stadium, you are celebrating the feast of the Chair of Saint Peter.

b Jesus has founded his Church upon the solid rock of the Apostle Peter. To Peter, Jesus has given the task of being the foundation of the Church and of safeguarding all her truth. For Peter, Jesus has prayed, that his faith might remain intact throughout the whole course of human history. To Peter, He has given the sure guarantee of his victory: *the powers of hell will not prevail.*

c —*The powers of hell will not prevail.* The task entrusted to Peter is handed down to his successors. Thus the Pope becomes today

896

the foundation upon which the Church is built, the center where there converge her charity and assurance to ever maintain intact the deposit of faith.

d   —*The powers of hell will not prevail,* despite the fact that Satan has broken loose, sowing divisions and schisms, these deep wounds which have shattered the unity of the Church, the Mystical Body of my Son Jesus. All the various Christian confessions, which in the course of the centuries have separated themselves from the Catholic Church, represent a victory of the Adversary against the unity of the Church, that unity willed by Christ and ardently implored of the Father.

e   And now the effort is being made to rectify all these errors by walking the path of reconciliation and ecumenism. However, the coming together of all the Christian confessions in the Catholic Church will take place with the triumph of my Immaculate Heart in the world.

f   —*The powers of hell will not prevail,* despite the fact that my Adversary has broken loose in order to bring you to a breakdown of charity. For this, he launches a strong attack on the Pope, who presides over all the charity of the Church. And so, division has entered into her very own structure. Above all in the division which often sets bishops against bishops, priests against priests, faithful against faithful, Satan has succeeded in building up his triumph.

g   But the powers of hell will not prevail, because, after the painful period of the purification and the great tribulation, the Church will shine forth in all her light of charity, of unity and of holiness. And this will be one of the greatest benefits which my motherly love will bring to the Church.

h   —*The powers of hell will not prevail,* even if now they have reached the point of contesting the Pope, of opposing him openly and of rejecting his Magisterium. Thus, errors are being spread about which draw many away from the true faith, and sects are being propagated which draw to themselves many children of the Church. Never as in Latin America has the great spread of the sects represented such a victory on the part of the powers of hell, who appear to have the upper hand.

897

i But I am calling all my children to the greatest fidelity to the Catholic Church; I am instilling in them a love for the Church, zeal for her unity, passion for her holiness, and strength for her work of evangelization.

j And thus, through those who are consecrating themselves to my Immaculate Heart, I am bringing to nothing all the effort which Satan is exerting, in his attempt to draw many of my children away from the one and only Church instituted by my Son Jesus. And by means of my extraordinary and motherly intervention, once again, the powers of hell will not prevail.

k The power of Christ will be revealed, when He brings his reign of glory into the Church, and then all the powers of hell will be imprisoned, so that they will no longer be able to do any more harm in the world. Then the holy Church of God will be able to pour out upon all the nations of the earth the greatest splendor of her truth and her holiness."

566 *Montevideo (Uruguay); March 7, 1996*

The Task I Have Entrusted to You

a "Continue this very wearying journey of yours to hold cenacles in so many cities of this continent of Latin America, where the heavenly Mother is loved and more and more glorified. You see how the triumph of my Immaculate Heart is becoming here a marvelous reality.

b What you are succeeding in doing is humanly impossible; I am supporting and leading you; I am giving you strength and comfort, because the times of my triumph have come, and you must carry out the task which I have entrusted to you, the task of bringing all into the safe refuge of my Immaculate Heart.

c — *The task I have entrusted to you* is that of bringing into my motherly garden the children, exposed to many dangers, subjected to so many acts of violence, set on the sorrowful road of sin and impurity. This perverse and wicked generation is daily setting snares for these little ones, whom Jesus is protecting in the enclosure of his divine love and to whom He is making known the secrets of his Heavenly Father.

d   — *The task I have entrusted to you* is that of leading to the consecration to my Immaculate Heart the youth, in order to rescue them from the great danger of straying away from Jesus and me. How greatly has the wicked world in which you live seduced the young people by offering them the poisoned bread of sin and evil, of pleasure and impurity, of entertainment and drugs.

e   I am leading the young people into the safe refuge of my Immaculate Heart, so that they may be defended by me and protected from all the dangers, instructed and led along the road of love and holiness, of mortification and purity, of penance and prayer. Thus I am forming for myself the cohort of my young people, called to enter into the new times, which the heavenly Mother is preparing for the Church and for all humanity.

f   — *The task I have entrusted to you* is that of bringing into the bright enclosure of my Immaculate Heart Christian families, that they may be assisted by me to live in unity and faithfulness, in prayer and love, open to the gift of life, which must always be welcomed, protected and jealously guarded.

g   — *The task I have entrusted to you* is that of leading into the safe refuge of my Immaculate Heart the priests, who are the sons of my maternal predilection, that they may be consoled and encouraged by me and assisted in becoming fervent ministers of Jesus, whom they must relive in life and faithfully announce in his Gospel.

h   — *The task I have entrusted to you* is that of bringing into my Immaculate Heart all this great continent of Latin America which belongs to me and which I guard with motherly jealousy.

i   Go, my little child, for yet a little while, along all the roads of the world, to peoples and nations so far away, to whom I am bringing you with love and joy. You must now enter into the second phase of your existence and prepare yourself to live out, in love and in suffering, whatever I ask of you, however great it may be, so that your mission might be accomplished and thus you might bring to fulfillment the task which I have entrusted to you."

Protector and Defender

a   "Today you are bringing to an end your long journey through-out Argentina, with a great cenacle which you are holding with the priests and many seminarians of my Movement. In this way, you are celebrating the liturgical solemnity of my most chaste spouse, Joseph. You have seen, in this great country, how I am loved and glorified by so many of my children. This land is especially loved and protected by me, and I cultivate it with special care in the safe refuge of my Immaculate Heart.

b   I desire that here my Marian Movement of Priests be spread even more. I ask that family cenacles be multiplied everywhere, these cenacles which I offer you as a powerful aid in saving the Christian family from the great dangers that threaten it.

c   Entrust yourselves to the powerful protection of my most chaste spouse, Joseph. Imitate his industrious silence, his prayer, his humility, his confidence, his work. Make your own his docile and precious collaboration with the plan of the Heavenly Father, in giving help and protection, love and support, to his divine Son Jesus.

d   Now that you are entering into the painful and decisive times, entrust also my Movement to him. He is the protector and defender of this, my work of love and mercy.

e   *Protector and defender* in the painful events that are awaiting you.

f   *Protector and defender* against the numerous snares which, in a subtle and dangerous way, my Adversary and yours is setting for you with increasing frequency.

g   *Protector and defender* during the moments of the great trial, which now awaits you, in the final times of the purification and the great tribulation.

h   As I express my gratitude to this country of Argentina, for the homage of love and of prayer which I have everywhere received, with Jesus and my most chaste spouse, Joseph, I bless you in the name of the Father, and of the Son, and of the Holy Spirit."

The Chalice of Comfort

a   "Beloved sons, live within the safe refuge of my Immaculate Heart this day of Holy Thursday. This is your feast. This is your pasch.

b   Gathered about your bishops, you are renewing today the commitments and the promises which you made on the day of your priestly ordination. And you are recalling, with joy and gratitude, the institution of the new Priesthood and the new Sacrifice, which took place during the Last Supper.

c   It is the Supper of love: 'Jesus, having loved his own who were in the world, loved them to the end.' (cf. Jn 13:1)

d   It is the Supper of the institution of the sacrament of love: 'Jesus took bread, and blessed, and broke it, and gave it to his disciples and said, "Take, eat; this is my body." And He took a cup, and when He had given thanks He gave it to them, saying, "Drink of it, all of you; for this is my blood, which is poured out for many for the forgiveness of sins." ' (cf. Mt 26:26-28)

e   It is the Supper of the new commandment of love: 'A new commandment I give you: to love one another. As I have loved you, so also are you to love one another.' (Jn 13:34)

f   It is the Supper of service given as an act of love: 'If I then, your Lord and Teacher, have washed your feet, you too should wash one another's feet.' (Jn 13:14)

g   But it is also the Supper which opens upon the sorrowful mystery of his passion. And thus comes the moment of his agony in Gethsemane, of the sweat of blood, of the weeping and mortal anguish, of the abandonment on the part of his disciples, of Peter's denial, of Judas' betrayal. Beloved sons, live, in my Immaculate Heart, the painful hours of Gethsemane.

h   How I would have wanted to be at Jesus' side to console Him in the moments of his interior agony, but the absence of the Mother was ordained by the Heavenly Father so that the agony of the Son would become all the more painful.

i   Behold Jesus burdened with all the sin of the world; upon his fragile body there weigh the rebellions, the violence, the injustices, the impurity and all the wickedness of man. He feels Himself crushed in the press of divine justice, and from his body there begin to ooze forth drops of sweat and blood.

j   When He goes to seek comfort from the three Apostles, He finds them sleeping. So then the Father sends Him the angel with the chalice of his comfort, which Jesus drinks with immense gratitude. In this chalice, I have placed all the love, the prayer, the suffering, the tenderness of my motherly Immaculate Heart. And thus Jesus, at the supreme peak of his abandonment, is comforted by the spiritual presence of the Mother.

k   My Immaculate Heart becomes today the *chalice of comfort*, which I want to offer to the Church and to all my children in the moments of their greatest suffering. For this reason, I invite you to enter, with your act of consecration, into the safe refuge of my Immaculate Heart, because I want to make of you today, my beloved sons, my chalice of comfort:

l   — *Chalice of comfort* for Jesus who relives in his Mystical Body the very events of his passion. How many are those today, even among his ministers, who abandon Him, deny Him and betray Him! In the sorrowful Gethsemane of your time, beloved sons, be the chalice of comfort which the Mother wants to offer to her Son Jesus. Place in this chalice all your love, your fidelity, your zeal, your apostolate, the precious drops of your priestly suffering.

m   — *Chalice of comfort* for the Church, which today is living the very hours of agony of Jesus, in her sorrowful Gethsemane of these last times. How the Church is crushed and beaten, abandoned and betrayed, struck and crucified in the agony of her great tribulation! Place in the chalice the comfort of your priestly fidelity; be zealous ministers of the divine word and of the sacraments; walk with courage along the painful way of love and holiness.

n   — *Chalice of comfort* for my Pope, who is now consummating his sacrifice, on the Calvary of an immense suffering; for the bishops, who have so much need of the love and assistance of their priests, that they may be comforted in their difficult and painful ministry; for your brother-priests, whom you must love, help, take by the hand and share the burden of all their difficulties. In these last times, how many dangers and subtle snares are being set each day in the life of many priests, who are the sons of my motherly predilection.

o   — *Chalice of comfort* for all this poor humanity, ill and so far from God, crushed under the weight of sin and evil, of hatred and violence, of injustice and impurity.

p   Then, in the Gethsemane of these last times, you become the *chalice of comfort*, which the heavenly Mother offers today to the Church and to humanity, so that they may live, in confidence and in great hope, the hours of the painful passion that have now arrived."

569   *Capoliveri (Livorno, Italy); April 5, 1996*
Good Friday

His Wounds

a   "Climb Calvary with me today, beloved sons, that you may be of assistance and comfort to my Son Jesus, condemned to the gibbet of the Cross. Led by the hand of John, who supports me as a son, I meet Jesus as He is climbing with great difficulty toward the summit of Golgotha. At this instant my Heart becomes pierced by the sword of an immense suffering, to which I do not succumb, because as Mother I must give the utmost assistance to my Son.

b   From the flagellation He has received, Jesus is reduced to one single wound. The terrible Roman scourges have incised deep lacerations in his body, and from them flows his life's blood which covers Him entirely. The thorns of his crown have opened up wounds in every part of his head, and from them flow rivulets of blood which descend and cover his whole face.

c   On Golgotha, his hands and feet are pierced with nails, and the jolting impact of the Cross, as it is dropped into the earth, cause Jesus unspeakable pains and make his living blood pour out continuously from his torn wounds. Today, look, one and all, upon Him whom they have pierced. Today, contemplate my Son Jesus, now reduced to one single bloody wound.

d — *His wounds,* open and bleeding, are a sign of his love for you. They are the price of your ransom. They are the flowers of a new springtime of life. They are the precious gift of divine mercy, which brings to all of you the paschal joy of redemption and salvation.

e — *His wounds,* beloved sons, cover them with love and with kisses, together with me, sorrowful Mother of the Passion and desolate Mother of the Crucifixion. Draw close with filial love and place the kiss of your immense gratitude upon each of his wounds: upon the wounds of his head, opened by the thorns of his crown; upon every laceration of his immaculate flesh produced by the flagellation; upon the wounds of his hands and his feet inflicted by the nails, by which He is hung from the Cross. Upon every one of his wounds, let the homage of your kiss of love be deposited, a kiss which makes amends, at least in part, for the gesture of the one who has betrayed Him, of the one who has denied Him, of the one who has abandoned Him, who has abused Him, who has crucified Him.

f — *His wounds* are for you the safe refuge in which you take shelter from the tempest of sin and evil. In his wounds you find your safe dwelling place, the new house which the Heavenly Father has built for you, the new house of communion with God and of salvation, the new house of purity and holiness, the new house of love and prayer, the new house of confidence and hope.

g Within his wounds, hide yourselves from the world and its seductions, from the Evil One and his temptations, in order to live in sweet intimacy of life with your divine Brother Jesus, who is today immolated for you.

h — *His wounds* become a fount of living water which springs up to eternal life. Wash yourselves in the fountain of grace and of divine mercy, springing from the open and bleeding wounds of my Son Jesus, today lifted up and dead, for you, on the Cross.

i Thus, you are washed from every stain, freed from every form of slavery, redeemed from every sin, withdrawn from the kingdom of Satan, brought to full communion with the Heavenly Father, open to love and goodness, illuminated by grace and purity, renewed in the fount of divine mercy.

j Beloved sons, hasten today, each and all, to Jesus Crucified and, with me your sorrowful Mother, kiss his wounds with love and gratitude. Hide yourselves in the safe refuge of his wounds; wash yourselves in the fountain of living water, which now flows forth forever from the open and bleeding wounds of my Son Jesus.

k And with the whole Church Militant, Suffering and Triumphant, on earth, in purgatory and in heaven, let there rise up to Jesus our act of profound adoration and immense gratitude: 'We adore You, O Christ, and we bless You, because by your holy Cross You have redeemed the world and by your holy wounds we have been healed.'"

570

Capoliveri (Livorno, Italy); April 6, 1996
Holy Saturday
First Saturday

Assuage My Sorrow

a "Beloved sons, stay close to your sorrowful Mother, on this one day when I remained without my Son. His body, hastily arranged and covered with purest linen, rests lifeless in his new sepulchre. I keep watch in sorrow and in prayer, in confidence and hope, in the certain expectation of his resurrection.

b —*Assuage my sorrow.* See if there is any sorrow like mine. My eyes again see with dismay all the cruelty, the wickedness, the inhuman ferocity of the crucifixion and the death of Jesus on the Cross.

c And I go back in my thoughts to the joyful moment of the Annunciation; to the heavenly songs of the angels and to the glad announcement given to the little ones and to the poor, the announcement of his birth in a cave; to the blessed time of his infancy threatened by snares; of his boyhood and youth as He bent over his daily work; to the brief and intense years of his public mission, when He proclaimed the Good News to all and was followed and listened to by the little ones, the poor, the sick and the sinners. My life has always been marked by the presence, close to me, of my Son Jesus.

d *—Assuage my sorrow.* Precisely to offer sweet company to my solitude, there spread — from the very first years of the Church — the pious custom of dedicating Saturday to a special veneration of your heavenly Mother. And at Fatima I asked that the five first Saturdays of the month be offered to me, as a sign of filial and loving reparation. And by means of my Marian Movement of Priests, this request of mine is now being accepted in every part of the world. And this gives great comfort to the sorrow of my Immaculate Heart.

e *—Assuage my sorrow.* This is also the first day of my new and spiritual motherhood. And so I look at all my children, whom Jesus has entrusted to me from the Cross, and I invite them to welcome into their own lives the precious gift of his redemption.

f How many there are, still today, who reject Him and who walk along the road of sin and evil, of violence and hatred, of pleasure and impurity. How great is my sorrow in seeing thus that the suffering of Jesus has been endured in vain, because the blood which He has shed for your salvation is being trampled underfoot by many.

g *—Assuage my sorrow.* I ask you to bring into the safe refuge of my Immaculate Heart all those who are far away, the atheists, the sinners, the slaves of sin and evil, those who are being seduced by the subtle snares of my Adversary and yours.

h For this reason, I want you all here today with me, on the one and only day when I have been left without my Son. Learn from me to believe, to hope and to love. Learn from me to entrust yourselves, with unshakable confidence, to the truth of

906

the word of God. In moments of doubt and of darkness, ask of me the assistance to keep vigil in prayer and expectation.

i   When Jesus will return to you in the splendor of his divine glory, then this poor sinful and wounded humanity, which is lying in the sepulchre of corruption and death, will come forth to begin at last the new times of its renewed life."

571   *Capoliveri (Livorno, Italy); April 7, 1996*
Easter Sunday

His Glorious Return

a   "Let your hearts be opened to joy, on the day in which my motherly Immaculate Heart was filled with such a fullness of blessedness that it cancelled out even the trace of her every suffering.

b   You too, beloved sons, live the moment when my Son Jesus, in the dazzling splendor of his glorified body, has presented Himself before me and has surrounded me with his most powerful light, has embraced me with filial tenderness, has placed his kiss on my wounded Heart and led me by the hand into the celestial kingdom of his divine glory.

c   Thus I became the first announcement, silent and motherly, of his resurrection. I was the first living witness of his glorious return to life. For this reason, I invite you to look today, with confidence and sure hope, to his glorious return.

d   — *His glorious return* gives new force of life to all humanity, redeemed but subjected to the terrible snares set for you by him who is a murderer from the beginning and who still wants to spread sin and death in the world.

e   — *His glorious return* gives comfort and consolation, courage and confidence to the Church, born in the sepulchre from which Christ came forth victorious and which is walking along her painful way of the definitive encounter with her Lord and Master.

f   — *His glorious return* gives a new light of grace to all of you, my poor children, who are subjected to the terrible and painful experiences of these last times of the purification and the great tribulation.

g   Never as in your days does it become so necessary to live this stupendous truth of Easter: Christ Risen is living in your midst and is guiding the events of individuals and peoples toward their ultimate fulfillment.

h   Turn today your gaze towards Him who is risen from the dead to lead you all into his kingdom of life.

i   Turn today your gaze upon your heavenly Mother, who is surrounded by the light of the purest paschal joy and who becomes again for you the silent and motherly proclamation of *his glorious return."*

572   *Shrine of Caravaggio (Bergamo, Italy); May 13, 1996*
Anniversary of the First Apparition at Fatima

The Sure Road

a   "Priests and faithful of my Movement from the region of Lombardy, you are gathered today for a great cenacle of prayer and fraternity in this venerated shrine, and in this way you are observing the anniversary of my first apparition, which took place in the Cova da Iria in Fatima on the thirteenth of May 1917.

b   I came down from heaven to point out to you the way along which you must journey in this century, in order to attain peace: that of conversion and of a return to the Lord, through prayer and penance. I came down from heaven to give you my Immaculate Heart, as a refuge in which to take shelter and *the sure road* which leads you to the God of salvation and peace.

c   — *The sure road* in these times, when many other roads are being pointed out, easier and traveled by many, but which are unsafe and do not lead to an encounter with the God of salvation and the Father of divine mercy.

d   — *The sure road* which leads you to accept all the truth contained in the Gospel of my Son Jesus. Along this road, pointed out by me, you are drawn by the splendor of the truth and become profoundly transformed by grace, which brings into your life the divine fragrance of sanctity.

e   Thus you become shining examples of the lived-out Gospel and courageous witnesses of Christ, who draws you to follow Him, in the daily actualization of his divine word.

f   — *The sure road* which leads you to renounce every form of sin and evil, to have a concrete experience of grace, of love and of purity.

g   In the pagan world in which you live, submerged by materialism and hedonism and by the feverish search for pleasure and impurity, you spread the light of holiness and purity, of the mortification of the senses and of penance, and thus you offer to all the help which my Immaculate Heart gives you, in order to attain a communion of life with God, your Redeemer and Savior.

h   — *The sure road* which opens up for the full communion of love among you all, made brothers by the bond which unites you as children of one and the same Father, redeemed by one and the same Son, sanctified by one and the same Spirit, and become children of one sole Mother.

i   My Immaculate Heart, above all in these times, becomes *the sure road* which leads you to a reciprocal communion, to an understanding, to a rejection of egoism and every kind of division, so that the new commandment which my Son Jesus has given you might at last become a reality: 'Love one another as I have loved you.' (Jn 15:12)

j   As you celebrate today this great cenacle of the Marian Movement of Priests, in this region from which it has spread to every part of the world, and as you recall my first apparition which took place at Fatima, where it was born, I want again to offer you my Immaculate Heart as your refuge and the sure road which leads you to God.

k   *It is the sure road* which leads you to the God of salvation and of peace, to the God of truth and holiness, to the God of communion and of unity.

l   On this *sure road*, walk — each and all — with me, in confidence and in certain hope, in joyous expectation of the greatest triumph of God which will take place with the triumph of my Immaculate Heart in the world."

573 *Madrid (Spain); May 22, 1996*

The Time of the Cenacle

a   "My little son, for a week you find yourself holding wonderful cenacles with the priests and the faithful of my Movement in the principal cities of Spain, particularly stricken and ensnared by my Adversary, but guarded and protected by me in the safe refuge of my Immaculate Heart.

b   Live then, with particular intensity, the liturgical time which occurs between the solemnity of the Ascension and that of Pentecost, which is *the time of the Cenacle*.

c   Call to mind the period of time which I spent together with the Apostles in the Cenacle of Jerusalem, united in prayer and in ardent expectation of the fulfillment of the prodigious event of Pentecost. And with what great joy did I contemplate the descent of the Holy Spirit, under the form of tongues of fire which came to rest over each one of those present, working the miracle of their complete and total transformation.

d   This is, for the Church and for all humanity, *the time of the Cenacle*.

e   — *It is the time of the cenacle* for the Church, invited by me to enter into the cenacle of my Immaculate Heart. In this new and spiritual cenacle, all the bishops must now enter, so that they may obtain, through prayer made incessantly with me and by means of me, a special outpouring of the Holy Spirit, who opens minds and hearts to receive the gift of divine wisdom; thus, they attain an understanding of the truth, whole and entire, and come to give their full witness to my Son Jesus.

f   The priests must enter into this new spiritual cenacle so that, by the Holy Spirit, they might be confirmed in their vocation and, by prayer made with me and by means of me, they might obtain power, assurance and courage to announce the Gospel of Jesus in all its integrity and to live it to the letter with the simplicity of the little ones who are nourished with joy by every word that comes from the mouth of God.

g   All the faithful must enter into this new spiritual cenacle, that they may be assisted in living their baptism and receive from the Holy Spirit light and comfort in their daily journey towards sanctity. Only in this way can they become today courageous witnesses of Jesus, risen and living in your midst.

h   — *It is the time of the cenacle* for this poor humanity, so possessed by the spirits of evil, impelled along the road of pleasure and pride, of sin and impurity, of egoism and unhappiness. Humanity must now enter into the cenacle of my Immaculate Heart: here, as Mother, I will teach it to pray and to repent; I will lead it to penance and conversion, to a change of heart and of life.

i   Within this new and spiritual cenacle, I will prepare it to receive the gift of the second Pentecost, which will renew the face of the earth. For this reason, I am asking today that the Church and humanity enter into the cenacle which your heavenly Mother has prepared for you.

j   The period of the purification and the great tribulation in which you are living must be for you *the time of the cenacle*.

k   Enter, all of you, into the new and spiritual cenacle of my Immaculate Heart to recollect yourselves in an intense and incessant prayer made with me, your heavenly Mother, in expectation that the great miracle of the second Pentecost, now close at hand, will be accomplished."

574   *Shrine of Latas (Santander, Spain); May 26, 1996*
Solemnity of Pentecost

The Second Pentecost

a   "With an extraordinary cenacle of prayer and fraternity, you celebrate today the solemnity of Pentecost. You recall the prodigious event of the descent of the Holy Spirit, under the form of tongues of fire, upon the Cenacle of Jerusalem, where the Apostles

911

were gathered in prayer, with me, your heavenly Mother.

b   You too, gathered today in prayer in the spiritual cenacle of my Immaculate Heart, prepare yourselves to receive the prodigious gift of the second Pentecost.

c   — *The second Pentecost* will come to bring this humanity — which has again become pagan and which is living under the powerful influence of the Evil One — back to its full communion of life with its Lord who has created, redeemed and saved it.

d   Miraculous and spiritual tongues of fire will purify the hearts and the souls of all, who will see themselves in the light of God and will be pierced by the keen sword of his divine truth.

e   — *The second Pentecost* will come to lead all the Church to the summit of her greatest splendor. The Spirit of Wisdom will lead her to perfect fidelity to the Gospel; the Spirit of Counsel will assist her and comfort her in all her tribulations; the Spirit of Fortitude will bring her to a daily and heroic witness to Jesus. Above all, the Holy Spirit will communicate to the Church the precious gift of her full unity and of her greatest holiness. Only then will Jesus bring into her his reign of glory.

f   — *The second Pentecost* will descend into hearts to transform them and make them sensitive and open to love, humble and merciful, free of all egoism and of all wickedness. And thus it will be that the Spirit of the Lord will transform the hearts of stone into hearts of flesh.

g   — *The second Pentecost* will burn away, with the fire of his divine love, the sins which obscure the beauty of your souls. And thus, they will return to the full communion of life with God; they will be a privileged garden of his presence; and in this resplendent garden there will blossom all the virtues, cultivated with special care by me, your heavenly Gardener. Thus the Holy Spirit will pour out upon the earth the gift of his divine holiness.

h   — *The second Pentecost* will descend upon all the nations which are so divided by egoism and particular interests, by antagonisms which often set them one against the other. And thus are

912

spread everywhere the wars and fratricidal struggles which have caused so much blood to be spilt on your streets. Then, the nations will form part of one single great family, gathered together and blessed by the presence of the Lord among you.

i   Today I invite you to enter into the cenacle of my Immaculate Heart, to recollect yourselves in prayer with me, your heavenly Mother. And thus, together let us implore the gift of the Holy Spirit, and together let us await the descent of the second Pentecost, which will renew the world and change the face of the earth."

575

Valdragone (San Marino); June 27, 1996
Spiritual Exercises in the Form of a Cenacle
with 25 Bishops and 300 Priests of the M.M.P.
from Europe, America, Africa, Asia and Oceania

My Motherly Plan

a   "How pleased I am to see you here, gathered together in a continuous cenacle of prayer and fraternity, bishops and priests of my Movement, who have now come from every part of the earth. Never as in this year has your participation been so great; never as in this year has the response to the request of your heavenly Mother been so generous.

b   I am gazing upon you with the delight of a mother who feels herself listened to and followed by her children. I unite myself with your prayer, and I deepen your priestly unity. As Mother, I help you to meet each other, to come to know each other, and to love each other; and I make your priestly fraternity greater. Thus you are formed by me to respond in a perfect manner to *my motherly plan.*

c   — *My motherly plan* is to lead you along the road of holiness and immolation. For this reason, I help you to set yourselves free from sin and from the evil which is within you. And so I lead you along the road of purity, of love and of holiness.

d   It is my task to uncover for you the subtle snares of my Adversary and yours, who seduces you in order to lead you along the way of evil and sin, of impurity and infidelity.

e   And so, I descend from heaven to set myself on the journey with you along all the roads of the world. And I call you to enter, each and all, into the safe refuge of my Immaculate Heart: here you will be formed by me to a great sanctity.

f   — *My motherly plan* is to give comfort to you in your sorrow, to pour balm on each of your wounds, and to give confidence and great hope to you in your discouragement. How difficult are the days in which you are living! This is the conclusive period of the purification and the great tribulation. In fact, all humanity is possessed by the spirits of evil, and my Church is shaken by the impetuous wind of errors, of divisions, of unbelief and of apostasy.

g   You must bear the painful weight of this situation. You are being called to carry the cross of all the Church. For this reason, you are destined to experience, as never before, the gentle comfort of my motherly tenderness; in my arms you will be caressed and consoled by me. Thus, I ask you to enter, once and for all, into the refuge of my Immaculate Heart.

h   — *My motherly plan* is to assist the Church along the painful way of her crucifixion and martyrdom. And I am making use of you, my little sons, whom for years now I have called and formed with the words of the messages which I have poured forth from my Immaculate Heart.

i   Be my very motherly and merciful presence in the Church. Close each of her wounds; wipe away her every pain; gather up the drops of her precious blood; place your priestly kiss on her every open and bleeding wound.

j   I ask you to love and console the Pope, who is living through the painful hour of his immolation. Be a filial support to the bishops with your love and your docility. Stay close to all your brother-priests, above all to those who are succumbing under the weight of the trial, which is now reaching its most painful peak. Therefore, you must now find shelter in the safe refuge of my Immaculate Heart.

k   — *My motherly plan* is to protect all humanity in the painful time of its salvation. The time is close when justice will espouse itself to divine mercy, for the purification of the earth. Prepare

914

yourselves, all of you, to bear the pain of the great purifying trial.

l You are the rays of love, which come down from my Immaculate Heart to brighten up the painful hours of the merciful chastisement. Illuminate with my maternal and merciful light the hours of gloom and of the great darkness which has come down upon the world. Give the balm of my motherly tenderness to the little, the poor, the sinners, the sick and those far away.

m I want to live in you and to act by means of you. The remedy that I am giving for the salvation of all, at the culminating moment of the great trial, is my very self, who will manifest myself to all, to the Church and to the world through you, my little sons, called by me and formed for this great task which I now entrust to you.

n Enter then, one and all, into the safe refuge of my Immaculate Heart, and never again leave it. Go out from this cenacle with joy and with a great hope. The graces which you have received here have been great, and you will come to understand them soon.

o The Most Holy Trinity has bent over you with pleasure, and God has granted you the gift of a change of heart. In the place of your little hearts filled with sins, I have put my Immaculate Heart. Be now the new heart of the new Church which Jesus is forming for Himself each day in the garden of his divine and merciful love. Go down from this mountain in peace, and become instruments of my peace in every part of the world.

p With those dear to you, with those who are entrusted to your priestly ministry, I bless you, each and all, in the name of the Father, and of the Son, and of the Holy Spirit."

576

Dongo (Como, Italy); August 15, 1996
Solemnity of the Assumption
of the Blessed Virgin Mary into Heaven

Look Up to Heaven

a "Live today with me, beloved sons, in paradise where I was assumed with my soul and my body, to participate in a perfect manner in the glory of my Son Jesus.

b — *Look up to heaven.* Your heavenly Mother was assumed into heaven at the very moment when she closed her eyes to her earthly life. And then, surrounded by a multitude of the angelic host, who exalted and venerated me as Queen, I was raised up to the glory of paradise.

c The Most Holy Trinity has bowed down, delighted and glorified, and in me has reflected the rays of its eternal and divine splendor. My Son Jesus, who had already ascended into heaven to take his seat at the right hand of the Father, has welcomed me with filial love and joy and has wanted me at his side, to share in his royal power in subjecting all things to Himself.

d Thus have I become Queen, because the Most Holy Trinity has confirmed me in my glorious role of beloved Daughter of the Father, Mother of the Son, and Spouse of the Holy Spirit.

e — *Look up to heaven.* In paradise, I exercise fully my maternal power. As Mother, I am close to Jesus in order to intercede for you. I cause to descend from my Immaculate Heart the graces of which you have need, in order to walk with me along the painful road of these last times. Thus you also can arrive here in paradise, where, with Jesus, your heavenly Mother awaits you.

f I am close to Jesus to offer my motherly work of reparation to the Most Holy and Divine Trinity. For this, I gather in the chalice of my Immaculate Heart all your sufferings, the great sorrows of all humanity in the time of its great tribulation, and I present them to Jesus, as a sign of reparation for all the sins which are committed each day in the world.

g And thus, I have again succeeded in postponing the time of the chastisement, decreed by divine Justice, for a humanity which has become worse than at the time of the flood.

h — *Look up to heaven.* From heaven, you will see my Son Jesus returning on the clouds in the splendor of his divine glory. Then finally the triumph of my Immaculate Heart in the world will be accomplished.

i To prepare for this divine prodigy, I want to establish my motherly triumph in the hearts and the souls of all my children. For this, I have caused my Marian Movement of Priests to spring

916

up within the Church, and I have brought my little son to every part of the world; and, in him and by means of him, I have manifested myself to all. For this reason, I continue to ask him to go to remote and distant places, in order to help you enter, through your consecration, into the safe refuge of my Immaculate Heart.

j   Thus you too, with your soul and heart, are living in paradise where I dwell, even if with your bodies you are still dwelling on this earth. In this way you too share in my maternal glory. And thus, you too unite yourselves in my work of intercession and reparation, and prepare, in prayer, in silence and in suffering, for the awaited moment — so hoped for — of the triumph of my Immaculate Heart in the greatest and most glorious triumph of my Son Jesus."

577   *Prague (Czech Republic); September 2, 1996*

The Evil of Your Century

a   "Once again you find yourself here, my little son, to conduct cenacles with bishops, priests and faithful of my Movement, in these countries of eastern Europe, which have lived for many years in the terrible bondage imposed by communism and who have obtained their liberation by one special intervention of my Immaculate Heart.

b   How many persecutions, acts of oppression and sufferings have these children of mine had to bear! My Church here has also been oppressed and persecuted, despoiled of its goods, crucified and led to martyrdom.

c   But now you are being menaced with an even more serious and insidious danger. It is practical atheism, *the evil of your century.*

d   — *Practical atheism* spreads by false ideologies, by the sects, by the errors which are spreading more and more, even within the Church.

e   — *Practical atheism* has led humanity to build a civilization without God, characterized by a feverish search for material goods, for pleasures, for entertainments, and by the worship given to money and to its great power.

f   — *Practical atheism* has destroyed in many the thirst for God, has impiously led to withdraw from Him the worship due Him, to give it to creatures, even to Satan, and to live as though God did not exist.

g   — *Practical atheism* has spread everywhere the wound of unbridled egoism, of violence, of hatred and of impurity. Impurity is proposed as a value and a good, and it is propagated throughout all the mass media. Sins of impurity are presented as a way of exercising one's personal freedom, and so impure sins against nature, which cry for vengeance in the sight of God, become justified and even exalted. The world has now been reduced to an immense desert, completely covered with filth.

h   You are living under the yoke of this terrible slavery. For this reason, only the pain of the merciful chastisement will be able to free this poor humanity from the great evil of practical atheism, which has spread everywhere.

i   It is my motherly duty to help you in the hours of the great purifying trial. As Mother, I am close to you to protect and assist you. And I am close to you also because my work, which I have begun in these countries, must be brought by me to its complete fulfillment.

j   And this will be done when, with the triumph of my Immaculate Heart in the world, you will be completely liberated from every form of practical atheism, which has been the *greatest evil of your century.*"

578

With the Strength of the Little Ones

a   "Gather together, like fragrant flowers of love and purity, about the cradle in which I am placed at the moment of my birth. Because I am little, I am pleasing to the Lord. Because I am little, I have been destined by my God to guide the cohort of his children against the terrible army of Satan, of the rebellious spirits and of their powerful followers. With my little children, I will in the end achieve my greatest victory.

b   — *With the strength of the little ones,* I will conquer the great power of Satan, who has set up his reign in the world and has seduced, with the cup of pleasure and lust, all the nations of the earth. For this reason, with my Marian Movement of Priests, I am gathering together, from everywhere, my little children, and with joy I see that they are responding to me with generosity and in ever increasing numbers.

c   — *With the strength of the little ones,* I will bring back to God this poor humanity, deceived and seduced by false ideologies and particularly ensnared by the great error of atheism. With it, Lucifer, the ancient serpent, Satan, has wanted to renew before God his proud challenge, bringing humanity to repeat his gesture of rebellion against the Lord: '*Non serviam:* I will not serve Him.' And so, I gather in the garden of my Immaculate Heart the great cohort of my little children, and I offer them to the perfect fulfillment of the Will of the Heavenly Father.

d   Thus, in them and by means of them, I repeat my gesture of humble and perfect availability to his Will, repeating again my *Fiat:* let your holy and divine Will be done.

e   — *With the strength of the little ones,* I will heal this humanity, ill and wounded by sin, by pride, by violence and by impurity. For this, I lead with gentle firmness all my little children along the road of holiness, of humility, of love and of purity.

f   And then this world will go back to being the garden, in which the Lord can once again be loved, enjoyed, served and perfectly glorified. Thus will be achieved the great victory foretold and sung in the Sacred Scriptures: 'Out of the mouths of babes and sucklings, You have asserted your power against your adversaries, to silence the enemy and the rebel.' (cf. Ps 8:3)

g   I bless this little country which, in these days, has given such joy and comfort to my Immaculate Heart.

h   You have seen, my little son, with what enthusiasm the priests and faithful have responded to my invitation to take part in the cenacles: how many graces have come down upon so many children in this country, where the heavenly Mother has received one of the greatest responses to her invitation to belong to the Marian Movement of Priests, in order to form part of the victorious cohort of my little children."

Share in My Sorrow

a   "*Share in my sorrow,* beloved sons. A sword continues to pierce the soul of your heavenly Mother. To the little children to whom I appeared at Fatima, I have wished to show my Immaculate Heart surrounded with a crown of thorns, in order to make them understand how numerous and painful the wounds are which cause my motherly Heart to bleed.

b   — *Share in my sorrow,* you who, through your act of consecration, are called to enter more and more into the refuge of my Immaculate Heart.

c   — *Share in my sorrow,* for the great spread of materialism and hedonism in these countries, which have lived for decades under the painful yoke of atheistic communism. My Immaculate Heart has obtained the great grace of their liberation. But the diabolic and masonic forces are being unleashed, causing to enter, into them also, the evil which now contaminates the whole world, such as materialism, the mad quest for pleasure and money, the dissolute and obscene entertainment, the pornography and prostitution. And thus these poor children of mine are again even more threatened and are running a greater danger of being lost.

d   — *Share in my sorrow,* for the spread of a subtle and insidious anticlericalism. The Church here has, for years, been persecuted, imprisoned, crucified and brought to martyrdom. I wish to recall, among all others, my beloved son, Cardinal Joseph Mindszenty, who has been a symbol and the precious victim of this bloody persecution.

e   Now the Church is apparently free, but she is still being obstructed in her mission by the flood of practical atheism, by the sects, by indifferentism and nihilism among the youth, because of which many of them flee from religion and thus new vocations to the priestly and religious life are far too scarce.

f   — *Share in my sorrow,* because here Freemasonry, with its hidden power, is in control, which leads to dissoluteness, to a loss of the sense of morality, to the exaltation of sexual liberty, to the destruction of the family through divorces, birth control and these abortions which are becoming more and more widespread and legitimized.

g   And so then you understand how the fall of communism, which took place here in 1989 through a special intervention of my Immaculate Heart, becomes only a sign and anticipation of my one complete and greater victory.

h   This victory will take place with the fall of practical atheism throughout all the world, with the defeat of the masonic and satanic forces, with the destruction of the great power of evil, and with the full triumph of God in a world, then completely purified by the great merciful chastisement.

i   For this reason, I exhort you to filial abandonment, to confidence and to a great hope. My Immaculate Heart is your safe refuge, in which by me you are consoled and defended, protected and prepared to live out the longed-for and awaited hours of the triumph of divine mercy upon the world."

580   *Zagreb (Croatia); September 20, 1996*

Do Not Fear, Little Flock

a   "How happy I am with the cenacle which you have held here, with the priests and the faithful of my Movement, presided over by the Cardinal Archbishop, whom I so love and protect.

b   In this country, my Adversary is on a rampage, bringing into it the painful trial of violence and war. How many sufferings these children of mine have had to undergo! I have intervened to obtain for them the great gift of liberation and peace.

c   But still graver tribulations are now awaiting you.

d   — *Do not fear, little flock.* The Heavenly Father has been pleased to give you the reign of my Immaculate Heart. I have manifested myself to you, and you have welcomed me with the generosity of my little children.

e   Now I can lead you along the road of purity, of love and of holiness, with the exercise of all the virtues which I cultivate, as a heavenly gardener, in the resplendent garden of your souls. Thus each day I offer you, as victims of reparation, to the justice of God, so that He may pour out upon the world the purifying grace of his divine mercy.

f   — *Do not fear, little flock.* Your heavenly Mother has made you the gift of drawing you together from all sides into her victorious cohort. The hour of the decisive battle has come. Satan has now reached the summit of his power, and now, even in the Church, he will bring to fulfillment that which the Lord has permitted him for her most painful purification.

g   The hours which you are about to live are among the most important, because all the events, which I have foretold to you, will reach their fulfillment.

h   — *Do not fear, little flock.* Jesus has gathered you into the heavenly enclosure of his divine love. He leads you to the perfect fulfillment of the Will of the Father. Jesus wants to be glorified by you. The hour has come when Jesus will be perfectly glorified by you. You are the consolation to Him in his abandonment; you are the profound joy of his divine Heart.

i   — *Do not fear, little flock.* You are my little children, whom I have gathered together from every part of the earth for the great battle between God and Satan, between the forces of good and those of evil. The Lord will conquer by means of me, his little servant. I will conquer by means of you, my little children.

j   What has taken place in this country becomes a sign for all. Because of its fidelity to Jesus and to your heavenly Mother, to the Church and to the Pope, Satan has been unleashed against it in an attempt to destroy it. With this object in mind, all the satanic and masonic forces have come together.

k   But I myself have marked the hour of their defeat. And thus it will be for all humanity. For this reason, I bid you to have confidence and a great hope.

l   — *Do not fear, little flock.* To you has been entrusted the mis-

922

sion of bringing to completion the triumph of my Immaculate Heart in the world."

581

Tokyo (Japan); October 13, 1996
Anniversary of the Last Apparition at Fatima
Spiritual Exercises in the Form of a Cenacle
with the Priests of the M.M.P. from Japan

A Great Sign

a   "With great joy I gaze upon you, priests of my Marian Movement of Priests of Japan, who have come here to live with me these days, in a continuous cenacle of prayer and brotherhood. You are bringing your cenacle to an end today, on which you are observing the anniversary of my last apparition which took place at Fatima and which was confirmed by the miracle of the sun.

b   There appeared in the sky *a great sign: signum magnum.*

c   I am the great sign which appeared in the sky: I am the Woman Clothed with the Sun, with the moon beneath my feet, and with a crown of twelve stars upon my head.

d   — *A great sign* in the terrible struggle against all the forces of evil, which have joined together against God and against his Christ. And so, close to the great sign of the Woman Clothed with the Sun, there appears also that of the Red Dragon, of the ancient serpent, of Satan, who is now manifesting himself in all his extraordinary power. It appears that the great Dragon has won his victory, because he has led humanity to build a civilization without God; he has spread everywhere the cult of money and pleasure; he has seduced minds with pride and with errors; he has violated souls with sin and evil; he has hardened hearts with egoism and hatred; he has corrupted all the nations of the earth with the cup of lust and impurity. Satan has succeeded in bringing his wicked kingdom upon the entire world.

e   But in the furious struggle of these last times, this struggle between heaven and earth, between the heavenly spirits and the demons, between the Woman and the Dragon, I appear as a great sign of my greatest victory.

923

f — *A great sign* of the victory of God over every form of atheism, theoretical and practical, of good over every form of evil and sin, of love over every form of violence and hatred, of truth over every form of error and falsehood.

g For this great victory, I have formed for myself the cohort of all my little children who, from every part of the world, have responded to me with a *yes*. With my Marian Movement of Priests, I have brought my invitation to the farthest confines of the earth, and I have formed for myself my victorious army.

h Even in this great country, almost completely pagan, my little children have responded to me with joy and great generosity. My motherly Heart trembles with love and tenderness for them. I open up for them, also, the way of salvation, and with the triumph of my Immaculate Heart, they will enter into the one sheepfold of which my Son Jesus is the Good Shepherd.

i — *A great sign* of light in these times of dense darkness. For this, I invite you to walk along the road of prayer and penance, of confidence and of your very great abandonment. Once again, I have sent you this little son of mine, to bring you the gift of my motherly tenderness. By means of him, I offer to your Church and to your fatherland a sure sign of my assistance and of my motherly protection.

j With those dear to you, with those entrusted to your ministry, I bless you in the name of the Father, and of the Son, and of the Holy Spirit."

582 Nagasaki (Japan); October 18, 1996

In This City

a "Today you are bringing to a close here the journey which you have made through all Japan, where you have been able to see the marvels of love and mercy of my Immaculate Heart. And you are bringing it to an end precisely *in this city,* especially loved by your heavenly Mother.

b — *In this city,* the work of evangelization was begun by Saint

924

Francis Xavier, the great apostle and missionary, who opened the way in this distant continent to the first announcement of the Gospel.

c — *In this city,* there were led to their martyrdom twenty-six of my children, heroic witnesses of Christ, to whom they offered their lives on the altar of my Immaculate Heart. You also were here to celebrate Holy Mass in the shrine, raised upon the spot of their terrible execution.

d — *In this city,* there also lived my son, Saint Maximilian Kolbe, and it is that he constructed the city of the Immaculata, which still today brings my shining presence to many of my Japanese children, who so love and honor me.

e — *In this city,* there also exploded the atomic bomb, causing tens of thousands of deaths in a few brief instants, a chastisement and terrible sign of what man can do when, distancing himself from God, he becomes incapable of love, of compassion and of mercy. This is what the whole world could become if it does not welcome my invitation to conversion and return to the Lord. From this place, I renew my anguished appeal to all the nations of the earth.

f — *In this city,* I manifest my maternal work of salvation and of mercy. I again invite all my children to journey along the road which, during these years, I have traced out for you with the messages which I have given to the heart of this, my little son.

g For this reason, I have wanted you here again, so that you might offer to this city and to all Japan, the safe refuge of my Immaculate Heart. Enter, each and all, into this refuge. Thus, you will be protected and defended by me, when the great and terrible day of the Lord comes upon you."

Seoul (Korea); October 31, 1996
Spiritual Exercises in the Form of a Cenacle
with the Bishops and Priests of the M.M.P. from Korea

A Land Blessed and Threatened

a   "How consoled I am by you, beloved sons, in seeing you gathered together here from many parts of Korea, to live these days in a continuous cenacle of prayer and brotherhood under the delighted gaze of your heavenly Mother. I unite myself to your prayer and make the bond of your priestly unity stronger.

b   Love one another as Jesus has loved you. Put into practice his new commandment to become one, and in this way you will give joy and comfort to the pierced Heart of my Son Jesus.

c   Carry in your heart and in your prayer the needs, the concerns and the apprehensions of your Church and of your fatherland, Korea, this land blessed by me and so threatened.

d   — *A land blessed,* because here my Church is prospering and spreading, thanks to the blood of the martyrs which has become fertile seed of so many new Christians.

e   — *A land blessed,* because the faithful are ardent in the faith, fervent in prayer, and united with their shepherds. Here, I am especially loved, invoked and glorified, above all by the little ones, the simple, the poor, the humble. And from these are springing up numerous vocations to the religious and priestly life.

f   — *A land threatened,* because here too the errors which distance one from the true faith are being spread; the sects which represent a grave threat to many of the faithful are undergoing a great expansion. And so I urge you, my beloved priests, to a great unity with the Pope and with your bishops who are united to him. Listen to and follow the hierarchical Magisterium of the Church, in order to resist the subtle snares of error and infidelity. Spread with courage the words of the Gospel, and form the faithful in the growth of their faith through a zealous work of catechesis, so necessary today for the Church in Korea.

g   Above all, I ask you, my beloved ones, to be zealous in your priestly ministry, persevering in prayer, ardent in love for the

Eucharistic Jesus, who must become the center of your apostolate and the great love of your life, open to the needs of the poor, of the humble, of the little ones, and, above all, of my children who live in the darkness of paganism and who do not yet know the light of the truth and of salvation which my Son Jesus has given you.

h — *A land threatened* in its peace and unity. This people has, in fact, become separated and divided. It has borne the weight and the bloody trial of a fratricidal war, and still today, great is the danger which threatens its tranquility and peace.

i Priests consecrated to my Immaculate Heart, be the instruments of my peace and of my motherly assistance to this nation, where I am so loved, invoked and glorified. Korea is a land particularly loved and protected by me; it is the garden in which your heavenly Mother gives extraordinary signs of her continual presence among you.

j I am leading you along the road of unity and peace. This unity and peace will come to your Church and to your fatherland as a special gift of my Immaculate Heart.

k Leave this cenacle in joy, and spread everywhere my invitation to be consecrated to my Immaculate Heart, in order to live in confidence and in a great hope.

l Through you, the comfort of my motherly presence also reaches my children of North Korea, of China, of Vietnam and of all this immense continent of Asia, still in great part pagan, but whom your heavenly Mother is leading along the way of truth and salvation.

m With those dear to you, with those who are entrusted to your ministry, I bless you all in the name of the Father, and of the Son, and of the Holy Spirit."

584

With Joy and with Immense Hope

a   "Look today, *with joy and with immense hope,* at your immaculate Mother.

b   — *With joy,* because I am the cause of your joy. This is how you invoke me, with the prayer which is so pleasing to me, in the litany of Loreto. On this day, I invite you to look to me with joy.

c   — *With joy,* you contemplate me in the light of my Immaculate Conception. Because I was destined from eternity to become the Mother of the Incarnate Word, the Most Holy Trinity has exempted me from any sin whatsoever, even from original sin, which each and every creature contracts at the moment of its human conception.

d   Thus, you see reflected in me the original plan of the Father, who has created man in his own image and for his greatest glory. And the Heavenly Father bows down over me with particular delight.

e   — *With joy,* you see me become the Virginal Mother of the Word, who becomes Man in my most pure womb. My Son Jesus is born of me to become your Savior and your Redeemer. In Him alone all humanity has the possibility of being set free from slavery to sin, to join in a communion of life and of love with the Heavenly Father.

f   — *With joy,* I manifest myself to you, completely filled with the Holy Spirit, who unites Himself to my soul by a true bond of spousal love, because only through his work does the human conception of God-made-man take place within me, and only by his divine action do I become the Mother of God. Because I am beloved Daughter of the Father, Mother of the Son and Spouse of the Holy Spirit, I can truly become the cause of your joy.

g   But today look at me also *with immense hope.*

h — *With immense hope,* in the days in which humanity knows the sorrowful experience of being far from God, having built up a civilization without God, in which his Law is continually violated and openly rejected. There have arrived for it the hours of the great trial and of its merciful chastisement.

i Then, as Mother, I make myself present, in a strong and continuous way, in order to help it in its journey of conversion and of return to the Lord. Thus, to all humanity, I open the door of my Immaculate Heart, *a safe refuge,* wherein it must enter for its salvation.

j — *With immense hope,* the Church looks to me as she lives out the purifying hour of her greatest crisis. She is being permeated with the smoke of Satan, lacerated in her unity, darkened in her holiness, threatened with the loss of faith and with a great apostasy.

k For this reason, I manifest myself to the Church, with the tenderness and the mercy of my motherly love, and thus I myself am helping and comforting her, in the painful moments of her great purification. My presence in the Church is, from now on, becoming stronger, continuous and more manifest. In the Marian Movement of Priests, the whole Church will see the extraordinary assistance which the heavenly Mother is offering her, to lead her into *the safe refuge* of her Immaculate Heart, where she will know the bright hour of her second Pentecost.

l — *With immense hope,* look to me, my little children, so afflicted, wounded and stricken by the impetuous wind of the great tribulation.

m Come to me, all of you, my little children.

n Come to me, because you have need of being consoled, encouraged, protected, defended and saved by your heavenly Mother.

o For this purpose, I have built for you the Ark of the New Covenant, into which you must enter to attain the new times which are now awaiting you. For this purpose, I invite you again today to enter, one and all, *with joy and with immense hope,* into the *safe refuge* of my Immaculate Heart."

God with Us

a   "Live with me the mystery of this holy night, in silence, in prayer, and in expectation. Share in the deep joy of your heavenly Mother, who is preparing herself to give you her divine Infant.

b   The Son who is born of me is also my God. Jesus is the only-begotten Son of the Father; He is the Word through whom all things have been created; He is Light from Light, God from God, consubstantial with the Father. Jesus is outside of time; He is eternal. As God, He carries within Himself the synthesis of all the perfections. By means of me, this God makes Himself true man.

c   In my virginal womb, there came about his human conception. In this holy night, He is born of me in a poor and un-adorned cave; He is placed in a cold manger; He is adored by his Mother and by his legal father; He is surrounded by the humble presence of shepherds; He is glorified by the heavenly cohort of the angels, who sing the hymn of glory to God and of peace to the men who have been loved and saved by Him.

d   Bow down with me to adore the Infant Jesus, just born: He is the Emmanuel; *He is God with us.*

e   — *He is God with us,* because in the divine Person of Jesus are united the divine nature and the human nature. In the Incarnate Word, there is realized the substantial unity of the divinity and of the humanity. As God, Jesus is above time and space; He is immutable and impassible.

f   But as man, Jesus enters into time, undergoes the limitation of space, subject to all the fragility of human nature.

g   — *He is God with us,* who makes Himself man for our salvation. On this holy night, the Savior and the Redeemer is born for all. The fragility of this divine Infant becomes remedy for all human fragility: his cry is alleviation for all sorrow; his poverty is wealth for all misery; his pain is comfort for all the afflicted; his gentleness is hope for all sinners; his goodness becomes salvation for all the lost.

h — *He is God with us,* who makes Himself redemption and refuge for all humanity. Enter with me into the bright cave of his divine love. Allow yourselves to be placed by me in the gentle and sweet cradle of his Heart, which has just begun to beat.

i Bow down with me, in an ecstasy of supernatural blessedness, to feel its first beatings. Listen to the divine harmony that rises from them with heavenly notes of love, of joy, of peace, which the world has never known. It is a song which repeats to each man the eternal and sweetest rhythm of love: I love you; I love you; I love you. Each of its beats is a new gift of love for all. Listen with me to his first sounds of crying. It is the cry of a little baby, just born; it is the sorrow of a God, who carries upon Himself all the sorrow of the world.

j — *He is God with us,* because, even in his human fragility, Jesus is truly God. Jesus Christ is God, outside of changes of time and history: He is the same yesterday, today and forever. During this year, when the Church is inviting you to enter into the contemplation of the mystery of Christ, enter, each and all, into the refuge of my Immaculate Heart. As Mother, I am leading you to understand the great gift of this holy night.

k The Father has so loved the world that He has given it his only-begotten Son, for its salvation. The Holy Spirit has made my virginal womb fertile, because the Son born of me is nothing else but the precious fruit of his divine action of love. Your heavenly Mother has given her maternal assent, so that there might be fulfilled the divine prodigy of this holy night.

l Beloved sons, bow down with me to kiss my newborn Son, and love, and adore, and give thanks because this frail Infant is God-made-man; He is the Emmanuel; He is *God with us.*"

586 Milan (Italy); December 31, 1996
Last Night of the Year

Pray and Make Reparation

a "I invite you to spend the last hours of this year, recollected with me in prayer, in silence, in a spirit of intercession and of reparation.

b   *Pray and make reparation.*

c   — *Pray,* to obtain from the Lord, through the maternal mediation of my Immaculate Heart, the graces of which you have need in these conclusive days of the purification and the great tribulation. With this coming year, enter into the time of immediate preparation for the great jubilee of the year 2000.

d   This special preparation which the Pope is urging of you through his apostolic letter, '*Tertio Millenio Adveniente,*' is to make you understand that this date is important and significant for the Church and for all humanity.

e   This date should be particularly significant for you, because I have previously announced to you, for that date, the triumph of my Immaculate Heart in the world.

f   — *Pray* in intimate union of faith with your heavenly Mother, who is carrying out her motherly work of intercession for all her children. I ask of you an incessant prayer, humble, persevering, trustful. And so I renew again my request to spread everywhere the cenacles of prayer and fraternity. Let these cenacles be spread among the priests, who are my beloved sons, and among the faithful.

g   I await a generous response from the little children, so that they may be defended and protected by me from the great perversion which has contaminated all the world. I ask the young people to gather together in these cenacles, that they may attain the new times which I have prepared for them. Above all, in these cenacles, Christian families must gather together, so that they may be helped by me to live in perfect communion of love, always open to the gift of life which must be desired, protected and defended.

h   — *Pray* to obtain the great gift of the second Pentecost, implored and awaited by you. It will be the Holy Spirit who will give to the world his full and perfect witness to Jesus.

i   *Jesus Christ* must be welcomed, loved, adored and followed by all humanity as your one and only Redeemer and Savior. The

Holy Spirit will open the minds and hearts of all to receive the light of truth. And thus there will be one single flock under one single Shepherd.

j — *Make reparation* for the sins of this poor humanity, which finds itself completely under the power of my Adversary. See how it has rejected God! It has built a pagan civilization, founded on the unbridled quest for pleasures and material well-being. The Law of the Lord is being completely subverted, and even the gravest moral disorders are being legitimized. Pride has seduced minds; impurity has corrupted hearts; the darkness of sin and evil has obscured souls.

k As of now, this poor humanity has touched the bottom of its misery. It can no longer succeed in recovering if a great act of mercy does not raise it up.

l Pray that the great miracle of divine mercy come upon this world.

m — *Make reparation* for the infidelities of so many sons of the Church. The lack of faith is spreading among its very shepherds, and the flock is being stricken by the impetuous wind of apostasy. Errors are being spread, taught and followed; the sects are multiplying everywhere.

n Who will still remain firm in the faith in Jesus and his Church?

o — *Make reparation* for my poor sinful children. I ask of you that which I asked of the three children to whom I appeared at Fatima. Do you wish to offer your life in a spirit of prayer and reparation for the salvation of all the sinners, especially those who have most need of divine mercy?

p So form, with me, a great network of love and salvation, spread out over the whole world.

q This then is the Ark of the New Covenant, the safe and awaited refuge, into which must enter those far away, the atheists, the sinners, the poor, the sick, the despairing, so that they may all enjoy the light, the peace and the joy which only the Immaculate Heart of your heavenly Mother can give you.

r Never as in these final three years, which separate you from the great Jubilee, will it become clear to the Church and to humanity, in an increasingly powerful way, how *my Immaculate Heart will be your safe refuge.*

s   For this I ask you to spend the last hours of this year, not in dissipation and amusements, but with me in prayer and in recollection.

t   *Pray and make reparation*, my beloved sons. Your heavenly Mother is causing her bright rays of purity and holiness to come down upon you.

u   I am preparing you to receive the new days which are awaiting you as gifts of grace and mercy, because, through you, my Immaculate Heart desires to attain its pre-announced triumph."

1997

JESUS CHRIST IS THE ONLY SAVIOR

Jesus Christ Is the Only Savior

a   "Today you are beginning the new year by celebrating the feast of your heavenly Mother, and you are contemplating me in the mystery of my divine maternity. I am true Mother of God, because the Son, to whom I have given flesh and blood for his human conception, is the Eternal Word of the Father and is true God.

b   *In the beginning was the Word*, that is to say, from all eternity. The Word is in the bosom of the Father, as his only-begotten Son, begotten, not created, consubstantial with Him. He is God almighty, omniscient, eternal.

c   *The Word was with God,* as his perfect image, reflection of his glory, eternal and subsistent Word, Son in whom the Father is forever pleased.

d   *The Word was God.* Through Him all has been created; everything that exists in the universe bears his indelible imprint.

e   *The Word took flesh and came to dwell among us.* I have been chosen as Mother, to give human nature to the Word, thus I have become true Mother of God.

f   My Son Jesus, a few moments before dying, has given me as Mother to all of you. My maternal task, in respect to you, is exercised in leading you to understand the mystery of his divine Person.

g   *Jesus Christ is the only Savior.*

h   *He is God with us.* In the mystery of the holy birth, you come to understand what a degree of abasement God has chosen to become completely one with all of you. He has assumed human nature; He has imposed upon Himself the limitation of time and space; He is born like every other creature; He has been placed in a manger; He has lived according to the pattern of life of every human being. He has become a child, like you; He has grown through the stages of adolescence and youth; He has experienced the very same feelings as you. He has become sensitive to love and been wounded by pain. He has delighted in friends; He has suffered because of enemies.

i   *He is God for us.* He has chosen to be one with us in all things, except for sin, in virtue of the love which God has for his creatures. From God, He became man, to become *the only* Savior of man. And so, I have been called to be the Mother of the Redeemer, united to Him in a special way, in the painful work of your salvation.

j   *He is God in us.* The precious fruit of his redemptive work is the return of man to a full communion of life with God. God can live in you with his love, with his grace, and with his very own life. God has become man in order to live in the life of each man. Thus humanity is brought back to a full communion with its Creator and Savior.

k   My motherly task is that of leading you all to Jesus Christ, your God and your Redeemer. Only thus will humanity be able to enjoy the inestimable blessing of peace. Jesus is your peace: peace between God and humanity; peace among all of you, called to be children of God and to form one single family.

l   Peace is the fruit of love.
     Peace is born of good will.
     Peace brings us to harmony and to the brotherhood of all.

m   To build true peace it is therefore necessary to receive Jesus Christ, who is the King of Peace. 'To all who received Him, who believed in his name, He gave power to become children of God; who were born, not of blood nor of the will of the flesh nor of the will of man, but of God.' (Jn 1:12-13)

n   During this year, in which you are beginning the spiritual preparation for the Great Jubilee, I invite you to follow me along the way of a deeper understanding of *the mystery of Jesus Christ,* true God and King of eternal glory.

o   *Jesus Christ is the only Savior.*
p   His word, contained in the Gospel, leads you to salvation, because it is a word of truth and of life. I will lead you to a full understanding of his divine word; I will cause you to love and live the Gospel of my Son Jesus.

937

_q I want to lead you to love Jesus, with my very own motherly Heart; for this, I ask you to consecrate yourselves to my Immaculate Heart. In this way, you come to be prepared by me to receive Jesus Christ with joy, when He returns in the splendor of his glory.

_r And then you also, my little children, will be able to behold '...his glory, glory as of the only Son from the Father, full of grace and truth.' (Jn 1:14)

_s On this day, I look upon you with maternal predilection, and I bless you all in the name of the Father, and of the Son, and of the Holy Spirit."

588

Vacallo (Switzerland); February 2, 1997
Feast of the Presentation of the Child Jesus
Eve of my Journey through South America

Upon the Way of the Beatitudes

_a "Contemplate me at the moment when I present the Child Jesus in the temple of Jerusalem. He is so small, delicate and fragile; it is only forty days since He was born. I carry Him in my arms; with love I press Him to my Heart; enraptured, I contemplate his eyes, which gaze at me and enfold me in his divine light.

_b Thus I myself come to be carried by Him *upon the way of the beatitudes.*

_c *Blessed are the poor in spirit.* The Lord, omnipotent and omniscient God, is totally present, reduced to nothingness as it were, under the appearance of this, my little Son.

_d He is born amidst great poverty, in a cave; He is placed in a manger; He spends his first days of life in a poor and bare dwelling place. And now I am bringing Him to the temple of the Lord, supported by my most chaste spouse, Joseph, and we offer for his ransom two little doves, which is the established price for poor people.

_e *Blessed are the afflicted.* When my Child is given back to me

by the priest and placed in my arms, the aged Simeon, enlightened by the Spirit of the Lord, reveals to my soul that his plan is, above all, one of a great suffering: 'Behold, He is here for the fall and rising of many in Israel, a sign of contradiction, that the thoughts of many hearts may be revealed. And for you also, a sword shall pierce your soul.' (cf. Lk 2:34-35) As Mother, I am thus associated with Him on the road of affliction.

f   *Blessed are the meek.* Contemplate in this Child of mine the reflection of meekness and goodness. His hands are opened as a divine caress upon every human suffering; his eyes cause light to shine down upon every shadow of sin and evil; his feet are formed in order to journey along barren and insecure roads to seek out those far away, to find the straying, to help those in need, to heal the sick, to welcome back sinners, to give hope and salvation to all. His Heart beats with throbs of divine love to fashion the hearts of all in meekness and compassion.

g   *Blessed are the merciful.* See in the Child, whom I bring to the temple of his glory, the Father's merciful love made man. The Father has so loved the world that He has given it his only-begotten Son, that it might be saved by means of Him. So then, in the fragile semblance of this Child, contemplate the victim, chosen and prepared, who must be immolated for your salvation. It is He who brings into the world the merciful love of the Father. It is He, the merciful Love, who renews the hearts of all.

h   *Blessed are the pure of heart.* God is present in my Child Jesus. His Heart is the Heart of God. He has assumed human nature from me, but his Person is divine. Thus the Heart that beats in this Child is the very Heart of God. See God in the Son, whom I carry in my motherly arms. Feel the beating of the Heart of God in his, which beats, and learn to love. Purity of heart is born from the perfection of love. Therefore, only one who loves can attain to purity of heart, and only one who is pure of heart can see God.

i   *Blessed are the peacemakers.* Here for you is the Child who is Peace itself. His name is Peace. His mission is to bring peace between God and humanity. His plan is to pacify the whole world. Only He can bring peace and render peaceful the hearts of all, called to form part of one single family of the children of God. If it rejects Him, the world will never know peace.

j   *Blessed are those persecuted for the sake of justice.* See in this Child the Victim, called to journey along the road of rejection and persecution. As a little one, He must flee into exile, for Herod orders that He be killed; as a youth, He lives in a poor house and is subjected to humble and heavy labor; during his public mission, He is obstructed, marginalized, and threatened, even to the point of being arrested, tried and condemned to death. It is He, the persecuted and stricken One, who brings healing to all.

k   And so today, as I carry Him in my arms to the temple of his glory, I gaze into his eyes, from which there appears the light of an immense beatitude.

l   This is He, your one and only beatitude.

This is He who points out to you *the way of the beatitudes,* along which everyone must travel in order to attain salvation and peace.

This is the Eternal Word of the Father, under the appearance of this little Child, who traces out for you the way of truth and of life.

This is the only-begotten Son in whom the Father, from all eternity, is well pleased.

This is the Son of the Virgin Mother, whom today I carry to the temple of his glory, and to all of you, I repeat: *Listen to Him.*

m   My little son, you find yourself again on the eve of a long and wearisome journey, which you must undertake for me in some countries of Latin America. Do not be fearful of the very heavy program which they have prepared for you. My angels of light are at your side at each moment, and in your very weakness, the power of your heavenly Mother will be the more manifest. Bring all into the refuge of my Immaculate Heart, so that I may help you to journey along the difficult way of your beatitudes."

940

The Immaculate Conception

a   "Today, with a great cenacle which you are holding in the stadium of this city, you are celebrating the anniversary of my apparition at Lourdes. I appeared as *the Immaculate Conception.* I wanted to confirm, through my words, the great privilege which the Lord had granted me, exempting me from the power of Satan and of sin, from the very moment of my human conception. Thus, I have been conceived without original sin.

b   *I am the Immaculate Conception.* The Father reflects in me the perfect plan which He had at the moment of the creation of the entire universe. The Son takes flesh and blood from me, for his human birth, assuming a nature which has never been, not even for an instant, subject to the power of the Evil One. The Holy Spirit makes fruitful this, his maternal and virginal garden, with the fullness of all his gifts. The Most Holy Trinity is well pleased to reflect Itself in me.

c   *I am the Immaculate Conception.* This I am for you, my poor children, so overwhelmed by sin and evil, stricken and wounded by my Adversary and yours, subjected to the gloomy yoke of enslavement to him. And so, today I invite you to follow me along the road of innocence and love, of prayer and mortification, of purity and holiness.

d   See how all the world has now been reduced to an immense desert, where there spring up in great numbers the wicked weeds of sin and egoism, of pride and hatred, of pleasure and impurity. Impurity becomes extolled and spread by all the means of propaganda, and thus the innocence of little children begins to be ensnared, leading then to the destruction of purity among youth and of chastity within family life. Over this world, the demon of lust rules as the master and succeeds in seducing, with the cup of pleasure, all the nations of the earth.

e   *I am the Immaculate Conception.* It is my motherly task to lead all my children along the road of mortification of the senses, and of prayer, of purity and of charity. Only thus can you penetrate into the mystery of love of my Son Jesus. Jesus holds purity very dear. Only to the pure of heart does Jesus reveal the secrets of his divine Heart. To little children of pure hearts, Jesus reveals the plans of his merciful love, which purifies and transforms everything.

f *To penetrate into the mystery of the life of Jesus and of his Gospel of salvation, you must live the virtue of purity.*

g Today, my little son, you find yourself in this great country of Venezuela, so ensnared by my Adversary, but so loved and protected by your heavenly Mother. How many of my children are being ensnared with the poison of corruption, of impurity, of error, of violence and of hatred!

h But in this great nation, your heavenly Mother is being more and more loved, implored and glorified by many of her children. And so I promise to gather all of you under my motherly mantle in the safe refuge of my Immaculate Heart.

i I express to you my joy in seeing my Marian Movement of Priests so widely spread here. Its strength lies in the little ones, the poor, the simple, and in those who have responded generously to my invitation to spread everywhere the cenacles of prayer for which I have asked.

j I promise never to abandon you, but to be ever your secure defense and your heavenly Shepherdess. I bless you all in the name of the Father, and of the Son, and of the Holy Spirit."

590   *Capoliveri (Livorno, Italy); March 27, 1997*
Holy Thursday

Into the Cenacle of His Divine Love

a "Enter into the cenacle of the divine Heart of Jesus, my beloved sons. Today is your feast. Today is your Passover. You are recalling the institution of the new Sacrifice and of the new Priesthood.

b Enter with me *into the cenacle of his divine love.* 'I have earnestly desired to eat this Passover with you before I suffer.' (Lk 22:15)

c *'I have earnestly desired.'* His entire life had always been di-

942

rected towards this ineffable moment. Jesus was reaching out in thought and desire to the summit of this holy mountain, Sion, where He would consummate his Passover. 'I have desired to eat this Passover with you.'

d   Enter *into the cenacle of his divine love*, to savor all the sweetness of this Last Supper. Jesus gives his body and his blood as spiritual food and drink for your new life. He wants thus to unite Himself intimately with each one of you, to the point of becoming totally one with you.

e   Love demands communion; love leads to unity. Jesus brings about a very profound unity with you, even to the point of becoming flesh of your flesh and blood of your very own blood. As Jesus is in the Father and the Father is in Him, so too, by means of the Eucharistic Communion, you are in Him, and He is in you.

f   Enter *into the cenacle of his divine love*, to understand how Jesus is Love which gives Itself, is Love which immolates Itself for you. There follows upon the Passover Supper, consumed with the Apostles, the agony of Gethsemane, the betrayal by Judas, the abandonment by the disciples, the denial of Peter, the outrage and the affront of the servants of the high priest.

g   No one has greater love than he who gives his life for those he loves. Jesus offers his life for love of you.

h   Beloved sons, give thanks with me to Jesus for this, his great gift. Soothe his great sorrow with your priestly love; kiss each of his wounds; guard each of his words in your heart; respond with generosity to your vocation. Your priesthood forms part of this, his gift; your ministry enters into the depths of his mystery of love.

i   *In the cenacle of his divine love*, learn to serve. Love which gives itself, love which immolates itself, is also love which puts itself at the service of others. Thus, Jesus washes the feet of his disciples. The Creator places Himself at the service of the creature; the first becomes the last; the Lord becomes a servant.

j   My beloved priests, place yourselves at the service of all. Be the hands of Jesus which close wounds, heal the sick, pardon sinners, lift up the fallen, support the weak, console the despairing, guide the straying and give to all peace and salvation.

k   *In the cenacle of his divine love,* live your priesthood in a spirit of gratitude and joy. You are called to be the ministers of the love of Jesus. Allow yourselves to be set afire by the flames of his divine charity, to become meek and humble of heart. Be faithful priests.

l   For this, I invite you to consecrate yourselves to my Immaculate Heart. As Mother, I am able to form you as priests according to the Heart of Christ, ministers of his love and of his holiness.

m   Thus by means of you, Jesus is able to continue to observe his Passover each day with you, even to the end of time."

591
Capoliveri (Livorno, Italy); March 28, 1997
Good Friday

I Will Draw Everyone to Myself

a   "'And I, when I am lifted up from the earth, *will draw everyone to Myself.'* (Jn 12:32)   Beloved sons, live, together with me, this day of the passion and death of my Son Jesus.

b   'When I am lifted up from the earth.' For this, the Word of the Father came down into my virginal womb; for this, He was formed for nine months in my motherly womb; for this, He was born of me in a poor and bare cave; for this, He lived through the days of his threatened infancy, of his adolescence and of his youth, bent over his daily work.

c   As I would watch Him grow in the beauty of his divine body, my thoughts would often go with trepidation to the place where He was to be immolated, as the victim prepared and awaited by the Father. And with Jesus, together we would gaze at this summit of Golgotha, where now his bloody Sacrifice is about to be accomplished.

d   'I will draw everyone to Myself.' The Father has so loved the world that He has given it his only-begotten Son, that the world may be saved by means of Him. Jesus offers Himself as the price of your ransom. Jesus immolates Himself for your salvation. Jesus is put to death on the Cross, so that the gift of his redemption may reach all humanity.

e See in Jesus Crucified the living icon of the divine mercy of the Father. It is mercy which impels the Father to give you his only-begotten Son. It is mercy that leads Jesus to immolate Himself on the Cross for you. It is mercy that causes all the blows, insults and outrages of this day to fall upon his divine body.

f See with me the new buds of divine mercy as they open upon his immolated body. Bend down with me to kiss the fragrant flowers of mercy, as they blossom from all his suffering. Let us kiss his body, reduced to one single wound; let us kiss his head, pierced by the penetrating thorns; let us kiss his face, stricken and disfigured; let us kiss his hands and his feet, transfixed by the nails; let us kiss his Heart, rent by the lance. Let us kiss, with love and sorrow, the true Lamb of God, immolated upon the Cross for our salvation.

g *'I will draw everyone to Myself.'* All humanity is drawn into his love of Savior and Redeemer. From Him is born the new humanity, brought to full communion of life with his Heavenly Father. From his pierced Heart, divine mercy descends with water and blood. From here is born the Church and gush forth the sacraments of your salvation.

h And thus the divine mercy becomes a defense for the innocence of the little ones, firmness for the vigor of youth, support for the weakness of the great, comfort for the suffering of the poor, pardon for the guilt of the sinners, hope for the fear of the dying, salvation and life for all.

i In Jesus, raised up from the earth upon the Cross for you, see *the triumph of Divine Mercy* over all humanity, redeemed and saved by Him.

j *'I will draw everyone to Myself.'* I participate as Mother in this, his plan of salvation. For this reason, I am close to my crucified Son today, and I look upon Him with profound compassion, as He is raised up from the earth. I share in his every suffering; I feel upon myself the weight of his Cross; the nails transfix my soul; the lance of the Roman soldier pierces also my motherly Heart. And thus I participate, as Co-redemptrix, in the work of your redemption.

945

k　I unite my motherly sorrow to all the suffering of my Son, because I have been called to be the Mother of Divine Mercy. For this reason, redeemed humanity is entrusted by my Son to my motherly love as well. Jesus has given me as true Mother to all humanity.

l　All of you, let yourselves be drawn into the cradle of this, my new and spiritual motherhood. Enter into the safe refuge of my Immaculate Heart.

m　With his triumph, foretold by me at Fatima, you will see accomplished the greatest miracle of the divine mercy upon the world."

592

Capoliveri (Livorno, Italy); March 29, 1997
Holy Saturday

Mother of the Redeemer

a　"Keep watch with me, beloved sons, on this day when I remained without my Son.

b　*I am the Mother of the Redeemer.* His mission is completed. His body, cruelly reviled, abused and crucified, now rests in his new sepulchre. The Victim has been immolated. The Sacrifice of the new and eternal Covenant has been offered. The new humanity, reconciled to God, is born in the cradle of an immense suffering.

c　The Mother remains still alive. I keep vigil in the sorrow which enwraps me and takes complete hold of me, and I continue to offer Him to the Heavenly Father, in an unceasing prayer, in a firm faith, in a hope which is about to become a certitude.

d　My Son Jesus, slain upon the Cross and laid in the sepulchre, is preparing to rise in the splendor of his divine glory. He who is the Author of Life cannot remain in death. He who is the light of the world cannot be subject to darkness. He who has set you free forever from your bondage to evil cannot bear upon himself the consequence of sin.

e　*I am the Mother of the Redeemer.* This day of my great sorrow

946

prepares the dawn of the greatest joy for all humanity, because my Son, who today lies lifeless in the sepulchre, is your only Savior, is your only Redeemer.

f   And so spend this day together with me, your immaculate and sorrowful Mother.
   Live it with faith in his divinity.
   Live it with hope of his definitive victory.
   Live it with love and in the grace which He has given you.

g   Today is the first day of my new and universal motherhood. I have become Mother also of the whole of humanity. The sepulchre, which receives the remains of my Son, becomes the cradle for your new birth.

h   Enter into the new sepulchre of my Immaculate Heart. This is the cradle in which I want to place all my children. Here, I help you to put aside the old man of sin and evil, of egoism and pride, of wickedness and impurity. Here, I form you into the new man of grace and goodness, of love and humility, of holiness and purity.

i   Second my motherly action, which brings you to an ever more perfect resemblance to your divine Brother, Jesus. And thus, Jesus sees with joy the fragrant flowers of his suffering coming into blossom, and in you, He is able to gather up the precious fruits of his redemption.

j   Beloved sons, live with me this day of the holy Sabbath. Participate in my maternal sorrow. Share with me my firm hope. Let my sure faith be your comfort.

k   He who today lies in the sepulchre is preparing for his greatest victory, at the moment when He will come forth in the splendor of his divine glory."

593

Capoliveri (Livorno, Italy); March 30, 1997
Easter Sunday

Witness of the Resurrection

a   "Live, together with your heavenly Mother, the profound joy of this Easter Day. Christ is alive! Christ is risen!

b When Jesus, in the light of his glorified body, appeared to me in all his divine splendor and, as a Son, bent over to close each wound of my motherly sorrow, my Heart was submerged in the fullness of Easter joy. Christ is risen! Christ lives forever!

c I have become the *first and silent witness of his resurrection*. The first witness, because Jesus has willed to share above all with his Mother the first fruits of this Easter joy. I am however a silent witness, because it is to the pious women and to the disciples that the task of announcing to the world this stupendous and divine prodigy has been entrusted.

d *I am a witness of the resurrection*. My task is that of sustaining and increasing the faith in those who have come to believe in Him. I have given new courage to those who were thinking that all was now finished; I have asked the pious women to go quickly to the sepulchre, which I knew was already empty; I have confirmed the faith of the Apostles, telling them how Jesus had first shown Himself to me in the splendor of his divine glory.

e The Gospels have not spoken of this, because my task as Mother is that of being the *silent witness of the resurrection*.

f As I had been a silent presence at the word announced by Him during the years of his public mission, so too I had to be a silent presence at the word which now had to be proclaimed by the Church.

g But there has been entrusted to the Mother the joyous task of bearing witness in life that *my Son Jesus Christ has risen and is sitting at the right hand of his Heavenly Father in the glory of paradise*.

h *I am today a witness of the resurrection*. In these times, when the historical fact of his resurrection is being denied or placed in doubt by many, I charge you, my beloved ones, to announce with force and to give witness with courage to the wonderful event of *Christ Risen*.

i If Christ had not risen, vain would be your faith.

If Christ had not risen, useless would be the announcement of his Gospel.

If Christ had not risen, there would be no reason for you to believe any longer in the truth of his word.

j *Christ is risen*, because He is God.

Christ is risen, because He had predicted it.

Christ is risen and has appeared in the divine splendor of his glory to the witnesses, chosen by Him beforehand.

Christ is risen and has appeared first of all to his Mother.

k I have contemplated Him, more resplendent than the sun, white as the snow, and his divine beauty has so impressed itself upon my life that, from that moment, I have begun to live paradise here below.

l And so, above all in your days, I invite you all, my dearly beloved ones, to announce with courage his death, to proclaim with force his resurrection, to await with certitude his coming in glory."

594 Fatima (Portugal); May 8, 1997
Twenty-fifth Anniversary of the Birth
of the Marian Movement of Priests

The Message of Fatima Is Reaching Its Fulfillment

a "I receive with joy the homage of the Marian Movement of Priests, which you are offering to me, on this day which recalls the twenty-fifth anniversary of its birth. You are here in the very same place, before the little Chapel of the Apparitions, where I have revealed to your heart the great plan of love and mercy of my Immaculate Heart. I have chosen you, my poor little child, to be, you yourself, the instrument of this plan of mine.

b Thus, during these years, I have led you through all parts of the world, and with toils and sufferings without number, you have visited several times many of the countries of the five continents.

c Now my plan is about to be completed. With my Marian Movement of Priests, I have called all my children to consecrate themselves to my Immaculate Heart.

d *It is the message of Fatima which is reaching its fulfillment* and is being realized everywhere, through the merciful action of your heavenly Mother. Through it I have asked for the consecration to my Immaculate Heart, as a sure means of obtaining conversion of heart and of life, and of leading humanity back along the road of its full return to the Lord.

e   By means of my Marian Movement of Priests, this consecration, willed and requested by me, has now been made in every part of the earth. Thus I have been able to form for myself the cohort of my little children, with which I will bring to completion my greatest victory.

f   *It is the message of Fatima which is being fulfilled* in the spread, now on a world-wide level, of the cenacles which I have asked of you, in order to gather you together in prayer, made with me and through me. With great joy I accept today from your hands, my little son, the homage which you are offering to me in these cenacles, which are being multiplied everywhere, among priests and faithful, among children, youth and above all in families.

g   With these cenacles, you are able to obtain the grace of conversion for many poor sinners, especially for those most in need of divine mercy.

h   With these cenacles, you offer a great force of intercession and of reparation to your heavenly Mother, who has intervened many times, in an extraordinary way, to shorten the painful time of the great purifying trial.

i   With these cenacles, you invoke the gift of the second Pentecost, which is now close at hand, because my Immaculate Heart has become the new spiritual cenacle, where this divine prodigy for the Church and all humanity will be accomplished.

j   *It is the message of Fatima which is being fulfilled* in your pledge of love, of prayer and of unity with the Pope and with the Church united to him. Here, I have predicted and have shown in a vision to the little children to whom I appeared, the sufferings, the oppositions, and the bloody trials of the Pope. These prophecies of mine are being fulfilled above all in this Pope of mine, John Paul the Second, who is the masterpiece formed in my Immaculate Heart.

k   With your pledge of love and prayer, you are his comfort and his consolation at the moment of his greatest sacrifice. With your docility and obedience, you become his most effective means of assistance, in order that his Magisterium be everywhere received, heeded and followed. With your unity with him, you are confirmed in remaining in the true faith, in the present times foretold here by me, when the faith is being lost by many of my children, because of the errors which are being taught and spread about more and more.

l   I have caused to spring up here, for twenty-five years now, my Marian Movement of Priests, *so that the message of Fatima, often contested and rejected by many, might in your days come to its complete fulfillment.*

m   Its fulfillment is necessary for you, my children, threatened and stricken, so that you may attain salvation. Its fulfillment is necessary for the Church, so wounded and crucified, so that from its painful and bloody trial it might emerge all beautiful, without spot or wrinkle, in imitation of its heavenly Mother. Its fulfillment is necessary for all humanity, so that it may return to the arms of its Father and come to know the new times of its full communion of love and of life with its Lord and God.

n   As of now, this plan of mine is being fulfilled with the triumph of my Immaculate Heart in the world.

o   I bless you, my little son, together with my Pope, with the bishops, the priests and the faithful of my Movement, spread through every part of the world. I bless you with love and joy. I bless you with the gratitude of a Mother, who has been listened to, followed, consoled and glorified by you."

595
Marseille (France); May 18, 1997
Solemnity of Pentecost

In the Light of His Truth

a   "My little son, continue this wearying journey throughout all of France, in order to hold everywhere wonderful cenacles with the priests and the faithful of my Movement. This is my hour. This is the hour when I want to gather you all into the spiritual cenacle of my Immaculate Heart. Here, the prodigy of the second Pentecost for the Church and for all humanity will soon take place.

b   *The Holy Spirit will give his perfect testimony.*

c   It is the testimony of the Holy Spirit which will convince the world of sin.

d   *In the light of his truth,* all humanity will understand the abyss into which it has allowed itself to be led by Satan who, in it [humanity] and by means of it, has wanted to repeat the proud gesture of his rejection of God and of his Law.

e   Thus humanity has arrived at building a civilization without God, has given itself a morality contrary to his Law, has justified every form of evil and of sin, and has allowed itself to be seduced by materialism, hatred, violence and impurity.

f   By the divine fire of the Holy Spirit, humanity will be completely purified, that it may again become that new garden where the Most Holy Trinity will receive its greatest glory.

g   It is the testimony of the Holy Spirit which will profoundly renew the Church.

h   *In the light of his truth,* the Church will see herself in all her human weakness and will be healed of her crisis of faith; she will be set free from the snares of errors, which have spread the deep wound of apostasy and infidelity within her.

i   Renewed by the divine fire of the Holy Spirit, the entire Church will reflect the glory of her Lord and will again become a faithful and chaste Spouse, all beautiful, without spot or wrinkle, in imitation of her heavenly Mother.

j   It is the testimony of the Holy Spirit which will bring you to an understanding of the whole and entire truth.

k   *In the light of his truth,* there will become apparent to all the saving power of the Gospel of Jesus, which will spread his divine splendor everywhere. And thus, Jesus will be listened to in his word, followed on the way traced out by Him, imitated in his life, and glorified in his Person.

l   *The hour has come when my Son Jesus must be glorified by all.* With the prodigy of the second Pentecost, humanity will acknowledge Jesus Christ as its Redeemer and as its only Savior.

m Then the Holy Spirit will open hearts and souls to welcome Christ, who will return to you in the splendor of his divine glory.

n Thus my Immaculate Heart will finally attain its great triumph."

596
Valdragone (San Marino); June 24, 1997
Solemnity of the Birth of St. John the Baptist
Spiritual Exercises in the Form of a Cenacle
with 28 Bishops and 300 Priests of the M.M.P.
from Europe, America, Africa, Asia and Oceania

Jesus Christ Is the Only Savior

a "You have come again this year to this mountain to live these days in a continuous cenacle of prayer and fraternity with your heavenly Mother. You have come in such large numbers, bishops and priests of my Movement from every part of the world.

b I look upon you with the delight of a Mother, who is listened to, followed and glorified by you. I unite myself to your prayer, which I gather up in my hands to present at the throne of the Most Holy and Divine Trinity. I help you to love one another as brothers, so that Jesus may have the joy of seeing his new commandment lived among you. I cause to descend into your souls the heavenly dew of grace, mercy, comfort, joy and peace.

c Follow me on the way that leads you to the Great Jubilee, along the path that has been indicated to you by my Pope, John Paul the Second. Let yourselves be carried in my Immaculate Heart to the encounter with Jesus Christ, your Redeemer and your only Savior.

d *Jesus Christ is the only Savior,* because He is the Eternal Word of the Father, who was incarnated in my virginal womb, was born, grew up and died upon the Cross for your redemption and your salvation.

e *Jesus Christ is the only Savior,* because He is the *Truth.* The perfect image of the Father, his Eternal Word, brings you the gift of the divine truth. His truth is contained in the Gospel. Beloved sons, be faithful and powerful proclaimers of the Gospel.

953

f See how the truth contained in the Gospel is obscured by rationalism and torn by the errors that are more and more widely spread about. Thus many are moving away from the true faith.

g Live to the letter the Gospel of my Son Jesus. Proclaim to the letter the Gospel that you are living. Do not stop spreading the light of the truth in the world, pervaded by the darkness of error and apostasy. Be the apostles of the new evangelization in a world that has become pagan, after almost two thousand years since the first proclamation of the Gospel.

h *Jesus Christ is the only Savior,* because He is the *Life.* Life is possessed by Him because He is God. Life is given to all by Him because He has obtained it for you by immolating Himself on the Cross for you. Life comes to you with grace, which makes you participate in the divine nature itself.

i Beloved sons, become the ministers of grace; become the bearers of life. For this reason, I ask you to be solicitous in the administration of the sacraments which Jesus has entrusted to you. Be, above all, available to minister the sacrament of Reconciliation, today so greatly neglected in many parts of the Church.

j Be the ministers of divine mercy. Through you, priests consecrated to me, let my motherly tenderness come down upon everyone. Seek out those who are far away; sustain the weak; pardon the sinners; console the afflicted; bring comfort to the sick; guide the uncertain; protect the little ones. Take everyone into your priestly arms, and carry them to the secure refuge of my Immaculate Heart.

k *Jesus Christ is the only Savior,* because He is the *Way.* He leads you to the Father in his Spirit of Love. He brings you along the path of perfect and eternal happiness. He prepares for you the longed-for final moment of your encounter in splendor with his divine glory.

l Jesus Christ is the only way that leads you to paradise. There is no other name given under heaven in which we can find salvation. Humanity is traveling along the way of its encounter with Him, which will take place when Jesus will return in glory to bring his reign into the world. Walk in the joyous expectation of his coming. Cross the threshold of hope, and live in peace, in joy, in serenity, in trust and in your filial abandonment.

m In these days of the cenacle, the Spirit of the Lord has descended upon each one of you and has placed in your hearts and souls the charism of his gifts. The Holy Spirit has confirmed you in your vocation and has given you light and strength in the fulfillment of your priestly ministry. Be faithful proclaimers of the truth; be solicitous bearers of life; be the light of hope and trust for everyone.

n During these days, I have healed so many wounds; I have placed the balm of comfort on much bitterness; I have dried hidden tears; I have inspired good resolutions; I have transformed hearts.

o Beloved sons, go forth from this cenacle in peace and joy. Become instruments of my peace in every part of the world. I am with you always. By means of you, I reveal myself to the Church and humanity. Through you, the triumph of my Immaculate Heart in the world is accomplished each day.

p With your loved ones, with those who have been entrusted to your ministry, I bless you in the name of the Father, and of the Son, and of the Holy Spirit."

597

Rubbio (Vicenza, Italy); August 6, 1997
Feast of the Transfiguration of the Lord

King of Eternal Glory

a "Climb with me the holy mountain of grace and holiness, that you may be illumined and transfigured by the glorious light of my Son Jesus. He is the only-begotten Son of the Father. He is the Word, eternally generated by the Father, consubstantial with Him, his perfect image and reflection of his divine splendor. He is the King of eternal glory.

b As He was transfigured on Mount Tabor in the presence of the three Apostles, Peter, James and John, so also will He manifest Himself to you in the splendor of his divine glory, if you climb with me the holy mountain of humility and littleness, of love and purity, of silence and prayer.

c The Father manifests his secrets only to children and little ones, while He hides them from the great and the learned. The Son reveals his divine splendor to you, little children formed and led by me with motherly kindness, upon the summit of holiness.

d   *King of eternal glory.* When the Word became flesh in my virginal womb, his divine splendor was completely veiled by the humanity He assumed. Thus his divinity was hidden by his humanity.

e   Look at the newborn Child placed in the manger, the little one in need of everything, the adolescent in the rhythm of his human development, the youth bent over his daily work, the man of sorrows who bears the weight of weakness, the rejection by his own, the condemnation to the gibbet, the scourging, the crowning with thorns, the crucifixion and death on the Cross!

f   See how his divinity becomes truly reduced to nothing under the painful limitations of his humanity. And still, with an act of unceasing and heroic faith, I adored my God in my Son Jesus, and with my soul, I always contemplated Him in the splendor of his divinity.

g   *King of eternal glory.* It is at the moment of his resurrection that his divinity is made manifest in all its splendor, in such a way as to assume into it even his humanity. In Jesus Risen, his humanity becomes divinized, because his is now a glorified body, just as it appeared to the three Apostles on Mount Tabor. 'And He was transfigured before them, and his face shone like the sun, and his garments became white as light.' (Mt 17:2)

h   In paradise, Jesus is now seated at the right hand of the Father, in the refulgence of his divinity. Today you must look more at the eternal glory of Jesus Christ. Many entertain doubts concerning his divine nature; they make of his word a matter of debate; they deny the historical fact of his resurrection.

i   Beloved sons, announce to all with courage the divinity of my Son Jesus. Let yourselves be surrounded by the splendor of his truth. Remember his death; proclaim his resurrection in the expectation of his coming in glory.

j   *King of eternal glory.* When Jesus will return in his divine glory and appear to all humanity, each one will be called to undergo the same experience as Peter, James and John underwent on Mount Tabor, because Jesus will manifest Himself in his splendor and his humanity will be completely transfigured in the most brilliant light of his divinity.

k   Then the whole universe will proclaim Jesus Christ as the

Son of God, the perfect Image of the Father, the Word made man, the one and only Savior, He through whom all things have been made and who has the power to subject all things to Himself. Jesus will bring his glorious kingdom into the world, and it will be a kingdom of holiness and grace, a kingdom of justice, of love and of peace.

l   Beloved sons, live in the joyous expectation of his glorious return. For this, I invite you to walk with me along the road of littleness and humility. In this way, the Father will reveal to you the secret of his Son; the Holy Spirit will lead you to an understanding of the whole and entire truth; Jesus Christ will manifest Himself to you in the splendor of his divine Person, so that He may be adored, loved and glorified by all as the *King of eternal glory.*"

598

Dongo (Como, Italy); August 15, 1997
Solemnity of the Assumption
of the Blessed Virgin Mary into Heaven

Resplendent Is the Queen at Your Right Hand

a   "Beloved sons, look today, with confidence and sure hope, at your heavenly Mother assumed into the glory of paradise, with body and soul. All the cohorts of the heavenly spirits prostrate themselves in profound veneration before their Queen, as I am raised to the highest part of heaven and am placed at the right hand of my Son Jesus. And all Paradise, with sweetest harmonies of lights and songs, which no one here below on earth could possibly hear, exalts me and proclaims: Resplendent, O Lord, is the Queen at your right hand.

b   *Resplendent is the Queen at your right hand.*

c   A person who is worthy of a very particular honor is placed on one's immediate right. When my Son Jesus, after having consigned Himself to death to obtain for you an eternal redemption, rises in the splendor of his divine glory and ascends into heaven, the Heavenly Father places Him at his right hand.

d   *At the right hand of the Father,* because there is bestowed upon Him that honor which is due to Him alone, as his only-begotten Son.

e   *At the right hand of the Father,* because, having completed the work of redemption, He has brought back all humanity, made a slave of sin, to full communion of life with God.

f   *At the right hand of the Father,* because Jesus is the only conqueror of the Evil One, of sin, of wickedness and of death.

g   *At the right hand of the Father,* because through Him the universe was created, and only to Him is given the power to subject all things to Himself, after having conquered and annihilated his enemies. 'The Lord says to my Lord: Sit at my right hand, till I make your enemies your footstool.' (Ps 110:1)

h   *The Heavenly Father,* placing Jesus Christ at his right hand, thus attributes to Him the greatest honor which is due to his only-begotten Son, to the Word made flesh, to the Redeemer, to the one and only Savior, and to the King of all the universe.

i   *Resplendent is the Queen at your right hand.*

j   When I am assumed to the glory of paradise, I am placed at the right hand of my Son. Jesus thus acknowledges the greatest honor that is due to me as his Virgin Mother, intimately associated with Him in the work of redemption, sharing in all his sufferings, called now to share in his divine power in glory.

k   *At the right hand of the Son,* because, with my *yes,* I gave my consent for Him to assume human nature in my most pure womb.

l   *At the right hand of the Son,* because I had been at his side during every moment of his life, drinking together with Him the chalice of much bitterness.

m   *At the right hand of the Son,* because beneath the Cross, with my immaculate and maternal sorrow, I have become true Coredemptrix, offering my Son Jesus to the Father as the price of your ransom.

n   *At the right hand of the Son,* because, in Him and by means of Him, I have achieved the victory over the Evil One, over sin and over death which entered into the world as a chastisement for the sin committed by the first parents.

o   *At the right hand of the Son,* because now I share in his divine power to subject all things to Himself.

p   *At the right hand of the Son,* that I may exercise close to Him my spiritual function as Mother of the Church and of all humanity.

q   *At the right hand of the Son,* I pray for you, intercede on your behalf, assist you and help you in the terrible struggle against Satan and all the wicked spirits, against evil and sin, so that one day Christ may conquer the power which death still has over you.

r   Thus, at the end of the world, when Jesus will raise you up for his final and universal judgment, you too, my children, may ascend up here into paradise, and then, you will be placed at the right hand of the Son and of your heavenly Mother to enjoy with them forever perfect and eternal happiness."

599

Milan (Italy); September 8, 1997
Feast of the Nativity of the Blessed Virgin Mary

Round About My Cradle

a   "Beloved sons, celebrate with love and confidence the feast of my nativity, and join in the joy of all the Church, which gathers in an act of profound veneration about the cradle where I am placed after my birth. Let yourselves be drawn by my sweet and heavenly fragrance.

b   *Round about my cradle,* all Paradise gathers in exultation, because the Most Holy Trinity is receiving its greatest glory. The Heavenly Father contemplates with pleasure the masterpiece of his love, which from all eternity He had decreed in the plan of his divine wisdom. The Word rejoices because He can at last see that creature whom He Himself has prepared as Mother for his birth in time. The Holy Spirit exults, because I am possessed by Him as his sacred and inviolate temple for his divine plan.

c   *Round about my cradle,* there gather all the heavenly spirits, because they contemplate in the little child just born, she who is destined to become their Queen. And they compose sweetest harmonies of songs and lights, which fill my soul with joy and cause my Heart to tremble, this Heart which has hardly begun to give forth its first throbs of love.

d *Round about my cradle,* gather today, all of you my children, called by me to consecrate yourselves to my Immaculate Heart, to be part of my victorious army. Learn from me to be little. Let yourselves be formed by me in order to become servants. Enter into my cradle, that you may experience with me the beauty and the delightfulness of littleness and humility. You must all walk today along the way of littleness.

e Satan is at the peak of his great power and feels that he is now the sure victor. He can now be defeated only by humility and the littleness of children consecrated to my Immaculate Heart. For this, I am leading you along the way of humility, of littleness, of simplicity, of innocence, of trust and of your greatest filial abandonment.

f *Round about my cradle,* in which I place all of you today, Jesus experiences the great joy of feeling Himself listened to, loved and followed by you. He knows that only the little and pure of heart know how to listen with docility to his words and to put them into practice. He gathers into the precious garden of his divine love the humble, the poor, the simple, the weak. He sees Himself ever followed with faithfulness by my little children, who are poor in spirit and in goods, and with them He is forming his disciples, who again today will remain with Him even to the end.

g *Round about my cradle,* there are reflected today the powerful rays of trust and of firm hope, to brighten up the painful days in which you are living and to give you motherly comfort in the sufferings and in the great agony of these last times.

h Allow yourselves to be enveloped by my light; welcome with love and docility the words which I give you, because with these I lead you along the road of goodness and holiness.

i In you, I am being consoled and glorified, because, by the

960

response which you have everywhere given me, I now see close at hand the dawn of the new times for the Church and for all humanity."

600

Sale (Alessandria, Italy); October 1, 1997
Feast of St. Therese of the Child Jesus

Merciful Love

a "Beloved sons, enter into the spiritual cenacle of my Immaculate Heart, so that I may have you penetrate into the divine mystery of the merciful love of my Son Jesus.

b *Jesus is Merciful Love,* because in Him is reflected the divine mercy of the Father, who has so loved the world that He has sent it his only-begotten Son for its salvation. In Jesus, the mercy of the Father becomes personified and realizes itself in the plan of salvation. By means of Him, the Father causes his pardon to descend upon humanity, which had wandered away because of sin, and brings it back to a full communion of love and of life with its Lord and its Creator.

c *Jesus is Merciful Love,* because, by making Himself man, He takes upon Himself the fragility, weakness and the suffering of all humanity. When a baby, He carries in his Heart the wails and the sighs of all the babies of the world; as a youth, He lives through all the vicissitudes and difficulties of youth, so fragile and exposed to the impetuous wind of the passions; when He reaches maturity, He carries within his divine Person the problems, the anguish, and the pains of everyone.

d He bows down over the poor to announce to them the Gospel of salvation; He proclaims freedom to prisoners; He comforts the abandoned, pardons sinners, heals the sick, consoles the afflicted, and drives out Satan from those he had possessed.

e *Jesus is Merciful Love,* because He is meek and humble of heart. Let yourselves be drawn after his meekness. See how He is gentle, tender, and compassionate to all; docile and meek, He lets Himself be led by his enemies, like a lamb which is being carried to its bloody sacrifice.

f   Let yourselves be possessed by his humility. The first becomes the last; the Master becomes the disciple; the Lord puts Himself at the service of all. The fullness of his divinity becomes hidden in Him under the human veil of his humility. 'Learn from me; for I am gentle and lowly in heart, and you will find rest for your souls.' (Mt 11:29)

g   *Jesus is Merciful Love,* because He wants to draw all into the burning furnace of his divine love. Allow yourselves to be drawn by Him. Do not resist his calls. Walk with me along the road of his divine love. Beloved sons, you too must make your own the sweet experience of your love for Jesus.

h   Today you are celebrating the liturgical memorial of Saint Therese of the Child Jesus, which is occurring on the first centenary of her birth into heaven. Today I give her to all of you as your little sister. It was she who consecrated herself as a victim to the merciful love of Jesus. It was she who allowed herself to be completely consumed by the burning furnace of his divine charity.

i   Imitate her in this, her little way. You too must become little, simple, humble, meek and gentle. You must become, all of you, little children, traveling along the way of spiritual childhood which she has traced out for you.

j   You too must offer yourselves as victims to the merciful love of Jesus, so that, through you, He may very soon shed upon the world the great prodigy of divine mercy."

601   *Sale (Alessandria, Italy); November 21, 1997*
Feast of the Presentation of the Blessed Virgin Mary

Conformed to Jesus Crucified

a   "Beloved sons, let yourselves be carried into the heavenly temple of my Immaculate Heart, so that I can make you more and more conformed to my Son Jesus. Your priestly life must be conformed in all things to that of Jesus. He wants to live in you in all his fullness. You must become his word, lived out and proclaimed to all with courage and fidelity, in such a way that the light of the Gospel may brighten up the dense darkness which envelops the world.

b   His merciful love wants to manifest itself and to draw all souls into the burning fire of his divine charity, especially those furthest away, the straying, those who are lying prostrate under bondage to evil and sin. Jesus works the prodigy of divine mercy, above all through your priestly suffering. For this, the moment has come when I wish to render all of you conformed to Jesus Crucified.

c   *Conformed to Jesus Crucified*, in your daily priestly ministry. The times have come when you, my beloved sons, must drink to the dregs the bitter chalice which the Heavenly Father has prepared for you. Interior sufferings are increasing, those caused by your own limitations, by human misery, by feeling in life the weight of your very great weakness. Also increasing are the intimate sufferings caused by the misunderstanding and rejection, often on the part of those close to you. I am asking you to taste, you also, the painful hour of Gethsemane.

d   *Conformed to Jesus Crucified*, especially in your many exterior sufferings. I have need of your priestly suffering. For each one of you also, I have prepared the moment of your own particular crucifixion.

e   For this reason, my little son, I have asked of you much suffering, caused by the painful heart operation which you have had to undergo. You have offered everything to me with great docility and filial abandonment, and this has greatly supported the plan of my Immaculate Heart.

f   It is above all with the physical sufferings, borne by you with docility and love, that I am conforming you to my Crucified Son, while I am at your side with the same motherly concern with which I stood close to Jesus in the bloody moments of his passion and his immolation on the Cross.

g   *Conformed to Jesus Crucified*, beloved sons, now that you are approaching the fulfillment of my plan, for which I have been forming and cultivating you for years with motherly urgency and jealousy.

h   Take courage, resume the journey in trust and hope. You are approaching moments of grace in which you will see flow out upon the world the torrents of divine mercy. The world will then be purified by this divine fire of love, and it will be completely renewed, so that Jesus may bring into your midst his kingdom of grace and of holiness, of justice, of love and of peace.

i   For this, I am asking you to second, each day, my motherly action, which seeks to make you all more and more *conformed to Jesus Crucified.*"

602   Vacallo (Switzerland); December 8, 1997
Solemnity of the Immaculate Conception

Open the Doors to Christ

a   "Look today at the heavenly splendor of your immaculate Mother, and let yourselves be drawn, each and all, by the waves of my sweet fragrance.

b   I am the Immaculate Conception.

I am all beautiful: *tota pulchra.*

I am the living tabernacle of the Most Holy Trinity, where the Father is everlastingly glorified, the Son perfectly loved, and the Holy Spirit fully possessed.

I am the door which opens upon your salvation. My motherly task is that of preparing you to receive my Son who is coming.

c   *Open the doors to Christ.* Jesus has come into your midst on the day of his earthly birth, by means of me, his virginal Mother, in order to become your Savior and your sole Redeemer.

d   Contemplate Him with purity of heart and with a look of love, at the moment when He is born of me and placed in a manger, feeling the rigors of the cold and the chill of a world which ignores and rejects Him. This little Child who is crying is God-with-us, is the Redeemer of the world, is the only Savior. Without Him, it is not possible for man to find salvation.

e   *Open the doors to Christ.* Open the doors of your mind, to receive his divine word with humility and docility. In the deep darkness which envelops the minds of a humanity submerged in errors, only his word brings you the light of truth. Make the announcement of his Gospel shine forth in the world. Carry out the task of a new evangelization which has been entrusted to you.

f   Bring, once again today, his word to the poor, the sinners, the sick, the prisoners, so that they may all walk in the light of the truth.

g   *Open the doors to Christ.* Open the doors of your soul to receive Him in a worthy manner at the moment when He communicates Himself to you under the Eucharistic species. It is Jesus in his divine Person, with his glorious body and his divinity, whom you receive when you approach Holy Communion. You must prepare in your souls a dwelling place which should be worthy of Him.

h   For this reason, I urge you to flee from sin, to not allow yourselves to become possessed by sin, to live always in the grace and love of God. If ever it should happen that you fall into mortal sin, sacramental confession is necessary before receiving Holy Communion. Today my Heart bleeds to see how *sacrilegious communions* are spreading more and more, because many come to receive Jesus in the Eucharist in a state of mortal sin without having gone to confession.

i   Therefore, let your souls be filled with grace and holiness, so that you may receive Jesus in a worthy manner when He gives Himself to you in the sacrament of his love.

j   *Open the doors to Christ.* Open the doors of your heart, that you may welcome Him with the firmness of your love. Jesus brings you to the perfection of love. He loves in you; by means of you, his love spreads to all. He wants to love each person whom you meet along your way. By means of you, his divine charity spreads, and thus you become the instruments of the triumph of his merciful love.

k   *Open the doors to Christ.* Open the doors of your life to Christ when He returns in the splendor of his glory. The Christian life must be ever oriented to this expectation. And so, I invite you to live in trust and in a great hope. Let yourselves be carried with filial abandonment in the arms of your Heavenly Father.

l Then, each day of this painful time will be lived by you in serenity and joy. Because the sufferings of the present moment are not comparable to the glory which awaits you, when Christ will manifest Himself and you will see Him as He is, in the blazing light of his divine splendor."

603

Enter with Me

a "*Enter with me*, beloved sons, into the cave where, on this holy night, my divine Child is born. Do not be disturbed by its squalor; do not be dismayed by its poverty; do not be saddened by its solitude. This cave is a sweet shelter for our weariness; it is a safe refuge for our pilgrimage; it is a cradle chosen by the Heavenly Father for the human birth of his only-begotten Son.

b *Enter with me* into the cave in silence and in an act of profound adoration. The Eternal Word of the Father is born to his human life; He is placed in a manger; He is glorified by the angels, adored by the shepherds, comforted and loved by me, his Virgin Mother, and by my most chaste spouse, Joseph.

c Understand, beloved sons, how much God has loved the world, so as to give it his very own Son. Contemplate with astonishment the manger: the Son of God has chosen to be born in poverty, in humility, in solitude, in pain and in tears.

d Feel with me the intense desire to cover Him with every kind of gratitude; warm Him with the kiss of your priestly love; clothe Him with the white garments of your virtues; wipe away his tears with the precious linen of your immolation; adore Him together with the shepherds, with the purity of your prayer; clasp Him to your heart as your only and greatest treasure.

e *Enter with me* into this dark cave, if you wish to share in the splendor of his divine dwelling.

f *Enter with me* into the fullness of time. This holy night brings time to its fullness. The time has been ordained by God in which to prepare for the human birth of the Son. From Adam to Noah,

966

from Abraham to David, from the patriarchs and the prophets, time has been marked by a long and ardent waiting for his coming.

g   On this holy night, the time of the first Advent is fulfilled, because a Child is born to you, Emmanuel, God-with-us. The very Son of God shares in the human fragility, which becomes apparent in a particular way in his birth, in his growth, in his adolescence, and in his youth. He carries the burden of all sufferings and offers Himself, as a gentle lamb, in his cruel Sacrifice for your redemption and your salvation.

h   Humanity is redeemed; man is saved; time reaches its apex when it marks the precious moment of universal redemption. As of this night, a new journey begins for humanity, illuminated by the hope and expectation of his second coming in glory.

i   *Enter with me* into the fullness of time, which will take place when Jesus returns in the splendor of his divine glory. This, his first coming, will reach its full significance only at his second coming. This holy night is ordained to the radiant day that will have no dusk.

j   My divine Child, whom you now contemplate in the manger and who cries and shivers from the cold, will one day return in the power of his divine glory and will bring time and history to its fullness. Time and history will reach their completion; with his divine and glorious presence, He will make all things new.

k   You are living out the mystery of this second Advent, which is preparing you to receive Jesus, when He returns to you on the clouds of heaven.

Only then will the second Advent through which you are living reach its fulfillment.

Then time will attain its fullness.

Then will the Immaculate Heart of your heavenly Mother attain her triumph, in the definitive and glorious triumph of her Son Jesus.

l   *Enter with me* into the fullness of time, and prepare yourselves to live the Great Jubilee, for which my Pope is preparing you, which will cause the ineffable light of the Divine and Most Holy Trinity to come down upon the world."

All Has Been Revealed to You

a "Beloved sons, in silence and in prayer, spend with me the final hours of this year which is about to end. Do not spend them in dissipation and entertainments, as so many of my children do.

b This year has been particularly important for my plan. You are now entering into my times. For this, I have traced out for you a light-filled way, along which all of you must walk, in order to live the consecration which you have made to my Immaculate Heart.

c *Now all has been revealed to you.*

d *All has been revealed to you:* my plan has been prophetically announced to you at Fatima, and during these years, I have been carrying it out through my Marian Movement of Priests. This has been revealed to you *in its gradual preparation.*

e This century of yours, which is about to end, has been placed under the sign of a strong power conceded to my Adversary. Thus, humanity has been led astray by the error of theoretical and practical atheism; in the place of God, idols have been built which everyone adores: pleasure, money, amusement, power, pride and impurity.

f Truly Satan, with the cup of lust, has succeeded in seducing all the nations of the earth. He has replaced love with hatred; communion with division; justice with many injustices; peace with continuous war. In fact this entire century has been spent under the sign of cruel and bloody wars, which have claimed millions of innocent victims.

g So then, the Most Holy Trinity has decreed that your century be placed under the sign of my powerful, maternal and extraordinary presence. Thus, at Fatima I pointed out the way along which humanity must journey for its return to the Lord: that of conversion, prayer and penance. And as a safe refuge, I offered you my Immaculate Heart.

h   *All has been revealed to you:* my plan has been pointed out to you even *in its painful realization.* Humanity has fallen under the domination of Satan and of his great power, exercised with the satanic and masonic forces; my Church has become obscured by his smoke which has penetrated into it. Errors are being taught and propagated, causing many to lose true faith in Christ and in his Gospel; the holy Law of God is openly violated; sin is committed and often even justified, and thus the light of grace and of the divine presence is lost; unity is deeply split apart by a strong contestation directed against the Magisterium, and especially against the Pope; and the wound caused by painful lacerations becomes ever wider.

i   In order to give the suffering and crucified Church of your time my motherly help and a safe refuge, I have brought the Marian Movement of Priests into being and have spread it through every part of the world by means of my book, which traces out for you the road along which you must journey in order to spread my light. With this book, I teach you to live the consecration to my Immaculate Heart with the simplicity of children, in a spirit of humility, of poverty, of trust and of filial abandonment.

j   I have now been guiding you for twenty-five years, with the words which I have spoken to the heart of this, my little son, whom I have chosen as an instrument for the realization of my maternal plan. During these years I myself have carried him several times to every part of the world, and he has allowed himself to be led with docility, small and fearful but totally abandoned to me, like a little baby in the arms of his mother.

k   As of now, all that I had to say to you has been said, because *all has been revealed to you.*

l   Therefore, on this night, there come to an end the public messages, which I have been giving you for twenty-five years; now you must meditate on them, live them and put them into practice. Then the words which I have caused to come down from my Immaculate Heart, as drops of heavenly dew upon the desert of your life, so threatened by snares, will produce fruits of grace and holiness.

m   From now on, I will manifest myself through the word, the person and the actions of this, my little son, whom I have chosen

969

to be your guide and whom I am now leading to the painful summit of his mission.

n   *All has been revealed to you:* my plan has been foretold to you especially *in its wonderful and victorious fulfillment.*

o   I have announced to you the triumph of my Immaculate Heart in the world. *In the end my Immaculate Heart will triumph.*

p   This will come about in the greatest triumph of Jesus, who will bring into the world his glorious reign of love, of justice and of peace, and will make all things new.

q   Open your hearts to hope.
Throw open the doors to Christ who comes to you in glory.
Live the trembling hour of this second Advent.

r   Become thus the courageous heralds of this, his triumph, because you — little babes consecrated to me who live from my very own spirit — are the apostles of these last times.

s   Live as faithful disciples of Jesus, in contempt for the world and for yourselves, in poverty, in humility, in silence, in prayer, in mortification, in charity and in union with God, while you are unknown and despised by the world.

t   *The moment has come for you to come out from your hiddenness in order to go and shed light upon the earth.*

u   Show yourselves to all as my children, for I am with you always. Let the faith be the light which enlightens you in these days of darkness, and let zeal alone consume you, zeal for the honor and glory of my Son Jesus.

v   Fight, children of the light, because the hour of my battle has now arrived. In the harshest of winters, you are the buds which are opening up from my Immaculate Heart and which I am placing on the branches of the Church to tell you that her most beautiful springtime is about to arrive.

w   This will be for her the second Pentecost. For this reason, I invite you to repeat often in the cenacles, the prayer that I have asked of you:'Come, Holy Spirit, come by means of the powerful intercession of the Immaculate Heart of Mary, your well-beloved Spouse.'

x   With the love of a Mother who, during these years, has been listened to, followed and glorified by you, I bless you all in the name of the Father, and of the Son, and of the Holy Spirit."

970

Vatican, Dec. 20, 1989: Encounter following the concelebration of Mass in the Holy Father's private chapel.

Vatican, Dec. 21, 1995: After having concelebrated Mass
with the Holy Father in his private chapel.

REPUBLIC OF SAN MARINO (ITALY)

June 22 - 28, 1997: International Retreat/Cenacle in San Marino. In attendance were 1 Cardinal, 24 bishops and 300 priests and national directors of the M.M.P. from five continents.

REPUBLIC OF SAN MARINO (ITALY)

June 22 – 28, 1997: Cardinal and bishops in attendance at the Retreat/Cenacle in San Marino.

REPUBLIC OF SAN MARINO (ITALY)

June 23 - 29, 1996: Spiritual Exercises in the form of a cenacle with one Cardinal, 21 bishops, and 328 priests, mainly national and regional directors of the MMP from five continents.

June 25 - July 1, 1995: Spiritual Exercises in the form of a cenacle with bishops and national and regional directors of the MMP from around the World. (Mass)

Effingham, IL – Oct. 10-14, 1994: Spiritual Exercises in the form of a cenacle with bishops and priests of the MMP of the North American continent.

U.S.A.

Effingham, IL – Oct. 10-14, 1994: Conference during the Spiritual Exercises in the form of a cenacle with bishops and priests of the MMP from North America.

Providence, RI – Oct. 25, 1994: Fr. Gobbi with bishops, priests and deacons following Cenacle and Mass at Cathedral of SS. Peter and Paul.

U.S.A.

St. Petersburg, FL – Nov. 10, 1994: Consecration of infants during cenacle at Cathedral of St. Jude the Apostle.

Marietta, GA – Nov. 4, 1994: Consecration of infants during cenacle at St. Ann's Church.

Cincinnati, OH – Oct. 17, 1994: Fr. Gobbi presides over cenacle with priests and deacons of the MMP.

U.S.A.

Waterbury, CT – Oct. 26, 1994: Fr. Gobbi presides over cenacle with bishop, priests and deacons of the MMP.

Lewiston, ME – Oct. 29, 1994: Cenacle with priests and laity.

Santa Fe, NM – Sept. 28, 1994: Cenacle at Paolo Soleri,
Indian School with 5,000 in attendance.

Greenville, SC – Nov. 3, 1994: Cenacle with priests and laity.

Birmingham, AL – Nov. 9, 1994: Cenacle with Mother Angelica and sisters.

Combermere, Ontario – Aug. 1983: Fr. Gobbi with bishops, priests and the national director from English-speaking Canada.

Edmonton, Alberta – September 19, 1994: Cenacle with priests and laity.

Montreal, Quebec – Sept. 14, 1990: Concelebration of
the Mass during cenacle with priests and laity.

AUSTRALIA

Melbourne – Dec. 4, 1993: Clergy Cenacle with Fr. Gobbi.

Jakarta (Cisarua) – Oct. 19-22, 1993: Spiritual Exercises in the form of a cenacle with priests of the MMP from Indonesia.

MEXICO

Guadalajara – Nov. 28, 1994: Cenacle with 400 Seminarians.

Leon – Nov. 27, 1994: Cenacle with 20,000 faithful of the MMP in the city stadium.

Loreto – Basilica of the Holy House – April 2, 1981: Fr. Gobbi and MMP priests following regional cenacle with 150 priests and 3,000 faithful.

GERMANY

Altötting – Aug. 26-31, 1984: Spiritual Exercises in the form of a cenacle with the priests of the MMP of the German language.

Oita (Japan), June 2, 1978: Cenacle with priests and nuns.

Nairobi (Kenya), Dec. 3, 1979: Cenacle with seminarians.

Jerusalem – March 5, 1982: Fr. Gobbi during the Eucharistic concelebration with 17 priests of the MMP from Jerusalem at a cenacle for priests and laity.

Tabga – March 3, 1982: Fr. Gobbi concelebrating Mass with priests of the MMP.

Onisha (Anambra State, Nigeria) – Nov., 1983: Eucharistic
procession during cenacle with priests and faithful.

Kinshasha (Zaire) – May, 1981: Cenacle with Seminarians.

SOUTH AMERICA – BRAZIL

Sao Paulo – March 26-29, 1992: Spiritual Exercises with Fr. Gobbi
and 250 lay apostles, 4 bishops and 60 priests from all of Brazil.

Jauru – Feb. 3, 1990: Cenacle with 4,000 children from neighboring villages.

Córdoba (Argentina) – March 22, 1992: Cenacle with 6,000 faithful.

Santiago (Chile) – March 11, 1992: Cenacle with bishops, priests
and seminarians at the Church of the Blessed Sacrament.

SOUTH AMERICA - ECUADOR/BOLIVIA

Ibarra (Ecuador) - Feb. 28, 1992: Cenacles with Fr. Gobbi, Archbishop B. Echeverria Ruiz (now Cardinal) and seminarians of "La Esperanza" Major Seminary.

La Paz (Bolivia) - March 25, 1990: Cenacle in Santa Cruz de la Sierra with 7,000 faithful and the Auxiliary Bishop, Mons. Tito Solares, who did the translation.

Lima (Peru) – March 5, 1992: Cenacle with Fr. Gobbi and groups of religious from various communities of contemplative life.

Caracas (Venezuela) – Cenacle with the faithful in "El Paradiso" stadium.

CENTRAL AMERICA – EL SALVADOR/HONDURAS

Ilobasco (El Salvador) – Feb. 13, 1994: Outdoor cenacle
with the bishop, and priests and laity of the MMP.

Managaya (Honduras) – Feb. 11, 1994: Cenacle with priests and laity of the MMP.

Masaya – Feb. 9, 1992: Cenacle with the faithful.

Managua – Feb. 7, 1992: Private audience with the President of the Republic, who with Fr. Gobbi consecrated her country to the Immaculate Heart of Mary.

Seoul (Korea) – Oct. 1, 1987: Cenacle with the faithful.

Santiago (Dominican Republic) – Dec. 8, 1994: Cenacle with the faithful.

DOMINICAN REPUBLIC

Santiago – Dec. 8, 1994: Cenacle with the bishop and priests of the diocese of Santiago.

Santo Domingo – Dec. 13, 1994: Cenacle in the major seminary with two bishops, priests and seminarians.

ACTS OF CONSECRATION TO
THE IMMACULATE HEART
OF MARY

ACT OF CONSECRATION
TO THE
IMMACULATE HEART OF MARY
(for Priests)

Virgin of Fatima, Mother of Mercy, Queen of Heaven and Earth, Refuge of Sinners, we who belong to the Marian Movement of Priests, called to form the cohort of your priests, today consecrate ourselves in a very special way to your Immaculate Heart.

By this act of consecration we intend to live, with you and through you, all the obligations assumed by our baptismal and priestly consecration.

We further pledge to bring about in ourselves that interior conversion that will free us of all human attachment to ourselves, our career, our comforts, or to easy compromises with the world so that, like you, we may be available only to do always the Will of the Lord.

And as we resolve to entrust to you, O Mother most sweet and merciful, our priesthood, so that you may dispose of it for all your designs of salvation in this hour of decision that weighs upon the world, we pledge to live it according to your desires, especially as it pertains to a renewed spirit of prayer and penance, the fervent celebration of the Holy Eucharist and of the Liturgy of the Hours, the daily recitation of the holy rosary, the offering of Holy Mass in your honor on the first Saturday of every month, and a religious and austere manner of life, that shall be a good example to all.

We further promise you the greatest loyalty to the Gospel, of which we shall always be genuine and courageous heralds, even, if necessary, to the shedding of our blood. We promise loyalty to the Church, for whose service we have been consecrated.

Above all, we wish to be united with the Holy Father and the hierarchy, firmly adhering to all their directives, so as thus to set up a barrier to the growing confrontation directed against the Magisterium, that threatens the very foundation of the Church.

Under your maternal protection, we want moreover to be apostles of this sorely needed unity of prayer and love for the Pope, on whom we invoke your special protection.

And lastly, we promise to lead the faithful entrusted to our care to a renewed devotion to you.

Mindful that atheism has caused shipwreck in the faith to a great number of the faithful, that desecration has entered into the holy temple of God, not sparing even many of our brother-priests, and that evil and sin are spreading more and more throughout the world, we make so bold as to lift our eyes trustingly to you, O Mother of Jesus and our merciful and powerful Mother, and we invoke again today and await from you the salvation of all your children, O clement, O loving, O sweet Virgin Mary.

(with ecclesiastical approval)

ACT OF CONSECRATION
TO THE
IMMACULATE HEART OF MARY
(for Religious and Laity)

Virgin of Fatima, Mother of Mercy, Queen of Heaven and Earth, Refuge of Sinners, we who belong to the Marian Movement of Priests consecrate ourselves in a very special way to your Immaculate Heart.

By this act of consecration we intend to live, with you and through you, all the obligations assumed by our baptismal consecration. We further pledge to bring about in ourselves that interior conversion so urgently demanded by the Gospel, a conversion that will free us of every attachment to ourselves and to easy compromises with the world so that, like you, we may be available only to do always the Will of the Father.

And as we resolve to entrust to you, O Mother most sweet and merciful, our life and vocation as Christians, that you may dispose of it according to your designs of salvation in this hour of decision that weighs upon the world, we pledge to live it according to your desires, especially as it pertains to a renewed spirit of prayer and penance, the fervent participation in the celebration of the Eucharist and in the works of the apostolate, the daily recitation of the holy rosary, and an austere manner of life in keeping with the Gospel, that shall be to all a good example of the observance of the Law of God and the practice of the Christian virtues, especially that of purity.

A4

We further promise you to be united with the Holy Father, with the hierarchy and with our priests, in order thus to set up a barrier to the growing confrontation directed against the Magisterium, that threatens the very foundation of the Church.

Under your protection, we want moreover to be apostles of this sorely needed unity of prayer and love for the Pope, on whom we invoke your special protection.

And lastly, insofar as is possible, we promise to lead those souls with whom we come in contact to a renewed devotion to you.

Mindful that atheism has caused shipwreck in the faith to a great number of the faithful, that desecration has entered into the holy temple of God, and that evil and sin are spreading more and more throughout the world, we make so bold as to lift our eyes trustingly to you, O Mother of Jesus and our merciful and powerful Mother, and we invoke again today and await from you the salvation of all your children, O clement, O loving, O sweet Virgin Mary.

(with ecclesiastical approval)

ACT OF CONSECRATION
TO THE MOST BLESSED VIRGIN MARY

For Young People
(In the spirit of the Marian Movement of Priests)

Virgin of Fatima, my dearly beloved Mother,
I who belong to the Marian Movement of Priests,
consecrate myself today, in a very special way,
to your Immaculate Heart.

By this solemn act, I offer my whole life to you;
my heart, my soul, my body
and especially this time of my youth in which I am now living.

Guide me along the way
that Jesus has traced out for us:
the way of love, of goodness and of sanctity.

Help me to flee from sin, from evil
and from egoism, and to resist temptations
to violence, to impurity and to drugs.

I promise you to go to confession often
and to receive Jesus into my heart
as my spiritual food of life,
to observe the commandments of God
and to walk along the road of love and purity.

I want to be a witness of unity
by my great love for the Pope,
for my bishop and for my priests.

I love you, O sweetest Mother of mine,
and I offer you my youth
for the triumph of your Immaculate Heart in the world.

(with ecclesiastical approval)

IMMACULATE HEART OF MARY
International Hymn of the M.M.P.

Music: adaptation of
Portuguese Hymn
Lyrics: Fr. Stefano Gobbi

1. Im- ma-culate Heart of Ho — ly Ma — ry.
2. Your faith - ful priests of - fer you their con - se - cra - tion.
3. The faith- ful of - fer you their con - se - cra - tion.
4. And when our life here on earth is fin' - ly o - ver,

1. Im- ma-culate Heart of Ho — ly Ma — ry.
2. Your faith - ful priests of - fer you their con - se - cra - tion.
3. The faith- ful of - fer you their con - se - cra - tion.
4. And when our life here on earth is fin' - ly o - ver,

1. You are the light and way, You are the light and way,
2. Look down with your sweet love, hold - ing them near your heart.
3. Bring them to - ge - ther now, read - y for bat — tle,
4. Come and do not de - lay, Come and do not de - lay.

1. You bring God's light to your chil - dren on earth.
2. Make them to be just like Je - sus your Son.
3. So that your heart soon may tri - umph and reign.
4. Come, don't de - lay, lead your chil - dren to heav'n.

1. chil - dren on earth.
2. Je - sus your Son.
3. tri - umph and reign.
4. chil - dren to heav'n.

A7

DIARY INDEX

1973

THE MOVEMENT IS NOW BORN

1974

CENACLES OF LIFE WITH ME

1975

BE JOYOUS

1976

YOU MUST BE LITTLE

1977

IN EVERY PART OF THE WORLD

1978

YOUR PUBLIC MISSION

1979

THE SIGNS OF THE PURIFICATION

1980

YOUR VICTORIOUS MOTHER

1981
THE LIGHT AND GLORY OF THE LORD

1982
I AM A CONSOLING MOTHER

1983

OPEN WIDE THE GATES TO CHRIST
(Extraordinary Holy Year of the Redemption)

1984

I ASK THE CONSECRATION OF ALL

1985

I AM THE BEGINNING OF THE NEW TIMES

1986

QUEEN OF PEACE

1987

THE RISING DAWN
(Marian Year)

1988
SHED LIGHT UPON THE EARTH
(Marian Year)

1989

COME, LORD JESUS

1990

MOTHER OF THE SECOND ADVENT

1991

THE ANNOUNCEMENT OF THE NEW ERA

1992
YOUR LIBERATION IS NEAR

1993
THE TIME OF THE GREAT TRIAL

1994

OPEN YOUR HEARTS TO HOPE

1995
MOTHER OF MERCY

1996
IN MY SAFE REFUGE

1997

JESUS CHRIST IS THE ONLY SAVIOR

CENTERS OF DISTRIBUTION
FOR THE
ENGLISH LANGUAGE EDITION

AUSTRALIA & OCEANIA
THE MARIAN MOVEMENT OF PRIESTS
P.O. Box 636
Castle Hill, N.S.W. 2154, Australia

Rev. Fr. Lino Valente
St. Joseph's Parish
114 High St.
Stanthorpe Q. 4380, Australia

WEST AUSTRALIA
I. Nardizzi
5 Keaney Place
City Beach 6015 Perth, W. Australia

SOUTH AUSTRALIA
THE MARIAN MOVEMENT OF PRIESTS
P.O. Box 209
Belair, S.A. 5052
South Australia

CANADA
THE MARIAN MOVEMENT OF PRIESTS
Rev. Lawrence J. Faye, C.S.B.
1515 Bathurst Street
Toronto, Ontario M5P 3H4
Tel. 416-653-6814

DENMARK
Rev. Fr. Tran Duc Thanh
Sankt Marie Kirke
Mariegade 8
6100 Haderslev, Denmark

ENGLAND
THE MARIAN MOVEMENT OF PRIESTS
Rev. Michael J. Gaughran, S.S.C.
"Lyndhurst"
Park Road
Waterloo,
Liverpool, England L22 3XE

FIJI ISLANDS
THE MARIAN MOVEMENT OF PRIESTS
P.O. Box 1320
Suva, Fiji, South Pacific

GHANA
THE MARIAN MOVEMENT OF PRIESTS
Rev. Albert Kretschmer, S.V.D.
St. Kizito's Rectory
P.O. Box 3285
Accra, Ghana, Africa

GIBRALTAR
THE MARIAN MOVEMENT OF PRIESTS
Rev. George McGrail
Church of St. Paul's
Varyl Begg, Gibraltar

HONG KONG
Fr. Melchiorre Arnoldi
11, On Yin St., Chai Wan Kok
Tsuen Wan, Hong Kong

INDIA
THE MARIAN MOVEMENT OF PRIESTS
Rev. Rosario Stroscio, S.D.B.
Auxilium Parish
8A, Mahendra Roy Lane
Calcutta 700 046, India

THE MARIAN MOVEMENT OF PRIESTS
Rev. Anastasio Gomes, O.C.D.
Carmelite Seminary
Peddem, Mapusa
Goa 403 507, India

INDONESIA
Mgr. V. Kartosiswoyo
c/o Mrs. Naniek Hadibowo
Prof. Supomo SH No. 11A
Jakarta 12810, Indonesia
Tel. 830-3209

INDONESIA (Cont'd)
Rev. Fr. Hubert Hady
Seminari Menengah
Roh Kudus Tuka
Kotak Pos 18
Sempidi 80351, BALI, Indonesia

IRELAND
THE MARIAN MOVEMENT OF PRIESTS
Rev. Michael Maher, S.M.
Chanel College
Coolock, Dublin 5, Ireland

KENYA
THE MARIAN MOVEMENT OF PRIESTS
Rev. Richard Woulfe, C.S.Sp.
P.O. Box 40369
Nairobi, Kenya

LIBERIA
Rev. Larry Gilmore, S.D.B.
Salesians of Don Bosco
8th St., Sinkor
P.O. Box 2751
Monrovia, Liberia

MALAWI
Rev. Fr. V. Nzolima
Box 607
Zomba, Malawi, Africa

MALTA
Rev. Michael Agius, OFM Cap.
Capuchin Friary
Azzopardi Street
Marsa HMR 14, Malta

NEW ZEALAND
THE MARIAN MOVEMENT OF PRIESTS
P.O. Box 838
Wanganui, New Zealand

NIGERIA
THE MARIAN MOVEMENT OF PRIESTS
Rev. Charles Ohaeri
Holy Ghost Cathedral
P.O. Box 302
Ogui, Enugu, Nigeria

Rev. Ernest Simple Okoli
Christ the King Parish
P.O. Box 411
Onitsha, Anambra State, Nigeria

PAKISTAN
Rev. Tareq Rehmat
St. Patrick's Cathedral
Sadar
Karachi, Pakistan

PHILIPPINES
THE MARIAN MOVEMENT OF PRIESTS
Rev. Antonio B. Olaguer, S.J.
P.O. Box 17610, San Juan CPO
1500 San Juan, Metro Manila, Philippines
Tel. (02) 4104117

SAMOA
THE MARIAN MOVEMENT OF PRIESTS
Rev. J.M. Pusateri, S.M.
P.O. Box 751
Apia, Western Samoa

SCOTLAND
THE MARIAN MOVEMENT OF PRIESTS
Rev. Benedict O'Keeffe
St. Andrew's
Auchmead Road
Greenock (Renfrewshire)
Scotland PA16 0JU

SIERRA-LEONE
Rev. Cyprian N. Nwachukwu, M.S.P.
St. Teresa Catholic Church, Yonibana
P.O. Box 1
Makeni, Sierra-Leone

SINGAPORE
c/o Dr. Victor Wee Sip Leong
Kin Mun Clinic
Blk 66
Toa Payoh Lor 4
#01-319
Singapore 1231

SOUTH AFRICA
THE MARIAN MOVEMENT OF PRIESTS
Rev. Ronald Cairns, O.M.I.
Catholic Church Alexandra
P.O. Box 39084, Bramley
2018 Johannesburg, South Africa

SOUTH KOREA
THE MARIAN MOVEMENT OF PRIESTS
Rev. Joseph A. Slaby, M.M.
124 Uam 2-dong
Nam gu
Pusan 608-062, Korea

SRI LANKA
THE MARIAN MOVEMENT OF PRIESTS
Rev. Jude Nicholas Fernando
National Seminary
Ampitiya, Kandy, Sri Lanka

TANZANIA
THE MARIAN MOVEMENT OF PRIESTS
Rev. Msgr. Second Arbogast, V.G.
Moshi Cathedral
P.O. Box 3041
Moshi, Tanzania, Africa

THAILAND
Rev. Fr. Surin Chunfong
Bishop's House
31/2-4 Somboonkul Road
Ratchaburi 70000, Thailand

Mr. Sonthy Saratham
75 Soi Kingplu, St. Louis 3 Road
Sathorn, Bangkok 10120, Thailand
Tel. 286-5858 / Fax: 287-2751

TRINIDAD
THE MARIAN MOVEMENT OF PRIESTS
Rev. Dwight K. Merrick
20 Rust St.
St. Clair, Trinidad, W.I.

UGANDA
THE MARIAN MOVEMENT OF PRIESTS
Rev. Evarist Ssempijja
P.O. Box 14125
Mengo-Kampala
Uganda, E. Africa

UNITED STATES OF AMERICA
THE MARIAN MOVEMENT OF PRIESTS
Rev. Albert G. Roux
P.O. Box 8
St. Francis, Maine 04774-0008 U.S.A.

ZAMBIA
Rev. Clement Mwiila
Monze Parish
Box 660200
Monze, Zambia, Africa

ZIMBABWE
Rev. Peter Meiring, SJ
Braeside Catholic Church
PO Cranborne
Harare, Zimbabwe, Africa

CENTERS OF DISTRIBUTION
FOR EDITIONS
IN OTHER LANGUAGES

ARABIC

P. Jean Saadé
Collège Central
Jounieh, Lebanon
Tel. (0) 9-910900 / 914266 / 932850

M. Elie Rahal
Jounieh, Lebanon
Tel. (0) 9-290468

The Marian Movement of Priests
P.O. Box 8
St. Francis, Maine 04774-0008, U.S.A.

CHINESE

Fr. Melchiorre Arnoldi
Church of the Annunciation
11, On Yin St., Chai Wan Kok
Tsuen Wan, Hong Kong, R.O.C.

Rev. Joseph Siao
69 Kuitzu Rd.
Taishan, Taipei
Hsien (243) Taiwan, R.O.C.

Rev. Thomas Chen
Tahsi Franciscan Friary
305 Kangchuang Road, Tahsi
Taoyuan Hsien, Taiwan, R.O.C.

Rev. Ernesto Rescalli
Yuet Wah College
18, Estrada da Vitoria
Macau (Via Hong Kong)

The Marian Movement of Priests
P.O. Box 8
St. Francis, Maine 04774-0008, U.S.A.

CROATIAN

Rev. Mihajlo Dudas
Radicev Trg. 5
41.000 Zagreb/Gornjig, Croatia

P. Izidor Jedvaj, S.J.
Jordanovac, 110
HR-10.000 Zagreb, Croatia

CZECHOSLOVAKIAN

Joseff Vlcek
Cernockova ul. 7
77200 Olomouc, Czechoslovakia
Tel. (420) 68-5223.763

FLEMISH-DUTCH

P. Silvester De Munter, O.F.M.
Minderbroedersstratt, 5
B-3800 Sint Truiden
Belgium

Rev. P. Arnold Spauwen
Houtlaan, 4
NL6525 XZ - Nijmegen
The Netherlands

FRENCH

Le Mouvement Sacerdotal Marial
Secrétariat
13, Rue des Vieux Prés
F-54120 Bertrichamps, France
Tel. 03/83714322 / 83714432

Le Mouvement Sacerdotal Marial
Secrétariat
C.P. 127, Succursale Limoilou
Québec, Québec GlL 4Vl, Canada

P. Georges Flieg
2, Rue des Quatre Saisons
F-68200 Brunstatt, France

P. Joseph Schwizer
Ermitage de Longeborgne
CH-1967 Bramois, Switzerland

R. P. Arthur Delhaye, S.D.B.
Rue Dubois, 2
B-4540 Amay, Belgium

P. Silvester De Munter, O.F.M.
Minderbroedersstratt, 5
B-3800 Sint Truiden, Belgium

Abbé Pierre Diallo
Paroisse du Sacré-Coeur
B.P. 163, Toma, Burkina-Faso, Africa
Tel. (226) 53-60.03

P. Élie Koma, S.J.
Centre Spirituel de Kiriri
B.P. 2130, Bujumbura
Burundi, Africa

Son Eminence le Cardinal Frédéric Etsou
Archdiocèse de Kinshasa
B.P. 8431, Kinshasa I, Congo, Africa

P. Edmond Kahindo
B.P. 1240
Bukavu, Congo, Africa

Mgr. Norbert Rakotondrasoa
Evêque
38100 Antsirabe
Madagascar, Africa

P. Christian Soudée
Ambozontany
B.P. 1440
301 Fianarantsoa, Madagascar, Africa

P. Jean Jblondo
Celes B.P. 8
Abidjan 80
Ivory Coast, Africa

Abbé Laurent Kalibushi
Centre St-Paul, B.P. 405
Kigali, Rwanda, Africa
Tel. 250-76371 / 76589

R. P. Jacques Pagnoux
Foyer de Charité
Cap-des-Biches, C.P. 60
Rufisque-Dakar, Senegal, Africa

P. Emmanuel Weîssan
Evêché d'Atakpamé
B.P. 11
Atakpamé, Togo, Africa

The Marian Movement of Priests
P.O. Box 8
St. Francis, Maine, 04774-0008, U.S.A.

GERMAN

Heidi Bartha
Marianische Priesterbewegung
Blumenfeld
D-7706 -Tengen 2, Germany

Pater Herman Netter, SVD
Schrutkagasse, 48
1130 Wien, Austria

P. Helmut Maria Gressung
Kath. Pfarrhaus Sankt Marien
Reisbach - Kirchplatz 12
D-66793 - Saarwellingen - Germany
Tel. 06838/84401

P. Paul Suso Holdener
Redemptoristen Mariawil
Bruggerstrasse, 143
CH-5400 Baden, Switzerland
Tel. 056-222295

HUNGARIAN

Erdos, Máthás
Mindszenty Ter 2
2500 Esztergom, Hungary
Tel. 33/11288

P. Otto Gellert
Matraverebèly Dózsa Gyorgy u. 10
3077 Matraverebely, Hungary

INDONESIAN

Mgr. V. Kartosiswoyo
c/o Mrs. Naniek Hadibowo
Prof. Supomo SH No. 11A
Jakarta 12810, Indonesia
Tel. 830-3209

Rev. Fr. Hubert Hady
Seminari Menengah
Roh Kudus Tuka
Kotak Pos 18
Sempidi 80351, BALI, Indonesia

JAPANESE

Fr. John Hayashi
Catholic Church
Kita 4, Nishi 23, Chuo-Ku
064 Sapporo
Hokkaido, Japan

Fr. Francis Uchiyama Keisuke, C.P.
II Nazareth Convent, Cho-Me 5-7
Katase Kaigan 2-57
251 Fujisawa, Japan

KOREAN

Rev. Joseph A. Slaby, M.M.
124 Uam 2-dong
Nam gu
Pusan 608-062, Korea

LITHUANIAN

Rev. Kestutis Trimakas
2830 Denton Ct.
Westchester, Illinois 60154, U.S.A.

Mons. Vincentas Jalinskas
Raguvos 20-10
Kaunas, Lithuania

MALAYALAM
V. Rev. Andrew Fernandez, O.C.D.
Mount Carmel Ashram
Perumkulam P.O.
Kottarakara 691 506
Kerala, India

POLISH
Anatol Kaszczuk
Szymonowo 14–330
Maldyty, Poland

PORTUGUESE

Padre António Cardoso Cristóvão, C.S.Sp
Apartado 106
2495 Fátima, Portugal
Tel. 0931 53 83 56

Pe. Nazareno Lanciotti
Caixa Postal 25
Cep. 78.255-000
Jaurú Mato Grosso, Brasil

Casa das Irmãs Servas de Maria Reparadoras
Rua do Coração de Maria
Cova da Iria, Fátima, Portugal

Sr. Otavio Piva de Albuquerque
Rua Freire da Silva, 98 – Cambuci
01523-020 São Paulo, SP., Brasil
Tel. 270-7533

RUMANIAN
P. Pietro Tocamel
Piazza SS Apostoli, 51
00187 Rome, Italy

SLOVAKIAN
Don Marian Vojtko
Jasikova, 20
82103 – Bratislava, Slovakia
Tel. 07/67-647

SLOVENIAN
Rev. Ivan Pojavnik
1 Dolnicarjeva
61.000 Ljubljana, Yugoslavia

SPANISH

Mons. Rubén H. di Monte
Calle Ameghino 907
1870 Avellaneda, Argentina
Tel. (01) 222-4381 / 222-5184

Sr. Federico Ferreira Achával
Quintana 308
1014 Buenos Aires, Argentina
Tel. (01) 812-1815

Sra. Gina Terrazas de Alaiza
Casilla 146
Santa Cruz, Bolivia
Tel. (03) 42-0745 / 42-6616

Sr. Otavio Piva de Albuquerque
Rod. Raposo Taveres, Km 26.5
06700-000 Cotia / SP
São Paulo, Brazil
Tel. (011) 7922-1255 / Fax: 7922-1447

Padre Antonio Gril S., S.D.B.
Oratorio Don Bosco
San Isidro 848
Santiago, Chile
Tel. (02) 635-3086

Padre Roberto Icarte Encina
Séptimo de Linea S/N
Casilla 17
Puerto Montt, Chile
Telefax: (65) 25-8642

Mons. Reynaldo Iriarte Ríos
Carrera 45 N° 53-122
Barranquilla, Colombia
Tel. 340-5248 / 340-3298

Padre Francisco Nuñez Gómez
Avenida 81 N° 48-95
Apto. 204
Santafé de Bogotá, Colombia
Tel. 225-0893

Sr. Fernando Leiva
Calle 114A N° 3821
Santafé de Bogotá, Colombia
Tel. 214-4275

Dr. Farid Jattin Vivero
Dra. Hortensia Jaraba de Jatin
Carrera 47 N° 85-101 Apto. 3B
Barranquilla, Colombia
Telefax: 357-6284

Movimiento Sacerdotal Mariano
Padre Juan José Gamboa Cordero, S.D.B.
Apdo. Postal 762 - 2010 Zapote
San José, Costa Rica
Telfs. 225-2396 / 283-7650

Sra. Merle Castro de González
Apartado Postal 2112-1000
San José, Costa Rica
Tel. 232-0707

S. Emcia. Bernardino Cardenal Echeverría
Ruiz, O.F.M.
Avenida América 1805 y la Gasca
Quito, Ecuador
Telfs. (02) 223-137 / 223-138 Ext. 21

Movimiento Sacerdotal Mariano
Padre Fabio Colindres
Apdo. Postal 01-345
San Salvador, El Salvador C.A.
Telefax: 260-5991

C14

Padre Miguel de Marchi, C.R.S.
Apdo. Postal 01-345
San Salvador, El Salvador C.A.
Telefax: 260-5991

Sr. Gerardo Borja Ferguson
Apdo. Postal 01-345
San Salvador, El Salvador C.A.
Telefax: 260-5991

Mons. Eduardo Aguirre Oestmann, F.M.M.
Apdo. Postal 623-I° 1907
Guatemala, Guatemala
Tel. (02) 592-0575 / 592-0292

Padre Elmer Son, F.M.M.
Seminario Fraternidad Misionera de Maria
6ª Calle 48-98 Zona 7
Colonia El Rosario
Guatemala, Guatemala
Tel. (02) 592-0575 / 592-0292

Mons. Geraldo Scarpone, O.F.M.
Obispo de Comayagua
Apartado Postal 41
Comayagua, Honduras

Padre Maximiliano Orellana
Calle Minas de Oro 319
Colonia Las Minitas
Tegucigalpa, Honduras
Tel. 232-5663 / Telefax: 239-4762

Sra. Ligia de Mayer
Calle Minas de Oro 319
Colonia las Minitas
Tegucigalpa, Honduras
Tel. 232-5663 / 239-4762

Pbro. Félix Pinoncely Proal
Apdo. Postal 1 Sucursal de Correos 3
Centro Comercial La Fuente
31021 Chihuahua, Chihuahua, México
Tel. (14) 10-5880 / 16-5298

Movimiento Sacerdotal Mariano
Padre Ismael Serrano
Apdo. Postal E-11
Managua, Nicaragua
Tel. (02) 65-8729

Movimiento Sacerdotal Mariano
Fray Vicente Morgante, O.F.M.
Apartado 6-5241, El Dorado
Panamá 6A, Panamá
Tel. 61-1692

Parroquia Ntra. Sra. del Perpetuo Socorro
Srita. Pabla Martinez
Tacuary y 4ta. (Blás Garay)
Asunción, Paraguay
Tel. (21) 71-056

Movimiento Sacerdotal Mariano
Padre Fernando Chang Valverde
Casilla Postal 01-444
Callao, Perú
Tel. (01) 429-0713

Sra. Ana Maria Sarmiento Díaz
Casilla Postal 01-444
Callao, Perú
Tel. (01) 429-1723

Movimiento Sacerdotal Mariano
Mons. Herminio de Jesús Viera
Apartado Postal 205, Estación 6
Ponce, Puerto Rico 00732
Tel. (787) 848-5265

Mons. Juan Antonio Flores Santana
Apartado Postal 308
Santiago de los Caballeros
República Dominicana

Sra. Carmen Rosa Alvarez de Crow
Apartado Postal N° 308
Santiago de los Caballeros
República Dominicana
Tel. 583-8677 / Fax: 582-6042

Pbro. Adolfo Solá-Sert Juliá
Muntaner 318, 2° - 1a. Dcha.
08021 Barcelona, Spain (España)
Telefax: (03) 414-7526

Pbro. Andrés González Plaza
Apartado 992
38400 Puerto de la Cruz
Tenerife, Spain (España)
Telefax: (22) 38-3200

Padre Nuble Alonso Rodriguez
Parroquia Santa Teresita del Niño Jesús
Pedro de Mendoza 6267
Montevideo, Uruguay
Tel. (02) 22-3217

Sr. Horacio Captevilla
Boulevard España 2175
Apartamento 602
11200 Montevideo, Uruguay
Tel. (02) 43-0283

The Marian Movement of Priests
P.O. Box 8
St. Francis, Maine 04774-0008, U.S.A.
Tel. (207) 398-3375

Pbro. Alexander J. Mendoza C.
Apartado Postal 69090
Caracas 1060, Venezuela
Tel. 265-3323 / 753-1148
Fax: 753-7112

SWAHILI

Fr. Edmond Kahindo
Pharmakina-Congo
B.P. 122
Cyangugu, Rwanda, Africa

TAGALOG

The Marian Movement of Priests
Rev. Antonio B. Olaguer, S.J.
P.O. Box 17610, San Juan CPO
1500 San Juan, Metro Manila, Philippines
Tel. (02) 4104117

TAMIL

V. Rev. Andrew Fernandez, O.C.D.
Mount Carmel Ashram
Perumkulam P.O.
Kottarakara 691 506
Kerala, India

Rev. Anthony Xavier
S.H. Sanatorium
Tuticorin - 628 002
Tamilnadu, India

VIETNAMESE

The Marian Movement of Priests
P.O. Box 8
St. Francis, Maine 04774-0008, U.S.A.
Tel. (207) 398-3375

FEAST INDEX

D2

FEAST	CH	MO DA YR	TITLE	CITY, REGION	COUNTRY
Advent	367	11 28 87	Prepare Yourselves With Me	Dongo, Como	Italy
All Saints	025	11 01 73	My Faithful Cohort		
All Saints	235	11 01 81	The Communion Of Saints	Quito	Ecuador
All Saints	276	11 01 83	Leader Of A Single Cohort		
All Saints	338	11 01 86	Your Place In Paradise	Dongo, Como	Italy
All Saints	413	11 01 89	The New Jerusalem	Dongo, Como	Italy
All Saints	436	11 01 90	Paradise Will Be Joined To Earth	Dallas, Texas	U.S.A.
All Saints	530	11 01 94	In The Splendor Of The Saints	St. Francis, Maine	U.S.A.
All Saints	556	11 01 95	Paradise Is United With Earth	Pouso Alegre, Minas Gerais	Brazil
All Souls Day	163	11 02 78	Do Not Feel You Are Alone		
All Souls Day	481	11 02 92	At The Hour Of Your Death	Dongo, Como	Italy
Anniv. Of The Apparition Of The "Virgin Of The Poor" At Banneux	069	02 15 75	The Joy Of Making You Grow		
Annunciation Of Our Lord	094	03 25 76	Mother Of Jesus, And Yours		
Annunciation Of Our Lord	173	03 25 79	Your Interior Equilibrium		
Annunciation Of Our Lord	196	03 25 80	My Yes And Yours		
Annunciation Of Our Lord	223	03 25 81	"Yes, Father"		
Annunciation Of Our Lord	243	03 25 82	Yes To The Gospel Of Jesus		
Annunciation Of Our Lord	261	03 25 83	Open Wide The Gates To Christ		
Annunciation Of Our Lord	287	03 25 84	I Ask For The Consecration Of All		
Annunciation Of Our Lord	401	03 25 89	In The New Sepulchre	Dongo, Como	Italy
Aparecida, Our Lady Of (Patroness Of Brazil)	555	10 12 95	I Am Glorified	Jauru, Mato Grosso	Brazil

Ash Wednesday	222	03	04	81	Mortify Your Senses	Dongo, Como	Italy
Ash Wednesday	347	03	04	87	On This Luminous Pathway	Recife, Pernambuco	Brazil
Ash Wednesday	374	02	17	88	Be Converted And Return To The Lord	Fatima	Portugal
Assumption Of The BVM	055	08	15	74	In Heaven To Be More A Mother		
Assumption Of The BVM	107	08	15	76	Live In Paradise With Me		
Assumption Of The BVM	206	08	15	80	My Glorified Body		
Assumption Of The BVM	228	08	15	81	Refuge Of Sinners		
Assumption Of The BVM	269	08	15	83	In The Light Of Paradise		
Assumption Of The BVM	292	08	15	84	Walk In The Light		
Assumption Of The BVM	312	08	15	85	Do Not Be Afraid		
Assumption Of The BVM	331	08	15	86	You Will Give Peace Of Heart	Bagni Di Tivoli, Rome	Italy
Assumption Of The BVM	386	08	15	88	I Have Intervened Forcefully	Rubbio, Vicenza	Italy
Assumption Of The BVM	409	08	15	89	Here Must Appear The Constancy Of The Saints	Rubbio, Vicenza	Italy
Assumption Of The BVM	429	08	15	90	The Way Of Light	Rubbio, Vicenza	Italy
Assumption Of The BVM	453	08	15	91	The New Era	Rubbio, Vicenza	Italy
Assumption Of The BVM	475	08	15	92	The Rays Of My Splendor	Rubbio, Vicenza	Italy
Assumption Of The BVM	499	08	15	93	Close To All Of You	Rubbio, Vicenza	Italy
Assumption Of The BVM	524	08	15	94	The Feast Of Joy	Rubbio, Vicenza	Italy
Assumption Of The BVM	549	08	15	95	A Sign Of Sure Hope	Rubbio, Vicenza	Italy
Assumption Of The BVM	576	08	15	96	Look Up To Heaven	Dongo, Como	Italy
Assumption Of The BVM	598	08	15	97	Resplendent Is The Queen At Your Right Hand	Dongo, Como	Italy
Blessed Michael Rua	060	10	29	74	How Much You Have Need Of A Mother!		

FEAST	CH	MO DA YR	TITLE	CITY, REGION	COUNTRY
Blessed Michael Rua	138	10 29 77	Doubts And Perplexity		
BVM Appears To	027	11 27 73	Only For My Son Jesus		
St. Catherine Laboure (Anniv.)					
Cenacle (Nat'l Directors' Retreat)	178	07 07 79	In This Cova Da Iria	Fatima	Portugal
Cenacle (Nat'l Directors' Retreat)	227	07 01 81	This Is The Hour Of My Victory	Valdragone	San Marino
Cenacle (Nat'l Directors' Retreat)	248	06 30 82	The Secret Of My Immaculate Heart	Valdragone	San Marino
Cenacle (Nat'l Directors' Retreat)	267	06 29 83	Why I Wanted You Here	Valdragone	San Marino
Cenacle (Nat'l Directors' Retreat)	291	07 05 84	Mother Of Jesus, The Priest	Valdragone	San Marino
Cenacle (Nat'l Directors' Retreat)	311	07 05 85	Instruments Of My Peace	Valdragone	San Marino
Cenacle (Nat'l Directors' Retreat)	327	07 04 86	A Spirit Of Joy And Of Consolation	Valdragone	San Marino
Cenacle (Nat'l Directors' Retreat)	357	07 03 87	My Times Have Arrived	Valdragone	San Marino
Cenacle (Nat'l Directors' Retreat)	408	06 28 89	Bear Within Yourselves	Valdragone	San Marino
			The Witness Of Jesus		
Cenacle (Nat'l Directors' Retreat)	428	06 28 90	The Second Pentecost	Valdragone	San Marino
Cenacle (Nat'l Directors' Retreat)	452	06 26 91	In You I Manifest Myself	Valdragone	San Marino
Cenacle (Nat'l Directors' Retreat)	474	07 01 92	Your Priestly Love	Valdragone	San Marino
Cenacle (Nat'l Directors' Retreat)	498	07 01 93	The Mission Which I Entrust To You	Valdragone	San Marino
Cenacle (Nat'l Directors' Retreat)	523	06 30 94	My Immaculate Heart Will Triumph	Valdragone	San Marino
Cenacle (Nat'l Directors' Retreat)	547	06 28 95	For The Salvation Of The World	Valdragone	San Marino
Cenacle (Nat'l Directors' Retreat)	575	06 27 96	My Motherly Plan	Valdragone	San Marino
Cenacle (Nat'l Directors' Retreat)	596	06 24 97	Jesus Christ Is The Only Savior	Valdragone	San Marino
Cenacle (Priest Retreat)	236	11 12 81	The Great Trial	Puebla	Mexico
Cenacle (Priest Retreat)	293	08 30 84	Mother Of Faith	Altotting	Germany
Cenacle (Priest Retreat)	294	09 13 84	In Cenacle With Me	Strasbourg	France

Event	No.	Date	Title	City	Country
Cenacle (Priest Retreat)	295	09 20 84	Be My Apostles	Fatima	Portugal
Cenacle (Priest Retreat)	296	10 24 84	Do Battle, Beloved Sons!	London	England
Cenacle (Priest Retreat)	298	11 14 84	My Urgent Invitation	Zagreb	Yugoslavia
Cenacle (Priest Retreat)	340	12 03 86	My Remedy For Your Illnesses	Dallas, Texas	U.S.A.
Cenacle (Priest Retreat)	361	09 08 87	The Great Marvels Of The Lord	Tokyo	Japan
Cenacle (Priest Retreat)	364	09 29 87	Heaven And Earth Are Uniting	Inchon	Korea
Cenacle (Priest Retreat)	387	08 31 88	The Eyes Raised To Mary	Vienna	Austria
Cenacle (Priest Retreat)	390	09 29 88	To The Angels Of The Churches	Madrid	Spain
Cenacle (Priest Retreat)	392	10 27 88	This Is Your Hour	Zagreb	Yugoslavia
Cenacle (Priest Retreat)	419	02 08 90	Mother And Queen Of Brazil	Brasilia	Brazil
Cenacle (Priest Retreat)	430	08 22 90	Queen Of Love	Budapest	Hungary
Cenacle (Priest Retreat)	437	11 15 90	The Hour Of The Great Trial	Malvern, Pennsylvania	U.S.A.
Cenacle (Priest Retreat)	443	02 26 91	Not By Bread Alone	Brasilia	Brazil
Cenacle (Priest Retreat)	454	09 03 91	Apostles Of The New Era	Olomouc, Moravia	Czechoslovakia
Cenacle (Priest Retreat)	459	10 16 91	The Gift Which I Am Making To The Church	Birmingham	England
Cenacle (Priest Retreat)	467	02 27 92	Mother Of The Second Evangelization	Quito	Ecuador
Cenacle (Priest Retreat)	468	03 27 92	Go And Evangelize	Sao Paulo	Brazil
Cenacle (Priest Retreat)	501	09 15 93	A Cause Of My Great Sorrow	Tokyo	Japan
Cenacle (Priest Retreat)	503	10 21 93	Have Confidence And Great Hope	Jakarta, Cisarua	Indonesia
Cenacle (Priest Retreat)	506	11 23 93	Your Light Will Shine	Sydney	Australia
Cenacle (Priest Retreat)	514	02 22 94	On The Rock Of The Apostolic Faith	Bogota	Columbia
Cenacle (Priest Retreat)	529	10 13 94	My Times Have Arrived	Effingham, Illinois	U.S.A.
Cenacle (Priest Retreat)	531	11 23 94	Let Your Trust Be Great	Lago de Guadalupe	Mexico
Cenacle (Priest Retreat)	540	03 22 95	I Am Consoled By You	Madrid	Spain

FEAST	CH	MO DA YR	TITLE	CITY, REGION	COUNTRY
Cenacle (Priest Retreat)	557	11 15 95	Spread My Light	Barretos, City Of Mary	Brazil
Cenacle (Priest Retreat)	563	01 24 96	Go In My Name	San Salvador	El Salvador
Cenacle (Priest Retreat)	581	10 13 96	A Great Sign	Tokyo	Japan
Cenacle (Priest Retreat)	583	10 31 96	A Land Blessed And Threatened	Seoul	Korea
Cenacle (Priests/Faithful)	375	02 25 88	My Motherly Message	Sao Paulo	Brazil
Cenacle (Priests/Faithful)	388	09 11 88	Love Is Not Loved	Paris	France
Cenacle (Priests/Faithful)	389	09 18 88	A Period Of Ten Years	Lourdes	France
Cenacle (Priests/Faithful)	456	09 12 91	In The Name Of Mary	Sastin, Slovakia	Czechoslovakia
Cenacle (Priests/Faithful)	532	12 05 94	The Apple Of My Eye	Mexico City	Mexico
Cenacle (Priests/Faithful)	539	03 11 95	My Secret	Fatima	Portugal
Cenacle (Youth)	522	06 11 94	Your Refuge	San Leonardo, Sardinia	Italy
Chair Of St. Peter	514	02 22 94	On The Rock Of The Apostolic Faith	Bogota	Columbia
Chair Of St. Peter	565	02 22 96	The Powers Of Hell Will Not Prevail	Cusco	Peru
Christ The King	339	11 23 86	The Way Which Leads You To His Kingdom	Ft. Lauderdale, Florida	U.S.A.
Christ The King	482	11 22 92	An Oracle Of The Lord	San Marco, Udine	Italy
Christ The King	505	11 21 93	The Glorious Reign Of Christ	Sydney	Australia
Christ The King, Vigil	164	11 25 78	My Motherly Action	Fatima	Portugal
Corpus Christi	176	06 14 79	Jesus In The Eucharist	Garabandal	Spain
Czestochowa, Our Lady Of	270	08 26 83	Mother Of The Purification	Toronto, Ontario	Canada
Dedication Of The Basilica Of St. John Lateran	086	11 09 75	Live Your Consecration		
Easter Sunday	263	04 03 83	Let Nothing Disturb Your Peace!		
Easter Sunday	324	03 30 86	Jesus Is Your Peace	Dongo, Como	Italy

Event	No.	Date	Title	Location	Country
Easter Sunday	380	04 03 88	Rejoice With Me	Dongo, Como	Italy
Easter Sunday	402	03 26 89	In Expectation Of His Glorious Return	Dongo, Como	Italy
Easter Sunday	424	04 15 90	The Second Pasch In Glory	Rubbio, Vicenza	Italy
Easter Sunday	447	03 31 91	Mother Of Joy	Rubbio, Vicenza	Italy
Easter Sunday	472	04 19 92	The Victory Which Conquers The World	Rubbio, Vicenza	Italy
Easter Sunday	493	04 11 93	The Pasch Of The New Times	Rubbio, Vicenza	Italy
Easter Sunday	518	04 03 94	It Is The Paschal Joy	Capoliveri, Livorno	Italy
Easter Sunday	544	04 16 95	The Triumph Of Divine Mercy	Capoliveri, Livorno	Italy
Easter Sunday	571	04 07 96	His Glorious Return	Capoliveri, Livorno	Italy
Easter Sunday	593	03 30 97	Witness Of The Resurrection	Capoliveri, Livorno	Italy
Exaltation Of The Holy Cross	551	09 14 95	Jesus Crucified Is Your Salvation	Milan	Italy
Fatima, 1st Apparition	099	05 13 76	Consecrate Yourselves To My Immaculate Heart		
Fatima, 1st Apparition	153	05 13 78	My Hour Has Come	Florida	U.S.A.
Fatima, 1st Apparition	175	05 13 79	The Woman Clothed With The Sun		
Fatima, 1st Apparition	200	05 13 80	The Times Of Battle	Cologne	Germany
Fatima, 1st Apparition	225	05 13 81	I Have Come Down From Heaven	Lome	Togo
Fatima, 1st Apparition	245	05 13 82	Look To The Pope!	Munich	Germany
Fatima, 1st Apparition	289	05 13 84	Be Converted!		
Fatima, 1st Apparition	351	05 13 87	Into What An Abyss You Have Fallen!	Milan	Italy
Fatima, 1st Apparition	382	05 13 88	These Are The Times	Marienfried	Germany
Fatima, 1st Apparition	425	05 13 90	I Am Coming Down From Heaven	Fatima	Portugal
Fatima, 1st Apparition	449	05 13 91	The Pope Of My Secret	Salzburg	Austria
Fatima, 1st Apparition	473	05 13 92	The Sign Of My Presence	Bologna	Italy
Fatima, 1st Apparition	495	05 13 93	The Bloody Years Of The Battle	Caravaggio, Bergamo	Italy

FEAST	CH	MO DA YR	TITLE	CITY, REGION	COUNTRY
Fatima, 1st Apparition	520	05 13 94	An Apocalyptic Message	Caravaggio, Bergamo	Italy
Fatima, 1st Apparition	545	05 13 95	Pray For The Pope	Perpignan	France
Fatima, 1st Apparition	572	05 13 96	The Sure Road	Caravaggio, Bergamo	Italy
Fatima, 2nd Apparition	406	06 13 89	The Beast Like A Lamb	Dongo, Como	Italy
Fatima, 3rd Apparition	004	07 13 73	The Reason For My Tears	Ravenna	Italy
Fatima, 3rd Apparition	156	07 13 78	Your Public Mission	Rome	Italy
Fatima, 3rd Apparition	203	07 13 80	The Work Of Co-Redemption		
Fatima, 4th Apparition	249	08 13 82	Instruments Of My Mercy		
Fatima, 4th Apparition	359	08 13 87	The Pope Of My Light	Dongo, Como	Italy
Fatima, 5th Apparition	294	09 13 84	In Cenacle With Me	Strasbourg	France
Fatima, Last Apparition	020	10 13 73	A Way Of Acting Different From Yours		
Fatima, Last Apparition	137	10 13 77	The Miracle Of The Sun	Fatima	Portugal
Fatima, Last Apparition	161	10 13 78	The Hour Of The Apostles Of Light		
Fatima, Last Apparition	211	10 13 80	Do Not Sin Any More	Manila	Philippines
Fatima, Last Apparition	233	10 13 81	An Interior Wound	Buenos Aires	Argentina
Fatima, Last Apparition	252	10 13 82	I Am The Dawn	Fatima	Portugal
Fatima, Last Apparition	314	10 13 85	The Two Cohorts	Fatima	Portugal
Fatima, Last Apparition	366	10 13 87	I Will Put An End To Your Slavery		Hong Kong
Fatima, Last Apparition	391	10 13 88	I Am Opening For You The Sealed Book	Fatima	Portugal
Fatima, Last Apparition	412	10 13 89	The Angel Of The First Plague	Dongo, Como	Italy
Fatima, Last Apparition	435	10 13 90	I Reveal My Secret	Mexico City	Mexico
Fatima, Last Apparition	458	10 13 91	The Great Sign In Heaven	Birkenhead	England
Fatima, Last Apparition	480	10 13 92	Lift Up Your Eyes To Heaven	Milan	Italy
Fatima, Last Apparition	529	10 13 94	My Times Have Arrived	Effingham, Illinois	U.S.A.

Fatima, Last Apparition	581	10 13 96	A Great Sign	Tokyo	Japan
First Saturday	001	07 07 73	I Will Always Be Near You		
First Saturday	028	12 01 73	The Spirit Of Rebellion Against God		
First Saturday	033	01 05 74	My Heart Will Be Your Refuge		
First Saturday	054A	08 03 74	The Decisive Moments Are Near		
First Saturday	063	12 07 74	Revealed To The Little Ones	Dongo, Como	Italy
First Saturday	067	01 04 75	Faithful To My Voice And That Of The Pope		
First Saturday	073	06 07 75	Respond To My Supreme Call		
First Saturday	095	04 03 76	Your Light Will Shine Resplendently		
First Saturday	102	07 03 76	Your Most Necessary Witness	Lourdes	France
First Saturday	106	08 07 76	Only With The Pope		
First Saturday	113	12 04 76	Of What Are You Afraid?		
First Saturday	116	01 01 77	Walk In My Light		
First Saturday	133	08 06 77	My Property		
First Saturday	136	10 01 77	It Is Not Given To All	Nijmegen	Holland
First Saturday	139	11 05 77	Everything Is About To Be Accomplished		
First Saturday	149	03 03 78	You Will Be Consoled		
First Saturday	154	06 03 78	The Whole Church In My Refuge	Nagasaki	Japan
First Saturday	158	08 05 78	In The Heart Of The Church		
First Saturday	171	03 03 79	The Fourth Sign: Persecution		
First Saturday	180	08 04 79	The Five First Saturdays		
First Saturday	193	02 02 80	Offered To The Glory Of God		
First Saturday	195	03 01 80	With Jesus In The Desert		
First Saturday	229	09 04 81	Mother Of Mercy	Sao Paulo	Brazil

FEAST	CH	MO	DA	YR	TITLE	CITY, REGION	COUNTRY
First Saturday	257	01	01	83	Mother Of Hope		
First Saturday	260	03	05	83	The Path Of Penance		
First Saturday	271	09	03	83	Ministers Of The Redemption	Vancouver, B.C.	Canada
First Saturday	303	02	02	85	I See Your Littleness		
First Saturday	326	06	07	86	Anchor Of Salvation		
First Saturday	332	09	06	86	My Heart Is Bleeding	Dongo, Como	Italy
First Saturday	338	11	01	86	Your Place In Paradise	Dongo, Como	Italy
First Saturday	379	04	02	88	Into The Sorrow Of My Desolation	Dongo, Como	Italy
First Saturday	403	05	06	89	The Two Wings Of The Great Eagle	Sant' Omero, Teramo	Italy
First Saturday	405	06	03	89	The Beast Like A Leopard	Milan	Italy
First Saturday	442	02	02	91	The Road Which Leads To The New Era	Milan	Italy
First Saturday	448	05	04	91	The Times Of Your Witness	Milan	Italy
First Saturday	494	05	01	93	My Motherly Presence	Sant' Omero, Teramo	Italy
First Saturday	502	10	02	93	The Task Of The Guardian Angels	Milan	Italy
First Saturday	510	01	01	94	Open Your Hearts To Hope	Milan	Italy
First Saturday	517	04	02	94	The Sabbath Which Is About To End	Capoliveri, Livorno	Italy
First Saturday	548	08	05	95	White Flakes Of Snow	Sant' Omero, Teramo	Italy
First Saturday	554	10	07	95	My Victory	Uruacu, Goias	Brazil
First Saturday	570	04	06	96	Assuage My Sorrow	Capoliveri, Livorno	Italy
Good Friday	071	03	28	75	The Way Of The Cross		
Good Friday	097	04	16	76	See If There Is A Greater Sorrow		
Good Friday	124	04	08	77	With Me Beneath The Cross		
Good Friday	151	03	24	78	How Much Blood!		
Good Friday	174	04	13	79	Near My Son And My Sons		

Good Friday	197	04 04 80	In His Greatest Abandonment		
Good Friday	224	04 17 81	Today His Passion Is Repeated		
Good Friday	244	04 09 82	This Is How I Found My Son		
Good Friday	262	04 01 83	All Is Accomplished		
Good Friday	288	04 20 84	Close To Every Altar		
Good Friday	308	04 05 85	Your Sorrowful Passion	Dongo, Como	Italy
Good Friday	323	03 28 86	Why Have You Abandoned Me?	Dongo, Como	Italy
Good Friday	349	04 17 87	On The Calvary Of This Century	Dongo, Como	Italy
Good Friday	378	04 01 88	Behold Your Mother	Dongo, Como	Italy
Good Friday	400	03 24 89	Remain With Jesus On The Cross	Dongo, Como	Italy
Good Friday	422	04 13 90	The Son And The Mother	Rubbio, Vicenza	Italy
Good Friday	445	03 29 91	The Man Of All Times	Rubbio, Vicenza	Italy
Good Friday	470	04 17 92	Let Us Adore Jesus Crucified	Rubbio, Vicenza	Italy
Good Friday	491	04 09 93	His Sorrowful Passion Is Being Renewed	Rubbio, Vicenza	Italy
Good Friday	516	04 01 94	The Bright Cross	Capoliveri, Livorno	Italy
Good Friday	542	04 14 95	Tears And Blood	Capoliveri, Livorno	Italy
Good Friday	569	04 05 96	His Wounds	Capoliveri, Livorno	Italy
Good Friday	591	03 28 97	I Will Draw Everyone To Myself	Capoliveri, Livorno	Italy
Holy Archangels	183	09 29 79	The Angels Of The Lord	Nijmegen	Holland
Holy Archangels	232	09 29 81	Queen Of The Angels	Montevideo	Uruguay
Holy Archangels	274	09 29 83	The Role Of The Angels	Curacao	Netherlands
Holy Archangels	335	09 29 86	With You In The Combat	Naples	Italy
Holy Archangels	364	09 29 87	Heaven And Earth Are Uniting	Inchon	Korea
Holy Archangels	390	09 29 88	To The Angels Of The Churches	Madrid	Spain
Holy Archangels	433	09 29 90	The Hour Of The Angelic Powers	St. Albert, Alberta	Canada

D12

FEAST	CH	MO DA YR	TITLE	CITY, REGION	COUNTRY
Holy Archangels	528	09 29 94	The Angels Of Your Time	Omaha, Nebraska	U.S.A.
Holy Archangels	553	09 29 95	The Times Will Be Shortened	Rio de Janeiro	Brazil
Holy Guardian Angels	210	10 02 80	A Great Design On This People	Cebu	Philippines
Holy Guardian Angels	478	10 02 92	The Announcement Of The Three Angels	Milan	Italy
Holy Guardian Angels	502	10 02 93	The Task Of The Guardian Angels	Milan	Italy
Holy Innocents	031	12 28 73	My Church Will Be Renewed		
Holy Night	064	12 24 74	Moments Of Anxiety		
Holy Night	089	12 24 75	Do Not Fear		
Holy Night	114	12 24 76	I Ask The Gift Of Your Love		
Holy Night	141	12 24 77	You Too Beget My Son		
Holy Night	166	12 24 78	His Second Coming		
Holy Night	189	12 24 79	How Great A Light		
Holy Night	217	12 24 80	About The Crib		
Holy Night	238	12 24 81	In The Cradle Of Suffering		
Holy Night	255	12 24 82	God Is With You		
Holy Night	279	12 24 83	His New Birth		
Holy Night	300	12 24 84	Everything Has Already Been Revealed		
Holy Night	318	12 24 85	A Great Silence	Dongo, Como	Italy
Holy Night	342	12 24 86	The Crib At His Glorious Return	Dongo, Como	Italy
Holy Night	369	12 24 87	An Announcement Of Joy	Dongo, Como	Italy
Holy Night	395	12 24 88	In The Night Of Your Time	Dongo, Como	Italy
Holy Night	415	12 24 89	The Time Has Reached Its Fullness	Dongo, Como	Italy
Holy Night	439	12 24 90	Receive The Prophetic Announcements	Dongo, Como	Italy
Holy Night	462	12 24 91	The Bright Cave	Dongo, Como	Italy

Holy Night	484	12 24 92	The Morning Star	Dongo, Como	Italy
Holy Night	508	12 24 93	This Holy Night	Dongo, Como	Italy
Holy Night	534	12 24 94	The Mystery Of This Night	Dongo, Como	Italy
Holy Night	559	12 24 95	Merciful Love	Dongo, Como	Italy
Holy Night	585	12 24 96	God With Us	Dongo, Como	Italy
Holy Night	603	12 24 97	Enter With Me	Dongo, Como	Italy
Holy Saturday	350	04 18 87	The Sabbath Of My Great Sorrow	Dongo, Como	Italy
Holy Saturday	379	04 02 88	Into The Sorrow Of My Desolation	Dongo, Como	Italy
Holy Saturday	401	03 25 89	In The New Sepulchre	Dongo, Como	Italy
Holy Saturday	423	04 14 90	Keep Watch With Me In Expectation	Rubbio, Vicenza	Italy
Holy Saturday	446	03 30 91	In The Long Holy Saturday	Rubbio, Vicenza	Italy
Holy Saturday	471	04 18 92	The Sepulchre Of Your Slavery!	Rubbio, Vicenza	Italy
Holy Saturday	492	04 10 93	Close To Every Sepulchre	Rubbio, Vicenza	Italy
Holy Saturday	517	04 02 94	The Sabbath Which Is About To End	Capoliveri, Livorno	Italy
Holy Saturday	543	04 15 95	Keep Watch With Me	Capoliveri, Livorno	Italy
Holy Saturday	570	04 06 96	Assuage My Sorrow	Capoliveri, Livorno	Italy
Holy Saturday	592	03 29 97	Mother Of The Redeemer	Capoliveri, Livorno	Italy
Holy Thursday	307	04 04 85	The Hour Of A New Agony	Dongo, Como	Italy
Holy Thursday	322	03 27 86	A Divine Mystery	Dongo, Como	Italy
Holy Thursday	348	04 16 87	Enter With Jesus Into Gethsemane	Dongo, Como	Italy
Holy Thursday	377	03 31 88	The Johns Of The Eucharistic Jesus	Dongo, Como	Italy
Holy Thursday	399	03 23 89	Jesus Comes	Dongo, Como	Italy
Holy Thursday	421	04 12 90	He Loved Them To The End	Rubbio, Vicenza	Italy
Holy Thursday	444	03 28 91	The Pasch Of Love And Of Sorrow	Rubbio, Vicenza	Italy
Holy Thursday	469	04 16 92	You Will Be Faithful Priests	Rubbio, Vicenza	Italy

FEAST	CH	MO DA YR	TITLE	CITY, REGION	COUNTRY
Holy Thursday	490	04 08 93	A Service Of Love	Rubbio, Vicenza	Italy
Holy Thursday	515	03 31 94	Let Yourselves Be Possessed By His Love	Capoliveri, Livorno	Italy
Holy Thursday	541	04 13 95	I Have Ardently Desired	Capoliveri, Livorno	Italy
Holy Thursday	568	04 04 96	The Chalice Of Comfort	Capoliveri, Livorno	Italy
Holy Thursday	590	03 27 97	Into The Cenacle Of His Divine Love	Capoliveri, Livorno	Italy
Holy Tuesday	096	04 13 76	Look At My Crucified Son!		
Holy Year Of The Redemption (Opening)	261	03 25 83	Open Wide The Gates To Christ		
Immaculate Conception	088	12 08 75	I Will Be Victorious		
Immaculate Conception	140	12 08 77	The Immaculate One At Your Side		
Immaculate Conception	165	12 08 78	Mother Of The Church		
Immaculate Conception	188	12 08 79	Mother Of All	Douala	Cameroon
Immaculate Conception	216	12 08 80	Great Mercy		
Immaculate Conception	237	12 08 81	On The Road Of Perfect Love	New York City, N.Y.	U.S.A.
Immaculate Conception	254	12 08 82	My Plan		
Immaculate Conception	278	12 08 83	The Medicine You Need	Grand Bassam	Ivory Coast
Immaculate Conception	299	12 08 84	The Will Of God	Dongo, Como	Italy
Immaculate Conception	317	12 08 85	Your Motherly Shepherdess	Perth	Australia
Immaculate Conception	341	12 08 86	My Candor Of Heaven	Santiago	Dominican Rep.
Immaculate Conception	368	12 08 87	Do Not Allow Yourselves To Be Deluded	Rubbio, Vicenza	Italy
Immaculate Conception	394	12 08 88	A Sign Of Hope And Of Consolation	Rubbio, Vicenza	Italy
Immaculate Conception	414	12 08 89	A Crown Of Twelve Stars	Rubbio, Vicenza	Italy
Immaculate Conception	438	12 08 90	Open Your Hearts To Hope	Sao Paulo	Brazil
Immaculate Conception	461	12 08 91	The Gate Which Opens	Milan	Italy

Category	No.	Date	Message	Location	Country
Immaculate Conception	483	12 08 92	The Holy City	Sant' Omero, Teramo	Italy
Immaculate Conception	507	12 08 93	The Years Of My Triumph	Perth	Australia
Immaculate Conception	533	12 08 94	Apostles Of The Last Times	Santiago	Dominican Rep.
Immaculate Conception	558	12 08 95	My Plan	Puerto de la Cruz, Tenerife	Spain
Immaculate Conception	584	12 08 96	With Joy And With Immense Hope	Milan	Italy
Immaculate Conception	602	12 08 97	Open The Doors To Christ	Vacallo	Switzerland
Immaculate Heart Of Mary	001	07 07 73	I Will Always Be Near You		
Immaculate Heart Of Mary	073	06 07 75	Respond To My Supreme Call		
Immaculate Heart Of Mary	154	06 03 78	The Whole Church In My Refuge	Nagasaki	Japan
Immaculate Heart Of Mary	177	06 23 79	In My Immaculate Heart	San Miguel	Azores
Immaculate Heart Of Mary	201	06 14 80	A Torrent Of Water		
Immaculate Heart Of Mary	247	06 19 82	In You The Mother Is Glorified	Split	Yugoslavia
Immaculate Heart Of Mary	266	06 11 83	The Gate Of Heaven		
Immaculate Heart Of Mary	290	06 30 84	The Mystery Of My Immaculate Heart		
Immaculate Heart Of Mary	326	06 07 86	Anchor Of Salvation		
Immaculate Heart Of Mary	384	06 11 88	The Great Apostasy	Monastery Of Le Bouveret, Vallese	Switzerland
Immaculate Heart Of Mary	405	06 03 89	The Beast Like A Leopard	Milan	Italy
Immaculate Heart Of Mary	427	06 23 90	My Immaculate Heart Is Glorified	Rubbio, Vicenza	Italy
Immaculate Heart Of Mary	451	06 08 91	Apostles Of The Last Times	Dongo, Como	Italy
Immaculate Heart Of Mary	497	06 19 93	My Work	Monastery Of Le Bouveret, Vallese	Switzerland
Immaculate Heart Of Mary	522	06 11 94	Your Refuge	San Leonardo, Sardinia	Italy
LaSalette, Our Lady Of	016	09 19 73	The Mother Must Be Loved And Lived		

FEAST	CH	MO DA YR	TITLE	CITY, REGION	COUNTRY
Last Night Of The Year	032	12 31 73	They Become Intoxicated With Emptiness		
Last Night Of The Year	066	12 31 74	The Seed Is Beginning To Germinate		
Last Night Of The Year	090	12 31 75	The Gift Which I Give To The Church		
Last Night Of The Year	115	12 31 76	True Poverty Of Spirit		
Last Night Of The Year	142	12 31 77	The End Of A Period		
Last Night Of The Year	190	12 31 79	Your Last Hour		
Last Night Of The Year	218	12 31 80	The Greatest Cry		
Last Night Of The Year	239	12 31 81	A Gentle And Sad Voice		
Last Night Of The Year	256	12 31 82	Watch In Prayer		
Last Night Of The Year	280	12 31 83	Return To Your Redeemer		
Last Night Of The Year	301	12 31 84	The Signs Of Your Time		
Last Night Of The Year	319	12 31 85	Your Prayer With Me		
Last Night Of The Year	343	12 31 86	And Peace Will Come To You	Dongo, Como	Italy
Last Night Of The Year	370	12 31 87	The Great Tribulation	Dongo, Como	Italy
Last Night Of The Year	396	12 31 88	Mother Of Intercession And Of Reparation	Dongo, Como	Italy
Last Night Of The Year	416	12 31 89	Open Your Hearts	Rubbio, Vicenza	Italy
Last Night Of The Year	440	12 31 90	My Tear Drops	Rubbio, Vicenza	Italy
Last Night Of The Year	463	12 31 91	Prostrate Yourselves With Me	Rubbio, Vicenza	Italy
Last Night Of The Year	485	12 31 92	The End Of The Times	Rubbio, Vicenza	Italy
Last Night Of The Year	509	12 31 93	Great Is My Concern	Milan	Italy
Last Night Of The Year	535	12 31 94	A Sorrowful And Concerned Mother	Milan	Italy
Last Night Of The Year	560	12 31 95	The Great Sign Of Divine Mercy	Milan	Italy
Last Night Of The Year	586	12 31 96	Pray And Make Reparation	Milan	Italy

Last Night Of The Year					
Lourdes, Our Lady Of	604	12 31 97	All Has Been Revealed To You	Milan	Italy
	038	02 11 74	Let Them Live Out The Trust Of The Present Moment		
Lourdes, Our Lady Of	092	02 11 76	The Perfume Of Your Purity		
Lourdes, Our Lady Of	120	02 11 77	Pure Of Mind, Of Heart, Of Body		
Lourdes, Our Lady Of	148	02 11 78	You Must Prepare Yourselves Now		
Lourdes, Our Lady Of	170	02 11 79	The Third Sign: Division		
Lourdes, Our Lady Of	194	02 11 80	Under My Immaculate Mantle		
Lourdes, Our Lady Of	221	02 11 81	I Look Upon You With Pleasure		
Lourdes, Our Lady Of	259	02 11 83	Love One Another		
Lourdes, Our Lady Of	373	02 11 88	The Lord Is Sending Me To You	Manaus, Amazonas	Brazil
Lourdes, Our Lady Of	466	02 11 92	I Set You Free From Slavery	Managua	Nicaragua
Lourdes, Our Lady Of	488	02 11 93	The Dangers Which Threaten You	Sao Paulo	Brazil
Lourdes, Our Lady Of	512	02 11 94	I Am Consoled	Tegucigalpa	Honduras
Lourdes, Our Lady Of	538	02 11 95	Wash Yourselves At The Fountain	San Marco, Udine	Italy
Lourdes, Our Lady Of	589	02 11 97	The Immaculate Conception	Caracas	Venezuela
Marian Year (Closing)	386	08 15 88	I Have Intervened Forcefully	Rubbio, Vicenza	Italy
Marian Year (Opening)	355	06 07 87	Come, Lord Jesus	Detroit, Michigan	U.S.A.
Mary, Mother Of God	116	01 01 77	Walk In My Light		
Mary, Mother Of God	143	01 01 78	It Will Begin With The Church		
Mary, Mother Of God	167	01 01 79	The Plan Of Merciful Love		
Mary, Mother Of God	191	01 01 80	Your Victorious Mother		
Mary, Mother Of God	219	01 01 81	The Only Possibility Of Salvation		
Mary, Mother Of God	240	01 01 82	I Am The Mother Of Consolation		
Mary, Mother Of God	257	01 01 83	Mother Of Hope		

FEAST	CH	MO DA YR	TITLE	CITY, REGION	COUNTRY
Mary, Mother Of God	281	01 01 84	Have Courage		
Mary, Mother Of God	302	01 01 85	I Am The Beginning Of The New Times		
Mary, Mother Of God	320	01 01 86	Queen Of Peace	Dongo, Como	Italy
Mary, Mother Of God	344	01 01 87	I Am The Rising Dawn	Dongo, Como	Italy
Mary, Mother Of God	371	01 01 88	Shed Light Upon The Earth	Dongo, Como	Italy
Mary, Mother Of God	397	01 01 89	Come, Lord Jesus	Dongo, Como	Italy
Mary, Mother Of God	417	01 01 90	Mother Of The Second Advent	Rubbio, Vicenza	Italy
Mary, Mother Of God	441	01 01 91	The Announcement Of The New Era	Rubbio, Vicenza	Italy
Mary, Mother Of God	464	01 01 92	Your Liberation Is Near	Rubbio, Vicenza	Italy
Mary, Mother Of God	486	01 01 93	The Time Of The Great Trial	Rubbio, Vicenza	Italy
Mary, Mother Of God	510	01 01 94	Open Your Hearts To Hope	Milan	Italy
Mary, Mother Of God	536	01 01 95	Mother Of Mercy	Milan	Italy
Mary, Mother Of God	561	01 01 96	In My Safe Refuge	Milan	Italy
Mary, Mother Of God	587	01 01 97	Jesus Christ Is The Only Savior	Milan	Italy
Miracle Of The Tears (Anniv.)	332	09 06 86	My Heart Is Bleeding	Dongo, Como	Italy
Mount Carmel, Our Lady Of	005	07 16 73	I Will Be Your Leader		
Mount Carmel, Our Lady Of	103	07 16 76	In The Spirit Of Filial Surrender		
Mount Carmel, Our Lady Of	204	07 16 80	Mediatrix Of Graces		
Mount Carmel, Our Lady Of	268	07 16 83	The Holy Mountain		
Nativity Of The BVM	109	09 08 76	You Must Be Little		
Nativity Of The BVM	135	09 08 77	I Have Been Pointing Out The Way To You		
Nativity Of The BVM	160	09 08 78	Your New Birth		
Nativity Of The BVM	182	09 08 79	An Anguished Appeal	Altotting	Germany

					Location	Country
Nativity Of The BVM	208	09 08 80	He Will Come To You As Fire	Inverness, Florida	U.S.A.
Nativity Of The BVM	230	09 08 81	By The Power Of The Little Ones	Brasilia	Brazil
Nativity Of The BVM	250	09 08 82	It Will Be Saved	Nijmegen	Holland
Nativity Of The BVM	272	09 08 83	The Smallest Of My Children	Montreal, Quebec	Canada
Nativity Of The BVM	313	09 08 85	The Hour Of Public Witness	Fulda	Germany
Nativity Of The BVM	333	09 08 86	My Birth	Milan	Italy
Nativity Of The BVM	361	09 08 87	The Great Marvels Of The Lord	Tokyo	Japan
Nativity Of The BVM	410	09 08 89	The Mark On The Forehead And On The Hand	Dongo, Como	Italy
Nativity Of The BVM	431	09 08 90	The Task Which I Have Entrusted To You	Milan	Italy
Nativity Of The BVM	455	09 08 91	The Crown Of The Slavic Peoples	Velehrad, Bohemia	Czechoslovakia
Nativity Of The BVM	476	09 08 92	Your Priestly Fidelity	Milan	Italy
Nativity Of The BVM	500	09 08 93	Along The Way Of Humility	Beppu, Oita	Japan
Nativity Of The BVM	526	09 08 94	With The Littlest Ones	Ottawa, Ontario	Canada
Nativity Of The BVM	550	09 08 95	Light, Love And Motherly Tenderness	Sale, Alessandria	Italy
Nativity Of The BVM	578	09 08 96	With The Strength Of The Little Ones	Bratislava	Slovakia
Nativity Of The BVM	599	09 08 97	Round About My Cradle	Milan	Italy
Palm Sunday	150	03 19 78	The Hour Of Darkness!		
Pentecost	226	06 07 81	"Come, Holy Spirit!"	Tananarive	Madagascar
Pentecost	246	05 30 82	The Hour Of The Holy Spirit	Blumenfeld	Germany
Pentecost	265	05 22 83	New Heavens And A New Earth		
Pentecost	310	05 26 85	Come, Spirit Of Love	Cagliari, Sardinia	Italy
Pentecost	355	06 07 87	Come, Lord Jesus	Detroit, Michigan	U.S.A.
Pentecost	383	05 22 88	The Holy Spirit Will Come	Heede	Germany

FEAST	CH	MO DA YR	TITLE	CITY, REGION	COUNTRY
Pentecost	404	05 14 89	The Huge Red Dragon	Shrine Of Tindari, Sicily	Italy
Pentecost	426	06 03 90	The Time Of The Holy Spirit	Vacallo	Switzerland
Pentecost	450	05 19 91	The Understanding Of The Whole And Entire Truth	Berlin	Germany
Pentecost	496	05 30 93	Comfort Amidst Mourning	Notre Dame de Laus, Gap	France
Pentecost	521	05 22 94	Come, Holy Spirit	Berlin	Germany
Pentecost	546	06 04 95	Tongues Of Fire	Vacallo	Switzerland
Pentecost	574	05 26 96	The Second Pentecost	Shrine Of Latas, Santander	Spain
Pentecost	595	05 18 97	In The Light Of His Truth	Marseille	France
Presentation Of The BVM	185	11 21 79	In The Temple Of My Heart		
Presentation Of The BVM	277	11 21 83	Along The Roads Of Africa	Enugu	Nigeria
Presentation Of The BVM	460	11 21 91	In The Temple Of My Immaculate Heart	Cagliari, Sardinia	Italy
Presentation Of The BVM	601	11 21 97	Conformed To Jesus Crucified	Sale, Alessandria	Italy
Presentation Of The Child Jesus	091	02 02 76	A Sign Of Contradiction		
Presentation Of The Child Jesus	119	02 02 77	I Am Carrying You In My Arms		
Presentation Of The Child Jesus	146	02 02 78	You Will Be Immolated In The Temple		
Presentation Of The Child Jesus	169	02 02 79	The Second Sign: Lack Of Discipline		
Presentation Of The Child Jesus	193	02 02 80	Offered To The Glory Of God		
Presentation Of The Child Jesus	220	02 02 81	The Light And Glory Of The Lord		
Presentation Of The Child Jesus	241	02 02 82	The Light Of Love And Of Hope		
Presentation Of The Child Jesus	258	02 02 83	I Am Asking You For A Spiritual Childhood		

Presentation Of The Child Jesus	285	02 02 84	The Soul Transpierced		
Presentation Of The Child Jesus	303	02 02 85	I See Your Littleness		
Presentation Of The Child Jesus	321	02 02 86	The Way To The Divine Will		
Presentation Of The Child Jesus	345	02 02 87	The Way To Divine Revelation	Dongo, Como	Italy
Presentation Of The Child Jesus	372	02 02 88	In You I Am Glorified	Porto Alegre	Brazil
Presentation Of The Child Jesus	398	02 02 89	I Am Bringing You To Jesus	Milan	Italy
Presentation Of The Child Jesus	418	02 02 90	Only In The Hearts Of Little Ones	Jauru, Mato Grosso	Brazil
Presentation Of The Child Jesus	442	02 02 91	The Road Which Leads To The New Era	Milan	Italy
Presentation Of The Child Jesus	465	02 02 92	To Meet The Lord Who Is Coming	San Salvador	El Salvador
Presentation Of The Child Jesus	487	02 02 93	In The Temple Of My Immaculate Heart	Jauru, Mato Grosso	Brazil
Presentation Of The Child Jesus	511	02 02 94	The Gift Of My Trust	Sant' Omero, Teramo	Italy
Presentation Of The Child Jesus	537	02 02 95	The Hour Of Your Immolation	Sale, Alessandria	Italy
Presentation Of The Child Jesus	564	02 02 96	In The Spiritual Temple	Managua	Nicaragua
Presentation Of The Child Jesus	588	02 02 97	Upon The Way Of The Beatitudes	Vacallo	Switzerland
Queenship Of Mary	056	08 22 74	My Reign		
Queenship Of Mary	108	08 22 76	Your Queen And Your Leader		
Queenship Of Mary	181	08 22 79	Faithful, Prompt And Obedient		
Queenship Of Mary	430	08 22 90	Queen Of Love	Budapest	Hungary
Ransom, Our Lady Of	018	09 24 73	I Will Do Everything For You		
Rosary, Our Lady Of The	082	10 07 75	What It Means To Be A Mother		
Rosary, Our Lady Of The	184	10 07 79	Your Rosary	Lourdes	France
Rosary, Our Lady Of The	275	10 07 83	The Dragon Will Be Shackled	Ft. Lauderdale, Florida	U.S.A.
Rosary, Our Lady Of The	336	10 07 86	The Rosary Brings You To Peace		
Rosary, Our Lady Of The	434	10 07 90	My Greatest Victory	Quebec, Quebec	Canada
Rosary, Our Lady Of The	479	10 07 92	The Angel With The Key And The Chain	Blumenfeld	Germany

FEAST	CH	MO DA YR	TITLE	CITY, REGION	COUNTRY
Rosary, Our Lady Of The	554	10 07 95	My Victory	Uruacu, Goias	Brazil
Sacred Heart Of Jesus	050	06 21 74	In The Furnace Of The Heart Of Jesus		
Snows, Our Lady Of The	077	08 05 75	The Priests Are Responding To Me		
Snows, Our Lady Of The	158	08 05 78	In The Heart Of The Church		
Snows, Our Lady Of The	548	08 05 95	White Flakes Of Snow	Sant' Omero, Teramo	Italy
Sorrows, Our Lady Of	081	09 15 75	Offer And Suffer With Me		
Sorrows, Our Lady Of	209	09 15 80	The Sufferings Of The Church	Chicago, Illinois	U.S.A.
Sorrows, Our Lady Of	231	09 15 81	Mother Of All Sorrows	Ponta Grossa, Parana	Brazil
Sorrows, Our Lady Of	251	09 15 82	A Great Force Of Reparation	Paris	France
Sorrows, Our Lady Of	273	09 15 83	I Am Beneath The Cross	St. Francis, Maine	U.S.A.
Sorrows, Our Lady Of	334	09 15 86	I Am Forming You To Suffering		
Sorrows, Our Lady Of	362	09 15 87	Why Am I Still Weeping?	Akita	Japan
Sorrows, Our Lady Of	411	09 15 89	Great Is My Sorrow	Fatima	Portugal
Sorrows, Our Lady Of	432	09 15 90	The Travail Of The New Birth	St. David, Maine	U.S.A.
Sorrows, Our Lady Of	457	09 15 91	Great Is My Sorrow	Budapest	Hungary
Sorrows, Our Lady Of	477	09 15 92	The Hour Of My Great Sorrow	Sant' Omero, Teramo	Italy
Sorrows, Our Lady Of	501	09 15 93	A Cause Of My Great Sorrow	Tokyo	Japan
Sorrows, Our Lady Of	527	09 15 94	The Pierced Soul	Saskatoon, Saskatchewan	Canada
Sorrows, Our Lady Of	579	09 15 96	Share In My Sorrow	Debrecen	Hungary
St. Agnes	145	01 21 78	Help Me, O Sons	Rome	Italy
St. Agnes	282	01 21 84	My Book	Castelmonte, Udine	Italy
St. Alphonsus Ligouri	010	08 01 73	It Will Be A New Church		
St. Augustine	014	08 28 73	Night Has Fallen Upon The World		
St. Augustine	057	08 28 74	Pray For The Holy Father		

Saint	No.	Date	Title	City	Country
St. Augustine	525	08 28 94	Vigilant Sentinels	Milan	Italy
St. Bartholomew, Apostle	013	08 24 73	The Great Goal Of Sanctity		
St. Bartholomew, Apostle	134	08 24 77	The Decisive Move		
St. Catherine Of Siena	126	04 29 77	My Plan		
St. Francis Xavier	187	12 03 79	Look At The Heart	Nairobi	Kenya
St. Ignatius Of Loyola	105	07 31 76	Your Difficulties		
St. John The Baptist, Birth Of	051	06 24 74	I Have No Need Of Human Means		
St. John The Baptist, Birth Of	596	06 24 97	Jesus Christ Is The Only Savior	Valdragone	San Marino
St. John Vianney	132	08 04 77	Love Always		
St. John Vianney	180	08 04 79	The Five First Saturdays		
St. Josaphat, Martyr	236	11 12 81	The Great Trial	Puebla	Mexico
St. Josaphat, Martyr	315	11 12 85	My Path	Auckland	New Zealand
St. Josaphat, Martyr	393	11 12 88	You Will Be Persecuted	Dongo, Como	Italy
St. Josaphat, Martyr	504	11 12 93	In The Heart Of The Little Ones	Suva	Fiji Islands
St. Joseph	150	03 19 78	The Hour Of Darkness!		
St. Joseph	286	03 19 84	Look At My Spouse Joseph		
St. Joseph	567	03 19 96	Protector And Defender	San Luis	Argentina
St. Joseph The Worker	264	05 01 83	This Month Of May	Pescara	Italy
St. Joseph The Worker	381	05 01 88	Offer Me Fragrant Flowers	Dongo, Como	Italy
St. Joseph The Worker	494	05 01 93	My Motherly Presence	Sant' Omero, Teramo	Italy
St. Joseph The Worker	519	05 01 94	The Hour Of Calvary	Rome	Italy
St. Luke The Evangelist	083	10 18 75	Be Joyous		
St. Mark The Evangelist	072	04 25 75	Do Not Grieve Me By Your Doubt		
St. Martin de Porres	214	11 03 80	Mother Of The Poorest	Calcutta	India
St. Paul Of The Cross	212	10 19 80	The Marvels Of Love And Of Light	Sydney	Australia

FEAST	CH	MO DA YR	TITLE	CITY, REGION	COUNTRY
St. Pius X	012	08 21 73	Close To My Heart In Prayer		
St. Pius X	360	08 21 87	Mother Of Adoration And Of Reparation	Rubbio, Vicenza	Italy
St. Rose Of Lima	079	08 23 75	You Will Have Them Walk Toward Me		
St. Stephen	030	12 26 73	The Caress Of A Mother		
St. Stephen	065	12 26 74	The Power Of The Spirit		
St. Therese Of The Child Jesus	136	10 01 77	It Is Not Given To All	Nijmegen	Holland
St. Therese Of The Child Jesus	600	10 01 97	Merciful Love	Sale, Alessandria	Italy
St. Thomas Aquinas	036	01 28 74	What A Mother Can Do	Rome	Italy
St. Thomas Aquinas	068	01 28 75	The Time Left To You		
St. Thomas Aquinas	284	01 28 84	My Gift To You	San Marco, Udine	Italy
St. Vincent de Paul	019	09 27 73	Foolishness To Confound Wisdom	Milan	Italy
Sts. Joachim & Ann	104	07 26 76	My Time		
Sts. Peter And Paul	202	06 29 80	The Desert Where I Withdraw	Fatima	Portugal
Sts. Peter And Paul	267	06 29 83	Why I Wanted You Here	Valdragone	San Marino
Sts. Peter And Paul	385	06 29 88	With The Faith Of Peter	Knock	Ireland
"Supplica" To The Blessed Virgin Of Pompei	199	05 08 80	The Same Dimensions As The World	Salzburg	Austria
Transfiguration Of Our Lord	133	08 06 77	My Property		
Transfiguration Of Our Lord	329	08 06 86	Climb The Mountain	Rubbio, Vicenza	Italy
Transfiguration Of Our Lord	597	08 06 97	King Of Eternal Glory	Rubbio, Vicenza	Italy
Victory At Lepanto (Anniv.)	082	10 07 75	What It Means To Be A Mother		
Victory At Lepanto (Anniv.)	184	10 07 79	Your Rosary	Lourdes	France
Victory At Lepanto (Anniv.)	275	10 07 83	The Dragon Will Be Shackled	Ft. Lauderdale, Florida	U.S.A.
Victory At Lepanto (Anniv.)	336	10 07 86	The Rosary Brings You To Peace		

Occasion	Number	Date	Title	City	Country
Victory At Lepanto (Anniv.)	434	10 07 90	My Greatest Victory	Quebec, Quebec	Canada
Victory At Lepanto (Anniv.)	479	10 07 92	The Angel With The Key And The Chain	Blumenfeld	Germany
Victory At Lepanto (Anniv.)	554	10 07 95	My Victory	Uruacu, Goias	Brazil
World Day Of Peace	587	01 01 97	Jesus Christ Is The Only Savior	Milan	Italy
World Day Of Prayer For Peace	337	10 27 86	The Task Entrusted To The Church	Sant' Omero, Teramo	Italy
25th Anniversary Of The MMP	594	05 08 97	The Message Of Fatima Is Reaching Its Fulfillment	Fatima	Portugal
	002	07 08 73	The Movement Is Now Born		
	003	07 09 73	Your Mission Is Taking Shape		
	006	07 21 73	Let It Be I Who Act		
	007	07 24 73	Only And Always Mother	Spotorno	Italy
	008	07 28 73	Watch And Pray		
	009	07 29 73	The Heart Of My Priests		
	011	08 09 73	The Purpose Of Your Life		
	015	08 29 73	For All My Priest-Sons		
	017	09 23 73	These Are My Priests	San Vittorino	Italy
	021	10 16 73	I Want To Save Them		
	022	10 20 73	The Light Of The Gospel		
	023	10 30 73	Always With The Pope		
	024	10 31 73	From The Hands Of My Adversary		
	026	11 14 73	The Demon Fears And Hates Them		
	029	12 19 73	The Triumph Of My Immaculate Heart	Dongo, Como	Italy
	034	01 17 74	Cenacles Of Life With Me		
	035	01 23 74	The Sign That I Will Give To Each One		
	037	02 10 74	Rely On Me Alone		

FEAST	CH	MO DA YR	TITLE	CITY, REGION	COUNTRY
	039	02 18 74	It Is Time That I Myself Gather Them Together		
	040	02 23 74	It Will Begin With My Priests		
	041	03 11 74	Great In Love		
	042	03 23 74	I Give You The Joy Of The Cross		
	043	03 27 74	Place Them In My Maternal Heart		
	044	04 01 74	Let Them Offer Me Their Sufferings		
	045	04 18 74	I Will Give Them This Water		
	046	04 30 74	My Beloved Children	Lourdes	France
	047	05 20 74	The Prayer Of My Priests		
	048	05 27 74	The Work I Am Accomplishing		
	049	06 08 74	I Want To Make Jesus Live Again		
	052	07 10 74	I Accept Your Crown Of Love		
	053	07 24 74	My Triumph And That Of My Children		
	054	07 30 74	I Will Lead You By The Hand		
	058	09 16 74	No One Passes Beyond This Point	Arcade	
	059	10 23 74	Prayer And Docility To My Voice		
	061	11 19 74	The Altar On Which They Will Be Immolated		
	062	11 30 74	The Sign Which God Gives		
	070	03 15 75	Without Thinking Of Tomorrow		
	074	07 09 75	Your Heaviest Cross		
	075	07 24 75	Serene In This Time Of Your Repose		
	076	07 29 75	Behold The Handmaid Of The Lord		

078	08	13	75	Satan Breaks Loose		
080	09	12	75	Little To Others, Great To Me		
084	10	24	75	Your Silence		
085	10	30	75	I Am Calling Them All		
087	11	25	75	These Hours Will Be Shortened		
093	03	07	76	The Perfect Consolers		
098	05	03	76	You Will Be Capable Of Loving		
100	05	28	76	Follow Me On The Path Of My Son		
101	06	19	76	Say With Me Your Yes		
110	09	25	76	This Is Why I Speak To You		
111	11	08	76	Look At Your Mother!		
112	11	20	76	The Time Of The Purification		
117	01	13	77	I Will Teach You To Love		
118	01	15	77	You Will Be Completely Renewed	Rome	Italy
121	02	18	77	In Every Part Of The World		Mexico
122	03	10	77	Your Martyrdom Of The Heart		
123	03	21	77	The Angel Of Consolation		
125	04	23	77	Do Not Let Yourselves Be Led Astray		
127	05	18	77	My Battle		
128	07	08	77	The Snares Of My Adversary		
129	07	14	77	United In Love	Montegiove	Italy
130	07	25	77	Your Docility		
131	07	29	77	Enter My Garden		
144	01	06	78	You Can Love Us This Way Too		
147	02	10	78	Only Then Will You Understand		

CH	MO DA YR	TITLE	CITY, REGION	COUNTRY	FEAST
152	04 10 78	You Will Be The Witnesses			
155	06 12 78	This Immense Nation		Hong Kong	
157	07 28 78	A Sign For All	Czestochowa	Poland	
159	08 09 78	The Death Of The Pope			
162	10 17 78	The New Pope, John Paul II			
168	01 28 79	The First Sign: Confusion			
172	03 09 79	Your Liberation Is Near			
179	07 29 79	Your Response			
186	11 28 79	The Desert Will Blossom			
192	01 22 80	A Great Net Of Love			
198	04 24 80	Have Confidence	Rome	Italy	
205	08 08 80	The Powerful Weapon			
207	09 02 80	The Rock Of The Great Division	New York City, N.Y.	U.S.A.	
213	10 27 80	The Way Of Unity	Melbourne	Australia	
215	11 14 80	The Power Of The Gospel	Bangalore	India	
234	10 22 81	Peace Will Come To You	Santiago	Chile	
242	03 05 82	The New Jerusalem	Jerusalem	Israel	
253	11 20 82	Obedient, Chaste And Poor	Rome	Italy	
283	01 24 84	My Signs	Zompita, Udine	Italy	
297	11 09 84	My Messages	Castelmonte, Udine	Italy	
304	02 09 85	My Word	Castelmonte, Udine	Italy	
305	02 14 85	My Purity And Yours	Castelmonte, Udine	Italy	
306	03 16 85	The Fast Which I Ask Of You	Dongo, Como	Italy	
309	05 02 85	Your Reparation	Pescara	Italy	

			Melbourne	Australia
316	12 01 85	Blessed In Expectation		
325	05 08 86	Mother Of Grace And Of Mercy	Merine, Lecce	Italy
328	07 30 86	Ark Of The New Covenant	Rubbio, Vicenza	Italy
330	08 08 86	Mother Of The Eucharist	Rubbio, Vicenza	Italy
346	02 24 87	My Rays Of Light	Rubbio, Vicenza	Italy
352	05 17 87	Your Light Will Return	Washington, D.C.	U.S.A.
353	05 23 87	The Deep Wounds	Denver, Colorado	U.S.A.
354	06 02 87	How It Makes His Divine Heart Suffer!	Seattle, Washington	U.S.A.
356	06 10 87	This Marian Year	Ottawa, Ontario	Canada
358	07 23 87	The Families Consecrated To Me	San Quirino, Pordenone	Italy
363	09 27 87	To All The Peoples Of The World	Seoul	Korea
365	10 09 87	The Children Most Loved By Me	Taipei	Taiwan
376	03 22 88	The Glory Of Mary	San Marco, Udine	Italy
407	06 17 89	The Number Of The Beast: 666	Milan	Italy
420	03 13 90	When The Son Of Man Returns	Sao Paulo	Brazil
489	03 15 93	I Have Wanted You Here	Fatima	Portugal
513	02 13 94	I Fill The Poor With Good Things	Ilobasco	El Salvador
552	09 17 95	Ever Farther	Manaus, Amazonas	Brazil
562	01 19 96	A Work Of Love And Of Mercy	Milan	Italy
564	02 02 96	In The Spiritual Temple	Managua	Nicaragua
566	03 07 96	The Task I Have Entrusted To You	Montevideo	Uruguay
573	05 22 96	The Time Of The Cenacle	Madrid	Spain
577	09 02 96	The Evil Of Your Century	Prague	Czech Republic
580	09 20 96	Do Not Fear, Little Flock	Zagreb	Croatia
582	10 18 96	In This City	Nagasaki	Japan

TABLE OF CONTENTS